Presumed Incompetent

Presumed Incompetent

The Intersections of Race and Class for Women in Academia

Edited by

Gabriella Gutiérrez y Muhs
Yolanda Flores Niemann
Carmen G. González
Angela P. Harris

© 2012 by the University Press of Colorado
Published by Utah State University Press
An imprint of University Press of Colorado
5589 Arapahoe Avenue, Suite 206C
Boulder, Colorado 80303

The University Press of Colorado is a proud member of

The Association of American University Presses.

The University Press of Colorado is a cooperative publishing enterprise supported, in part, by Adams State College, Colorado State University, Fort Lewis College, Metropolitan State College of Denver, Regis University, University of Colorado, University of Northern Colorado, Utah State University, and Western State College of Colorado.

Cover art: Color Block Face by Bernadette Elszy-Perez
ISBN 978-0-87421-869-5 (cloth), ISBN 978-0-87421-922-7 (paper)
ISBN 978-0-87421-870-1 (e-book)

"Where's the Violence? The Promise and Perils of Teaching Women of color Studies," by Grace Chang, reprinted from *Black Women, Gender, Families*. Copyright 2007 by the Board of Trustees of the University of Illinois. Used with permission of the author and the University of Illinois Press.

"The Making of a Token: A Case Study of Stereotype Threat, Stigma, Racism, and Tokenism in Academe," by Yolanda Flores Niemann, reprinted from *Chicana Leadership: The Frontiers Reader*, edited by Yolanda Flores Niemann, with Susan H. Armitage, Patricia Hart, and Karen Weathermoon. Copyright 2002 by Frontiers Editing Inc. Used with permission of the University of Nebraska Press.

An earlier version of the essay now titled "African American Women in the Academy: Quelling the Myth of Presumed Incompetence," which subsequently was revised, appeared in *Dilemmas of Black Faculty at US Predominantly White Institutions in the United States: Issues in the Post-Multicultural Era*, edited by Sharon E. Moore, Rudolph Alexander Jr., and Anthony J. Lemelle Jr. Copyright 2010 by Edwin Mellen Press.

Library of Congress Cataloging-in-Publication Data
Presumed incompetent : the intersections of race and class for women in academia / edited by Gabriella Gutiérrez y Muhs ... [et al.].
   p. cm.
 Includes bibliographical references and index.
 ISBN 978-0-87421-869-5 (hardcover) – ISBN 978-0-87421-870-1 (e-book) – ISBN 978-0-87421-922-7 (pbk.)
1. Women college teachers. 2. Women college teachers—Social conditions. 3. Minority college teachers. 4. Women in higher education. 5. Sex discrimination in higher education. 6. Feminism and higher education. I. Gutiérrez y Muhs, Gabriella
 LB2332.3.P74 2012
 378.1'2–dc23
2012022578

Contents

Part II: Faculty/Student Relationships

Part III: Networks of Allies

Acknowledgments

For several years and at different junctures in the evolution of this book, Aldo Ulisses Reséndiz Ramírez, Brittny Nielsen, Rae Wyse, and Marianne Mork helped me consolidate, format, and manage this monumental manuscript. From the first stages of formulating lists of contributors and calling for papers to the very last-minute changes and revisions, as well as assisting with some of the intellectual work of organization, their help was invaluable. I thank Jennifer Evans for her work on the last leg of this project. I am sure that this is the first book of many that each of them will work on. I also thank Eric Muhs for making beautiful spaces for me to work in and Enrico and Eleuterio for letting me have the many hours it took to complete this project, instead of spending the time in front of the tube with them. I also wish to thank my intellectual mentors—Yvonne Yarbro-Bejarano, Jacquelyn Miller, Helena María Viramontes, Mary Pat Brady, Norma Cantú, Francisco Alarcón, Karen Mary Dávalos—and my friends: Susana Gallardo, Shirley Flores Muñoz, Antonia García, Lucy Ramírez, Melyssa Jo Kelly, Graciela Vega Carbajal, Lupe McKeithen Vega and especially, Sally Hawkridge for mothering and educating my children in her mariachi ways. In memory of Don Luis Leal, Adrianna Castillo-Berchenko and Lila Martin-Geldert.

Gabriella Gutiérrez y Muhs

I owe a special debt of gratitude to people who have supported and encouraged my personal and professional development over the years. There are no words to describe the difference that these cherished family members, friends, and mentors have made in my life. I do not name them here for fear of unintentionally omitting someone who has contributed to my success and quality of life, but they know who they are. I especially appreciate Barry, my husband, and our two children, Russell and Mychaelanne. Their unconditional love and support of my career goals for making the academic environment a place where every person can thrive have given me courage. I value their insistence that I take the time to nurture my physical and psychological health. I am truly blessed.

Yolanda Flores Niemann

I would like to thank my research assistants, Ursula Owen and Tamara Rogers, for their work on this project. I am also deeply grateful for the support and encouragement that I received from Richard Delgado, Jean Stefancic, Eileen Gauna, Gloria

Valencia-Weber, Maritza Reyes, and Juan Martínez. Finally, I want to acknowledge the many women who expressed enthusiasm for the book and contributed thoughts and ideas, but requested that their identities be kept anonymous.

Carmen G. González

I would like to thank all the women academics of color who participated in focus groups under the auspices of LatCrit, Inc. during the preparation of this book, for their honesty, insight, humor, and savvy. I would also like to thank the informal faculty group of black women organized by Ula Taylor at the University of California, Berkeley, for their support. My deep appreciation goes out to my fellow panelists and the audience at the session on storytelling and the law at the Association of American Law Schools' 2011 meeting, where I presented a version of the introduction to this volume. Last but not least, I would like to thank my coeditors for their commitment and vision in bringing this important project to fruition and for asking me to participate.

Angela P. Harris

Foreword

When *This Bridge Called My Back*, edited by Cherríe Moraga and Gloria Anzaldúa, was first published in 1981, women of color in the movement and universities across the country greeted it with deep joy and near reverence because it so accurately reflected and validated the realities with which they had been contending for a very long time. Although intellectually we understand institutionalized systems of domination, study them, and teach their details and histories, in our hearts and innermost selves we may also—at the same time—somehow internalize the ideas about our presumed incompetence that are so pervasive in our everyday lives. In this light, the stories and analyses drawn from the lived experiences of the supremely competent and brilliant women in this book will have an effect similar to the joy that greeted *This Bridge*. We are in the university. We are in the labs. We are in the law schools and courtrooms, medical schools and operating theaters. We prevail, but sometimes it is at enormous costs to ourselves, to our sense of well-being, balance, and confidence. This book should go a long way toward healing wounds, affirming sanity, and launching renewed determination.

When we view the history of the United States, the discrimination against women of all races and ethnicities, men of color, and working-class people is amply and repeatedly demonstrated, ranging from the slave codes of the eighteenth and nineteenth centuries that made learning to read a capital offense for slaves, to the segregation of the public schools in the late nineteenth and much of the twentieth centuries based upon race and the various systems of tracking meant precisely to leave certain children behind. The abrogation of more than 375 treaties between the United States government and Native American tribes and nations in the nineteenth and twentieth centuries led to their loss of sovereignty and homelands and the forced removal of children from Native families and communities by the age of five. The children were mandated to attend mission schools and forbidden to wear their traditional clothing or speak their own languages. These schools were staffed by ignorant, racist, and often brutal priests and teachers. These were terrifying experiences for tens of thousands of Indian children well into the mid-twentieth century.

Repeated US violations of the Treaty of Guadalupe Hidalgo that ended formal hostilities between the United States and Mexico in 1848 resulted in the loss of Mexican land rights and the use of the Spanish language in newly conquered territories. Signs in public parks, restaurants, and many other locations in Texas, Arizona, and Colorado throughout the 1950s and into the 1960s read, "No dogs and Mexicans allowed." Even today darker-hued people experience a thousand and one indignities at border crossings when trying to enter the United States.

Women, too—simply because they were women—were denied access to higher education, law schools, and medical schools until the middle of the twentieth century. Barbara McClintock, for example, who entered Cornell in the 1920s, could not major in genetics simply because women were not permitted to do so. She ended up in botany, which turned out to be just fine with her because all she ever wanted to do was work in her lab, and she figured out how to do genetics anyway. And when her (white, male) colleagues overwhelmingly and repeatedly dismissed her findings in genetics—only one or two really stuck by her—she nevertheless persevered. McClintock was, in fact, the founder of the field of molecular biology before it existed and lived long enough to be awarded the Nobel Prize in physiology in 1983 after laboring in virtual obscurity for almost sixty years!

At the turn of the twentieth century, an African American teacher and scholar, Anna Julia Cooper, published an inspired book she titled *A Voice from the South*. In it she issued a clarion call for the higher education of women, challenging the racist prejudices in white society and the sexist ones among some of her colored brethren. The essays in the book also dealt with many philosophical issues of her day, including a sophisticated challenge to positivism that was then making itself felt in the fledgling social sciences. In 1925 Dr. Cooper became one of the first three African American women to complete a PhD. It could not be done in the United States; she graduated from the Sorbonne in Paris. Her dissertation was titled "L'Attitude de la France à l'egard de l'esclavage pendant la Revolution" ("The attitude of France toward slavery during the Revolution"). In it Cooper focused on the Haitian and French revolutions, arguing that France's economic dependence on slavery and its commitment to colonial expansion undermined its egalitarian ideals.

At about the same time that Cooper was publishing her *Voice*, W. E. B. Du Bois was entering Harvard, only the sixth African American ever admitted to the college. It was 1890. While living in Cambridge, he decided to visit the Boston Museum of Natural History. There he came upon a crude exhibit purporting to depict Darwin's theory of evolution. Heavily influenced by the social Darwinism of the time, a profoundly racist and conservative movement, the exhibit was a visual representation of an ascending order of intelligence from the smallest of beings to the most advanced. At the very top was a white, European man and below him, an African man, who appeared just above the apes. Shocked and grieved, Du Bois fled the museum. He describes that moment in the first of his autobiographies, *Dusk of Dawn*, published in 1940.

Like Cooper, Du Bois also saw in slavery a system that debased democracy and undermined America's egalitarian ideals. In his monumental study, *Black Reconstruction in America*, Du Bois described the period following the Civil War (before racial segregation was fully institutionalized in the South) as "the finest effort to achieve democracy for the working millions which this world had ever seen" ([1935] 1998). And he wrote that the shibboleth of race was used to divide poor whites from their black counterparts, allowing the former slaveholders and plantation owners to reassert their stranglehold on the political economy of the South. Our country has struggled with the consequences of this ultimate betrayal of Reconstruction for more than a century and a half and continues to do so today, even with a black president in the White House.

In the face of this history, it is stunning to read the essays in this volume showing the repeated efforts by contemporary white academics, lawyers, and politicians to manipulate statistics and feign liberal intentions while denouncing affirmative action, claiming "reverse discrimination"—as if there even were such a thing—and blaming students of color and women for their presumed "failures." In fact, the people who gained the most from affirmative action by any statistical analysis were white women! And many of the training programs and paths to advancement established by affirmative-action programs benefited white workers as well as people of color. But again, as in previous historical periods, racism was used to divide people, not only white from black but among racialized minorities as well. Asian Americans were seen as the "model minority," "illegal aliens" became a term that divided the Chicano/Hispanic community within itself and from African Americans, and so on.

However, as in any great movement for radical social change, there are many examples of successful pockets of resistance and challenges to this backlash against affirmative action and prodemocracy efforts. For example, back in the mid-1970s, a small organization called SACNAS (Society for the Advancement of Chicanos/Hispanics and Native Americans in the Sciences) was founded. As the story goes, four or five Chicano scientists were attending a national academic conference and found themselves in the same elevator. They joked that if the elevator crashed it would wipe out the presence of Chicanos in the sciences, and they decided then and there to do something about it. SACNAS is, according to its statement of purpose, "a society of scientists dedicated to fostering the success of Hispanic/Chicano and Native American scientists—from college students to professionals—in attaining degrees, careers, and positions of leadership."

From these modest beginnings, SACNAS has grown into a unique national organization. Beginning in junior high schools and high schools through undergraduate and graduate programs, its supporting members, including many white faculty and professionals, mentor hundreds of students a year. SACNAS excludes no one from membership, and many African and Asian American young people, as well as white working-class students, benefit from its mentorship programs and support. In addition, although the sciences are at the core of its programs, there are many of us from the social sciences and humanities who participate. In 2009 SACNAS had a national membership of 3,150. This included 1,600 undergraduates, 600 graduate students, and hundreds of precollege teachers, postdocs, and professionals. There were 3,500 registered participants at its 2010 national conference, which was one of the most inspiring conferences I have ever attended. I witnessed young people growing in enthusiasm, confidence, and self-esteem as they moved among different presentations on all levels of scientific and social inquiry. I marveled again at how resilient human beings are and how little it takes to nurture our young people and provide them with visions of purpose and success.

Despite this history and these inspiring movements, America's public discourse on race often remains entrenched in fear, self-delusion, denial, and cooptation, including the presentations, papers, and essays by some very powerful academics and politicians. Some, who even declare themselves liberals or feminists, continue to deny every statistical, sociological, and political study of actual, verifiable discrimination based on race and/or gender. It is truly mind-boggling arrogance and ignorance. The contributors to this volume—each in her own way—analyze, dispute, challenge, and rouse us to resist in every way we can. Their work brings us to new levels of understanding about how insidious racism and sexism are, its workings in daily life, and the ways in which we may more effectively and joyfully persevere.

Bettina Aptheker

INTRODUCTION

Angela P. Harris and Carmen G. González

As editors who are also women faculty of color, we produced this volume to provide a framework for understanding the contradictory culture of academia. On the one hand, the university champions meritocracy, encourages free expression and the search for truth, and prizes the creation of neutral and objective knowledge for the betterment of society—values that are supposed to make race and gender identities irrelevant. On the other hand, women of color too frequently find themselves "presumed incompetent" as scholars, teachers, and participants in academic governance. The essays collected in this volume examine the ways that higher education reflects and reproduces—yet also sometimes subverts—the social hierarchies that pervade American society, including race, gender, class, and sexuality.

The United States continues to be a nation profoundly marked by racial, gender and economic inequality. The US has among the highest levels of income inequality in the developed world and the lowest rates of upward mobility (Massey 2008; Herz 2006; Scott and Leonhardt 2005; Keister 2000; Schor 1992). Notwithstanding the accomplishments of the social movements of the 1960s and 1970s, white women and people of color continue to experience covert and unconscious bias in the job market that depresses earnings and restricts social mobility (Tsang and Dietz 2001; Castilla 2008; Lempert 2010). Recent studies confirm pervasive bias against people of color in employment, housing, credit, and consumer markets (Massey 2008; Pager and Shepherd 2008).

Despite this evidence of persistent inequality, the belief in meritocracy and the narrative of upward mobility through hard work and self-sacrifice continue to serve as defining national myths (Delgado 2007; Hochschild 1996). Higher education, in particular, is widely regarded as the ticket to social advancement. Higher education exerts a powerful pull on the American imagination. Armed with studies showing that college graduates have far higher incomes than those who only hold a high school diploma or less, policy makers frequently exhort young people to earn a college degree (Gates Foundation 2010). Education and nondegree training programs are similarly urged upon older workers as a solution to unemployment and underemployment. And education is not only an individual advancement strategy. An educated, skilled workforce, we are told, is essential to sustain corporate investment in US research and development and prevent capital flight in a fully globalized economy. Thus, higher education is deemed essential in the United States for economic advancement and success, both individual and national (Lewin 2010b).

However, a large body of social science research indicates that higher education is not immune from the inequities that plague the rest of American society. Most of this research focuses on the experiences and outcomes of college and university students and indicates that Latino/a, African American, and Native American students have lower rates of college enrollment and retention than white students. The National Center for Education Statistics, for example, reports that in 2001–2, Asians/ Pacific Islanders had the highest six-year graduation rate, followed by whites, Hispanics, blacks, and American Indians/Alaska Natives. Approximately 67 percent of Asians/Pacific Islanders, compared with 60 percent of whites, 48 percent of Hispanics, 42 percent of blacks, and 40 percent of American Indians/Alaska Natives graduated with a bachelor's degree or its equivalent within six years (National Center for Education Statistics 2010). Underrepresented students of color also report higher levels of stress and anxiety, caused partly by straitened economic circumstances and partly by the alienating environment of predominantly white institutions (Schwitzer et al. 1999). For many students from a working-class or impoverished background, whether they are students of color or not, college and graduate school is a mystifying—even hostile—place, full of opaque cultural codes and academic challenges for which they are poorly prepared (Terenzini, Cabrera, and Bernal 2001). Finally, for students of color, racism in the form of daily "microaggressions" is another constant concern (Solórzano, Ceja, and Yosso 2000). As psychologist Claude Steele's research indicates, for instance, even the fear that one will be judged according to extant stereotypes can depress academic performance (Steele 1997).

Although full-time, tenure-track faculty at US colleges and universities have been less well studied, at first glance they would seem to have little to complain about. These academic workers have reached the top of the privilege and status hierarchy. Although the ivory tower itself is under assault from the same economic and social pressures that have made so many American jobs increasingly precarious—an issue to which we return later—by all external measures, full-time faculty enjoy levels of autonomy, prestige, and economic reward that are unusual indeed.

This book demonstrates, however, that the women of color who have managed to enter the rarefied halls of academe as full-time faculty find themselves in a peculiar situation. Despite their undeniable privilege, women of color faculty members are entrenched in byzantine patterns of race, gender, and class hierarchy that confound popular narratives about meritocracy. Far from being above the fray, faculty at institutions of higher education are immersed in the daunting inequities and painful struggles taking place throughout an increasingly multicultural America.

For many women of color on college and university campuses, the problems begin with numerical representation. While the nation's student population is becoming increasingly diverse, the overwhelming majority of full-time faculty positions continue to be filled by white men and women. From 1997 to 2007, for example, the percentage of students of color enrolled in US colleges and universities climbed from 25 to 30 percent (Ryu 2010). However, the percentage of full-time faculty positions held by people of color increased only slightly—from 13 percent in 1997 to 17 percent in 2007 (Ryu 2010). Women of color, in particular, continue to be underrepresented. In 2007, women of color held only 7.5 percent of full-time faculty positions. Moreover, the percentage of women of color declined steadily with rising academic rank. Women of color comprised 10.4 percent of instructors and lecturers, 9.9 percent of assistant professors, 6.6 percent of associate professors, and only

3.4 percent of full professors (Ryu 2010). In addition to being concentrated in the lower academic ranks, women of color are also overrepresented in less prestigious academic institutions, such as community colleges (Jayakumar et al. 2009; National Center for Education Statistics 2009).

These statistics, however, tell only part of the story. Although quantitative data and statistical measurements are crucial in understanding the experiences of women of color in academia, we have made the choice in this volume to focus instead on personal stories and qualitative empirical data, such as surveys and interviews. In our view, qualitative research is particularly important in the investigation of social hierarchies. As feminist scholars and those in the critical race theory tradition have established, personal stories may bridge the epistemological gap that frequently appears between the lives of people with a particular privilege and those who lack that privilege (Delgado 1989; Montoya 1994). Storytelling by individuals, when done well, packs an emotional punch and provides the psychological detail necessary to understand a person with very different life experiences (Delgado 1989). Qualitative empirical research, in similar fashion, creates a frame in which to interpret the quantitative data. The narratives collected in this volume reveal that not only the demographics but the culture of academia is distinctly white, heterosexual, and middle- and upper-middle-class. Those who differ from this norm find themselves, to a greater or lesser degree, "presumed incompetent" by students, colleagues, and administrators.

The essays collected in this volume explore the presumption of incompetence through a series of interrelated themes that place the contradictory predicament of women of color faculty in a larger historical and cultural perspective. One of these themes is the negotiation of identity in the academic world—the privileges and challenges that arise from the intersections of race, gender, class, and other claimed and assigned identities. These essays illustrate what critical race theorists have called "working identity" (Carbado and Gulati 2000b; Houh 2006; Onwuachi-Willig 2007; Yoshino 2006). Social identities are not static but emerge in the context of interaction. And in the field of everyday interaction, identity performances may clash with stereotypes and expectations held by others (Carbado and Gulati 2000b).

Thus, students want their black women professors to be more "motherly." White faculty may feel comfortable learning salsa with their Latina colleague or treating her like the maid, nanny, or secretary who ministers to their personal needs. Yet faculty and students of all ethnicities and genders may feel threatened when their colored female colleague acts like a serious intellectual rather than a mascot, cheerleader, or seductress (Pleck 1990). When an academic woman of color's behavior thwarts expectations, the result may be what Peggy Davis calls *microaggressions* (P. Davis 1989): subtle or blatant attempts at punishing the unexpected behavior. These pages are filled with stories of microaggressions and responses to them, including attempts by the person disciplined to accommodate, resist, or perform a kind of jiu-jitsu with others' demands. In the process, the faculty member in question may find herself embracing a new identity, clinging tenaciously to an old one, or some combination of both (Carbado and Gulati 2000b). Or the result may be a subtle and complicated palimpsest of identity as new identifications are written over old ones.

These identity performances take place against a backdrop of institutional privilege and subordination. The obvious dimensions of structural injustice include race, gender, class, and sexuality (and we could add disability, not represented in this volume). The contributors to this book find themselves disciplined by colleagues, students, or administrators whenever their assigned and/or claimed identities do not match cultural stereotypes. As the cognitive psychology literature explains, unconscious bias plays a part in the way teachers and students are perceived by others (Chang and Davis 2010). Given a climate of shared cultural stereotypes and images, it is not surprising that although each of these stories is unique, the authors also describe strikingly similar barriers to their success.

However, just as every unhappy family is unhappy in its own way (as Tolstoy wrote), each workplace structured by caste has unique features. In the academic workplace, judgments of worth tend to be extremely subjective. Reputation is the coin of the realm, and reputations are built not only by objective accomplishments but through images and sometimes outright fantasies—individual or collective—that cling to the nature of the work and the person being evaluated. Academic judgments, then, are especially susceptible to unconscious bias, although the precise forms this bias takes varies from one institution to another.

This point brings us to a second theme that connects these essays: the link between agency and structure, the individual and the collective. As feminist consciousness-raising groups recognized long ago, the personal is political. Predominantly white and male employment and educational institutions systematically disfavor women of color, not solely through individual bias but as part of larger systems of education, employment, media, and other civil society institutions that perpetuate and extend the privileges created by group subordination. It is important, then, to read even the most seemingly personal stories in this collection as symptomatic of a larger, structural problem, rather than solely the issues of any one woman or department, college, or campus.

A third theme raised in many of the essays in this volume is the nature of academic culture itself. Academia, as a legion of satirical novels has pointed out, has its own culture in which certain faculty qualities and attitudes—brilliance, rigor, seriousness, rationality, objectivity—are greatly prized. The origin of academia's reverence for these qualities can be traced back to the birth of the scientific method. As scholars of the university have noted, the campus has had a long love affair with science or, perhaps more accurately, with the idea of science. Within the pecking order of the university, the most valued pursuits are those that most easily claim rigor, objectivity, and, these days, technocratic mastery. Thus, there has been a long struggle between the sciences and the humanities, and within the sciences, between the "hard" and "soft" ones. The qualities that are valued in scholarly endeavor are also esteemed in professional life. Research universities are more prestigious than teaching ones; research is valued over teaching at nearly all universities, and teaching is valued more than community service (Wisniewski, Ducharme, and Agne 1989). Among researchers and scholars, the romance of the brilliant, lonely genius in pursuit of Truth—even if the heavens should fall—still lingers around promotion reviews.

These revered characteristics, however, are not only associated with the hard sciences. They are also traditionally linked with masculinity and are understood as the opposite of femininity. For instance, rationality is prized at the expense of recognizing—or being able to deal with—emotion (Harris and Shultz 1993). On every campus, tasks associated with femininity—such as teaching—are valued less than those associated with masculinity, and the most prestigious disciplines are those with the fewest women. This means not only that people with female bodies or feminine self-presentations are likely to be excluded from certain disciplines or understood as inferior. It also means that the disciplines themselves—forms of knowledge and the methods of producing them—are understood and pursued in gendered terms (McCloskey 1998; Keller 1983; Resnik 1989–90). Methods of knowledge production that do not fit the model of the brilliant genius who works alone and possesses learning inaccessible to the masses, such as participatory action research, are marginalized or actively denigrated. And methods of knowledge production that challenge the idea of value-free academic inquiry are bitterly attacked. For instance, in the 1980s in the discipline of law, a storytelling movement pursued by critical race theorists drew harsh (one might say hysterical) criticism because of its departure from the norms of objectivity and neutrality (Farber and Sherry 1993).

Racial hierarchy also pervades the history of academic culture, although its influence is harder to see. Scholars in the hard sciences often protest that their work is value neutral and politics-free and, therefore, that questions of social hierarchy and caste are irrelevant. The history of science, however, shows this is not the case. One need not take up the extreme claim that there is no such thing as objective truth to see that cultural, social, and political interests shape what people investigate and, therefore, what they find (Blackburn 2005). For example, from their inception, Western scholarly disciplines as distinct as geology, botany, and tropical medicine flourished, to a great degree, in service of Europe's colonial enterprise. These disciplines enabled Europeans to exploit the mineral riches of the colonies, profitably cultivate tropical cash crops in far-flung colonial plantations, and protect the colonizers from the ravages of tropical disease (McNeill 2010; McClellan 2010; Brockway 2002; Drayton 2000). Meanwhile, the so-called natives were pronounced uncivilized and stripped of their natural resources in the name of scientific conservation or sustainable resource extraction (Drayton 2000; Harding 1998). This, of course, does not make tropical medicine and botany false. It does mean, however, that political interest shapes scientific knowledge in subtle and occasionally blatant ways.

Again, the issue is not only the use of scientific knowledge for political ends. Nor is it only the exclusion of people of color from the ranks of those engaged in the pursuit of scientific knowledge. What is insidiously troubling about Western intellectual culture is its espousal of "value-free science" to mask the ways that the idea of pure and interest-free truth has been and continues to be used to perpetuate unjust social hierarchies. Perhaps the most obvious example is the scientific literature on race. Stephen Jay Gould, in his book *The Mismeasure of Man,* skillfully shows how leading scientists in the late nineteenth century produced scholarship that was woefully deficient, even by its own standards, yet remained highly regarded because it confirmed the prejudices Anglo-Europeans held about white supremacy and black inferiority (Gould 1981).

As we move further into the twenty-first century, these debates about whether and under what conditions knowledge can be value free may be overshadowed by changes in the institution of the university itself. Many scholars argue that American colleges and universities today, influenced by neoliberal ideology and struggling with financial burdens, have embraced corporatization (Nussbaum 2010; Slaughter and Rhoades 2004; Washburn 2006; C. Nelson 2010; Nelson and Watt 2004; Giroux 2009; Saunders 2010; Johnson, Kavanagh, and Mattson 2003; Bok 2003). Features of this corporatization include closer and more explicit partnerships, especially in the hard sciences, with private industry; the adoption of business models for university governance (including the move to abolish tenure), instead of traditional shared governance; and a focus on short-term financial returns, which privileges revenue-generating ventures in business, science, and engineering, over disciplines like the humanities and the arts that do not generally generate profit.

The corporatization of the university has also facilitated a marked shift in the academic labor market away from full-time, tenure-track positions and toward contingent labor, including greater reliance on adjunct and part-time faculty and graduate students for teaching. Data collected by the American Association of University Professors (AAUP) from the period including the 2008 recession reveal a telling pattern in full-time appointments: the total number of faculty members grew, but most of the new appointments were in non-tenure-track positions. Just in the two years between 2007 and 2009, the growth in full-time, non-tenure-track and part-time faculty positions outstripped the increase in tenure-track jobs (American Association of University Professors 2010–11). According to federal data analyzed by the AAUP, graduate student employees and faculty members serving in contingent appointments made up more than 75 percent of the total instructional staff in 2009. These trends suggest that the market for full-time, tenure-track academic work may become a winner-take-all market, with a handful of academic superstars at the top and an enormous underclass for whom academia is a classic "bad job," featuring low pay, few or no benefits, and low job security or input into shaping the rules that govern one's working life. The data also suggest that women of color are likely to be disproportionately represented at the bottom, exacerbating the presumption of incompetence.

The advancing corporatization of the academy also presages a number of cultural changes that may adversely affect women faculty of color. Colleges reportedly are coming to treat their students more and more like customers, and arguably students have adopted that attitude for themselves, coming to higher education to buy the commodity of credentials, rather than to learn (of course, it is not clear there ever was a golden age when most students did come to learn!) (Giroux 2009; Saunders 2010). It is possible that this shift will also exacerbate the presumption of incompetence by encouraging the disciplining (through poor evaluations or micro-aggressions) of faculty members whose identities, authority, insights, pedagogical approaches, and/or failure to conform to stereotyped expectations challenge entrenched racial, gender, class, or other hierarchies. If academic women become service workers who must please, rather than educate, their students, their career advancement will likely be determined to a greater extent than before by their ratings on "customer service" evaluations.

A 2009 study conducted by researchers at the universities of Wisconsin–Milwaukee, British Columbia, Michigan, and Washington and at the US Military Academy at West Point highlights the pitfalls of this service worker model. The researchers found that volunteers who viewed videos featuring a black male, a white female, or a white male playing the role of a bookstore employee assisting a customer consistently rated the performance of the white male as superior even though the actors in the video read the same script, performed the same tasks, and were filmed in the same location. This preference for white males was exhibited by white men and women viewers as well as viewers of color of both sexes. Surveys of patient satisfaction with the performance of doctors and customer satisfaction with country clubs belonging to a large hospitality company revealed the same bias (Hekman et al. 2010). The results of this study bode ill for female academics of color.

A fourth theme in these essays is mechanisms for change. The restrictiveness of American academic culture has its origins in the history of American education. The nation's most prestigious universities were not established to educate women, people of color, or the working class. On the contrary, they were designed to serve the interests of wealthy white men (Karabel 2006; Saunders 2010). Not until the decades following the Second World War did social movements, federal legislation, judicial decisions, and presidential decrees pry open the doors of the nation's universities to large numbers of women, people of color, and members of the working class (Brubacher and Rudy 1997). While many of the formal barriers have been lifted, academic institutions remain, at their core, profoundly inhospitable to the experiences and points of view of those formerly excluded. The Third World Feminist movement of the 1970s on college campuses around the country succeeded in planting women's studies and ethnic studies departments where there had been none (Hu-DeHart 1993; Sandoval 2000). Yet, in the end, the values that animated the founding of these departments were at least partly eclipsed by the larger culture of the university.

Regrettably, the culture of academia overall remains not only remarkably blind to its own flaws, but deeply invested in a thoroughgoing denial. Most faculty of color on predominantly white campuses, if they have worked for more than a year or so, are familiar with the committee appointed to investigate diversity concerns. Such committees tend to spring up like mushrooms after a rain in the wake of racist incidents and create files of paper that are then stored until the next scandal. The culture of academia, ultimately, is impervious to change because its power structure is designed to reproduce itself. Here we return to our first theme: the links among race, gender, sexuality, and class. When the people in power receive a mandate to search out excellence, the first place they look is to people like themselves, and too often that is also where the search ends. Social science literature, for instance, abounds with studies demonstrating that "employers assign higher subjective ratings to male or white employees than they do to women or minorities with comparable work records" (Merritt and Reskin 1997, 229 n. 98).

In addition to underscoring the need for meaningful structural change, these essays highlight the need for individual women of color to recognize and honor the connections among body, mind, culture, and spirit—connections that are denied by the rationalist and masculine-dominated culture of the academy—to survive and thrive in a hostile academic environment. The women who tell their stories in this collection individually and collectively experience physiological and psychic effects from being presumed incompetent. Mounting public health evidence suggests that chronic stress—like the pressure of being continually misperceived or belittled or having to fight off microaggressions—can result in higher levels of hypertension, cardiovascular disease, and coronary heart disease (Lewis 2006; Lepore 2006; Peters 2006). At a subtler level, the antiracist psychiatrist Frantz Fanon wrote decades ago about the psychic strain white supremacy places on people of color (Fanon 1967). More recently, Patricia Williams has described the effects of constant racist belittling as "spirit-murder" (P. Williams 1991).

Within academic culture with its masculine bent, there is no easy way to articulate or deal with the emotional, the psychic, or the spiritual. Many of the authors in this collection, however, have developed resources for naming their wounds and healing them, including friendship, alliances, and poetry. Similarly, some of the authors in this collection have found ways of combating the relentless individualism of academic culture to reclaim community and solidarity in their professional and personal lives.

The remainder of this introduction provides an overview of the essays in this book. It also discusses the "silences" within this collection—the stories that women of color shared with us about their experiences in academia but, for various reasons, decided not to publish at this time.

Part I: General Campus Climate

The articles in Part I lay the book's foundation by examining—from a variety of perspectives—the ways that academic institutions create an inhospitable climate for women faculty of color. The authors analyze the dissonance between the intersecting identities of women of color (including gender, race, ethnicity, nationality, and class) and academia's white, male, middle- and upper-class, heterosexual norms. Through personal narratives, interviews, and traditional academic research, these authors describe and explain how cultural stereotypes distort the ways women faculty of color are perceived, evaluated, and treated by students, colleagues, and administrators. The problem often begins during hiring when unconscious bias triggers greater scrutiny of the presumptively incompetent applicants of color while the flaws of white male applicants are minimized or disregarded. Women of color must perform their social identities carefully and selectively to avoid being criticized, marginalized, dismissed, or rejected by colleagues and students. This performance may be particularly treacherous for women teaching or writing in disciplines (such as ethnic studies and women's studies) that challenge dominant ideas about equal opportunity. The essays lament that white faculty and administrators, despite personal and institutional commitments to social justice, often fail to recognize or address the demoralizing and potentially career-threatening microaggressions that routinely confront women faculty of color. This denial is particularly troubling to the extent that the increasing commercialization of higher education encourages students to see themselves as customers and treat their professors as service workers who must cater to their needs and preferences. As the authors explain, hiring additional faculty of color is necessary but does not solve the problem. Rather, what is required is transforming academic culture so that it welcomes and embraces those who are currently regarded as "other" and increases the opportunity for alternative points of view to challenge dominant ideologies and deep-rooted social hierarchies.

Part II: Faculty-Student Relationships

Part II examines faculty-student relationships, specifically the social environment of aspiring academics and the challenges that women faculty of color experience in the classroom. These authors analyze the obstacles that female students of color must overcome to enter the professorial ranks, including lack of mentoring or encouragement, the need to counter negative stereotypes, and the presumption that they were admitted to competitive academic programs or hired as faculty only because of their race and gender. In addition, women from working-class or impoverished backgrounds often struggle with the disorientation associated with stepping into middle- and upper-class working environments and the nagging sense that they have abandoned their communities of origin or "sold out." The authors also explore the experiences of junior faculty as they find their voices in the classroom, grapple with student demands and expectations (including the internalization of racial, class, and gender stereotypes by their students of color), and experiment with novel pedagogical strategies designed to transform conventional approaches to the study of race and gender. Finally, the essays examine gender and racial bias in teaching evaluations and the procedures that might ameliorate this bias.

Part III: Networks of Allies

The articles in Part III examine the supportive (and not-so-supportive) relationships that academic women of color form at work. The research indicates that building networks is crucial to professional success in academia. These essays suggest that allies are also essential for individual well-being and the work of making the campus climate more hospitable for women faculty of color. At the same time, building networks on campus can be challenging for academics. The authors in this part identify two broad challenges to building networks. The first is institutional—the structure and culture of academia. As graduate students, women of color may be hesitant to establish strong relationships with junior faculty, who may share their interests but also may lack the power to mentor them effectively or may not receive tenure. When women of color enter the ranks of junior faculty, their challenge is to overcome the competitive nature of academia. Establishing relationships of openness and trust is crucial, these authors suggest, even if it means violating norms of secrecy around issues like salary and perks. Racial solidarity can help establish this openness and trust, but the authors also note that even in a racially homogenous group, hierarchies of status connected with the rank of the school or role within the institution (tenured versus untenured, for example) may appear. Joint appointments raise another kind of institutional challenge to, and opportunity for, networking. Participation in two departments can facilitate network building, but it can also place intolerable demands on a faculty member's time and energy.

The second broad challenge to building networks for academic women of color is overcoming social privilege. Several of the essays, for instance, address the issue of organizing as women. Organizing and supporting one another as women faculty members requires white women to identify and work through their racial privilege. Another, more subtle issue related to privilege is being the first or the only person of one's community in academia. This position brings with it the heavy burden of needing to serve a specific community without becoming overwhelmed by the demands for one's time and attention.

Part IV: Social Class in Academia

The essays in Part IV, "Social Class in Academia," analyze class consciousness and bias in higher education. Women from the lower or working class face enormous obstacles in the academy, due not only to material deprivation but also to the alienation of working-class academics from their origins and native communities. These academics face enormous pressures to pass as middle- or upper-class, and they must carefully evaluate the potential repercussions of "coming out" as working class— much like the risks of coming out as gay in the larger society.

The essays analyze the ways that race, class, and gender reinforce the marginalized status of women faculty of color. For example, these authors examine the condescension that characterizes the way white faculty and other diasporic immigrant academics treat American-born or American-raised Latinas because of their families' actual or presumed lower-class origins. Another manifestation of class and racial bias is the preferential treatment some white faculty and administrators give middle- and upper-class Asian American and elite Indian, African, and Latin American immigrant faculty at the expense of "presumptively incompetent" US–raised Latinas and African Americans thought to come from the working class. Finally, as anti-immigrant hysteria sweeps the nation, Latinas are vulnerable to being perceived as "illegal aliens" and linguistic traitors and may face not only marginalization in academia but verbal and physical harassment by students. These essays present a sobering account of the intersections of race, class, and gender for academics from the working class.

Part V: Tenure and Promotion

The articles in the fifth part, "Tenure and Promotion," are among the most gripping in the book. Here, in a series of often harrowing personal narratives, women faculty of color tell candid stories about their own paths to tenure and beyond. Although each woman's story is different—a common saying in academia is that "all tenure is local"—some disturbing connections are evident. These women faculty of color experience academia as a foreign space and wonder whether they really belong there, despite their qualifications. Self-doubt and shame are constant threats. These essays also suggest that women faculty of color too often face belittling, sometimes openly racist, comments about their qualifications, their activities, and their research, especially when that research involves race and/or gender. According to these authors, women faculty of color are overburdened with externally—and internally—imposed demands that they do everything better than their colleagues, and they are also singled out to fulfill special demands, such as being the "face of diversity" for their departments or campuses or mentoring all students of color.

These essays also reveal the workings of aversive racism in academic institutions. Many of the women who tell their stories in this section were hired, promoted, and given or denied tenure in ways that violated normal campus procedure. Hostile white colleagues, in some of these accounts, went to great lengths to sabotage the women they felt did not belong in their institution. Also destructive were those colleagues who professed support for the professor under fire but encouraged her to accede to unreasonable demands to appease the attackers or leave the institution "for her own good." In an environment where great lip service is given to diversity and federal affirmative-action policies apply, overt racism is discouraged. Therefore, battles over racial and gender hierarchy are fought through individual women's bodies and minds.

The essays in this section, however, are not only shocking and sad. They are also filled with humor, wisdom, and inspiration as the authors draw insights from their own experiences and give advice to those still walking the path through hiring to tenure. These essays are also filled with the hope and faith that solidarity among women faculty of color and their allies will ease the way for the next generation of academics.

A Note on the Silences Shouting from Within
This Anthology

One of the most telling experiences that we, the editors, had concerns the essays that are not in this collection. Although the essays included are rich, varied, and multilayered, many women who responded to our call for papers expressed enthusiasm for *Presumed Incompetent* coupled with reservations about contributing. Some of these potential contributors finally decided not to have their experiences included for several reasons.

First, some would-be contributors felt too wounded spiritually and psychologically to write about their experiences. Several women asserted that it would take years to fully process the covert and overt acts of hostility that they encountered on a regular basis from students, colleagues, and administrators. Many women described stress-related physical and psychological symptoms and disorders, including high blood pressure, asthma attacks, autoimmune disorders, significant weight gain, depression, post-traumatic stress disorder, and cancer.

Second, a significant number of women decided not to contribute to the anthology for fear of retaliation. They believed that they would be penalized for airing their home institution's dirty laundry in public, and they were not prepared to become pariahs. One woman felt that writing about her experiences would not only burn bridges at her current institution but also undermine her future career prospects. She described the vilification and rejection that her home institution had lavished on a highly qualified applicant who had published an article detailing the bias she had experienced as a woman of color at another university. Rather than being moved by the applicant's gut-wrenching tale, her prospective colleagues dismissed the narrative as a fabrication, and declined to hire her.

Third, many women believed the problems they encountered at their home institutions were part of a pattern or practice experienced by many others. In their view, it was impossible to write about their individual experiences without disclosing the experiences of others. Unwilling to publicly embarrass colleagues already burdened by institutional inequities, these women informed us that they could not participate, even anonymously.

Fourth, several women reported that trusted mentors had warned them that publishing an essay based on personal experience would be regarded as "un-intellectual" and would subject them to personal and professional ridicule. Several potential contributors hold prominent positions in university administration and public service in addition to their accomplishments as teachers and scholars. They informed us that describing their personal experiences in academia would harm them professionally and impede their efforts to create opportunities for students and colleagues. Sadly, for these would-be contributors the price of individual success was, apparently, silence about the ways in which academic attitudes and institutional practices reproduce hierarchies of race, gender, and class.

Fifth, a number of women expressed apprehension about writing in an area outside their professional specialization. These potential contributors explained that they were trained to do analytical work in their respective disciplines but lacked the requisite theoretical background to examine fully the complex ways that race, gender, sexual orientation, and class had shaped their professional lives. Other women—under constant pressure to prove themselves in their academic disciplines and overwhelmed by service obligations as the representative of color on multiple university committees—simply decided they could not afford to devote the necessary time and effort to this project.

Sixth, many women privately told us their stories in great detail but declined to put them in print to avoid exacerbating already tense and fractured professional relationships at their home institutions. For instance, several of these women reported having been recruited by prominent liberals who seemed genuinely excited at the prospect of increasing the diversity of experiences and perspectives at their universities and who offered mentorship and support. However, after the women's arrival these faculty members treated their protégées in a condescending manner—boasting about how much they had done to help the women succeed, taking credit for their accomplishments, and/or publicly expressing worries about whether they could satisfy the university's promotion and tenure requirements. In addition, a few women reported that they were penalized when they expressed opinions that diverged from those of their patrons. Stunned at being cast in the role of charity recipients by colleagues they had regarded as supporters, these women declined to contribute until they could figure out how to do it in a manner that would prompt self-reflection, rather than defensiveness, from their misguided "benefactors."

Seventh, a few women feared that making their stories public would undermine fragile coalitions among faculty of color in their department by exposing the complicity of certain colleagues in perpetuating the presumption of incompetence. For example, stories like this one emerged, which we couch in general terms to protect confidentiality:

> A troubling pattern that plagues many educational institutions is the tendency of faculty and administrators to adopt a faculty member of color as the official pet or mascot. The pet may be a key administrator's personal favorite, who serves as the official spokesperson for all faculty of color. She may be the "exceptional" woman of color whose accomplishments (real or imagined) or compliant attitude put other faculty of color in a negative light. In public, the pet makes a dramatic display of her selfless efforts to support colleagues of color. In private, the pet is harshly critical of the teaching and scholarship of these same colleagues, thereby reinforcing the race- and gender-based presumption of incompetence.

As this narrative suggests, academic institutions may pit faculty of color against one another by bestowing lavish rewards on one faculty member to avoid accusations of racism when they denigrate another. This behavior is consistent with broader societal patterns. As Richard Delgado observes, when racialized groups coexist in a particular location, whites often maintain racial hierarchies by giving one group preferential treatment at the expense of those less favored (Delgado 1999). Regrettably, some members of the favored group, including those who describe themselves as feminists and critical race scholars, may enhance their own status by collaborating in characterizing other faculty of color as inferior. Feeling unable to describe these dynamics without exposing other women of color, many potential contributors opted for silence.

Eighth and relatedly, several women declined to participate because their stories raise uncomfortable questions about what will happen as faculty of color achieve critical mass in higher education. Will they reproduce the dysfunctional racial and gender hierarchies of predominantly white institutions, or establish a new paradigm? In a handful of institutions where faculty of color have achieved critical mass, women faculty of color reported that the internalization of long-standing societal norms has simply reconfigured the racial and gender hierarchy, rather than eliminating it. In other words, the dominant racial group subordinates other racialized groups—often in alliance with white faculty, who continue to enjoy high status. Women of color remain at the bottom of such hierarchies and may even be worse off than in majority-white institutions because they feel unable or unwilling to denounce oppressors who also happen to be people of color. One woman described this situation as "the Anita Hill paradox at the institutional level." Institutional transformation therefore requires that all faculty—white and of color—acknowledge and demolish conscious and unconscious biases, rather than replicate divisive survival strategies of the past.

Finally, several women felt that their experiences in academia, though personally challenging, had been relatively benign in comparison to those of friends and colleagues in other departments and at other institutions. In some instances, particular women were treated well precisely because their home institution was seeking to overcome its (well deserved) reputation as a hostile environment for women faculty of color. It is important to keep in mind that the essays collected in this anthology reflect a range of experiences and institutional settings, and do not presume to represent the experiences of all women of color in all institutions at all times.

These silences and omissions magnify the importance of the essays in this volume as timely and valuable contributions to our knowledge about the current state of higher education. As a group, these essays add texture and nuance to the big pictures conveyed by empirical research, and provide the intimate details of lived and felt experience that only personal narrative can offer. Moreover, these essays go beyond simply providing a critique. Read together, they yield a multitude of lessons for administrators and faculty, both white and of color. Thus, in the conclusion to this volume, Yolanda Flores Niemann condenses and summarizes these lessons and offers concrete recommendations for moving forward.

A final editorial observation may be necessary regarding the impact of affirmative action on the presumption of incompetence. A popular argument against affirmative action is that it contributes to the stigmatization of those who are its beneficiaries—and even those perceived to be beneficiaries. Certainly the successes of women faculty of color are often met with envious grumbling about affirmative action, and some social science research confirms that white men and others use this rationalization to justify their discomfort about female success (Heilman, Block, and Lucas 1992; Heilman 1996; Krieger 1998). It is conceivable, therefore, that the essays in *Presumed Incompetent* could support the conclusion that affirmative action is damaging those it attempts to help.

However, we do not believe the converse is true—that eliminating affirmative action will erase the presumption of incompetence. Evidence of condescension and belittlement long predates affirmative-action policies in academia. For instance, in the autobiographical book "Having Our Say: The Delany Sisters' First 100 Years," two African American schoolteachers born in 1893 and 1891 relate their experiences of being challenged because of their race despite their qualifications as professionals (Delany and Delany 1997). Nor has the termination of affirmative-action programs in recent years at several universities eliminated the presumption that students of color are less qualified and capable. Indeed, one recent study found that students in states that had abolished affirmative action reported more stigma and hostility than students going to school in states with such programs (Bowen 2010). The stigmatization effect appears to be a complex phenomenon not directly dependent on the presence or absence of affirmative-action programs (Krieger 1998; Bowen 2010).

More importantly, the potentially stigmatizing effects of affirmative action must be weighed against the alternatives. Krieger, surveying the research, concludes that the abolition of affirmative action would significantly reduce the presence of women and people of color by eliminating an important mechanism that compensates for discriminatory disadvantage. Abolishing affirmative action also sends a message to the larger society that racism and sexism have been overcome and that there is no need to examine one's attitudes and behavior for unconscious bias (Merritt 2010). We therefore believe that the benefits of affirmative action far outweigh its drawbacks.

The essays in *Presumed Incompetent* point, finally, toward the Third World Feminist recognition that the business of knowledge production, like the production of tea, spices, and bananas, has an imperialist history that it has never shaken. Inventing the postcolonial university is the task of the twenty-first century. We can only hope that this task of decolonizing American academia is completed before the tenure track itself disappears. Otherwise, scholars in the next century may confront another ironic example of women finally rising in a profession just as it loses its prestige and social value.

Part I

General Campus Climate

INTRODUCTION

Brenda J. Allen

When I told a young black woman faculty member I was writing a foreword for a book about women of color in the academy, her response surprised both of us. She slowly repeated the title—*Presumed Incompetent*—and tears sprang into her eyes. "That was exactly my experience in grad school," she said softly. "You just don't know what I went through," she added as the tears slid down her cheeks. She shook her head from side to side and whispered, "I can't believe how much this still hurts." She then told me a few of the subtle and blatant ways that interactions with her professors and peers exemplified the premise of this book. She hadn't told anyone but her father what she had gone through during grad school.

I was caught off guard because I had served as an external reviewer on her committee, and she had passed her dissertation defense with flying colors. Moreover, she had gotten a tenure-track position at a nearby institution and had recently earned early tenure and promotion. I had no idea of the strife she had endured. I was dismayed to learn about her struggles, even as I was impressed with her resilience. Knowing only too well that her experiences were not at all unusual, I realized more than ever the significance of this book.

I'm sad to report that in the more than thirty years that I've been in higher education, I've met countless other women of color graduate students and faculty members who have shared stories similar to this young woman's. And I've personally experienced moments of presumed incompetence. When I became an assistant professor at a predominantly white university, I was one of only three black women in the tenure track on that campus, along with one Native American female assistant professor and two Latinas. Throughout the years, I watched as women faculty of color came and left for varying reasons usually related to feeling unwelcome. As a communication scholar, I became so intrigued by race and gender dynamics that I began to focus my research and writing on socialization experiences of female graduate students and faculty of color. Their/our experiences seemed to counter theories in my field about the way newcomers "learn the ropes" of their roles in organizations.

Based on interviews with women of color in various academic settings (including an historically black university), I applied a social-constructionist approach to expose and explain inequities based on or related to social identities. I critiqued extant theory, and I developed and disseminated practical insights based on the women's experiences. I developed a body of scholarship that incorporated my experiences and applied theories from organizational-communication studies (see, for example, Allen 1996, 2000, 2011). This area of inquiry fulfilled me much more than my original research focus. Thus, as I came up for tenure, I changed from concentrating on computer-mediated communication to becoming a critical scholar of social identity and organizational communication. I became committed to critical theory's commitments to investigate social conditions and excavate hidden power dynamics, raise consciousness, and explore how and why people comply with—as well as how they and their allies resist—dominant belief systems.

I eventually moved to another campus, where I was promoted to full professor and later became a department chair. Currently I am an associate dean, and one of my areas of responsibilities is faculty development. I also serve as Master Mentor of the Tenure-Track Faculty-Mentoring Program on my campus. From the standpoints of these various roles, I am excited to discern the wonderful gift that this volume offers to higher education.

Presumed Incompetent provides a wealth of information and insight about diverse, yet similar, ways that women of color experience how others judge them unfit for academia. The authors—a rich sample of women of color from across the broad terrain of the academy—eloquently express their lived experiences through provocative personal narratives and qualitative empirical data. They describe and depict complex characteristics and consequences of enacting and negotiating their identities. They expose problems related to being outsiders within[1] that reveal the ubiquitous power of numerous dominant ideologies in US society, including white supremacy, patriarchy, heteronormativity, classism, ethnocentrism, and rationality. Their combined narratives illustrate ways that members of the academy routinely and robotically rely on these prevailing belief systems as they indoctrinate one another into specific roles. Thus, they form a compelling mosaic of higher education as a crucial site of struggle where various groups compete to shape institutional reality to serve and preserve their own interests. They also illuminate macro- and microlevel issues as they detail systemic challenges and unveil everyday nuances of bias and discrimination.

In addition to depicting many of the difficulties that women faculty of color encounter, the authors also describe ways that they and their allies resist power dynamics. They share specific strategies for deconstructing dominant systems that can inspire and empower other women of color while also providing recommendations to our faculty colleagues and administrators. In the concluding chapter, Yolanda Flores Niemann draws upon their narratives and scholarship on tokenism, stereotyping, cultural diversity, and intersectionality to present a detailed overview of lessons learned. She focuses this comprehensive summary on five interrelated aspects of academic life (general campus climate; faculty/student relationships; social class, tokenism, and the search process; tenure and promotion; and networks of allies and mentors) and offers more than a hundred specific recommendations for administrators and women of color.

In conclusion, *Presumed Incompetent* far exceeds the editors' objectives to expose experiences of women faculty of color and suggest remedies for redressing this persistent, prevalent problem. I commend the editors and the authors for their

---

1   Black feminist scholar Patricia Hill Collins (1998) coined this term "to describe social locations or border spaces occupied by groups of unequal power" (p. 5).

courage and indomitable spirits. They have created a viable, valuable resource for *all* current and aspiring faculty and administrators in academia. Anyone who has the privilege of reading this volume will deeply benefit from the wisdom, insight, and practical advice that it offers. *Presumed Incompetent* holds tremendous potential to transform the academy so that no other women of color will experience the indignities that the authors and my young colleague endured. Rather, they will be free to contribute their unique knowledge and perspectives to help higher education meet the demands of our ever-changing world.

Chapter 1

Facing Down the Spooks

Angela Mae Kupenda

Early in my academic career, a white male administrator scolded me during my annual pretenure evaluation. He did not have any problems with my teaching or service or scholarship. The problem he stated was that I did not tell him and my colleagues enough about my personal life. He said I was beginning to be much too private, just like the other woman of color on the faculty. I assured him that my coworkers did know all the relevant information about me. More importantly, they knew at least as much about me as I knew about them. He wanted me to trust them more with the intimate details of my life. I explained that they already knew those details: I was single, had no children, was close to my family and friends, lived a quiet life, was active in my community, attended church, and enjoyed travel, my books, and the arts.

Growing increasingly frustrated, he leaned forward in his chair, looked me straight in the eye, and, with his ordinarily pale face turning red, he yelled, "You must trust us more if you want to succeed here; there are no spooks behind the door!" That night when I recounted this story to one of my best friends, he said I should have replied, "You're right; there are no spooks behind the door because right now the spooks are staring me in the face." I wish I had thought of that retort, but instead I was uncharacteristically speechless.

When I think back now to this experience, I wonder if the white male administrator was thinking of some stereotype that black women—especially perhaps southern ones—are afraid of ghosts and goblins and engage in all types of magic to rid their homes and lives of these pesky creatures. The thing about an imagined, or even real, ghost is that it is not actually blood and bones that you can get your hands on and rid yourself of easily. The belief is that although they are not physically present, ghosts have a haunting power and can appear from anywhere (especially behind doors or under beds) without any notice and at inopportune moments.

As a black female academic with more than twenty years of experience in academia, to tell the truth, ghosts *have* haunted me: the ghosts of Jim Crow; the goblin of slavery-like, white, presumed superiority; and ghouls of sexism, racism, and classism just will not leave me alone! Beneath the surface of seemingly innocent encounters with supposedly well-meaning white administrators or colleagues or students, these ghosts linger and haunt me with words and acts that torture my very soul and keep me from being able to experience academia the way a white male with similar credentials can.

In this chapter, I plan to share with you some of these haunting encounters. I will recount the stories and what people said. Then, together, we will expose and examine the spirits behind the words that leave me struggling daily—even with all my experience—to maintain not only more than competence but also its appearance, yet seem never to receive an automatic presumption of competence because I am an academic who is black, female, southern, and from an economically disadvantaged background.

The Spooks in the Story I've Just Told

Although this story is just the beginning, it is very telling. The white male administrator knowingly or unknowingly seemed to say blacks must be entertaining to have a place with other faculty; they must share private details to appeal to the voyeuristic interest that some whites feel about blacks; and they are always afraid of what may be hiding behind the door. On the other hand, maybe he had just finished reading a book about spooks and did not mean anything, or had heard some rumor about me and wanted to know if it was true. I prefer to think that the more rational explanation is that this evaluation encounter was a visit from the enduring ghost of the slavery and postslavery treatment of black women and that academia is not immune from this ghost haunting its ivory towers.

During slavery black women were not allowed any privacy, not even for their bodies, which were inspected, prodded, used for experiments, and vulgarly displayed for the economic profit of whites. Their innermost parts were available at the whim of the white master for his own personal exploration, even for his sick pleasure. There was no such thing as the crime of rape against a black woman slave; if a crime at all, sexual violence was regarded only as a trespass on the white master's property.

White females, on the contrary, had their bodies cloaked, placed on pedestals, and protected to an oppressive degree. Even if they personally and freely chose to reveal their uncloaked bodies—to black men, for example—such sexual or marital alliances were unlawful and could lead to their black male lover hanging from a tree. Custom as well as law protected white women's privacy. For example, as a girl, I was always amazed that documentaries about countries where black women were commonly topless always showed their full black and brown nakedness, while films about similarly unclothed white women always seemed to cover their most provocative parts. It appears that for a black female academic to choose to protect some aspects of her life as private—not for display to the casual white colleague or administrative observer—is still a radical step. In contrast, the radical step for a white female academic might be to reveal private aspects of her life, especially about her sexuality.

My experiences in the workplace seem to suggest that even in academia, black women have limited choices. One is to tell white colleagues all they want to know and more, to be as comic as these people's misconceptions desire, to represent one's sexuality in a free way that whites may then claim confirms the truth of the lies told during and after slavery that black women are like animals. Following this path is most problematic, though, because whites may then argue that the black female professor's behavior confirms their presumptions that she is not fit for intellectual work, that she is incompetent. Sometimes, even when black females are carefully professional and competent, white colleagues claim they see the black behavior their minds envision because they so want to see it, even when there is little evidence of it.

For example, I mentored a pleasant, black female student who groomed herself very well and was struggling in her classes. One of my white male colleagues would walk back and forth past my office door looking in at us whenever she was there. His obvious, spooky facial expressions greatly disturbed me and made me feel very protective of, and helpless to defend, the young black woman. She took her midterms and did not do exceptionally, but her grades were salvageable. This colleague, who was one of her teachers, came to me one day after I had met with the young woman at length to develop a strategy for her success. He gloated, "That girl who just left your office is not going to pass; she wears her nails too long and pretty to be smart enough to be a lawyer. I know she is going to fail."

I could not believe that he would actually make such a racist/sexist remark and directly to me! After I stopped my neck from jerking around in disbelief of his haunting presence, I told him that his statement revealed some troubling things about him as both a professor and a colleague and he should never repeat what he had said to me or anyone else. Now I had not noticed her fingernails at all, but subsequently I saw that they were well groomed; however, it was nothing like what he was trying to suggest. However, her attempt to be an attractive black woman somehow gave him an excuse to call up this ghost and actually bring it to life with his words and perhaps in grading her papers, too.

A second choice for a black woman is to try to project an image of competence and professionalism. Nevertheless, even then a haunting is inevitable. I made a habit of going to my classes well prepared and organized. Students in my predominantly white male class commented favorably on these and other points. However, the major troubling point they expressed was that they were scared of my face when I was serious as we discussed the law. Many suggested if I came into class and gave them a big, warm smile every morning and continued smiling throughout the class, then perhaps they could accept me—a black female teacher—better. [Today I am embarrassed to admit that when younger, I caved in to their incessant pleas, started smiling more, and even told a few jokes.] The students seemed to like me better, and my class evaluations improved, but unfortunately, I found I had fallen through a trap door that led to one of the most troubling ghosts for a black female academic hoping to become a scholar: the "I want my mammy" ghost.

"I Want My Mammy" Ghosts

As the white students became more and more comfortable with me, I—like any good academic—directed some of my attention to my research and scholarship. Publications and developing a national reputation were critical if I hoped to be promoted and get tenure. The problem for me was a summer program the school had for beginning students who needed a little extra help. I agreed that the program was necessary, but as a beginning instructor, I knew that teaching in the program during the summer would ultimately mean I would not be promoted because I would not be able to devote the summer to my writing the way my white male colleagues who were assistant professors could. Therefore, after discussions with several black and white female teachers far more senior, I painstakingly—in email and then later in person—explained to my white academic dean why I would not be able to take over running the program in my first year on the faculty. I even used some of the language that the far-more-seasoned women faculty had helped me construct. I suggested that if all the professors took a turn teaching during the summer, I would be happy to take mine many summers down the road after all the senior faculty.

He did not like that. He said that some of our colleagues were not good teachers, although he admitted that they made far more money than I did. I then suggested that I could teach in the summer program and have the fall semester off to write. He did not like that proposal, either. That is when the spook really came from behind the door. He said, "We know you are concerned about becoming a scholar and getting tenure, but we can't afford for you to work on your research this summer. . . .We need you to teach all summer. . . .Yes, there are others who can teach and who already have tenure. . .but we need and want you. . . .We need you to teach in the summer program because you are black, you are a woman, you are a great teacher, and you nurture, mother, feed, and nurse all the students."

Years later in evaluating the reply I gave him, I admit I could have been more delicate. However, I had originally been viewed as lacking teaching competence and had struggled to overcome that, and now the only thing needing attention was my scholarship, and I knew that, and he did, too. So I could not restrain myself. I repeated his statement to him word for word. He was nodding in smiling agreement. And then I added, "Listen to what you are describing. . . . You just described a mammy. . . . I guess I will have to be a mammy for you nine months a year, but I will not be a mammy twelve months a year. Three months a year I must try to be a scholar."

In a way, I felt as if I had played a role in awakening the "I want my mammy" ghost and therefore had contributed to my own oppression. I had become a mammylike, fully accessible stereotype to make the white students more comfortable. Moreover, I had done this at great cost to my complete self and my abilities as an academic. I had participated in the séance that called forth the "I want my mammy" ghost.

Subsequently, I was talking with my mother on the phone from work and telling her about my tiring day and about how depleted I felt. She thought for a few minutes, and then she told me that what she was about to say would sound harsh, but it would explain the inner rumblings I felt. She said, "You are so tired because you feel like a clown. You smile when you do not feel like smiling. You bite your tongue and make no sound when you want to speak. You try to make the casual and watchful observers so comfortable with you, but now you are uncomfortable with this false self. You take care of others' feelings, instead of your own."

She was right. The "be my mammy" ghost and "be my clown" ghost are close kin. In both kinds of haunting, black female academics are asked, or required, to focus on presenting a comforting appearance for whites who miss the blacks of the "ole South," those whites who dreamily sing, "I wish I were in Dixie," instead of focusing on their careers as scholars, activists, and teachers. In the slavery—and even postslavery—South, for example, black women were required to place the needs of the white families they worked for over those of their own children. Unfortunately today, black women in the South still face these ghosts. When we try to ignore their ghoulish calling, we may be punished for allegedly lacking collegiality or harboring irrational anger.

I was even punished by a black female student, who insisted I "would be liked more by the white students if I would get a really good perm in my hair," thus looking more familiar. (Interestingly, this black female student did not have a good perm, either.) Black students also endure punishment for adopting hairdos that look unfamiliar to whites. Years later, I went natural with my hair. Then, many years after that, several of my black female students went natural. White classmates accosted them regularly and accused them of joining "Kupenda's agenda" by stopping perming their hair and making themselves look more natural, which the white students felt was unnatural.

Almost as troubling as seeing the rights that others believe they possess to set the boundaries of a black female academic's personal space is the loneliness that academic often feels within the female community at large.

Flying with the White Female Ghosts and Their Disappearing Acts

A junior white female colleague approached me and said, "I know everything you go through because I am a woman, too." I assured her that women do have struggles in academia. However, I told her she has one thing I do not have, and that is her white skin with its automatic, unearned privilege. I reminded her that she seems to count on my support on gender-based issues, but she and some other white females disappear and leave me standing alone on racial or racial/gender-based issues. She said she understood, but that did not stop her disappearing acts.

I am not arguing that black and white female academics cannot be allies and friends; one of my closest friends is a white female who teaches at a historically black school. I am just saying that white females have to avoid disappearing at critical points for a mixed-race female friendship to be real, instead of just an illusion. As I prepared to be reviewed as a nontenured faculty member, I had four conversations that led to my believing that there are usually spooks right behind the door—or inside the door, holding it tightly shut so the black female cannot enter—when a black female professor tries to get a white female colleague to support her on racial issues.

First, when I went to a feminist white female colleague to discuss some issues, she related to me well but confessed she had no personal experience with being a racial minority. However, she did believe that in academia there were active issues of racial and gender oppression. Second, when I talked to a very conservative white female, she angrily declared there were no gender or race problems and that idea was definitely all in my mind. Months later, this same white female tried to get me to be at the forefront of a gender battle. When I reminded her of her earlier remarks, she had a lapse of memory and looked as if she were seeing a ghost. Finally, the feminist white female told me that she would not be there to support me. She said, "You are on your own; we white women can't help you with any of your problems with racism. But it is going to be fun to watch how it all turns out." Fun to watch?! I cannot recall ever watching anyone's battle with sexism, classism, racism, or any other -ism and having fun doing it. What is even more amazing, though, is that this same white female told me that they needed me at that school to help "lead the white women in the battle over sexism." In my academic career, I have often found better support among a few white males.

At the core of the lack of unity between black and white female academics, I think, is that some white females refuse to see race or racism as a real problem. In addition, some refuse to consider that the white female experience is not the only gendered experience among women. One day—after teaching a tense class where I as the teacher was the only black in the room—I retreated to the faculty library to have a cup of strong coffee. A smiling, white female colleague invited herself to join me as I relaxed. She then incessantly urged me to accept her theory that most of the situations I faced at her school were prompted by my gender and not my race. "Admit it," she argued, "you suffer more here because you are a woman and not because you are black!" Wearily I questioned—almost pleading—with her, "How am I to know whether my oppression is because of my race or my gender?" I added, "When people oppress me here or anywhere, I don't generally ask them to clarify whether they are oppressing me because I am female, black, a black female, or a black female from the South." She sighed that she would have to ponder what I had just said. And putting my coffee cup down, I made a mental note to try to relax next time in the privacy of my office.

A number of years ago, several of my white female colleagues obtained information that women as a group were being underpaid compared to male colleagues. At that same time, I had acquired information that I was the lowest-paid faculty member in my division, even lower than those far more junior. My white male supervisor refused to make an equitable adjustment to my salary, first claiming he could not figure out what alteration to make. After I utilized my Ivy League business degree and historically black college finance degree to explain how he could do it, he just flatly refused. He did promise to give me a good percentage raise that he hoped I would keep as quiet as possible. That year the white females wanted all of us to agree to disclose our percentage raises. I explained my issue was about the nonequity of my salary, period. I assured them, though, that if the other women disclosed not only their raises but also their salaries, I would also disclose both of mine. I never received a response as they quietly disappeared.

Although white women and black women professors can do much to create better academic lives for all women, it seems that the ghosts of slavery still keep us at odds with one another. During slavery white women did not have full rights either. Nevertheless, they, as a group, were definitely regarded as human beings, albeit female ones. At times today white women seem to force even their peers into cookie-cutter images. At one school, a very intelligent Jewish woman was interviewed for a position. I privately asked some of the white women why they were not supporting her. Their answer: they did not think she looked enough like the other white women on the faculty, and she seemed a bit too strong for them. I talked with one young, white female for hours about diversity and made a point that—even among white women—different types should be included, for otherwise, white women are discriminating against themselves. She promised me she would think about our conversation.

I was not privy to the meeting, and later I heard that the Jewish woman would not be hired. The sharply dressed young white woman with whom I had talked (who also had told me she had started to wear more makeup and more feminine clothes as she approached her tenure review) told me, "I know you wanted us to be more open and diverse in our hiring. Nevertheless, we will not be extending an offer to the Jewish applicant. In our discussions about her, someone remarked that she is like a Jewish you." I replied to my pleasant white female colleague, "I'm really confused now because surely she should have received an offer if she reminded you of me."

As a black female academic, I learned early on that many white females easily come and go on justice issues. They may enjoy some presumption of competence based on their race as compared to nonwhites. However, in the absence of non-whites to project incompetence onto, this presumption may fizzle away when the question turns to gender. Therefore, as my mother would say, some resort to "throwing a rock and hiding their hand." They look for black women to be at the forefront of the gender issues so that they, as white women, can still benefit and yet be protected by white males who do not regard them as threatening. As a result, building trust is hard, for black females may not know whether their white female colleagues will stand by their side or will disappear and reappear according to their own interests and whims or for their amusement.

"Just Be Our Negro" Ghosts

Many spooks exist in academia, but an equally troubling one, and the last one to be chased in this chapter, is the "just be our Negro" ghost. Perhaps these ghosts are present in almost all workplaces, but they especially rear their scary heads in academic institutions where there is little diversity but people want to pretend that there is more.

My annual evaluation seemed to be going well. I had documented my work and felt quite proud of my accomplishments for that year. At the end of a session that seemed to signal a great direction for the next year and a long-awaited raise, the white male administrator congratulated me, then said he had one little problem to discuss.

I saw the shadows of a ghost developing when he told me that he liked black people and some of his best friends were black. He went from there to remind me that he himself had suggested I attend a black conference to help with my scholarship and had signed the papers approving my funding for the trip. This was true, I acknowledged. Then he said that I was spending too much of my time with people of color. He wanted to show me off more to white people. He tried to assure me that black people would love me, even if I did nothing for or with them. He laughed eerily as he explained that he wanted me to shun black folks and focus on white folks to help my image and that of the school.

Oh no, I was staring in the face of the "just be *our* Negro" ghost. I had seen this ghost before when a previous white male supervisor had brought me newspaper clippings about black people he admired—generally articles about people who often publicly expressed very negative views about other blacks. Now, this ghost had followed me to the academy!

This "just be our Negro" ghost is very complicated. The story I've just told emphasizes the "our" part. Be our Negro means to act in ways some whites deem appropriate for black people to behave: obedient, submissive, and silent unless joking. In other words, this ghost compels, "Do not be a Negro's Negro, and do not be your own Negro." This ghost calls for black females to act solely at the command of and for the pleasure of whites. Moreover, this ghost also calls on a black woman to be labeled "Negro." In other words, this ghost chants, "Don't be black and proud, don't be nationally and internationally a person of color, and certainly don't claim a dual entitled status, as an African American, in the mother continent of Africa and the privileged state of America." This ghost whispers and screams, "Just be our Negro, a pre-civil-rights Negro who knows her place—the one designated for Negro women—and stays in that place."

During my early years of teaching, a big, tall, white male athlete earned a grade below a C in my course. I had tried and tried to help him, but he would not accept any tutoring or extra instruction. When he saw his posted grade, he came and stood over me at my desk demanding a grade change. I stood my petite—at the time—self up and declined to make the grade change, explaining how it had been calculated. My grades were coded and ready for me to walk over to the campus computer system when my white male administrator sent for me. He explained that the white student could lose his scholarship if he did not pass. We discussed several options for the young man, none of which he thought the athlete would find acceptable. The administrator acknowledged that the student had had other grade problems with white professors, but my grade was the one he was choosing to focus on. He pressured me then just to change the grade and give the student an unearned higher mark.

At that point, I placed my coded grades on the administrator's desk and told him that I was not going to do that. However, I said I would give him my grades and he could then do whatever he pleased with them and submit them himself. He jerked his hands from the papers as if he had spotted a ghost and yelled, "That would be breaking the rules, and I could get in trouble." Being a Negro woman in this situation obviously meant that I was supposed to yield to the administrator's pressure, then take the full rap for the trouble when the improper grade change was later revealed.

Black women academics may find themselves compared to romanticized versions of nurturing, mammylike, comic Negro women from the ole South. "Just be our Negro," these ghosts cry. When I was growing up, my own dear mother worked hard as a cook, a maid for white people, and a saleswoman for Avon products. She worked whatever jobs were necessary to get all six of us through school. Her work was honest, but her hope was that we would all obtain our educations and never have to clean the homes of white people for a living, as she had.

Therefore, I thought the letter I received from an older white female who had helped me rather strange. After she helped me, she expressed an interest in our being close friends. I was delighted and reached out to her often. When she became distant and disrespectful, I realized our friendship would never be close and equal, but I remained professionally respectful and appreciative of her. I then received a letter from this white female describing a wall she perceived as dividing us. She went on to tell me that I should be more like Lulu. Lulu had been her black nanny and later her maid for many years, and she was the best Christian the woman had ever met. My white female acquaintance wondered aloud why I could not be just like Lulu for her.

Just as with the first story in this chapter, I was rendered speechless. I am speechless still about what this all means for black female academics and the institutions that employ them. I think the ghosts will fade when—instead of becoming speechless—we identify them for what they are. The more we give voice to a reality that suppresses these illusions, the closer we will move to being able to function together in the real world.

No, the spooks are not behind the door! They are present and dwell in our lives and structures and institutions, in a society that pretends that racism, sexism, and all the other -isms do not exist. Just remember: what we face down cannot harm us.

As a final story, when I was working in an extremely oppressive environment, my sleep was regularly disturbed by dreams of being chased by something scary. When

I told my mother about these fitful dreams and scary characters, she said the next time I had that dream I should make myself acutely aware of their presence, stop running, turn around, and face them down. I did, and these nocturnal creatures went away. I stood up to them in my dreams and also, subsequently, found courage and words to confront them in my nightmarish work situation. Somehow facing them minimized their power over me and enlarged my own power. Therefore, the first step we have to take is that all of us—with courage (which is not the lack of fear but rather action in the face of it)—must begin to admit that the spooks are there and face them down!

CHAPTER 2

WAKING UP TO PRIVILEGE

Intersectionality and Opportunity

Stephanie A. Shields

A metaphor best expresses the way my understanding of white privilege has operated and changed over the years. I think of white privilege as lighting my path of professional development. Over the course of forty years of academic life, I have come to see how this light made travel over the rocky and difficult road possible, how it lit up opportunities at many critical junctions, and how it blinded me to what was just outside my own experience.

Whatever the image or metaphor, I spent much of my career, especially the early years, without seeing the unearned white privilege that has been accorded to me and has buoyed and advanced my professional status. I am a baby boomer and therefore unaccustomed to having anything unique happen to me. Ours is such a huge bulge in the population distribution that I know that if I have had an experience—any experience—I can guarantee that I am not alone. That gives me and my generation a sense that our personal experiences define the norm. Media representation of boomers as a monolithic block obscures the great variety within our generation: early boomers compared to late ones; women of color compared to white women; those who benefited from a growing national economy compared to those who could not. What is normal for one intersectional group is worlds apart from others. The tendency to identify one's own behavior as normative, as we know from much research on social cognition, is quite common. But in the case of white boomers, this belief tends to function like a foundational truth.

I explain my generational profile as a preface to dealing with the challenge that Yolanda Flores Niemann has given me to think through for this chapter. She observes that most white women are extremely uncomfortable distinguishing between the realities of their lives and those of women of color. White women become angry when they use the word "woman," and she interjects, "You mean white women." Yolanda asked me to think about why this happens. What does my position as a senior white woman in the academy help all of us understand about this denial of privilege? I will return to the question later because first I want to describe my own intersectional position and the way it relates to my consciousness of white privilege at specific points in my adult development, location, and place in history.

There are many ways in which I experience unearned privilege—for example, I am able-bodied—but in this essay I want to focus specifically on that bright light of white privilege and the cascade of additional benefits that it has brought me. For much of my life, I have honestly thought about my good fortune without awareness of the central role that race privilege has played in creating the many opportunities I have enjoyed. My awareness of privilege was a simple "how fortunate I am in the universe" view of life. I think it wasn't until the 1980s that I fully grasped that being a member of a particular intersectional group—in this case, white and educated—on its own conveyed a door-opening, step-to-the-front-of-the-line status associated with privilege, particularly the white advantage that I had neither earned nor asked for, yet benefited from.

My experience of both recognizing and not recognizing privilege is, I believe, a feature of being the last generation that was directly told that "you cannot do this because you are a woman." I tell the story in episodes because they reveal, I believe, the way my understanding of intersections of privilege has changed and grown over the years. The first two episodes are set in a stunningly white world, and though any reader would notice this, the fish swimming in the water doesn't. I begin with these episodes because I see them as important points in my journey toward understanding my intersectional position and the role of unacknowledged white privilege in defining that position.

Because intersectionality is central to the way I understand my experience, I want to be clear about how I understand this construct. I subscribe to the idea that social identities are organizing features of social relationships that mutually constitute, reinforce, and naturalize one another (Collins [1993] 2000; Crenshaw 1994b; Nakano Glenn 1999; Anthias and Yuval-Davis 1983). Intersections create both oppression and opportunity (Baca Zinn and Thornton Dill 1996). The white privilege that I focus on here, for example, offers more than avoiding disadvantage or oppression by actually opening up access to rewards, status, and opportunities unavailable to other intersections. While I experience a set of intersections as my individual social identity, those intersections also reflect a complex operation of power relationships among social groups. In other words, intersectionality not only defines who I am as a social individual but also reflects my relative position of power and status because of the social groups that define my identity.

Seeing and Not Seeing Privilege

I was a first-generation college student. I went to college on scholarship and federally funded work-study, and was acutely aware that my working-class background differed from that of most other students at the small, selective, and almost totally white private university I attended. Within that milieu, social class was the axis of privilege. I was grateful for the support of scholarships to be there but didn't see my situation as privileged. Rather, it seemed to me, at the age of eighteen, that I was the happy beneficiary of terrific luck. I was deeply grateful for that luck, but I did not grasp that privilege stood behind it.

My luck was not luck at all but a great social experiment: California's 1960 Master Plan for Higher Education. That investment in higher education extended the privilege of postsecondary education to a broader social and economic class than any state ever had before. Among other features of the plan, the Golden State guaranteed that residents could attend—through scholarships based on need and ability—any accredited college or university in California. The doors of community colleges were free and open to all residents "capable of profiting from the instruction offered" (California Legislature 1973, 33). Indeed, my parents had moved our family to California from Nebraska precisely because of the lure of free college for their four children. In light of higher education's precarious position today, it is almost unbelievable that any state ever made such a commitment.

Privilege, in the form of opportunity for postsecondary education, was extended to a wide swath of the California population and coupled with a commitment to include students from underrepresented groups. Since it was a state program, access to post-high school education fashioned a normal, natural, and desirable goal. Of course, you had to be in a position to grab the opportunity and hold on to it. My high school was no great shakes, but it gave me an adequate enough education to qualify to continue, unlike other students, predominantly those of color, whose high school experience was a barrier, rather than a pathway, to such opportunity. In my own case, the full scholarship offered by the state paid not only my tuition in California but also fees for a transformative year of study abroad in Rome. Unbelievable. Without that support, study outside of the United States would have been completely out of my reach. That a state would pay for an educational opportunity of this kind does not compute in today's political atmosphere. That year abroad changed my life deeply and permanently in a most positive way.

At the time, I knew that that my university education was a great privilege and that I had had to work hard to make it a reality; what I did not see was that women of color from a similar class background to mine would be less likely to be exposed to this opportunity and thus even less likely to enjoy its long-term benefits. Poverty is overrepresented among people of color, so the disproportionate advantage that whites enjoy relative to other racial ethnic groups was further exaggerated. The Master Plan extended the privilege of higher education to many who would never before have had access, yet like another important door-opening social experiment—the post-World War II GI Bill—beneficiaries were disproportionately white, male, and middle class. In the case of the GI Bill—sexist and racist discrimination was built into the legislation, and classist discrimination into its execution (Humes 2006), whereas the Master Plan explicitly rejected potentially discriminatory measures. Nevertheless, groups that had been underrepresented in higher education (rural; poor; women of all race and ethnicities; men of color) remained that way. The ten-year evaluation of the Master Plan soberly pointed out that "our achievements in extending equal access have not met our promises . . . we have made considerable progress [but] equality of opportunity in postsecondary education is still a goal rather than a reality" (California Legislature 1973, 45).

The slogan of the political action committee Emily's List is "Early money is like yeast." The version of the Master Plan open to me was exactly the extra boost, the yeast that made so much more possible down the road. Today I am convinced that this great, life-changing program made my career possible, and that my whiteness and able-bodied status continued to open doors. In these days of the Great Recession and the near collapse of California's economy, the original 1960 Master Plan for Higher Education seems a fantasy, too good ever to have been true. It has been replaced by a system with a much-reduced potential for broad impact. Higher costs to students and fewer sources of scholarships and low-cost loans now create even greater social and economic distance between those who can find a way to higher education and the majority of women and men of color who cannot.

Coming to Terms with (White) Women's Marginalization

One of my clearest recollections from the first weeks of grad school at Penn State is being told that women don't finish the PhD program. Ours was the first graduate cohort in psychology at Penn State where the proportion of women was not limited to two or three in an entering class of fifteen to twenty. Another first-year woman and I were meeting with the faculty member to whom we had been assigned as teaching assistants. As he smoked his pipe, he shared with us his observation that— whatever our ambitions—it was a "fact" that women pretty much all dropped out of grad school.

So Pamela and I decided to get the data. The graduate staff assistant generously pulled out the records for us, and we discovered that women, indeed, dropped out of the program at a high rate. But there was more to the story. Men were highly likely to drop out, too, but 50 percent of two is a lot more noticeable than a comparable percentage of fifteen or more male students. We didn't yet have the construct of "chilly climate" (Sandler, Silverberg, and Hall 1996) or research on tokenism (e.g., Niemann 1999, 2003; Yoder 1985, 2002) to explain what might be going on, but it seemed clear to us that the environment was not conducive to enhancing women's success. We did not think to ask which of the women and men who had dropped out were students of color. And I am not sure that the department would have had that data if we had requested it. The overwhelmingly white context and the clear, in-your-face sexism overwhelmed my capacity to see that the sea change in the department's admissions policy had largely benefited white women.

Our experience as white women in a psychology doctoral program was certainly different than that of women who had begun grad school just two or three years ahead of us. Rhoda Unger (1998) writes about the almost-generational difference of experience that separated cohorts of women who were only a few years apart in age. Half of our class was women, and most of us had already embraced women's liberation. That first year was a watershed for women in the program in many ways. Women grad students, lecturers, and one of the two women faculty members began to meet occasionally.[1] Those meetings led to a graduate seminar on the psychology of women the following year and ultimately to the establishment of a women's studies program.

Change was in the air, and the magnitude of what needed transformation could not be ignored. Carolyn W. Sherif and Ellen Piers were the only tenure-line women in a department of thirty-some all-white faculty.[2] And I recall only three African

---

1   Phyllis W. Berman, then a well-known developmental psychologist and one of several lecturers in the department, initiated this first local activism. Her husband was a tenured professor in another department, but she was a lecturer because Penn State at that time was averse to hiring both members of a couple into tenured positions. Phyllis recruited me to help her invite all women faculty, lecturers, and grad students to meet to discuss "mutual interests as women psychologists" (I still have a copy of that invitation).

2   Carolyn's actual experience was far more difficult than we graduate students could see. In

American grad students and no other women or men of color among the sea of white faculty, staff, and grad student faces. Penn State's location in then all-white rural central Pennsylvania offered no real diversity. Most telling, in my view, is that the department conducted searches for six tenure-line positions that year, and *every one* was filled by a white man. Graduate students were at that time not included in any aspect of the search process—I don't think we understood what had happened until the following fall, when there were six new white male faculty faces. Had that search taken place the following year—once women in the department began to organize—I would like to believe the outcome would have been different.

Working against us in pressing for change was the low proportion of white women and miniscule proportion of women and men of color in the pool of potential faculty applicants. In 1971–72 (the year of that job search), the proportion of PhDs going to women and men of color and white women was only beginning to rise above more than token levels. In 1970 just over 20 percent of the PhDs awarded in psychology went to women (Cynkar 2007). By 2008 70 percent of new PhDs were women (National Science Foundation 2010). In 1978 only 6.8 percent of PhDs awarded in psychology went to women and men of color, and by 2008, the proportion had only increased to 20 percent (Thurgood, Golladay, and Hill 2006; National Science Foundation 2010). (It should be noted that I could not find psychology data reported for gender by racial ethnicity, from either APA or NSF even for recent years.)

I was aware that I occupied a suspect and precarious position in the academic citadel. Yet I had been admitted and saw that I could have an effect. What made us successful was critical mass. Though I don't have the data for the five women in the clinical half of my cohort, of the five women in experimental psychology who started together, four of us completed the PhD program, a huge improvement over women's situations in previous years. Our critical mass and an optimistic belief in opportunity for women made a world of difference in the way our cohort fared; we did not see ourselves as isolated tokens but as the leading edge of a new wave.

Was I aware of my privilege as a woman in this monochromatic world? Absolutely. I was reminded at every turn that I was entering a space where women's entrance had previously been restricted. Was I aware of my privilege as a *white* woman? I am not sure, but I believe I did not fully consider the racial privilege of my position. I believe my lack of consciousness did not arise from an exclusionary impulse but from a limited experiential horizon, a lack of consciousness that contributed to a false sense of normalcy. I was preoccupied with feeling like an interloper. As a first-generation college student I had learned to "do college" pretty well, but to "do graduate school" was something else—I hadn't known anyone who had gone to graduate or professional school, so I had no clue what was involved in graduate work.

Looking back now—as out of my depth as I felt—I understand how my race and other characteristics that made me look as if I fit in as a graduate student smoothed the way for me. I had arrived into this overwhelmingly white, Judeo-Christian, heteronormative, nonimmigrant world from another that was just as overwhelmingly white, Judeo-Christian, heteronormative, and nonimmigrant. I didn't notice anyone missing as I moved from one environment to the next. This, of course, is the essence of privilege. At that time, my sense of both comparative privilege and lack

her autobiography (Sherif 1983), she recounts, for example, how resistant the department was to promoting her to full professor despite her substantial research record and international visibility in social psychology.

of privilege was completely defined by the way that I differed from the highly visible dominant group: white male PhDs.

Today I understand this strange juxtaposition of marginalization and privilege as deeply connected to that historical moment and geographic location (Roth 2004). A few years earlier, it would have been unlikely that I would have been admitted to graduate school. A few years later, the inclusion of white women—as graduate students at least—would be taken for granted, not the transformation that my cohort represented. This raises the question of what it takes to expand our consciousness to include groups outside of the realm of our immediate experience. When do other intersections—invisible to those enjoying privilege—become noticeable by their absence? And once they have been noticed, what do those of us who have made it through the door do to ensure that it doesn't swing shut behind us?

Owning Up to White Privilege

I was in a white world in Pennsylvania, and it wasn't until my return to California to take a position at the University of California, Davis, in 1977 that I fully realized the impact of white privilege as a significant factor in every aspect of my everyday life. Through teaching the psychology of gender, I had begun to grapple with intersections of social identity, though I did not have the theoretical language that has since developed. While finishing my dissertation, I had taught at the Altoona campus of Penn State, where diversity meant first-generation adult students: rural white women who were trying to juggle child rearing and college and mostly white male Vietnam veterans.

Preparing for classes in northern California, however, brought the previously unexamined dimension of race and ethnicity into the equation with a sizeable number of Latina/o and Asian American students in classes. Teaching compelled me to revise my understanding of women and gender in a fundamental way, not only through continually revealing the diversity of experience within the conventional (and thereby presumed white) female/male gender categories but also by demonstrating that gender is inseparable from the meaningful, salient social identities that intersect with it. The times were changing, too. The backlash against affirmative action (UC–Davis School of Medicine admission practices led to the Bakke case) made the reality of privilege much more salient.

In my first years as an assistant professor, though, I had the tunnel vision fostered by a publish-or-perish environment. As other contributors to this volume know better than I do, one of the most energy-draining aspects of being on the margins is the constant requirement to justify your existence: Why are you here? In my untenured years, my professional survival was on the line, and justification of presence was an ordinary part of my life in my "tenure home" department, with respite coming only through links with other women (women of color and white women) across the campus. It is hard to see your own privilege when everything points to your marginalization. It seems almost unbelievable now that I could have felt so vulnerable as a woman faculty member and because of what I studied, but—as with my graduate school cohort—timing was everything. A few years earlier, I would have never been hired because of my research on gender; a few years later, it would not have been an obstacle.

Even with tunnel vision directing my actions, however, the diversity of the state and undergraduate population created a reality that demanded engagement. Though I didn't yet have the concept of intersectionality—that idea would not make its way to the psychology of gender for another ten years—I began to understand—in a way I had not before—that social identities inseparably define one another. There was no great epiphanic moment when I realized this. Rather, my understanding evolved over time as the cumulative effect of individual moments and sometimes difficult conversations, especially classroom discussions. Most important, I think, was a growing awareness that I should not assume that my existing knowledge about another group's experiences was sufficient for me to presume that I understood that experience. In other words, I learned that one of the most important things I could do to understand my relative privilege and others' relative lack of it was simply shut up and listen. I also discovered that understanding your unearned privilege contains a responsibility for action.

Another significant factor in coming to terms with my relative privilege was seeing firsthand what Latina and Native American women colleagues who had been hired before or about the same time as I had were forced to deal with. This was in the late 1980s and early 1990s. I already knew that their scholarship and teaching were constantly under the microscope. Students were especially vocal in demanding their attention and often challenged their racial and ethnic loyalty whenever a conflict arose between the administration and the students, which, at that time, was often. Especially striking was the paternalism that these colleagues encountered at almost every step when dealing with university administration. Institutional paternalism did not seem simply to be the style of a single, particular administrative unit but occurred across the entire organizational structure.[3]

One particular situation a few years later stands out. In connection with the inauguration of a campus-wide consortium for research on women and gender, I organized an event in the new alumni center. As planning advanced, Chicana colleagues told me that the room I had reserved for the event was unacceptable to them. It bore the name of a fraternity that some years earlier had had a lewd song about a young Mexican woman as its drinking anthem. My colleagues wanted no part of a celebration where they had to enter a room with that fraternity's name. I did not know about this history and was grateful that they trusted me enough to tell me (rather than just boycott the event). I was able to change the venue for the event, but the room in the alumni center still carried the name, so the fundamental problem was not resolved. With my colleagues' permission, I tried to make some headway with the alumni association and administration to listen to the problem and work with us to fix it. Not only did I get nowhere in evoking interest in hearing the complaint, but when I got any response at all, it implied that these Chicana faculty were simply digging up irrelevant history (subtly implying that it was for obscure political reasons). I had encountered plenty of administrative indifference throughout the years, but in this case, there wasn't even any willingness to go through the motions of listening. I would say that I let my colleagues down, but we were all shut down and shut up before we even had a chance.

Of course, understanding something in one area may fail to generalize it into others. What did I fail to see? Probably the most blatant example of blindness to white privilege was lurking at the heart of my own research. Much of my work focuses on

---

3   This same sort of paternalism occurred in response to women faculty's demand for a salary equity study and adjustment in the early 1990s. Throughout the process—from delays in conducting the study to the final grotesque procedure for petitioning for redress—we were met with obfuscation and a patronizing dismissal of our concerns.

the connections between gender and emotion. Some of my early work in the 1980s addressed the question of gender-emotion stereotypes. Surprisingly, at that time, there was next to no research on beliefs about the connection between gender and emotion. Unthinkingly, I began the way that most gender-stereotype researchers did—by using descriptions of a generic woman and generic man to explore the stereotypes. And—as research has shown time and time again—*generic* in the US academic world signals white.

Interestingly none of the probably all-white audience of editors, conference attendees, or other colleagues who assessed my work stopped to ask "which woman? which man?" It was only as I worked to develop the theoretical framework of this line of research that I saw what I had failed to notice before—my own work was being built on a psychology of exclusion, an approach that I had long critiqued. I wish that I could say it was easy to remedy the problem, but to this day, I continue to grapple with ways to make my research methods effectively and efficiently define significant intersections in social identity. My writing explicitly acknowledges my own experiential and epistemological position, but that feels less and less an adequate response as time goes on.

Making Something of Privilege

Promotion to full professor is the most liberating experience of academic life. I vividly recall talking with a friend from the German department who had also been promoted that year. We realized that we were now "the senior women"—the people that we had always assumed exercised some presence and power within the university. It was, indeed, a position of privilege because it brought tremendous freedom to speak your mind. In addition, the proportion of women (across racial ethnicity and departments) to men was increasing: the university had hired some key senior women (mostly white women), so there were more of us to shoulder the responsibility of pressing for change. I also had the luxury of a secure position from which to see that old problems lingered, whether because of misogynistic department culture or tokenism or both.

Overall, however, white women faculty had reached a critical mass that collectively could have an impact. The power of white women in the academy, relative to other groups, has grown, I believe, largely through the power of numbers. There are simply more of us proportionately than any group other than white men. As we know from research on tokenism in organizations, once a group can reach the critical mass of 30 percent or so, individuals have more opportunities to exercise their power as a group and are also more likely to be seen as individuals.

What did we want to change? We pressed for salary equity. We pushed for on-campus child care. We pressed for bringing women into academic leadership. And we achieved most of these goals in some form or another. I think it was the University of California culture that made some ambitious goals totally noncontroversial (e.g., bringing women of color and white women into leadership positions). Action on other issues, however, was at the mercy of oppositional, angry, white male faculty (e.g., addressing gender-based salary inequity).

We pushed for more diversity in faculty hiring. Fortunately the university administration was on board with that idea even when departments were not. For example, search committees were expected to review and pay attention to data on the proportion of women of color, white women, and men from underrepresented groups who were in the national applicant pool (typically recent PhDs), and compare it to the composition of their applicant pool at each stage of the search process. It would be great to say that this was enough to inject diversity into the short list of applicants or offers made, but more often it took additional search money and prodding from the dean's office to get some departments to consider a candidate who had been overlooked in the first round or interview a candidate from the longer short list who had not made it to the interview stage. At all steps of the search—from writing the ad through final deliberations—the words "qualified candidate" were often used as a kind of code by obstructionist faculty who meant "substantially better than other candidates I would be comfortable with." In other words, "qualified" when applicants from under-represented groups meant "spectacular but nonthreatening." Although many faculty saw through these word games, I do not remember any open discussion of this verbal duplicity.[4]

Essentially, we wanted to change the face of the faculty, but this is easier said than done. It takes years to alter faculty composition because of the low turnover rate and late average age of retirement. Even though tenure could be cast as a villain here because it contributes to the slow rate of turnover, its presence makes the academy a safe place to propose, discuss, and follow through on ideas and actions that challenge the status quo. To challenge and change the academy for the better, multiple intersectional perspectives must be represented. This requires that those of us who enjoy the privilege of tenure explicitly broaden the way we think about and conduct faculty searches.

My concern is that there is not enough room to change the composition of the faculty fundamentally without some radical restructuring of the way we hire and reconsideration of what we value in promotion and tenure. Of course, my concern may become a moot point through the increasing reliance on temporary, part-time faculty—which creates another growing problem of a two-tier faculty class system, one likely to have a preponderance of women of color and white women in temporary positions. It is assuredly easier on our comfort zone to admit temporary hires—with less status and salary than our own—into our realm, as demonstrated by research on aversive racism (Pearson, Dovidio, and Gaertner 2009).

What didn't I see or acknowledge? If anything, I underestimated the need for coalition building to create the desired change in faculty culture. Especially in my early years, when the campus was smaller and there were few faculty women, any woman who wanted to be known by other faculty women was visible. There was a general sense of connectedness. I think I knew all of the faculty women of color, including the one African American woman in the medical school and the only African American woman in the law school. But the campus and the proportion of women grew, and I found myself working for change most closely with the women faculty I already knew best, and with few exceptions, we were white. At the time, I saw myself as working for the benefit of all women faculty. I witnessed and understood the extra demands and scrutiny that women of color endure, but I believe I presumed too much about the collective position of women and did not think sufficiently that the added layers of oppression that women of color experience may require a different approach to objectives and priorities.

4   Our university avoided a strategy for ersatz diversification that I have seen more recently, namely, recruiting (or appointing) to visible administrative positions women and men of color from outside the US.

Yolanda asked me how "white women's unwillingness to see their privilege leads to continued marginalization and oppression of women of color." I would say that, for many of us, it is not unwillingness to see privilege, but unthinkingness, a kind of taken-for-granted state. To escape from it first requires insight into our position relative to others and then careful and consistent watchfulness not to settle back into a comfort zone. It may seem strange to view change-seeking as a comfort zone, even if it is, because there is nothing comfortable about lobbying for a pay-equity study, child care leave, and on-site child care, and the list goes on. That said, it is easy to get wrapped up in the action and miss how narrowly that action is defined; thus, some colleagues are better served than others.

Whatever our victories, constant vigilance is needed to prevent not only our own backsliding but regression by the institution itself. Studies of salary equity, for example, have shown that old gender-based inequities reappear within a few years of administrative correction. Equally as chilling is the fact that gains in diversifying faculty composition can vanish almost overnight. The experience of the University of California is telling here. Challenges to California's affirmative-action laws in the mid-1990s resulted in the passage of an anti-affirmative-action initiative in 1996. Martha West (2000, 2007) reports that the impact on the composition of the University of California faculty across its ten campuses was striking and immediate, resulting in a precipitous drop in the proportion of women faculty (both women of color and white women). Without attentiveness to hiring and retention practices, the proportion of tenure-line women faculty fell drastically below the number available in the national hiring pool.

New Intersections, New Marginalization, New Privilege

I just turned sixty-one. Identities are not static but change or, more optimistically, evolve over one's life course. Aging has lately introduced me to yet a new view of my privilege. It now includes recognition of my comparative financial security, an awareness heightened by the lingering effects of the Great Recession. It is ironic that I am back to where I started: social class is a significant personal intersection, but now it has a very different meaning than it had years ago. My social class position today exaggerates the unearned white privilege that has always benefited me and that I trace back to the critically important, privilege-linked opportunity to attend university. I have also come to be much more aware of age as a salient intersection. In the US youth-oriented culture, age is not an intersectional identity that is advantageous, especially not for women of any ethnic or racial group. In some situations, age is a ticket to social invisibility; in others, it evokes patronizing behavior; in still others, it elicits fear of women's strength and potential power.

These changes in my intersectional position lead me back to the question that Yolanda asked me to consider in this essay: why are white women uncomfortable distinguishing between the realities of their lives and those of women of color? Why, when white women use the word "woman" and she interjects, "You mean white women," do they become angry? What is happening? What does my position as a senior white woman in the academy help us understand about this denial of privilege? I cannot speak for other white women, but I can say what I have observed and what I have experienced.

Some people's reactions are, I believe, simple to explain: there are some white women who just don't get it—not only don't they get it about women of color, they don't get it about white women. In fact, they don't get gender politics at all, whether it is because they believe they live in a postracial, postgender, everybody's-fine world or for other reasons. They are offended by any reminder that unearned privilege and undeserved inequity exist in the world they move through. This position is patently defensive at the core: what, me privileged? These women, I hope, are the minority.

But what about other white women in the academy? I think there are layers of explanation for what appears to be or is an angry reaction. Sometimes these women may hear "you mean white women" as an accusation, whatever the speaker intends. By this I mean that they hear that they are personally to blame for their unearned privilege. This reaction exposes their ambivalence about their position. These are their demons, not a problem in communication, and they must resolve their issues. I think it is not unlike what white male students in psychology of gender classes have to overcome—a sense that if we are talking about male privilege, the intent is not to blame them individually (after all, they signed up for the class, and other men did not) but to push them to acknowledge their unearned privilege and exercise the social responsibility that follows that acknowledgment.

At other times, the reaction is to a person's own inattention or embarrassment at being caught for overgeneralizing ("Yes, I meant to say . . . "). Or it may reflect fears and insecurities because prejudice has surfaced when this attitude fundamentally goes against the person's self-concept as a nonprejudiced person ("I didn't mean to say . . . "). My level of awareness and how I interpret it is directly connected to the context where these interactions take place, my position in that social environment, and what I have learned or failed to learn before. Of course, it isn't the job of my women of color colleagues to correct my inattention, but, frankly, we live in a world that encourages forgetting at every turn, and I may need help to remember what I know and believe.

At a deeper, more complicated level is another message that "you mean white women" appears to convey. Singling out whiteness defines my intersectional position solely as unidimensional white privilege, a position only interested in and capable of seeing the world through that lens. "Wait a minute," I want to say, "you don't know who I am." The combined facets of my social identity connect me in complex ways to relative privilege and relative disadvantage. I am more than my whiteness. My class background, sexual orientation, age, gender, ability status, and more—not just race—are all points of intersection that define my social identity at this moment. Yet, at the same time as I mentally raise this protest, I know that the facets of my social identity—each intersection—mutually constitute, reinforce, and naturalize one another. Thus, the thread of whiteness is inevitably woven through gender, age, and every other significant dimension that defines me.

The construct of intersectionality thus both clarifies and complicates my understanding of my white privilege. In my research and writing, it complicates my study of women and gender, forcing me to spell out to whom my conclusions apply and under what conditions (Shields 2008; Shields and Bhatia 2009). On a personal level, an intersectional perspective provides a scaffold to construct my understanding of the advantages and relative disadvantages that I experience. It enables me to understand the way those positions have shifted over the years and gives me a language to describe the connections and uniqueness of different intersectional points. It acts as the reminder that I so often need to keep me from settling into the unexamined complacency of privilege.

CHAPTER 3

A PROSTITUTE, A SERVANT, AND A CUSTOMER-SERVICE REPRESENTATIVE

A Latina in Academia

Carmen R. Lugo-Lugo

> *Write what should not be forgotten.*
>
> Isabel Allende, *Paula*

> *If I didn't define myself for myself, I would be crunched into the other people's fantasies for me and eaten alive.*
>
> Audrey Lorde, *Sister Outsider*

> *Freeing yourself was one thing; claiming ownership of that freed self was another.*
>
> Toni Morrison, *Beloved*

Introduction: Or, Allow Me to Illustrate the Title of My Essay

During my first time teaching introduction to comparative ethnic studies as a newly hired, tenure-track faculty member, I was about to begin class one day when a white male student raised his hand. I acknowledged him, and the following exchange ensued:

> Student: Can we cancel class today?
> Me: Why should we cancel class?
> Student: I don't feel like being in the classroom today, and since my parents pay for your salary, I think it is only fair you do what I say.

Though I was momentarily taken aback, I also chuckled at his reasoning (and audacity) a bit, after which I explained to him that by paying his tuition (which is what I suspected he meant), his parents were actually paying for his SEAT in my classroom, not my salary, since that is actually paid by the Washington state legislature. Up to this point, the other students in the class were following this exchange very closely, like a tennis match. Perhaps interested in seeing how I handled their classmate's request, and thus how seriously they should take me, the students were as attentive as I had ever seen them, some on the edge of their seats looking anxious, others wearing a horrified look on their faces. I finally concluded the exchange with the following statement: "and, regardless of who pays for my services, I am your professor, not your personal prostitute." The class let out a collective, sizable gasp, followed by uproarious laughter, which helped dissipate the tension somewhat.

My admittedly awkward final comment was an attempt at highlighting the fact that although I might have been there to provide a service for them (I was there to teach him and his classmates about race relations), I was not at their disposal, so they could not dismiss me whenever they weren't in the mood for class. I then proceeded to preempt the material for that day to have a discussion about entitlement and white privilege, even though I am fairly certain we had covered those topics before (nothing like a real-life, just-happened example to provide insight and drive a point home).

As I reflect back on that encounter and the class discussion that followed, I can identify three elements that were operating in that one request: (1) I was a woman of color; (2) I was teaching a subject that many consider unnecessary (I keep hearing that racism is now a thing of the past) or academically flawed (meaning too critical of whites); and (3) I was teaching at a historical juncture marked by the relentless corporatization of the university, a process that has turned teaching into a marketplace (or shopping mall of sorts), where students feel like self-entitled customers and faculty and staff are forced to play the roles of either clerks, checkout cashiers, or customer-service representatives. Something to keep in mind is that although these three elements may have had different origins, as I discovered in the conversation that ensued afterward with the entire class, they were operating simultaneously in that one exchange.

As I recall, our class discussion that day was pretty fruitful, and after much processing and back-and-forth analysis by the students, a female student of color—still baffled by the incident—challenged her classmates to "just think of the kind of nerve that it takes" for any student not only to think that he owns his teacher but to feel free and secure enough to tell her in front of forty-nine classmates that he, in fact, does. Aha! Exactly. After that comment, I let the class go an entire five minutes before the bell rang, not because I wanted to honor in any way the original request that class be dismissed early, but because I did not want any other comment to taint that final insightful observation. I wanted it to linger in their minds (haunt them perhaps) until the next class period. The important thing is that the sense of entitlement the female student of color was talking about is the result of the three elements I listed. And because I believe they still inform many of my interactions with students (for I still teach that class at the same institution), I shall spend the rest of this essay discussing these elements in detail.

A Latina in the Ivory Tower

Although the university is often seen as a space detached from the rest of society (hence the term "ivory tower"), as a trained sociologist I know full well that the same ideas we find in society at large operate within the confines of the university, because it is part of and develops from that very society. That is why my position within both US society and academia is an important component of this discussion, a position that is described something like this: I am a woman. A woman who is of color. A woman of color who is a Puerto Rican (which means I am viewed as a Latina). And those markers mean something at the beginning of the twenty-first century in and outside the US academy. As identities, they inform the way I position myself in relation to other gendered and racial subjects, but as markers, they provide my students with a lens through which to look at, interpret, and treat me. This lens, of course, is created by the current understanding that our society has about Latinos/as at this historical juncture.

Since the United States is such a segregated society, it is fair to assume that its mainstream culture does not derive any understanding of Latinos/as from daily interactions. According to the last census, Americans tend to live in neighborhoods with people who are like them in both race and social class. Moreover, according to a data-analysis report released by the US Bureau of the Census, the national index of residential segregation for Latinos/as rose 1.5 percent between 1980 and 2000 (US Bureau of the Census 2008). It is then only fair to conclude that mainstream (white) Americans obtain their understanding of Latinos/as not from personal experience or face-to-face encounters but from social institutions, including, of course, pervasive and omnipresent ones such as the media and popular culture.

What does it mean, then, for mainstream white America to understand Latinos/as through an institution like the media? Since the Latino/a explosion of the 1990s, US popular culture has systematically sold specific images of Latinos/as. According to music, film, television, and other venues, Latino males are hot, dark, handsome womanizing law enforcement officers or criminals (see, for instance, most of the characters played by Jimmy Smits, Benjamin Bratt, or Benicio del Toro), while Latinas are just hot and sexy (see, for instance, most of the characters played by Eva Longoria, Jennifer Lopez, or Eva Mendez). Magazine covers are full of phrases like "sizzling hot" and "hot tamale" or the word "sexy" when describing Latinos/as. When I wrote this essay in September 2009, a general search on Amazon.com under the keyword "Latina" produced hundreds of results. What's really telling is that of the first ten, nine were DVDs with the following titles: *Sizzling Latinas*, vol. 2; *Joe Pusher's Latinas*, vol. 1; *Joe Pusher's Latinas*, vol. 5; *Latina Pole Queens*; *Muy Caliente: Nude Latinas*; *Joe Pusher's Latinas*, vol. 4; *Latina Party*; *Sexy Latinas del Reggaeton*, vol. 2; and *Latina Girls Going Bananas*, vol. 2. I assume I don't have to describe the pictures on the covers of these DVDs, but I will say that they match the titles beautifully.

Similarly the first two hits in a Google search under the keyword "Latinas" produced the following: "Sizzling Latinas" and "Sexy Latinas, Spanish Girls, Hot Latin." I can't say for sure—because I dared not go to those sites—but I suspect they were pornographic, giving us a good idea of the forceful ways that Latinas and their supposed hotness are sexualized and turned into commodities. Similarly, an advanced Google search with the keywords "handsome Latinos" produced more than two hundred hits, most of them related to gay porn. These results are important, because they tell us a story of the commodification (by way of sexuality) of Latinos/as at the beginning of the twenty-first century. Though some may be skeptical about my using pornographic websites to show or measure Latino/a commodification, I would like to point out that just like academia, the porn industry reflects the society from which it emerges.

For more than ten years now, these views on Latinos/as have permeated US mainstream society and culture, creating archetypes of these groups. These archetypal images are then superimposed on the bodies of flesh-and-blood Latinos/as, like a cloak of expectations. In fact, these portrayals and descriptions have become ingrained in people's minds to the point where they are part of the collective understanding of Latinos/as in the United States and create a reality. The results of my hasty searches in Amazon and Google ring true to that collective understanding and reality. As a white female student once told me when I was talking about stereotypical representations of Latinas in popular culture, "But Latinas *are* hot."

Mainstream understandings of Latinos/as affect the way they are treated and thus, the way they live their lives. Though this may seem like a simplistic conclusion, its simplicity should not be mistaken for banality. After all, with that statement, I am suggesting that mainstream understandings of Latinos/as (as flawed, inaccurate, and even misguided as they may be) have a direct impact on their material existence. That is why when looking back at some experiences I have had over the years, I must remember that this society sees me through a specific lens. For instance, as a graduate student in the 1990s, I had to contend with being viewed as a hot commodity by some of my professors, including one who once intimated in a hopeful tone that he had never been with a "hot Latin lover." As a graduate instructor close in age to the students I was teaching, I also had to deal with similar comments from my students, along with invitations to hang out or have a few drinks or fun in town. For better or worse, I learned to deal with all that as part of who I was within the academy and the well-rounded education I was getting.

Now that I am a professor—dealing with both my identity and the perceptions that others have of me—dealing with who I am within the academic setting has a great deal to do with who I am not: a white male, the archetypical expectation for a college professor. This white male is supposed to be knowledgeable, wise, and capable. And it is clear to my students—from the moment they step foot on my classroom for the first time—that I am neither white nor male. Being a college professor is difficult enough for any woman because women are still, to this day, not seen as prone to reason or even possessing intelligence; in fact, many people continue to regard them as volatile creatures dominated by their feelings, their "hearts." If you think I am exaggerating, a female white student said just this semester in class that as she understands it (that is, as she's been told), women "do not have the brain capability to understand engineering." If this society can get a white woman to believe she does not have the brain to do engineering, I can only imagine what things you can get her to believe about other people, especially those with whom she has only a few, if any, interactions.

Given all this, a Latina in the classroom is sure to evoke a different set of images, many of which, I would imagine, led the student in the original story I told to think he could command me to stop class without any repercussions. After all—as he admitted in the postexchange discussion—he would not have thought about asking his math professor (who he conveyed was male and white) to dismiss class. That is why it is difficult not to cringe when students write in the course evaluations at the end of the semester things like "she is really knowledgeable," "she knows what she is talking about," "she's really smart," or the one I got last semester: "Carmen is the woman of my dreams; she is intelligent and funny." I know that they mean those accolades as compliments, but I also know that in many cases, they say these things because those were not their expectations when they walked into the classroom and saw me (a Latina) on the first day of class. They did not expect an intelligent, knowledgeable person, which is why I suspect they feel the need to write those comments, as if implying "she is not what I expected," or "I was pleasantly surprised with the way things turned out." But regardless of the way things ended up, I am still teaching classes that many of my students think (at least when they enroll in them because they must so they can get their diversity credits) are not necessary (at best) or a waste of their time (at worst).

A Latina in the Ivory Tower Teaching Ethnic Studies

Racism and racial inequalities are alive and well. That is the basic tenet of the classes I teach and the discipline of ethnic studies in general. As simple and intuitive as that statement may seem to some, however, it goes against contemporary understandings of race relations that are ingrained in our students' minds, namely, that racism is a thing of the past. Apparently, somewhere among the march in Washington, the Freedom Summer, the urban riots, the assassination of Dr. Martin Luther King Jr., the war against Vietnam, the war on drugs, the continual reelection of staunch segregationist Strom Thurman to the US Congress, the Rodney King incident, the voracious expansion of the prison industrial complex, the welfare reform, the lynching of James Byrd, No Child Left Behind, the creation of the Department of Homeland Security, the Patriot Act, the invasions of and wars against Afghanistan and Iraq, Abu Ghraib and Guantanamo, the three nooses hanging from a tree in Jena's high school, and the Secure Fence Act, we overcame racism.

And, if there is a problem, it is an individual one (i.e., a few bad apples), which means it is definitely smaller than it was before, which means things will work themselves out with time. Students are quick to declare (as if it were a badge of honor) that they learned not to see color (the color-blind mentality Eduardo Bonilla-Silva [2009], talks about in his work), and that we actually live in a society where race does not matter anymore (the so-called postracial society, also addressed by Bonilla-Silva [2009]). After all, we have a black president (one whom many suspect was not born in the United States because his father is Kenyan, is a Muslim, and hates America, but a black president nonetheless). So when I actually tell them, as I stated in the sentence opening this section, that racism and racial inequalities are alive and well, their understanding of the world where they live is threatened. By me. A woman. Of color.

The color-blind mentality leads them to conclude, then, that ethnic studies classes are unnecessary and a squandering of time, energy and resources. The translation: my job is a waste of their (parents') money. What can an ethnic studies professor teach them about racial inequality when that problem has basically evaporated from our society? Those of us working on ethnic studies and calling students to reflect on racism, they often argue, are stuck in history—because for students, history is something that happened a long time ago and has no relevance today. From their perspective, we just need to let go of the past, stop bitching about it, and move on.

As a student so expressively (if inaccurately) put it in an introductory class when trying to respond to an author's point that racism affects people's livelihoods, "Slavery ended like hundreds of years ago. We need to like forget about it and like move on."

At the same time that they trumpet the complete elimination of racism and racial inequality, however, students also talk about *reverse racism:* "immigrants who can't even speak English" taking American jobs, people of color playing "the race card" to get their way, and, of course, hot Latinas. The fact that they can parrot the nonsense that conservative pundits rehearse daily in the media is, of course, not surprising. We do have to put this in a context, though, because this is the generation that came of age with a color-coded terror alert and a government telling them to be vigilant about threats. The words of former President Bush following the September 11, 2001, attacks—"either you are with us, or you are with the terrorists"—resonated for seven years and informed the way these students understand their position in the world. As this message made it clear, not only was there an "us" and a "them," but obviously, more importantly, the "them" was always and without question a threat to the security and safety of "us."

Ethnic studies turns all those concepts upside down by forcing students to understand the genesis of an us/them binary and analyze its consequences. In addition, ethnic studies is different from disciplines like sociology, political science, and anthropology, which tend to hide behind the curtain of scientific objectivity and present issues by discussing numbers and an array of calculated theories designed to provide some explanation for the numbers. In fact, listening to my colleagues and friends in those disciplines discuss their student evaluations, it appears that if professors in any of these (and related) disciplines try to move beyond mere presentation of facts, they are told to "shut up and teach." Because of its transdisciplinary methodology, ethnic studies is not a shut-up-and-teach kind of discipline. Ethnic studies does not hide behind the veil of objectivity, and in fact, to be effective, it has to advocate and strive for a fundamental transformation of race relations. Stating that there is inequality is not enough. And here is where I come in: I am a Latina telling my mostly white students that racism, discrimination, and inequality still exist and affect all our lives (theirs included), both in ways that can be measured and ones that cannot. I also tell them that they are implicated in those things, that they must do something about them, and that their comforts come at the expense of others. And, of course, they do not want to hear that. Especially not from me.

A Latina in the Corporatized Ivory Tower

The global market forces that have shaped and characterized our contemporary society spare no one and nothing. That includes the academy. Seeking a corporate model of efficiency, universities are restructuring academic and administrative units and running them like departments within a corporation. This is why the last two presidents at our university have proclaimed without raising many eyebrows that they are the CEOs. In addition, the devaluing of education and the resulting lack of funding recently experienced by universities in the United States have turned places of higher learning into symbolic (and sometimes even literal) shopping centers. For instance, Barnes & Noble owns the bookstore at our university, and it has its own Starbucks stand. Starbucks also owns (or its coffee is sold in) most coffee stands on campus, and the food court at the Student Union Building features fast-food chains like Subway and Panda Express, among others. As in any shopping center, customers need currency, and at our institution, students can use their identification badges as debit cards in any of these establishments. Also the gear sold by the athletic department is sponsored by Nike, turning athletes and students wearing the school clothing into walking billboards for their company. It is then no surprise that college students behave not like people seeking a higher form of knowledge but like customers of academia. They walk into the bookstore as customers, and they walk into my classroom, latte in hand, as customers as well. Why should they behave any differently when my classroom is only a few steps away from the bookstore?

Within this new structuring of the academic institution as a corporate marketplace, students begin to treat their professors and other university workers as clerks or cashiers at a department store, who are there to serve and satisfy their every need. Because of this, professors must accommodate their preferences: "Can we have more discussion? I learn better when I talk things out." Or, "Can we have less discussion? I like it better when you lecture." Trying to accommodate the "I like it better this way" or "I like it better that way" turns professors into customer-service representatives, kowtowing to the demands made by customers and making sure they are satisfied with the product. As the business cliché goes, "The customer is always right."

In the marketplace academy, students shop for classes that suit their schedules, professors that they like, and experiences that satisfy them. Asking to be added to my class two weeks after the semester started last spring, a student told me that for that time period, she had been "shopping for a class" that fit her schedule and available time, and mine would be "just perfect." When I told her it was too late to add my class, her response was quite telling: "But I want this class." Students also, as illustrated in the opening story, think they are paying for all that with their (or their parents') tuition money.

As customer-service representatives with email addresses and office phone numbers, we are also supposed to be available always (at all times and any time) to satisfy our students' demands and appease their concerns. I can't even begin to count the number of times a student has told me, "I sent you an email last night, and I never heard back from you." This usually means the person sent the electronic message around 10:00 p.m., and it is 10:00 a.m., and I still have not replied to the message. I have also had many instances where a student seriously expected me to reply to a message he or she sent on Sunday evening asking me to give him or her ideas for a paper that was due the next morning. And they seem genuinely baffled when I tell them that I am not on call twenty-four hours a day and that I do not check my messages on Sundays. In fact, I said just that to a male student once, and his response was this: "What do you mean you don't check your messages on Sundays?" Even JCPenneys gets to have store hours.

The Classroom as a Stage

As Jim Farrell tells us, shopping is "the great American pastime" (Gage 2003). Moreover, consumerism has turned into entertainment. It is only logical to assume, then, that if students are learning to treat the university as a marketplace, they also want to regard it as a place to satisfy their entertainment needs. That may be why, a few years ago, a white female student told me that according to her boyfriend's calculations, each class period was costing them the same as a ticket to the movies (full price, not matinee). In a similar fashion to the student who asked me to cancel class, she made her observation as I was getting ready to start class, perhaps commanding me (in a more subtle way than the male student did) to be entertaining. By turning the academy into a marketplace (a shopping mall), universities have (inadvertently perhaps) turned professors into clerks. In addition, because of the relationship between consumerism and entertainment, coupled with the performative aspect of teaching, the academy as marketplace has also transformed into the academy as Hollywood. And as we know, within our celebritydom, not all performers are created equal. That is to say, a white performer is not treated in the same way as a nonwhite one. I will use two Hollywood actors to illustrate this point.

Let us analyze the expectations our society has of actress Angelina Jolie and those it has of actress Penélope Cruz. Even though they are approximately the same age, and both are Academy Award winners, it seems fair to argue that we expect different things from them, and those differences are (at least in part) the result of Jolie being perceived as white and Cruz as nonwhite. And before anyone raises the point that as a Spaniard, Cruz is a white European, I would like to remind everyone that because of her dark looks, name, and accent, and the weird ethnic classifications involving Hispanics and Latinos/as in the United States, she is, in fact, considered a Latina, and thus nonwhite. Although Jolie and Cruz are both sex symbols, if we look at media reports about both of them, Jolie is consistently portrayed as a human being with depth, whereas Cruz is consistently described only in relation to her perceived ethnicity: within this context, she is another hot Latina (who may be a good actress but who is definitely, and first and foremost, hot). The mainstream, online magazine AskMen.com provides the perfect means of analysis.

Let us begin with Jolie. According to AskMen.com,

> When she's not busy adopting third-world children and making the world a better place, Angelina Jolie is making the world a prettier place . . . [and] when both men and women consistently rate you as the woman they'd most like to sleep with, you know you're sexy, possibly even the sexiest woman alive. Esquire at least thinks so, and People magazine once voted her the Sexiest Person Alive. Whether she's a blonde [or] a brunette . . . , Angelina Jolie always looks hot, even when she's not trying. . . . She is the epitome of beauty whether she's wearing a headscarf in an African refugee camp or she's donning a designer gown on the red carpet. And those lips. . . . (AskMen.com 2009)

And here is what the magazine says about Penélope Cruz:

> Able to jump from Spanish to English with ease, Penélope is the ultimate Hollywood Latin beauty, with oodles of talent to boot. . . . Cruz's status as a bona fide sex symbol has been firmly in place for well over a decade now, as the actress established herself early on as the textbook definition of a sultry Spaniard. Her willingness to doff her top has certainly won her a legion of male fans across the globe, though there's little doubt it's her genuine abilities as an actress that's ensured the endurance of her career. . . . It's just as clear that, no matter what her future holds, Penélope Cruz has earned a permanent place in our hearts as one of Hollywood's most indelible, exotic beauties. (AskMen.com 2008)

As we can gather from these two accounts, while Jolie is hot, Cruz is Latina hot (i.e., an exotic beauty). In addition, and perhaps more importantly, Jolie is granted a humanity to which Cruz does not have access. We can find that humanity in Ask-Men.com's descriptions of Jolie's humanitarian work. Statements such as "when she's not busy adopting third-world children and making the world a better place," and "she is the epitome of beauty whether she's wearing a headscarf in an African refugee camp or she's donning a designer gown on the red carpet" present Jolie as something more human than a sex symbol. Cruz, who has also done humanitarian work in Africa, publically supported organizations seeking to eliminate poverty, AIDS, and weapons of mass destruction, and provide, clean and fresh water, is obviously not granted the same courtesy.

It follows, then, that if students see the classroom as a stage and their professors as performers, they have different expectations for their professors, based not only on the classes they teach but also on their race and gender. Thus, the performance of a white male professor teaching ethnic studies will be received differently than that of a Puerto Rican female with an accent.

A Few Concluding Remarks

Regardless of all the things I have discussed and the complicated interactions I may have with my students, I love being a college professor. I see it as a contribution to improving this most incomprehensible society. I also see it as my way of helping leave this place in a better condition than I found it. I take racism and racial inequalities seriously, and because I do, I spend an inordinate amount of time providing my students with the tools they need to understand what those things are, the shapes they take, and the impact they have on all of us, regardless of our racial background.

Still, I wish I did not have to pleasantly surprise my students by showing them I have a brain because after they walked in my class and saw me, they were expecting me not to have one. Relatedly, I wish my students would not dismiss me because I am not white and male. And I sure as hell wish they would not tell me they think I am the woman of their dreams. But I know that—in the light of the reality of race relations in our country—my wishes will remain only that. After all, dealing with all that is part of the reason why I have to teach my classes in the first place. As I already said, I have accepted my reality, and I can live with it. I also know I am not the only professor in the United States who has had to deal with these situations. Because of conversations I have had with colleagues and the literature I have read, I know my experiences are similar to those of other faculty of color and white female faculty members teaching unconventional disciplines.

What I have not accepted yet, still troubles me tremendously, and will continue to peeve me for as long as it is a reality in my life, is the rampant and unabashed corporatization of higher learning and its effects on students. I resolutely refuse to be my students' personal assistant. I will not be their brown-faced entertainer. And I will not check them out like a cashier as they make their way to the rest of their lives. I do understand that the corporate mentality is also part of our society, and since, as I discussed earlier, what happens in society at large also operates within the confines of the university, I can only expect the corporatization of society to be part of academia.

However, I also know that the university (especially a state, land-grant university such as the one where I teach) can resist the pressure to become another corporation.

I believe it should have the moral imperative to do so. Instead of advancing market-place ideologies, as a place of higher learning, the university can privilege learning over money, students over corporation, and people over profit. The university can become a place where people go to seek knowledge, not one where they go to buy their diploma. In the end, it would be just a tad easier to be able to talk to students about race relations, racial inequality, and racism without having to contend with an institution that puts a price tag on me, my class, and my lectures.

CHAPTER 4

BLACK/OUT

The White Face of Multiculturalism and the Violence of the Canadian Academic Imperial Project

Delia D. Douglas

> *There are moments in my life when I feel as though a part of me is missing.*
> *There are days when I feel so invisible that I can't remember my own name,*
> *when I feel so lost and angry that I can't speak a civil word to the people*
> *who love me best. Those are the times when I catch sight of my reflection in*
> *store windows and am surprised to see a whole person looking back.*
>
> Patricia J. Williams, *The Alchemy of Race and Rights*

Critical race scholar Patricia J. Williams is only one of many who have poignantly argued that racism achieves a violence that is psychological, embodied, and cultural (P. Williams 1991, 228; see also Alexander and Knowles 2005; Essed 2002; S. Hall 1996; Myers 2005). This essay is both a personal narrative and an analytical discussion of the myriad of ways that expressions of racial hostility and racism surface in the academy through the often-intangible, but ever-present, values, norms, and practices that are felt and lived in the daily lives of Canadians. A related topic is the way racial ideologies and strategies of exclusion become operational in various organizations. It is precisely because institutions of higher education remain key sites to reproduce social power, privilege, and prestige that I want to draw attention to the ways that everyday/mundane forms of racial violence (e.g., language, attitudes, social relationships, and loyalties) are revealed in this setting. In sum, following Ruth Roach Pierson, I want to "reflect on how deeply racism and imperialism/colonialism remain institutionalized within the academy and academic professional circles" (2004, 90).

At present the subjects of systemic racism, the culture of whiteness, and the ongoing exclusion of Aboriginal and racialized minority women remain marginalized in Canadian universities (see for example, Henry and Tator 1994; C. E. James 2007;

Kobayashi 2006, 2007a; Luther, Whitmore, and Moreau 2003; M. S. Smith 2007). In Canada we find ourselves at a key moment: despite twenty years of an equity policy, the representation of Aboriginal and racialized minority women remains deplorably low, and the Employment Equity Act is under review (Canadian Association of University Teachers 2007; Henry and Tator 2007). In response to the current climate, in 2007 a Coalition of Academics of Colour and the Equity portfolio both asked that all member associations of the Canadian Federation for the Humanities and Social Sciences organize sessions at their May–June 2008 meetings around equity hiring, retention, and accountability in Canadian universities.

This call to action is significant because it challenges nationalist beliefs that assert that Canada's multiracial and multiethnic population, in combination with the institutionalization of the policies of multiculturalism and bilingualism, preclude the possibility of racism in Canada (Bannerji 1996; Razack 2000; Stewart 2004). As Dionne Brand summarizes, "Unlike the United States, where there is at least an admission of the fact that racism exists and has a history, in this country one is faced with a stupefying innocence" (1998, 191). The refusal to believe that there is a connection between prejudice and violence is one of the consequences of official accounts that deny and trivialize Canada's history of genocide, slavery, segregation, and racist immigration policies (see T. L. Cooper 2006; Monture-Angus 2003; Nelson and Nelson 2004; Thornhill 2008). Additionally, Canada's proximity to the United States has contributed to the idea that its national identity is based on racial virtue (Razack 2002; Schick and St. Denis 2005). As a result, the denial of the conditions that created this white settler colony has created a social climate that sanctions expressions of violence and normalizes white domination. Thus, representations of Canada's past remain a key source of conflict in relation to the production of public discussions of cultural difference, citizenship, and belonging in the present.

My interest in issues of identity, education, and equity are the result of my particular history as a black Canadian woman who was born in Britain in the 1960s and raised on Canada's prairies by my father in a single-parent household. I attended graduate school in both Canada and the United States and received a PhD in sociology in 1994. Although I had become disenchanted and dispirited by the alienating and antagonistic culture and structure of the academy, after graduation I did apply for several jobs at Canadian universities. However, when I was unable to secure a position, I decided to seek employment outside of the university. In 2002, I finally realized that my aspiration and commitment remained in postsecondary education, and I began the (seemingly never-ending) journey to garner a tenure-track position at a Canadian institution. To date, I have been unable to secure a full time position; I continue to labor on the margins as part-time faculty and an independent scholar.

What follows draws on my experiences as a part-time instructor, an equity consultant, and a research associate. I discuss the various forms of violence that are the direct result of the failure to take seriously the race, class, and gender structure of Canadian universities. I argue that the current atmosphere implicitly and explicitly affirms and supports the culture of whiteness, which ultimately maintains the status quo, namely the attitudes of white entitlement and racial superiority. I also address the difficulty and trauma that are a result of my conditional/marginalized position and the ways I negotiate these institutional restrictions. In particular, I describe the hardship that accompanies my financial instability, namely, a future without a pension and the torment of knowing that I cannot make up the wages that I have lost in the years since I received my doctorate. I contend that we need to take seriously the consequences of years of structured racial exclusion and the power of unmarked whiteness so that we can better respond to the complex and varied manifestations of racial oppression and the incalculable damage that these forms of discrimination have caused.

I begin with a discussion of the organization and content of racial discourses in Canada. I then outline the particular history of black settlement, followed by a brief description of the academic imperial project. Subsequently, I examine a number of my experiences in postsecondary institutions to illuminate the breadth and complexity of the operation of power and privilege that maintain inequality in these settings.

Canada, White Settler Nation

> *Canada is a land troubled by questions of race and space, whether we are speaking of First Nations land claims, Quebec nationalism or the absented presence of Canada's others.*

> Rinaldo Walcott, *Black Like Who?*

Rinaldo Walcott's description of Canada captures the ambiguities and contradictions that define its history and national identity. Canadian cultural and political identities have been shaped by its geographical proximity to the United States and the ongoing struggles between the competing voices of the two founding colonial powers, Britain and France. The ambivalent ties that exist between the province of Quebec and the rest of Canada most persuasively illustrate a key source of this tension. Moreover, in 2007, following moves made by Russia and Denmark, Prime Minister Stephen Harper continues to assert Canada's claim on the Northwest Passage and the country's right to sovereignty of the Arctic. This bid to extend the boundaries of Canadian territory, combined with the unremitting conflict over land and social justice among First Nations communities, is further evidence of the ways that Canada continues to negotiate unequal and unresolved geographies.

The historical privileging of the white ethnicities of English and French has produced a public consciousness predicated on negating the fact that the pattern of white settlement that produced Canada is a direct result of the social practices, institutional structures, and ideologies that were directed against those groups who were marked as racial subordinates (Backhouse 1999; Monture-Angus 2007; Walker 1997). For example, the history of the violence of European conquest that produced Canada includes the enslavement and displacement of Aboriginal people from their land, the indentured labor of the Chinese workers who built the railroad, and the internment of the Japanese during World War II.

In 1985 the Canadian government passed the Multiculturalism Act, a statute that endorses the full and equitable participation of all communities in society and recognizes their right to maintain, share, and enhance their cultural heritage. Correspondingly, Canada's official policy of multiculturalism is readily understood to indicate the charitable disposition of its citizens as well as the improbability (if not the absence) of overt racial conflict (Bannerji 1996; Mahtani 2002). However, as George Elliott Clarke decries, "The price of this flattering self-portrait is public lying, falsified history, and self-destructive blindness" (2006, xiii).

On the rare occasion that racism is acknowledged, it is typically understood as subtle and covert (i.e., less harmful), thereby sustaining the popular view that expressions of racial hostility and violence in Canada are unusual occurrences; it is widely believed that if you encounter racism, it is not as bad as what is happening south of the border (Nelson and Nelson 2004; Stewart 2004). Thus, if you describe an experience of racism/racial hostility, you are likely to encounter expressions of disbelief and disclaimers, which assert that one would "expect that kind of situation to occur in the US, not here." In short, our nearness to the United States has long shaped the content and interpretation of Canadian racial discourses. In addition, whilst, national discourses remain organized around the interests of the former imperial powers of Britain and France, the racial composition of Canada has undergone profound changes as Aboriginal and racialized minority groups have become the fastest-growing members of the population (Statistics Canada 2007, 2008).

Furthermore, there has been a substantive rise in economic and social disparities as prohibitive poverty levels prevail among both urban and rural Aboriginal communities along with many recent immigrants who reside in our metropolitan centers. Thus, amid dominant claims that the nation values the contributions of all of its members, the marginal positions these groups occupy within Canadian society demonstrate that this is not really the case.

Furthermore, owing to these recent demographic changes, whites are demonstrating a new consciousness and disquiet over the meaning of Canada's national and cultural identity (Mackey 1999; M. S. Smith 2007). The character of the dominant response to these shifts in the national landscape is revealed in a number of moves made by the federal government. Specifically, in 2006 Canadian Prime Minister and Conservative Party leader Stephen Harper issued a formal apology to the Chinese Canadian community for the head tax and offered financial compensation, but only to the thirty surviving widows of the tens of thousands who participated in building Canada's railway. In June 2008 in the House of Commons, the prime minister also apologized to Aboriginal, Métis, and Inuit students for the abuse, violence, pain, and suffering that Indigenous peoples experienced in the residential school system for more than a century. In 2007 Canada was one of four countries (along with Australia, New Zealand, and the United States) that did not support the United Nations Declaration on the Rights of Indigenous Peoples. However, in November 2010, the Canadian government reversed its denunciation of the declaration and currently endorses the United Nations's affirmation of the rights of Indigenous peoples. In August 2008, while attending a Sikh festival in the Vancouver suburb of Surrey, Prime Minister Harper expressed regret for the Komagata Maru incident that took place in 1914, when 376 South Asians were denied entrance to Canada. Lastly, this government also refused to participate in the 2009 United Nations antiracism conference that was held in Durban, South Africa, in April.

Moreover, in an attempt to curb the gains made through decades of activism and struggle against oppression and stifle continued demands for social justice and equity, the Harper government instituted debilitating cuts to the already-modest budget for the federal government organization Status of Women Canada, forcing many of its offices across the country to close. There have been a number of related moves such as planned changes to the Immigration and Refugee Protection Act that would give the immigration minister more power to give priority to immigrants with job skills that are deemed in demand in Canada. In a related matter, the prime minister has also proposed amendments to immigration laws that would change the criteria for international claimants to seek entrance to Canada based on humanitarian and compassionate grounds. The federal government has also recently withdrawn millions of dollars of funding dedicated to artistic and cultural programs. What is more, this cabinet aligned itself with the Bush administration's so-called war on terror, first by extending Canada's military presence in Afghanistan, and second by refusing to secure the release of Canadian citizen Omar Khadr from US custody at Guantanamo Bay.

In sum, while some of the federal government's decisions appear to acknowledge Canada's history of racial violence and demonstrate a spirit of respect for the humanity and rights of Aboriginal people and the contributions of racialized minorities, these actions are largely symbolic. Because these gestures do not address ways that the legacies of Canada's past continue to exert their influence in the present, they merely reinforce the status quo of inequality. Thus, for all intents and purposes, these "conservative closures" (A. Y. Davis 2008) undermine Canada's commitment to domestic and global struggles for equality and social justice and signal the emergence of what Patricia Hill Collins describes as a "new politics of containment" (1998, 35), which disproportionately affects the status, privileges, and opportunities available to Aboriginals and racialized minority Canadians.

Black/Out

> *Slavery is Canada's best kept secret, locked within the national closet. And because it is a secret it is written out of official history.*
>
> Afua Cooper, *The Hanging of Angelique*

In this discussion, I am using the term *black/out* to refer to the incalculable erasures and disavowal of a black presence in Canada. For example, few know that slavery was practiced in New France and British North America for more than two centuries and that the pattern of black settlement extends across the country and dates back to the 1600s. Rather, a narrative that is oft repeated is that upper Canada/Ontario was the final destination of the Underground Railroad; claiming it was the place where slaves escaped to freedom promotes the claim of Canada as a space of safety and liberty (A. Cooper 2000; Pabst 2006). Along with the institution of slavery, this legacy of systemic discrimination includes the repudiation of land grants to black settlers by the British government and segregation (Backhouse 1999; Thornhill 2008; Walker 1997). Additionally, racialized immigration policies were implemented to regulate the entry of black women from the Caribbean. They were recruited to work as domestic laborers and nurses, but were not afforded the opportunity to enter the country as potential legal immigrants. Rather, they were only granted access to the Canada country through temporary visas (A. Cooper 2000). In conjunction with the exclusion of blacks from Canadian histories, black geographies have also been hidden or expunged through practices such as the renaming of Negro Creek Road in Holland Township in Ontario to the name after a white male settler, along with the destroying of black communities in Africville, Nova Scotia, and Hogan's Alley in Vancouver, and the destruction of black cemeteries, such as the Old Durham Road Pioneer Cemetery in Ontario, and the slave cemetery in

Saint-Armand, Québec (Ihnatowycz 2007; Mackenzie 1991; McKittrick 2002, 2006; Starr 2000).

Expunging Canada's histories of antiblack racism from our national consciousness has had permanent consequences. For example, black Canadians are not considered real members of the nation. Our presence is regularly interpreted as an anomaly or exception, and we are commonly regarded as being from "elsewhere." Most often we are assumed to be immigrants from the West Indies, the United States, or the African continent (see A. Cooper 2000; J. Nelson 2008; Walcott 2000, 2003). Moreover, Canada's closeness to the United States, in conjunction with its overwhelming symbolic and material presence, has exerted great pressure upon expressions and interpretations of blackness in Canada as black American cultural practitioners, athletes, celebrities, and products have attained overarching visibility and currency in the country. This visibility has contributed to the notion that the United States is constitutive of the authentic figure of blackness (Pabst 2006). All told the varied ways that blacks have been excluded from the imagined community of the Canadian nation physically, symbolically, and discursively continue to undermine the ways that Canada's past informs its present. In sum, processes of racialization and racism in Canada work alongside policies of multiculturalism to frame blacks and blackness as outside the boundaries of the nation and, by extension, the academy, in a way that McKittrick describes as the "erasure and existence" (2002, 28) of a black Canadian presence.

The Academic Imperial Project

As I mentioned at the outset, two decades following the introduction of employment-equity measures, the proportion of Aboriginal and racialized minority groups within Canadian universities remains deplorably low. What is more, universities do not consistently gather data on the racial composition of their staff; the only national equity data on academic staff is supplied by the Canadian census. In addition to the absence of data on the racial and ethnic composition of their full-time employees, universities provide no information on part-time staff, sexual minorities, or persons with disabilities (Canadian Association of University Teachers 2007; Drakich and Stewart 2007). Consequently, outside of the ever-growing number of personal accounts that confirm the dearth of Aboriginal and racialized minority groups, there is no adequate official report of the standing of these groups in Canadian postsecondary institutions (Kobayashi 2006; Luther, Whitmore, and Moreau 2003; Moghissi 1994; Mukherjee 2001; Ng 1993). The unwillingness of universities to collect comprehensive information on Aboriginal and racialized minority groups is noteworthy because it undermines conversations about equity while simultaneously validating public discourses which suggest that race is no longer relevant and, furthermore, that racism is not an issue in Canada's de facto multiracial and multiethnic society (Henry and Tator 2007).

With few exceptions, equity in postsecondary institutions across Canada has related to gender. The data indicate that the majority of the women hired have been white and able-bodied. As a consequence, white women are increasingly becoming the new gatekeepers (Henry and Tator 2007b; hooks 1994; M. S. Smith 2007). Thus, white men, and to some extent white women, have unquestionably benefited from informal and unstated "affirmative" selection (Bonilla-Silva 2003; McKinney 2005). Steadfast resistance to critical analysis of hiring patterns maintains the current state of racial inequity, however. There continues to be limited recognition and discussion about the absence of Aboriginals and racialized minority groups and the implications of their exclusion (Henry and Tator 2007b; Kobayashi 2007b).

I want to make a connection here between the current racial climate and nation building. In this context, I am using the phrase "the white face of multiculturalism" to draw attention to the ways that white racial domination (and its attendant culture of whiteness) coexists with public recognition and celebration of Canada's multiracial and multiethnic status (Mackey 1999). I contend that at this sociopolitical juncture, the recent public acts of contrition actually open the door for the kinds of strategic closures that the federal government and other Canadian institutions are currently employing. As Pierson summarizes, in the face of the growth of Aboriginals and racialized minority groups, "exclusion and erasure are important to maintain regimes of racist and imperialist knowledge, instruments wielded in the service of the psychological, cognitive, and affective processes of denial and disavowal" (2004, 96).

Multicultural Myths and Racial Realities: The Cultural Politics of Everyday Life

In the next section, I offer examples of my experiences in the academy to illustrate the way institutions and individuals participate in reproducing racism and social inequality. Borrowing hooks's phrase, the "passion of experience" (1994, 91), I include a variety of vignettes to illuminate the painful and embodied nature of my experiences to bear out how race, gender, and class are both material and symbolic components of my subjectiveity struggle (Alexander and Knowles 2005). I speak about the economic and social exclusions, emotional anxiety, and interconnected character of the racialized and engendered aggression that I have experienced as a result of my subordinate position as a black Canadian woman who is also a contract faculty member.

Who's Afraid of a Young Black Woman?

> White people [along with other racialized groups] fear black people in big ways, in financial ways, in small ways, . . . in utterly incomprehensible ways.
>
> Patricia Williams, *Seeing a Color-Blind Future*

Several years ago I taught a class in a women's studies program that explored literature of the diaspora and narratives of race, gender, and nation. This class was comprised of both graduate and undergraduate students, all of whom were white women. Several of the undergraduate students were struggling with the course materials largely because they had no background in the intersections of gender and race or critical race scholarship. I had instructed the students to write essays responding to the readings. Given the lack of engagement and meaningful analysis in their assignments, I told the students that they could rewrite and resubmit them without penalty. Nevertheless, there was a growing tension and hostility among the students because they were frustrated and angry about their low grades.

One morning several weeks into the term, as I was preparing to leave to teach this class, the director of the department (a white woman) came into my office to tell me that one of the students had approached her to say that she was dropping the class. During their conversation, the student had asked the chair why I "hated them." When the director relayed this conversation to me, she assured me that this student's comments had "nothing to do with race." Moreover, while she acknowledged that the student's educational background was "weak," she told me that—upon reviewing the student's paper—she would not have given her a failing grade. She then informed me that she had advised the student that she could do an independent study with her during the summer to make up the credits she was losing as a result of dropping my course.

I want to identify this communication as symptomatic of a form of racial hostility, namely, the everyday violence of white domination in the form of gendered racism (Essed 2002). I contend that the white student's revulsion toward me was transformed into my so-called hatred of "them." Her resistance to the course material and the demands of the assignment (in addition to my feedback and her grade), as well as her profound discomfort with me as an authority figure, led her to construct herself as a righteous white person who was being attacked by the threatening black female other. In this situation, she acted from her position of white racial privilege; her effort to denigrate me confirmed that she felt she was superior to me and that she recognized that she had the ability to challenge my authority. In short, the student's complaint to a senior administrator, combined with the director's undermining my authority and granting the student an independent study as compensation, are instances of systemic racism (Kobayashi 2007a; Stanley 2006).

Moreover, the director's rush to deny the relevance of race illustrates the way whiteness is inextricably linked to power, namely masking the interconnectedness of race and gender (Williams 1997). Her negation of the significance of the interracial component of this faculty-student interaction stifled consideration of the possibility that the student's opposition and resistance were due to the fact that I was a black female instructor. As bell hooks observes, "White women can't even face their hostility at having to listen to a black woman talk when she's saying what they don't want to hear. They think it's just the ideas. Most of them have never listened to a black woman, or taken anything a black woman says seriously" (1997, 222).

I contend that in the academic culture of domination, the (gendered) racism of this student's actions was not acknowledged (hooks 1994). Rather, the white female director supported (and arguably bonded with) the white student in a manner that maintained the racist status quo (McKinney 2005). Additionally, the director's decision to tell me of this encounter as I was on my way to teach this very class showed a lack of regard for the kind of racial hostility that I was confronting. She did not ask me about the course or anything specific related to this student; she merely provided me with her evaluation and assessment and communicated what she believed was my inadequate handling of the situation. In short, the fact that the director recognized only the student's perspective as relevant revealed her sense of duty (i.e., racial loyalty) toward the young woman. Given the white student's racial pronouncement, the director's failure to consider the complexities involved when a black woman teaches a course that focuses on race and its connection to gender and power indicates a lack of awareness (or denial?) of white resentment and resistance, as well as this student's categorization of me as the racial other (Bérubé [2001] 2003). The director ignored my point of view and failed to recognize my class as a hostile space where the students had formed racial alliances to support their sense of injustice. This rebuff (by the director of a women's studies department) suggests an "indifference to the effects of racialization" (Kobayashi 2007a) and illustrates the void between a scholarly/organizational commitment to social justice and the inequitable personal relationships that are experienced every day within the academy (Kobayashi 2007b).

Job Wanted

After I had completed my PhD, a white male friend in the United States told me that—owing to the implementation of affirmative action—his employment opportunities were severely limited. In light of the political climate, he believed that I would have no problem getting a job. It has been fourteen years since that conversation, and that friend is now an associate professor while I have yet to secure a tenure-track position. His claim that white male applicants were being supplanted by the supposedly less-qualified Aboriginal or racial-minority candidates reflects an unceasing sense of entitlement that is a fundamental component of attitudes about white racial superiority. Despite the academy's lack of diversity, his unwillingness to recognize the circumscribed employment prospects of racial and ethnic minorities conveys the ever-present certainty that white males have the right to the best jobs. As a consequence, unspoken racial preferences continue to influence hiring and promotion, although they are not identified that way (McKinney 2005).

Correspondingly, a white Canadian female colleague characterizes my career path as "unique" and describes me to others as someone who has "slipped through the cracks." A senior white faculty member recently told a research colleague of mine (a white female) that I chose not to have a job in the academy. He proceeded to tell her that when I graduated, many scholars in the United States were "salivating" at the prospect of hiring me. I wonder if they have had a good look at the composition of their departments lately. These two examples illustrate the resistance and hostility that I continue to encounter from those who assume that if I really wanted a full-time job, I could find one. As I have already mentioned, I left the academy following my inability to secure employment; no one sought me out as a potential colleague or a desired/desirable candidate.

Both of these exchanges confirm a disengagement from racial reality. In particular, they reinforce the notion that the existence of employment-equity policies will ensure that equality is achieved (C. E. James 2007). They also bolster prevailing mythologies that declare that racism is an unusual occurrence, rather than widespread and "intentional" (Kobayashi 2007a, 5). As Patricia J. Williams cogently argues, for whites this form of "racial denial tends to engender a profoundly invested disingenuousness, an innocence that amounts to the transgressive refusal to know" (1997a, 27). Few are willing to acknowledge that Aboriginal and racialized minority groups have lost job opportunities as a result of discrimination. In this instance, the existence of employment equity and multicultural policies masks the operation of white racial power.

At a conference in 2008, I met a Canadian Aboriginal scholar who teaches in the United States. When she learned of my difficulties finding full time employment, she suggested I look for work in the United States because, in her words, I would be "appreciated more" south of the border. I am often asked if I am willing to go to the United States, the assumption being that once I garner experience I will then have a better chance of securing full-time employment in Canada. For the record, I have applied to American institutions and have not been successful at getting a job.

Moreover, aside from the not-so-small issue of relocation, there are what I regard as much more critical issues, namely, that my leaving will not contribute to an expansion of Canadian curricula, nor will it address the absence of racialized minority mentors and pedagogic diversity. There is much to uncover and make public about the histories and experiences of black Canadians and other groups. Considering the history of disavowal of the legacy of a black presence in Canada, the suggestion that I should go to the United States can also be interpreted as further evidence of the ongoing difficulty Canadians have recognizing blacks as members of the nation. Because the politics of race and racism are not on the agenda in Canadian universities (or in any other Canadian institution, for that matter), I have an investment in contributing to the transformation of the current culture and structure of both the academy and Canadian society. Thus, if we are to construct more equitable and just learning environments, white domination and racial inequality must be reckoned with.

Furthermore, I regard my part-time/subordinate standing in the academy as a manifestation of gendered racism/violence. My financial stability is inextricably linked to my emotional security. The many years of economic hardship and the constant energy that it takes to look for work have taken a toll on my physical well-being and my sense of self. My job insecurity remains a considerable source of distress, and as a result, it has been difficult for me to plan my life. I am not financially independent, and I (along with thousands of other Canadians) do not have a pension plan or extended medical and dental benefits. I have also expended a great deal of time creating new courses (primarily special topics courses), conducting my own research projects, and writing for publication. It has been exceptionally difficult to balance the need to generate an income with carving out time to write. I need to teach to live, and I need to write to get full-time work. Moreover, when I work as a part-time instructor, I do not have access to travel funds or money to support research or attend conferences, where I could develop networks and share knowledge. In short, securing full-time employment requires financial certainty coupled with the time to write and do research.

The absence of diversity in academia suggests that people who look like me do not belong; students and faculty are being socialized through the exclusion of a range of voices, experiences, and perspectives, and this further reduces their opportunity to interact with marginalized or underrepresented groups. As a consequence, "intellectual impoverishment" (St. Lewis 2007) will be reproduced along with inequality (Margolis and Romero 1998). Correspondingly, the inability to achieve substantive change in the academy reveals the ardent investment in maintaining the culture of whiteness through strategies of racial exclusion, indifference, and silence. In short, the antipathy toward Aboriginal and racialized minority groups in postsecondary institutions is emblematic of "the white face of multiculturalism," namely, the coexistence of the workings of white racial domination alongside the actuality of Canada's multiracial and multiethnic population.

Another issue that disproportionately influences part-time faculty is the restriction regarding the number of registered students necessary for a course to be taught. Class size typically shifts at the start of the term, and the official number of students is not known until the drop/add deadline has passed. Of late deans and other senior administrators are enforcing stricter requirements on student enrollment in courses. If a course does not have the requisite number of students, it will be canceled.

Thus, in an effort to ensure that the mandatory numbers of students sign up for a class, instructors are expected to promote their courses. While universities vary in the extent that faculty is expected to create and post advertisements, the marketing of courses (and the nebulous idea that they must be appealing to a range of students) requires additional time and energy and produces more anxiety. In contrast to full-time faculty, we are not guaranteed payment for these services. At one institution, my contract stipulated that if the course did not have enough students by the term deadline, I would receive only three hundred dollars for all my efforts. In this current corporate and bureaucratic academic environment where pragmatism reigns, students want the quickest path to an A or material that they deem relevant, which usually means courses that will guarantee them stable employment, rather than enlighten them about the history of race relations in Canada. Similarly, in a country where national discourses typically promotes the policy of multiculturalism as evidence of open-mindedness, the relevance of race and racism is a tough sell.

To Be Black, Female, and Dis/Embodied

> *Encounters are moments when realities of domination and oppression become embodied, but they are simultaneously opportunities to disrupt meta-narratives.*
>
> L. Peake and B. Ray, "Racializing the Canadian Landscape"

In my initial efforts to return to the academy, I met with a number of administrators and faculty. I want to recount one encounter with a senior administrator of a sociology department (a white woman) since our conversation is emblematic of the kinds of privileges and power that are available to white women in societies structured by racial domination (hooks 1994). During our meeting, she told me that it was too bad that I didn't have more experience. I had left the academy only because I was disillusioned and had not been able to find work after I received my PhD. It is indeed a bitter irony to have people ask me where I have been or tell me that I don't have enough experience. (Unemployment does limit your ability to practice your craft.)

At one point during our conversation, she told me that we are all feminists in the academy, and when I mentioned that it has been difficult to negotiate my identity as a black female in the classroom, she downplayed our differences, saying it was also difficult when she was in front of the class. The lack of empathy (or indifference) she conveyed about our different situations contributes to the reproduction of the academy's culture of whiteness (Pierson 2004). As antiracist scholar and activist Tim Wise argues, the "ability of whites to deny nonwhite reality . . . is as strong as any other evidence of just how pervasive white privilege is in this society" (2005, 59). The homogenization of our differences took an interesting turn when the discussion turned to course content. She conceded that the kind of material that is used to teach an intro (or first-year) group of students about racism and sexism is very different from what is selected to teach more advanced students. "You can't offend them," she said.

In a department of sociology, surely words like sexism and racism are fundamental to any introductory discussion and analysis of the social world. What is feminist about avoiding a dialogue about power and discrimination and the implications of systemic oppression and inequality? Yet again I was reminded that having privilege/ power means certain individuals can choose if, when, and under what conditions to move away from the security of their own positions (Kimmel 2003). When I later described the exchange to a racialized minority friend, she found it curious that the administrator did not offer to mentor me; she then suggested that perhaps in future meetings with "these white women" I should not expose my vulnerabilities.

The violence that is a consequence of misrecognition and exclusion is at the very least, exhausting. I remember feeling so disheartened by our conversation that afterward, even though it was lunchtime, I went home and went to bed. I describe this encounter to illustrate the brutality of erasure (and marginalization) as well as the ongoing battle to speak out "against the insistence that being female is all that matters" (hooks 1997, 98). This meeting exposes the operation of white denial in the reproduction of racial power; the interaction was unwelcoming. I felt out of place. I was not heard, and this senior administrator dismissed as inconsequential my position as a black female Canadian academic and my experiences of racism (Kobayashi 2006). Moreover, her declaration of a shared feminist identity while refusing to acknowledge the way race and class shape how we differ as women confirms what bell hooks has described as the "inability of white women to get a handle on the meaning of 'whiteness' in their lives . . . or the white supremacy that shapes their social status" (1994, 104). In sum, this interaction illustrates the way white women have taken up the position of gatekeepers of the racial status quo (i.e., the culture of whiteness) of the academy.

The Paradox of Power in the Academic Empire

Years ago, I taught an upper-division course on ethnography in a sociology department. In addition to studying research methods, we considered some of the ongoing and emergent dilemmas, such the insider/outsider debates, the politics of interpreting and recording data, and the relationship between researchers and their subjects of study. The course emphasized the intersections of race with gender and class and the impact of the multiple components of our identities on the entire research process. The majority of the students were female. Half of the class consisted of members of racialized minorities, most of whom were Asian. The other half was made up of members of the white majority.

From the outset, the racial tensions in the room were appreciable. The white students struggled to reconcile the preponderance of racialized minority students and the fact that their professor was a black woman. Specifically, while a number of the white students recognized the importance of gender to ethnography, they could not see the relevance of race to the process of field research. They did not want to think about race and its link to gender and class. They did not think these issues were important to their ways of thinking and being; they did not trust me or my framing of the course material. Race, they believed, was a property of those typically marked as the racial other, and consequently, it did not apply to members of the racial majority (Carby 1992).

The white students never wavered in their sense of superiority and entitlement, and they frequently sought to silence and intimidate me through their behavior. A racialized minority female friend of mine who had recently received her undergrad- uate degree had wanted to sit in on a couple of the lectures, but after two classes, she stopped, saying that she could no longer stand to watch the white students treat me with such disdain. For example, several of the white students told me that I was vague and that my method of evaluation was subjective. On one occasion, a white female student told me that she really liked my lecture, and on another occasion, she asked me if this was my first time teaching. After I returned their second assignments, one of the white male students who sat in the back row confidently told the class that he had received a better grade because "he had said more about himself." As he hurled his accusation toward me, he had a look of incredulity, petulance, and the presumed expectation that he was not alone. In contrast, the majority of the racialized minority students incorporated the multiple components of their identities into their work without hostility. Throughout the semester, my discussions of the centrality of race (and its intersections with other social formations) to the relationship among researchers' identities, their research, and the dilemmas they encountered gaining access and establishing trust seemed to disrupt the white students' sense of themselves and their interpretation of what matters (Schick and St. Denis 2005).

On the last day of class—when I asked the students to share their thoughts on the course—an exchange student from Norway stated that the course was not worth the money. In contrast, several of the racialized minority students simply said that they had gained helpful knowledge about the dynamic and complex nature of fieldwork. Later—outside of the classroom—I encountered several of the white women who had been hostile throughout the term. They told me that while they liked the course, they felt that the behavior of the Asian students had prevented it from being as good as it could have been. Overall my experience teaching this course confirms the fundamental divisions between white and racialized minority students and underscores the urgent need for education about the impact of race and racism in Canada (Henry and Tator 2007a; Kobayashi 2007b, M. S. Smith 2007).

What's in a Name?

A number of years ago, I had a conversation with another part-time sociology instructor (a young white female) about age, respect, and students' behavior. She told me that students are frequently surprised when they first see her and assume that she is gullible. She told me that in light of the students' treatment of her, she had changed the way she dresses, and she now writes on the board the way she wants to be addressed in the classroom. A female colleague who is Japanese told me that she writes Dr. on the blackboard on the first day of class to encourage more respectful treatment from the students.

In contrast, I have noticed that in many women's studies programs, a number of the white female faculty encourage students to call them by their first names. I have never given my students this option. In light of the black/out or the erasure of the history of slavery and black settlement in Canada, combined with the scarcity of black female lecturers, I am not readily recognized as a legitimate faculty member or a Canadian citizen; students are frequently surprised when they learn that I am their instructor (Messner 2000; Stanley 2006). Similarly my skin color, tone, and personal style do not correspond with students' perceptions and experiences of academic staff in Canadian postsecondary institutions: for many students, black remains a suspect category (Crenshaw 1997). In this context, I ask students to call me professor; the majority of them comply with my request. However, there are always one or two who (selectively?) forget or—in the event that they become agitated or disgruntled with me—attempt to assert themselves by calling me by my first name.

Undoubtedly the subject matter that I teach has the potential to elicit an intense reaction from the students. Moreover, given the dearth of racialized minority and Aboriginal faculty, students rely upon extant ways of thinking to make sense of their social worlds. Consequently, social relationships in the classroom are also shaped by the world outside the university setting. As Carl James (1994) explains, "That I am a professor does not make me immune to the stereotypes and concomitant issues and problems that go along with being a racial minority, and a black person in particular in this society" (cited in Henry and Tator 1994, 84).

To summarize, these vignettes illuminate the ways that racial violence in its myriad forms is pervasive and cumulative. Crucially, they identify "the ways in which racial categorizations impact upon the body as a material object and of the complex and often painfully contradictory ways in which identities are actually lived out at the level of embodied experience" (Alexander and Knowles 2005, 10). In an article where she reflects on her life as a black female law professor, Taunya Lovell Banks uses the term "ethical fear" (1997, 100) to describe her realization that being feared is part of the "black experience" (98). She argues that blacks have "adapted to the fear of being feared and the dangers implicit in generating this fear" (98).

The simultaneity of being invisible and hypervisible has meant that I customarily operate in a state of alertness. I watch/observe while I am being watched/observed. In the classroom, I am mindful of every look or stare, of every whisper, and I am cognizant of the ever-present undercurrent of white allegiances/alliances that often commence partway through a course and continue until the end. White students in particular feel entitled to be discourteous, arrogant, and abrasive. They feel very comfortable lashing out. There have been many days when I feel incompetent, disconsolate, and enraged, and in those moments, I simply want to give up. Aboriginal scholar Patricia Monture-Angus's words describe why I remain in the academy: "I am not necessarily courageous, just determined to have a right to survive. And I am surviving in the way I know how, in the way I was taught—by writing, telling and exposing" (2003, 48).

White Canada Forever? Empire Building and Canada's Multicultural Color Line

What I want is to acknowledge that racism has damaged reason, damaged academic and civic freedoms and damaged the project of education itself. Admitting this means pursuing a kind of resolute and ongoing reckoning with whiteness.

Les Back, "Ivory Towers? The Academy and Racism"

In this discussion, I have offered some examples of what it means to be a black Canadian woman living under the multicultural sign in an effort to illuminate some of the structures, ideologies, and social relationships that "bring about and sustain racism and imperialism" (Pierson 2004, 91). My examination of the embodied intricacies of our everyday lives in a Canadian context is meant to encourage rethinking the ways that various systems of domination intersect and are experienced at a time where discussions and analyses of race and racism are being marginalized (Collins [1993] 2003).

In conjunction with a broader resistance to equity and social justice, Canadians find themselves at a time of diminishing diversity (M. S. Smith 2007) as universities have responded to shrinking budgets and a decade of retirements by increasingly turning to corporations for financial support and making sure they have a steady supply of contingent faculty to fill their needs. At the same time, departments/programs claim that they can barely teach their core curriculum and that they have no money to teach anything new or diversify their faculty. Consequently, the gap between the academy and the community is increasing as the homogeneity of faculty stands in stark contrast to the changing composition of Canadian society. Amid the nation's increasing diversity, the predominance of whites in the academy simultaneously confirms white supremacy by reinforcing the belief that those who are there are effectively the top candidates for the job. Consequently, whites are readily understood as authorities, and they unquestionably believe themselves to be best suited for their respective professions.

Thus, Canadian universities remain key sites of enculturation for whites since they are the places where the values and norms of the dominant culture are taught, affirmed, and taken for granted. The resultant privileges and confidence that whites take for granted are evidence of the wages of the academic empire (Du Bois [1935] 1998). Thus, it is not surprising that few whites have had the courage to speak out and challenge these structured exclusions (Henry and Tator 2007a; hooks 1994; Kobayashi 2007b; M. S. Smith 2007). Furthermore, the absence of a critical mass of Aboriginal and racialized minority faculty also makes it difficult for objects of repression to speak up for fear of reprisal. In this context, we must ask ourselves, at what point does the absence of racial diversity become what Baker (1993) describes as "willful ignorance and aggression" (cited in Pinar 1993, 62)?

Overall these moves are integral to the psychological, symbolic, and material production of empire and examples of expressions of violence upon which the academy and society rely (Razack 2008). Understanding these connections is imperative, for as Goldberg states, "violence, accordingly, is threatened or experienced in or as the everyday in societies the multicultural character of which has been produced out of postcolonial politics" (2005, 223). Indeed, behind the patina of claims of a harmonious (i.e., white) multiculturalism lies a much harsher racial reality; universities—indeed all Canadian institutions—remain racially structured environments where whites predominate (Canada Task Force 2000). In general, postsecondary institutions continue to foster race, class, and gender exclusivity that simultaneously obscure and advance the Canadian imperial project. As Pierson summarizes, there are two purposes to racist and imperialist practices and thought processes, namely, to "secure and maintain the hierarchy, and a group's or individual's dominant place in that hierarchy, as unproblematic; and two, to redeem for the dominant an unassailable character" (2004, 99). In closing, we are undeniably living in a "vicious moment" (A. Y. Davis 2008) as local and global practices become more ruthless, intensifying existing inequalities (Mohanty 2003). Nothing less than a collective response will do.

CHAPTER 5

THEY FORGOT MAMMY HAD A BRAIN

Sherrée Wilson

Of all groups, as bona fide intellectuals, [African American women] are the furthest removed from society's expectations of their place, the least expected to succeed on merit, and the most vulnerable to insult.

Nellie Y. McKay

Introduction

In one of the earliest studies that examined the climate for African American women scholars at predominantly white institutions (PWIs), Moses (1989) declared that their professional development or job satisfaction was not achieved without constant struggle. The findings noted some of the typical problems experienced by African American women faculty and administrators:

1. constant challenges or being viewed as "other" and therefore believed to be inferior;
2. lack of professional support systems;
3. excessive scrutiny by peers, superiors, and students;
4. an unstated requirement to work harder to gain recognition and respect;
5. assumptions that positions were acquired through affirmative action and that therefore the faculty members lacked the necessary qualifications;
6. tokenism, that is, being viewed as a symbol of race rather than as an individual; and
7. denial of access to power structures normally associated with their position(s).

The last decade of the twentieth century seemed to foster an increase in research specifically focused on African American women in academe and the way the intersection of race and gender impacts their experiences (Benjamin 1997; Berry and

Mizelle 2006; Collins [1993] 2000; Cooper 2006; Gregory 1999; Mabokela and Green 2001; Turner 2002b). African American women scholars are often faced with multiple marginality (Turner 2002b), where they may be accorded a particular status or subjected to certain treatment due to their race and gender. As a result, the experiences of African American women scholars at PWIs are distinct from those of their male counterparts.

Additionally, the fact that the "double minority" status (Stevenson 1993) of African American women may be perceived as an advantage in the hiring process may result in the presumption that gender and race were the primary reasons for these women securing positions in academe, rather than their competence as scholars, teachers, and/or researchers. As a consequence, the actual skills, expertise, and accomplishments of African American women scholars may be dismissed or ignored. That presumption may also affect the way students see African American female faculty at PWIs. hooks (1994) asserts that white students view African American women faculty as the "mammy" and, because of that, expect that they—regardless of their educational attainment or occupational status—will assume various caretaker roles. Daufin (1995) concurs and explains that since some white students can only imagine African American women as servants or caretakers, they may be unable to accept or adjust to the idea of having to work for African American women faculty. Those students may resent an African American woman who has power over them and is in a position of authority; the result may be lower-than-average student evaluations and an increased number of complaints regarding assignments and overall teaching competence.

Subtle messages of inferiority and incompetence from university administrators and faculty may reinforce the students' negative perceptions of women of color (Stevenson 1993). As a result, women faculty of color may encounter deans and department chairs who fail to support them when faculty/student conflicts arise. Wright and Dinkha (2002) found that some women faculty of color were pressured to make grade changes to accommodate students who voiced strong objections, which only succeeded in creating a hostile and unhealthy climate. As Gregory stated, "It is evident that we still have much work to do to encourage the permanence of African American women scholars; regardless of talent, a faculty member cannot reasonably function in an inhospitable academic environment" (1995, 96).

It is critical that the experiences of African American women scholars be prominently featured and recognized, given the challenges that they may face as a result of what Stanley (2006b) terms "double bind" syndrome—the combination of being a woman and a woman of color. By conducting and advancing research on African American women in higher education, institutions can become more aware of their challenges as well as their successes. This essay gives voice to the experiences of "Professor Andra," an African American female faculty member. Andra was the only female among the sample participants of a study that explored the experiences of African American faculty who were formerly employed at Urban University (the pseudonym assigned to the institution), a PWI. The narrative describes Andra's encounters in her former academic department at Urban, her presumed incompetence, and her eventual decision to leave the institution. The essay also highlights the strategies that helped Andra to cope in what was sometimes a hostile environment and offers recommendations that may lead to creating a more welcoming climate.

Methodology

Johnsrud and Sadao (1998) addressed the difficulty of designing and conducting research that has as its focus ethnic and minority faculty members (which they defined as Japanese, Chinese, Korean, Hawaiian, Filipino, black, Hispanic, Native American and Pacific Islanders). The number of respondents is often small; therefore, quantitative methods are not always applicable to this kind of research because accurate conclusions cannot be drawn. Additionally, simply categorizing and reporting findings based on ethnicity, gender, rank, or discipline can lead to a loss of the individual aspects of the participants' experiences, as well as their differences.

The potential loss of the unique aspects of ethnic and minority faculty members' experiences is particularly serious with African American women because much of the research on this population has traditionally been subsumed under such topics as women, women and minorities, or people of color (Carter, Pearson, and Shavlik 1987–88; Moses 1997; Rains 1999; Turner 2002b). As Hine pointed out, historians assumed that the experiences of black men applied to black women and the history of white women likewise related to black women. As a result, "it was left to the small number of black women scholars to insist that black women's experiences, precisely because of their race, gender, and class, were different and distinct in fundamental ways from those of black men and white women and deserved to be studied in their own right" (1997, 333).

Gordon (1992) suggested that voice scholarship helps to illuminate the experiences of persons of color in the academy, and the use of qualitative methodology responds to critical questions raised by scholars of color about the way research is conducted in communities of color since the lack of voices there reduces the usefulness of the knowledge that we can gain from the individuals' experiences (Ladson-Billings and Tate 1995). Errante (2000), hooks (1994), Kvale (1995), and Lincoln (1995) also emphasized the value and significance of using qualitative and interpretive inquiry to listen to persons of color. Lincoln (1995) declared that researchers must strive to "fairly listen to and portray voices, particularly disenfranchised ones" (283) so that those previously silent voices can be heard. Delgado (cited by Tate 1997) concurred and argued that the stories of persons of color come from a different frame of reference, which therefore gives them a voice that is different from the dominant culture and deserves to be heard.

To facilitate exploration of the faculty experiences, open-ended interview questions in a semistructured format were used. The initial interview with Andra was conducted in person at the institution where she is currently employed; the interview was audiotaped and lasted approximately ninety minutes. A follow-up interview, which was also audiotaped, was conducted via telephone and lasted sixty minutes; the interviews were transcribed, coded, and analyzed to identify themes and determine the meaning that Andra attached to the experiences. Analyses were conducted immediately so that data collected from the initial interview could help to formulate the questions for the follow-up session.

Participant Profile

Prior to her employment at Urban University, Professor Andra was working as a faculty member at an institution in the southeastern part of the country; during her fourth year of employment, an administrator of Urban University's School of Health and Human Services (SHHS) visited Andra in an effort to recruit her.

Andra stated that the opportunity sounded very attractive and that—in terms of the recruitment process—she received a "full court press." The offer came along at a time when Andra was ready to advance her career and professional development:

> I started as a lecturer, and you know you're worried about your contract all the time; then eventually I was an assistant professor, and then I just thought, okay. I was just ready to leave the institution when the representative from Urban showed up. It was a good opportunity. I thought, 'Oh, okay. This is not bad.' And, at that time, the program I was in was a very small program, and I wanted to spread my wings a little bit, so I did want to be at a larger institution. So that was it. That and the kind of interest they showed looked very attractive.

And so, armed with fifteen years of practical experience in the mental health field, a PhD from an institution on the East Coast, and prior teaching experience at a large public university, Andra accepted the position at Urban. Her research interests included community mental health practice, program development and evaluation, clinical practice with overwhelmed families and individuals across the life span, and diversity. When Andra joined the faculty as a tenure-track assistant professor in the SHHS at Urban, she was recruited as one of a cohort of several other African American faculty members by the dean of the school at the time: "They did something very smart at the School of Health and Human Services, and you have to give Solomon a lot of credit for this; he decided enough talking about we can't find any minorities, and eight of us were recruited at the same time, and so those early years it was really wonderful to have such a nice cohort of African Americans." Note: At the time of our first interview, Andra was completing her first year after leaving Urban as a tenured associate professor at a small private institution on the East Coast where she was the only African American faculty member in her department.

Although she had more than ten years experience as a professor, Andra indicated that the first year at her current institution had probably been the best that she had ever had; she attributed that to her positive interactions with her colleagues, as well as the affirming nature of the institution:

> People have extended themselves in ways that I've found unbelievable; in fact, I found it hard to trust. Because after the Urban experience, you know, you're waiting for the knife to come out or the other shoe to drop. There is a sense of community, and there is a mission that's been fused throughout the institution. The janitor can tell you what the mission of the college is— very proudly; every student here can tell you what it is. Its mission is service to humanity by developing students' spirits, minds, and bodies. And they're dead up serious about it. Anybody who comes to this college has to do some community service as a student.

Narrative

Andra was employed at Urban University for nearly ten years, where she achieved tenure and was promoted to associate professor one year prior to leaving the institution; and while the move to Urban was initially a positive one for Andra, it became more stressful over time: "The early years were not nearly as stressful as the later years. I think at first you're just trying to know each other, and we did have this supportive network. We were so happy just to be with each other learning the system. Then after a while, you begin to see little things."

Wright and Dinkha (2002) stated that women faculty of color undergo a number of experiences that may affect their productivity and ability to develop professional identities. "Environmental stressors not only influence their ability to make valuable contributions but may over time encourage them to seek positions elsewhere or to leave the academy altogether" (102). After nearly ten years at Urban, Andra reached the point of no return and determined that she needed to leave the institution:

> It was so stressful, and after a while I had no hope for change. There are just some things that need to be done at the school, and I didn't see them happening. By the time I was going up for tenure, I knew that this was probably not a place that I could stay. But then you're committed. It's like, okay, I did all this work, you do this tenure thing, so I might as well. So the year after, I was just tired. I just could not—after going up; do you know what I mean? Start a big job search after all that, so I don't know how else it could have played out, but the thing I did learn is to leave a place sooner, rather than later. So all of those things played a role; I just didn't have any hope anymore.

Despite the fact that Andra left a department at Urban, where she was one of a five-member cohort of African American faculty, to work at an institution where she is now the only African American faculty member, she indicated that the trade-off was worth it because of the differences in climate of the two departments: "When you would tell people your reality at Urban, it would always be denied. You know, it was really kind of the cheese stands alone—it wasn't as if you felt that you had any allies. We often talked about when we get off the elevator at the school, you could feel yourself just tensing up and just, okay, let me get ready to do battle. I don't need this. And when I talked to this faculty [at her current institution], there was such a sense of camaraderie." That image of preparing to do battle is also portrayed by an African American woman faculty member in the video *Through My Lens* (University of Michigan 1999), which captured the experiences of women of color faculty at the University of Michigan. In the video, the faculty member relates that each day she had to make decisions about what things are worth dying for and what things she needed to walk past or ignore in her work; Andra expressed similar sentiments as she reflected on her work life at Urban.

Working in a Challenging Climate

When faculty of color experience an academic workplace that is chilly and where they feel alienated, they will be less satisfied with nearly all aspects of their positions and work environments (Turner and Myers 2000; H. Astin et al. 1997). Establishing a critical mass of faculty of color in academic institutions is frequently cited and recommended as a strategy for minimizing feelings of alienation and cultivating a more welcoming climate (Branch 2001; Moody 2004; Stanley 2006a,b; Turner 2002a). The rationale behind this recommendation is that the very presence of other faculty of color in the workplace helps the scholars to become part of the campus community (Laden and Hagedorn 2000) and lessens their feelings of isolation. This was undoubtedly the thinking behind recruiting the faculty cohort of which Andra was a member; and in fact, Andra did emphasize that—in terms of the relationships that she formed—her time at Urban was invaluable: "I really learned a lot there. I really learned a lot of the pitfalls of academic life. I developed some relationships there that I'll have the rest of my life. So I'll never regret that. I would say that in the beginning you're hopeful. I think there's a kind of honeymoon period and so that was okay. And then you start to say, 'huh; something's wrong with this picture' as your awareness grows. The last few years were really painful, and I stayed too long."

While hiring a critical mass of faculty of color to avoid placing one of them in solo status is recommended to facilitate their retention (Stanley 2006a, b; Moody 2004; Turner 2002a), the fact that a campus or department is ethnically and racially diverse in number doesn't necessarily translate into an environment that is positive for faculty of color. Johnsrud and Sadao (2002) found evidence that a campus that had three times the number of minority faculty members than most institutions of its type still experienced instances of intolerance and exclusion. For women faculty of color at PWIs, that may mean encountering what Thompson and Louque (2005) termed a "culture of arrogance": a climate that is hostile or unwelcoming. In Andra's case, despite being a member of a cohort of other African American faculty, she reported incidents of invisibility, salary inequities, lack of support from administrators regarding students, and stereotypical comments and racist behavior from colleagues as well as students. Andra's description reveals the climate that she and other faculty experienced in Urban's SHHS:

> It felt hostile, and you know some very directly racist incidents happened. At one point, people in the school—it was African Americans, and I think gays and lesbians—got Ku Klux Klan notes under our doors. Or sometimes just plain old racist things were said. Or they'll tell you about how their momma and poppa and uncle and everyone else in their family hates niggers, but they don't—that's a quote. You just would be amazed at how direct it would get. So there were just some overtly, very challenging things that went on, and then there were some more subtle things.

William A. Smith contends that African Americans and other people of color experience *racial battle fatigue* as a result of encountering racism on a continual basis; specifically Smith characterized racial battle fatigue as "a response to the distressing mental/emotional conditions that result from facing racism daily (e.g., racial slights, recurrent indignities and irritations, unfair treatments, including contentious classrooms, and potential threats or dangers under tough to violent and even life-threatening conditions)" (2004, 180).

Andra detailed another incident that occurred while she was at Urban that would seem to contribute to racial battle fatigue and was very telling about the climate within her department:

> We had a faculty member who really should have been asked to retire some time ago, and we were in a committee meeting. I was chairing, and Debra was sitting next to me, and we're trying to move forward. He takes out the *USA Today* newspaper and begins to read a column, and I thought, you know, I don't think this is appropriate. He's reading it out loud, and it was tangential really—had nothing much to do with what the meeting was about—and so I asked him to put it away, copy it and send it around if you really want people to read it, and he went off. He went totally off on me.

Stood up, started spitting in my face, talking about "you people": "What's wrong with you people? If an African American person was reading next to you, you'd let it go on, and I just think that when you people get a little power, you abuse it." And Debra is sitting next to me, and her leg is shaking. My white colleagues left the room—ran out. Yes, they did. Debra, bless her heart, she stayed and tried to defend me, but then he started attacking her. And that had a profound impact on me. I said, "Okay, I'm getting the picture." This faculty member had just been bizarre, just had done awful things, and it was tolerated.

St. Jean and Feagin (1998) explain that while the phrase "you people" may not appear harsh to white speakers addressing African Americans, it can be offensive because it signals a lack of civility, and in this case, implied disdain for Andra as an African American. St. Jean and Feagin went on to report that "the US Court of Appeals for the Third Circuit handed down a decree that pervasive use of such phrases as 'you people' and related epithets are enough to prove that a workplace has a racially hostile climate" (129).

The respect that faculty of color garner from their peers may also play a role in creating a positive work environment. However, Andra indicated that some of her colleagues at Urban did not recognize that her expertise extended to areas beyond diversity: "I have twenty-seven years experience in mental health with people of color; I had this conceptualization about overwhelmed families, so I had lots of interests, but the only interest that I was ever given credit for was diversity. You just sit down and be black and you better be black in the way we were comfortable with." Turner and Myers (2000) argue that one of the greatest frustrations for African American faculty is the realization that their visibility in their departments or at their institutions may be based solely on race.

On the other hand, Andra felt that there were times when Urban used faculty of color for its own gain, to reap the benefits of the cultural tax (Padilla 1994): "You're used a lot for your race, and that just comes with the territory. They are going to trot you out and trot you around as their African American person, but that's not considered in terms of your workload. It doesn't count. They are going to expect you to mentor and take care of students of color, but you're not going to get credit for that, either. I learned a lot. They wanted our visibility in the service arena, but they didn't want to reward you for it."

As Padilla stated when explaining the concept of cultural taxation, while there is an expectation that faculty of color will accept various service activities, the institution may fail to appreciate and/or recognize the service, particularly when it comes to promotion and tenure. While the service performed by African American faculty may significantly impact students' success, Andra communicated the feeling that it was not appreciated by the institution: "I can tell you that if it was not for some of us, many of the students of color and some of the white students would have left. We were very student-centered, but that's not rewarded, and there are so many things you do that aren't recognized."

Interaction with Students

A diverse faculty can provide all students with role models that represent various racial and ethnic groups. However, prior to entering college, students receive subtle and not-so-subtle messages regarding persons from other racial and ethnic groups. Smith, Yosso, and Solórzano (2007) stated that the vast number of race-specific ste-reotypes to which white students are exposed prior to entering college likely affect their view of people of color. Andra described the way that hooks' (1981) conten-tion that African American women are viewed as the mammy stereotype applied to her own experience with students at Urban: "I always felt that many of them kind of underestimated me. It was almost like the mammy syndrome. They wanted me to be their mammy. 'Oh, Mammy, I feel bad; take care of me, mammy.' But they forgot Mammy had a brain and the same kind of PhD as others. Some nasty little things have happened in the classroom. You're supposed to always be chuckling and nurturing no matter what they do. You're not supposed to demand the same level of performance. 'You's the mammy.'"

Aguirre (2000) suggested that faculty of color often encounter white students whose perceptions are biased. One of the most prevalent biases is that the faculty member is simply an affirmative-action hire and, as a result, he or she becomes mar-ginalized in the eyes of those white students. For some white students, their entrée into higher education may provide the first opportunity to interact with persons of color. Andra felt the issue should have been broached on her teaching evaluations: "Things went on in the classroom . . . . Very often we had people from Podunk, USA, who had never seen a person of color in any role of authority. That was very chal-lenging, and when we would try to talk about that—I even wanted to put an item, a question of my own, on the teaching evaluations that tried to address that, but I was told absolutely not."

Also in terms of classroom experiences, African American women faculty often describe instances of having their credentials questioned or challenged by students; this resonated with Andra: "Well, some people had a harder time than others, but I think you're challenged about things like 'how do you know that?' or there is more testing and sort of questioning your right to give them anything less than an A."

Lack of Support for Faculty

Stevenson (1993) asserted that women faculty of color may encounter administra-tors who sabotage the interactions that teachers have with students. Andra expressed discomfort with the school's culture of valuing students over faculty: "The boundar-ies between faculty and students were really blurred in lots of ways, and that was something that we just were not comfortable with. It comes down to taking your word or a student's word. In terms of faculty of color, the student is going to win that battle. The other thing is sometimes when you had to make very hard decisions and flunk a student, both directors would override that decision, so we would have just ridiculous people who never should have graduated; they would get out." Stevenson (1993) also noted that department chairs and deans sometimes undermine faculty when asked to intervene in student/faculty or faculty/peer conflicts, particularly when they rebuff the explanations offered by faculty of color. An incident when Andra was facilitating a diversity group with students while at Urban illustrates the point:

> I got pushed into doing this diversity group with these students, and it was one of the most painful experiences I've ever had with students. This stu-dent challenged me all the way down the line. In one meeting, the student got so angry [that] she threw down her knapsack and stomped out of the

room and slammed the door. It was awful. In fact, this student told me that African Americans didn't know much about their own experience and that I ought to read Robert King's *Oliver* because in her experience, whites have helped more. This is a lesbian student, and there was always the comparison. I even tried to say oppression is oppression. The shape is different. It's apples and oranges, but they're both fruit. And this is a filthy rich student, by the way, and nobody has ever suffered like she did, and there was some real poignant sharing by some of the African American students in the school, and she dismissed it.

So I went to the director of the graduate program, who had been one of the people kind of pushing me into it. I said, "I'm really having a problem." She told me, "I don't want to be triangulated." And I thought, "What?" It just hit me that my word was not as good as that of this student. And the final slap in the face was that after this awful experience that was very painful for some of the African American students in the group, the director nominated this student for graduate student of the year, and she got that award at graduation. And frankly, that was the end of my relationship with that faculty member.

Thus, not only did the white student make disparaging remarks to a faculty member, but administrators discounted the effect of the incident on Andra as well as the African American students. The student's behavior was subsequently reinforced and essentially validated when she was nominated for and eventually received an award.

Interactions with White Female Colleagues

While the comments from students cannot be excused, there was the expectation that white women faculty colleagues would be more culturally aware. Andra recounted patronizing comments from white female colleagues who believed their limited experience with the civil rights movement and work in an African American housing project meant that they were experts on matters of diversity:

There is one faculty member, for example, who is always saying how she worked with Dr. King and she marched in the '60s. That's her image of herself. She doesn't want to hear about anything she's doing now that is subtly racist . . . but you scratch underneath that surface, and the same stuff is there. We had another faculty member who'd say—and this used to drive us to distraction—"I worked in Cabrini Green Projects for one year, and therefore I know it all. There is nothing you can really tell me that I haven't experienced." I mean she would say things like this, and it takes more than a year in the projects to understand what's going on.

St. Jean and Feagin asserted that negative comments and actions that African American women receive from white women are as numerous as those endured from white men, and that those comments are "one more way whites manipulate or demean the status and lives of African American workers" (1998, 127).

When Race and Gender Collide

As has been demonstrated, when race and gender intersect, there are challenges that distinguish the experiences of women faculty of color from those of her male colleagues. As a result, African American women faculty may be marginalized, as illustrated by this experience Andra had:

> There was a faculty meeting, and I was making comments, and it would be pretty much ignored. A white male would then make the same comment, and then everybody heard it—oh, isn't that brilliant. So those kinds of things would happen quite frequently. You're not heard, and myself and two other African American women faculty colleagues, we made the most noise, but people would literally not hear what we said, and then we would have a white faculty member repeat it, and they would react as if it was the second coming.

The double marginalization that African American women face can make it difficult to determine whether the reactions and behaviors directed at them are due to race, gender, or a combination of both (St. Jean and Feagin 1998). When asked whether she perceived the incidents she encountered resulted from race or gender, Andra stated unquestionably that she felt they were due to race: "I think when people look at us, they see a black woman, not a woman who is black, and so the first thing that they relate to is your race." Indeed, St. Jean and Feagin (1998) found that in the majority of cases of gendered racism against black women, the women concluded that the discrimination was due to race, rather than gender.

Conversely, Andra also experienced what Rains (1999) calls *designated visibility*— unwanted visibility that is solely a function of skin color: "Well, your mistakes are noticed, very much so. And whatever shortcomings you have, they're very, very visible. It's just when you get to your achievements, somehow you become less visible, but any shortcoming you have is magnified to the nth degree."

Support Systems

As a faculty member at Urban University, Andra was subjected to students who challenged her teaching methods, questioned her credentials, and disputed grades that they received; additionally, interactions with some of her colleagues were less than optimal. When Andra turned to administrators in her school for support, she either encountered resistance and/or felt that her concerns were ignored. As a result, Andra endured a work environment that was hostile and unwelcoming and fostered alienation. So how does a person cope? Two primary sources of support—a faculty cohort and peer mentoring—were vital to Andra's professional survival during her years at Urban University.

The Faculty Cohort as a Counterspace

When Andra was recruited to Urban's SHHS, she was one of an eight-member cohort of African American faculty members; at the time of her departure, five of the members remained. That group provided a venue for the African American faculty to share their common experiences, receive support, and engage in the collaboration that is often sought by African American faculty working at PWIs. Andra emphasized the importance of receiving support from and engaging with individuals who shared common histories, cultures, and experiences and who could truly be empathetic:

> I think there is a common experience, so we really have and still do have—I mean we bonded very intensely through going through that same

experience. I mean Talia Newman is more like family; I speak to her mother on a regular basis, and she calls me "baby"—you know it's like that. Grace Tilton and I are still very much in touch; Gianna and her whole family—we are still very much in touch. So I really developed some relationships there that I'll have the rest of my life. So I'll never regret that. Our kids are very close. So really, some profound relationships came out of that. So it was just wonderful not just personally but in terms of the kinds of ideas that we were able to exchange—we learned so much from each other.

It is not unusual for individuals to seek out other persons with whom they share similar backgrounds, cultures, and experiences (Bennett 1998; Feagin, Vera, and Imani 1996); this may be particularly significant for African American faculty at PWIs since they look to one another for support, validation, and reassurance. As a result, the faculty may create *counterspaces*, a term coined by critical race theorists Solórzano, Ceja, and Yosso (2000); these are safe areas or relationships with other individuals with whom they share common experiences and where they will be encouraged and nurtured. That natural seeking of others with whom we have an affinity (Bennett 1998) explains why Andra indicated that for her, the cohort needed to be comprised of other African Americans: "You are more relaxed; you are more yourself, and you're not doing the bicultural dance; you're not watching every little thing you say when you have a good supportive network of your same group, there's just nothing that can replace that."

Mentoring

Mentoring as a form of support is believed to be essential to the career advancement and success of African American faculty (Diggs et al. 2009; Stanley 2006a, b; Tillman 2001; Turner and Myers 2000). For African American women faculty, it can be difficult to develop mentoring relationships (Cooper 2006: Woods 2001); however, Andra was the beneficiary of mentoring from a senior faculty member as well as peer mentoring.

Andra spoke highly of a senior faculty member at Urban who provided invaluable support and guidance, particularly during her preparation for promotion and tenure: "Yeah, I just would not have made it if it wasn't for Grace Tilton. But you know, isn't that an unfair responsibility to put on one person? I mean she did it gladly—I think because we really are good friends—but yeah, it was Grace, and my sense is that some of us would not have been tenured if Grace had not been on the committee." The peer mentoring was a benefit of Andra's membership in the faculty cohort; it also provided a venue for collaboration: "I think one of the things that did help me was having people—the cohort; again Talia and I are very close, and we write together; we have an article coming out, and we're working on another one. Grace and I have presented together; we've got a really nice presentation that we do. Lola and I have presented together, so that's what helped—the collaboration."

Discussion

Mentoring relationships are particularly crucial for African American women faculty at PWIs since they can help to offset the challenges that the women will likely face as they move up the academic ladder (Cooper 2006; Gregory 2001; Locke 1997); mentors can provide needed encouragement and guidance, particularly when the women find themselves in less-than-optimal academic settings. While Andra's mentors were African American, there is literature that suggests mentors and mentees are not required to be the same race or ethnicity (Cooper 2006; Thompson and Louque 2005). In fact, Stanley (2006b) advocates the establishment of cross-race faculty mentoring relationships, stating that they aid retention and also prepare the mentees for conflicts that may arise when discussions about diversity occur.

Ultimately, African American female faculty scholars must determine which mentoring relationships work best for them. Ideally, several different relationships will be established, based on various factors (scholarship, interests, cultural experiences, race, and ethnicity) since one mentor cannot (nor should try to) meet the complex needs of the faculty member.

Harvey's (1994) assertion that simply increasing the numbers of faculty of color is not enough to retain them is evidenced by Professor Andra's experiences. Institutions must also work to change climates and cultures to ensure that they feel welcoming to persons of color. As long as departmental and/or campus climates fail to welcome faculty of color, retaining those faculty will remain a challenge (Yoshinaga-Itano 2006).

Andra described racist incidents and a hostile climate, which she felt the leadership of the school failed to acknowledge or address. She had worked at Urban University for ten years when she made the decision to leave; she came to Urban as an assistant professor in the SHHS but had earned tenure and promotion to associate professor one year prior to her departure. Andra was one of a five-member cohort of African American faculty in her school while at Urban and touted the benefits of working with and having the support of other African American faculty. The cohort aided her professional development and survival and helped her to cultivate and establish what she characterized as lifetime friendships. However, despite having the benefit of a same-race cohort, Andra cited the climate in the school as her primary reason for leaving the institution. She emphasized that her earlier years at the institution, under the dean who initially recruited her, were positive ones. However, a change in leadership altered the racial climate, and Andra felt that ensuring a climate that nurtured all the faculty was not a priority for subsequent deans.

While faculty of color often encounter climates that are hostile and less than ideal, Turner and Myers (2000) state that faculty generally leave unwelcoming institutions, rather than the profession entirely. They attribute this pattern to the high levels of satisfaction associated with an academic career. Andra's experiences at Urban did not diminish her interest in teaching; rather, she sought a more welcoming environment at another institution. Although Andra is now employed at a school where she is presently the only African American faculty member in her department, she indicated that the environment is far more positive than the one she experienced near the end of her tenure at Urban University.

Summary and Recommendations

While at Urban, Andra had various support systems at her disposal, including a faculty mentor and membership in a cohort of African American faculty. However, her experience at Urban suggests that these personal and institutional support systems may not be enough to overcome a climate hostile to women of color. Therefore, the following is recommended:

1. prior to initiating search and recruitment, it is critical that administrators and leaders conduct cultural audits to assess the "temperature" of the climates in their academic units;
2. institutional administrators must accept responsibility for cultivating and providing an educational environment that welcomes and supports all its participants, regardless of race, ethnicity, or gender;
3. academic administrators and leaders must demonstrate that all faculty are valuable and competent members of the campus community;
4. administrators should examine their own knowledge regarding women faculty of color and the challenges that they may face at PWIs;
5. administrators should demonstrate their commitment to cultural competence and faculty diversity by modeling skills and behaviors that can be emulated; administrators should commit resources for faculty development that includes mentoring and community building; to counter or alleviate feelings of isolation, administrators need to explore ways that women of color faculty can become connected within academic units on campus and/or within the community;
6. since African American women faculty, as well as other women faculty of color, may be in departments or disciplines where they are the only minority member or one of a few, the institution should provide resources so that the women can attend conferences and/or join professional organizations where they can cultivate and build a community of support;
7. campus administrators should conduct exit interviews with departing faculty to determine the reasons they are leaving institutions and consult with faculty who have remained to identify factors that can aid retention.

Conclusion

Because gendered racism separates the experiences of African American women in higher education from those of their male colleagues, it is important to analyze the distinct experiences of African American women faculty and increase the awareness of the double marginalization that they face on campus. In addition, studying the experiences of African American women faculty may reveal successful strategies for thriving and surviving that may be useful to other women faculty of color as they advance professionally and can lead to thinking that will eventually presume that these valuable faculty members are anything but incompetent.

CHAPTER 6

PRESENT AND UNEQUAL

A Third-Wave Approach to Voice Parallel Experiences in Managing Oppression and Bias in the Academy

Kimberly R. Moffitt, Heather E. Harris, and Diane A. Forbes Berthoud

The Presence of Women Academics of Color

> *How do the excluded engage the apparently dominant order? Does progress entail that the marginalized accept mainstream norms and abandon transformative possibilities? These questions . . . become more complicated once we realize that the excluded are never simply excluded and that their marginalization reflects and determines the shape, texture, and boundaries of the dominant order and its associated privileged communities . . . the outside is always inside: invisible perhaps, implicated and disempowered, unrecognized but omnipresent.*
>
> Richard Iton

Ruminations on questions similar to those posed in the opening quote by political scientist Richard Iton guided the inquiries and resonated with the voices of the black and Latina women professors who shared their experiences of recognizing and responding to the complexities at the four traditionally white universities (TWIs). Through the exploration of their interlocking identities, these women share their experiences from a place of empowerment in spite of their marginalization on numerous levels. Each one has made a conscious decision to center herself in an institution that views her as "other" because she is more than a woman—she is a woman of color.

According to the July 3, 2002, issue of the *The Chronicle of Higher Education*, a dismal 8 percent of full-time faculty members in the United States are African Americans and persons of Hispanic origin. This figure is compounded by the experiences shared by professors of color, who feel "excluded from networks," "must work twice as hard . . . to get half as far," and find themselves "unappreciated and unused" (Bonner 2004, B11). Although the numbers for women academics are overwhelmingly higher—39 percent by 1999—there still remain significant disparities that make the reality for these professors gloomy. For instance, an American Council of Education (2001) study stated that most female professors had only attained the rank of instructor/lecturer (53 percent) and were largely teaching at public community colleges (51 percent). Though present in the academy more than at any other time in history, these women of color still struggle to come to terms with their exclusion and lack of participation. Rather than being interwoven into the fabric of their respective institutions, they seldom benefit from the privilege of their class status as a professor or education in the ways their colleagues, who are members of the dominant culture, do. Instead, they navigate their often-confounding and implicitly biased organizations not just in the formal and informal cultures of the academy, but also in a parallel one where policies and procedures are created, changed, and/or made so opaque that there is scant opportunity to remain abreast or benefit from them.

Most often women of color in the academy have been studied from the critical perspective of feminist theory (Essed 2000; Yokomizo Akindes 2002; Vargas 1999, 2002). Many of these studies have concentrated on the classroom, rather than the overall institutional experiences of the women. For instance, Vargas (2002) found that the issue in the classroom was not her teaching techniques, but rather the sociopolitical dynamics that surrounded her. This position was supported by Turner, who asserted that "many faculty women of color see themselves as reflecting and projecting their realities in the work that they do" (2002, 88). The realities that are reflected include their multiple marginalization and intersecting identities such as their gender, race, ethnicity, nationality, and class. The feminist readings of these marginalized identities result from the writers focusing on gender in their explorations of the women's experiences. The outcome is a tension between gender and another characteristic such as race or class (Segura 2003; Vargas 2002; Wilson 2006). According to Vargas, women of color challenge "hierarchical systems of social distinctions" (2002, 9). Yokomizo Akindes added, "How do college professors, for example, help students to unlearn what the dominant culture has conditioned them to believe; that class differences are nonexistent in the United States?" (2002, 163). There is no doubt that these marginalized identities are perceived as influential factors impacting the experiences of women of color academics.

Birthed out of the frustration, alienation and isolation of the academy are support systems that recognize the women's unique needs, both within and outside of the workplace (Wilson 2006). Turner observed, "By bringing ourselves through the door and supporting others in doing so as well, we can define ourselves in and claim unambiguous empowerment, creating discourses that address our realities, affirm our intellectual contributions and seriously examine our worlds" (2003, 89). While the support systems may appear to perpetuate the marginalization of the participants, they actually strengthen the women as they navigate what are at times hostile environments (Turner 2002; Vargas 2002). That is because it is within such groups that the women are able to share stories from their past that illuminate their present.

The literature on women academics of color is compelling. The critical lenses used to frame the experiences are fundamental. Yet there remains room for studies that interlock, rather than bifurcate, the sociopolitical identities of the women.

Though complex, balancing the experiences in the classroom with institutional ones as they are impacted by the multiple ways the women are marginalized provides a more holistic understanding of their day-to-day reality in TWIs.

This study adopts a third-wave feminist approach to manifest the diversity, collectivism, and inclusiveness of minority women's voices. In this chapter, we ground our parallel experiences as women of color within the dominant culture of the academy and unveil their marginalized experiences. The study lifts their narratives out of the realm of what some may perceive as oversensitive imaginations and, in fact, privileges their positions as valid and significant. The intersectionality of race, ethnicity, class, and gender is colored by the different nationalities of the women. Since the women come from Argentina, Colombia, Jamaica, Canada, the United States and its territory, Puerto Rico, their countries of origin and the influence of those cultures frame their perceptions of their experiences in the academy. Many of the women compare and contrast their experiences in their home countries to those in the United States to make sense of the types of marginalization they currently encounter.

The chapter is divided into four themes that acknowledge these women's positions as characterized by the complex intertwining of their multiple types of marginalization and identities. The first section examines the often-unspoken, but influential, area of class. The second section explores the role of mentorship by and for women academics of color. The third section highlights the tension that results from the intersecting identities of race, ethnicity, nationality, and gender. And the final section reveals how or if the women adjust themselves as they navigate TWIs. Finally, the essay offers insight into ways the women's race, ethnicity, class, and gender may act as gateways to healing by making recommendations that perhaps move them, and us, closer to being both present and equal in the academic institutions where they have chosen to serve.

Third-Wave Feminism

Third-wave feminism serves as the framework of this study because of its commitment to the diversity of women's experiences and its critical foci on the multiplicity of intersecting oppressions in global contexts. In its attempt to build upon and fill the gaps that exist in the second wave of feminism, third-wave feminism steers clear of essentialist notions of femininity to embrace the experiences of all women, rather than only those of a particular race and class (e.g., upper, middle class, white women) (Ortega 2006). Heywood and Drake explain that third-wave feminism is concerned with "the development of modes of thinking that can come to terms with the multiple, constantly shifting bases of oppression in relation to the multiple, interpenetrating axes of identity, and the creation of a coalition politics based on these understandings" (1997, 3). Second-wave liberal and cultural approaches sought to unify diverse women by appealing to universal sisterhood while the third wave recognizes the racist, heterosexist, classist, and other implications of the erasure of difference (Lotz 2003, 5). The move from the second to the third wave began in the late 1980s and by the mid-1990s was distinctly consolidated as a movement that focused on a continuation of second-wave concerns, recognition and representation of cultural diversity, political activism, and global consciousness (Pender 2004; Whittier 2006).

Rebecca Walker, daughter of womanist Alice Walker, wrote a seminal article entitled "The Third Wave" in 1992 for *Ms.* magazine that marked the launch of the movement. Her outrage at the Clarence Thomas hearings urged other young women not to become complacent or forgetful but to continue to engage in political activism. Walker's work also highlighted a characteristic of the third wave—a unique focus on individualism and respect for multiplicity as she spoke in her own voice and stayed away from making a collective definition of the movement. Orr describes this feature of the third wave: "Feminist practices become matters of personal style and individual choice" (1997, 34). Third-wavers may then respond to sexism in distinct and confrontational ways as they encounter it in their personal worlds, whereas second-wave feminists responded to gender oppression as systemic and institutionalized (Shugart 2001).

Although individualism has been noted as a defining characteristic, third-wave feminism has important historical and political roots in collective action. In the mid-1980s and early 1990s, when the term "third wave" was first used, feminists of color engaged in theoretical and philosophical debates about race and sexuality through their writings and discussions, and Dulin records the New York City gathering of a hundred young feminists, who organized into an activist network that they named the third wave: "The vision was 'to become a national network for young feminists; to politicize and organize young women from diverse cultural and economic backgrounds; to strengthen the relationships between young women and older feminists; and to consolidate a strong base of membership able to mobilize for specific issues, political candidates, and events'" (1993, 33). Orr (1997) points out that the emphasis of the third wave was organizing young feminists as evidenced in the network's first project, the Freedom Ride 1992, a bus tour to register voters in poor communities of color.

Third-wave feminism by no means represents a coherent, stable, or unified set of ideologies. It embraces contradiction and paradox and explores and celebrates our increasingly pluralistic world. Women of this generation have been raised in a global economy and political climate that has been shaped by technology that provides them with easy access and closer distance between themselves and others (Cox, Dicker, and Piepmeier 2003; Kinser 2004).

This study responds to the critique of third-wave feminism as individually focused and exclusive (Diaz 2003; Lotz 2003). Although we represent the third wave by virtue of our ages and growing up with so-called feminist issues of women's freedom and voice, working motherhood, and work/life balance (Springer 2002), we seek to challenge and expand third-wave assumptions by exploring global dimensions, political activism, and the centering issues of social identity, such as race, class, gender, nationality, and age, as evidenced in our experiences of academic life. We believe that these foci will enrich our understanding of third-wave feminism as it exists in the dominant culture of the academy. What we propose is a more expansive and integrated approach to feminism in this third-wave generation that acknowledges our diversity and the complexity of connectedness with other women.

Methods

While numerous studies have reflected on the experiences of women academics of color (Aguirre 2000; Vargas 2002; Turner 2002; Segura 2003), research that explores the combined voices of Africana and Latina academics is lacking. To add to this literature, in the spring of 2009, we conducted semistructured focus groups that allowed women to share narratives about their lives as persons of color in the dominant culture of the academy. We felt that utilizing such a method allowed the participants to express themselves openly with the support and camaraderie of those sharing their experiences at TWIs, thus providing richer data than could be garnered from other methods (Stout, Staiger, and Jennings 2007, 126).

The goal of this study was to unveil the marginalized experiences of women academics of color. We solicited participants via personal contacts, snowballing, and area campus listservs. Our only prerequisite stated that the faculty member had to be a woman of color who taught at a TWI. A total of twelve women, including the three authors, was selected and participated in two separate focus groups. These sessions were held on two university campuses in an effort to sample a broader range of women. The women represented four TWIs in the northeastern part of the United States, ranging from small, private, liberal-arts universities to large, state-supported institutions.

In each session, the same core questions were asked: first, participants were asked to share why they had chosen the academy as a profession; subsequent questions explored their interlocking identities—race, ethnicity, nationality, class, and gender—and the mechanisms they rely upon for support. The focus groups were digitally recorded and notes were taken to ensure accuracy of the participants' stories. After transcribing the session data, we were able to ascertain the themes apparent within each session and across both of them. Those four themes are discussed next.

Class: "The Last Frontier of Our Denial"

The women's narratives revealed complex and multilayered attitudes about class. Their reflections about their consciousness of socioeconomic class in the academy encompassed their education, wealth, expectations and standards of excellence, ideas about dress, hobbies, and modes of speech. Many acknowledged that the United States society was structured and focused more around race and ethnicity than on class. Many of the non-US-born participants or second-generation immigrants, in particular, spoke distinctly about the stark absence of social and intellectual discussions about class structure in the United States and specifically in the academy. Anita, a Latin American professor, observed,

> I think that class in our society is the last frontier of our denial. Because here, you know, we have this narrative in the United States of everybody's created equal—ha-ha-ha—and you know everybody who works hard—ha-ha-ha—[everybody] can get to where they go . . . American dream . . . and clearly, there are dual narratives; there's multiple narratives in terms of the American experience, and class, I think, is the final frontier . . . because we don't want to admit it—that we have a class system.

Irena's reflection further underscores the absence of class in our frame of reference in the United States:

> I came to this country before 9/11, so I used to say, "Americans see the world through a pink-tinted glass." You know, they don't understand poverty because they have not seen it, or if they have seen it, they don't want to admit it. They have not seen hunger, and if they have seen it, they don't want to admit it. They just don't—never wanted to admit the realities of the world. After 9/11 that pink glass was shattered . . . . And now they have

seen the outside and now they are seeing that those realities exist in this country, too.

Gabriella, a middle-aged Latina professor, spoke about her upper-class upbringing in her home country and her perception of the difficulty white colleagues have with relating to her as a Latina from another country who comes from the upper class—well-educated, with limousines and drivers in her home country, and someone who owns property there and in the United States: "In terms of class, it's a lot of work for the gringo [American], in my case, because it is not a question . . . . Because you're [her nationality] . . . . How can you be rich? That's not right." Gabriella's statements highlight her perceptions of the ways that she has experienced members of dominant groups in the academy struggling with the apparent contradictions of a Latina academic from the upper class in an international country who maintains those seemingly upper-class behaviors in a society where many in academia are not persons of privilege.

Karyn, an African American professor in her mid-thirties, reported a conversation with a student that also highlighted complexities caused by socioeconomic class and perceptions of people of color. In her discussion with her student, she stated that it was important for brown people to explore the outdoors and be involved in multiple activities: "And he [the student] said, 'Well, what's your goal with it?' and I said, 'Well, for me, you know, I do a lot of camping and hiking.' And he said, 'You don't have to answer this question, Dr.——, if you don't want to, but can I ask you, is your husband white?' And I said, 'No, he's the color of my Blackberry. What's your point?' And he was like, 'Because black people don't do those things.'" The student's association with his professor's activities was framed around race so that her choice of outdoor activities naturally meant she was married to a white man. Karyn also addressed the social and cultural restrictions that she thought were imposed on African Americans in this society and noted that her body is read in particular ways because she is an African American woman.

Means of Access and Legitimization

Some women described using aspects of their socioeconomic status (SES) as a means of gaining access or legitimizing their presence in the academy. Danielle, a Caribbean woman academic in her mid-thirties, stated,

> I think I use my "class narrative" to gain access to some white parts of this institution. And that—I didn't really think about it as very outstanding . . . but in this context—having gone to private school my entire life all the way through college—I realize that that's a big thing in America . . . pre-K all the way up to college. And that helps me to enter the narrative here with a lot of white Anglo-Saxon . . . people because then I can enter the discourse of privilege, of social justice, of diversity, of high-quality education, of an I-belong-here-and-I-deserve-to-teach-these-students. And I didn't realize how important that was because I used to think about nationality primarily.

Danielle's statements reflect a sense of alienation and difficulty in socializing professionally that women faculty of color experience when working in academic cultures (Aguirre 2000; Thomas and Hollenshead 2001). However, to negotiate these dynamics, she has found that identifying with elite components of US social structures—such as private, religious education—and other factors in her upbringing help her access dominant ways of thinking in the academy.

Denise's statements reflect similar ideas and further connect this privilege of her education and experience to her work with her students in supporting their goals: "So I tell myself, 'Okay, I can use the titles Dr. and PhD to, you know, maintain access to certain class spaces—upper-class spaces—to academia, but I can never forget about all of these other class spaces that I've come from and that inform my students' lives.'" Denise views her multidimensional experiences with class and understanding of the ways that her current class provides her access as a tool to connect to her students and her work—central tenets of the third wave—and to engage in collective action and individually participate in political activism for global good.

Class, Connection, and Advancement

Participants' stories also reflected complex ideas about their class and their students' class. They spoke about standards of excellence that they believed were important for them to uphold for their students, as well as their own personal expectations that were in some ways linked to their place in academic society. Gabriella, for example, a middle-aged Latina professor, said she thought that class meant that you were "classy . . . you were engaged in excellence." She also stated that the first time she taught about certain European scholars in her discipline, her colleagues described that as elitist: "They're telling me . . . this drive for excellence is very classist. And I'm totally confused by all of this . . . and I'm trying to get the students to see . . . and the other faculty are telling me, 'Do you understand that that's very classist?' And I didn't get it. I still don't get it. Because I see—I see in each one of them this possibility of the imagination that I have to make room for."

In this instance, Gabriella's narrative weaves class with high standards of excellence expressed through a desire to share various aspects of her discipline with her students. Her pedagogical approach is also informed by her own education and introduction to her discipline in elite institutions.

Other women academics also spoke about their perceptions of their students' class but said they refrained from making destructive assumptions:

> I've found that I'm purposely mindful of not adopting certain class assumptions that dominant power structures would want you to adopt. And I specifically mean that in terms of how I read and interpret my students and where they're coming from and what their capabilities are. So I don't want to be that professor who says, "Oh, well, you know, you're from——, so you must probably 'have prepped' yourself like this" . . . because those, ironically, turn out to be some of my best students. So I purposely remind myself and find myself telling my students, "This is my own life history and background." I've been—I think I've been almost every class except uber-rich.

Closely connected to the women's awareness of both their students' and their own class is their sense of responsibility toward each student, to treat them as valuable individuals with tremendous potential. As women academics of color, they bring a keen awareness of the dangers of stereotyping and exclusion, and their narratives reveal how their own experiences of and education about class influence their continued work. Sandra, for example, an African American professor in a large state university, stated,

And this society is less focused on class, to a certain extent, than race. Race is predominant here. However, the subtleties are class based, and, yes, I do think about class. . . . I didn't come from a wealthy class; I came from a working class with excellent, very intelligent parents who were forced by the society to have to stay at a certain place—they should have been elsewhere. So I see that in my students. I see the impact of class on them and race in their dynamics, in their aspirations, in their assertiveness or lack of it in the classroom, and this is across all of the races and all of the genders—all of the genders. And I often think about that, and my thought about the class issue is I don't want to interject that into—I have to discipline myself not to inter-ject any judgments on students based on where their life—where they're coming from. What I need to really work on myself about is . . . because this society encourages people—you putting people into pigeonholes. I think to have the responsibility to educate a mind . . . is a tremendous responsibil-ity. It doesn't need to have any more chains or barriers or oppression put on the mind. So I have to control myself; that's what I do.

Jennifer, an African American professor in her thirties, works in a large private university that is predominantly white and has previous teaching experience in a historically black university. Her narrative about class also intersects in complex ways with race, education, and pedagogical approaches:

I think class is very present for me as well. I'm from Ohio, and I was raised in the midst of the steel belt. And so—coming from a working-class back-ground—I really did not realize what that meant until I went to a working-class university and a professor said in class, "I am going to treat you as if you are students at an Ivy League university." Her syllabus was very dif-ferent. Her expectations of us were very different. The readings that she included were very different. At that point, I realized that information is distributed on your class and on race. And heaven forbid that you come from both. And that was probably the turning point for me in terms of what I wanted to do with education, not for myself, but for others and getting others to understand how information is limited to them even after they get this degree and these letters behind their names. It's not equal to what you're getting from these other universities.

Jennifer's awareness of her class and educational background profoundly influ-ences her approach to teaching. Her class identification also informs her approach because she connects with those students from a working-class background; it also shapes her understanding of her mission and teaching style as a woman academic of color: "And I prepare my classes in that way and have come to find that the students that I'm with now expect that and appreciate that, whereas the students I was with before [African American students] were not sure what I was attempting to do . . . . As I developed a relationship with them, they could comment to me that I was teach-ing like a white professor and that I was attempting to show off my intellect."

Again her narrative reveals a complex interrelationship among class, race, per-ceptions of competence, and educational standards, also found in other women's comments. As an African American professor, she must confront students' percep-tions of black professors' work and expectations and ideas that there are "white" ways of working in the academy that are not accessible for African American academics. Yet amid the contradictions and paradoxes of her journey, she continues to engage in a commitment to their advancement by maintaining the same standards her previous professor upheld for her and that have influenced her pedagogical approach with students of all races. Segura's findings about Chicana academics support aspects of these narratives as well: they contest limitations placed on their communities and see themselves as agents of social change fighting for sustainable intellectual agendas (2003, 47).

Jennifer continued, "They began to see me as a colleague, and I would tell them, very simply, 'I'm giving you the same education that they're getting somewhere else so that you can compete with them. This population is not your competition . . . . This is not your competition.'"

Mission and Mentorship: "Standing in the Gap"

Third-wave feminist goals are very connected to political activism and collective action. The women's narratives also explored their missions as academics. Their social identities are very intimately interwoven with their commitment to engage in social action and change and a sense of shared responsibility to contribute to the intellectual and academic advancement of their students. Anita, a Latina professor in her midforties, stated, "If you love your job, you don't have to go to work. And I mean, you know, when . . . we have a student that's accepted to Columbia University, . . . I just go, like, 'Wow, I'm so happy that I can make money doing something that I love and promoting the people that I love and mentoring these students to go on and find their place in the world and maybe they don't have to scrap quite as hard.' I mean, a lot of our students have already scrapped plenty hard." Anita speaks about a love for her students and a genuine interest to mentor them so that they can have access to better educational and career opportunities. Her love of her work and passion for promoting her young students remain paramount in her focus as a woman academic of color.

Gabriella's earlier statement also reflects that idea of contributing to students' development as humans in the world and intellectual beings with potential: "Because I see—I see in each one of them this possibility of the imagination that I have to make room for." As a Latina professor, she also mentioned her gratification when a Latina student had accomplished a goal. She stated that if she was able to work with a Latina student who might have been quiet for three years and yet successfully presented a paper at a conference or applied to a school that is "just slightly out of reach," she felt happy. She framed her narrative amid the social expectations that many Latina women are resisting—expectations from their families that marital and child-caring responsibilities will take priority over educational and professional goals. Her mentorship of such students is central to her work.

Denise's statements encompass the multidimensional vision she has of her work: she views herself as an instrument of learning and teaching and a person who serves as a "bridge" and "stands in the gap." This view of mission is active and agentic and enhances third-wave feminism in profound ways: "So I see my position in the classroom, and even as I walk around the halls here, or I visit other campuses for whatever reason, as that kind of intermediary to bridge that knowledge difference; to maybe stand in the gap and say, 'Okay, these are some experiences that I bring as a transnational black woman and a PhD that you might not know about and I can tell you—beyond just what I give you as a textbook reading.'"

Sandra's particular approach is to mentor and seek other African American students whom she believes may be isolated or marginalized in a larger college setting: "From my perspective, what I have to do is mediate—I mediate a lot for African-American students . . . . When I'm in the classroom, one of the things that I really do make the point to say is 'please see me. Please see me no matter what. Please go into my office hours. I welcome you coming.' So that's with the whole class, but I really, really do mean it for the African American students, and I look at them, and I learn their names first, and I know—and I can tell when they're either engaged or not . . . . "

Jacqueline, a senior African American professor, who teaches in a large predominantly white state university, also stated that she sought the African American students and enjoyed mentoring them during her years of teaching. As she reflected on her mission and service, she said that in the last decade, she had contemplated returning to teaching in a historically black university as a way to be of greater service to her community, yet she also wondered how she could serve the small population of minorities who were in her program.

The Intersection of Race, Ethnicity, and Gender: "I Am a Human Being"

The voices of the women in the focus group testify to the fact that the complexity and consequences of marginality in the academy increase when race, ethnicity, and gender intersect. Because the discrimination and bias they experience is often directed at a number of their identities as "other" simultaneously, it is difficult to discern the target of the discrimination. Furthermore, the participants tended to regard their gender as a given and highlight the impact of their race and ethnicities in addition to the fact that they are women professors when sharing their experiences in the academy. Their focus reinforces what T. M. Harris (2007) and Turner (2002) define as historical and multiple marginality, respectively. The manifestation of these types of marginality for professors of color in this study was often an acute, unyielding, and emotionally draining prejudice by members of the dominant culture at TWIs. One participant, for example, wondered how much students are really open to the idea of a black or Latina professor in the classroom in this supposed era of diversity. Irena also voiced her curiosity about the state of the academy as it relates to women of color: " . . . I think what I am striving for, what I am trying to do is to get rid of the label. I dream of the day that nobody will ask, on a form, 'What is your gender?' and 'What is your ethnicity?' I just . . . completely dislike it . . . I mean, I am a human being. What else do you need? Smart enough to have a PhD in chemistry. What else do you want? . . . "

Her query was supported when another participant said she feels like an outcast due to her South American accent and origins. Salma is a middle-aged Latina from Argentina: " . . . Having a foreign accent in Argentina is normal. Having a foreign accent like me, people treat you like shit just for having a foreign accent. And I don't consider myself that you cannot understand my English. You may have trouble understanding because you are not used to my—you know I don't speak perfectly, but I think you can understand me . . . . But the barrier and the horrible things you hear from monolingual speakers is like whoa!"

Nevertheless, Jacqueline, an African American woman also in midlife, discussed the way she is able to transcend the negativity that many of the other participants experienced as a result of their intersecting identities in the academy:

> I don't know; maybe I'm blind or something, but I don't—like I said, I don't think about the gender; I don't think about the class thing. I think it may have something to do with where I'm from. I'm from, like I said, a rural—not rural; it wasn't really rural; there was the rural part outside the little town. But I'm from the segregated South. I mean, I grew up in the segregated South, and I was in a neighborhood community school where everybody was kind of told that you're cute and you're smart and you can do whatever you want to do in life. And so you could be like a monkey and be dumb as a doornail, but you're told this throughout the community, your church—you're told this in your school. I mean, my mom would say it, but my father would always say—you know, people would say, "You have such pretty girls, . . . and he'd say, "And they're smart." So I can always remember his saying, "And they're smart"

While not as unaffected as Jacqueline, Jennifer said that her identity issues centered more on age and stature: "I am conscious of my need to assert myself more due to height and age"

However, these women were the exception. The majority of the focus group participants expressed deep frustration because of their perceived difference primarily due to race, ethnicity, and class in the academy and life generally. Anita offered,

> My family's mixed. But having this complexion, you know I've sort of had to doubly stand up for people who were being—you know—and to continually point that out . . . a lot of times people look at me and make assumptions that I'm going to be like that, which is understandable, but it also can hurt, and it's like, yeah, this skin gives me some privilege; I don't freaking want it, but they're trying to just hand it to me, and you can't hand it back. You know, it's like, "Take this damn privilege back." I mean and they—you know, you can't; it's impossible. So it's very—but this is not at all to take away from the discriminatory experiences that darker-complected people go through. God, I mean I've—like I said, I've seen it. You know it's awful; I mean it's horrible.

Acceptance: "I Have to Adjust My Way of Being"

Consistently the women participants reflected on the adjustments required of them inside and outside the classroom. Many shared that they were unable to exhibit their identities fully and, in turn, felt that the academy was willing to accept only those aspects of their identities that the institution deemed palatable. This adjustment (or lack thereof) was manifested in two distinct ways: a) code switching, and b) the need to convey information in a multiperspective manner.

Code switching, as interpreted by several of the women, necessitated communicating without the markers of "Latina-ness" and/or "Africana-ness." And to do that meant these women had to leave part of themselves behind to be embraced by the academy; otherwise, there were repercussions. In her study on Chicana women academics, Segura attests that we must not "forget that the academy is littered with the bodies of those who could not adapt or whose institutional configurations were not conducive to even token inclusion" (2003, 48). This resonates well with Anita's reflection, where she stated,

I'm talking about with my way of being. I have to adjust my way of being. And I think that's what I mean by punishment. It's not really punishment that I meant. I think what I meant is more like we have to adjust our way of being to fit into a structure; they don't. They don't have to adjust their way of being to me. I mean, I would love—if I were a dean—to make everybody come into my office and act Latina or act black; you know, whatever that means. Okay? However, I know that—being the person that I am—I'm going to accept them for who they are. That's not true for me. I have to code-switch. I mean, I have to go in, and I have to speak their language, and I have to structure my—and they can't—it's like they don't hear me if I'm the way I am.

You may argue that none of us are able to bring our whole selves into the classroom. And this stance has merit when you consider the multitude of issues impacting a professor's success in the classroom. However, Vargas problematizes this notion by outlining "risk factors" of faculty who are seen as "other." "Others" on a traditionally white university campus deviate from the norm of a college professor, who is most aptly featured in the portraits hanging in the halls of university administration buildings. This otherness is compounded by the individual's multiple identities; as you add risk factors such as sexual orientation, race, or class onto a female body, you are then "adding a weight. So, those make it far more challenging to survive" (1999, 365).

This is a different experience from that of faculty members who are, in fact, closer to the norm. As Anita noted, "I think I was like in second grade when it suddenly occurred to me—and I don't know if I'd probably started absorbing this—when it suddenly occurred to me that I was like an 'other' in this world on so many different dimensions, and that—because of that—I was going to have to fight and scrap and claw for every damn thing. And so for a long time, I became alienated; I mean from about second grade until I started, actually, college, I was pretty alienated."

Salma highlighted her risk factors as a Latina immigrant when she shared her experience as a professor teaching English and intercultural communication: "I found that students didn't like me because of my accent. They said, 'You don't even speak English correctly. You cannot be a professor' . . . and [then] I put a C on a paper for a lady that was a disaster. It was a disaster, but I didn't want to put an F because I wanted her to revise the paper. Do you know what she said? 'You don't even speak English. How do you know my paper is bad?'"

Jennifer agreed with the points raised about having to adjust yourself, but she revealed the apparent complexities of this process by comparing different types of institutions:

> I'm not bringing my whole self to this environment because there are certain cultural elements that don't agree with the setting, and it's difficult for me to give all that I am to the students because there's something I'm gonna have to stop and translate about these cultural differences; whereas at an HBCU [historically black college and university], you're able to bring your whole self to the table at all times. There are colleagues who are there in an academic setting and in a social setting, so it always felt like a community. So for me that identity is an ever-pressing question and challenge in transitioning in those different settings. I continue to wonder whether

or not . . . this idea of diversity and that we're moving into this new age, but whether or not the students are really open to that or understand what that means to them to have the benefit of an African American or Latina faculty member in front of them.

Jacqueline challenged the opinions offered here by stating that she did not feel cultural constraints in the classroom and—because of her discipline—her students were, in fact, encouraged to "be honest about what their feelings are." To that end, Jacqueline suggested that the classroom was the space created to exchange ideas and learn from one another, including those "multicultural differences" she represents.

Yet—even in the midst of "checking their identity at the door"—several participants felt they were also expected to be multiperspective in their approach. Denise offered, "I feel, oftentimes, in our classroom experiences and even talking to other—some other colleagues—that you are forced—because of being a person of color—to adopt interdisciplinary moves in ways that our other colleagues, who are not of color, do not have to do . . . . Like I have to—I don't just teach a literature class. In that class, I have to know about geography; I have to know about history; I have to know about philosophy; I have to know about a lot of other things that are informed"

Gabriella continued this line of thinking when she remarked, "As a philosopher, I have to know about biology; I have to know about physics; I have to know about rhetoric, about just the interplay of what has gone on between you and Irena . . . and one of the most interesting ways of learning to respect one another came when we collaborated in interdisciplinary ways; where some of the faculty were more recalcitrant in these areas."

Jacqueline agreed that issues of diversity were paramount in the classroom; however, she often used the literature of her field to assist students with their exploration and provide validity for points of contention she raised. Sonja, on the other hand, did not feel that her self-proclaimed Afrocentric identity influenced her classroom in any way because she spent most of her class time focusing on abstract concepts about business and economics. But because of her identity, she was cognizant of the racial/ethnic backgrounds of her students. And for that reason, she found herself willing to engage them on multiple issues that might reflect the different cultural groups represented in her classroom.

What Does It All Mean?

The experiences shared by these women academics of color highlight complex interlocking systems at play—class, race, ethnicity, and nationality; however, it is gender that functions as the given among all of these women. They easily embrace the idea that the interpretations of their experiences in the academy are firmly grounded in their gender and only become convoluted when coupled with other interlocking identities. In fact, the women found it unnecessary to reference their experiences as women specifically and, as a result, focused most of their attention on the identities that seemed to offer the most tension, inequality, and inspiration in their efforts to succeed in the academy.

Our study reiterates findings from other studies of women and academics of color (Vargas 1999; Aguirre 2000; Turner 2002; Segura 2003). Yet issues pertaining to class, nationality, and support seemed to resonate in ways not found in previous studies. Specifically this mix of Africana and Latina women academics believed that their class consciousness and nationality influenced how they taught, what they taught, and why they taught issues of SES. Many of the participants found the perception that all women academics of color reside in the same SES troublesome and felt that their willingness to explore those issues with their students (and colleagues) was an opportunity to isolate class beyond racial boundaries and recognize the role that nationality plays in these discussions. Several of the women affirmed their position of privilege as a result of their class status in their home countries and struggled with the constraints placed upon them by the stereotypes of women of color in the United States. Although they articulated their concerns differently, those American-born participants shared these frustrations and noted that attention was given to class through their style of dress and activities they engaged in outside of the classroom, as well as their commitment not to prejudge their students' class status.

These women also exhibited commitment when they discussed "why do you do this work?" Most participants believed the marginal status of women academics of color meant the academy was not a conducive environment for encouraging and bolstering others who shared their phenotype. In fact, they found the academy oppressive and feared minority women who wanted to be teachers might choose another career or be forced to leave the academy. Nevertheless, the women appeared empowered in their status and felt compelled to remain to help others. This commitment was exhibited in stories shared about their interactions with colleagues as well as students of color. Participants stated that studies such as ours had become a space for sharing and connecting with people with similar experiences. They also saw opportunities to engage with one another as an outlet for their occupational frustrations and an opportunity to fortify themselves for future experiences that might question and/or challenge their existence in the academy. Buddy systems, research and/or teaching mentors, and first-year faculty programs were all mentioned as activities established to offer support to faculty of color. Most of the women concurred that such programs were a means to mentor and empower these women to remain successful in the academy.

This success also applied to students of color in the classroom. The participants frequently conveyed their diligence in mentoring students of color in particular because they saw themselves reflected in their students. Many of the women told stories of being the sole student of color in a classroom or even an entire department or feeling isolated and frustrated by course material that never explored issues applicable to their race, ethnicity, or culture. Yet through their teaching and advising roles, they informed their students that they were a resource cheering for their academic success.

In this study, we sought to hear the voices of women academics of color who teach at TWIs. Additionally, we filtered these experiences through the lens of third-wave feminism, which provides a space to hear the perspectives of those outside of the movement's normative boundaries (i.e., upper, middle class, white women). What has been shared here exhibits and broadens the tenets of third-wave feminism in profound ways. These women's stories come together to create a means of thinking, understanding, and negotiating their interlocking identities and the oppression they experience within the academy.

These women utilize their narratives also to center themselves and other women academics of color. Their connection to others who have experienced oppression in the academy was necessary to share strategies and offer advice about ways to remain successful. Although this counters a significant feature of third-wave feminism, which suggests there should be no unified interpretation of our experiences, it is significant that feminists of color thought it important to "strengthen [the] relationships . . . and mobilize for specific issues" (Dulin 1993, 33). Our study uniquely explores that recommendation and finds that collective action is essential and advantageous to women academics of color. New and continued efforts for Africana and Latina academics to collaborate on projects that address their concerns in the academy are crucial. It is through this approach that we can build upon the third wave and embrace the voices of women of color in the academy.

CHAPTER 7

NAVIGATING THE ACADEMIC TERRAIN

The Racial and Gender Politics of Elusive Belonging

Linda Trinh Võ

When considering whether to write this chapter, I had all the reservations so eloquently articulated in the introduction to this book, cognizant that I should be spending my time laboring on that single-authored book that will contribute to my next promotion.[1] However, reflecting upon the journey that led me to a life in the academy and the opportunity to make the path more welcoming to a future generation was too inviting to pass up. Women of color, like most who attend graduate school hopeful of achieving faculty status, are motivated by lofty goals to make a contribution to some original form of knowledge.

Growing up, I had no aspirations to become an academic since I did not know that this was a profession and had no contact with professors. The high school teachers I knew well discouraged me from the teaching profession since they disliked the stressful conditions they endured in an underfunded district with one of the lowest college attendance rates in California. At my large public university, the books I devoured captivated my imagination, and the research papers I wrote inspired me to query my professors about their career choice. Having labored at minimum-wage jobs, I was persuaded by the fact that being a faculty member meant you had flexible hours and did not have to wear a uniform or clock in, so I idealistically entered graduate school. In those early years, I received little mentorship and busied myself with adjusting to the mechanics required of my coursework, so it was not until later that I truly became aware of the competitiveness, elitism, and cronyism embedded within the academy and had to seriously contemplate if I belonged or wanted to devote my life to this profession.

---

1   I thank Yolanda Flores Niemann for encouraging me to write this chapter and for her incisive comments on an earlier draft.

I know women of color, full of self-confidence, who have forged successfully ahead in their careers and encountered few glitches. I have not lived that life. My mother, like so many rural women displaced by the violence of war in Vietnam, was forced to leave her children behind to be raised by relatives while she gravitated to urban areas to find employment. In her case, she worked as a maid for US government employees, one of whom became my stepfather and whom I met when I was five. We moved to a different country, mainly in Asia and Europe, almost every other year, and this augmented my intellectual curiosity as a scholar and forced me to adapt quickly and blend into my new schools and surroundings. Growing up in a multiracial, multicultural family in various countries presented some interesting challenges and definitely contributed to my endurance in the academy.

As a child, I was puzzled by the socioeconomic inequalities that surrounded me and have always been curious about the enormous expenditure of energy and the vast consumption of resources needed to establish and maintain entrenched racial, class, gender, and sexual hierarchies, even when common sense indicates that eradicating such systems of inequalities are more productive and fruitful. I am still perplexed by the way academic institutions, which can claim some significant gains in advancing diversity, continue to create an inhospitable environment for white women and men and women of color. In this chapter—drawing from research as well as personal experiences and observations—I intend to analyze institutional barriers that persist, evaluate reactions and decisions, and explore viable strategies that can make the academy a more accommodating and welcoming place. I will examine racial and gender discrimination and obstacles, focusing especially on hiring, mentoring, and promotion processes. In the last couple of decades, the demographic transformations in this country, along with the accompanying changes in the university population, make it imperative for universities, both private and public, to reconsider and adjust their policies and practices if they want to remain relevant and meaningful to the communities they serve (D. G. Smith 2000). This is the larger context in which I constructed this chapter and the spirit in which I hope it is read.

Learning Promotional Skills

Academic institutions are not neutral racial and gender spaces, and female and male faculty of color experience them differently from their white counterparts (Garcia 2000). For example, studies show that females are hesitant to exercise self-promotion, a necessary skill set to advance in the profession (Winkler 2000). Women of color have to learn the skill of self-promotion and also become comfortable with being boastful, flaunting our accomplishments, and ensuring we receive due credit for our work. For some this means having to overcome the fear of being perceived as arrogant, egotistical, self-serving braggarts and being able to ignore the negative labels associated with "aggressive" women. There are countless instances where I have observed women in positions of power undermine their authority or expertise by prefacing their opinions, suggestions, or ideas with "I'm not sure if this makes sense" or some similarly dismissive remark, only to follow it with a brilliant thought. This is hardly a statistically significant observation, but it does indicate we need to be conscious of the way we are socialized and its influence on gendered behavior patterns.

Studies show that the salary differential between men and women is not solely a result of employers purposely being discriminatory; it exists because men are more forceful in negotiating their salaries (Brown 2003). It appears that men automatically believe they deserve the job and negotiate harder based on their assumed worth. It seems women are just so thankful to land a job that they fail to negotiate sufficiently before they accept their positions. Although I may be speaking from limited administrative experience, I have observed this gender disparity in action. Most noticeable is that women seem more hesitant to go on the job market to acquire counteroffers than their male counterparts, and this seems to play a role in the salary differential. At many institutions, much of the negotiation process is cloaked in secrecy with various factors being considered, such as salaries, research funds, teaching load, and other resources, so women of color have to be astute enough to be informed about the variables. Male colleagues seem more adept at this entitlement game and as a result advance in their careers and also are more generously rewarded. We need to overcome our reservations about negotiations, recognizing that our base salary is the foundation for future incremental increases and, if it is too low, this disparity can add up to a sizeable share of lost income during a career.

Self-aggrandizement is an acquired habit for those who have been socialized to be nurturers and are unaccustomed to being the center of attention. It is inaccurate to assume that Asian American women share some kind of common culture or characteristic when we have such diverse histories and backgrounds. Broad generalizations about ethnic or racial groups should be avoided; rather, the focus should be on the intersection of varying factors, ranging from Asian cultural expectations and US cultural norms that shape our lives to the context of structural barriers and constraints that impacts the pragmatic personal decisions we are forced to make. Over the years, I have watched as promising women of color, including Asian Americans, abandon their professional ambitions to defer to the careers of their male partners, some whom are academics, while others accept non-tenure-track positions.

We may be averse to taking risks because of familial expectations and economic predicaments that make it more difficult for us to pursue prestigious fellowships in other locales or vie for enviable positions that require relocation. Some Asian American women from low-income immigrant families financially support their parents and, at an early age, assumed adult responsibilities because their parents spoke limited English, and they continue to shoulder these burdens as graduate students and faculty. For those of us who are immigrants or whose family members are recent immigrants, strong cultural expectations dictate that we defer to and respect our elders (Eng 1999).

Although some of the countries from which we immigrated had or have female rulers (e.g., India and the Philippines), there is still a gender and age hierarchy that assumes that females will be subservient to males and to their parents.[2] The gendered culture in the United States also reinforces traditional roles associated with marriage and motherhood, even though increasing numbers of women are in the workplace and single, female-headed households are commonplace. Being nurturing and humble does not translate well into the competitive academic cultural environment, so adapting mandates some cultural retooling for many of us.

At the beginning of my career, I lacked the confidence that I saw in my classmates. This self-doubt was compounded by the fact that I was conscious that my

---

2   From my cursory conversations with female faculty members in Asia and my own observations visiting their institutions, I know they face incredible barriers in the academy.

parents had only finished grade school and also because there were so few faces of color, particularly female ones, in any graduate program on my campus. Compared to the majority of graduate students of color, who were often first-generation college attendees, I noticed that a number of my white classmates had close or distant relatives who were scholars, so these peers appeared rather comfortable around academics and savvier about university culture. Regardless, graduate school and the stressful tenure process can generate incredible self-doubt, even shattering the confidence of some of the smuggest scholars. At the time, there was one token female representative from each group—Native American, African American, and Latina—in my graduate program, and I recall them struggling as well, but because we were in staggered cohorts and vastly different stages of our education, we could only support each other from afar.

Post-tenure status and the academic freedom that accompanies it, as well as becoming an administrator, changed my level of confidence to some extent. As I was finishing my dissertation, I eyed a prestigious fellowship but thought I would never be selected, so I procrastinated in completing the application and turned it in at the post office only five minutes before closure on the day it had to be postmarked. I received this career-changing fellowship, and it helped to ease some of my lagging self-doubt about becoming an academic. I can now appreciate my contributions to the academy and the community, ones I could not imagine myself making as a young graduate student. My confidence still wavers at times, and I still encounter instances when others question whether I belong. However, I no longer dwell on these drawbacks; rather, I focus on my capacity to improve the academic environment and strengthen its institutional promise.

Tackling the Job Market

Faculty hiring is one of the crucial areas where we can transform the academy, yet given the entrenchment of academic practices, it is one of the most contentious aspects to change (D. G. Smith et al. 2004; D. G. Smith 2000).[3] On one search committee, we were discussing the candidates so we could compile a short list of people to invite for a campus visit. I found noticeable the ways that the weaknesses of a male candidate's file were perceived as permissible in comments such as, "That's something he could learn on the job," or "Well, that is counterbalanced by his other qualifications." At the same time, the strengths of a female candidate's file were overlooked or belittled: "Well, that experience would be irrelevant to the job," or "That's really unimpressive." At one point, most of the senior voices on the committee took turns dismissing a candidate's qualifications until one of them, in closing the discussion, commented that including a woman and a minority member would make the pool look diverse. He implied that it would be a positive reflection on the committee to include her. The other males agreed, and she was added onto the short list. I articulated that she was a strong candidate from the beginning and deserved a campus visit, and now she was only included as a token in the short pool of candidates. Consequently, I was extremely uncomfortable with their justification to include her. As the only face of color in the room and the most junior member of that committee, I said nothing in those few seconds, in part because of the shock of what was transpiring.

---

3   There are all kinds of misperceptions—some that are contradictory—that do not withstand the empirical evidence, such as there are no diverse faculty available or they have all been hired.

I have been that token minority candidate before, a position where you know from the initial meeting that the committee members have another candidate in mind and are merely going through the motions of interviewing you. During your campus visit, you meet with the few graduate students of color in the program, who inform you quite bluntly that you are not a serious contender since the department would never hire a woman of color whose specialty is on "race." After describing their personal experiences encountering racial bias as graduate students in the program, they further inform you that, in recent history, the department has failed to tenure any faculty of color. I have actually experienced versions of this scenario more than once. In one memorable interview, I learned that several Latino faculty members had just left and were filing discriminatory grievances against the department and institution. A white faculty member, in charge of diversity in the department, earnestly informed me that the African American students in his classes just could not learn, no matter how much time he devoted to them. Other faculty members, including a senior female, asked me questions about my age, the number of children I had, and my marital status, all inappropriate and illegal questions for interviews. There are instances where the token candidate is offered the position for one reason or another; however, being associated with this distinction is an inauspicious beginning for any faculty member.

Transforming the hiring process means reeducating our colleagues about the hostile climate they create, whether intentionally or inadvertently, for women of color. In the example I described, I am still unsure in hindsight if my silence was the right choice. I could have protested the process at the risk of eliminating her from the pool, as well as alienating potential allies, but I was more intent on opening the door to the possibility of a woman of color being hired. As a faculty equity advisor, a part-time administrative position, I tried to counter that experience by working proactively to implement new hiring and recruiting policies with the intention of altering entrenched attitudes, which contribute to academic departments being complacent about their hiring practices.[4] It was challenging the first year to instruct colleagues on best practices to increase their applicant pool, seriously consider how they could diversify the short list of candidates that came for campus interviews, and create a more hospitable environment for these candidates. As expected, some senior colleagues vehemently protested what they charged was intrusive oversight and changing traditions. It became easier with each successive year as faculty became accustomed to the new procedures or practices and some of the most resistant departments became more responsive.[5]

---

4   I shared this funded position with a white woman faculty member for the first year and for a year and a half held this position by myself in conjunction with my chair responsibilities. The mission statement reads: "The UCI Advance Program carries out the campus commitment to gender equity and diversity in the professoriate." A National Science Foundation Institutional Transformation Award originally funded the program in 2001 to increase women in the science, technology, engineering, and mathematics (STEM) fields on campus; then the executive vice chancellor and provost institutionalized the UCI Advance Program and extended its mission to include diversity in July 2006. More information is available at UCI Advance Program for Faculty Equity and Diversity at http://advance.uci.edu//.

5   There is now national racial and gender data on the availability of new PhDs and tenured faculty in a wide range of disciplines, and administrators of the UCI Advance Program make this annual data available to all search committees. Faculty are required to attend workshops on strategies for creating search committees, planning outreach efforts, composing a short list, arranging campus visits, and making the final selection. While there are still areas we

Finding Mentors and Building Networks

A crucial strategy women of color faculty should adopt early on is avoiding becoming isolated and staying in our silos. Graduate school is supposed to prepare us to be scholars, namely to conduct research and publish.[6] If we are fortunate, graduate school provides us with some training to teach. However, it often fails to prepare us for many aspects of our careers. Consequently, we find ourselves stumbling along as faculty members and, later, as administrators. There is often a steep learning curve for new faculty members. The anxiety is reduced if you have supportive colleagues who protect you from burdensome committee work, present you with suitable teaching assignments, and genuinely support your research agenda. Yet there are cases where colleagues, for a wide range of reasons—for example, you were not their candidate of choice for the position—treat new arrivals as rivals and attempt to sabotage their careers. A good mentor can help you navigate the political landmines, and studies consistently find that well-planned mentoring correlates with the success of female and male faculty of color (Turner, González, and Wood 2008).

However, advocating for mentorship programs for faculty can be controversial. At an administrators' meeting when my colleague and I announced a new mentorship program we planned to institute, a senior white faculty member near retirement dismissed the idea. We suspect that he was hostile because our program not only targets retaining all junior faculty but was especially created to support women faculty and faculty of color. He stated that our program was useless since mentors can misdirect junior colleagues, and he elaborated that new faculty should know what to do; otherwise they should not have been hired. We defended the program and, fortunately, we did not need his approval to implement it. The program pairs junior faculty members with a senior mentor outside their department. We developed this external mentoring program to supplement the support junior faculty were supposed to receive from departmental colleagues. However, it is difficult to trust colleagues in your department when they are the reason for your grievances. I have been able to observe the way direct and indirect intervention and assistance from senior mentors has helped to contest the unfair treatment of junior colleagues, especially in egregious merit and promotion cases.

When I found myself at a large campus in a rural location, I was fortunate to have the chance to participate in a support group for junior women of color faculty. Since we came from different disciplines, our focus was not on reading or critiquing each other's work, a practice that I had engaged in at other institutions. We just gathered over delicious meals (you are compelled to learn how to make your favorite ethnic foods in these locations) and shared stories about overcoming isolation. We shared advice on campus policies, networking opportunities, and the promotion process. It was one of the few opportunities I have had to participate in a sustained effort to

---

can improve to diversify the faculty, it may be difficult to demonstrate a direct correlation between these policies and the hiring of diverse faculty. The program has made faculty more aware of best practices in terms of equity and transparency. This program has also implemented changes to career advancement by including recognition of diversity activity in research, teaching, and service in the merit and promotion review.

6   Faculty are expected to provide feedback to students on their projects or dissertations, but only some take the time to offer any substantial guidance about the intricacies of applying for jobs, negotiating job offers, publishing their research, presenting at conferences, etc. Preparing white female graduate students and male and female graduate students of color for their faculty careers should be specifically tailored.

bring junior African American, Asian American, Latina, and Native American faculty women together. There was only a handful of us on campus, and although we came from different backgrounds and fields, this was one of the few spaces where we felt we belonged. We made considerable effort to create a productive and collegial group, which counter to some assumptions, does not automatically occur when women of color come together.

Additionally, in the early stages of my career I attended professional conferences and made a concerted effort not just to present my research or serve on committees but also to find peers and mentors, predominantly women of color, from various institutions and academic levels. I was fortunate to find people willing to share advice about ways to manage the job market, publish a book and prepare for tenure, balance a career and family, and deal with racial and gender discrimination. It is to these friends that I still turn for encouragement, wisdom, and emotional replenishment as I continue to advance in my career since each stage brings new challenges.

Yet I have seen numerous instances when competitive graduate students of color dissociated themselves from other minority students to distinguish themselves or purposely avoided working with faculty of color or women. They consider it more advantageous for their careers to have white, male faculty endorse them and their research, even when these individuals are poor mentors or only marginal experts in their area of study. They will replicate this pattern as faculty members, disassociating themselves from certain kinds of graduate students. It is ironic when some later face racial or gender barriers in their careers, despite employing "strategic gender and racial avoidance" tactics. Many of us know women of color or white female faculty who, once they have advanced, exclude other women from entering their domain. They fear that these newcomers will become their competitors or feel that because they advanced in a harsh environment, others should endure similar struggles to prove themselves. Some do not want their male colleagues to accuse them of favoritism, so they go out of their way not to intervene on behalf of female colleagues.

In contrast, I have also been at institutions with white women presidents, one who sponsored informal gatherings at her residence for women faculty of color to network and to provide input on how to make the campus culture more supportive of their needs. I have also worked with white males who signed up for administrative responsibilities to diversify the gender and racial composition of the faculty. I have not always agreed with their tactics, yet I recognize that they possess certain forms of privilege that can be crucial to the tasks at hand. In reality some women of color faculty advocate to implement race- or gender-neutral plans and prefer the status quo. So, as a pragmatist, I recognize that allies should not be measured simply by their race or gender. We simply cannot assume that other women of color will unite with us, and it is essential that we create possibilities for new alliances.

Contending with Criticism

It is easy to obsess on our disappointments in the academy. However, rather than dwelling on the number of jobs we felt we deserved, publications that should have been accepted, grants we should have received, or awards where we were overlooked, it is more productive to consider what we have accomplished in spite of the barriers. It is worth pausing to recognize that there is room for improvement and consider what you can learn from each experience, but the quicker you can move on, the better. Now that I have been on a number of hiring, promotion, award, and fellowship committees, I realize that political wagering takes place in all these situations: a fair amount of subjectivity taints many decisions. Dwelling on the negative and trying to figure out if our ethnic, gender, class, or sexual orientation led to the rejection can be counterproductive. Not only is it difficult to ascertain the reasons, but it also wastes precious time.

Blatant incidents of racism and sexism or other personal affronts can be devastating, yet if we allow the anger to eat away at us and force us to leave the academy, then institutions will conclude that we are incompetent, even if this is irrational. Without a doubt, I have had moments when I thought if I quit or failed at a particular task, then people would assume that other Asian American women would behave similarly, justifying our exclusion in the future. In some cases, I was motivated to prove them wrong. This was a reaction I had throughout graduate school when a number of faculty in my department expressed skepticism that my dissertation on such an obscure topic as Asian Americans would earn me an academic job or a publisher. I ignored their comments and found support from faculty and graduate students on other campuses who shared my research interests.

Being sensitive to criticism does not produce a good academic. I remember one time in graduate school when a male committee member critiqued one of my oral exam papers and asked me to rewrite it and, to my embarrassment, I began crying. I took his criticism personally, rather than professionally. After reflecting on this incident, I realized that such criticism is harsher for those of us who experience marginalization to contend with because it is compounded by covert and subtle messages we receive that convey that we do not belong and should leave the academy. I do not always agree with critiques of my work and now am more astute at dismissing misguided feedback, but I also have developed thicker skin and am grateful when a scholar is willing to take the time to read my work and provide me detailed and thorough feedback. In addition, I have been on the other side, serving as a reviewer for manuscripts as well as a series editor for a university press, and know how time consuming it is to provide meticulous and constructive feedback on manuscripts, sometimes even on multiple drafts, rather than spending time on my own publications.

Achieving Tenure

Over the years, I have become familiar with numerous cases of white female faculty and male and female faculty of color who have faced major obstacles at their institutions, with some finding new opportunities at other universities or leaving academia altogether. I have known faculty who have committed suicide or been homicidal, battled alcohol and drug addiction, struggled with mental illness, or faced debilitating health problems. Some of these afflictions were inherited or triggered by personal problems, but many were aggravated or brought on by their academic careers. These problems may be similar to what happens in other professions, but it seems in many ways that academics have ideal careers with flexible hours, opportunities for lifelong learning, and the cliché of making a difference, which should lessen these problems. It is difficult to determine the reasons for the problems, but it seems that considerable attrition occurs along the way and the tenure period is the crucial time when problems are likely to arise (Cooper and Stevens 2002).

Each tenure case varies: some colleagues sail through while others encounter major obstacles. The tenure experience depends on the faculty, the department, the higher levels of reviews required, and the year a person goes up for review. Some institutions are notorious for denying tenure to faculty of color, particularly women. As a graduate student, I was keenly aware of the reports that Asian American women were the least likely to receive tenure and their absence was noticeable at the professional conferences I attended (Hune 1998). Over the years, I have listened to stories about tenure struggles, read about the legal battles many fought to gain tenure, and signed petitions or written letters of support for those denied tenure.[7] Almost every year in my discipline, Asian American faculty, mainly women, have been denied tenure. My last letter of support was for an Asian American woman faculty member denied tenure at a prestigious private institution. This woman had a forthcoming book from a university press, was honored with teaching and service awards, and received prestigious grants, but that was not enough to gain her tenure.

I watched many scholars leave the academy, both of their own volition and involuntarily. The mantra that people of color have to work twice as hard as their white, male colleagues to prove themselves has stuck with me. At times, even against my better judgment, I have furiously tried to live up to this maxim. I definitely have become more adept at multitasking over the years, but the result can lead to unnecessary anxiety and unhealthy working hours. The expectations for tenure become too overwhelming for some, and this can affect their ability to focus on their publications. They withdraw because they are reluctant to seek advice or ask questions that may make others perceive them as incompetent.

This behavior is counter to the notion that self-advocacy is necessary for survival. If, for example, you have colleagues purposely attempting to undermine your promotion, you must be proactive and vocal, find allies, and do your research so you are familiar with university policies and the parameters available to defend yourself. As the faculty equity advisor, my responsibilities included providing faculty with advice on procedures, directing them to available resources and, at times, advocating on their behalf with administrators. I found that in the cases where faculty contending with problematic colleagues or chairs, contentious merit and promotion cases, or other inequity issues contacted me early on, prior to the situation becoming too contentious and the participants becoming too embattled, I was able to intervene and strategize with them more effectively, and we were more likely to reach a satisfactory outcome.

I am the kind of person who always asks "what if" questions. I like to be equipped with multiple scenarios when plans A and B do not come to fruition. I was a post-doctoral fellow, a visiting assistant professor, and an assistant professor at two institutions, so I took a circuitous route not addressed in the faculty manuals about the typical timeline for tenure. I had to make sure I was familiar with all my options for promotion, including going up for early tenure or requesting an accelerated review or discovering how much progress faculty members actually have to make on a second book project. I sought advice from my mentors and chair but also contacted higher-level administrators and staff who handle faculty promotion files, and I continue to advise others to do the same since both formal and informal policies can change in such a subjective evaluation process. What I learned over the years is that ours is a mobile profession: faculty and administrators change positions and universities, so institutional memory can be fleeting. Those in positions of authority

---

7   Don T. Nakanishi (1993) discusses one of the major tenure battle cases that address some of the obstacles that remain today.

or who are gatekeepers may be unfamiliar with intricate policies, rules, or precedents, such as stopping the tenure clock or postponing the tenure process, so it is incumbent on faculty to advocate for themselves.[8]

Contesting Gender and Sexual Harassment

Power comes in various forms in the academy, and even in places that are supposedly governed by egalitarian principles, there are cases of gender and sexual harassment. For example, women of color may experience gender harassment from colleagues, but it can manifest itself in the classroom setting as well (Stanley 2006b). I have seen the way teaching obstacles affect the morale of some of my colleagues as well as the emotional costs of teaching controversial materials and theories, distracting them from their publications and delaying their promotions, or derailing their careers altogether. I understood this predicament when I faced difficulty teaching ethnic studies to a mainly white student population who had little exposure to communities of color. At my previous campus, I had won teaching awards, but at this one, I had to prepare myself mentally for the hostile teaching environment I faced every time I walked into the lecture hall. Those who were antagonistic made their opposition clear from their body posture to the blatantly racist comments they made in class, greeted by other students clapping and cheering in agreement. They did not bother to hide the fact they resented being taught American history by a "foreigner" or "refugee," even if I spoke English without an accent. I was the first Asian American many of these students had ever encountered, especially a female in a position of authority, and hostile students labeled even white colleagues teaching ethnic studies as "race traitors."[9] Other women of color faculty teaching more race-neutral classes, such as economics, also encountered nonverbal and verbal challenges to their authority in the classroom.[10]

It is disheartening to hear about the number of cases where female graduate students and faculty have had to contend with severe forms of sexual harassment or naïvely submit to compromising relationships that became detrimental to their careers. I have had male graduate students and faculty make inappropriate sexual statements and advances toward me, and I know I am not alone. These are difficult cases to prosecute, and all too often, institutions fail to educate faculty about proper conduct, enforce appropriate punitive action, or provide support or resources for those who come forward. Avoiding male colleagues who are notorious for making female colleagues uneasy or making sure you meet with them in public spaces are

---

8   This is especially true of department chairs, where there is usually high turnover. In some cases, there is conflicting information, so it is incumbent on faculty to check on the accuracy of the advice they receive.

9   At the time, my perception in the classroom was compounded by the racial incidents and hate crimes that occurred on campus and in surrounding towns, which were havens for white supremacists.

10   In the years I taught there, I broadened my pedagogical approach, taking into consideration the background of the student population by reframing the theories, using new readings and videos, and experimenting with discussion formats in the classroom and online; without a doubt, those approaches expanded my teaching skills. I also focused on the students who were intellectually engaged with the material and found sustenance working with the diverse student organizations on campus. When I left the lecture hall, I felt assured that I had done my best and did not dwell on the rough teaching days; I moved on to other tasks at hand, such as my research and publications, and that sustained me.

precautionary tactics. However, I recognize that there is often nothing we can do to ward off unwanted sexual advances if the perpetrator is intent on making them. We are all too familiar with female students who come to us distraught about our male colleagues who have made inappropriate advances to them or who ask us quite innocently, "Is it normal for a faculty member to invite a student to his house for a private dinner to discuss her research paper?" We are also aware of cases when untenured female faculty members intervened on their students' behalf only to have their own careers disrupted.

While campus workshops or presentations by performance troupes that traverse college campuses to educate staff and faculty about sexual and gender harassment can be effective, they can also be improperly implemented. I attended presentations on sexual harassment in the workplace at large public campuses that intermix all ranks of faculty and staff, as well as ones specifically for supervisors across the campus, from faculty in charge of large laboratories to those managing facilities maintenance staff, and found a number to be ineffective. Attendees select from a choice of time slots for generic workshops, rather than occupationally specific ones tailored to their respective roles.[11] There is such variation in the responsibilities associated with these roles, and these mandatory workshops fail to address this with any diligence. One workshop I attended on improper behavior seemed more like a comedy show, I assume to bring some levity to a serious topic, but when significant time is spent catering to an older, white, male attendee, who was defending what was obviously depicted as offensive behavior in the skit as benign, there are definitely drawbacks to this format. Universities should take more preventative measures, which include providing formal and informal guidelines about unacceptable behavior, making sure all new graduate students, faculty, staff, and admistrators are aware of these at their orientations, and reinforcing them by detailing some of the legal cases individuals and institutions face regarding sexual harassment or gender discrimination. Training needs to be conducted in a serious manner and with attention to differences within units and diverse populations on campus.

Ideally, we should not have to worry about being harassed in the workplace by our colleagues or forced to take action, but the reality is that gender and sexual harassment in both mild and severe forms occurs much more often than is officially reported. I say this because I know the number of anecdotal stories women have shared with me, but they have never officially filed grievances, acknowledging that the repercussions would be more damaging to them. These situations occur too frequently for these women even to consider pressing charges and many fear that the university would not protect them.[12] How should you react when a male faculty

---

11   Some years, I choose to attend the workshops in lieu of completing the timed online tutorial. California State Assembly Bill 1825 (AB1825) is the first sexual-harassment law of its kind to actually detail the requirements for effective compliance training, setting the standard for not only California but the rest of the country as well. All supervisors, including all faculty members, are required to complete two hours of sexual harassment prevention training every two years with the first deadline in December 2005. The challenge has been figuring out ways to conduct this training en masse with limited resources.

12   I realized how ill prepared universities can be at dealing with both gender and sexual harassment when I saw firsthand in two separate incidents the way those in positions of authority handled the cases improperly and ineffectively. In the gender harassment case, the male chair informed me that he had taken care of the problem and that I had to excuse the behavior of the male minority faculty member since he had been working long hours. The

member chairing the search committee informs you that he is the primary decision maker and pressures you to have a cocktail with him at the hotel bar after the official job interview dinner has ended and the other colleagues have gone home? The simple answer is to say no and consider that, if you are offered the position, this may not be an ideal job if he will be your senior colleague. Of course, this choice is based on the assumption that we have options in an extremely competitive marketplace.

I acknowledge that same-sex harassment can occur, as well as females targeting males, but it is not the sexual orientation or gender that matters as much as the power relationship: those who are harassed usually have less power in these situations. This is compounded by the fact that women of color are newer populations in the academy, so they are most likely concentrated in the lower ranks. The preponderance of sexualized and racialized stereotypes about Asian Americans and other women of color can make us vulnerable targets. The converging perceptions of Asian American woman as exotic and docile "model minorities," who are less likely to file a complaint, increases the chances of us becoming victims of "racialized sexual harassment" (Cho 1997).[13] Without becoming overly paranoid, we must take preventative measures, be aware of those who have been repeatedly accused of improprieties, and continue to work toward contesting these inequities, whether it is to create effective policies to curtail this behavior or take appropriate punitive action.

Changing Policies

Academic careers can be taxing, as the narratives in this book reveal. In retrospect I survived the harsh academic terrain because of sheer luck, determination and, most importantly, carefully selecting which battles I am willing to entangle myself in, constantly weighing the potential gain versus the likely career repercussions and personal costs. Faculty can tackle a plethora of meaningful causes or institutional transformations. For example, some transformations involve committee work while others include confronting administrators. There is no formula about whether it is best to speak up or stay quiet, but evaluating the energy we have to expend and the viability of a satisfactory outcome is crucial. On a pragmatic level, we may make some allies in the process, but we also have to weigh the number of individuals we might anger and their ability to retaliate.

Even though universities are places of learning and enlightenment, there are times, unfortunately, when they can be reactionary and entrenched. At a large public university where I was employed, I distinctly remember my reaction when I opened up a printed copy of the university directory and saw my home address and phone number listed next to the generic information about faculty. I immediately contacted the office that had compiled the directory and was told that they included personal information unless faculty members went into the computer system, used

---

chair also told me that he had recommended to the faculty member under duress to "go see a movie or go to a bar to relax." This was after a police report had been filed, and I learned campus specialists were contacting him to offer counseling, but no one contacted me to offer assistance or follow up. I left the institution shortly thereafter.

13   Cho explains that "military involvement in Asia, colonial and neocolonial history, and the derivative Asian Pacific sex tourism industry established power relations between Asia and the West which in turn shape stereotypes of Asian Pacific women that apply to those in and outside of Asia" (167).

their passwords, and requested to have it removed. I explained that as someone who teaches large lecture classes, often ones that fulfill general education requirements on topics of race, ethnicity, gender, and sexuality, I have taken precautions to acquire an unlisted phone number and home address. I am comfortable with intellectual debates in the classroom, but when an aggressive student threatens you over a grade or is using misogynist or racist language to argue that sexism and racism do not exist, you hardly need to be reminded that you are vulnerable. The supervisor dismissed my suggestion to have their policy reversed and instead have faculty request to have their personal information included.

Even as a new assistant professor, I was determined to change this policy regardless of the repercussions. I tried to recruit some colleagues to complain as well, but although they were sympathetic, they were unwilling to become involved. I then wrote a petition, and with the support of my chair, an African male, we sent it out to all the department chairs to distribute to their faculty. I was surprised by the high number of colleagues in the sciences who immediately sent back the signed petitions, compared to some chairs in the liberal arts who refused even to distribute it to their faculty. Some faculty contacted me, scolding me for trying to change a perfectly fine policy that allowed faculty to create a student-friendly environment in a college town and denying that any safety issues were involved. I sent the petition and signatures off to the administrators, and after some time, there was a public announcement that they would reverse the current policy, perhaps prompted by the safety and liability issues I had raised, but no one bothered to contact me directly. The lesson I learned was that even if the university has always enforced or implemented a certain policy, it can be reevaluated and changed as new populations enter the academy.

Although some may consider this a minor triumph, it is these small victories that make the academy more welcoming to diverse populations on campus. Studies indicate that female faculty members encounter more stress than their male counterparts in balancing parenting with their academic careers (O'Laughlin and Bischoff 2005). The workload for pretenure faculty at research institutions can be intense, and the pace of life does not accommodate women faculty who plan to have children. Developing family-friendly policies that allow modified teaching responsibilities and an extension on the tenure clock during pregnancy and after the birth or adoption of a child can relieve some of this stress.[14] Providing affordable and accredited childcare on campus is another accommodating measure. It is not uncommon for women as graduate students or early in their faculty careers to opt for non-ladder positions (lecturers, adjuncts, and part time faculty) or leave the academy because they cannot fathom balancing motherhood and a full time career (Mason and Goulden 2002). For women faculty of color, fears are compounded by the burden of contending with a racially uninviting institution.

At my own university, when I organized a campuswide workshop on family-friendly policies targeted to educate junior faculty on their options, led by staff whose job it was to assist faculty with things like requirements for requesting a modified teaching schedule or stopping their tenure clock, few people attended. I learned that some were afraid to attend: they did not want their colleagues to know they were

---

14   For general resources on work and family, see American Association for University Professors at http://www.aaup.org/AAUP/issues/WF/ and the UC Faculty Family Friendly Edge at http://ucfamilyedge.berkeley.edu/ucfamilyfriendlyedge.html.

planning to have children, instead of focusing on their publications. The two times I informed my department chairs, one a male and one a female, that I was expecting a child, their immediate reaction was to ask how my classes would be covered or which department tasks I would fail to complete with only begrudging words of congratulations afterwards, and these felt more like a scolding. Perfectly sound policies may be in place; however, there are problems if they are not widely advertised or employed. A stigma is still associated with utilizing these policies, and promotional-review committees must be educated on how to evaluate these files without bias, so in addition to revisiting formal policies, changing the academic culture is essential as well.[15]

Becoming a Skillful Administrator

While undergraduate student populations are shifting, in some cases rapidly, across the country, the change among the faculty and administrative ranks is incremental or even stagnant.[16] Asian American undergraduate students make up close to half the population at many University of California campuses, yet the system, as well as many of the individual campuses, are unsure about how to handle these changing demographics. Some institutions treat these students as "model minorities" and consider them a good substitute for white students. Others are wary of the encroaching minoritization of their campus and have tried to curtail student admissions (Takagi 1992). When I walk around my campus, it is the norm to hear students speaking a range of ethnic languages mixed with English, which should be expected since the majority of Asian Americans are first- or 1.5-generation immigrants or the children of immigrant or refugee parents. We know from previous immigration patterns that heritage-language retention decreases with future generations, but the current younger generation also brings with them a diversity of cultures and customs. Even pronouncing their names produces tongue twisters, so they are definitely dissimilar from the college students of a generation ago.

The higher one advances in the academic hierarchy, the smaller the number of men and women of color. In the past two decades, the numbers of white women in academic administration have increased significantly, including those who are serving as presidents of research universities. However, the changes for people of color have been barely noticeable, and there is a paucity of women of color, including Asian American, in senior administrative positions across the country (Chan 2005).[17] My current campus has an African American male chancellor, one of the

---

15   In both public sessions and private conversations, I have heard women faculty express apprehension over utilizing family-friendly policies, such as modifying their teaching duties, since they are afraid that their peers will resent having to shoulder their responsibilities, which could lead to repercussions later. And if they extend their tenure clock, they are fearful that when they are evaluated for tenure, they will be expected to produce more publications, or that subconsciously, their colleagues will judge them more harshly since they received more time. From my experience as a mentor, and given what I do know about infamous cases across the country, I cannot say with conviction that the fears of these untenured female faculty are unfounded.

16   "Although diversity of both the state college-age population and the national pool of doctoral candidates is increasing, the diversity of the UC faculty has remained flat" (Task Force 2006, ii). The report concluded that underrepresented minority faculty are concentrated in certain fields and departments with almost a quarter in just three areas—education, languages, and ethnic studies.

17   Chan is one of the few Asian American women administrators from my discipline.

few in the country, and more than 50 percent of the students are Asian Americans; however, there are no senior Asian American administrators on campus.[18] There has been minimal to no concerted effort to increase the number of Asian American administrators at various ranks on the University of California campuses.[19]

Ideally, when someone accepts an administrative position, he or she should be a senior faculty member who is entering a workplace environment surrounded by supportive colleagues and being provided with an efficient bureaucratic structure and a robust budget. Instead, as an associate professor, I reluctantly assumed the chair in a period of departmental rebuilding after senior faculty members had to be removed for their administrative failings and the global economic downturn had decimated university budgets. Unsure if I had the ability to chair, I found the work manageable, although at times draining. I befriended supportive administrators on my campus, as well as other institutions, who generously provided me with guidance. As much as possible, I slowly learned not to take matters personally. I accepted the reality that being an administrator can make you unpopular, even among former allies. Educating myself about the formal policies, as well as informal rules, particularly learning who had real decision-making power and access to resources, was critical. I was often one of the few or the only woman or person of color in the room, which is something that I became accustomed to as I advanced in the academy. On the positive side, you can make a memorable impression on administrators because you do not blend in at meetings.

Leadership roles can be treacherous for women of color since their authority is often challenged more than that of white males or females (Turner 2002b). I was all too familiar with male and female faculty of color being removed from such positions early for political reasons or because they could not adjust to the responsibilities. In other cases, they found themselves unwilling to deal with the racism and sexism they experienced, with some stepping down because they became physically ill from the strain of the job. Asian American women still have to work against the prevalent stereotypes of them as submissive and subservient, which can undermine their authority and prevent them from being considered for leadership positions (Hune 1998). I can only speculate about the perceptions my colleagues have of Asian American women and was more intent on observing their behavior in dealing

---

18   I am considering administrators above the rank of department chair. Born in China, Chang-Lin Tien, a thermal engineer, was executive vice chancellor at the University of California, Irvine, from 1988 to 1990, and, to my knowledge, the last high-level Asian American academic administrator at my campus. He was appointed chancellor at the University of California, Berkeley, from 1990 to 1997, making him the first Asian American to lead a major research university in the United States (University of California 2002).

19   Henry T. Yang, a mechanical engineer, was appointed the chancellor of the University of California, Santa Barbara, in 1994, and Steve Kang, an electrical engineer, was appointed chancellor of the University of California, Merced, from 2007 to 2011. For the most part, the faculty data on Asian Americans and Asian nationals, who often first are international students, is not disaggregated, and the majority of them are concentrated in the STEM fields. Data on underrepresented minority faculty (if Asian Americans are included) often lists them as the largest group, with Asian American men as the largest number of male faculty of color and Asian American women as second in size for female faculty of color. Richard Tapia (2007) and Jo Ann Moody (2004) discuss the difference between diversity and representation as it relates to ways to improve "domestic-minority representation" and the importance of disaggregating this data.

with the few women of color administrators on campus.[20] I am still taken aback by the level of incivility and disrespect female administrators experience, behavior that male colleagues do not seem to direct at male administrators. I can say that some colleagues are very supportive in offering advice and resources, while others are skeptical and wary and keep their distance. I can definitely attest that I improved my negotiation abilities, acquired diplomatic skills, and developed more patience. Being chair of a department, even a small one, is a risky venture, and I accepted the sacrifices to my research that resulted. I have yet to decide if this posed a worthwhile risk to my career in the long term.

Conclusion

Institutions of higher education need to consider a holistic approach to hiring, retaining, and promoting diverse faculty, and this means reconfiguring institutional practices. Simply encouraging departments to diversify their recruitment process does not ensure that a wide range of faculty will be hired. If institutions encounter difficulty retaining diverse faculty, administrators need to determine if there is a pattern for these departures and this assessment should include a comprehensive evaluation of the workplace culture and environment at their institutions. A department or institution that acquires a reputation as a revolving door for white women and male and female faculty of color, especially those perceived as unfairly dismissed, can find it difficult to attract diverse candidates (Moreno et al. 2006). In addition, this reputation creates an inhospitable climate for diverse colleagues on campus. An institution that permits their colleagues to be mistreated instills doubt among faculty of color that they will be treated fairly when it is their turn to be evaluated.

Creating equitable policies, along with transforming a hostile workplace culture, benefits all faculty (Kerber 2005). Most university administrations espouse the rhetoric of diversity or multiculturalism, and some may have even set aside specified resources to support such efforts. Yet if these efforts at inclusiveness are tokenized or not enforced, they will fail to create equal opportunities or change the campus environment. As administrators and faculty, it takes courage and finesse to bring about meaningful, foundational transformation. It means knowing basics, such as ways to bridge differences, build unlikely coalitions, and take strategic risks. There are ways to institute change not only by taking punitive measures, but also by rewarding the accountability of administrators who are attentive to gender- and racial-equity practices and policies that foster a more supportive climate for faculty.

Lastly, institutions of higher learning cannot disassociate themselves from larger demographic and racial transformations in our society or remain complacent by resting on their laurels. California is now a "majority-minority" state, and more states will be following this pattern as well. Some whites are wary about what this will mean for institutions of higher learning in terms of the curriculum as well as the composition of the students, staff, faculty, and administrators. National political debates over affirmative action and immigration, which are explicitly about race, as well as policy reforms that are not about race per se but have been framed as racial debates, such as health care and welfare programs, can impact the way people of color are perceived and treated in the academy. As a democratic society, we are grappling

---

20   In academic affairs, there are a fair number of white women in full time, high-level administrative positions; however, there are few men and women of color or none at any given time.

with how to ensure that access, allocation, and distribution of limited resources are equitable, and these struggles over scarce resources are mirrored in the universities where we work. As renowned academicians who pride ourselves on research that hopefully will contribute to alleviating or resolving some of society's most complex problems, as well as shaping the minds of future generations of leaders, it seems our intellectual reputation depends upon us completing our "homework" first.

Part II
Faculty/Student Relationships

INTRODUCTION

John F. Dovidio

Presumed Incompetent: The Intersections of Race and Class for Women in Academia is not a book just for women of color: it is a volume *about* women of color but one that is *for* men and women of all races and ethnicities. It provides rare insights for those of us who are not women of color into the experiences, perspectives, goals, and realities of a significant constituency in academia.

The perspectives offered in the chapters of *Presumed Incompetent* challenge our beliefs about what academia stands for and inspire us to work to achieve the ideals of the profession. The narratives are rich and textured, highly informative even to those of us who study these topics and work "in the trenches" of academia. For the past thirty-five years, my research has focused primarily on issues of racism, sexism, and intergroup relations. I have held faculty positions at a liberal arts college, a large public university, and a private research-intensive institution. In addition, I spent five years as a department chair and almost ten more years in central administration, including being dean of faculty and provost. Much of what is in these pages reinforces the empirical literature on racism and sexism generally, as well as my own scholarship on contemporary bias. These narratives also confirm what I have witnessed personally as a faculty member and administrator. Even more importantly, although experienced researchers often believe that we already have a comprehensive understanding of a topic, and administrators often feel that we have seen it all, the particular value of this book for me is that it makes it clear that there has been so much that I have actually failed to see.

This volume gives voice to women of color in academia and illuminates the challenges they face. These narratives contain deeply personal examples of those challenges. The messages are difficult to hear for anyone who believes in fairness and equality, particularly those of us who hold that academia is responsible not only for intellectual progress but also for moral leadership. The psychological evidence suggests that readers—both women and men—will be inclined to dismiss the events described as exaggerations or illustrations of "oversensitivity." Others will believe the incidents are real and accurately portrayed but will attribute the problem to rare and unusual "bad actors." However, the examples the authors describe, which may startle those of us who live a different social existence, typify life for a woman of color in academia. In addition, the chapters illustrate scientifically documented processes of bias—sometimes blatant, but often subtle—that pervade our society. It is important that we all listen.

The frequent questioning of competence that is directed at women of color, which may sometimes be echoed by women and men of color themselves, is not new. In the past, their competence was openly questioned, but now it is whispered about or held in silent suspicion. But this is not social progress. Research in psychology, sociology, and political science demonstrates significant declines in overt expressions of racism, sexism, and other forms of -isms as egalitarian principles become more widely endorsed. This trend does not mean that bias is disappearing, however; it is being replaced by prejudice and discrimination that may be less conscious and intentional and manifested in more subtle ways. For instance, our research consistently reveals that whites tend not to discriminate against blacks in situations where appropriate behavior is clearly defined, but they do systematically discriminate in situations where the standards for action are less clear or negative responses to blacks can be justified on the basis of factors other than race.

For example, our research and the work of others show that blacks, Asians, and white women who have impeccable qualifications may be hired or promoted at rates comparable to those of white men, but when their record is anything short of perfect, they are victimized by discrimination. In these cases, decision makers weigh the strongest credentials of white men most heavily while they systematically shift their standards and focus on the weakest aspects of racial minorities. The process often occurs unconsciously, even among people who believe that they are not racist or sexist. Moreover, because people justify their decisions on the basis of something other than race or sex—how a particular aspect of the record falls short of the standards, for example—they fail to understand the way racism or sexism operated indirectly to shape the qualities they valued or devalued and, ultimately, what they decided.

Nevertheless, even though the bias may occur without conscious malevolence and be expressed subtly, the practical consequences can be just as severe as those of blatant prejudice—in this case, the failure of a person of color or white woman to get hired or promoted. Subtle bias can also have deeper psychological consequences. Whereas people of color and white women may be buffered from the negative psychological consequences of failure (e.g., depression, lowered self-esteem) when they attribute it to someone else's prejudice, subtle bias can erode self-confidence and psychological well-being because people of color and white women are more likely to believe that they are personally responsible for their failure.

One very distinctive component of this book is its emphasis on intersectionality—a woman who is also a person of color. While there is a large amount of scholarly literature about bias against white women and members of disadvantaged racial and ethnic groups, the unique *intersectional* experience of women of color is less well-understood. Perhaps part of the bias in the literature is grouping women as if the experiences of white women and women of color can be treated as one collective. For years, women of color have been an extremely attractive group to administrators in academia. Besides the ideological benefit of providing female and minority students with successful role models, they have had the practical advantage of counting as a "twofer" in affirmative-action accounting. However, once they have been brought through the doors of the university, their experiences belie their value to the academy, as reflected in the essays in this book.

Beyond the biases and obstacles that women of color face for being both women and people of color, they confront an additional challenge: being invisible. Members of minority groups are perceived primarily through standards exemplified by the men of their group, and women of color are typically judged by standards that are tailored to white women. It is thus more difficult to understand what a woman of color means psychologically; she often "falls between the cracks." As a consequence, what she says and does is more easily overlooked or forgotten. When women of color are visible—often because of their distinctive token status—the consequences are largely negative. Women of color may compensate by asserting their difference and demanding recognition. Unfortunately, respect cannot be demanded, and complainers are punished.

The alternative response is to try to fit in by not acting different and avoiding calling attention to the qualities that make you distinctive. Although women of color may be entering academia in increasing (albeit incrementally small) numbers, they often feel that the only way to succeed, or even survive, is to assimilate to prevailing norms and cultures—to blend in so they can be heard and seen. But by blending in, they abandon identities that define who they are and buffer them psychologically and socially in the face of discrimination. In addition, when they attempt to blend in, women of color lose their distinctive voice, and our students, institutions, and society miss the opportunity to benefit from diversity. Harmony achieved in this way also reduces the likelihood that institutions will change to become more inclusive and truly innovative. Colleges may achieve diversity in numbers, but the true meaning of difference is lost, and the opportunity to capitalize on new perspectives is forfeited.

The chapters in this volume are cautionary and instructive, not pessimistic. In the midst of the challenges the women of color describe in their chapters, there is indeed a very bright spot. These are all stories of resiliency. These women have succeeded because of their ability to overcome obstacles, and their chapters chronicle that success. There is no simple solution or recipe for overcoming bias. Certainly talent and perseverance are necessary—but not enough. What this book provides is a multidisciplinary and multicultural perspective on the challenges facing women of color in academia, an intellectual understanding of the ways bias is manifested, and concrete examples of what can be done to thrive in spite of discrimination. These chapters reassure other women of color in academia that they are not alone and that they can succeed—in fact, that they can be leaders.

But, as I said in the beginning, this book is for people other than women of color, too. It is for people like me, a white male, because no matter how long I study bias, I can never really experience and understand it until I listen to the voices of those who are victimized daily by it. This book is about our future: what it can be, and ways that we, as the academy and a society, can embrace the profound benefits of diversity.

CHAPTER 8

VISIBLY INVISIBLE

The Burden of Race and Gender for Female Students of Color Striving for an Academic Career in the Sciences

Deirdre M. Bowen

> *The emotional, sexual, and psychological stereotyping of females begins when the doctor says, "It's a girl."*

Shirley Chisholm

The twin themes of too few students of color and too few female students in the pipeline for careers in science, engineering, or mathematics are certainly not new. Many have written expressing their concern and warning of the effects of not having these populations properly engaged in these fields. However, the intersection of race and gender creates additional burdens for women of color striving to stay in the pipeline and develop an academic career in the sciences. This third theme—the experiences women of color endure while majoring in the sciences—is the focus of this essay.

The limited studies conducted on underrepresented minority women majoring in the hard sciences describe a consistent set of factors that provide unique challenges for them. While females are generally more likely to switch fields before entering graduate school than males and exit the science and engineering pipeline at every stage more than males, women of color experience isolation and stigma more than white women or minority males do (Alper 1993). They carry the burden of three major challenges.

First, women must overcome the stereotypes associated with their scientific and mathematical abilities based on their race and gender. In a study at Stanford University (Moses 1989), the respondents stated that others continually tested their qualifications. A general perception that they did not deserve to be in graduate school surrounded them.

Second, the mentoring women of color receive is severely lacking, even though we know support is essential to a student's continued success in academia (Moses 1989, 9–10). Female faculty of color are scarce, and those who do exist are often overburdened. While male faculty are plentiful in the sciences, and even male minority faculty may be more numerous than women of color, black female students report that minority male faculty appear to hold the same views as their white colleagues: they perceive females as less committed, less capable, and too aggressive (Moses 1989). As Moses notes, black male mentors may be aware of the challenges that black students face, yet they do not know the barriers that impede black female students.

Moreover, relationships and informal interactions with faculty seem particularly to elude female minority students. Certainly minority students generally feel isolated and outside the department "in" group (Allen, Haddad, and Kirkland 1984), but black female graduate students are less likely to have informal interactions with advisors such as spontaneous conversations or invitations to lunch or the advisor's home (Moses 1989). The issue seems to be one of indifference, rather than outright hostility.

Third, women of color are further challenged by the educational setting where they find themselves. For example, Fleming's (1984) work examining the experiences of African American women at historically black universities and colleges (HBUC), compared to those at predominantly white colleges and universities (PWCU), found different types of negative experiences in each setting. Women at HBUCs demonstrated greater academic achievement than their counterparts at PWCUs but at the cost of greater passivity, thus limiting their ambition and motivation. On the other hand, African American women at PWCUs developed greater skills in independence, assertiveness, role modeling, performing under pressure, coping, and developing ambition (L. R. Jackson 1998, 361). However, these students didn't make the same academic gains as their counterparts at HBUCs.

Furthermore, the composition of the campus, as well as the structural support offered to female and minority students, plays a significant role in the way women of color activate their sense of self. For example, Lisa Jackson (1998) found that schools tend to address gender and race as two separate attributes that force women of color to choose one trait over the other. The result is that race becomes much more salient because gender issues are focused on a white female construct that alienates women of color. Thus, women of color are limited in their ability to confront the connection between their gender and race in an academic setting.

The complexity of the interaction between gender and race demonstrates the careful attention faculty must give to opening up opportunities for women of color. It may be tempting to create structural support for women of color, generally, in the sciences, yet Steward, Gimenez, and Jackson's study (1995) of male and female students from four racial and ethnic groups at predominantly white universities revealed that very little overlap in values, motivation, or personal preference crossed gender lines or within racial or ethnic groups. According to Reid and Kelly (1994), however, there appears to be a tendency to define the female experience as universal and the minority female experience as an anomaly.

Unfortunately, most of this research is more than ten years old. More recently, Richard Tapia wrote in *The Chronicle of Higher Education* (2009) of the success some top-tiered research universities have had in producing underrepresented minority PhDs in the math and sciences by providing strong commitment and support from the faculty and the institution generally. However, the question still remains: How do women of color fare in programs designed to support students based on their underrepresented racial status?

Methodology

The research I conducted comes from a larger study I completed testing the validity of the arguments of the anti-affirmative-action camp with regards to higher education admissions. The present study examines the narrower question of whether underrepresented minority female students who are majoring in the sciences and attending strong mentoring programs have different experiences than underrepresented minority male students attending comparable mentoring programs. In other words, how do minority female students' experiences compare to their male counterparts when both are being nurtured for careers in the sciences? The results indicate that while race is a salient feature of both genders' experiences within higher education, certain gendered differences do appear that are not entirely consistent with previous research.

I sampled more than 330 students attending the Annual Biomedical Research Conference for Minority Students held in Anaheim, California, from November 8 through November 10, 2006. More than 1,233 undergraduate and 300 graduate students who are underrepresented minorities in their respective fields of study attended the conference.

I collected data during three phases at the conference. First, I approached students when they checked in at the registration center; second, I approached students during their poster sessions on the second day of the conference; and finally, I distributed surveys at a professional development session on the third day of the conference. On all three occasions, students were first asked if they would like to participate in the survey and were told its goals. I assured students that participation was completely optional and confidential. They were free to stop filling out the survey at any time. In addition, after students dropped their surveys in the envelope, they were given the option to provide contact information for a follow-up interview. Of the students that my research assistant and I were able to approach at the conference, only twenty-two declined to fill out the survey.

In addition to the surveys, I collected additional data through telephone interviews with twenty-two respondents, twelve of whom are females. These interviews lasted between forty-five minutes and an hour. I took detailed notes on respondents' answers, but I did not tape the interviews. They provided additional insight into the trends that emerged from the survey data.

I measured the students' experiences using seven variables that fit into two main categories: student interactions and faculty interactions. Within student interactions, I examined overt racism by students, pressure to prove oneself because of race, having one's qualifications questioned, whether students felt they fit into the campus population, and whether they thought the school's affirmative-action policy influenced the way other students perceived them. As for faculty interactions, I measured overt racism from faculty, lower expectations by faculty because of their race, and encouragement by faculty to speak about their career aspirations. Finally, I asked whether the students believed that faculty and students or just students agreed with the following statement: minority students can only get accepted to college with the help of affirmative action.

Using the software program Statistical Program for the Social Sciences (SPSS), I analyzed these variables for the entire population but split the sample by gender. Next, I analyzed the same set of variables but split the sample based on gender and race or ethnicity for Latinos/as and African Americans. Finally, I conducted the analysis again with the gendered and race/ethnicity split sample using the same variables, looking for patterned differences based on class by measuring their parents' educational attainment. I ran cross tabs and a chi-square analysis. Here are the results.

Results

I begin with a description of the demographic variables for the sample split by gender. Remarkably, 65.3 percent of the sample is made up of females. However, on other key variables, the sample is surprisingly evenly divided. As table one reveals, the mean age for both groups is twenty-one years. Across both groups, the mean college GPA is 3.49. About 80 percent of both females and males attend schools in states that allow affirmative action. In addition, 96 percent of females and males are considering applying to graduate school. Moreover, this sample represents a highly privileged segment of the population where more than 50 percent of the students have at least one parent with a college or graduate degree. Finally, the distribution for racial group membership is quite consistent across genders, with African Americans making up the majority of the sample—60 percent for males and 58 percent for females, followed by Latinos/as—25 percent and 23.7 percent, respectively. The next multiracial group makes up a much smaller percentage for both genders—6.8 percent for males and 9.5 percent for females. While I collected data on Asian Americans, Native Americans, Middle Easterners, and Pacific Islanders, each of these groups represented no more than 5 percent of the sample. Thus, while they are included in the aggregate data, these groups are not part of the individual race/ethnicity analysis.

I began the analysis by examining differences in gender in the racial aggregate for both student and faculty encounters. While table two presents the results, several significant trends emerged that are worth reporting. Consistent with what one might expect, despite substantial faculty support for minority students generally, females were slightly less likely to report that faculty encouraged them to speak about their career aspirations. Specifically, 81.8 percent of females responded positively to this question compared to 90.7 percent of males. These differences are statistically significant. Again, faculty should be commended for overwhelmingly engaging students of both genders, but the fact remains that women of color receive a little less support.

Despite somewhat fewer interactions with faculty, no differences existed between males and females regarding their perception that faculty had lower expectations of them because of race. In both cases, only about 20 percent of respondents answered this question positively. While the survey did not ask whether faculty had lower expectations of them based on gender, other variables—as well as interview responses—suggest that females perceive faculty as having lower expectations of them. For example, when asked whether minority students are only accepted because of affirmative action, 35.2 percent of females, compared to 23.1 percent of males, responded that both faculty and students felt that way. On the other hand, 15.4 percent of males, compared to 9.3 percent of females, stated that mostly students but not faculty felt this way. These differences are also statistically

Table 1: Demographic Variables

	Female		Male	
Gender	65.3%	(190)	34.7%	(103)
Mean age	21years		21years	
College GPA	3.49		3.49	
Attending school in an affirmative-action state	80.4%	(161)	81.2%	(85)
Considering applying to graduate school	95.6%		96.3%	
Race/ethnic group				
African American	57.9%	(110)	60.2%	(62)
Hispanic/Latino/a	23.7%	(45)	25.2%	(26)
Bi-/Multiracial	9.5%	(18)	6.8%	(7)
Asian American	4.2%	(8)	3.9%	(4)
Native American	1.6%	(3)	1.0%	(1)
Pacific Islander	2.1%	(4)	2.9%	(3)
Middle Eastern	.5%	(1)	0%	(0)
Highest level of education for a student's parent				
High school	19.3%	(39)	13.0%	(14)
AA	6.4%	(13)	4.6%	(5)
BA	25.2%	(51)	19.4%	(21)
MA/MS	17.8%	(36)	17.6%	(19)
PhD/JD	9.4%	(19)	18.5%	(20)

Table 2: Faculty Encounters by Gender and Race Aggregate

	Female		Male	
Faculty encourages them to speak about aspirations	81.8%*	(166)	90.7%	(98)
Faculty had lower expectations of them because of race	21.4%	(43)	20.2%	(21)
Minority students can only get accepted to college with the help of affirmative action				
Faculty and students believe this	35.2%*	(68)	23.1%	(24)
Just students believe this	9.3%	(18)	15.4%	(16)
They have experienced overt racism from faculty	14.0%	(28)	14.2%	(15)

*p = < .05 chi-square test

Table 3: Encounters with Other Students by Gender and Race Aggregates

	Female		Male	
They experienced overt racism from other students	20.8%*	(41)	31.1%	(33)
They felt pressure to prove themselves because of race	40.8%*	(82)	54.7%	(58)
School's affirmative-action policy did not influence the way others perceived them	68.0%**	(68)	43.6%	(24)
They were able to fit in with college population	80.3%	(163)	75.0%	(81)
Their qualifications were questioned	26.6%	(54)	30.6%	(33)

*p = < .05 chi-square test　　**p = < .01 chi-square test

significant. Finally, about 14 percent of both groups had experienced overt racism from faculty.

While gendered differences emerged that indicated faculty interactions were more negative for females, gendered differences also occurred in relation to student interactions. However, they appeared to be much more significant for male students. For example, it was quite disturbing that almost a third of male students reported overt racism from other students compared to a fifth of female students. Moreover, while more than half of male students stated that they felt pressure to prove themselves because of race, about 40 percent of females felt this same pressure. Furthermore, 68 percent of female students stated that their school's affirmative-action policy did not affect the way other students perceived them, while only 43.6 percent of males agreed with this statement. All of these differences are statistically significant. On the other hand, almost a third of female and male students reported that other students questioned their qualifications.

Given these results, it is not surprising that slightly more female students (80.3 percent) feel that they fit in with their college population compared to male students (75 percent).

The results reveal that both male and female students must navigate issues of race in their student and faculty spheres; however, females are saddled with one additional yoke—their gender. The way in which gender and race interact for females in the hard sciences is quite complex and is explored in the next section. In the meantime, the way women from different racial groups experience faculty and student interactions adds further nuance to this story.

While I collected data on a number of different racial groups, the samples are quite small. Thus, the reported analysis offers only an exploratory glimpse into the experiences of African American and Latino/a or Hispanic students. I conducted an analysis of the same set of variables—based first on faculty encounters and then student encounters—that I did for the sample as a whole, but this time I analyzed the sample based on gender and racial or ethnic groups.

Table four shows the results for faculty encounters. While both Latino and Latina students reported a slightly lower rate of racism (11 percent) than did African American students generally, male African American students (18 percent)

Table 4: Faculty Encounters by Race and Gender

	Female	Male
There was overt racism by faculty.		
African American	14.5%	17.7%
Hispanic/Latino/a	11.1%	11.5%
Faculty encourage you to speak about your career aspirations.		
African American	81.8%	91.9%
Hispanic/Latino/a	86.5%	88.5%
Faculty had lower expectations of you because of race.		
African American	20.9%	21.7%
Hispanic/Latino/a	18.2%	11.5%
Minorities can only be accepted because of affirmative action? Yes, but mostly students and not faculty believe this.		
African American	8.5%	18.0%*
Hispanic/Latino/a	9.5%	16.7%
Minorities can only be accepted because of affirmative action? Yes, both students and faculty believe this.		
African American	36.8%	21.3%
Hispanic/Latino/a	35.7%	25.0%

* p = < .05 chi-square test

reported overt racism from faculty at a higher rate than African American females (14.5 percent).

Differences also appeared with the variable *faculty encourages you to speak about your career aspirations*. Specifically, Latino and Latina students reported virtually similar rates of faculty encouragement: 88.5 percent and 86.5 percent, respectively. On the other hand, while African American males reported the highest rate of faculty encouragement (92 percent), African American females reported the lowest rate (82 percent).

Quite remarkably, the opposite trend emerges with the variable *faculty had lower expectations of you because of race*. African American students across gender lines responded in a consistent manner, with only about 20 percent of females and males answering yes to this question. However, Hispanic or Latino male students reported the lowest rate (11.5 percent) of perceiving that faculty had lower expectations of them because of race. Latina or Hispanic women reported at rates closer to African American students of both genders (18.2 percent).

Finally, a pronounced gender—rather than racial or ethnic—split occurs when students were asked whether faculty and students or just faculty agreed with the statement that minorities can only be accepted to college with the help of affirmative action. Specifically, more than a third of African American females and Latina students thought that both faculty and students agreed with the statement while only a fifth of African American males and Latino students felt the same way.

Table 5: Encounters with Other Students on Campus by Gender and Race

	Female	Male
Pressure to prove oneself because of race		
African American	42.7%	60.7%
Hispanic/Latino/a	34.1%	46.2%
Overt racism from other students		
African American	17.0%	29.0%
Hispanic/Latino/a	20.5%	24.0%
Ability to fit into the college population		
African American	82.7%	79.0%
Hispanic/Latino/a	84.4%	69.2%
Qualifications questioned by other students		
African American	27.3%	35.5%
Hispanic/Latino/a	15.9%	30.8%
School's affirmative-action policy did not influence the way other students perceived them		
African American	58.7%	43.3%
Hispanic/Latino/a	39.1%	43.2%

Students' interactions with other students on campus uncover similar trends to the general gender differences already reported, but they reveal greater variance across gender lines within racial and ethnic groups. For example, gender differences are greatest among African American students for the variable *pressure to prove oneself because of race* and the variable *overt racism from other students*. Specifically, while males in both groups were more likely to report feeling pressure to prove themselves, African American males reported the highest rate (60.7 percent) with a greater disparity from their female counterparts (42.7 percent) compared to Latinos/Hispanics. Latina students reported the lowest rate of 34.1 percent while Latino students responded with 46.2 percent.

In a similar way, females were less likely to report overt racism from students than males, but African American males reported the greatest incidence at 29 percent with African American females reporting the lowest rate of 17 percent. On the other hand, Latina and Latino students reported fairly consistent rates of 20.5 percent and 24 percent, respectively.

On the other hand, greater disparity exists between Hispanic/Latino/a students than African American students on the two variables: *ability to fit into the student population* and *qualifications questioned by other students*. Significantly, Latina students reported fitting into their campus population at the highest rate (84.4 percent) while Latino students reported fitting in at the lowest rate (69.2 percent). African American female students stated they fit into their population at a similar rate to Latina students (82.7 percent). However, African American male students were close behind with a rate of 79 percent.

These results make sense in light of the results from the other variable, *qualifications questioned by other students*. Minority students may feel less likely to fit in if they perceive that their peers doubt their ability to succeed in college. Again, interestingly enough, Latina students were substantially less likely to perceive that their qualifications were questioned (16 percent) than their male counterparts (30.8 percent) or African American students generally. On the other hand, African American female students reported that their qualifications were questioned at a rate more consistent with Latino students—27.3 percent, which is more than African American male students. Conversely, African American males reported the highest rate of having their qualifications questioned (35.5 percent).

The last variable, *school's affirmative-action policy did not influence the way other students perceived them*, tells an interesting story through both gender and racial differences. African American females were most likely to agree with this statement (58.7 percent) while Latina students were least likely to agree (39.1 percent). However, this twenty-point spread also represents the largest difference across gender lines among racial/ethnic groups of all the variables. Remarkably, the males responded identically across racial groups on this variable with 43% agreeing that the school's admission policy did not influence the way others viewed them.

The story becomes even more complex when one adds parents' educational attainment as a measure of class. I divided the sample based on those students who had at least one parent with a college degree and those who did not. The results appear in table six.

Let's begin with an examination of the two faculty variables. For the variable, *lower expectations by faculty because of race*, intersecting class with gender reveals an interesting pattern. For the population as a whole, males whose parents had a college degree were more likely than females in this category to answer yes to this question. Yet for the sample whose parents did not have a four-year college degree, females were more likely to answer that faculty had lower expectations of them because of their race.

The same pattern holds true when examining this variable for each racial or ethnic group. However, the distinction is greatest for Latinas and Latinos. Parental educational attainment seems to influence the way females and males interpret ethnicity as it applies to faculty interactions.

On the variable measuring *encouragement by faculty to speak about their aspirations*, gender differences appear to give way to class differences. Specifically, both males and females who had at least one parent with a four-year degree answered this question positively at twice the rate of students of both genders whose parents did not have a college degree. Once again, though, class mediates gender and racial understandings of faculty interactions.

Beginning with the population of students who had at least one parent with a college degree, African American females and Latinas were less likely than males to report that faculty encouraged them to speak about their aspirations. For African Americans, a 25 percent disparity exists between females and males, and for Latinos/as, it's a 16 percent disparity. On the other hand, for the sample where neither parent had a college degree, females from both racial and ethnic groups were more likely to report that faculty encouraged them to speak about their aspirations.

With regard to the remaining three variables, parents' educational attainment continues to influence gendered constructions of one's educational experiences.

Table 6: Class, Gender, and Race for Select Student and Faculty Variables

	Parent with less than a four-year degree		Parent with at least a four-year degree	
	Female	Male	*Female*	Male
Overt Racism from others				
General Population	53.3%	22.7%	46.7%	77.3%
African American	41.7%	25%	58.3%	75.%
Latino/a	75%	20%	25%	80%
Qualifications questioned by other students				
General Population	38.1%	21.7%	61.9%	78.3%
African American	25.1%	28%	74.9%	72%
Latino/a*	80%	0%	20%	100%
Pressure to prove oneself because of race				
General Population	42.4%	23.8%	57.6%	76.2%
African American	38.5%	22.2%	61.5%	77.8%
Latino/a	75%	22.2%	25%	77.8%
Lower expectations by faculty because of race				
General Population	36.7%	23.5%	63.3%	76.5%
African American	35%	25%	65%	75%
Latino/a	66.7%	0%	33.3%	100%
Encouragement by faculty to speak about their aspirations				
General* Population	31.6%	22.3%	67.4%	67.7%
African American	44.4%	19.5%	55.4%	80.5%
Latino/a	38.7%	22.3%	61.3%	77.7%

*= p<.05

For example, while males—generally and across racial and ethnic lines—were more likely to report experiencing overt racism from students, having their qualifications questioned, and feeling pressure to prove themselves, once parental educational attainment is taken into consideration, females with parents without a college degree responded more consistently with the group of males who had at least one parent with a college degree than with females, generally.

This pattern is consistent in both the general population as well as across racial and ethnic lines, too. For example, African American females whose parents didn't have a college degree were almost 18 percent more likely to report encountering overt racism than their male counterparts. Even more markedly, Latinas were 55 percent more likely to report overt racism than the Latinos in this category. On the other hand, females with a parent who had a college degree were less likely than males to report encountering overt racism.

Furthermore, both males and females with at least one college-educated parent were more likely to indicate that other students had questioned their qualifications. Class alone, rather than gender, was a better predictor of whether African American students perceived that their qualifications were questioned. On the other hand, class mediated gendered responses for Latinos. Specifically, Latinas without a college-educated parent, like Latinos with a college-educated parent, responded at much greater rates that students questioned their qualifications.

Finally, the theme remains consistent with the last variable: *pressure to prove oneself because of race*. Class, much more than gender, mediates responses to this variable. Once again, students of both genders with a college-educated parent felt more pressure to prove themselves because of race than their counterparts whose parents didn't have a college degree. However, more females without a college-educated parent were likely to experience this pressure than their male counterparts regardless of racial and ethnic identity.

When examining this variable across racial and ethnic, as well as gendered, lines, Latinas without a college-educated parent encountered this pressure at rates consistent with males of both ethnic and racial groups who did have a college-educated parent. On the other hand, although African American females without a college-educated parent certainly felt this pressure more than their male counterparts, this disparity is far greater among Latinos and Latinas (16 percent for African American students, 50 percent for Latino/a students.)

As the data suggest, while gender alone certainly plays a role in understanding female college experiences for those in the sciences, race/ethnicity and certainly class intersections add a much richer understanding of the multifaceted identities female students must navigate as they pursue their careers. The next section explores some explanations for these trends.

Discussion

Recall that this study sought to examine differences across gender and racial/ethnic lines for underrepresented minority students who are in mentoring programs and majoring in the sciences. The results explored these differences based on both faculty and student interactions. This discussion section is divided into the same two sections.

Faculty Interactions

The discussion begins with the results for faculty interactions based on the intersections of gender, race, and class. The question of faculty interaction is an important one because significant disparities exist between the number of male and female professors and especially male and female professors of color who teach in the sciences. As we consider how to keep the pipeline flowing for students of color, and particularly for female students of color, a consistent theme emerges from prior research: good mentoring and positive faculty interactions are critical to students' academic success (Moses 1989; Ellis 2001; Nettles 1990; Nolan 1999; Golde 2000; Nerad and Miller 1996; Herzig 2004).

Yet therein lies the conundrum. On the key variable that measures faculty mentorship or advising, females reported receiving slightly less encouragement to speak about their career aspirations. To be sure, most faculty are doing an admirable job, yet a statistically significant disparity exists. This difference is important because all the students in this study are in programs specifically designed to mentor students. However, these results are consistent with other scholars' work. Both Moses (1989) and Herzig (2004) report that women are affected negatively by the sex of their advisor more often than men. Specifically, male professors are more likely to mentor males than females.

More recently, Carrell, Page, and West (2009) found that while a professor's gender has little effect on male students, having a female professor has substantial impact on female students in relation to their performance on introductory math and science courses and their likelihood of continuing to study math and science, as well as graduating with a degree in one of these fields.

The question is, why does this gender difference, however small, still remain? Based on the research results, I theorize that two main factors may be at work. First, male professors may never have considered possible gendered and racial attitudes they may possess and how these attitudes affect their interaction with female students of color. In other studies, female students consistently reported that male professors appeared to question their commitment to the field (Moses 1989). While that question was not asked in the survey portion of my study, interview data suggest that male professors in the sciences may still harbor questions about female commitment to the sciences. The fact is that male faculty in the sciences have extremely limited interactions with female colleagues of color. Thus, a self-fulfilling prophecy may result.

Because male professors do not encounter many female professors of color (after all they make up only 2.6 percent of all professors in science and engineering), they may come to believe female students of color are not committed or capable. Female science professors of color act as role models for not only other females in their discipline but for the entire population—reminding all parties, other faculty and students alike, of what is possible. So the faculty may not engage female students of color in the same way because of their unconscious, unquestioned, gendered construction of who becomes a scientist.

One female respondent explained, "I know they think that I may do science for a while, but eventually I will get off the career track, so I am not really worth investing in the way the male students are. The professors would never say that outright, but you can tell that's what they think because not one of them has ever said, 'Once you become department chair . . . ,' or 'Once you have tenure . . .' to me." The female students also pointed out that I did not ask in the survey whether I felt faculty had lower expectations of them because of their gender. The interview data, however, suggests that female students certainly perceived that while faculty did not necessarily have lower expectation of them because of race at a rate greater than male students, they did sense lower expectations because of their gender.

A corollary that emerges from the interviews and data about the faculty's (un)conscious racial and gender attitudes is the nature of what is communicated to female students of color. When I was examining why females were more likely to report that both students and faculty believed minority students could only get admitted with the help of affirmative action, an interesting pattern emerged.

Both Latina and African American female students often reported that faculty treated them as exceptions. In other words, they were the outliers while male students were the norm. Faculty attempted to pay female students compliments for their work, but they often sounded as if the faculty seemed genuinely surprised about what these students had accomplished. Yet, when male students achieved the same thing, it was taken for granted. Faculty made comments like these: "I am so glad you're here! Thank God for affirmative action!" "Wow! I had no idea you knew how to do that! I thought it was a small miracle that you were even here!" Again well-meaning faculty may not have taken the time to reflect on how their gendered and racial attitudes were affecting the way they treat female students of color. These results are consistent with what others have written regarding stereotypical challenges females face about their math and science abilities. Garcia notes in her personal narrative that "the absence of women in these fields, I believe, is a major reason why our stereotypes have not changed significantly" (2006, 244).

However, examining the aggregated data masks who feels the greatest disparity in terms of race and class. While African American females reported the lowest rate of encouragement from faculty with a clear distinction from African American males (unlike the minimal distinction between Latina and Latino students), the gendered differences become much more apparent once parents' educational level is incorporated.

The group of African American women who reported the greatest invisibility were those females who had at least one parent with a college degree. The disparity reached 25 percent. This disparity holds true for Latina students in this category, too, but to a lesser extent at 15 percent. Thus, perception of faculty interactions is significantly mediated by class.

On the one hand, the gendered difference among African American students may reflect the same pattern that Fleming (1984) found in her study. Recall that African American females were more passive at HBCUs where more African American males were present. Because these science programs group male and female students of color together, African American females in my study may have assumed a less assertive demeanor and thus become at greater risk for invisibility compared to African American males. However, it is unclear whether this same effect impacts Latinas as well.

Alternatively, this perception of invisibility among female students with a college-educated parent may reflect the higher set of expectations that they carry compared to students whose parents do not have a college degree. Specifically, female students with a parent who has a college degree may have more social capital and, therefore, greater and more specific ideas about what faculty encouragement looks like. On the other hand, female students without a college-educated parent may have lower expectations about both the quality and quantity of faculty interactions. Thus, any faculty interaction appears positive to them.

Furthermore, the results of the study show that females with no college-educated parents are more likely to report that faculty encouraged them to speak about their aspirations compared with their male counterparts. Again perceptions may reflect expectations, rather than reality. Latinas, in particular, may have different ideas about visibility and equality from their male colleagues. For example, Hurtado and Sinha's study on Latina and Latino doctoral students (2006) revealed that male privilege played a significant role in gender socialization of their families. The female students did not, generally, challenge this status quo within the family and may have carried this sensibility with them to school. Thus, females who expected to receive unequal treatment may have been satisfied with any encouragement from a mentor, even if it was less than what males received.

In the final analysis, one should think carefully about who is at the most risk for invisibility. Expectations may form perception, but in reality female students should receive the same level of support and encouragement from faculty as male students do. Race and class clearly mediate the perception of mentoring received and perhaps even reflect the actual mentoring faculty provide. However, faculty should carefully consider how class, race, and gender inform the way they interact with students and student expectations.

Understanding the nature of faculty interactions becomes deeper after examining the attitudes faculty and students possess about affirmative action and minority admissions, according to underrepresented students. While a sizeable difference in perceptions existed between Latino and Latina students, African American females were far more likely to report that faculty and students held the attitude that minority students could only get admitted to college with the help of affirmative action.

However, the story becomes a little more complicated when this variable is compared with another: *the school's affirmative-action policy did not influence the way other students perceived them.* African American females, by far, were most likely to report that the school's policy did not affect the way other students saw them. This result suggests that the stigma that African American females experience about affirmative action comes from faculty, rather than their peers. In other words, if the question regarding attitudes about minority students needing affirmative action had offered another choice: "faculty but not students believe this," African American females would have selected that answer. It appears that the intersection of race and gender is more powerful for when African American females are interacting with faculty than with students.

These results appear consistent with Ogbu's (1978) comparative educational theory of minorities and, more recently, McClelland's (2003) work on the integration of minority students on predominantly white campuses. Students from involuntary minority groups (enslaved racial groups) believed race relations to be worse than students from voluntary minority groups (those who immigrated to a host country by choice) based on perceived white student attitudes. Similarly, in my study, female African American students were more likely to report encountering negative attitudes from predominantly male professors than other students. Again these interactions might be the result of professors' lack of awareness or training in engaging students in a racially and culturally mindful manner. One African American female pondered, "I sometimes feel like they [faculty] automatically assume I cannot possibly be here on my own merit. They just look right through me because someone in the admissions office made a mistake. Girls don't do science, but black girls especially don't. If I ask a question, they sigh and say things like, 'Can anyone else answer this question? Anyone?' And you know what? No one can because it was a good question!"

The second major factor at play involves the gendered application of self-censorship by professors. For example, female student respondents observed that professors engaged in self-censorship with male students but not with them. Specifically, male professors were more likely to make comments about minority admissions and affirmative action in front of female students but did not do so with male students. The male professors might have felt more comfortable making offhand remarks like this in front of female students because they viewed them as invisible. In other words, these professors might have thought, "It doesn't matter what that female student thinks of me because she and I will never be colleagues." One female student of color sighed, "I can't tell you how many times I would be in a group of white students and faculty, and they'd let it slip on the affirmative-action thing. Even though I am in a state with no affirmative action! If my black brothers were there, stuff like that never happened. I just didn't exist."

How invisibility is understood certainly varies by race and class. In the general population in this study, both males and females who had a college-educated parent were more likely to report that faculty had lower expectations of them because of the students' race, although a disparity still existed between males and females. However, race became a much more crucial factor for African American students generally in the group that had at least one college-educated parent.

The burden of race may become an identifying feature motivating faculty interactions when other factors can be explained away. For example, students who have a college-educated parent are more likely to possess instrumental knowledge that gives them the information they need to navigate the institutional waters of the academy (Rendon 1992). Therefore, the students may be less likely to interpret some failure of this knowledge as the basis for the way faculty treat them, while students whose parents do not have a college degree may be more likely to see their failure to understand how college works as one of the reasons for the faculty's lower expectations.

The way class mediates racial understanding of faculty expectations does not completely eliminate gender. African American females who had at least one parent with a college degree were still 10 percent less likely to believe faculty had lower expectations of them because of race than males in this category. Moreover, both African American females and Latinas whose parents did not have a college degree were more likely than their male counterparts to report that faculty had lower expectations of them because of race.

However, Latinas whose parents did not have a college degree did not report in the same manner as the general population of females or African American women on this variable; instead, their responses were similar to the general population and African American females whose parent(s) were college educated. Thus, race, more than class, became a defining feature of the way Latinas from presumably lower-socioeconomic-status households interpreted faculty interactions. This phenomenon is worth examining further, but I must caution that the sample size is quite small.

Latinas without a college-educated parent may be more likely to respond in this fashion because of the bicultural identity that they uniquely possess (Torres 2006). Latinas whose parents are not educated may find it difficult to reconcile the ties to their ethnic identity with the new sense of self they must develop in an academic institution. Latinas can feel guilty for not assisting family, for the privileged academic life they lead, and for the sacrifices that others before them have made. As Torres observes, students with less acculturated parents are more likely to have difficulty maintaining a bridge to both their worlds, while students who have more acculturated parents are better equipped to fuse these dual identities. Overwhelmingly, parents who have a college degree tend to be more acculturated.

Thus, Latinas may interpret their strong ethnic identity as the basis for lower expectations by the faculty. Rendon (1992) points out that as Latina students move between a home environment and neighborhood that respect and celebrate their cultural identity to a predominantly white, male institution, they can feel a significant amount of dissonance and even culture shock. This situation is further exacerbated by what González et al. (2002) observed in their work: faculty were not particularly interested in ethnic-related research topics and seemed uninformed about affirmative action. Thus, Latinas struggling with bicultural identity may feel particularly marginalized because of their ethnicity. One student states, "I do not feel that anyone is interested in the types of things I am interested in. While professors may ask me what my goals are, and while they don't roll their eyes when I say I'd like to focus on the reproductive issues of young women, they do get that blank look on their face like 'whatever.' But for me, I live in a community where these issues are very real."

Student Interactions

On the question of student interactions, it would be easy to assume that women appear to be doing well compared with their male counterparts. After all, the statistically different responses on racism, pressure to prove oneself because of race, and affirmative-action policy suggest that males are encountering a more hostile environment. Nevertheless, female students may be processing these interactions differently from males. Research on gender socialization shows that when dealing with negative interactions, women are much more likely to reflect internally and blame themselves while males are likely to turn outward and blame others (Vikesland 1998).

Once again, relying on race and gender alone does not tell the complete picture. For all three of the student-interaction variables—overt racism, qualifications questioned, and pressure to prove oneself because of race—African American females with a college-educated parent feel the burden of race much more acutely than their Latina sisters. It could be that racial stereotypes become most pronounced for the population of females who possess instrumental knowledge, and the status cues are more difficult to avoid. Whereas for Latinas with social capital, who have fused a scholarly identity in the white world, ethnicity may play less of a role in the way others treat them. On the other hand, Latinas without instrumental knowledge may be more clearly defined by their minority status. Other students may place them in ethnically stereotypical categories more easily and treat them accordingly.

In other words, it is virtually impossible for African American females to hide their racial identity, regardless of the amount of social capital they possess. Other students may have difficulty determining the minority status of privileged Latinas with social capital because they may not fit the ethnic stereotypes where other students try to place them. As Goffman (1963) wrote, there are the discredited whose master status is readily identifiable, and the discreditable, where identity is not as easily discovered. In this second category, it is possible to pass as a member of the dominant, normative group.

One student wryly observed, "When I am at school, I act white. I dress conservatively. I avoid speaking Spanish. I study harder than them. It's that simple. I can't change that I am a female, but I can make them stop assuming I am a dumb Mexican. I am like an *Othello* game piece. You know that game? At least I know the game I have to play." In this case, this student uses social capital to make her ethnic identity invisible in the hopes of avoiding the marginalization she may otherwise experience from other students. The research suggests that the more visible one's master statuses are, e.g., race, gender, or class, the more invisible a female student of color becomes.

Conclusion

Garcia uses the metaphor "brown diamonds" in describing her experiences in a doctoral program in the sciences (2006, 243). Women of color come in a variety of hues, they are rare, and they need polishing for their brilliance to shine through. Any program that considers developing a support system for women in the sciences must address gender, race, and class differences in the ways each female finds to navigate her way through the academy. Neither gender, nor ethnicity, nor class allows for a one-size-fits-all approach. But if we are to truly change the nature of the field, mentors must think carefully about the way they engage female students of color so they no longer remain visibly invisible. Perhaps we should work to develop programs that better train professors in the art and science of effective mentorship for all students, not just the ones they see when they look in the mirror.

CHAPTER 9

STEPPING IN AND
STEPPING OUT

Examining the Way Anticipatory Career Socialization Impacts Identity Negotiation of African American Women in Academia

Cerise L. Glenn

Higher education has been a means for underrepresented groups to gain access to higher standards of living and better jobs in the United States, especially since the 1950s and the civil rights era. Often thought of as a key component of pulling ourselves up by the bootstraps, women, people of color, and/or those of a lower socioeconomic status have utilized colleges and universities to achieve our piece of the American dream. Although this has been a successful strategy for many people, women of color often find ourselves in precarious situations because of the way we modify and communicate our identities to others inside and outside of the academy as we begin our career paths. We often receive conflicting messages from varying sources about who we are, who we are becoming, and who we should be. Efforts to develop our professional selves often create tension about what it means to be a woman of color because our ideas of identity are influenced by family members, peers, and society. This can be particularly troublesome because we must not only negotiate sexism and racism but must also adjust to our changing ideas about socioeconomic status as we matriculate through institutions of higher education and initiate our careers.

This chapter elucidates challenges posed by intersections of race, socioeconomic status, and gender that African American women face as we learn our professional roles in academic settings while struggling to maintain connections with the communities from which we come. Although this issue impacts the way various women of color negotiate and communicate our identities, I have chosen to focus on African American women in particular because I have expertise with this subset of the population as a self-identified African American woman and my current research focuses on African American women in academic settings. I draw from the experiences of colleagues and friends, as well as my own, to explicate key points. In addition, I utilize participants' comments from a larger study I am conducting regarding ways that African American female graduate students negotiate their identities in academic settings. Pseudonyms ensure the confidentiality and anonymity of the women who kindly granted me permission to use their stories. Although multiple voices are heard in this chapter and these stories may resonate with other women of color, I do not attempt to speak for all African American women.

I center this analysis in perspectives that come from organizational and intercultural communication and black feminism; that vantage point allows me to merge ideas about anticipatory and early career socialization with the ways in which gender, race, and socioeconomic status (class) intersect to influence the construction and negotiation of cultural identities. Furthermore, this approach explains the difficulties African American women face as we negotiate changing ideas about our identities as we transition to careers in academia. Anticipatory career socialization causes many of us to feel that we must step outside of certain aspects of our identities to successfully move along our career paths in academia. The particular emphasis on transitions during anticipatory career socialization and changes in socioeconomic status contributes to scholarship on women of color, which focuses primarily on the intersections of gender and/or race, as well as studies of women who have already assumed their professional roles.

Fully addressing the ways that intersections of race, gender, and socioeconomic status impact African American women as they negotiate their cultural and professional identities during anticipatory career socialization requires an overview of identity negotiation, black feminism as it relates to African American women's identities, and anticipatory career socialization. I then discuss how anticipatory career socialization in educational settings can divert women from particular careers. Next, I specifically address anticipatory socialization—both within academia and in outside communities—for African American women who aspire to be professors. Finally, I discuss resistance strategies that can promote positive constructions of identity and some challenges that those strategies create.

Identity Negotiation

Identity negotiation is the process we use to define and understand our sense of self as we interact with others. This process is inherently communicative since discursive encounters with peers and family and community members impact the way we form, maintain, and modify our identities in various contexts (Hecht 1993; Hecht, Jackson II, and Ribeau 2003). We negotiate our identities through ways that others define us in addition to the ways we define ourselves. Jung and Hecht (2004) assert that the various influences on our identities cohere at times and create opposition at others. Through social interaction and conversations, we develop and maintain multiple and shifting identities and experience stress and fragmentation when messages about our identities are contradictory. These contradictions often take dialectical forms. Goodall and Goodall describe dialectics as the "interaction of two opposing arguments or forces called *tensions* . . . " (2002, 181). Thus, we create and modify our cultural identities through dialectical tensions as multiple influences on our identity push and pull us toward multiple definitions of our sense of self (Hecht, Jackson II, and Ribeau 2003).

Black Feminism: Understanding Identity Negotiation of African American Women

Black feminism provides a useful lens for examining identity negotiation in African American women in academia. As Ashcraft and Allen (2003) note, race has often been excluded when examining issues related to organizational communication. In her explanation of black feminist standpoint theory, Patricia Collins (1986, 2000a, 2000b) explicates the interlocking systems of oppression that African Americans face due to our racial, gendered, and socioeconomic backgrounds. The phrase "triple jeopardy" vividly describes the way women of color often occupy multiple subordinate positions in society simultaneously (Houston 1988). Black feminist thought creates a space for examining these sources of marginalization as they intersect, instead of considering them disparate phenomena. Furthermore, it centers the experiences of African American women who are often excluded from scholarship, which begins to fill in this gap in understanding the experiences of members of nondominant social groups.

Black feminism allows us to comprehend that African American women negotiate their identities in ways that differ from dominant social groups. According to Collins, "a subordinate group not only experiences a different reality than a group that rules, but a subordinate group may interpret that reality differently than a dominant group" (2000a, 184). Although African American women may operate with a different interpretation of our social realities, we must negotiate our sense of self and merge it with images projected onto us by others. Collins explains, "Black women's lives are a series of negotiations that aim to reconcile the contradictions separating our own internally defined images of self as African-American women with our objectification as the Other" (2000a, 99). Dialectical tensions manifest themselves as African American women strive to negotiate and resist oppressive notions of our identities—often stemming from stereotypes—through the way we define ourselves. Efforts to resist stereotypical constructions of our identities stem not only from our self-defined notions of identity but also from our creation of and involvement in safe spaces. These spaces can include our families, churches, beauty salons, and other places where we gather to discuss our challenges from our distinct vantage points (Collins 2000a).

Anticipatory Organizational Socialization

Organizational socialization describes the process by which people learn their professional roles in their occupational settings. Jablin's (1987, 2001) conceptualization of organizational socialization processes focuses on its communicative nature. Socialization into organizations consists of the following stages: a) anticipatory socialization, b) assimilation, and c) exit. For the purposes of this chapter, I will overview the first stage and briefly discuss the newcomer aspect of assimilation since it overlaps with anticipatory socialization. Anticipatory socialization consists of messages received and processed from numerous sources prior to choosing a career. Vocational occupational socialization refers to the process of learning about particular careers (Jablin 1987, 2001). Family members, peers, teachers, and other members of the communities to which we belong discuss occupations with us from early childhood to adulthood.

Organizational anticipatory socialization occurs right before accepting a job and officially beginning a career in a particular organization. It consists of recruitment and interviewing, during which prospective newcomers learn about their occupational roles within a particular setting. Upon accepting a position, new members begin the process of assimilation or the breaking-in period. This entails "learning the ropes" of their job positions and becoming a part of the organization's culture through learning its rules (Allen 2000). Through this process, organizational outsiders transition to becoming insiders (Bullis and Stout 2000). In academic professions, however, the lines between anticipatory socialization and newcomer assimilation often blur as graduate students begin assuming the tasks of their careers, such as teaching and publishing.

Anticipatory Career Socialization as Outsiders

Academic institutions serve as integral components of anticipatory career socialization. As students obtain degrees, they learn about their prospective fields, as well as begin to shape perceptions of their professional roles in those fields. Members of academic institutions can socialize those of us in nondominant social groups, however, in ways that render us occupational outsiders. Instead of being socialized into our careers, colleges and universities can socialize us *out* of desired occupations. The following discussion of vocational occupational socialization reveals the various ways African American women are discouraged from pursuing our career goals early in academic matriculation. This discussion emphasizes careers specific to academia to illustrate how those of us who have not been discouraged from stepping into this occupation continue to face challenges as we begin to cope with notions of identity that others project onto us.

Vocational Occupational Socialization

After choosing a career, we learn more about these occupations through education and internships. For marginalized Others, these experiences often serve as mechanisms for learning how colleagues and supervisors will treat us once we enter these professions. African American women learn that we will have to deal with stereotypes formulated by members of more dominant social groups, in particular being perceived as a mammy (a caregiver), a token, and/or the angry black woman (Allen 2000, 2004; Bonner 2001). Michele passionately recalls,

> Anything I did, um, not only was about black people but particularly about black women. So all of the stereotypes about black women that my peers and my professors had now got put, you know, put on me. So if there was a day I wasn't feeling well and might have been a little snappy— oooh, she's the angry black woman. If I was in a mood where I was nice and accommodating—oooh, now I'm the mammy figure. It was constant. Every day, every interaction for me . . . seemed to be an opportunity to fulfill a stereotype.

Michele further explains that in addition to having her instructors and peers see her as stereotypes of African American women, she also learned that her field did not include any African American figures. She states, " . . . [it was] really oppressive, very difficult as a black woman, as a young artist really trying to define who I am, who I was, in my craft. It was very frustrating that we didn't—I ended up majoring in photography, and my head of the photography program at no point never, *never* talked about any black photographers."

African American women also receive messages that we should not obtain advanced degrees and do not belong in the fields we have chosen. Natasha, a political science student, notes that she often encounters the perception that " . . . particularly black women are less intelligent, that we don't have any place, particularly in my field . . . that whole notion of why are you here."

Denise expresses similar sentiments when she states, "All of my professors were men, white men . . . . I often felt dismissed . . . and because of that I had to work harder to make myself be seen because I didn't want to be ignored . . . . So I really had to make a concerted effort to get to know these dudes, talk, go to their office, get in their face. And I was getting dissed . . . . It's just like you're invisible." Denise notes that in her field of public relations, most of her job relates directly to the contacts she makes as a student. The invisibility she encounters makes it difficult to be successful in her career, which has partly caused her to modify her goals and elect to pursue another profession. Even though the new field pays less than her first choice, she feels that she will be more likely to be successful.

Similarly to Denise, Angel discusses that being rendered invisible caused her to change her major from biology to psychology. She explains that in the natural sciences, African Americans and females are underrepresented. Because she was treated as if she did not belong in the natural sciences, she believed that switching to the social sciences would be the only way to have her voice heard in the classroom. She explains,

> I even had a professor—I walked into a organic chemistry class—he was just lookin' at me like you must be in the wrong place kind of thing. I was like, no, I'm not in the wrong place. Or I'd gone into a classroom, particularly my science classes, where I really had very weird experiences. And I knew that it was attributed to my race, in particular. It was, you know—professors have come in and have asked if I was there to change the light bulb on the projector, and I'm just like, why would you think that? I'm a student in the class, so . . . .

Angel adds that these interactions took place in front of her peers, and the professors did not believe their comments were inappropriate. She began to feel that her presence was unwelcome and that her professors would not be able to see her potential in her natural science classes due to her race and gender. The intersections of racism and sexism in covert and overt forms often cause African American women to decide to question or modify their career choices if they must negotiate stereotypes, feelings of invisibility, and disparaging comments.

Organizational Anticipatory Socialization

So far the discussion has focused on common difficulties African American women experience during the beginning years of pursuing degrees in preparation for our careers. To unpack the multiple and often-contradictory messages regarding occupational socialization, this chapter now turns to African American women who have elected to pursue careers as professors. Those of us who pursue our desired career paths must continue the difficult process of identity negotiation as we shape our professional selves. While completing the last years of graduate school, we eagerly and anxiously anticipate finding a job in academia. We begin the long and tedious process of filing job applications. Many of us are fortunate enough to be recruited by prospective employers. During the job fairs and phone interviews, disturbing trends emerge at many of the schools to which we have applied. We discover the following common assumptions among many of our interviews: (a) no matter how we frame our research agenda, prospective employers think our work will be connected to African American women; (b) we are eager to nurture and mentor other students of color, regardless of their majors or career interests; (c) we will incorporate race and gender into the courses we teach (despite the fact that many of us have no coursework on our transcripts related to these issues); (d) we will enthusiastically serve on any committee with the word "diversity" in the title; and (e) we are well equipped to "deal with" students from underprivileged backgrounds who are not as well prepared for college as they should be. All of us, including colleagues, research participants, and myself, experienced at least two of these expectations when we talked to a prospective employer.

These expectations can place African American women in double binds as we enter the professoriate. At times these preconceptions work to our benefit, sometimes they only seemingly do, and more often they work against us. Given the research interests and educational backgrounds of many of us (myself included), the first and third assumptions work to our advantage. After further thought, I began to question ways that these preconceptions also worked against us in some (not all) of our interviews. One of my colleagues, Tabitha, remembers being interrogated about her understanding of a course that the person interviewing her stated had nothing to do with race or gender. Despite the fact that she has a degree in this subject and has done equally well in courses where race and gender never came up, she was automatically presumed to be competent in anything related to race and gender but had to prove she was knowledgeable about core courses she would have to instruct.

During a conversation with one of her interviewers, Christine learned that he considered her ability to "be great with the 'underprivileged' students who do not come from supportive backgrounds" one of her greatest assets. When she looked at him quizzically, the interviewer explained, "You know, given your common background." When she still said nothing, the interviewer hurriedly changed the subject. I recall a similar remark that took place during a conversation with a professor. I—perhaps not wisely—asked what background she was referring to. She responded that many of the students of color at this particular university were first-generation students who came from "those neighborhoods." I replied—again perhaps not wisely—that I was a second-generation college student from the suburbs. This conversation ended uneasily, and I still ponder the meaning and significance of this dialogue (although we have spoken since then, and she has been very polite to me).

Tokarra reveals that during a phone interview, she was asked if she was willing to advise an organization for African American students, be part of two committees focused on diversity, and be a member of another committee that was developing curriculum for students interested in African American studies. When she asked how many committees junior faculty typically served on during their first year, she was told that they were generally dispensed from this obligation. In this instance, however, the faculty desperately needed people of color on these committees immediately. Feeling overwhelmed by the demands that would be placed upon her if she accepted this job, she declined the request for a campus interview.

Recruitment and interviewing serve as important information-gathering experiences as African American women gain a deeper understanding of the way others in higher education perceive and define their occupational goals, commitments, and expectations.

Anticipatory Socialization within African American Communities: Are You Still One of Us?

In addition to receiving responses from those inside academic institutions that African American women do not belong in our respective fields in academia as we obtain undergraduate and graduate degrees and begin interviewing for positions, these messages also come from our families, peer groups, and communities. Instead of challenging our intelligence and potential to achieve, this feedback focuses on what we may lose by pursuing academic careers. As we decide to enter the realm of occupations that earn higher wages, we will be stepping outside of the safe spaces that help us resist negative notions of our identity. Shanita, who aspires to be a professor and is currently applying to doctoral programs, has arguments with her boyfriend, who tells her she is becoming "too bourgeois" as she completes her master's degree. He has warned her that if she continues into a doctoral program, she will lose her ability to relate to black people. Leslie notes that when she told her friends that she was attending a doctoral program, they responded that "it's uppity . . . and you're bourgeois anyway, so you belong there." Celeste feels that obtaining an advanced degree may come at too high a cost. Although she receives support from her peers and family members as she works toward her goal of becoming a professor, she feels this support often comes with the question, "If you pursue this path, are you still one of us?"

Questions regarding inclusion and commitment to African American communities also reflect a newer stereotype that has not previously been discussed in literature about careers or work-life balance—the black lady. Unlike other stereotypes that are projected onto us by members of dominant social groups, this one comes from those with similar racial and ethnic backgrounds. It represents black women as educated and independent, yet emasculating and alienating. It says that these women do not know how to treat men or act like they do not need them; therefore, they pursue careers at the cost of romantic relationships (Collins 2000a).

The messages that educated African American women may become black ladies begin early in our anticipatory socialization experiences. In elementary school, my father encouraged me to maintain my high grades and to do well in school but also warned me that "no man likes a woman who is smarter than he is." These words stung, and I was very surprised to hear them from my father, who has always been supportive of my goals. LaTonya, an assistant professor, explains that she raised three kids on her own while pursuing her college degrees. One of her daughters dropped out of college and moved in with her boyfriend. When LaTonya asked her why she had made this decision, her daughter responded, "Because I don't want to end up like you—alone." LaTonya painfully recalls that her daughter told her that her friends in college were having a difficult time finding dates and she did not want "to educate herself out of a man." LaTonya sadly relates, "All I did to get myself where I am! I thought my kids looked up to me. I really wanted to inspire them to accomplish whatever they want . . . . All of this? And I'm an example of what you [referring to her daughter] *don't* want to be?" Tisha, who has given up on the possibility that she will ever get married at thirty-five, states that she is looking into adopting a child. She does not regret her career choice but feels that it cost her the possibility of being married and raising children with someone she loves.

African American women may also face backlash against the knowledge they have obtained in academic settings. Those from their communities sometimes feel that these women no longer value lived experiences and prefer the linear, more rigid knowledge of academia as ways to understand their identities. Smitherman discusses that "blacks are quick to ridicule 'educated fools,' they have 'book' learning . . . knowledge, but not wisdom" (1986, 76). Older relatives particularly challenge academic constructions of knowledge. Janessa observes that her aunts and grandmother often find the tone and content of her conversation disrespectful and full of "sass," and I have had an older relative ask me jokingly, "Do you know anything that's not written in some book?" Tyra notes that at times she feels that "I've become caught up in the Ivory Tower . . . and have lost my ability to communicate with the family as effectively."

Perceptions from loved ones that becoming a professor has reduced inclusion and commitment to African American communities, severely limited the possibility of romantic relationships, and challenged the validity of lived experiences can be painful to negotiate. Often the change in socioeconomic status for many African American women in academic positions causes us to face negative perceptions of our personal and professional identities outside of scholarly settings as well.

Identity Negotiation from the Margins: Resisting Projected Notions of Identity

As previously discussed, African American women face resistance to forming our personal and professional identities from people inside and outside of academic institutions, which can cause conflict and anxiety as we move from anticipatory socialization to assimilation in our careers. Despite contradictory career messages, we find ways to resist negative notions of our sense of self and professional lives through constructing and participating in safe spaces and creating social change and a way to express our inner selves in academia (Collins 2000a). These safe spaces include relationships with mentors, friendship groups, and family members. Mentors provide an important way for us to resist stereotypes and negative perceptions of our career advancement, as well as provide encouragement and successful strategies from those who have been in our shoes. Natasha states that "mentors provide important motivation and empowerment." Janice adds, "It helps just to see us in positions of power . . . negotiating academia successfully." In addition to mentors in the academic environment, family and friends also provide support. Leslie, who lives with her parents while completing her doctorate in anticipation of a career as a professor, states, "I bounce a lot of things off my family. We talk a lot when I come home from class . . . [we discuss] what happened in class . . . what I was feeling, some of my concerns."

In addition to safe spaces, we also utilize and create ways to be included in academia through our research and teaching. Leslie explains that she has "made peace [with] . . . class privilege" by using her "new social awareness to give back to those of us [African Americans] who are still oppressed." She assigns her students projects, such as community and civic engagement, to encourage them to give back to their communities and appreciate the privilege of obtaining a college education. Annika, whose mother is an in-home caregiver, centers her research on women of color in nursing professions. Tisha researches ways that African American college students use popular music to make decisions about their sexual practices. Like Annika and Tisha, I also conduct research on women of color to help make our voices known to others in my disciplines. Kayla points out that she adds a discussion on diversity no matter what class she instructs. Janessa uses class exercises, such as the privilege walk, to help her students understand that certain groups are privileged while others are marginalized in our society. I have also guest lectured women's studies and communication theory courses about black feminism and womanism. Opportunities such as these encourage our students to learn about themselves and different groups of people as they continue their journeys of anticipatory socialization.

Challenges of Resistance Strategies

Even though African American women utilize successful strategies to promote positive ideas about their personal and professional identities, I must also note that our solutions often present challenges of their own. Creating extra assignments and guest lecturing often create extra work that does not get compensated. Those of us who focus our research on women of color have learned that in certain disciplines, the presentation and publication outlets that are most advantageous for tenure are not as friendly to our work. Those that are accessible to us may cause us to publish extra manuscripts and travel to additional conferences to present our work because they do not carry as much weight for tenure. Many of the participants I interviewed elected to work at teaching colleges where their research interests would not count against them for tenure. Although this is an excellent option, it subtracts from the time they have to commit to research because they must spend most of their time engaged in teaching and service. Our family and peer groups often hold both positive and negative perceptions of our career identities, often causing us to take the bad with the good. Despite these challenges, we strive to continue on our career paths with fervor. In Annika's words, "Sure it's tough, but I wouldn't want to do anything else . . . and the joys often compensate for the negative things life brings."

Conclusion

The stories shared about the ways that race, gender, and socioeconomic status impact African American women as we negotiate our identities in academic settings and with outside family and social groups help us understand the role of anticipatory career socialization in shaping our personal and professional selves. Although previous literature has addressed the intersection of race and gender in influencing newcomer socialization, incorporating the impact of socioeconomic status on anticipatory career socialization contributes to a greater understanding of the issues African American women choosing careers in academia often face. Despite the difficulties we have encountered defending self-defined notions of identity against negative ideas and stereotypes, the participants feel that we have benefited from these experiences and that overcoming these obstacles will serve us well in our career paths and other settings throughout our lives.

CHAPTER 10

SILENCE OF THE LAMBS

Angela Onwuachi-Willig

Introduction

For an untenured faculty member, perception is everything. It matters how her students, her senior colleagues, the greater university, and outsiders at other institutions perceive her (Carbado and Gulati 2003b).[1] The way that an untenured faculty member uses those perceptions, or in the words of Professors Devon Carbado and Mitu Gulati, works her identity, is critical to her survival and the ultimate goal of obtaining tenure (2000b).[2] How should this young "lamb" signal to all that she is a dedicated teacher, a brilliant scholar, and a wonderful colleague who services her department, the university, and the community as a whole? In that signaling, how should she balance her own sense of self with her appraisal of the institutional values involved? In other words, how does a pretenure faculty member "resolve the conflict between [her] sense of identity and [her] sense of the identity [she] needs to project to signal to [the] employer that [she] exhibits the characteristics the employer values" (Carbado and Gulati 2000b, 1266)?

For outsiders, such as women of color, this task of negotiating and performing identity can prove rather burdensome because of the need to undertake extra identity work to counter negative stereotypes about groups based on race, gender, and class (Carbado and Gulati 2000b). As Carbado and Gulati explain, these burdens can be especially heavy in workplaces such as academia, where valued employee attributes, such as collegiality, are difficult to define and observe.[3] For many junior faculty members, a recurring conflict between these two identities is the longstanding tension between voice and no voice: to speak or not to speak becomes the question. Senior colleagues, even those who embrace antisubordination ideologies such

---

1   Devon W. Carbado and Mitu Gulati identify the three most important elements of the tenure decision as scholarship, teaching, and service and then analyze the problems that minority scholars face in negotiating their service obligations.

2   Carbado and Gulati describe identity as both phenotypical and performative.

3   The pressure that outsiders feel to negate stereotypes about their identities is a form of employment discrimination that is ignored by the establishment.

as Latino/a critical theory (Hernández-Truyol, Harris, and Valdes 2006), often advise their junior contemporaries to remain silent. For junior women of color who are engaged in critical legal studies such as feminist legal theory, critical race theory, LatCrit theory, and/or critical race feminism, this advice is a double-edged sword. On the one hand, silence may be key to their survival in academia. On the other hand, as Audre Lorde once proclaimed, silence may not protect them but instead work against them (1984, 41).

How then can women of color, especially those from poor or working-class backgrounds, draw the line between following advice for survival and resisting their own subjugation—between balancing the identity-affirming conduct that maintains their voices and the identity-negating conduct of remaining silent? In this chapter, I explore the balancing act that many untenured (and tenured) female faculty of color face between choosing to give in to hierarchy and working the system. In so doing, I do not offer any answers for ways to balance these actions. There is no one-size-fits-all answer. As the late Jerome McCristal Culp once asserted, all tenure is local (Chang and Davis 2010).[4] The rules that apply at one institution do not necessarily govern another.

Additionally, the decisions surrounding silence are deeply personal. The tenure process is an exhausting one, and each individual must do what allows her to sleep at night during the pretenure period. We all have to strive to be like Sister Pollard, who proclaimed during the Montgomery bus boycott, "My feets is tired, but my soul is rested" (King 1965). Finally, although I went through the tenure process recently and relatively unscathed, I have to admit that I constantly struggled with the issue of silence, both strategically and emotionally, pretenure and continue to do so now. Depending on the day, my soul may be rested, or it may not be, but, like many female faculty of color, I am always tired. Through it all, I have learned that there are good silences, bad silences, and unforgivable silences.

I. Silence as Action?

> *It is not the case that the man who is silent says nothing.*
>
> Apache maxim, quoted by Margaret Montoya, *Silence and Silencing*

Not all silences are bad. Although silences can often be self-negating, they also can empower. As Professor Margaret Montoya explained, for women of color, silence can have many meanings and can be used in a variety of ways (Montoya 2000, 859). Silence is not always negative. Outsiders, such as women of color, may utilize silence to "produce centrifugal forces that decentralize and destabilize . . . power and privilege," making silence a tool of resistance (852).

As an untenured professor, I learned firsthand about the power of silence by observing the conduct of a senior male colleague of color at the first law school where I worked. I recall my initial surprise at this colleague's silence during most and much of our faculty meetings, especially given his stature as a highly respected member of the faculty. His silence stood in stark contrast to that of

---

4   Chang and Davis note that Culp made the statement at the 1991 Southeast/Southwest Law Teachers of Color Conference and that the "phrase is often invoked at the LatCrit/SALT Junior Faculty Development Workshop" (35).

many of our white, male senior colleagues, some of whom voiced their opinion on every matter—two, three, even four times. I wondered about my colleague's silence, at times wishing for more of his voice. I wanted to learn from him through his opinions, but, in the end, I learned more from his silence. Eventually, I saw that I had misunderstood his silences in these meetings, mistakenly viewing them as a lack of passion for certain topics. As I watched him more and more through-out the year, I understood that his silences were, at least in part, strategic. His frequent silences gave him a powerful voice when he spoke in public settings. Because of his profile, colleagues would have listened to him in any event, but his usual silence gave him more voice—a thundering one—when he chose to speak in open forums. He was, as they say, E. F. Hutton; when he spoke, people listened—in part because of his silences.

Normally a quiet person myself, my colleague's silences taught me what Montoya conveyed so beautifully in her article *Silence and Silencing: Their Centripetal and Centrifugal Forces in Legal Communication, Pedagogy and Discourse*—that silence "can be a significant positive signal to [others] of color that [their] language patterns are not deficient" (2000, 856). The silences of my colleague also taught me about the importance of understanding silence within context and the need to study and comprehend silence as part of "an interactive process" (853). What I later learned was that my colleague's silences in public meetings were just part of the picture. He did much of his speaking outside of the public faculty eye in private settings. As Montoya would contend, he shifted the meaning of his silences depending on the context. It is in this sense that we, as educators, must "learn to hear silence in oral and written communications and inquire into its meanings" (911). We have to become comfortable with silences enough to read them when that is what they need to be read and nurture them when they should grow into spoken voice.

For example, as Montoya declared, we as professors, including female professors of color, should learn to use the silences in our classroom to allow less-vocal students, in particular those of color, the space they need to participate. As Professor Doro-thy Roberts explained, "One possibility is that by employing silence, the professor subverts the dominant style of speech in law school classrooms. By breaking through the fast paced aggressive banter, typically dominated by white male students, silence allows less aggressive students of color to compose their thoughts and to participate" (2000, 936–37). Undoubtedly, silence, or silences, can be good, powerful even, for female faculty of color. But two questions remain: When are the silences harmful? How can such harm be prevented—at the moment and in the future?

II. Effects of Silence

> In becoming forcibly and essentially aware of my mortality, and of what
> I wished and wanted for my life, however short it might be, priorities and
> omissions became strongly etched in a merciless light, and what I regretted
> most were my silences.

Audre Lorde, *Sister Outsider*

Just as all silences are not bad, they are also not all good. Female faculty mem-bers of color need to ask themselves about the effects of their various silences. After all, we—female faculty of color—can be silenced in so many aspects of our job as a result of our racial and class backgrounds. We can be silenced through our difficulties in saying no to extra service burdens that involve diversity, especially where we know our voices will not otherwise be represented or because we—especially working-class women of color—feel a need to pay it forward (Tokarczyk and Fay 1993);[5] through our shame in talking about the daily burdens and biases that we face in the classroom, biases that are often invisible to white colleagues without explicit explanation (Chang and Davis 2010); through our feelings that we are impostors and do not truly belong in the academic world, where our racial and class backgrounds make us minorities (Tokarczyk and Fay 1993, 17); and through our deliberate identity choices about when, what, and to whom we speak in the classroom (Chang and Davis 2010; Tokarczyk and Fay 1993, 24).[6]

Such silences can be deafening at times. At some point, we as female faculty of color, especially pretenure, have to ask ourselves about the costs of our various silences. At what point does our playing the game merely become giving in or giving up ourselves? How can we balance the act of not speaking without losing self and yet speak without losing the game?

This balance of silence and nonsilence is difficult to achieve. For a woman of color especially, this game of silences can become complicated by the fact that her silences may result in her unique outsider perspectives never being expressed within the classroom or confirm the stereotype that she, as a minority, has nothing to contribute. Take, for example, the black female professor who decides to invoke the names of the casebook authors as she poses questions regarding race, gender, and class in her assigned cases (even though the nuanced and fine points in the questions are really her own). On the one hand, because this professor may be the first black teacher for many of her students and students, often unaware of their own biases, tend to doubt the competency of minority professors, her strategic decision to attribute race, gender, and class discussions to other scholars can be wise. Such a strategy can actually add legitimacy to the professor's points in the eyes of her students, who will perceive the questions as legitimate because they come from the book. On the other hand, this same strategy can work against her, backfiring and causing the same doubting students to wonder whether the professor is making any kind of contribution to the course.

At the same time, that silence may be harmful within certain contexts, so, too, may nonsilence, or rather voice. For example, a female professor of color's decision to be vocal about issues of race and gender in the classroom may just end up exposing that professor to a form of ultravisibility, marking her as the representative of her race. Even as a tenured, full professor, I struggle with these worries and decisions.

Most recently, I struggled with these issues when I taught employment discrimination for the first time in the spring of 2009 at the law school to which I later made a lateral move. Having long desired to teach the course because of its relationship to my former practice and my pending scholarship, I began with a tremendous rush. I enjoyed challenging students to see the case facts and analyses

---

5   Michelle Tokarczyk and Elizabeth Fay explain that working-class women "are more likely to accept heavy teaching loads and committee work because of the psychological toll of crossing gender and class barriers" and because they feel the "need to 'pay back'" (16–17).

6   Chang and Davis discuss the way faculty of color "edit [their] own performances to try to render ones that will be acceptable to [their] students" (28).

from different perspectives. I also enjoyed having my students challenge me to see cases from unexpected angles.

Little did I know, though, that I was in for a surprise, one that emerged as I covered the law regarding workplace appearance codes and discrimination—in particular, those cases concerning the hairstyles, or rather the hair, of black women. When the class reached this section of our casebook, I first presented them with a hypothetical based upon the case *Rogers v. American Airlines* (1981, 229). In *Rogers*, a black female employee of American Airlines filed a discrimination lawsuit under Title VII, arguing that the airline discriminated against "her as a woman, and more specifically, a black woman" through a grooming policy that prohibited certain employees from wearing all-braided hairstyles (231).

I was pleasantly surprised by my students' initial reaction to the *Rogers*-based hypothetical. My students—none of whom were black and many of whom came from small, rural, predominantly white towns—readily voiced what they saw as unlawful discrimination. They argued fervently that the prohibition on braided hairstyles was a form of race discrimination.

I then revealed that my hypothetical was based on an actual case—*Rogers*—and detailed its outcome. I told them that the district court dismissed the plaintiff's race and sex discrimination challenge to the employer's appearance policy on the following grounds: (1) the contested appearance provision did "not regulate on the basis of any immutable characteristic," and (2) the challenged policy applied equally to both races and sexes (1981, 231–32). As I explained the court's rationale, my students slowly began to nod their heads in agreement. Their challenges to the hypothetical problem ended. I pressed them briefly with questions about race, hair, and stereotypes, but I never really dove into complex criticisms of the case. In essence, the challenges stopped on my end, too.

When I returned to my office after that class, I began to question my silence during this classroom discussion. Why had I remained on the sidelines, not pushing my students as hard as I normally would on this particular problem? My hesitation seemed to stem from more than just my usual worry as a woman of color: my concerns about working my identity in a way that could overcome the presumption of incompetence usually imposed on professors of color (Carbado and Gulati 2000b; Carbado and Gulati 2003a).[7] Additionally, my holding back was about more than my understanding that my status as a black woman made me more vulnerable to student perceptions as a professor lacking in objectivity and pushing my own agenda (P. Smith 2001; Carbado and Gulati 2003a; Chang and Davis 2010).[8] Finally, my

7   Carbado and Gulati describe the way women and people of color attempt to alter their racial identities to prevent discrimination and preempt stereotyping in the workplace. They claim that "the social meaning of, for example, a black person's racial identity is a function of the way in which that person performs (presents) her blackness" such that blacks can choose to accept or reject societal expectations of behaving "conventionally"—that is, in accordance with predominant stereotypes (2003, 1771).

8   Pamela Smith notes that, for black female law professors, legal academia can be an "environment that is hostile to [our] credentials, our appearance, our existence, our accents, our beliefs, our values, and our exercise of professorial and evaluative authority" (2001, 1128); Carbado and Gulati detail, through an example, "the negative relationship that might exist within a particular law school context between the stereotypes about [a black male] professor's identity, and the professional and social norms of the faculty" (2000b, 1280); and Chang and Davis describe the challenges faced by Asian Pacific American male and black female faculty in law school classrooms and their similarities.

reticence was about more than my class insecurities and my general feeling of not belonging in academia (Tokarczyk and Fay 1993).[9]

When I honestly interrogated my action in that class—or rather my inaction—I realized that my apprehension was the result of a mixture of feelings about voluntarily instigating a situation where I would both directly and indirectly be the subject of discussion and evaluation. I also was afraid to expose too deeply—to witness too boldly—my students' lack of understanding and awareness about black women and their experiences—our hair, our wants, our burdens in living up to an appearance ideal that is rooted in a white female norm. I had to concede that my reluctance was, in many ways, like that of Professor Paulette Caldwell, who nearly twenty years earlier described her reluctance to discuss the *Rogers* case during a class in an article entitled "A Hair Piece: Perspectives on the Intersection of Race and Gender." She wrote,

> My anger eventually subsided, and I thought little more about *Rogers* until a student in my course in Employment Discrimination Law asked me after class to explain the decision. I promised to take up the case when we arrived at that point in the semester where the issues raised by *Rogers* fit most naturally in the development of antidiscrimination law.
>
> Several weeks passed, and the student asked about *Rogers* again and again (always privately, after class); yet I always put off answering her until some point later in the semester. After all, hair is such a little thing. Finally, while participating in a class discussion on a completely unrelated topic, the persistent one's comments wandered into the forbidden area of braided-hair cases. As soon as the student realized she had publicly introduced the subject of braided hair, she stopped in mid-sentence and covered her mouth in embarrassment, as if she had spoken out of turn. I was finally forced to confront what the student had obviously sensed in her embarrassment.
>
> I had avoided private and public discussions about braided hair not because the student had asked her questions at the wrong point in the semester. Nor had I avoided the subject because cases involving employer-mandated hair and grooming standards do not illustrate as well as other cases the presence of deeply-ingrained myths, negative images, and stereotypes that operate to define the social and economic position of blacks and women. *I had carefully evaded the subject of a black woman's hair because I appeared at each class meeting wearing a neatly-braided pageboy, and I resented being the unwitting object of one in thousands of law school hypotheticals.*
>
> Discussing braided hair styles with students did not threaten me in places where I had become most assured. I was personally at ease in my professionalism after a decade of law practice and nearly as many years as a law professor. I had lost—or become more successful in denying—any discomfort that I once may have experienced in discussing issues of race and gender in the too few occasions in the legal profession devoted to their exploration. I had even begun to smart less when confronted with my inability to change being the only, or one of inevitably too few, blacks on the faculty of a traditionally white law school. *But I was not prepared to adopt an abstract, dispassionate, objective stance to an issue that so obviously affected me personally; nor was I prepared to suffer publicly, through intense and passionate*

---

9   Tokarczyk and Fay describe this feeling as "the impostor complex" (17).

advocacy, the pain and outrage that I experience each time a black woman is dismissed, belittled, and ignored simply because she challenges our objectification. (1991, 368–69; emphasis added)

Unlike Caldwell, my hair was not in a braided pageboy; instead, I wore and still wear it in long, thin locks down my back.[10] Like Caldwell, however, I discovered that I was nervous about voluntarily making myself both a subject and object—of being both highly visible and completely invisible at the same time: being visible as a piece of evidence on display but completely invisible in terms of understanding about my hair, my being. Because of this fear (coupled with my usual worries as a black female professor), I left many questions unasked, questions that I believed that judges and other lawyers had left unasked and unevaluated for many years. Although seemingly the most powerful person in the room, I felt somewhat powerless in my ability to press my students harder about a race-based analysis of this case—one that many courts have referred to dismissively as just a "hair" case.[11]

At the end of the day, my silences in that particular class hurt not only me but also my students. In a room with no other black people, my students lost the unique perspective that I had about understanding and interpreting hair as a defining feature of race for black women, a perspective rooted in my own understanding and knowledge about black hair.

A few weeks later, I received another chance in that course to come back to the hair issue. This time I spoke openly, explaining my theory about the way that braids, locks, and twists—in light of the prevailing gender ideal for women with long, straight hair—should be understood as natural hairstyles and thus a sign of race, just as Afros are viewed under antidiscrimination law. The students, many of whom had not fully considered the effects of the differences between black and white hair for women, were receptive to my challenges on this legal issue, nodding this time with me instead of the *Rogers* court.[12] Perhaps in doing so, they viewed me as subject, but I imagine that my openness to challenge them with my insights made it harder for them to view me as a delegitimized object, making my choice to speak a powerful one, even if somewhat stilted.

Only rarely, though, do we get second chances to make up for our silences, especially pretenure. Relying on the opportunity for a second chance is risky and unwise. After all, there are, at least in my mind, times when we have no choice but to speak—when silences may be unforgivable. But how exactly can we, female faculty of color, identify those times?

---

10   Locks describe "the style of hair that has permanently locked together and cannot be unlocked without cutting" (S. B. White 2005, 296 n3). In an earlier article, I also provide a definition for locks (Onwuachi-Willig 2006, 873 n3). A 1995 article in the *New York Times* defined locking as "allowing the hair to mat." According to White, the term "loc" or "lock" is preferred to "dreadlock" because "the term dreadful was used by English slave traders to refer to Africans' hair, which had probably loc'd naturally on its own during the Middle Passage" (2005, 296 n3).

11   Lani Guinier comments, "Those with outsider consciousness live with the peculiar sensation of always looking at one's self through the eyes of others. . . . In our insider roles, we are still outsiders. . . . For self-conscious, second-sighted outsiders, multiple consciousness centers marginality and names reality" (2003, 75).

12   Guinier observes, "Using her outsider perspective, a black woman law professor may take 'information from the margin to transform how we think about the whole'" (2003, 76).

III. Unforgiveable Silences

Silence has several prices that those [who] are afraid must pay. One price is that it keeps those in need isolated from those [who] can provide solace and affirmation.

Pamela J. Smith, "Tyrannies of Silence of the
Untenured Professors of Color"

I realized that there were unforgivable silences as I was preparing my tenure statement at my new institution. Before then, I had come to regret one of my silences during a pretenure meeting with the dean and associate deans at the beginning of my first fall semester. When I look back, I realize that my silence in that meeting was largely a result of shock.

I had just moved to this school as a pretenure lateral to join my husband, who had accepted a tenure track position at a different institution nearby, and I was scheduled to come up for review the following fall. As I sat down with the dean and the associate deans to discuss my plans for tenure and the expectations for my review file, one of the associate deans, a white, senior male, remarked, "What we really care about are your teaching evaluations here, not the ones at your previous institution." I was in my first semester of teaching at my second law school. I had no evaluations to speak of yet and—at least until that moment—had not been too preoccupied with them. That associate dean's statement, however, changed my feelings of relative comfort within the classroom. After all, I was aware—based on studies and articles, others' stories, and my own experiences—about the biases against women of color in the classroom.

I immediately thought in response, "Really? My record does not matter much?" I wanted to explain to him that—unlike him and many of my white male colleagues—I did not walk into a classroom with a presumption of competence; that students judged me more harshly than they did my white peers; that I effectively had to work twice as hard to get good evaluations; that it could take a while—at least two semesters—to build up the same credibility that my white peers so often automatically received; and that this struggle would be particularly arduous in my case because of the institution's overwhelmingly white student body, very few of whom had interacted with people of color, much less encountered a professor of color, and where there were few students of color and even fewer (almost none) in my courses. I wondered, "How could he so easily discount my hard work in building my credibility as a teacher at my prior institution?" I had not earned strong student evaluation scores overnight. "How could he—with just one statement—erase the additional burdens that I carried as a woman of color in the classroom?"

I then thought back to the same, pretenure meeting at my first school with my first dean, a meeting that had gone completely differently. In that meeting, as the dean, a white, senior male, explained the process for evaluating teaching, he said, "You should know that I am fully aware of the challenges that women of color face in the classroom. We fully consider these challenges as we evaluate your teaching." I remembered how soothing I had found his words at that time. They had left me with the feeling that at least the dean understood the struggles that many senior faculty of color had warned me about and had worked to prepare me emotionally to handle. My dean's words had relaxed me—at least as much as any pretenured person can be relaxed (which is not very much).

As I sat in my first pretenure meeting at my new school, I was struck by the stark differences in the approaches of the two schools' administrations. In that meeting with my new administration, I remained silent. I had not expected the associate dean's words, which were not at all intended to be disarming, and I did not know how to respond to them.

After that meeting, my comfort level in my classes declined. I understood that everything was riding on my evaluations in these courses (Bonner 2004). I engaged in my classroom teaching with the associate dean's words always stuck in the back of my mind.[13]

When I had a chance to speak about my classroom challenges as a female professor of color in my tenure file, I limited my words and thoughts. I had previously planned to discuss these challenges at length—to educate others from what I hoped would be a position of relative privilege. However, my evaluations in one of my classes, though not bad, were not as strong as my prior ones, and I was worried that my discussion of those challenges, including studies of proven bias against women of color, would sound too much like making excuses (Yuracko 2006). My silences before had affected my freedom to speak later. Although I went through the tenure process—as others repeatedly tell me—easily and unscathed, that incident and similar situations continue to haunt me. Just as I had worried in my employment discrimination class, this incident (and others) exposed me too deeply—made me witness too boldly—my colleagues' lack of understanding and awareness about black women and their experiences—our burdens in living up to an ideal rooted in a white male norm.

At the same time, however, this incident (and others) taught me much about unforgivable silences—about the times when we must speak, if not for ourselves, then for the sake of others. In speaking of these lessons, I am not focusing on my silence during that pretenure meeting; given my status as an untenured faculty member, my reaction was certainly understandable, even if I personally regretted it. For the same reasons, I am not referring to my muted voice in my tenure application.

Instead, I refer primarily to the tenured voices that formed the basis of my first dean's understanding words to me—the nonsilences of senior colleagues of color that together worked to create a space where my dean at my first institution could acknowledge my challenges and burdens as a female faculty member of color. My first dean had been influenced by the teachings of not only my silent, senior male colleague of color (in private settings) but also a senior female colleague of color; posttenure both of them had informed, educated, and conversed with my first dean about the classroom challenges of people of color, and women of color in particular.[14] My senior colleagues of color had used their power and status to create a space for those who came after them—teachers whom they knew would not have the same voice with which to speak. My senior colleagues of color understood that if they

---

13   Professor Linda Greene once wrote of her similar awareness of the dangers of being black and female in the classroom, noting, "I came to fear this almost daily assault on my psyche" (2003, 89). Similarly Professor Margalynne Armstrong wrote, "I feared the students, their judgment of me, and their power over me. Their assessment of my performance would determine my future as a law professor. Although I am sure that all new teachers are frightened of students at first, I felt my fears were enhanced because I was so noticeably different from most of my audience" (2003, 108).

14   My dean also formally learned of such challenges, which I later found out were taught during deans' school and then reinforced by my senior colleagues of color.

"allow[ed] . . . shame to keep [them] silent, then the historical record [would] never include [our] stories, and it [would] be as if these things never happened and law schools [would] never change" (Chang and Davis 2010, 12). As a result, they refused to engage in unforgivable silences that would have perpetuated a presumption that the average white male professor's experiences are the same as those of women of color. They exposed for their dean the reality that we—female faculty of color—do not function in a color- and gender-blind profession and that we who are female and colored are never presumed competent.

Voices like theirs are needed even more today as the tenure gap between majority and minority professors widens, rather than narrows.[15] They are needed to protect and overcome the silence of the lambs and effect change at institutions across the nation.

Now, as a tenured full professor, I think of these senior colleagues of color and the junior ones after me when I need encouragement and strength to speak and I feel too tired to explain the experiences of women of color during a faculty hiring meeting or an appointments committee meeting (and perhaps, in the future, at a tenure meeting). It is these colleagues—and my memories of them and their gifts to me—that often remind me that it is time to stop being a lamb, that it is my duty as one of relative privilege in the tenure game to educate and not remain silent, that the silences reserved for the young lambs are no longer my own.[16]

---

15   The Association of American Law Schools (AALS) explained in one of its studies concerning minority faculty recruitment and retention in 2004,

> Comparing minority and non-minority tenure track professors, we see two alarming trends—a wide racial tenure gap in each cohort and longitudinally, an increasing racial gap over time. Among those law professors hired in 1991, 74% of white law professors were awarded tenure by year seven, as compared to 60% of people of color. The racial gap is more striking for the 1996–1997 cohort, where 73% of white law professors but only 47% of minority law professors were awarded tenure by year eight. (2005, 3)
>
> The most disheartening statistic from this AALS report was that, out of the eleven Latino/as who became law professors in 1996–97, none of them had received tenure by their seventh year (2005).

16   Pamela Smith notes that "you may be just what that person [a junior faculty member of color] needs to defeat the tyrannies of silence that keeps us all in fear" (2001, 1132).

CHAPTER 11

ON BEING SPECIAL

Serena Easton

I think I thought I was special—immune to the realities of racial discrimination. Because I grew up in the heart of black middle-class privilege in a mostly white suburb of New Jersey, instances of blatant racism were few and far between. Moreover, because of my elevated social class, the "good family" I came from, and my penchant for getting good grades at a challenging high school, I was considered "different" from the other black kids in town. Thus, while other black kids my age might have had to deal with racism and discrimination from whites in the town, these things rarely touched my life in any meaningful way. And so—after graduating from the excellent public school system in my town—I entered a private university in New Jersey with a full academic scholarship, and at twenty-two, I matriculated with a 3.895 grade-point average. I was smart. I was ready to take on the world. I was special. After deciding corporate America wasn't for me (a decision based on several unpleasant summer internships at a major telecommunications company), I decided to sign up for more school—after all, I was pretty good at school. In addition, I had developed a serious love of sociology and knew that in college I had only scratched the surface of what I wanted and needed to know.

I began life as a sociology graduate student in the fall of 1998 at a large public university in the deep South. My first apartment was next to fraternity row. There I was in my parents' minivan with all of my boxes, passing by gigantic plantation-style houses, each with rocking chairs on the front porch and large confederate flags either hanging from the houses or draped across the front lawn. As I had lived my entire life in New Jersey and had only seen those flags on Klan vehicles in *Eyes on the Prize* films, to say that I was frightened is an understatement. This was where I was going to teach while I earned my degree? These were the people I was going to have to teach about race and racism? This place looked like some throwback to the 1950s. I knew that the school was more than 90 percent white, but somehow in my twenty-two-year-old brain and my infinite naïveté, I thought that they would be like the white liberals I'd known in the Northeast and wouldn't be overtly discriminatory. Moreover, I was special! That kind of racism wasn't going to touch me.

It turned out that the students at the university actually did think I was "special"—the way that people label learning-disabled children that way. In the eyes of these wealthy white eighteen-year-olds, I couldn't possibly be educated, qualified, or smart enough to be a teaching assistant. I was this northerner, this girl only a few years older than them, this large black woman who evoked a mammy image and reminded them of their nannies and maids who worked back home in their large houses ensconced in well-manicured subdivisions. And while I may have been as articulate as any white male professor, my race and gender were obvious barriers to their respect. I didn't realize that this was the case until I started talking to my fellow first-year TAs, all of whom were white. As we sat in the mailroom commiserating over how hard it was to teach four discussion sections and be first-year grad students at the same time, I began to realize that their stories sounded very different from mine. In my sections, everything I said was questioned, scrutinized, and cross-examined.

Fully expecting my cohort to complain about the same problems, I was stunned when they began looking at me as if I had just grown an eyeball on my forehead. They weren't having these difficulties in their sections—it was just me. Only I was forced to pull up statistics, photos, theories, graphs, and charts constantly as evidence that what I was saying was true. Valerie Ann Moore describes this phenomenon as the "inappropriate challenges" often posed to female professors and professors of color, where "students demand that 'certain kinds' of professors justify their teaching methods, defend their knowledge, and prove their grasp of the material" (1996, 202). She goes on to say, "As a result of these challenges, such professors must prove themselves each time they walk into their classrooms" (202). So while all of us TAs might have been balancing our four discussion sections with our own classes—requiring a reading load of more than a thousand pages a week—only I as the sole black member of the cohort had to overprepare every week for discussion sections that often made me feel as if I was being cross-examined on the witness stand. When I realized that I was the only one facing this reality, loneliness and anger quickly began to set in.

I would bear witness to their privilege over and over again, only reinforcing my loneliness in that six-year period and reinforcing my race as a master status in a way it hadn't been before. For most of my life, race was there and was a reality but not one that necessarily confronted me every day. Overnight it seemed my life became littered with what I began to call "racial interruptions" or moments where suddenly and without warning, the salience of my race snapped into focus, unable to be downplayed or ignored. It happened when suddenly a white male student came to my office hours wearing a confederate flag or Klan T-shirt. It happened when I was in the middle of a lesson on affirmative action and a young white woman informed me that since I was likely a product of this policy, I probably wasn't qualified to be teaching her discussion section. It happened when I found myself fighting every year for one of the better assistantship assignments to which the white students always seemed to have access. It happened when I found that faculty members took greater interest in and better care of my cohort members than they did of me (even though in the end, I was the only one from that cohort who graduated from the program). It happened when I needed somewhere to blow off steam and relax, but the only places available were unfriendly white bars where the white students in the department got drunk, thereby forcing me to be the perpetual designated driver on the rare occasions when I joined them. Racial interruptions were everywhere—constant reminders that I was different and unequal, and didn't belong. No one understood the situation, and no one cared. It was just me, a brown-skinned Jersey girl in the middle of the deep South, fending for myself.

Part of fending for myself included paying my own bills on a teaching-assistant-ship salary. I worked as many as three jobs at the same time during graduate school. Again, I naively thought that everyone in my cohort had the same problem. As it turned out, their parents were financing their houses, apartments, cars, groceries, cell phones, and trips to the movies. My parents told me early on that the best they could do for all of us girls was help us get our undergraduate degrees; after that we were on our own. Yes, my family was middle class, but we were *black* middle class. As Oliver and Shapiro (1995) so aptly note, middle-class blacks earn 70 cents for every dollar earned by middle-class whites, and possess only 15 cents for every dollar of wealth held by middle-class whites. So while we had some money, it could stretch only so far; it couldn't finance my life in graduate school.

One of the jobs I took to make ends meet was tutoring members of the football team, most of whom were young black men from small rural towns in poor areas. Really, we shared a similar position at the university: the school was exploiting all of us for cheap labor that we consented to perform in exchange for an education. The pay for the job was good, the hours were short, and when the student athlete didn't show, I could get some reading done for my classes and prepare for my discussion sections. This was seemingly a perfect solution to my money woes—except that I was reminded over and over again of just how unspecial I was and how unspecial we all were/are as black people. Moreover, in studying and researching inequality, I was all the more aware of its dynamics and manifestations.

The guys on the football team *really* thought they were special. Here they were on full tuition athletic scholarships at a big football school in the South. They were on television every Saturday, they were admired by the nearly all-white student body, they were sought after by all the women, and they were given special privileges by their professors. In every way imaginable, they were the big men on campus, or so they thought. As a tutor, I was "on the inside" of the athletic department's operation. What I saw was a modern-day plantation system where white directors, coaches, assistant coaches, and staff told young black men when to get up, practice, eat, go to class, go to sleep, do their homework, and anything and everything in between. Caught up in this system were eighteen- and nineteen-year-old black boys, many of whom would never have been able to get into the university without their athletic ability. They were boys who needed a lot of extra help in trying to compete with their wealthy, well-educated white classmates.

Some saw their athletic scholarships as an opportunity to get a bachelor's degree they otherwise wouldn't have. Most, however, saw it as an instant one-way ticket to the NFL, despite the incredibly long odds. Trying to get them to study and engage in their academic careers was a challenge, to say the very least. That challenge was only complicated by the fact that they practiced at least six hours a day, were sometimes in class five hours a day, and were only allotted two hours a day for homework. The homework time period wasn't nearly enough for young men who were largely unprepared to be in college. Essentially, it seemed that the university never meant for them to graduate; instead, they were pawns on the football field, running the ball and winning bowl games until perhaps their bodies became too injured for them to continue. They were being exploited.

Needless to say, when I brought this point up to the football players—particularly during sessions when I felt as if they weren't giving their all—it did not go over well. To them I was a black girl from the North who "talked like a white girl" and was all "high sadity" with her fancy education. My class and gender meant that I couldn't understand where they were coming from. On some level, I think they knew they were being exploited, but they surely didn't want someone like me pointing it out to them. Still, this was an injustice that became hard for me to swallow, particularly when in studying inequality, I became so hyperaware of the ways it manifested itself on a macro- and microlevel. Their exploitation became that much more difficult to ignore when I met a young man named JR. One night at the tutoring center, I discovered that he could barely read. I left the center that night enraged, with angry tears running down my face. How was JR ever going to graduate? It seemed that a football career was his only chance for long-term success. Sadly, however, a year later when he was still in his early twenties, JR had a stroke on a very hot day during practice: football career over, academic career highly questionable, and long-term success perhaps improbable.

The anger I felt was all-consuming. These boys thought they were special. The university pretended they were special. The athletic department pretended they were special. As it turned out, these poor black boys were only special insofar as they were useful. Within the long tenure of Africans in America, it was simply a case of "different verse, same as the first." So why was I so angry? How could I have possibly been surprised that this was the case? While I was angry about the inequality I was seeing, I was also mad at myself for having such a strong reaction to it. When you understand inequality, how can you possibly be surprised when it is happening either to you or those around you? Perhaps I felt that way because it is almost unfathomable to understand the cruelties of inequality and how humans can be so unkind to each other. Nevertheless, I didn't have time to pontificate over this situation; I had a program to complete.

It came time for my cohort to write our theses, and panic set in. As the black faculty were all junior faculty, they were unable to chair my committee. As a result, I had to turn to a white faculty member who had a history of less-than-stellar mentorship of graduate students. He ended up mentoring both me and one of my friends in the program who was white. Naively I didn't think twice about this. After all, I was still thinking I was a little special and that discrimination probably wouldn't touch my life the way it had so many others, so it didn't occur to me that race might enter this picture as well.

The fact was that it had already become a factor in my completing my thesis without my having realized it. My white friend had gotten a series of nonteaching assistantship assignments. While I and another person had gotten the standard classroom assignment of teaching four discussion sections a week, she was able to work for her assistantship in the computer lab, where she spent all of her time writing her thesis. I had begged the white graduate program director (notorious for his racial bias) several times for this assignment. After all, I had been killing myself teaching those four discussion sections! It didn't matter to him. He reasoned that since I was so good in the classroom and my evaluations were so excellent, I should continue the discussion sections. Ironically, I was being punished for my talents in the classroom. The decision was made that my white friend would stay in the lab while I would try to finish my thesis despite teaching four sections, taking three classes, and working two jobs on the side. My wealthy white friend, unencumbered with many of these constraints, finished her thesis three months early.

At the time she was getting ready to defend her thesis, I was still begging for a moment of our advisor's time. For my thesis, I had to implement some statistical methods that were somewhat unfamiliar to me, but my advisor assured me he would "walk me through" them. I kept asking for help, and he kept putting me off. Aggravated by this situation and not one to sit by and be ignored, I finally barged into his office and demanded some time. He gave it to me and began to teach me the method. After the lesson was over, he told me to crunch some numbers and write up an analysis to submit to him later that week. I did so and put it in his mailbox. I expected to get an answer by email about whether or not I had done the assignment right, but that wasn't quite the response that I got.

The mailroom in the department was a large room where all of the faculty and graduate student mailboxes were located. There was a small adjoining kitchen in the back, and there were tables where people chatted, caught up, and ate lunch. It was the departmental gathering place. Often gaggles of grad students headed there right after the class they had in a room next door. I was part of that gaggle one day when, after a research-methods class, we all headed to the mailroom to chat, gossip, and let off some steam. Without any warning, I saw my thesis advisor appear in the doorway holding up my paper that was full of red marks. He barged in and started barreling toward me, yelling, "Stop what you are doing. *Don't write anything else. Don't write another thing until we have talked!! This is all wrong!*"

Even as I write about this incident now, some ten years later, I can remember the tidal wave of shame and embarrassment that washed over me. I was only one of two black graduate students at the time. The other one had already been summarily written off by the students and faculty, and the jury was still out on my promise as a scholar. His yelling at me in a mailroom that at the time was full of white faculty and students felt as if my fate had been sealed—I wasn't as smart as everyone else. I couldn't cut it, and now it seemed everyone knew it. My face began to get hot, tears began to form, and I watched the white faculty and staff make a hasty exit from the mailroom so they did not have to witness any more of my humiliation. It never occurred to my advisor (even though he was a race scholar) that as one of the only black graduate students, this incident might discredit me in front of the entire department. When I brought this up to him later, he apologized, but the damage had already been done.

About five weeks before my thesis was due to the graduate school and in the middle of my process of writing and revising, my advisor left the country for two weeks, only telling me a couple of days before. Before he left, he made sure to inform me that he didn't believe that there was any way I could finish the thesis on time. However, I had to finish on schedule because I needed to teach a summer course for extra money, which I couldn't do without a master's degree. While he was away, my committee (consisting of one of the black faculty members) stepped in to help me finish the thesis.

When my advisor came back and read the draft, he hated it. He made sure again to make this declaration public. This time he came into the departmental computer lab—again full of white graduate students—where he proclaimed, "I hate your paper, and I want to throw it in my fireplace!" More hurt and humiliation. When I asked what he wanted fixed, it boiled down to a few writing and editorial issues.

Still, no matter what the problem was, it didn't require another public humiliation. Despite all of this, I finished my thesis on time but not without a great deal of resistance from my advisor. Immediately following the defense, he said, "I really didn't think you could do it." To which I replied, "Yes, and imagine how hard it was for me not to have your support." Two years later, the thesis was published in a peer-reviewed journal as my first scholarly article.

I now had a master's degree, which meant that I could be what was called the "Teacher of Record" for a class of my own. My very first assignment was teaching the Sociology of Race and Ethnic Relations to fifty students. To fifty white students. To fifty wealthy, white students. To fifty wealthy, white, native southerners between the ages of eighteen and twenty-two. This was not going to be easy. As I took the long walk up to the front of the classroom—one of the longest walks that professors of color ever have to take—I could feel the eyes of these white students boring into the back of my head. Often professors of color who teach race courses are automatically discredited because they are perceived as biased and self-interested, rather than experts in the field (see Moore 1996). In other words, it's personal. To depersonalize my connection to the material, I constructed a syllabus that completely framed the sociology of race within the history of the United States. I painstakingly went group by group, policy by policy, concept by concept. It seemed to work. It appeared that the students saw me as capable, smart, and professional—this wasn't personal; I was an expert. I even won two teaching awards for my race courses. But, as I would soon learn and as the old feminist adage goes, the personal is political, and the political is personal.

In these race relations courses, I took on a new "special" title—the black person who proves that things can't be as bad for blacks as sociological research suggests. After offering statistics, research, and anecdotes thoroughly explaining the sociological context that informs and shapes the oppressive lives of African Americans, I began to get resistance from students who either (1) didn't believe that the situation was as bad as I had explained to them, or (2) thought that if it was that bad, it was because blacks simply hadn't tried hard enough to get ahead. As I pressed them further for arguments about why what I was saying couldn't be true, I began to get comments that were some variation of "well, Ms. Easton, you're Colored, and you made it." Of course, that the term "Colored" was used to refer to me was horrifying in itself and shortly thereafter provoked a lesson on appropriate racial terminology.

However, there was clearly a larger issue at stake: the students saw me as "special" and different from other blacks and had decided that if I could make it, why couldn't they? While we had covered intersectionality (i.e., the intersections of race, class, gender, and other categories of difference), it seemed that they had difficulty applying this concept to real life. Discussion after discussion had to be held about (1) how growing up middle class gave me a lot of privileges that many blacks did not have, and (2) that I wasn't so special because anywhere from one-quarter to one-third of all blacks are considered middle class (Attewell, Lavin, Domina, and Levey 2004; Pinkney 2000). They said they understood. They nodded their heads. Still, I could see through the furrowed brows and confused visages that they were having trouble reconciling this information. My middle-class status made them believe that things couldn't possibly be as bad for blacks as I was telling them, and yet—if I had had a lower-class background—I would've been discredited as incompetent or incapable of being able to teach a college-level course. Some of them were making that judgment anyway because to them, black would always mean incompetent, regardless of social class, background, or education. It felt like a no-win situation.

Happily, after six years, my time in the program was drawing to an end. After working with a dissertation advisor who was the only black faculty member left in the department (and who had made it clear that he wasn't at all happy about working with me), I was finishing my dissertation and on the job market. I was expecting to have a very difficult time but as it turned out, I received four interviews and four offers. Still, there was only one job I wanted—the one in my home state of New Jersey. This was my chance to get back to my family. My only nephew (at the time) was three years old, and I was watching him grow up through e-photos and phone calls. My sisters needed some support, my parents were getting older, and it was important that I got back home. Unless something bizarre happened at the interview, I was going to take this job if it was offered.

But something bizarre did happen.

I arrived at the university on the day of the interview, full of excitement and ready to give it my all. I felt like the kids in *A Chorus Line* singing, "God, I hope I get it. I hope I get it. Please God, I need this job! *I've got to get this job.*" From the start, this interview felt different from the others I had been on. I noticed there weren't many faculty around to talk to, but I thought that maybe it was just early and they'd show up for my teaching demonstration (because it was a teaching school after all), and they'd certainly show up for my job talk. I got to the teaching demonstration, and no faculty (except the faculty member whose class I had taken over that day) were present. But I thought that maybe this was just a bad time for them, or maybe they were teaching at the same time. Still, I couldn't help thinking, why would they schedule my demonstration for a time that was bad? Oh well, no matter. I still had the job talk, and there I would dazzle them with my presentation and research skills, and they'd want me, and I could move back to New Jersey, and I could be with my family again!

Two faculty members and the department head (a white male) out of the eight faculty members on staff came to the talk—a slightly bigger turnout than the teaching demonstration. At all of the other interviews I'd had, even though the departments were small, nearly everyone turned up for the interview in addition to administrators and faculty in other departments. So this was a bit off-putting and reaffirmed the feeling I had had all day that maybe this department wasn't that interested in having me. My fears were subsequently confirmed when I finished the job talk and it was time to go home. On my way out, I somewhat casually asked the department head where they were in the process of interviewing candidates. He said that they hadn't seen any candidates before me and weren't going to interview any after me. I began to get excited, foolishly thinking that perhaps I was their only choice. I started mentally celebrating: *This is it! I can go back home! I've got this job!* But then the department head said, "Well, I'm just going to be honest with you. You're going to get this job because you're black and a woman. So we're going to give you this job. But we're going to hire someone else for the job we advertised." He went on to tell me that university policy stated that they could hire a strong minority candidate if one applied in addition to the person for whom the job ad was intended. In other words, I was their affirmative-action hire, and they were going to give me "special" treatment by gifting me with the position.

Feeling the beginnings of physical illness, I asked the department head if he was implying somehow that I was unqualified for the position. He said, "Well no, but in the ad, we asked for someone who uses quantitative methods." Fine, even though my dissertation was qualitative, I had published an article based on my master's thesis that utilized quantitative methods, and I had a background in it. When I mentioned this to him, he said, "Yeah, I told the dean that, but it didn't work, so we're going to give you this job because you're black and a woman." Utterly horrified and dejected (particularly by him using the word "give" over and over again), I said my thank yous and good-byes and was escorted to the elevator by the only other faculty member of color in the department, an Asian male. When we got into the elevator and the doors closed, he turned to me and said, "Don't worry about what the department head said. He said the same thing to me last year when I was hired."

See, it's not that we faculty of color don't know about the nationwide effort to diversify faculty at colleges and universities. It's not that we don't know that we may be beneficiaries of affirmative action. Of course we know. But no candidate or faculty member wants to feel patronized, humiliated, or treated with condescension as if they are wholly unqualified for the position they are seeking. They particularly don't want this kind of treatment after they have fought tooth and nail within a context of inequality to get where they are. And yet this department head had gone out of his way to treat me this way.

I went home later that evening to my parents' house, so upset that I could hardly speak. My sisters came over, and everyone was excited and overjoyed because I had gotten the job. I tried to tell them about what had happened and how upset I was. I had worked my butt off in graduate school and overcome seemingly impossible obstacles and still could present myself as a fairly strong candidate, but here was this white man intent on letting me know that I was only going to be hired because of my race and gender. As I was telling the story, I recall my father saying several times, "But you're still going to take this job, right?" My sisters and mother echoed his question. I didn't have the heart to tell them that there was no way I could take a job where the department head felt as if he was doing me a favor by gifting me with a position that he felt I didn't really deserve. I would have to turn the job down and stay away for a few more years. My family was very upset and sad, and one of my sisters said she felt as if I was abandoning her again. It absolutely broke my heart.

I ended up taking a job in a large midwestern city at an institution that seemed very happy to have me and had a larger percentage of students of color than any other school where I interviewed. It was an institution dedicated to social justice and because of that had very liberal admission standards. I didn't realize what that actually meant; I was just happy to be at a school with so much diversity (roughly 50 percent white and 50 percent minority, with black students comprising 22 percent of the population). A large portion of the students of color had come from the poor-quality public schools in the city. They were excited to see a young black faculty member whom they thought might understand their experiences better than the white faculty. For my part, I was happy to be teaching race at a social justice–oriented institution with actual black, Latino, and Asian students who could speak to their experiences. I was also happy to be teaching white students who had a much greater awareness of social inequality than the very privileged, wealthy white students I had taught in the South.

Things got tricky very early in my first job. I came into the job with five courses already prepped and taught as a graduate student, but my department head needed me to prepare four more because more race courses were needed in the department. That took up a lot of time, leaving very little for research. I then began to notice that I was swamped with black students during my office hours. The conversations never seemed to be about the material, even though some of them were doing very poorly in the class. Instead, they talked about abortions, abusive boyfriends, the struggles of coming out, losing welfare benefits, the difficulties of finding affordable childcare (prompting some young women to bring their children to class), and parental abuse. Apparently this is quite common: according to Guiffrida (2005), black students often expect black faculty to advise them not only on career guidance and academic issues but on personal problems as well. Essentially we are often asked to assume a parental or "other-mothering" role (Collins 2000) in these students' lives.

In this regard, one student was particularly memorable. He kept showing up during my office hours to tell me about the trouble he was having with his mother at home and seemed to be suffering from severe depression and anxiety. This prompted me to escort him to the mental health center three times. One day he came to my office threatening to kill himself after I wouldn't let him turn in late a one-page paper he'd had six weeks to write. In his anger at me, he attempted to push me down a flight of stairs but was stopped when a student jumped in to try and shield me from him.

When I reported the incident to the powers at the university, a white administrator told me that as a poor, black, gay male, he represented a key demographic in the student body. This of course made me wonder if my representing a key demographic in the faculty as a woman of color was equally important—at least enough to make sure my safety was a priority. The answer became clear when I was forced to give this seriously unbalanced student an independent study and he was allowed to remain at the university, where he graduated and then reenrolled as a graduate student, despite his attempted attack on a faculty member. For the rest of the time I was at that university, just the simple act of going to work became a terrifying experience.

While my being one of the few black faculty members meant that black students often flocked to my office hours and classes, they weren't always pleased with what they got from me. In large part, this was due to the difference in our class backgrounds. They were first-generation college students from ghetto neighborhoods, and they felt that their "she-talks-like-a-white-girl" instructor couldn't understand their struggle. It was a struggle I focused on in all of my classes on the black experience, and I always looked at it from a social justice perspective, concentrating on the structural inequalities that blacks face rather than reducing it to matters of personal responsibility. Essentially I wanted them to interpret their experience in sociological terms and communicate that I understood what they faced as much as I could without having lived some of their struggles. But to be sure, the problems of the black middle class are qualitatively different from those of our working-class brothers and sisters, and when you don't come from the ghetto, you can't really know what it is like. This created a sizable obstacle in my relationship with my students. Moreover, there was the authenticity issue: as others have noted (Cole and Omari 2003; Lacy 2007; Patterson 1972), "authentic" black culture and identity have become increasingly positioned as located among the lower class and are more likely to include stylized ways of talking, walking, acting, and thinking as the root of blackness (see also Peterson-Lewis and Bratton 2004). Thus, blacks like me who do blackness differently and don't have all of these characteristics are perceived as "acting white." That was the way my students saw me.

As if the class issue wasn't enough, I was younger than many of my black students (I started the job when I was twenty-eight), and this school had a large population of nontraditional students. Valerie Moore notes in her research that female professors often find that their students perceive younger-looking women as "inexperienced [and] easier to push around" (1996, 203). This was true in my case: where I had never gotten complaints from the black students at the white university where I had done my graduate work, all of the complaints I received at this university came from black students. Additionally, many of those challenges came from older, black, female students who didn't feel that they should be held accountable to me for things like their attendance or the quality of their academic performance. And so, inevitably, what my black students saw was a young black girl who talked like a white girl, had been given privileges that they could only dream about, and thus thought she was better than her students, even though that couldn't be further from the truth. Essentially the intersections of race, class, and age conspired to make my life rather difficult at my first job.

One of the students' major complaints was that I expected too much of them and my standards were too high. These standards included things like writing using proper grammar, spelling, and paragraph structure. Realizing that many of the students had come out of the city's public school system, which was notoriously inept, I dedicated entire class periods to how to write a paper and do library research, when to use commas and semicolons, and how to write an analysis (not a summary) of a course reading. Essentially, in a class of forty, I was often remediating at least half of the students.

When I told some of my white colleagues that I was holding my students to these standards, they told me that they didn't demand these things of them because they didn't think it was fair. When I inquired why, they argued—as is typical of those stuck in white liberal guilt—that it was unfair to penalize these students for writing in nonstandard English: because they were poor and of color, we shouldn't and couldn't expect as much from them. This idea infuriated me. They were telling me that my people couldn't learn and because of that, I should lower my standards for them. Because I couldn't do that and sleep at night, both students and faculty perceived me as too hard. Some students did appreciate my efforts to help them conquer the learning curve they were dealing with and even said that they began to get better grades on their writing in other classes because I was so hard on them. However, another contingent felt that I was unreasonable. At a teaching school, these perceptions actually matter quite a bit and seemed to color my teaching evaluations.

Still, no matter how important teaching may be at a college or university, more often than not research is one's currency in academia. For a tenure-track assistant professor, teaching three courses per semester that often reach maximum enrollment while remediating half of the students in each class means that there is very little time left for research. This situation was complicated for me by the excessive advising I was expected to do. As Guiffrida found in his interviews on black students' demands of black faculty, "Providing the level of personal advising, support, and advocacy that these students were seeking is time consuming and [detracts] from other, more traditional faculty responsibilities such as research, teaching, and professional service" (2005, 719). This was very true in my case. Moreover, because of the low salary at the institution and the huge amount of debt I had incurred while in graduate school, I had to teach summer school every year, which also bled into any time I needed for research. Yet research is central in academia, and I was falling behind. I had a book manuscript that was taking forever to complete, for all of the aforementioned reasons which made my tenure prospects questionable at best.

As I began to realize I was in trouble and was becoming increasingly unhappy in my career, I became furious. The anger had actually been building for the past ten years and was putting me in serious danger of turning into the "angry black woman" stereotype. The person I was angriest at was me. How could I have possibly been surprised that my life was being shaped by categories of difference and inequality? I knew what inequality looked like. I had researched it; I had taught it. But for some reason, when I was living it, and it was happening to me, I found it much more difficult to anticipate, negotiate, and react effectively. Did I just think that racism, classism, and sexism happened to other people? Was I really just thinking all of this time that I was special? Was this just arrogance or some other personal defect in my character, or was it something else?

As I thought about it, I decided that the surprise wasn't simply due to me being so blinded by my privilege that I thought I was immune to the dictates of racial inequality. It also stemmed from this: when you are fighting for your life within a context of inequality, you can become so busy trying to survive that you have no time to reflect on the system that is putting you in that position in the first place. I was in the trenches of the academic jungle, taking grenades. When you are fighting a war like that, you don't have time to reflect thoughtfully upon the structure of the war, whether or not it should be happening in the first place, or what has put you in the midst of it. No matter how much you may know in your head that you and your people are victims of a system that you didn't create, it doesn't really matter when you're taking grenades. You must react to stay alive. I had to stop being mad at myself for being angry and shocked by the inequality I witnessed and experienced on a daily basis as an academic. I had to release those feelings to move forward. Life is what it is. I am entrapped in this system where things beyond my control happen, and the only thing I can do is try my best to be successful in spite of the macrostructural problems that impact me on this microlevel. Just because the race is hard doesn't give me permission to stop running.

After all, when I place my struggles in the context of the historical ones experienced by my brothers and sisters, I realize that I have had opportunity beyond what they even thought was possible. Moreover, I have been given the extraordinary privilege and opportunity to educate a new generation on the complex manifestations of inequality so that the world may be a little bit better for their children and grandchildren. While there may be nothing particularly special about me, I have the chance to make sure that all of my students have a special, unique, thought-provoking, and soul-stirring experience every time they enter my classroom. When my students of color thank me for helping them to understand their own lives better through a sociological lens, for not giving up on them, for not letting them hand in substandard work, or for helping them stay on track when they want to throw the towel in, then I have my reward. When my white students write me at the end of the semester asking what they can do to make things better for students of color on campus, or when they decide they can no longer abide by the racist and ethnocentric comments they hear from their friends and family, then I have my reward. Thus, while my personal sacrifice has been great, the returns have been immeasurable. And at the end of the day, the experience of being a black academic is much like what old Sister Pollard said during the Montgomery bus boycott: "My feets is tired, but my soul is rested."

CHAPTER 12

ARE STUDENT TEACHING EVALUATIONS HOLDING BACK WOMEN AND MINORITIES?

The Perils of "Doing" Gender and Race in the Classroom

Sylvia R. Lazos

Teaching is important. Among the traditional three main responsibilities of the professoriate—teaching, scholarship, and service—teaching is probably the most important from the public perspective. The Association of American Colleges and Universities has recently challenged its members to focus more on student learning and develop better ways to measure it (National Association of American Colleges and Universities 2006), citing the well-reported statistics that the United States is slowly slipping behind other industrial countries in student performance in math, science, and writing.[1] In addition, demographics have changed the student population and its educational needs. Increasingly a greater proportion of the student population is less ready for college. Legislators, faced with shrinking state budgets, have become more prone to scrutinize what highly paid, tenured faculty members do with their time and routinely insist that they do more or better teaching. In sum, the current political climate where universities are operating demands that administrators carefully monitor faculty teaching effectiveness.

While there are many ways to evaluate teaching, universities have come to rely widely on student evaluations. According to a 1993 survey conducted by management expert Peter Seldin, 86 percent of universities used student evaluations of teaching in decisions about faculty retention, tenure, promotion, and merit pay

---

1   The National Assessment of Educational Progress (NAEP) reports on nationally representative samples of student work in reading, mathematics, science, writing, US history, civics, geography, and the arts. NAEP has recently stated that the achievement of US students in grades four, eight, and twelve has been slipping as compared to that of other industrialized countries. For details see http://nces.ed.gov/nationsreportcard.

(Seldin 1993). The use of student evaluations grew rapidly from 1970 to the 1980s. Since 1985, many institutions have used the SIR, the Student Instructional Report, which was developed by educational assessment expert John A. Centra at the Education Testing Service in Princeton, New Jersey, which also administers SATs. Although thoughtful commentators have persistently proposed additional methods of evaluating teaching (Arreola 2000; Seldin 2004; Braskamp and Ory 1994), no other method approaches the popularity of student evaluations (Seldin 1999). These evaluations have the advantage of providing a summary number that purports to assess teaching efficacy. This makes comparisons among colleagues easier. And the supposed objectiveness of numbers washes away any possible ambiguities and complexities. This is why many university administrators continue to be enamored with student evaluations (Seldin 1999).

The professoriate has produced an avalanche of articles critiquing and defending student evaluations.[2] The criticisms are startling. Methodological questions start with the most basic one: what do student evaluations actually measure? Professors Harry Tagamori and Laurence Bishop have concluded that the questions on student evaluations are so ambiguous that you can't even determine what they are asking. Tagamori and Bishop examined a random sample of student evaluation forms and found that more than 90 percent contained questions or items "that were ambiguous, unclear, or vague; 76 percent contained subjectively stated items, and over 90 percent contained evaluation items that did not correlate with classroom teaching behavior" (74–75).

Another statistician, Professor Valen Johnson, assembled a massive data set of student evaluations at Duke University and concluded that there was a significant statistical link between a professor's goal of receiving positive student teaching evaluations and grade inflation (Johnson 2003). Indeed a student's expectation of what grade he or she will get in a class is a strong predictor of how positive the instructor's evaluations will be for the instructor (Marsh and Dunkin 1992).

These studies make a point that upon reflection should be intuitively obvious. Evaluations may not be measuring teaching effectiveness as much as they are capturing students' subjective reactions at the moment that they are being polled, and their opinions reflect their feelings and thoughts about a range of things: whether they like the professor, whether their expectations about the course were met or they felt unsettled (perhaps because the professor deviated from the syllabus); and how well they imagined they were performing in school and in the class. Even student gossip becomes part of the picture (Feldman 1989a). Psychometric expert Mark Shevlin, comments that "students are not trained in rating or psychometrics"; rather he concludes that the main basis of their "global evaluation" of competency is "lecturer charisma" (Shevlin 2000 403). Statistician and assessment expert Professor Kenneth Feldman observes that student "ratings are designed not so much to obtain objective descriptions of teachers and courses but to measure the subjective reactions of students to them" (1989a, 257).

If student evaluations are subjective, are they then also subjective about the race and gender of the instructor? To what extent will a student's reaction to a professor's gender and race influence his or her evaluation? If student evaluations

---

2   According to Peter Seldin (1993), more than fifteen thousand articles have been published on the subject. Another set of researchers observes that this is one of the most common topics of research in higher education (Theall and Franklin 1999).

systematically produce lower ratings for women and minorities, then they may well be inhibiting these teachers' professional advancement. Consider that in most liberal arts colleges, a candidate's rating of satisfactory and most often excellent teaching is often the principal criterion for granting tenure. Empirical evidence irrefutably establishes that women and minorities gain tenure at lower rates than their majority counterparts and earn less in merit increases as well (Curtis 2005).[3] Student evaluations may well be holding them back.

Certainly, anecdotally many women and minorities blame student evaluations as a principal reason why they have not been able to get a foothold in academia. *New York Times* special reporter Mark Oppenheimer recently detailed the cases of two women, one teaching African American theatre at Wesleyan and the other teaching feminist studies. In the case involving the African American studies professor, she was told that her contract would not be renewed unless she received "the top two ratings (Outstanding and Good) by at least 85 percent of the students in both your courses." Her student evaluations were 76 percent outstanding and good (meaning a handful of students failed to rate her at the top two levels), and she lost her job. Although she received rave feedback from many students, she believed that the few students who were uncomfortable with her discussion of race and gender issues in class were very negative in their evaluations. The article also reports the case of a journalist professor at Antioch College who focused on race and gender issues in her classes and research. Her tenure case was derailed because her department chair focused on forty-three handwritten comments in her student evaluations that accused her of "having a political agenda" and "supporting gay rights." Because she failed to be rated excellent in teaching, she was denied tenure (Oppenheimer 2008, 24).

Part II discusses the psychology and sociology literature that establishes with robust empiricism that gender and race influence the way women and minorities are viewed in the classroom. Unconscious bias, stereotypes, and assumptions about role appropriateness are the subjective parameters that students unconsciously carry in their heads and use to shape the way they perceive their women and minority professors. These professors must walk a narrow pathway to manifest their gender and race and balance their teaching goals; they must maintain their individual authenticity in the classroom and yet avoid alienating students who—even at this late date—may not have encountered a minority authority figure in a professional setting. In sum, women and minority professors' performance in the classroom is fraught with potential land mines that they must navigate on the way to tenure.

Teasing out just how gender and race impact student evaluations from the empirical studies is a complex task. Part III of this chapter details that the empirical data as to whether subjective gender and race bias exists in student evaluations are equivocal. Some studies report that gender influences student evaluations in a positive way, and others show that gender and race have a negative effect. So if empiricism does not help resolve this issue, should we be satisfied to conclude that because we cannot detect large differences in the way women or minorities are

---

3   For as long as the American Association of University Professors' survey has collected data on tenure status—since the late 1970s—approximately 47 percent of women on the full time faculty have had tenure, while 70 percent of men have. The proportions of faculty with tenure have dropped slightly in recent years among both men and women, but the gap has remained consistent.

treated, university faculty should continue to rely on student evaluations in making personnel decisions?[4] Even though statisticians cannot yet resolve the tricky question of how gender and race influence student evaluations, that does not mean that gender and race are not present in the classroom and are not influencing the way students see their professors and react to them.

Part I:. Subjectivity in Student Evaluations: Like Me, Like My Teaching

There is robust and extensive literature that defends the use of student evaluations and finds student evaluations to be useful as both a formative feedback instrument for the professor and a reliable summative evaluation assessment tool for administrators (Centra 1979; W. E. Cashin 1995; Cohen 1981; Costin, Greenough, and Menges 1971). For example, in an exhaustive monograph published in 1987, Professor Herbert Marsh concluded that "student ratings are (a) multi dimensional (b) reliable and stable, (c) primarily a function of the instructor that teaches the course, rather than the course that is taught, (d) relatively valid against a set of indicators of effective teaching, (e) relatively unaffected by a set of indicators hypothesized as potential biases, and (f) seen to be useful to faculty as feedback" (1987, 255). Even so, there is also recognition that "student evaluations seldom make an optimal contribution to improving either teaching or [helping make accurate] personnel decisions" (McKeachie and Kaplan 1996). This dose of skepticism is justified by the substantial research on the subjectivity of student ratings.

Beauty and the Student

A 2003 empirical study by economists Daniel Hamermesh and Amy Parker examined a large sample of student instructional ratings at the University of Texas for a random group of professors.[5] Researchers assigned six independent measures of professors' beauty and found "that measures of perceived beauty have a substantial independent positive impact on instructional ratings by undergraduate students" (p. 373). Instructors who were judged better looking received higher student ratings, which moved them from the tenth to the ninetieth percentile. This impact exists within university departments and even particular courses and is larger for male than for female instructors.

Professor Hamermesh also found that perceptions of beauty among minorities have bigger effects—a bigger penalty in evaluations for ugly minorities, a bigger positive payoff for good-looking minority group members. Although the observations for minorities contain some "noise" (for example, since the evaluators were mostly white, they had a harder time judging the beauty of other races, and minorities were also disproportionately made up of non-English speakers, who—because of their accent—are generally penalized in student evaluations), it seems fair to conclude that bad looks negatively impact minorities more than whites, and good looks help them more than whites (email from Hamermesh, August 3, 2010).

---

4   This is the conclusion of John Centra, the father of the Student Evaluation Instructional Ratings (SIRs) form ("The differences in ratings, though statistically significant, are not large and should not make much difference in personnel decisions" (Centra and Gaubatz 2000, 32)).

5   The study covered a total of 463 courses and 94 professors (Hamermesh and Parker 2005, t. 1).

Seduction, Enthusiasm, and Charisma

No other experiment has received as much attention as the "Dr. Fox" ones. The original 1973 study by Donald Naftulin, a psychiatrist, and his coauthors asked an actor to give a lecture titled "Mathematical Game Theory as Applied to Physician Education" to three groups: grad students, practicing psychologists, and educators and administrators (Naftulin, Ware, and Donnelly 1973). Dr. Fox was a distinguished looking actor with a pleasant voice, who was entertaining, lively, and charismatic; conveyed warmth; and made jokes. The scripted content of his lectures was nonsense, full of "double talk, neologisms, non sequiturs, and contradictory statements" (631). He was rated highly by all three groups. As the authors note, not even the group of experts in the audience was able to resist the charm of Dr. Fox and detect that his lectures were "crap" (633). The phenomenon became known as the "Dr. Fox" effect or "educational seduction."[6]

Because the original study was criticized for methodological shortcomings, the Fox study spawned a series of follow-up ones. One of the original authors, professor of medical education John Ware, and his coauthor Reed Williams, set up another Dr. Fox experiment, where 207 students rated six lectures on substantive teaching points (1975). This time the groups were divided so that there was a control group (with no seduction effect), and students were randomly assigned. Each lecture varied in substantive content, from low (four substantive points) to high (twenty-four points), and students were subsequently tested by multiple-choice exams. The same professional actor gave all six lectures using various degrees (low and high) of educational seduction. The results showed that ratings did not reflect the substantive content of the lectures and were also unrelated to how well students did on the exam. The most important factor affecting student ratings remained the seduction effect. The researchers concluded that "faculty who master the Doctor Fox Effect may receive favorable student ratings regardless of how well they know their subject and regardless of how much their students learn" (Ware and Williams 1975, 155).

Almost ten years following the original Dr. Fox study, Professor Abrami and his coauthors conducted a quantitative review of the Dr. Fox literature (Abrami, Leventhal, and Perry 1982). They found that instructor expressiveness had a substantial impact on student ratings. They also found that lecture content had a substantial impact on student achievement but a small impact on ratings. This research and follow up studies concluded that good and effective teaching was a multidimensional skill and that students were rating specific features of teaching on the basis of their global evaluation (Abrami, d'Apollonia and Cohen 1990; Abrami, d'Apollonia and Rosenfield 1997).

Recent scholarship continues to reaffirm how much the Dr. Fox effect influences student evaluations. Something that can be called enthusiasm, charisma, or likeability, originally described in that effect, strongly impacts student ratings: what students believe that they are learning—but not necessarily what they actually learn (Williams and Ceci 1997). Note, however, that other research concludes that student ratings correlate significantly with the amount students learn (Abrami,

---

6   It should be noted that the original Dr. Fox study has been faulted for "serious methodological shortcomings"; specifically the research was a series of one-shot case studies with neither control groups nor objective measures of student learning (Marsh 1987, 331; Abrami, Leventhal, and Perry 1982).

d'Appolinia and Rosenfield, 1997; Abrami, d'Appolinia and Cohen 1990; Feldman 1989a, 1989b).

Twenty-five years after the original Fox experiments, an internationally known professor of psychology at Cornell, Stephen Ceci, attended a teaching skills workshop taught by a professional media consultant who trained faculty to improve their presentation skills (Williams and Ceci 1997). The media consultant provided hands-on coaching and suggested ways that faculty could improve individual presentation styles, for example by varying their voice pitch (in Dr. Ceci's case, he was encouraged to lower his voice), and using more hand gestures. The goal was for the teachers to be perceived as enthusiastic. Ceci proceeded to compare the results of his student evaluations pre- and postmedia training in his developmental psychology course. He tried to teach the course in the spring semester as much as possible in the identical way that he had taught it during the fall semester, which was before the training. He taught the course on the same weekdays and at the same time, had approximately the same number of undergraduates (more than two hundred), used the same syllabus and book, adopted the same lecture design, and did not vary his content.[7] In other words, the only difference was that Dr. Ceci had acquired seduction skills with which to charm his spring class.

His student evaluation scores increased significantly in every category. Ratings went up for instructor effectiveness—knowledge of the material; tolerance of diverse views; accessibility to students; organization of lectures; enthusiasm in the classroom. For example, on a question that had nothing to do with style or enthusiasm—"How knowledgeable is the instructor?"—Ceci's pretraining mean rating was 3.6 (out of a total of 5) for the fall semester and jumped after the training to 4.05—a highly significant statistical difference. Students' reception of his more enthusiastic delivery extended to what they believed they had learned in the course. For the question, "How much did you learn in this course?," before the training, Ceci received a mean score of 2.93; after the training the mean jumped to 4.05—a change highly significant change. He concluded that the students "*thought* they learned more, but in fact, they had not; the end-of-semester point totals for the identical sets of exams . . . were virtually identical" (Williams and Ceci 1997, 22; emphasis in original).

Some researchers argue that it is personality that the students are rating. The statistical impact of an instructor's observed personality is so large that evaluations "could most accurately be called a 'likeability' scale" (Clayson and Haley 1990). In various studies, being described on personality tests as an extrovert (McCroskey 2004; Murray et al. 1990; Feldman 1986), exhibiting "charming" behavior, and having charisma (Shevlin 2000; Ederle et al. 1985,) have been shown to statistically positively influence student evaluations positively. One researcher concluded that "This robust relationship between instructor extraversion and students' perceptions of teaching effectiveness could be interpreted to support the fear of some faculty that student evaluations are just personality contests and may not be valid measures of teaching effectiveness" (McCroskey et al. 2004, 206).

---

7   Specifically Ceci used (1) the same syllabus, textbook, and reserve readings; (2) the same overhead transparencies at the same relative points in each semester; (3) the same teaching aids (slides, videos, demonstrations) at the same points in each semester; (4) the identical exams and quizzes; (5) nearly identical lectures; (6) the same schedule and room (days of the week, time); and, finally, (7) the same ratio of teaching assistants to students each semester. (Williams and Ceci, 1997, p. 16).

These studies have not defined what the students mean by "enthusiasm" or "charisma." Certainly humor helps (Waters 2004). So does beauty (Hamermesh and Parker 2005). Reaching out to students so that they perceive that you care is also important (McCroskey et al. 2004). And not being boring but striving to be enthusiastic and engaging seems to be a major key to good student evaluations (Shevlin 2000; Ederle et al. 1985; Waters 2004). If you can't be charming or humorous, then telegraph to the students that you will give them all good grades (Marsh and Dunkin 1992; Johnson 2003; Oppenheimer 2008). If all else fails, give your students chocolate before handing out the evaluations[8] (Youmans and Jee 2007).

On the other hand, student evaluations have been found to relate negatively to deep student learning. A recent study by Professors Scott Carrell and James West (2010) used a longitudinal data set of 10,534 students who attended the US Air Force Academy from fall 2000 to spring 2007. At the academy, students are assigned randomly to all of their classes and have to follow a rigorous track of courses in mathematics, humanities, and the sciences after taking introductory classes so, for example, students will take Calculus I, Calculus II, and then more advanced math. For this experiment, instructors in the introductory courses used common syllabi, and all students took standardized exams that were graded by several professors. Using advanced statistical methods, Carrell and West created a value-added model for instructors, which allowed them to isolate each teacher's contribution to student achievement in the actual course taught (e.g., Calculus I) and the following courses (Calculus II). They found that instructors who produced higher student achievement in the courses they taught received better evaluations from their students. They were also more likely to be untenured and less experienced. On the other hand, instructors who received low student evaluations in the courses that they currently taught also increased student achievement in follow up courses. These instructors were more experienced and mostly tenured faculty. The study concluded that instructors who were highly rated by their students did not necessarily promote the deep learning that is necessary for students to do well in more rigorous course work. Rather, students' evaluations were negatively correlated with subsequent performance—"students appear to reward higher grades in the introductory course but punish professors who increase deep learning" (Carell and West 2010, 412).

These findings may appear paradoxical to some people. Professor Stanley Fish, without knowing about this study, blogged about what it takes to promote deep learning and the tension between this choice in pedagogy and positive student evaluations: "Sometimes (not always) effective teaching involves the deliberately inducing of confusion, the withholding of clarity, the refusal to provide answers; sometime a class or an entire semester is spent being taken down various garden paths leading to dead ends that require inquiry to begin all over again . . . . Needless to say that kind of teaching is unlikely to receive high marks on a questionnaire that

---

8   This experiment involved 98 undergraduates from the University of Illinois at Chicago from three different classes: two statistics classes (n = 34 and 29) and one research-methods class (n = 35). The same instructor taught all three classes. Each class required students to enroll in one of two Friday discussion sections of approximately equal size. The same teaching assistants led sections for each class (with different teaching assistants serving each of the three classes). Participants who were offered chocolate gave higher ratings on average (M = 4.07, SD = .88) than those who were not offered chocolate (M = 3.85, SD = .89) (Youmans and Jee 2007).

rewards the linear delivery of information and penalizes a pedagogy that probes, discomforts and fails to provide closure" (blog by Stanley Fish, June 23, 2010).

Thin-Slice Judgments: Instructors' Nonverbal Behavior and Student Evaluations

Malcolm Gladwell's book, *Blink,* brought into the popular mainstream the cognitive research on "thin-slice" judgments (2005).[9] As Gladwell describes in his opening chapter, unconscious, lightning-fast judgments that we make at a glance are very often correct and may be more accurate than if we stopped and reflected step by step on what is going on in our decision. People may not be able to articulate what is happening as they process information, but they are thinking very rapidly at an unconscious level. These "blink" or thin-slice judgments reflect what individuals have learned in their lives about the situation they are facing; more importantly, the mind is picking up on nonverbal behaviors that may be important clues about what they are observing. In lay terms, we refer to this kind of thinking as intuition or deciding from the gut, but the mind is thinking—it is just doing so very quickly and at an unconscious level.

To illustrate, Gladwell describes a research psychologist who has spent years studying the factors that keeps couples together in happy marriages or leads them to divorce. (It turns out that mutual respect and humor are key elements in a marriage's long-term survival.) This expert's thin-slice judgments are so accurate that he can observe forty-five seconds of a video of a couple's interaction—without sound— and accurately forecast whether husband and wife will stay together or break up (2005, 21–39).

Research of thin-slice judgments also has shown that our appraisal of others—even when based on very brief observations—can be remarkably accurate. As Harvard psychology professor Nalini Ambady and her coauthors describe, "many day to day judgments of people occur unwittingly and intuitively, . . . a fleeting glimpse or a mere glance can lead to an instantaneous evaluative judgment. Once made, such judgments provide the anchor from which subsequent judgments are realized" (2000, 20).

Thin-slice judges are surprisingly accurate about reading the nonverbal behaviors and emotions of the subject (by observing the face, the voice, and the body) (Waxer 1976, 1977); assessing interpersonal behavior (Bernieri et al. 1996); determining who is in charge or is dominant within the social group (Ambady, Koo, Lee and Rosenthal, et al. 1996); and assessing kinship or empathy (Constanzo and Archer, 1989). Thin-slice judgments are more likely to be accurate in assessing nonverbal behaviors and personality traits such as interpersonal skills (Ambady et al. 2000). As an example, Nalini Ambady's research has shown that observers' quick, thin-slice judgments of a surgeon's nonverbal gestures and tone-of-voice interactions with a patient are a better predictor of whether that doctor will get sued for malpractice than his or her education (Ambady et al 2000).

Women seem to be better at making thin-slice judgments (Hall et al 2000), perhaps because they are hardwired to read emotions more accurately on people's faces. Psychologists have found that the accuracy of thin-slice judgments is also subject to

---

9   As defined by Nalini Ambady and her coauthors, thin-sliced judgments are "brief excerpts of expressive behavior sampled from the behavioral stream . . . less than 5 minutes long . . . from any available channel of communication, including the face, the body, speech, the voice, transcripts or combination of the above" (Ambady et al. 2000, 203).

the observer's affective state. So for example, if the observer is depressed, he or she will project negativity about the subject's emotional state onto her thin-slice judgments (Forgas 1992; Ambady and Gray 2002). Thin sliced judgments are most accurate when made by well-adjusted and stable people (Ambady and Gray 2002).

Professors Ambady and Rosenthal (1992), as well as other researchers (Clayson and Sheffet 2006; Babad, Babad, and Rosenthal 2004), have found that observers' thin-slice judgments are highly predictive of student evaluations. Ambady and Rosenthal selected thirteen graduate teaching fellows (seven men and six women) who were instructing undergraduate courses at Harvard in the humanities, social sciences, and natural sciences. No section was larger than twenty students. They videotaped classes and then produced a thirty-second composite tape of ten-second snapshots taken from the beginning, middle, and end of the class. They instructed nine female judges to score the composite videotapes of the instructors—without sound—on observable characteristics (competence, confidence, professionalism, dominance, honesty, attentiveness, enthusiasm, likeable, optimism, supportiveness, anxiety, warmth) based on thin-slice judgments of nonverbal behavior—how often the instructors smiled, grimaced, bit their lips; how they held their hands (open hand, pointing, fists); their hand gestures; head shakes; and the positioning of their heads, legs, and torso (leaning forward or backward). The researchers then calculated a composite likeability rating (that excluded anxiety). They found their nonverbal composite variable correlated significantly with the instructors' student evaluations at the end of the course by a significant factor *(r =. 70).* A follow up study in 2004, with a larger data set, found the same relationship, but the magnitude was lower (Babad, Babad, and Rosenthal 2004).

Law professor Deborah Merritt from Ohio State University summarizes this research and its relevance to the wisdom of using student evaluations for important personnel decisions, such as retention, promotion, and merit pay:

> Students . . . rapidly form an impression of a professor's personality. An image based almost entirely on nonverbal behavior gels within the first few minutes of the semester. The students may refine their impressions as the semester progresses, but the initial image remains telling. The significant correlation between assessments completed after just five minutes of class and those offered at semester's end is . . . troubling. It confirms not *some* connection between a professor's style and student evaluations, but an *overwhelming* link between those two factors. Nonverbal behaviors appear to matter much more than anything else in student ratings. Enthusiastic gestures and vocal tones can mask gobbledygook, smiles count more than sample exam questions, and impressions formed in thirty seconds accurately foretell end-of-semester evaluations. The strong connection between mere nonverbal behaviors and student evaluations creates a very narrow definition of good teaching. By relying on the current student evaluation system, law schools implicitly endorse an inflexible, largely stylistic, and homogeneous description of good teaching (Merritt 2008, 251–52).

Summing up: Concerns and Questions

Professor Merritt's critique of student evaluations, based on her thorough research of the way the brain works and much of the research discussed here, is devastating and raises concerns of fairness. Should a professor's ability to contribute to the academy depend on how well he or she emotively presents him or herself to the students? For many defenders of student evaluations, the answer is yes—they argue that teachers need to unpack behaviors of warmth, rapport, and connection with the students and recreate themselves as enthusiastic Dr. Fox-like professors since this is a key strategy of good teaching (Matthews 1997).

Others, like Professor Merritt, argue that likeability, charisma, and warmth are rooted in an individual's "physiology, culture, personality and habit" (Clayson and Sheffet 2006, 158) which are difficult for a faculty member to change. Certainly no instructor can alter physical things about himself or herself like beauty, tone of voice, or whether a face seems warm. Professors Clayson and Sheffet, who replicated Ambady and Rosenthal's research of thin-slice judgments and student evaluations, concur and argue that "if . . . student perceptions are even marginally related to relatively long-lasting traits [in instructors], it may be true that some teachers never will receive consistently high evaluations in certain environments, irrespective of anything they do or possibly could do" (2006, 158). Instructors can "game" the system by manipulating the students' affective state and giving them chocolates just before administering evaluations and get better student ratings or telegraphing to the students that they will get good grades in the course. Regretfully, the recent Air Force Academy study argues that evaluations are negatively correlated to students' deep learning. It is no wonder that so much research exists on student evaluations. Yet these paradoxical findings indicate that there is still more research to be done.

Part II: Manifesting Gender and Race in the Classroom

Navigating the goal of getting good student evaluations is difficult for any professor seeking a foothold and advancement in the academy. In spite of the words of caution from proponents of student evaluations, they often are given too much weight in tenure, promotion, and pay decisions. The system is "crazy for everybody" (Grillo 1997, 748), but it is particularly dangerous for minorities and women who must also contend with the unconscious biases of their students who have role expectations that are anchored in gender and race stereotypes.

Unconscious Bias and Stereotyping

As Malcolm Gladwell notes, thin-slice judgments can be very accurate, and in many instances, such as the emergency room, wizened, experienced professionals should let go of step-by-step analysis and trust them. That saves time, and doctors should trust that their unconscious mind is making quick, accurate judgments that will be hard to replicate in step-by-step analysis (Gladwell 2005). But there is a dark side to thin-slicing, as Gladwell points out (71). The learned concepts in our unconscious cognition reflect stereotypes and unconscious biases of which we are unaware, and in fact, in many cases, our conscious values may be incompatible with our unconscious attitudes. Because we are all unconsciously impacted by stereotypes that we have learned from the culture around us, most of us unconsciously discriminate in one area or another. Intuitive thinking can be very accurate in certain situations, but thin-slice judgments shaped by stereotypes that we carry in our head about blacks, women, the disabled, overweight people, mothers who work, and "out" gay men and lesbians can be very wrong and lead us to make unconsciously biased judgments.

The Implicit Association Test (IAT) developed by Yale and the University of Washington in the mid-1990s is now widely recognized as a computer test that measures unconscious or latent cognitive associations and biases (Lane et al. 2007). The IAT works by asking participants by pressing a computer key to classify words into familiar categories. As the test progresses, participants are asked to sort words into categories that reveal associational bias, for example, cockroach/bad, flower/ good. Then the computer flashes images, and the ordering becomes more confusing when the sorting does not follow a pattern like cockroach/bad, flower/good, and it takes longer to do it. The test now asks the person to sort categories that require him or her to resist stereotypical associational bias—male/career, male/science, female/family, black/crime, fat/ugly. The longer that it takes the test taker to sort out categories by going against stereotype, the stronger the link to prior cognitive stereotypical associations (Greenwald, McGhee, and Schwartz 1998; Lane et al. 2007). Based on reaction times, the test reports back to the individual, for example, "Your data suggest a moderate automatic preference for thin people compared to fat people."

Over the course of the last fifteen years, the IAT has been shown to be consistent and reliable. As a group, the millions tested "demonstrated, on average, greater positivity for white over black, non-Arab Muslims over Arab Muslims, abled over disabled, young over old, and straight over gay" (Lane et al. 2007, 66). It has also measured stereotype-consistent associations between white/American, males/science, females/liberal arts, males/career, females/family, and blacks/weapons.

This is evidence of the hold that stereotypes have on unconscious cognitive processes. A person may not be aware of automatic negative reactions to a racial group and may even regard them as objectionable. Most test takers report themselves as unbiased and not holding prejudiced beliefs (Lane et al. 2007). However, most participants also possess automatic, unconscious negative feelings—in the case of whites, 97 percent have negative unconscious attitudes toward blacks; and in the case of blacks, 45 percent hold negative unconscious attitudes toward blacks (Dasgupta et al. 2000).

Stereotypes are "overgeneralizations and are either inaccurate or do not apply to the individual group member in question" (Heilman 1983, 270). Certainly many times stereotypes have some truth to them, but they also grossly overgeneralize (e.g., Latinos or persons with accents are illegals, blacks are associated with crime) and lead to distortions. As Professor Heilman notes, "Once an individual is classified as a member of a social group, perceptions of that group's average or reputed characteristics, and perceptions of behavior based on those characteristics, are readily relied on by those doing the classifying. It then becomes more difficult for the classifier to respond to the other person's own particular characteristics, making accurate, differentiated, and unique impressions less likely" (1983, 272).

Further research links unconscious negative attitudes based on stereotypes to discriminatory behavior. In a well-known study, for example, police officers whose IAT scores demonstrated strong associations between black and weapons were more likely in a video game to shoot at ambiguous black figures who popped up from behind buildings but had no weapons (Correll et al. 2007).

The prevalence of unconscious biases is connected to social structure, power, and the distribution of resources and opportunities. Specifically feminists and critical race theorists have argued that the academy is gendered and raced, meaning that power, resources, and opportunities are not distributed equally but are based on gender and class. Men and whites are privileged and have an easier time navigating obstacles to get through the door and then rise through the ranks of the professoriate (Valian 1998; Basow 1986; McGinley 2009; Maranville 2006; Delgado and Bell, 1989). Whites and men start from a presumption of competence; minorities and women do not and have to deal with a multitude of unconscious biases that put them at a disadvantage. The playing field is not level.

Empirical research backs this claim. Researchers have shown that unconscious bias impacts who makes it through the door of academic institutions. Professors Steinpreis, Anders, and Ritzke presented real-life curriculum vitas of successful academic psychologists to a panel made up of 238 male and female academic psychologists who were to review them and make hiring recommendations. The names on the vitas were changed to male and female at random. Both men and women judges were more likely to hire male job applicants over female candidates with an identical record. The panel also rated the teaching, research, and service records of male job applicants over those of women candidates even when they were identical (Steinpreis, Anders, and Ritzke 1999).

Recent research reflects just how hard it is for blacks to get that first opportunity. In a well-known study by economists Bertrand and Mullaithan (2000), researchers sent out 5,000 resumes in response to 1,250 Boston and Chicago employers' help-wanted ads. They used made-up identical resumes; one set had "white-sounding" names (e.g., Emily) and the other "black-sounding" names (e.g., Lakisha). Every employer was mailed four resumes: (1) average qualifications with a white-sounding name, (2) average qualifications with a black-sounding name, (3) highly skilled with a white-sounding name, and (4) highly skilled with a black-sounding name. The results were that resumes with white-sounding names got 50 percent more callbacks than those with black-sounding names. The high-quality resumes with black-sounding names attracted no more interest than the average black ones, and lower-skilled candidates with white names got more callbacks than highly skilled ones with black names.

The Dynamics of Gender and Race in the Classroom

As the curriculum vita experiments show, unconscious stereotypical beliefs create expectations about someone before that person walks in the door. When women and minorities enter their classrooms, their students, too, have expectations about them. Their majority counterparts do not face this obstacle. As women and minority instructors labor to make their classrooms friendly and warm (so that they can get decent student evaluations), they must ponder how their conduct will be perceived by their students in the context of their gendered and raced role expectations. From the get-go, the task is daunting.

Gender stereotypes place women in a double bind (Eagly, Makhijani, and Klonsky 1992). When women labor in roles and jobs that are viewed as male, they must fight the stereotypical presumptions that they are not competent, authoritative, or charismatic leaders (Valian 1998; Eagly, Makhijani, and Klonsky 1992). However, when women try to compensate for those perceived shortfalls, they can come across as more incompetent (because she lectures too much), insecure (because she keeps referring to her credentials), or self-promoting (because she tries to put herself in a leadership position). Further, if she does not fulfill the stereotypical expectations of being nurturing and caring and polite, she will experience backlash (Valian 1998). Women professors who behave counter to stereotypes and exhibit "non-lady-like" behavior receive lower evaluations than men (Basow 1998), and many see their careers placed in jeopardy. Moreover, if she is part of only a handful of women within her institution, below critical mass, she will stick out as a token, which will amplify stereotypical expectations (Kanter 1977).

Minorities also experience double bind stereotypic expectations. The presumption when a minority professor walks in the door is that he or she is not well credentialed (Harlow 2003). Showing irritation or anger backfires. Creating a comfortable learning atmosphere requires that the minority teacher put white students at ease in relation to issues of race. Yet African Americans must labor under the additional burden that white students have a harder time sorting out the emotions on their faces because generally whites cannot read black faces very well.

Numerous studies have attempted to determine how gender and race impact student evaluations. Surprisingly the results have been equivocal. Studies with large data sets across campus for a single large institution, like Dr. Hamermesh's University of Texas study (Hamermesh and Parker 2005) and the Air Force Academy's study (Carrell and Scott 2010), report that women are rated slightly lower (but still statistically significant) than their male counterparts. The Texas data set also showed that minorities fare slightly worse than white instructors (Hamermesh and Parker 2005).

Another set of studies reached the opposite conclusion. Professors John Centra and Noreen Gaubatz (2000) assembled a large data set made up of 741 classes in the humanities and sciences in twenty-one colleges and found no differences in the ratings of male and female instructors. Only in one area—course organization and planning—was there a slightly significant ratings difference in favor of male instructors. During the 1990s, Professor John Feldman published a two-part meta-analysis, and concluded that the differences that existed were slight, and not sufficiently significant to show gender bias (Feldman 1992, 1993). Peter Seldin's (1993) brief review as well concluded that gender has little or no effect on student evaluations. Yet other studies have had such mixed results that the authors hesitated to conclude whether their data showed gender bias (Hancock, Shannon, and Terntham 1993).

The sociological perspective offered by feminist researchers is helpful in resolving this apparent quandary. Gender and race affect student evaluations in more subtle ways than statistics reveal. Professor Anne Statham is unequivocal that students bring gender expectations into the classroom (Statham et al. 1991, 117), even though the statistics are deceptive in other studies (Basow 1998; Laube, Massoni, and Sprague 2007). Although in overall ratings, women appear to be, or are close to being, on a par with male professors, a more careful examination shows that women have to labor harder to satisfy student expectations (Basow 1998; Laube, Massoni, and Sprague 2007). Things can go wrong very quickly for women and minority instructors.

That is because two sets of expectations are in conflict: one is based on the social/role expectations that come from being a woman (warm, welcoming, nurturing), and the other relates to being a competent professor (knowledgeable, enthusiastic, and interesting) (Basow 1998; Valian 1998). In addition, expectations themselves are variable and are shaped by the discipline the woman is teaching—humanities and nursing, for example, are considered more female as compared to science, engineering, law, or medicine (Basow 1995, 1998). Finally, some institutions may have a history of being more friendly and welcoming of women and minorities than others (McGinley 2009; Basow 1986). For example, Professor McGinley (2009) discusses possible bullying that may occur in some institutions with a history of male dominance.

Women in academia are comparable to women managers in leadership positions. In the course of a semester, they must lead their students through a syllabus, somehow convince them that the materials are fun and accessible, and challenge them to challenge themselves through difficult passages. Women's leadership, both inside and outside the academy, is expected to embody both stereotypically feminine qualities of nurturing and relationship building as well as the stereotypically masculine qualities associated with competence and leadership (Valian 1998). In workplace settings, women in leadership positions are decidedly at a disadvantage. In a startling experiment with trained actors who pretended to be managers, women managers who took the lead in workplace discussions were unfavorably received by both women and men listeners as measured by their nonverbal facial expressions. Male managers, on the other hand, were always well received (Valian 1998, 130). In a meta-analysis, Professors Eagly, Makhijani, and Klonsky (1992) found that women in leadership positions were evaluated least favorably when they deviated from prescribed gender roles or acted in a masculine (or strict) manner.

Women have to navigate within narrow boundaries set by cultural stenotopic expectations. In workplace leadership settings, they must be sufficiently assertive to be listened to and taken seriously, and yet not be viewed too assertive or overly masculine. Professors Eagly, Makhijani, and Klonsky (1992) found that having a style that is too assertive or perceived as autocratic is especially costly for a woman. In such situations, women receive especially negative evaluations. While a man may get away with being snippy, not consulting those who work for him, or not always saying please and thank you, when a woman commits such errors, the backlash is severe and may result in rejection by her peers and being fired by her superiors (Eagly, Makhijani, and Klonsky 1992; Valian 1998; APA brief, Price Waterhouse 1988). In the notorious case of *Hopkins v. Price Waterhouse* (1988), Anne Hopkins, a woman who was very competent and worked as hard as any male manager, was not promoted at the time of partnership, and was advised by her superiors to "act more feminine."

Interpreting Student Evaluations and Gender Dynamics in the Classroom

Many women and minorities report that deciphering their student evaluations is confusing (Grillo 1997; P. J. Smith 2000). What does the research show are the keys for women instructors to do well in their student evaluations?

Presumption of Incompetence

Research shows that both minorities and women are presumed to be incompetent as soon as they walk in the door. Professors Miller and Chamberlain (2000) conducted a survey of three hundred undergraduates taking sociology classes in a department that had a critical mass of women faculty (25 percent). They found that students consistently underestimated the educational credentials and academic rank of women and minority professors. In a study of a public midwestern university where there were few African American professors, Professor Harlow (2003) reported that her interviewees—minority professors—said they were challenged

frequently about their qualifications to teach in the classroom. Most black professors interviewed felt that their classes always contained at least some students who
questioned their ability to be professors.

Different Strokes for Different Genders

An early field study by Professors Basow and Silberg matching male and female
professors of similar rank from comparable disciplines in a liberal arts college showed
that the gender of the student was a key variable in student evaluations. There was a
consistent pattern that male students rated their female professors lower on all measurements on the student evaluations—scholarship, clarity, student interaction, and
enthusiasm (Basow and Silberg 1987). Another recent study of evaluations gathered
in 741 different courses taught at twenty-one different institutions showed that women
faculty received significantly lower ratings from male students than from females
(Merritt 2008). Researchers have also found that male students in disciplines considered masculine, such as economics, business, and engineering, are more likely to rate
their women instructors negatively (Basow 1995). Professor Basow speculates that this
may be because male students in these disciplines hold more traditional views.

In a later study where Basow (1995) reviewed four years of student evaluations at
a liberal arts college, she found a strong pattern of student interaction with professors' gender. Women students consistently rated their women professors highest,
and male students were consistently hard on them. So particularly for women professors, the adage "you can't please everyone all the time" is particularly fitting. The
same lecture from the front of the class may be ringing all kinds of bells in a woman
student's brain while a male brain may be hearing just "blah blah blah."

In the Air Force Academy database put together by Professors Scott Carrell and
James West that mapped the progress of students over six years, researchers found
that women instructors had a highly positive value-added effect on female cadets.
Young women who were taught introductory courses in science or math by a female
instructor performed substantially better in the following advanced courses than
their counterparts who had male instructors. The researchers found that the female
students who had very high scores on their SAT in science and math benefited (by
performing at the highest level in the follow up courses) when they had woman
instructors in their introductory courses (Carrell et al. 2009).

The Carrell and West gender study may indicate that a reason that female students rate their women instructors higher is that they get something from interacting with a female teacher—inspiration, confidence building, female role modeling,
or a teaching style particularly tuned to female sensibilities—that they don't receive
from male instruction. This is a valuable kind of learning and goes beyond mere
in-group preferences.

Likeability and Warmth

For women instructors to be well recommended in student evaluations, they must
live up to the female-stereotyped expectations that they should be warm, friendly,
and supportive inside and outside the classroom and have good interpersonal skills
(Kierstead et al. 1988). One study found that women who smiled were rated much
more favorably than unsmiling ones. Men also gain standing by smiling frequently—
although not as much as women—and are not as heavily penalized when they do
not smile (Kierstead et al. 1988).

As Professors Sprague and Massoni point out, women function under a different scaling system than men. Stereotypes can influence the evaluators' understanding of a trait. Stereotypes shift not only their balance in expecting things from teachers but also their perceptions about what it entails to achieve those qualities. Students expect women to engage in a different set of behaviors to satisfy a particular trait (Sprague and Massoni 2005). To be considered caring, women had to spend more time meeting students outside of class and being accessible during office hours (Bennett 1982; Statham et al. 1991). Students were more harshly critical if their women instructors were not available (Bernstein 1995). In another study that looked at the way students described their best and worst male and female teachers, the best women teachers were called caring, helpful, and kind (that is, nurturing); in contrast, the best male professors were funny and friendly (that is, entertaining) (Sprague and Massoni 2005). In a study that actually observed women's interactions in the classroom, likeability increased more when they interacted with students, generated laughter, acknowledged contributions, and allowed students to interrupt comfortably for clarification and input (Statham et al. 1991). Feedback and correction from women were well received only when they were gentle and affirming (Statham et al. 1991).

Women who conform to stereotypical expectations of approachability, caring, and warmth are rewarded with good evaluations. Projecting warmth and putting in the time to be considered caring and kind and relieving tension by frequently smiling or keeping things light are traditional female behaviors; at the same time, these are class-management techniques that produce good teaching in general. However, women "outliers," whose personality is male oriented and who are not smiley or giggly, are more likely to be disliked by students because they do not exhibit these stereotypical behaviors (Statham et al. 1991). Professors Sprague and Massoni's (2005) study of the best/worst teachers found that students were particularly vitriolic against women who disappointed them by not seeming nurturing. The worst women teachers were chastised as cold, mean, and unfair; students sometimes used terms such as "bitch" and "witch." By contrast, these kinds of gender-specific phrases were not used to describe the worst male teachers. Indicating just how emotional students can get with female teachers who fail to be nurturing, disappointment can be so extreme that it results in death threats. Professor Pam Smith's ethnographic study of what can go wrong when an African American female is viewed by her students as overly demanding and harsh showed a divided student body where the teacher, not the material, became the focus of the class and student incivilities were extreme, ranging from personal comments on her dress and hairstyle to death threats and hate mail (Smith 1999).

Managing Authority

Being authoritative represents a particular challenge for women and minority professors. Recall that because of stereotypes, students assume women and minorities are under qualified to teach (Miller and Chamberlain 2000). Students have less fear of and respect for their female and minority instructors and are more likely to challenge their authority. Professor Statham and her coauthors (1991) observed the interactions of women and male instructors with students over the course of a year at a liberal arts college and found that women were challenged in class at least 10 percent more often than men. Challenges were more frequent when women professors were at the assistant and associate levels.

Both male and female instructors find maintaining authority in the classroom and at the same time keeping the atmosphere warm (necessary to get positive student evaluations) to be challenging. Instructor corrective strategies that students will accept from women are limited (Statham et al. 1991). Women must avoid being considered "mean" and having "no sense of humor"—descriptive terms that students reserve for their worst women professors (Basow 1998).

Professor Ann Statham's field study found that women instructors handled authority differently from men, namely, with a light touch and by seldom directly confronting the student. When students did not directly challenge the professor's authority (such as by talking in class or arriving late), women professors, particularly at the lower ranks, dealt with the problem by approaching them indirectly after class or ignoring the problem. Male assistant professors felt that they could confront the offending behavior directly, such as, for example, taking a newspaper away from a student who was reading during their lectures.

Professor Statham and her coresearchers found that women professors handled verbal challenges to their authority in class with a "considerable amount of patience, even when they thought that the students were wrong" (1991, 77). In one case, a woman associate professor patiently endured the objections to her presentation of the class materials by one student for three weeks. On the other hand, male assistant and associate professors felt that they could directly confront challenges by explaining to the student why he or she was wrong. Only when a woman professor had reached the rank of full professor did she feel that she could publicly stop a student's challenging behavior with a reprimand (Statham et al. 1991).

Another study examined student evaluations to determine the way students reacted to negative grades from women and minority instructors. In an empirical study of more than two hundred students and seven hundred course evaluations, students judged the quality of their instructors after they received their grades. Female instructors were evaluated much more harshly than males, and minority teachers were judged more severely than their white counterparts (Sinclair and Kunda 2000). The researches call this dynamic *motivated stereotyping*, which they say occurs because stereotypes allow students to be more dismissive of a disappointing grade from a female or minority instructor. Motivated stereotyping puts the blame for a student's disappointing performance directly on the female or minority instructor, who was judged incompetent to begin with (Sinclair and Kunda 2000).

In the Statham field study, women instructors often adopted positive reinforcement strategies in the classroom by, for example, pointing out what the students were doing well and correcting them by suggesting ways they could do better. Professor Statham and her coauthors call this feedback *modified control* that is partially positive. This soft student-professor interaction correlates with positive student evaluations for women professors in both competence and likeability. (No comparable correlation was measured for male professors.) By contrast, women professors' unspoken positive reinforcement in the classroom, for example, just nodding or smiling and not expressly saying, "I like the way that you are approaching that question," correlated negatively with the way the students rated their women professors' competence and likeability (Statham et al. 1991).

Professor Statham and her coresearchers concluded that women deal with the stereotype double bind by redefining the way they exercise authority in the classroom. The corrective strategies that many women professors use with mostly good effect does not stray too far from students' stereotypic expectations. Statham and her coauthors argue that women professors are remolding what students see as role-appropriate behaviors for women professors. However, exercising authority so subtly, where students are rarely directly reprimanded or embarrassed, can hardly be said to reshape students' gender-role expectations. However, Statham and others retort that women professors are changing role expectations because the interactive teaching style that many women adopt in the classroom is less hierarchical and more informal, and students are more directly involved in the process of learning. Statham argues that such a feminine approach to teaching "abolishes" women's power and authority. However, these transformation claims may be overstated because, again, a nonauthoritarian teaching approach is the kind of style that students come into the classroom expecting from a woman professor (Statham et al. 1991).

Feminist analysts like Statham, who write glowingly about a generally soft feminine approach in managing authority and teaching, are also rightly concerned about women instructors whose personality and style do not match these stereotypical feminine strategies (Basow 1998; Sprague et al 2007). It is clear that direct exercises of authority by a woman professor engender student backlash (see e. g., Maranville 2007; Smith 1999).

Competence and knowledge

To receive favorable evaluations from students, women professors are expected to act more experienced and professional, have a highly structured instructional approach, demonstrate more effort preparing for class, spend more time with students, provide a reduced workload, and give higher grades than men professors (Bennett 1982). However, when women overwork being competent or capable, they can receive student backlash. Professor Statham and her coauthors found that women instructors who spent more time presenting material in the classroom and going over substantive points got higher competency ratings but lower likeability ones. When women instructors checked on students' understanding and solicited input, they got higher likeability ratings, but their competency marks fell. As Professor Statham and her coauthors point out, this represents a particular double bind for women since likeability and warmth are key elements for women professors to get good student evaluations. Students may look down on women who labor to clarify difficult points (why is she trying so hard to teach me?) (Statham et al. 1991).

Perception as a "Partisan Hack" by Being a Woman Teaching Women's Studies

Recent research documents that a negative relationship exists between students' perceptions that their professors are ideologically driven and their evaluations. Professors Woessner and Woessner surveyed at random thirty political science instructors teaching undergraduate classes to 1,385 students. They found that students are more critical of a course when it is taught by an instructor that they view as highly partisan. The more that the professor's political views differ from the student's, the more likely students are to think that their professor is not competent and does not care about them. Students report not being comfortable in classrooms where the general ideological viewpoint differs from their own. The greater the differences between a professor's and student's ideological positions, the lower the student evaluations are (Woessner and Woessner 2006).

The case studies reported by journalist Oppenheimer (2008) of professors who lost tenure-track jobs because of student evaluations involved feminists who were presenting material from a feminist or an outsider viewpoint. In another study, minority faculty reported that they were more likely to be challenged by their students when they discussed issues of race in the classroom (Harlow 2003).

Several studies indicate that stereotypes predispose students to view their minority and women professors as ideological partisans when they are teaching controversial subject matter. Professors Moore and Trahan tested students' attitudes by asking students to rate a syllabus for a proposed sociology of gender course to be taught by a hypothetical woman professor. The students were asked to project what they anticipated the course experience would be like. The majority predicted that the professor would be biased and more than likely would have a political agenda. When the hypothetical teacher was a male professor, students did not believe that he would have an ideological agenda (Moore and Trahan 1997). Another study found similar results with a Racism and Sexism in American Society class when the instructor was African American (as opposed to white) (Ludwig and Meacham 1997). And a third study found this attitudinal bias when a hypothetical Latino professor was proposed to teach a course called Race, Gender, and Inequality (Smith and Anderson).

Some students react negatively to professors who challenge their ideological beliefs. Psychological research has shown that reviewers asked to read articles on the death penalty rated the authors most harshly when they differed from the reader's ideological belief (Lord, Ross and Leeper 1979). When the article contained divergent ideological views, the reader easily identified flaws in it and was more likely to question the credentials and authority of the author. These readers were much more likely to disparage the sources of information. When students sit in a classroom and have to hear a viewpoint from a feminist teacher or a critical race theorist that clashes with their worldview, he or she cannot escape so the most convenient way to deal with this unpleasant classroom experience is to disparage the professor, his or her abilities, and the teaching approach. The student evaluation provides a handy complaint form. As observers and researchers have noted, the vitriol that students express in forms that take aim at feminist, multicultural, or any outsider subject matter sounds extreme and highly emotional. Yet these outlier evaluations are averaged in with the other, more temperate student evaluations.

Part III: Minority Professors and Student Evaluations

This chapter has already discussed the kind of dynamics that minority and women professors share. In addition, critical race theorists Richard Delgado and Derrick Bell reported the following as part of their survey of minority law professors:

> Minority law professors' teaching evaluations, as reported, are generally at or near the institutional median. Substantial numbers reported that their evaluations vary greatly from subject to subject, are sometimes both positive and negative for a single course, or are best in technical subjects that do not call for much normative analysis. Some said that while they are treated politely by majority race students in class and around the law building, they are regularly "trashed" on evaluations. Some report increasing numbers of "bullets": students who give the professor the lowest rating

in all categories, thereby lowering his or her average as much as possible. (p. 355)

A study by Professor Harlow interviewing African American faculty found that they were highly aware of what they believed were students' (unconscious) biased perceptions:

83 percent believed that students immediately reacted to their race;

76 percent believed that students questioned their intellectual authority;

55 percent believed that they had to prove their competence and intelligence; and

34 percent experienced inappropriate intellectual challenges (2003, 352)

As a consequence, minority law professors must face racial performance burdens in the classroom that white professors do not encounter :

White Faculty	African American Faculty
Do not have to worry about race (instead hold white privilege)	50 percent believe race will have a negative effect on students' evaluations.
Do not have to worry about students questioning competence	Because minority professors fear that their competence will be questioned, 69 percent of black women and 44 percent of black men choose an authoritative demeanor, which in turn, may turn off students who reward likeable professors.
Do not have to deal with students' stereotypes that make negative assumptions about the professors' competence, knowledge, and qualifications	To be effective, black faculty must manage their own perceptions of students' behavior that is influenced by negative stereotypes, and not overreact by becoming unfriendly, sullen or angry.
The more white male professors interact with students, the more likely it is that they will be rewarded with positive evaluations.	White students are not able to accurately perceive the emotions behind the facial expressions of minorities, so misunderstandings about a minority professor's intentions, their emotional warmth, are very likely occur. As well, white students perceive professors with African American features as less attractive, which in turn negatively impacts student evaluations.
More range of choice as to the selection and emphasis of the subject matter	When minority professors talk about race in their classroom, students are more likely to say they are biased or "spend too much time" doing it. A minority professor can safely address controversial race issues, only if she positions herself as a "nonpartisan."

In sum, minority professors must negotiate many more burdens than non-minority professors from the first moment that they walk into the classroom. These additional burdens and potential risks are difficult to navigate even for the most experienced professor, but the risks are higher and the penalties even heavier for newly minted assistant professors who must also master new material, learn to teach effectively, and get a productive research agenda on track. New minority professors start their careers with a significant handicap not of their own making.

Professor Harlow reports that one in two minority professors anticipate that they will receive less favorable evaluations solely because of their race (Harlow, 2003). The classroom is filled with positive and negative emotions. Students enter the classroom with unconscious stereotypes about the professor's race, ethnicity or accent, which in turn informs how the student perceives, listens, and reacts to the professor. The student may well perceive herself as fair-minded and racially enlightened, yet these unconscious stereotypes influence cognition and emotions at an unconscious level; it is part of the brain's system of "blink" or automatic thinking.

On the other hand, a minority professor who has had to deal with a lifetime of racial slights might well react negatively to what he or she perceives as conscious or unconscious biased treatment from his or her students. The situation can quickly deteriorate. Students misread their minority professor, and the minority professor reacts with irritation. Now the students have reason to perceive the minority professors as not being as "warm," or, more damaging, as the "angry" minority who is overly sensitive about her race and eager to push a partisan ideological racial agenda. The professor reacts to what she perceives to be unjustified hostility by deploying more authority in the classroom and becoming even more formal and emotionally unapproachable. More students, in turn, become disconcerted, alienated or angry, and these reactions will be recorded in harsh and emotional evaluations.

Hence, minority professors must be able to closely monitor and manage their emotions, conscious and unconscious, from the first day they walk into the classroom. Minority professors cannot get caught up in anticipating that their students will be hostile, because the classroom atmospherics will deteriorate and become tense. Neither can a minority professor make an issue of students' lack of racial knowledge or sophistication, because it will sound like preaching, "talking down to," or partisan politics, all of which create a high likelihood of student backlash in her evaluations (Smith 1999).

In one of the early works of critical race theory, *The Alchemy of Race and Rights*, Professor Patricia Williams described ordinary blacks as consciously over-dressing to do routine tasks, such as going shopping, because they did not want to trigger white shopkeepers' and white security guards' negative unconscious stereotypes; for example, not being buzzed into a Benetton store or being shadowed by security when shopping for shoes (Williams 1992). In a similar manner, minority professors can choose to perform their race in the classroom so that they are not tapping into the most negative stereotypes about minorities (angry political racial partisan) but rather more benign or neutral stereotypes (such as middle class black professional). Not all discrimination is the same. According to survey data, the most acute kind of discrimination is aimed towards blacks who are viewed as militants, while middle class blacks are viewed more neutrally (more respect about their competence, and more warmth towards them as a social group) (Fiske 2010). Accordingly, the strategic minority professor will "perform" her race in the classroom so that students think about her more as a middle class professional, and stay away from the more negative stereotypes associated with minorities. So at one level, this means doing the basics well: being prepared, being knowledgeable, listening to students, and thinking about how to communicate well difficult concepts to students; in sum, teaching well (Bain 2004). However, as well, performing as a middle class professional minority may well mean staying away from racial hot button topics, until and unless the professor can figure out how to handle such volatile topics without seeming to be a racial partisan. Sadly, this final observation undermines the most compelling justification for diversifying faculties—the assumption that minority professors will be able to teach students more empathy and sensitivity about the racial issues that divide American society.

Conclusion

Individual minority and women professors can do a great deal to negotiate the stereotypes in the classroom that will influence how students see them and judge them. Many individual minority professors, including women, are able to manage the complex process of overcoming stereotypes, adopting effective teaching techniques, and making material accessible. Thus, they become highly successful teachers.

However, academia needs to make systemic changes to account for the factors that systemically negatively impact both women and minority professors. The question of what student evaluations measure should be framed productively. This is a systemic problem, not an individual (female, minority female) one. For example, the American Bar Association took responsibility (at least in its 2006 report) for the lack of black women's success in private law firms. The Association of American Law Schools should take such leadership. Only if academia adopts responsibility as an institution will the playing field become level for minority and women professors.

First, at a minimum, macroanalyses of bias in student evaluations are clearly needed by gender, race, and sexual orientation. In spite of decades of research, controversy continues to exist as to whether there are systemic biases that impact women and minority professors whose careers can too easily be negatively impacted by student evaluations.

Second, institutions should think about teaching and the evaluative process more creatively. Suggestions from Professor Merritt include: Use focus groups mediated by outsiders. Do evaluations less often but more deeply. Get students to think, not react intuitively. Each teacher should get feedback at least once during the semester and react to it. Think of teaching as an ongoing process, not an end product (Merritt 2008).

If decision makers do not take the time or care to fully understand the candidate's teaching file, including evaluations, and permit important personnel decisions to proceed on the basis of potentially misleading or biased data, then they ethically fail the professoriate, students, and the institution.

CHAPTER 13

Notes toward Racial and Gender Justice Ally Practice in Legal Academia

Dean Spade

The many ways that academia generally and legal academia specifically produce and reproduce hierarchical norms and standards of race, gender, sexuality, ability and class have been explored in the articles in this volume and many others. Because the university is both a location of the production of knowledge that is often central to sexist, racist, capitalist, and imperialist regimes of practices and a place where structures of laboring are articulated through these forces, what does it mean to practice ally politics in the university, and specifically, in the law school (Dean 2010)?[1] Race and gender norms in academia produce structural barriers for women and trans people of color in hiring and promotion.[2] These forces also create

---

1   I take the term "regimes of practices" from Mitchell Dean's discussion of Foucault's theory of governmentality, which is useful for thinking about the multiple locations of the production of racial and gendered systems of meaning and control. Such an analysis

> attend[s] to . . . the routines of bureaucracy; the technologies of notation, recording, compiling, presenting and transporting of information, the theories, programmes, knowledge and expertise that compose a field to be governed and invest it with purposes and objectives; the ways of seeing and representing embedded in practices of government; and the different agencies with various capacities that the practices of government require, elicit, form and reform. To examine regimes of government is to conduct analysis in the plural: there is already a plurality of regimes of practices in a given territory, each composed from a multiplicity of in principle unlimited and heterogeneous elements bound together by a variety of relations and capable of polymorphous connections with one another. Regimes of practices can be identified whenever there exists a relatively stable field of correlation of visibilities, mentalities, technologies and agencies, such that they constitute a kind of taken-for-granted point of reference for any form of problematization (Dean, 26–27).

2   I use the phrase "women and trans people of color" intentionally to mark those facing the intersections of gender and race-based harm. Like other trans scholars and activists, I understand that transphobia is an element of patriarchal systems of meaning and control. To the extent that trans people violate the basic rules of gender assignment and coercive

barriers to admission for students who are women and trans people of color as well as grade disparities and a hostile environment. These conditions contribute to the law profession's lack of accountability to populations who bear the brunt of violence and maldistribution structured and maintained through our legal systems. How can those of us who seek to engage our academic labor in solidarity with women and trans people of color codevelop interventions to address these concerns,[3] particularly learning from the methodologies and innovations of women of color feminism (Sandoval 2000)? How can we work to change the culture and impact of law schools and of the legal profession?

I entered legal academia from a background in grassroots activism and legal services. In the context of that work and the experiences that brought me to it, I learned the value of thinking critically about my privilege and power and cultivating awareness of opportunities for solidarity with people with differing identities and experiences. These frameworks became central method of my work. In fact, a significant part of my decision to pursue an academic job emerged out of my desire to leave a paid leadership position in the organization I had founded. The social movements in which I was working and that still guide my work have critiqued the concentration of nonprofit governance in the hands of lawyers and white people (INCITE! 2007; Mananzala and Spade 2007). As a white lawyer/founder of an organization that serves and organizes primarily low-income people of color and operates through a collective model committed to being governed by and for those we serve, I decided early in the organization's history to leave a paid staff role when the time was right in order to open that staff position to someone else. Developing new leadership from the constituency most affected by the work and redistributing power and money away from allies and toward directly impacted populations are key values in the organization and in how I understand my participation. The organization has race and gender quotas for collective membership to develop and centralize the leadership of trans people of color and features a flat pay scale to ensure that people with educational privilege (especially lawyers) do not receive more compensation than others.[4]

I sought work as a professor not only because I love teaching, reading, and writing but also because it is a type of work that allows flexibility and time for doing unpaid work in social movements. As a white person and lawyer, I want to provide support to social movements, not take resources (in the form of salary, for example) from them. When I was hired into a tenure-track law teaching job, I brought these sensibilities, which had been developed through years of activism, into a new

---

gender norming, we experience conditions of marginalization that produce high rates of unemployment (an estimated 70 percent nationally), housing and health-care discrimination, and disproportionate incarceration. As I have written elsewhere, these conditions are particularly severe for trans people of color. Trans scholars and activists use the term women and trans people when talking about a variety of situations and conditions where gender oppression produces disparities impacting people facing acute harm in various gendered systems of meaning and control.

3   As a new professor in only my second year on the tenure track, I am aware that the interventions I am working on are at a very early stage of development and also that much work has already been done on these issues that I am likely still to discover. I offer the tools shared in this article with a deep sense of humility and desire to find opportunities for further collaboration and mentorship.

4   See http://srlp.org/about/collective.

work environment. As I adjust to academia, I am confronted by norms of hierarchy, competition, and individualism and struggle to figure out ways of translating feminist and antiracist values of collectivity and antisubordination into the new work I am doing.

I entered legal academia with an interest in bringing the critical thinking and practices of grassroots activism to students. I believe this to be particularly important because the legal profession is especially hierarchical and trains attorneys in ways that are often problematic for social movements. Legal services follow service and reform models that have been critiqued by women of color feminists and others for replicating colonial dynamics and strengthening and legitimizing structures that produce harm (INCITE 2007; Spade and Mananzala 2007; Munshi 2009). Further, law reform often operates as a cooptive and containing force in social movements where radical demands for redistribution are translated into formal legal equality demands that preserve the status quo while creating the appearance of change (Siegel 1996; Harris 2006).

To move beyond legal services that primarily stabilize and justify systems of exploitation and to combat the colonial dynamic of lawyers understanding themselves as autonomous saviors of communities unconnected to meaningful collective struggle and unaccountable to the communities they serve, legal education needs to open more space for critical interrogation both of structural inequality and the complex role of law reform in social movements. I am interested in exploring how law schools frame leadership, how the law school classroom reproduces national mythologies about law and the power of law reform, how stories about transformation can more accurately reflect the histories of social movement, and how individualism and heroism can be disrupted as guiding ways to understand the role of lawyers in social change.

The ability of legal education to provide this kind of analysis—to produce learning communities that critically confront power, rather than solely reproduce conditions of domination—is integrally connected to who is in the law school—the students, staff, faculty, and administrators. The people who govern the school (faculty and administrators) determine key points regarding admission criteria, curriculum, and pedagogy. The people who teach classes engage or fail to engage with students in ways that build critical analysis and skills for understanding and addressing power and privilege. The students who attend classes and cocurricular activities and gather socially cocreate an environment that is more or less accessible and welcoming to traditionally underrepresented students and professors and also evaluate professors in the light of biases they have.

At each level, the presence or absence of traditionally underrepresented groups creates feedback loops that impact access to the institution, the curriculum, the environment, and the future of the profession. Ensuring that women of color faculty are hired, retained, and flourish in the legal academy requires addressing student racism and sexism that contribute to biased evaluations, introducing students to pedagogy focused on feminist and racial justice issues, and addressing admission criteria for students and other policies of the law school. Because white supremacy and patriarchy are produced and reproduced at all levels of legal education— from disparate pay scales for staff and faculty to admissions policies to pedagogy— opportunities for intervention are virtually everywhere. Figuring out how to take advantage of them is a complex and creative process requiring frequent reflection and revision. Allies working in solidarity with women and trans people of color must ensure that our actions are guided by relationships with those most directly impacted and are continuously reevaluated and open to critique.

Interventions

In both classroom and cocurricular settings, I seek to help students develop their ability to critically analyze the role of law in social change and the limitations and dangers of law reform as well as critically engage with their own social and political positions and behaviors. This process involves linking analysis of personal experiences of trauma, subjection, and privilege with structural understandings of power and distribution. Particularly, I find that developing a meaningful racial justice critical lens requires both classroom and cocurricular engagement because of the inherent limitations of mandatory/graded classes. For students to analyze their experiences of racial domination and oppression and unpack the trauma connected with them requires a non-graded space in addition to the intellectual and political discussions (and sometimes more) that can happen in the classroom.

In the rest of this chapter, I share examples of methods I use in the classroom as well as a project I codesigned called the Racial Justice Leadership Institute that offers students a cocurricular space for developing skills and capacities for racial justice work. The strategies I share constitute my initial efforts to intervene in some of the conditions that marginalize women and trans people of color in legal academia and perpetuate the cooptation of social justice work by legal reform.

Classroom Strategies

Group Agreements

I start all my classes with an exercise that is typical of many activist community meetings. The class generates group agreements about the ways we want to treat each other and create a learning environment that will support our work together. I find this exercise necessary and useful because of the competition and individualism that legal academia fosters through the Socratic method and curved grading. My concern is that the culture of the law school classroom actually makes lawyers into bad people—or worse people than they would have been otherwise—because it harms their ability to work in groups, to collaborate, to listen, to share power, and to be secure enough personally to withstand critical feedback. The group agreements offer an initial chance to address some of those problems as well as others that relate to oppressive dynamics in the classroom.

The first group agreement we discuss is "move up/move back." This agreement asks each person to gauge his/her own participation rate. It invites those who have a tendency to observe and volunteer less to take the risk and those who tend to be the first with their hand up to let others have more time to gather their thoughts. In discussing this agreement, I tell the students that I intend to create a space where guessing is invited and wrong answers are not a source of humiliation, hoping that those who are shy to volunteer based on bad classroom experiences will risk trying again under new conditions.

The second group agreement is "collaboration not competition." In this agreement, we discuss ways that the class will be a space where small group work and graded group assignments take place, and in each of those instances, we will all aim to make sure everyone participates equally and no one is left behind. I ask them to take responsibility for educating one another as well as themselves.

The third group agreement is "constructive feedback." In this one, I invite students to tell me how the class is working for them as it goes along and to post thoughts about it on a Web page that I have set up to allow anonymous entries so that I can continue to improve the class throughout the semester, rather than only getting feedback from them at the end. I encourage them to take responsibility for their experiences in the class by giving this feedback.

The fourth group agreement is addressing each other correctly with regard to name and pronoun. We agree to pronounce each other's names correctly (Lustbader 2006),[5] not to assume each other's pronouns until we have confirmed them,[6] and to call each other by the names we go by. Being misidentified by professors or fellow students, I have found, can be a major obstacle to student participation. Some choose to avoid speaking if it includes risking being misidentified. Other, more obvious group agreements that usually get included are "respect one another," "do not use the Internet for unrelated purposes during class," and "be punctual."

Starting the class with the idea that we are a community with a shared purpose, that there are guidelines to make the space open and accessible, and that these guidelines are something we are volunteering to share provides a significant departure from the professor-dominated, presumed-neutral space of the law school classroom. No doubt we are still in the law school. I am still the professor. In large classes, I still have to grade on the curve. These group agreements do not eliminate any of that, but they establish a critical entry point for conceptualizing our relationship to one another, an invitation to track our participation in those dynamics, and a space for questioning the way things are arranged. They explicitly disavow certain values (competition, individualism, self-promotion) and invite others (collectivity, cooperation, self-reflection). I also openly share the limitations of the group agreements and acknowledge the structural conditions that undermine them, encouraging the students to critique the grading system, the curve, law school pedagogy and other structures and suggesting that student activism can be mobilized to change these structures if they desire it. I hope that framing the context in these ways reminds them of the agency they do possess in a context that often feels stifling and disempowering.

---

5   Paula Lustbader's insightful article, "Walk the Talk: Creating Learning Communities to Promote a Pedagogy of Justice," addresses the hostility of law classrooms to students from groups underrepresented in legal education and recommends practices that foster an improved learning environment. Lustbader specifically addresses proper name pronunciation as a key element of creating a respectful and accessible environment.

6   One barrier for transgender and gender nonconforming students in the classroom occurs when professors and fellow students misidentify them by name or pronoun. Because pronouns are often based on appearance and many trans and gender nonconforming people have identities and appearances that depart from traditional expectations, being misidentified is a common experience. Professors can address this potentially embarrassing problem by ensuring that they refer to students correctly, rather than adding to the problem by forcing students to decide between trying to correct them or avoiding participation in class so they won't be misidentified (Spade 2010).

Grading Criteria

Another strategy I bring to the classroom is using multiple grading criteria in classes where the traditional method is a single final exam (Lustbader 2006).[7] In my Administrative Law course, 30 percent of the grade is based on the final exam, 30 percent is based on an assignment where students write a five-page comment on a current proposed regulation, 30 percent is based on a group project where students investigate an administrative agency as a group and create a fifteen-minute presentation, and 10 percent is class participation. This mix of assignments allows students to get training in collaboration, something rarely offered by a law pedagogy that centers on individualism, competition, and the myth of meritocracy.

I find that students have an enormous amount of anxiety about collaborating, and I ask them to confront it, establish a group process that ensures the work is evenly distributed and report on that to me, and take the risk of moving up and moving back in the group. I am clear about my desire to help them hone the kind of leadership skills that involve collaboration and collective participation. The group project and the paper also have the benefit of allowing students to focus on administrative-law issues that relate to their career interests and helping them get a more hands-on sense of material that can seem abstract. Perhaps the primary reason I choose this evaluation strategy, however, is that I believe that the exam-focused evaluation criteria that is common in law pedagogy contributes to racial disparities in law school performance (Lustbader 2006). My hope is that by providing opportunities to demonstrate a range of skills, rather than solely exam-taking ones, students who sometimes fare poorly in law classes may have an opportunity to excel.

Political Education Skills

In my Poverty Law course, we spend time critiquing the system-stabilizing role of legal services (Geoghegan 2008) and the dissent-quelling role of poverty programs more broadly (Piven and Cloward 1993). We look at critiques of the power dynamic between lawyers and poor people seeking legal assistance and discuss models for developing legal services as part of social movements that help build collective struggle against poverty, rather than individualizing harm and maintaining systems of wealth inequality. We discuss how attorneys can act as demystifiers of legal systems for communities organizing against harms that include enforcement of laws and policies. In analyzing how lawyers can support the demands of directly impacted communities, rather than framing and shaping demands in the name of those communities, we discuss ways lawyers can learn to communicate with people struggling in poverty differently and shift expertise and power through that communication.

As part of their graded work, the Poverty Law students do group projects where they create interactive political education workshops and lead them for their classmates. These workshops are not presentations; they are interactive activities designed to help the group engage in shared political analysis about some critical point from the week's readings. I share with them a range of tools, including sample political education workshops from United for a Fair Economy, which has developed very useful political education curricula on the racial wealth divide in the United States. These tools provide a sense of what it means to create a community

---

7   Paula Lustbader discusses the benefits of using multiple grading criteria rather than a single exam.

learning space not based on the idea that people are to be told the truth, but rather that they can collaborate to build shared analysis about their experiences (Chinen 2010).[8] I work with them as they create the workshops to help them think through their goals, logistical issues, and potential pitfalls. This project aims to help them move from conceptualizing poverty lawyering as saving poor people and leading change from the top to understanding that the poverty lawyer is an ally and servant to poor people's movements.

Focus on Governance and Participation

In my Poverty Law, Law and Social Movements, and Critical Perspectives on Transgender Law classes, I devote time to the analysis developed by women of color feminism and other intellectual traditions about the governance of social movement organizations and the role of mass participation and leadership development in social change. Moving beyond a doctrinal focus to analyze the relations of power that lead some harms to be addressed by litigation and services and others to go unaddressed and that privilege some strategies while others get overlooked is key to the critical engagement I seek to share with the students. Women of color feminism has developed analytical tools that examine how social issues get framed into narrow legal-equality struggles, often in ways that undermine and coopt struggle and even worsen conditions for those experiencing multiple vectors of subjection.[9] Helping law students analyze movement decision making, including understanding barriers to leadership development for people directly affected by marginalization, and conceptualize accountability strategies for movement organizations and professional workers provides tools for them to interpret their experiences of internships and jobs that are lacking in a focus on doctrinal analysis. Building an understanding of privilege (race, gender, education, age, class, ability, citizenship status) and sharing models of work that aim to redistribute decision making away from elites and toward large numbers of impacted people provides a framework for imagining transformative change that uses law reform as a tool, rather than defining itself through law reform. More broadly, the analysis developed by women of color feminism operates as a baseline for these classes, where an analysis of race, poverty, and gender is expected on every issue. Race, gender, and poverty are central, and students learn that they are expected to consider any problem we discuss through a critical lens that interrogates the impact of any issue and the effectiveness of any strategy through these dimensions.[10]

---

8   Mark Chinen cites Paulo Friere on the "banking" method of education.

9   Scholarship focused on the limitations of the white-led domestic-violence movement's focus on law enforcement is an example of this kind of analysis that I frequently use in classes (INCITE 2008; Bierra, Liebenthal, and INCITE 2007). Chela Sandoval's description of five forms of oppositional consciousness commonly employed by social movements in the United States is particularly helpful for understanding conflicts between legal equality demands and broader demands for social and political transformation (2000, 56).

10   Though the doctrinal focus of administrative law can make this project somewhat more challenging, I have found that inserting a few key critical materials on race and power into the beginning of the class and then refocusing discussions of various areas of doctrine using examples related to the administration of welfare, criminal punishment, and immigration helps to retain a critical lens for the course. Texts I have found useful include James C. Scott's *Seeing Like a State: How Certain Schemes to Improve the Human Condition Have Failed* (1999); Lisa Brodoff's "Lifting Burdens, Proof, Social Justice, and Public Assistance Administrative Hearings"; and Gabriel J. Chin's "Regulating Race: Asian Exclusion and the

Confronting the Valorization of Law and Lawyering

In the first half of the semester, students sometimes say my class is depressing. I think this is because of the work I am doing to shift their understanding of law. I find that many students have certain beliefs that both obscure their understanding of the role of law in structuring and addressing the maldistribution of life chances and lead to disappointment and alienation in the legal work they take up during and after law school. First, many of them worship the Constitution and other canons of law as sacred texts that will deliver equality and fairness if only they are interpreted correctly. Historicizing the conditions under which the American legal system was established and the founding documents drafted (slavery, genocide), and the meanings of the key terms that were used at the time ("equality") helps move students away from uncritical acceptance of the nationalist narratives that justify and legitimize racialization and maldistribution.

Second, I help them critically examine the hero and savior stories about lawyering and legal change that they bring to class and the progress narratives that anchor them. Relying on a range of critical tools, we raise questions about whether it is true that everything used to be worse (more oppressive/unfair/exploitative) than it is now and that it was fixed by changing what was legally permissible (passing antidiscrimination laws, establishing color-blind constitutionalism, creating minimum wage laws, etc.). We explore the limitations of formal legal equality and the ways that law often transforms just enough to preserve the status quo in the face of social movement demands or other disruption. We study theories of power that help us account for ways that harmful systems of meaning and distribution like racism and sexism operate through complex and diverse strategies and technologies that are mostly outside the scope of the laws that purportedly try to eradicate them.

These conversations question the theory that many law students arrive in class with—that changing the law will change people's lives and by being law reformers, they will be heroes to downtrodden people. By studying social change processes and the role of lawyers in them and exposing the false neutrality of American law and the false promise that tinkering with it is the path to liberation for people whose systematic exploitation and liquidation it was created to legitimize, we can move into an analysis of the potential for change that legal work *can* have and the meaningful roles that lawyers can play.

These initial disillusionments, however, are challenging. Perhaps the best resources for this work, I find, are the students themselves, who tend to arrive with different experiences, areas of awareness and myopia, and motivations. As we explore the materials in a participatory environment (both the classroom and the course Web page, where we have a dialogue that different students are assigned to lead each week), they tend to question each other's progress narratives and paternalistic assumptions, name their own and each other's conditions of privilege, and to coconstruct a new analysis strengthened by a collaborative process that includes conflict and disagreement.

Cocurricular: Racial Justice Leadership Institute

In addition to these approaches to classroom teaching, I have also sought to incorporate tools for developing a critical race lens based in a personal exploration of trauma, oppression, and dominance into the law school by collaborating on a

---

Administrative State."

cocurricular activity called the Racial Justice Leadership Institute (RJLI).[11] In the grassroots activist spaces where my work developed, intensive training on racial justice is a central tool for organizational development and movement building. It provides dedicated space to do deeper work to confront internalized oppression and dominance and build skills for identifying, talking and thinking about, and dismantling racism.

A key component of this work is the use of caucuses. The RJLI divides participants into a white caucus and a people-of-color caucus, and participants spend much of their time meeting in these caucuses. Caucuses have several benefits. First, they overtly disrupt the "people of color as educators" dynamic that often pervades racially integrated spaces. Creating separate caucuses acknowledges that white people and people of color have different work to do in healing and addressing racism. In these separate spaces, each caucus can focus on its particular work and the dynamics of internalized oppression or dominance. Often getting into the caucuses also provides an intensive entry point for talking about racial justice. As a white caucus participant in many similar trainings, I have consistently seen white people struggle with the idea of being grouped in a white caucus. Several key complaints tend to emerge. First, many struggle with seeing themselves as white people. These responses relate to their refusal to acknowledge white privilege. Also many white people feel uncomfortable in the caucus because they believe that the best way to learn about racism is to be with people of color who are talking about the effects of racism in their lives. They feel they are being deprived of key learning by being separated into a white caucus. Also white caucus members often point out that the people-of-color caucus is multiracial so it does not makes sense to separate only white people, and in fact it may be racist to do so.

All of these objections, and the underlying anxiety they reflect, are excellent starting points for talking about race and racism. For both caucuses, separating offers an opportunity to discuss how race and racism impact white people and people of color differently and therefore the work of dismantling racism has different obstacles and requires different capacities for white people and people of color. Breaking into caucuses also provides an opportunity to discuss the way people of color are commonly put in the role of educators of white people. The white caucus also creates a space where white people can begin to address competitive dynamics that often exist among self-identified antiracist whites. When white people are competing to show how aware they are, they often fail to build the trust and form the relationships necessary to do white-on-white work to dismantle racism. The white caucus is intended to be a space to build relationships among white people that may be a key resource for the white-on-white work that needs to be done in any institution or organization to address white supremacy.

The white caucus is also an important place to address key responses to being confronted about racism, especially guilt and defensiveness. At the RJLI, I start the white caucus with an exercise where members partner up and go over a worksheet about "one-ups" and "one-downs." The sheet, divided into two columns, identifies forms of privilege and categories of oppression such as age, socioeconomic class, education, religion/spirituality, ability, and physical size. It describes one-up groups

11   I codeveloped and cofacilitated the Racial Justice Leadership Institute with Jolie Harris, assistant director of the Office of Multicultural Affairs at Seattle University.

(e.g., US born, able bodied, age of thirty to mid-fifties, Christian, slender) and one-down groups (e.g., born outside the US; people with physical, emotional, or learning disabilities; Muslim, Jewish, agnostic, atheist, Buddhist, Hindu). I ask the students in their pairs to look at all the categories and tell each other where their experience is reflected. I start the session by sharing that I want them to have a chance to think through their different experiences of privilege and oppression because of an awareness that each of these connects to their race privilege and causes them to experience whiteness and access to its benefits differently. I introduce this to acknowledge that white experience is not uniform, even though our work in the session focuses on race and aims to help each of us learn more about how race and racism operate. My hope is that starting with this exercise allows students to feel heard and seen in their multiple identities and experiences but also realize that experiences of other kinds of oppression do not negate white privilege or mean that we do not need to account for and understand our roles as white people in a racist society. This, along with a discussion of people's concerns about being in a white caucus, provides an entry point for our work analyzing race and racism and beginning to address common defenses against acknowledging them.

Both the white caucus and people-of-color caucus of the RJLI are also assigned to read a short article called "Detour-Spotting for White Anti-Racists." The article outlines common habitual responses that dismiss or minimize the existence of racism, such as the assertion of color blindness, cultural appropriation, victim blaming, silence, requests to be educated, and the assertion of a white person's own oppression in another area (sexism, anti-Semitism, homophobia, etc.) (Olsson 1997). In the white caucus, the group goes over the article paragraph by paragraph, looking at each particular detour and discussing when we have seen it used and any reflections we have about it. We also make lists of manifestations of white privilege that we have seen to help us build skills and awareness about the way racism operates. We also go over a handout about cycles of socialization to help establish that racism is not an issue of individual wrongdoing but an immersive, systemic, formative experience that requires constant, active, reflective engagement to continually unlearn. This provides an opportunity to talk about guilt and blame as well and address the ways that white people often compete with each other to be the "most antiracist," rather than working together to support the lifelong process of reflection and action to address our co-production of white supremacy.

The white caucus also uses a handout called "Costs of Racism to Whites." The list includes things like "distorted, inaccurate picture of history," "feeling a false sense of superiority," "lost relationships with people of color," "lost relationships with family, friends, colleagues over fighting about racism," "tendency to live in fear of people of color, feel uncomfortable and tense around them," and other items. We go over the handout in the caucus and share experiences we are reminded of by the different items on the list. Again this gives the participants an opportunity to reflect on the role that racism plays in their lives, how deeply it shapes their experience and emotional reactions, and how significantly it organizes our social and professional interactions. For many this is also another moment to expose the prevalence of racism in a culture that pretends it has been resolved or is a problem of isolated aberrant individuals.

The white caucus also uses tools that directly address ways of responding to being confronted about racism that offer an alternative to defensive/evasive responses and stem from an understanding of the cumulative impact of racism and the difference between intent and impact. The caucus identifies cumulative impact as one reason to choose not to criticize the way that someone brings up racism. We discuss the fact that people on the losing end of white supremacy will have repeated experiences of racism throughout life and may have deep feelings of anger, fear, distrust, and frustration. Caucus members are encouraged to approach these conversations with openness and a desire to support these individuals in sharing their experience, rather than with a critical appraisal of the way they might have presented their point "better." When working with white law students, I include in this discussion the fact that white lawyers often occupy high-level positions in organizations where it is especially important that we provide space and support, rather than critiquing people who bring racism to our attention. I share stories of moments in my own life when such assertions prompted feelings of defensiveness, fear, and a desire to critique the way the message was delivered. I share how working with myself and/or other white people to process those feelings allowed me to make a more appropriate response that did not blame the victim, criticize the delivery, or evade the issue.

Similarly, when we discuss intent versus impact, we talk about the need for allies to apologize for and address impact, rather than defend their intent. During this discussion, members often share stories about their own mistakes in dealing with discussions of racism, their fears about being racist, and their difficulties in realizing that they cannot become perfect at antiracism and need to continue unlearning harmful approaches and behaviors and being accountable for mistakes throughout their lives. During this discussion, we also go over handouts that outline specific language to use in dialogues about race to avoid these issues, show respect and openness, and support people naming racism and seeking accountability and change.

The members of both caucuses are also given an assignment between the second and third sessions to track patterns of behavior by group identity in the various spaces of their lives. They are asked to watch the ways race operates in their workplaces, families, classes, and other parts of their lives. The tracking worksheet asks them to think about questions like "Who is talking? Who is silent? Who has eye contact with whom? What is being talked about? Who reacts to whom? Who seems to be shutting down or zoning out? Who initiates? Who supports?" These questions invite the students to look at the world through a racial justice lens and identify patterns. In the final session, the caucuses come together to discuss what patterns they have noticed. This activity builds shared analysis among the students and creates the possibility of collaborating to address problematic trends they see in the spaces they share.

The RJLI program takes place during three sessions; the first lasts all day, and the two others are three-hour evening meetings. At Seattle University, where we have begun this institute, students have expressed a desire that the program be mandatory for all students, faculty, and staff. It remains to be seen whether the training will be broadened to reach more or all of those constituencies, but our hope is that the success of the program will encourage the students to push for its expansion and the school to meet that demand over time. We believe that the depth of this curriculum, which extends far beyond diversity and inclusion rhetoric, provides vital tools to help students work for racial justice throughout their careers. This is particularly urgent in law, where racial disparity plays out, not just in the systems that deliver racial injustice (criminal punishment, public benefits, housing, immigration, child welfare) but also in the profession itself, where power and compensation are concentrated in white people, and in legal education, where racist admission practices and institutional norms produce unequal access to the profession.

In its broadest vision, perhaps such training could be one tool in addressing a range of issues we see in legal academia. Perhaps students with sharper racial justice perceptions will be less racist as evaluators of professors, will make more demands for racial justice in their law schools, and will participate in their classes differently. Perhaps an increased analysis of white supremacy in all members of the law school community can shift dialogue and decision making about admission criteria, tenure, compensation, curriculum reform, and other key issues that structure our profession.

There are many structural obstacles to working as a white ally in struggles for racial justice in legal academia. The pressures of professionalism promote silence and assent, perhaps especially in untenured professors. The white cultural norms that shape academic institutions—hierarchy, individualism, competition, scarcity—encourage us not to act as allies, not to endure the risks of taking unpopular action by naming oppression in our academic work or professional interactions with students, faculty, and staff. The structure of the law school encourages our students to emulate these qualities, compete, and abandon their preexisting values and "think like a lawyer." Legal scholarship includes long traditions of critique and counterpractice, and yet legal academia's limitations remain persistent and perhaps have worsened in the context of a rollback on affirmative action and a political climate of neoliberalism (Lewin 2010a). It can be difficult to take up ally work under such conditions, or that work can feel so compromised that it can be discouraging. However, a central tenet of this work is recognizing the opportunities that privilege provides to disrupt the creation of that privilege and the obligation to take action. My own practices in this realm feel incomplete and experimental and no doubt will be a source of reflection, mistakes, and adjustment for decades to come. My years in grassroots activism provide an anchor for the values I want to bring to this work, just as the example of radical academics intervening on these issues supplies inspiration.

CHAPTER 14

WHERE'S THE VIOLENCE?

The Promise and Perils of Teaching
Women-of-Color Studies

Grace Chang

When I am asked what I teach, I respond somewhat reluctantly that I teach women's studies and often add that I teach women of color studies. Recently I was asked by a white man, "What is that? White male bashing?" and I surprised myself with the directness of my answer. I said, "No, actually, it is probably more like white feminism bashing, or the critique of white, Western feminism." I was careful to specify that the target of my criticism is the body of thought and practice generally identified as white, Western feminism, rather than those who support its theories. The man asking the question expressed relief and continued to ask eagerly about what I taught. Unfortunately, some white women students in my classes are not similarly reassured by my stated focus and instead exhibit great defensiveness about my challenging their precious and sometimes newfound feminist ideals.

In fact, some students have expressed great anger and hostility toward me for what they see as my attacking or ridiculing them and all white people. One student wrote the following in an evaluation of my Grassroots and Transnational Feminist Movements class:

> This class was captivating and interesting. It definitely challenged my opinions and point of views [*sic*]. However, being a Caucasian I felt very uncomfortable and discriminated against. I have never been [a] racist of any kind as I was raised to respect all races. But, I felt that the instructor made several racist remarks regarding whites, "white privilege" and many derogatory things against the white class. The reason this bothered me was because it seemed pointless and not relevant . . . I felt like she was making fun of whites, and this made me feel attacked and this hindered my desire to read and come to class . . . I hope Chang realizes how much a turn off her teaching is for an open minded and liberal student.

Similarly I received this mixed review from one student on the "Rate My Professor" (or, as I call it, "Hate My Professor") Web site: "If you're white, be prepared to hate her. But if you aren't an ignorant dumb****, afraid to learn about the truth in an aryan-infested world where, yes, homosexuality and extremist patriotism exist, then . . . this is your class, knowledgeable colored person. THIS is your class." Another reviewer on the same Web site responded, "Actually, I'm white and I love her," but added, "You either love her or you hate her." These comments have led me to wonder what exactly it is that evokes such intense feelings toward my teaching style, my subject matter, and/or me. And which is it that students react to?

Perhaps one of the most gratifying teaching evaluations I ever received was a comment made the first time I taught a class called Women of Color in US Society at University of California, Santa Barbara (UCSB). The student wrote that I "make the white community feel unsafe and uncomfortable." I felt this was a great honor, signaling that I was able to unsettle the privileged place of comfort enjoyed by so many students at the institution where I teach—so much so that this student identified or invented a "white community" that he or she charged I was threatening. When I reported this comment to members of my community—including social justice organizers of all stripes in the San Francisco Bay Area—they congratulated me and asked me what I had done to wield so much power. In this chapter, I can only discuss what I attempt to achieve through my teaching style and choice of subject matter and speculate on what may be so threatening. I neither claim credit nor accept blame for the fear, anger, and hatred apparently inspired by my teaching.

A Career of Living Dangerously

I joined a women's studies department with certain hesitations about being identified as a teacher and scholar in that area. My training, disciplinary affiliation, and self-identification had always been with ethnic studies or a field that some may argue is still emerging—women of color studies.[1] In striving to develop women of color studies as a discipline distinct from women's studies and its attendant limitations of white, Western feminist biases, I feared that a women's studies department might not be the most fertile ground or amenable host. Indeed, the challenge of developing women of color studies and attempting to counter and overcome the limits of white, Western feminist racism and colonialism has been more than an abstract or academic endeavor. It has been a struggle fraught with many frustrations and one that has generated many questions along the way, including these: What function does women of color studies serve in a college curriculum? What forms does it take? How does it satisfy the desires and fantasies of white students and faculty? Does it meet the needs of women of color as students or faculty? How might it do so better?

I have developed and taught three core undergraduate classes over the past three years: Women of Color Studies; Women, Globalization and Resistance; and Grassroots and Transnational Feminist Movements. I believe I have learned a great deal from my students' responses about what American students are prepared to learn in college, what they expect—often simply to be entertained—and what they resist

---

1   I sometimes use the term "women of color studies" interchangeably with "transnational feminism" as they both address approaches to feminist thought and practice that center women of color. In my view, a transnational framework should encompass these bodies of theory and practice as they inform, illuminate, and impact the lives of women in the First and Third worlds, particularly as they relate to the dynamics of power between them.

or refuse to study or even consider.[2] I have also observed that students have much societal support to close their minds to troublesome issues in the current political atmosphere. In the context of the favorite American pastime of hunting down "dangerous professors" à la David Horowitz's hit list, this is a difficult climate for professors to undertake teaching controversial issues.[3]

Yet this is precisely what I teach in my classes, or so I am told. The description on the syllabus for my class entitled Women of Color Studies states the following: "Women of color in the United States live their lives and negotiate their identities and daily struggles at the intersections of race, class, gender, sexuality, disability and nation. That is, women of color experience and respond to the interlocking systems of racism, classism, sexism, homophobia, transphobia, ableism and colonialism on a daily basis. An enduring challenge for Women's Studies is to address the complexities of the lives and struggles of women of color at these intersections."

In practical terms, that has translated into a ten-week crash course in looking at how women of color experience these many forms of oppression and struggle in the face of them to forge their identities and fight for civil, immigrant, labor, welfare, queer, and disability rights and against globalization and reproductive and environmental racism, to name a few issues. An equally important component of the class is an examination of ways that traditional women's studies approaches and public discourses promoted by US media and government may fail to address these issues adequately or deliberately obscure them. In this chapter, I discuss my vision and efforts to address these issues, some of the methods I have used to introduce and illuminate them in accessible and acceptable ways, some of the resistances and backlash I have encountered from students, and finally, some of the strategies I have devised to deal with or move beyond those obstacles.

In developing a women of color studies curriculum, I have tried to build a framework that is intersectional, that looks at the experiences of women of color living within the structures of these systems of oppression and views them as inextricably linked, rather than as separate, multiple, and related only in an additive model (Baca Zinn and Dill 1999).[4] This approach also encompasses the way women of color have responded to and resisted these structures and calls attention to the many forms of opposition they employ, including their daily survival. As there is no established canon in this emerging field, I strive to build a core group of texts as a starting point for my students' common base of readings while making room for them to contribute their own selections and writing. In addition, my goal is to connect women of color studies with social justice work and make this link clear and viable for students.

Creating these new or emerging approaches to women of color studies necessitates new methods as well. I try to employ materials and methods in both my

---

2   This is not meant to be an indictment of UCSB students in general, or even of any particular students who have taken my classes, because I think that they may be fairly representative of all US college students.

3   In 2005 a campaign started at UCLA urging students to turn in their liberal professors, class notes, syllabi, etc., for a reward of a hundred dollars, presumably to identify and purge the campus of these threatening faculty members.

4   I have tried to avoid the "racial/ethnic-group-of-the-week" approach in my teaching in favor of a comparative one that addresses the common or related experiences and struggles of African American, Asian American, Chicana/Latina, Native American, and Arab American women. Thus, my syllabi are structured around issues and the ways that different groups have experienced and engaged these issues, responded and resisted.

teaching and scholarship that highlight the perspectives of and analyses by women of color. I privilege texts or testimony by women of color reflecting on, documenting, and analyzing their own experiences, rooted in their own values and social locations, and expressed in their own words. To emphasize the importance of testimony and analyses by women of color, I often tell the story of being interviewed by a white male economist for a job where I would be coteaching a political economy class with him. He asked why I had relied so heavily on interviews and testimony for my book and insisted, "You can't rely on people to analyze their own lives." This was a pivotal moment in solidifying my commitment to qualitative methods as the foundation of my research and teaching.

In my years of teaching since then, I have affirmed again and again my conviction that it is this mentality within academia—among many social scientists and perhaps many members of dominant US society in general—that makes it crucial to develop fields such as women of color studies and, beyond content, to design particular methods within that field as well. It is the notion that "experts" can understand the lives of those who experience oppression and exploitation in dominant society better than the oppressed and exploited themselves that necessitates the development of a whole new field, and even perhaps an ethic, of women of color studies.

Building a Women-of-Color Studies Method and Ethic

In an initial and ongoing attempt to develop such a method and ethic, I created a graduate-methods class: Participatory Research, Community Organizing, and Popular Education. I start with the premise that much social science research can be faulted for reproducing—in relationships between researcher and the researched—the very inequalities and exploitation that social scientists ostensibly set out to study and hopefully intend to eradicate. This is particularly relevant to women's studies because feminists have been some of the principal culprits of colonial, maternalist and racist feminism. Yet many scholars have articulated feminist principles of research in their attempt to offer strategies and ethics avoiding these pitfalls (Baca Zinn 1979, Mies 1983). Similarly activists and scholars have developed principles and models of participatory research within, or in support of, the work of community organizations. These efforts have aimed to bring research to the service of communities being studied, rather than the reverse.

As Saba Waheed, nguyen ly-huong, and Anna Couey suggest in their article, "Decolonizing Research," community-based participatory research is "about communities doing our own research for our own ends, instead of being researched by institutions outside our communities that use our knowledge for their ends. It is about challenging who controls and defines knowledge and creating our own liberatory system of knowledge" (2005, 1). This comment encapsulates exactly the principles around which I seek to build women of color studies as a new field and method of research. It addresses two central questions that challenge and guide my work at every turn: What is good social science research, and what is social science research good for?

Thus, in my classes, I ask students to read a number of texts proposing principles for good, ethical social science research, and we look at several models of how such research has supported community organizing for social justice. I focus on research undertaken by women of color as community members who seek to identify the needs of their own communities and contribute to meeting them through their research (Domestic Workers United 2006). In contrast, I show them examples of "white knight" models featuring white, Western men and women defining other people's problems and rescuing them from themselves. I ask students to question or cautiously approach research conducted by outsiders to the communities and be wary of the potential oppression or exploitation of subjects that can occur in the research process. As an alternative, I expose students to the principles of participatory action research and its benefits, including engaging subjects in the design and implementation of their own research agendas.

To demonstrate some of these principles in action, I bring guest speakers who are organizers and scholar/activists to share their experiences, but much can be achieved without the benefit of guest speakers through a variety of means. I often use testimonials and texts based on qualitative methods, particularly those generated by social justice organizations. For example, I regularly use the report, "Welfare Reform as We Know It," a collection of testimonials gathered by the Grassroots Organizing for Welfare Leadership (GROWL) project (GROWL 2000). These testimonials document the experiences of women of color from across the country in their encounters with the welfare state. The participants talk about their negotiations with case workers in their efforts to receive basic needs and services of housing, childcare, training, education, etc. and the many forms of racism, ableism and overwhelming discouragement, harassment, and obstruction they face.

Reading the testimonies of women who readily corroborate the scholarly feminist critiques of the welfare state greatly impacts the students. I have only had one skeptical student remark that the accounts of the women were so similar that the GROWL report seemed "formulaic." I responded that in standard social science research, when many people confirm a pattern across a broad spectrum, we call that evidence. That is the value of qualitative research and testimony. In addition, I sometimes ask students to offer their own testimonials. This has worked best in settings where I have taught greater numbers of nontraditional students, but it is feasible to do it in every setting, tailored to particular topics.

Students have volunteered to recount their experiences with the welfare state as children or parents in families receiving welfare, as sons and daughters of veterans receiving GI benefits and disability, and as men and women who have served in the military themselves. It has been powerful for students to hear their peers talk about their experiences with these oppressive systems in the United States beyond my lectures on socialist feminist critiques of the welfare state or the military-industrial complex. One white single mother described social workers making home visits to scrutinize her parenting, or advising her to quit school and go to work. Another woman recalled being humiliated as a child by grocery cashiers when her mother used food stamps. Men and women whose fathers were veterans and/or had done military training or service themselves shared their understanding of the military as low-wage work, part of the welfare state, and a harsh system of social conditioning where they encountered sexual harassment and homophobia.

Using student testimony and the general ground rules I set for class discussions has produced some surprisingly effective results. At the outset of my classes, I ask that students contribute to discussions by drawing from the readings or relate observations based on their own, direct experiences, rather than hearsay, secondhand accounts, or media reports. When we discuss issues such as discrimination in encounters with the welfare state and they are constrained by the requirement to speak from their own experience, privileged students are hard pressed to dominate the discussions as they often do otherwise. Of course, privileged students are often uncomfortable with this method because it doesn't allow them to focus exclusively on themselves or their own experiences and forces them to listen to others. Moreover, they have a much harder time dismissing the insights and accounts of oppression or discrimination of a peer when faced with a live person they have known in real life in class.

It is particularly powerful when students who have race and/or class privilege can talk about new perceptions about these privileges after analyzing some of their previous experiences. For example, one white woman who went to a clinic for birth control and abortion counseling recalled walking into a waiting room full of women of color, being seen and served immediately, then seeing the same women still waiting when she left the clinic. Another biracial Asian/white woman who was a sexual-assault survivor observed that the accused man of color was presumed to be and portrayed as a worthless predator during prosecution, while her attorneys played up her unquestioned character, higher education, and socioeconomic background. In each case, I believe it was truly invaluable for students to hear these women offer these analyses from the positions of greater social status or privilege they occupied and identify the workings of racism and classism, even when they worked to their benefit.

The feedback I have received from my students and teaching assistants reflects that these methods also have made those who have not usually enjoyed the privileges of the dominant society feel more confident or safe to voice their perspectives in my classes. They find that their experiences and analyses are recognized by their peers, valued by their professor, and mirrored in the texts they are reading. I believe that this is what we mean when we speak of making curricula relevant to students of color and the working class beyond a superficial and inadequate multicultural or cultural-sensitivity requirement. A relevant curriculum should enable students to relate their life experiences to the ideas and analyses they are studying, and, at the same time, it should challenge students to see beyond their own life experiences and social status to try to understand the position of others without presumption, judgment, pity, or antipathy. Furthermore, it should help students examine the impact of their life conditions on others. This, I would argue, is the connection that many US students don't want to see and thus often fail to make.

Western Feminist Fantasies of Other Women's Salvation

Students have very specific expectations when they seek to study the Other—namely women of color and Third World women—in women's studies classes, and they seek it with consumer vengeance. One of the classes I inherited when I arrived at UCSB was originally called Women's Struggles in Africa, Asia and Latin America. I revamped it to turn the focus on the sources and impact of United States–driven globalization in the Third World, its effect on communities of color within the United States, and resistance movements organized by women of color in response. Though I renamed it Women, Globalization and Resistance, many students still enrolled thinking they would hear a litany of women's struggles outside the United States, presumably against the backward cultures and brutal patriarchy of Other men. They fully expected to read and hear about bride burning, veiling, female genital mutilation, wife beating, and selling daughters for child prostitution—all as regular features of the brutality of Third World men and the devaluation of women and girls in traditional (read, backward and ignorant) Third World families and societies (Mohanty 1984).

Many students were disappointed that I did not fulfill this expectation. As I now understand, when people seek to hear about women of color around the world, they expect to hear grotesque and heart-wrenching tales of oppression, misery, and violence. For example, in a recent request from an antiviolence organization looking for a keynote speaker for an event, a colleague received this inquiry:

> I'm looking for someone to speak on the topic of the correlation between Discrimination/Oppression and Sexual Violence. I'm hoping that they will cover the Tootsi/Hutu issues in Africa with sexual violence against women, Indias Cast [*sic*] system and sexual violence, Color in America and Sexual Violence would be good—ie African American communities and the Latino community too. Can you give me a referral on this from the Women's Studies dept. that would be interested in volunteering their time . . . to speak on this topic for our organization.

The assumption is that men of color and Third World societies are inherently more predisposed to patriarchy and violence against women, and the corollary is that white, Western women are more liberated and free from this violence. After repeated encounters with this expectation among students, I now see the prevalence of this assumption and its insidious functions as it is embedded and promoted in much standard US women's-studies curricula, feminist discourse, and popular media.[5]

White, Western feminist discourse constructing women of color as more oppressed, exploited, and helpless than white, Western women are as useful to white, racist patriarchy as they are popular among some Western feminist schools. They imply the need for women of color to be saved, presumably of course by white, Western men and women, as individuals or representatives of their governments. This serves to distract Western women from their struggles against their oppressors and blinds them to their complicity in oppressing others. It also paves the way for the abuses that Western feminism wreaks against non-Western women and their nations in the name of liberation. Finally, it obscures the ways that Western imperialist, capitalist forces are often to blame for the ills of non-Western societies such as poverty, deliberate economic underdevelopment, environmental degradation, displacement from land, privatization of basic needs and resources, and other conditions stemming from the spread of global capitalism that do not help to liberate non-Western women by any stretch of the imagination. I think that anthropologist Laura Nader captures it best in her article, "Orientalism, Occidentalism and the Control of Women":

> A central dogma in both non-Western and Western states is that Western economic development and industrialization will improve the condition of Third World women. There is also a widespread belief that women in the

---

5   A woman-of-color colleague recently reminded me that often students of color—sometimes second- and third-generation immigrant women—have been so inundated with this philosophy and internalized it to such a degree that they, too, expect to hear stories about the "awful men of color," perhaps especially from a woman-of-color professor.

US and Western European countries are better off vis-à-vis their men folk than their sisters in societies that are not "developed." . . . A challenge to Western assumptions comes from women who are part of nationalist, religious or ethnic movements in the Third World. These women believe that they are better off than their exploited Western sisters (1989, 329).

I often use this passage in my lectures. Nader's point here, of course, is that identifying other women as more oppressed is a tactic used in both Western and non-Western contexts to suppress, threaten, and control local women and undermine local feminist struggles.

Similarly Leila Ahmed in *Women and Gender in Islam* calls the use of Western feminist rhetoric to justify or support imperialism "colonial feminism" and argues, " [If] feminism on the home front and feminism directed against white men was to be resisted and suppressed [at home] but taken abroad and directed against cultures of colonized peoples, it could be promoted in a way that admirably served and furthered the project of the dominance of white men" (1992, 153). Students often respond to this argument with confusion and disbelief. When I provide them with a few concrete examples of this phenomenon, they react with even less enthusiasm.

To illustrate colonial feminism, I often use the example of how rhetoric about the oppression of women under the Taliban was used to justify the US invasion of Afghanistan in 2001. I remind students that even though Afghani women had suffered oppression under the Taliban for many years prior to September 11, 2001, and had done so under previous and subsequent regimes as well, US forces seized the discovery of their plight after 9/11 to call for their liberation by bombing Afghanistan. Simultaneously US audiences were bombarded with images of Afghani women wearing burqas as the ultimate symbol of their oppression in limited Western understanding.

While many feminist authors and scholars of color have tried to undo this massive miseducation of the American public, I continue to see evidence of the damage done. One very powerful means and manifestation of this miseducation is the continued production of "Under the Burqa," part of *The Vagina Monologues* created and performed in 2001, which most American women's audiences consumed voraciously and adored. Because I would not dare to paraphrase or describe this gross misrepresentation, here is a section with its original introduction:

> Last year Eve Ensler had the opportunity to go to Afghanistan. There, she witnessed firsthand what the outcome of misogyny would be if it were allowed to manifest itself totally. Under the Taliban, women are essentially living the lives of walking corpses. This monologue is for the brave, tender, fierce women of Afghanistan. That we may all rise up to save them.

UNDER THE BURQA

imagine a huge dark piece of cloth
hung over your entire body
like you were a shameful statue
imagine there's only a drop of light
enough to know there is still daylight for others
imagine it's hot, very hot

imagine you are being encased in cloth,
drowning in fabric, in darkness.
imagine you are begging in this bedspread
reaching out your hand inside the cloth
which must remained covered, unpolished, unseen
or they might smash it or cut it off
imagine no one is putting rupees in your invisible hand
because no one can see your face
so you do not exist . . . .

imagine muttering as a way of talking
because words did not form anymore in the darkness
and you did not cry because it got too hot and wet in there.
imagine bearded men that you could only decipher
by their smell
beating you . . . .
imagine suffocating
while you were still breathing
imagine you could no longer distinguish
between living and dying
so you stopped trying to kill yourself
because it would be redundant

imagine me inside the inside
of the darkness in you
i am caught there
i am lost there
inside the cloth
which is your head
inside the dark we share
imagine you can see me

i was beautiful once
big dark eyes
you would know me.

In 2001 Oprah Winfrey performed this monologue for eighteen thousand people in New York's Madison Square Garden, ending the gala event by lifting a burqa from an Afghani woman onstage, just as French imperialist women had unveiled and thereby symbolically freed Algerian women in great public acts, attempting to reassert French dominance in Algeria in 1958 (Abu-Lughod 2002). Eve Ensler and Oprah Winfrey have unwittingly given us a perfect illustration of the uses of US colonial feminism to justify Western imperialist violence against women of color, colonized women, and their societies, all in the name of women's liberation. The problem is, however, that US students—like the women who comprised the enthusiastic audience at the New York extravaganza—would sooner defend colonial feminism than entertain thoughts about its uglier side.

This is what I found in my classes when I critiqued *The Vagina Monologues*, "Under the Burqa" specifically, and other pieces as both reflecting and promoting Western feminist racism. Students who were participating in the campus production of the play were outraged by my critique and insisted that Eve Ensler had removed and recanted the burqa monologue. Yet, in a recent quick Internet search, I found that any number of colleges, including Yale, the University of Michigan, Brandeis, MIT, and the University of California, Riverside, had listed "Under the Burqa" in their programs for productions of *The Vagina Monologues* during the last two years.

What accounts for the enormous popularity of *The Vagina Monologues* on college campuses as well as in countless benefit performances for women's-rights organizations? I suggest that they appeal to the Western feminist fantasy of the oppressed Third World woman or "other" woman, who can be relegated to the position of pitiful, helpless souls who need rescue. Eve Ensler says it all in her introduction to the "Under the Burqa" monologue: "That we may all rise up to save them." The appeal of *The Vagina Monologues* to many white female college students appears to be the promise of their starring roles as saviors.

Western Eyes Averting Their Own Gaze

It has been interesting to observe how much easier it is for white American students to recognize the oppression of women of color and Third World women by US-based and multinational corporations, white men, and men of color than to acknowledge the toxicity of colonial feminism, racism in US-based white feminism, or racism in general. One of the best examples of this phenomenon is the typical defensive and hostile response I get from students when I talk about the racism of the Abercrombie & Fitch Company.

I often use the recent follies of Abercrombie & Fitch to illustrate the function and impact of racism within global capitalism both here in the United States and abroad. The multinational corporation produced a line of arguably anti-Asian T-shirts, including the most notorious one, which depicted two caricatured Chinese men, complete with buck teeth and slanty eyes, and the slogan, "Wong Brothers Laundry Service: Two Wongs Can Make it White." I talk about these T-shirts in the context of their likely production in sweatshops in Saipan and marketing in catalogues filled with bronzed-but-white young Americans frolicking on exotic, tropical islands where these sweatshops could be located.

I also talk about the 2003 case brought against the corporation, an employment-discrimination class-action lawsuit[6] that argued that Abercrombie had discriminated against Latinos, Asian Americans, and African Americans to create the "Abercrombie & Fitch Look" through policies that recruited, hired, and maintained a disproportionately white workforce of public salespeople, discouraged people of color applicants, and channeled the few people of color who were hired to stockroom and overnight shifts, away from the public eye, or into back-of-the-house positions (Greenhouse 2004). In other words, the corporation's products and practices illustrate perfectly the links that connect the racism in the design and marketing of its products to its employment practices in US stores and its sweatshop labor practices.

---

6   On June 16, 2003, a coalition of four organizations, including the law firm of Lieff Cabraser Heimann & Bernstein, LLP, the Mexican American Legal Defense and Educational Fund (MALDEF), the Asian Pacific American Legal Center (APALC), and the NAACP Legal Defense and Educational Fund, Inc., filed an employment-discrimination class-action lawsuit against Abercrombie & Fitch.

The first time I lectured about these links, I was genuinely shocked at one white woman's response: she reported that Abercrombie & Fitch had recruited her sister and insisted that the corporation was just seeking an attractive, "all-American look." The comment spoke for itself. Fortunately another white woman student who apparently had the A&F look reported that she, too, had been recruited to apply for a sales position and went for an interview out of curiosity. She reported that a large sign greeted the potential employees, saying, "You're an Abercrombie girl if: you're athletic, you like boys . . . " etc. The student read between the lines and concluded that the corporation readily advertised its preference for skinny, heterosexual employees. This astute student and others have been able to make the connections among the racism, sexism, and heterosexism embodied in Abercrombie's practices at the levels of marketing, employment, and production, as well as in the products.

Other students, however, cling to their ideas that these practices merely reflect personal choices or tastes and good marketing tactics that individuals and corporations are fully free to exercise. Ironically, while many US students are very well programmed to see the evils of multinational corporations and sweatshops, which they presume are based outside of the United States always, those same students often resist seeing the problems with discriminatory employment practices, racist images, or their foundations in racist US ideology. To me this reflects the approach often taken in traditional women's studies curricula: focusing on predictable, oversimplified topics such as sweatshops as the only manifestation of US imperialism and locating the blame for all other forms of exploitation of Third World women on their local men and societies.

Identifying corporations, non-US cultures, white men, or men of color exclusively as the oppressors lets everyone else—including US society and government and those white women who create, maintain, or support US racist patriarchy—off the hook. It is much more palatable for US students, especially white women, to identify these other oppressors than to look at ways they may be contributing to the oppression of US women of color and immigrant women as employers, coworkers, or peers. For example, almost without fail, when I present the issues of immigrant women and women of color as domestic workers, students (including economically privileged students of color) muse about their beloved nannies who raised them and the mutually close relationships they believe they had with them.[7] Only reluctantly do some of them reexamine these memories and question whether these relationships were as affectionate or rewarding, materially or otherwise, from the employees' perspective.

Where's the Violence?

> *Without an emotional, heartfelt grappling with the source of our own oppression, without naming the enemy within ourselves and outside of us, no authentic, nonhierarchical connection among oppressed groups can take place.*

---

7   In a discussion at the University of Redlands with faculty from several disciplines who addressed paid domestic work in their classes, we were amazed to find that we had all encountered this experience with students' nostalgia for their nannies and a desire to spin a narrative of relationships of mutual love and beneficence.

*I have come to believe that the only reason women of a privileged class will
dare to look at how it is that they oppress is when they've come to know the
meaning of their own oppression.*

Cherríe Moraga, *"La Guera"*

In these passages from her classic essay, *"La Guera,"* Cherríe Moraga suggests
that it is difficult for us to recognize our own oppression—our condition of being
oppressed—yet we must understand it before we can understand the oppression
of others or our complicity in it. I have found, however, that many students do
not want to acknowledge their role or complicity in the oppression of others and
indeed—when confronted with this possibility—they would rather claim or focus on
their own experiences of being oppressed. This explains a curious demand among
students for violence to be covered in women's studies classes.

At a recent meeting of women's studies faculty from a number of campuses, several members reported this popular theme in their students' interests. Many students request or expect violence to be part of the standard women's studies curriculum as indicated by these common questions: "Why don't we talk more about violence?" or "Why isn't violence in the syllabus?" After further discussion, it becomes
clear that the students are asking for a focus on domestic violence and sexual assault,
issues that they believe belong in women's studies classes. Yet I believe this frequent
demand for violence signals something more than a concern for understanding
domestic violence and sexual assault as presumably common issues for women. I suggest that this curriculum appeals to women with white, middle- and upper class, or
heterosexual privileges because it gives them some claim to victim status as women.

I discovered this while teaching a class called Meaning to Survive: Women and
Violence that I had designed and taught at Evergreen State College with very positive results.[8] It indeed was about women and violence, yet some students as UCSB
said it was not what they had expected. I very explicitly introduced the course in
the announcement flier, syllabus, and first meetings as a study of violence against
women of color and other women marginalized in US society. I explained that
focusing on these target groups offered a unique lens through which we could
understand the intersections of sexism, racism, classism, ableism, homophobia, and
colonialism in dominant US ideologies and social, economic, and legal structures.
Yet many students repeatedly rejected the idea that racism, classism, and homophobia were forms of violence, or that women of color, poor women, queer women, or
Third World women might experience and respond to domestic, sexual, or other
forms of violence differently and under distinct conditions from privileged women.

Despite the prominent warning labels, I believe that many students who enrolled
in the course were unprepared to do the work or make the commitment to grapple
with these difficult issues. Others wanted to discuss exactly these controversial issues
for which they found little or no support or space in their other classes or elsewhere.
The class thus became a perfect environment to observe the persistent conflicts in
feminism emerge, in particular the persistent denial of racism or privilege by white
women. When I reflect back on this class, I often refer to it as my "laboratory" in
white feminist racism since these issues unfolded for us in living color in a way that
I could not have elicited if I had tried to stage it.

---

8   This is also the title of my book in progress, which addresses violence perpetrated against
      women of color, their children, and their communities through the family law state.

It will be helpful here to describe the physical dynamics of the class to understand the context where these difficult discussions took place or were at least attempted. The class quickly and visibly bifurcated so that mostly women and men of color sat on one side of the room while mostly white women sat on the other. This amplified a pattern of white women scowling and sending hostile glares at me during discussions while the women and men of color often looked pleadingly at me to respond whenever one of the white students made a racist remark or tried to insist that an issue was "not about race or racism." A large core of the white women students did not want to talk about racism—as violence or even in general—and expended great energy avoiding these discussions or shutting them down.

With these dynamics firmly established by midquarter, we embarked on a discussion of the controversial issue of reproductive rights abuses of women of color. Specifically students were assigned readings on the CRACK campaign, a privately funded program targeted to coerce mostly low-income black and Latina women to volunteer to be sterilized in exchange for a cash award, ostensibly to prohibit drug-addicted women from reproducing (Roberts 1999; Scully 2000). We had just finished studying the use of welfare and immigration policies to exert labor and social controls over women of color and immigrant women in the United States and assign different values to the lives of children of color. An interesting discussion began among three students: a black man and a biracial black/white woman, who supported the idea of the CRACK campaign; and a Middle Eastern woman, who argued against it.

The discussion was lively and predictably charged. A white woman who was very uncomfortable with the energetic and contentious exchange (and who also did not appear to have done the readings) tried to interrupt, exclaiming, "Can people not attack each other, please?" I responded that I was monitoring the discussion closely to ensure that people treated each other respectfully and that I heard nothing but healthy dialogue. I also asked the three students involved if they felt uncomfortable with the way the discussion was proceeding. None of them voiced any concern and instead eagerly expressed that they wanted to continue. The undergraduate advisor told me that one student that day had commented that I had made a great intervention in the class. The student who wanted to shut down this conversation that was uncomfortable to her for a variety of reasons—including, I believe, lack of preparation to participate—felt very aggrieved about the episode, however, and my unwillingness to let her stop it.

The following week students were assigned to read and facilitate a discussion on several articles addressing the historical use of the rationale that white women needed protection from black male predators to justify the lynching of black men. We read some highly problematic writings by Susan Brownmiller, selected from *Against Our Will: Men, Women and Rape,* and an article called "Rage before Race," which discussed the recently reopened Central Park jogger rape case (Brownmiller 1975; Combahee River Collective 1986; James 1998; Little 2002). My aim was to have students examine racism in mainstream US feminist responses to the case then and now and discuss ways to address the problem of racism in antiviolence rhetoric and practice. I hoped to discuss the challenge for feminists of color to counter the construction of men of color as sexual predators while, at the same time, breaking the silence about individual men of color who are perpetrators of violence in our communities. Moreover, I wanted students to contemplate the difficult position of black women who chose to defend the fair-trial rights of the men accused in the case and how this led to their condemnation by white feminists as traitors.

Two students were able to connect our discussions of this case with their observations of the criminalization of men of color at UCSB and the inordinate media attention on allegations of rape committed by men of color here and more broadly in US society. But the conversation deteriorated rapidly from there. Students reverted to the old stand-by topic, the media, and wanted to talk about Michael Jackson and Kobe Bryant and thus divert the focus to class and celebrity status, rather than race. Again, here, I suspect that students who had not done the reading had great interest in avoiding discussing it. Toward the end of the class, I stood up, closed the door, insisted that the default topic of the media was banned from our discussion, and announced that we were restricted to talking about rape and race for the last fifteen minutes. I encouraged students to go back to the questions raised by the student facilitators at the beginning of class that had been drawn from the readings.

At that point, one white woman who had desperately wanted to discuss the media quoted a statistic from one of our readings that most incidents of rape involve people of the same race and asked why, then, we were bothering to discuss the relationship between rape and race. When I responded with my original goals for the discussion, she demanded to know if I thought that instances of white men who raped women of color or men of color who raped white women were more important or egregious than same-race rape cases. I reviewed my original focus and goals for the discussion and my principle of trying not to hierarchize experiences of oppression or violence, but I believe that my words were largely lost on her. She and others had already identified me as suspect on many levels—certainly as racist—and undeniably aggressive in attempting to force her and other students to engage in uncomfortable discussions of topics best left untouched, in their view.

Other disappointing, yet fully predictable, moments in the class came when a woman with aspirations to become a police officer announced that she was "not racist at all" because she had dated "men of all colors," then proceeded to proclaim her complete and utter shock at a report I had given her on racial profiling and racist, anti-immigrant abuses by law-enforcement agents. She remarked that she was sure that most people had never encountered or even heard of such things. That was one of many moments in the class when the eyes of several students of color met mine in disbelief, anger, and a plea for me to intervene. Another moment came when two students gave a presentation on "female genital mutilation in *some* country in Africa" despite my extensive discussion of western constructions of Third World women's oppression and barbaric non-Western practices—all in the service of romanticized notions of white, Western women's liberation and justifying First World imperialist practices in the name of this feminism.

I think that many faculty of color face some version of this scenario in their classrooms when attempting to discuss racism or other forms of oppression in dominant US society. It is a tricky enterprise, trying to expose students' racism or other forms of ignorance while also protecting ourselves from becoming the targets of ignorant and hateful students who feel fully entitled to express their beliefs and deeply aggrieved at being challenged. I have sometimes been told that I "do not belong here," or that I "obviously don't want to teach here." I have often wondered whether this is in response to my usual opening statement that I am at UCSB to serve students of color, queer students, and low-income and first-generation college students. I remind myself that I am committed to serving students but not being served up to them.

Two students who were taking the women and violence class and other women's studies classes with white faculty, simultaneously, observed that there might be a good cop/bad cop phenomenon might be at play. That is, while white women faculty might introduce many of the same topics—including problems in white feminism, or reproductive rights abuses of women of color—the white students did not feel attacked or defensive vis-à-vis these white women professors. On the other hand, I have observed that white women faculty and teaching assistants I've worked with who challenge white students about racism are sometimes attacked viciously by defensive students as "race traitors."

Another student reported that she felt many of the students interpreted the presentation of problems in feminism outlined within a historical framework to mean that these problems, and "those bad white feminists," were literally a thing of the past. Yet these same conflicts have continued to rear their ugly heads in feminist movements, particularly in antiviolence and antiglobalization work, as well as many other social justice struggles. I am plagued by the thought that these conflicts will continue in feminist and other movement work if the students we are teaching leave our training grounds without positive influence or intervention from us; they are bound to be just as or even more deeply entrenched in these destructive dynamics and attitudes as when they arrived in our classrooms.

Perhaps some of the most frustrating comments I have received from students fall along the lines of "the readings were good, the topics were interesting, new, important, etc., but the professor was so offensive and racist that I couldn't get past that." Literally students have said they are so offended that they don't want to read or come to class. This is just another version of the passive "entertain me or give me my money back" consumer model of education that so many students seem to demand. It is a close relative of the "we just want to learn . . . " line that I get with regularity: it goes something like "Well, I don't have any experience with these issues, so I'm just here to learn from you and the other students in the class." Yet the students who spout that line consistently come to class without reading the assigned texts, ostensibly because I have offended their fragile sensibilities.

I have often wondered why students so certain they cannot benefit from my awful teaching remain in my classes. I received an email from a student outlining how she felt attacked and offended by my comments in class and a video I showed the first week. She ended with the following statements:

> I think this class is very informative and I am learning more in it than I do in most of my other classes . . . . However; I wanted to speak from the standpoint of a girls [sic] who is aesthetically white. Just as all Asians and Latinos do not want to be categorizied, hopefully neither do white peo-ple. I just ask you to be careful with who you point the finger at because I don't think it's productive to bitch about stupid white men. It's very disheartening to come to class and feel badly for being born white and priviledged [sic]. Also, I think it's wonderful to inspire activism in young people on any level, but it's also hard to be categorized as "white," and therefore "bad." I don't want to be damned if I do and damned if I don't. I hope you understand why I wrote this email and I will continue to come

to your class and learn about what I can do to be a better person . . . white or not . . .

I suppose I am to believe that this student bestowed some great favor upon me by condescending to stay in my class to receive disembodied information in spite of my onerous presence. bell hooks has identified this attitude and expectation as the "mammification" of faculty of color—who are adored and welcome to impart their knowledge until or unless they hurt the delicate feelings of privileged students by calling out their privileges. Then they are slapped back into place.[9]

I do gain affirmation from many of my varied teaching experiences and from students of color, queer students, and white and working-class students who express their appreciation for my work in real, tangible ways. I also take great pride in the possibility that I am challenging those students suffering from white, upper class, and heterosexual privilege. At other times, however, I feel disgusted and outraged that these same students can use these privileges to be hostile, exercise "contrapower harassment,"[10] and either dismiss my teaching in favor of a less-threatening, "nice," white professor or condescend to take (quite literally) from me the perspectives and knowledge I offer. More importantly, they can use their demand power to control the shape and direction of the curriculum, whether in women's studies or any other discipline that is subject to students' maligning, devaluing, or discrediting those identified as liberal professors or the subjects they undertake to teach.

Strategies of Counterresistance

In the context of such vulnerability and obstacles to our work, I believe women of color faculty and others wishing to engage these issues must develop methods to advance the work as well as strategies to counter the resistance we inevitably face. Over the past few years—in my efforts to develop the field of women of color studies—I have created and tested a few pilot strategies to implement this ambitious endeavor. While the results of these tests are not all in, I offer them here and invite suggestions for others.

The first strategy is to use political theater and various other modes of popular education to draw on the lived experiences of students and enliven the curriculum. True to my principle that we must create better alternatives to whatever we critique, I started a group to create a student production of the *Vagina Dialogues*,[11] our alternative to the ubiquitous *Vagina Monologues*. The *Vagina Dialogues* grew out of heated conversations with the exclusively white cast of *The Vagina Monologues*, many of whom were students in my class who were upset with my critiques and indignant that they had tried to recruit women of color to their group, yet bewildered that none had joined. The *Vagina Dialogues* proved to be a thoroughly rewarding means of creating a community among women of color and white allies on the UCSB campus.

---

9   bell hooks conveyed this in a public presentation and personal conversation at Evergreen State College in the fall of 2002 at a "Day of Absence, Day of Presence" event.

10 Katherine Benson coined the term "contrapower harassment" in 1984 to explain the dynamic when students, who ostensibly have no formal power over their teachers, draw on sociocultural power based on race, class, gender, etc. to harass them (Buchanan and Bruce 2004–5).

11 We changed the name of the group to Women Of color Revolutionary Dialogues (WORD).

It also served as a support group and space for students to articulate and share their understanding and experience of feminist issues through powerful analyses and expression in the pieces they wrote, performed, and directed. Our multiracial cast chose to address issues of race, rape, sexual harassment, adultery, anger, racism in the academy and nonprofit world, capitalist "development," sex work, trafficking, self-identity, survival, and communities of resistance. Most importantly, each piece reflected women's analyses and understandings of their experiences with oppression and the ways they resisted without casting themselves as the caricature of the hyperoppressed woman of color or Third World woman.

A second strategy I have tried is to tackle the issues of racism and internalized racism among people of color or other oppressions within and between racial groups. Thus, I draw on the work of mixed-race studies scholars such as Carol Camper, a mixed, black Canadian woman, who speaks of "colourism" as the "legacy of colonization" and the history of colonizers "giving local mixed race people access to things their unmixed sisters and brothers would never have" to recruit light-skinned, mixed-race people into the role of oppressors (2004, 180). I draw a comparison here between mixed-race people and white women, who are each given a small measure of privilege for agreeing to uphold or conform to society's racial hierarchy, yet are never given the full privileges of equality with white men.

We venture into even more delicate and dangerous territory when we discuss, for example, class conflicts within racial groups or conflicts among communities of color. I am often a bit reluctant to introduce these issues in an already embattled or unequipped group of students, but whenever I hesitate, I am immediately reminded that there is no way to avoid these issues, and we cannot afford to do so. Thus, in our discussions of welfare rights or reproductive rights abuses of women of color, more often than I'd wish the situation arises where a black man or woman student eagerly advocates or defends the very social controls I am attempting to expose and critique.

For example, in the discussion of the CRACK program I described earlier, a black man and biracial black/white woman were both singing the praises of this racist, ableist, and eugenicist campaign based on the usual specter of "black women crack addicts leaving their babies in garbage cans," as one student put it. When I asked where these images had come from and whether these students had ever had personal contact with someone who was addicted to crack, one student recalled a distant relative, and the eyes of the other students in the class grew bigger. Yet I suspect that neither of these students have much basis for personal empathy or even an abstract understanding of the lives of drug-addicted women of color since their exposure has been mostly limited to the prevailing representations, whether through media images or the policy and academic discourses that serve to demonize, pathologize, and criminalize poor women of color. Nevertheless, I believe that when these two black students voiced their perspectives, it had at least two results: (1) for some students, perhaps, it validated the criminalization of women of color, convincing them that if even black people advocate these social-control measures, they can't be racist or wrong; (2) for some students, I can only hope, it demonstrated the destructive power of racist images to influence people of color to blame other people of color for the host of social problems for which US society and government have already indicted them.

In the past year—in the context of the immigrant-rights and immigration-policy debates—I have had many teachable moments or opportunities to discuss how people of color are vilified and scapegoated in similar ways, and the broader phe-nomenon of how poor people of color are deliberately and systematically divided against each other. For example, in the wake of proposals to criminalize undocu-mented immigrants as felons, a Chicana student was outraged to learn of the images of the pregnant Latina target in the *Grand Theft Auto* video game. I responded that the character was a creation of the US government before it became the twinkle in any entertainment corporation's eye. This gave me an occasion to review the history of Native and black women (alongside women with disabilities) being por-trayed as hyperfertile or unfit for reproduction to justify their forced sterilization and reproductive control and the denial of public support and basic needs for their devalued children.

The same student went on to say that she was very upset whenever she heard people making comments about Latinos allegedly stealing jobs from African Ameri-cans. Several students in the class—both black and white—had adopted an anti-immigrant position on the basis of this myth. Again this was an opportunity not only to dispel the myth but to use it as a potent illustration of the way government, media and private-citizen groups like the Minutemen perpetuate such images to try to pit poor people of color against each other ideologically, while, at the same time, liter-ally dividing them through workfare, contract labor, guest worker, strikebreaking and other bad labor practices (Hutchinson 2006; Chang 2000).

It is important for students of color to know the histories of these divide-and-conquer tactics so they may see the effects—such as black/Latino conflicts—as the result of these racist policies and practices, engineered by the state rather than inherently or inevitably preordained as a feature of multiracial society, as some would like us to believe. I have also found that this focus can be a useful strategy in teaching white students because it takes the lens away from white people without "letting them off the hook." It does not allow white people to be unaccountable, but perhaps it lets them externalize the inquiry and better recognize patterns of racism at an institutional level and in historical context. Moreover, it expands the possibilities for both white people and people of color to take leadership in con-fronting state abuses of power and interrupting media representations or academic discourses that enable these abuses.

To return to my starting point in this essay, my aim is not to identify individual white men or women as the enemy but to challenge students to identify the sites and structures of power that have been used to perpetrate violence and injustice against women of color and their communities. Western feminism as an academic discourse and practice has often been such a site. I share a hope with several of my colleagues that women of color studies—as a field, a method, an ethic—can be more subversive than what women's studies has become.

I believe we must look very closely at what our students demand to be served in their women's studies curriculum and the manner in which they demand to be served as well. When they derail discussions about racism and default to the media as villain and the celebrity "vagina warriors" as heroes,[12] when they resist qualitative methods because they leave rich white people out of the center for a moment, when they refuse to see the links between the privileges they enjoy and the exploitations

---

12   Celebrities and others who have participated in the *The Vagina Monologues* are often awarded
      the title of "vagina warriors."

others suffer, yet they still insist on discussing violence—without consideration of race, class, sexuality, disability, and nation—as a staple of women's studies courses, something has gone terribly awry.

At the core, I believe the demand for including violence in the women's studies curriculum—alongside the inability to see racism, classism, homophobia, ableism, and imperialism as forms of violence—is both a reflection of and a mechanism to solidify US white women's privilege. Privileged white women cannot stand not being able to claim status as victims of gender oppression when race, class, sexuality, dis/ability, and nation complicate this status. While I have suggested that privileged white, Western women also enjoy the role of savior and will readily cast women of color and Third World women in the victim role to capture the liberator role for themselves, when confronted with their possible collusion in the oppression of others, they quickly claim the status of the victimized.

Audre Lorde asks in her classic essay, "The Uses of Anger," "What woman here is so enamoured of her own oppression that she cannot see her heelprint upon another woman's face? What woman's terms of oppression have become precious and necessary to her as a ticket into the fold of the righteous, away from the cold winds of self-scrutiny?" (1984, 132).

What woman indeed? As I've observed, there are far too many for comfort. Yet if white, Western women truly want to cling to the identity of the victim, then let them identify clearly who the victimizer is. Like Laura Nader, I believe that white, Western women are indeed no better off than women of color or non-Western women in certain terms. I suggest that many of the white women I've encountered are victims of US racist, imperialist ideologies and have been largely duped into believing they are more liberated than other women by the very system that enables US racist, capitalist, patriarchal, imperialist violence to be visited upon people all over the world.

My hope is that women of color studies can provide a viable, powerful, radical alternative to these ideologies that have been deeply embedded in traditional women's studies to date and brought feminist thought and practice to a perilous impasse. The promise of women of color studies is open up new possibilities for US feminists beyond the old tired roles of victim or savior. Gayatri Spivak brilliantly describes the racist colonial project in and outside the academy as violence done under the banner of "white men saving brown women from brown men" (1988, 784). We must be equally wary of being violated by white women who wish to save us against our wills. As I often tell my students, women of color are fully capable of saving our own damn selves.

Epilogue

The year I wrote "Where's the Violence?" I was in the throes of preparing for a tenure review and had survived the first few years of teaching in a new, often-hostile context where my characterization of my profession as a "career of living dangerously" hardly felt like hyperbole—and still doesn't. I have witnessed some of my dearest and most respected friends and colleagues—men and women of color— lose their physical health and spiritual well-being from the blows of navigating these treacherous waters as faculty of color.

I have also experienced waves of surprising job satisfaction and pride and joy in my work on all levels: teaching in many modes as a professor and mentor and community building through my spoken-word/political-theater group WORD

(Women Of color Revolutionary Dialogues). These alternate with waves of supreme dissatisfaction, disenchantment, and anger as I try to advocate for and advise my undergraduate and graduate students along the way. I find that many women of color graduate students who have studied and taught with me read this piece with recognition, if not dread, and both see their experiences in the trenches as teaching assistants affirmed and foresee with some trepidation the long road ahead of them. I simultaneously encourage and caution them as they navigate their own ways through this dangerous territory of the academy, often saying, "I will support you 100 percent if you stay, but if you choose to leave, I'll support you in that also," and we joke about the street in Santa Barbara ominously named Salsipuedes, translated roughly as "get out while/if you can."

What has changed since the year I wrote this piece? I have received tenure and—more significantly to me—been nominated for a number of teaching and service awards. I have also earned the dubious distinction of having David Horowitz list me and post the syllabi for my undergraduate courses on his Web site under the heading "Indoctrination Studies" as examples of the way I and other left-wing faculty are poisoning the minds of young, innocent students with our propaganda. Upon finding these, a colleague wrote to congratulate me, saying that he hadn't yet made it onto the list. I even received a hateful email from a UCSB alumnus who had seen the Horowitz post and wanted to let me know that he would not be donating to the university because of the likes of me. But I have also received real affirmation from students who truly appreciate my teaching and scholarship. And one parent whose daughter asked him to visit my class with her took the time to write this:

> You are obviously passionate about and knowledgeable of the subject matter, but I was mesmerized by the interaction with your students. Even in a large lecture hall, you have attracted the attention of these young minds to the importance and (unfortunately) the prevalence of racism and gender bias in our government's "welfare" programs and immigration legislation. Thank you for positively contributing to my daughter's education by providing a very special and valuable insight into our society. You are one of the reasons that UCSB is a world-class university.

While these various forms of praise (intended or not) are heartening, I am still constantly reminded that I cannot afford to rest on my laurels and expect to preach to the converted.

I have certainly seen a noticeable shift after the huge budget cuts to the University of California/California State University system and public education at large that took effect in the past two academic years and continue to be visited upon us. They have had devastating effects on the quality of life for students as well as for staff and faculty struggling to serve more students with fewer resources and less support for the hard work of teaching against the tide of hate. The racist, sexist, homophobic, ableist, anti-immigrant, antilabor, and antipoor forces mounting rapidly under populist banners do not represent an abstract backdrop to our teaching but are the scary realities of our lives and those of our students.

Yet I have found during these years of cutbacks that the more obstacles students across the board face, and the more that students have to struggle to receive and create a quality education for themselves, the less distance there seems to be between the concepts I am presenting about social justice and community organizing and the struggles that they face every day. Recently, at least, it seems that as I am ranting against the state and capitalism, I look out in my undergraduate lecture halls and see less disbelief in my students' faces and more recognition, more rage—as well as more sorrow. I feel that this effect may already be fading some, however, as the effects of the budget cuts manifest in those students whose only means to education is financial aid vanish as quickly as the aid does. It remains to be seen how the cuts to federal and state student aid and loans will change the face of the student body in our classrooms on California public campuses.

One response I still get from students regularly in course evaluations is some variation of this: "I left class crying every time. It was just so depressing to hear about all of these terrible things happening. I wish the professor had focused more on how we could help these people." Recently I have also had a rather hostile, defensive version of this question directed at me in a lecture class: "Well, what are we supposed to do if we ARE privileged? Are we just supposed to sit there and do nothing?" This remark came in response to my critique of certain paternalistic and maternalistic figures—academics, journalists, or organizers—operating in what I call "white knight" or "sister/savior" mode. I responded by putting my planned lecture on hold and opening up the discussion to comments from other students in the class. Several students have since remarked that it was one of the most important and engaging discussions they've had in a college course.

As I responded in class that day, my answer to these questions is both complicated and very simple. In some cases, it is "yes, sit there and do nothing except step back and educate yourself." This is part of some basic principles of community organizing and good allyship that I try to teach. The idea is to do no harm but also to get out of the way and leave it to those communities that are impacted to identify and define what the problem is and how to solve it. I ask students to consider then—and only then—how they as true allies may offer whatever resources, access, and labor their privilege affords them to contribute to the movement work, if they are invited.

But on another level, my response is another question that I may direct back to these students: Why do you insist on fashioning yourself as the one who can or should help? Is the problem solely that of the poor, downtrodden others that you imagine are waiting or in need of your help? Or is this very attitude the problem—or, perhaps I might ask less threateningly, is the problem also yours? Isn't the point of working for social change to make a more just society where all people can expect to have their basic needs met and live free from exploitation, persecution, and exclusion? Poet and activist Sonia Sanchez cautions us to scrutinize all theory or practice that some claim to be liberatory and asks, "But how do it free us?" (Uh Huh; But How Do It Free Us?, 1974). And by this she means all of us. Is it liberatory for all people? Because if we work for our freedom to live in a better world, ideally it is neither a selfish nor a magnanimous thing but the right thing to do.

Part III
Networks of Allies

Introduction

Nancy Cantor

Stereotypes and oppression manifest themselves in a multitude of ways. Attuned to the power structures of the day, they operate simultaneously at overt and subconscious levels that are both deeply personal and profoundly political. Their targets and victims are thwarted and injured as individuals and as members of groups. Even those who struggle for social justice are vulnerable to cruel divisions and to being played off against each other and against themselves. The premise of this volume, as Sylvia R. Lazos captures it, is that "whites and men start from a presumption of competence" and "minorities and women do not and have to deal with a multitude of unconscious biases that put them at a disadvantage. The playing field is not level." To read *Presumed Incompetent* is to confront with painful clarity the forces that divide and diminish our society on the basis of race, gender, class, sexual orientation, and disability. In many of these chapters, the authors have been courageous enough to disclose the "thousand paper cuts" that afflict their personal lives as women of color (Mason and Goulden 2002, 21-27), as well as the great gaps and barriers that have afflicted their hopes, families, communities, and careers.

It is particularly important that their arena is academia because higher education is playing a vital role in shaping the present and the future. Colleges and universities offer a potent opportunity for transformation because women have reached something like a critical mass in these places. Now we need the vision that this book offers to move ahead with the reasonable measures it recommends. While it's true that women have become the majority population on campus, earning 60 percent of the undergraduate and half of the PhDs and professional degrees awarded each year (Shriver 2009), the aggregate figures fail to reveal the dire situation of women of color. As this volume makes clear, they are subject to two, three, or even four levels of stereotyping and discrimination. They are in a position, as the National Academy recently reported, that can only be described as "extreme" (2007, 14). Between 1989 and 1997, the proportion of tenured minority women went down (National Academy 2007, 19). Donna Shalala has observed that "women scientists and engineers with minority racial and ethnic backgrounds are virtually absent from the nation's leading science and engineering departments" (National Academy 2007, xi–xii). As recently as five years ago, there were no African American, Hispanic, or Native American women in tenured or tenure-track faculty positions in the nation's "top 50" computer-science departments (D. J. Nelson 2005; National Academy 2007, 19). And in the "top 50" physical sciences and engineering departments, no Native

221

American woman and only one African American woman held the position of full professor (National Academy 2007, 19).

Delia D. Douglas, a black Canadian independent scholar, argues in her chapter that the culture of whiteness has created an atmosphere that maintains the status quo, "namely the attitudes of white entitlement and racial superiority." "We need to take seriously the consequences of years of structured racial exclusion and the power of unacknowledged whiteness," she maintains, "so that we can better respond to the complex and varied manifestations of racial oppression and the incalculable damage that these forms of discrimination have caused." She and other authors are responding to third-wave feminism, with its orientation to the diverse experiences and oppression of women, in contrast to earlier feminist forms that sought to appeal to ideas of universal sisterhood and have ended up favoring white women, particularly if they are upper or middle class. It is within the fabric of difference—the authors of the chapters in this book argue—that progress can be made.

Talking across differences among groups requires them to acknowledge the vast differences within them, differences that are both rich and problematic for many of their members. We have both a moral and a practical obligation to recognize—not deny—that other group-based markings—race, sexual orientation, class, and disability—are at work among women. It's both difficult and important that women who are white—the relatively privileged ones who have been the primary beneficiaries of feminism—perceive, acknowledge, and then act against the additional forms of discrimination experienced by women of color without feeling defensive. While it's true that most white women of a certain age have been "presumed incompetent" at one time or another, women of color continue to suffer far more. We are overdue for a change.

The struggles for women's rights and racial justice are historically intertwined. Many of the early suffragists were radicalized by the discrimination they experienced as women in movements for temperance and abolition.[1] Elizabeth Cady Stanton and Lucretia Mott were both refused seats at the World Anti-Slavery Convention in London in 1840. Susan B. Anthony, who was president of the Daughters of Temperance in Rochester, New York, was not allowed to speak at the state convention of the Sons of Temperance in Albany. From the beginning, women have realized that justice makes many demands. Anthony was also an agent for the American Anti-Slavery Society. (For these efforts, she was hung in effigy, and her image was dragged through the streets of Syracuse.) Jane Addams, the founder of Hull House in Chicago, was also the first president of the Women's International League for Peace and Freedom and went on to support the founding of the NAACP and, later, the American Civil Liberties Union. Nannie Helen Burroughs, the prominent black educator, suffragist, and church leader who set up women's industrial clubs all over the South, captured this spirit in her motto for the school for African American women and girls she founded in Washington, D.C., in 1909: "We Specialize in the Wholly Impossible."

In many respects, the genius of the women's movement and the transformative legacy of its leaders have been the persistent call from outside the walls of "normal institutions" for those inside to change their ways, along with the willingness of

---

1   The stories of these women and many others are available from the National Women's History Museum online at http://www.nwhm.org/.

women to get inside and show them how. This outside-inside dialectic is worth our attention today as we push to make higher education more inclusive, more innovative, and more valuable, working from both the outside and the inside.

In this effort, we also have modern-day heroines to inspire us. Anita Hill, who was courageous enough to speak publicly about sexual harassment and the abuse of power in the workplace during the confirmation hearings for Supreme Court Justice Clarence Thomas in 1991, has described this transformative role as "Insider Women with Outsider Values," using as her subjects two other exceptional women—Coleen Rowley and Sherron Watkins, who challenged highly respected male-dominated institutions—the FBI and Enron—and pushed for reform as insiders (Hill 2002). As Hill noted, these two outstanding women, as leaders, had access to information and authority over others, as well as heightened awareness of the resistance within their institutions to any efforts at change. It's likely that this knowledge deepened their resolve to speak out—in their cases, "to blow the whistle." Hill articulated a critical contrast between *insider* status—positions of authority and leadership within previously male-dominated institutions—and *outsider* values. At any given moment, we may all be insiders or outsiders, depending on the circumstances. To transform the world of academia, we must hold on to our outsider values when we get inside, making spaces to bring in others who are on the margins or still outside.

To build diversity and inclusion in our institutions and disciplines—to construct what the legal scholar Susan Sturm calls an "architecture of inclusion" (2006, 247-334)—we need more than numbers. As the authors in this volume argue, we must create a healthy academic climate. This requires a culture of collaboration where issues of intersectionality can be addressed. Inclusion requires justice and due process. It also needs the give and take of social support, of flexibility of models and respect for individual and group differences, and, perhaps most daringly, of risk taking where leaders and others are free to make mistakes and change course. Yolanda Flores Niemann's conclusion deserves careful reading, discussion, and action. We have an opportunity to create a "new normal," to establish policies and foster practices that will become second nature in the culture of departments and units because they truly expand the possibilities of excellence for everyone.

CHAPTER 15

WORKING ACROSS RACIAL LINES IN A NOT-SO-POST-RACIAL WORLD

Margalynne J. Armstrong and Stephanie M. Wildman[1]

Both women of color and white women may face a presumption of incompetence when they enter the law school classroom as professors. Due to centuries of excluding women and people of color from the professoriate, white men "receive a benefit of the doubt, a little chip of 'you belong here,' that others may not receive" as they approach the podium (Wildman 1996, 165). Presumptions of the competence of white men and the incompetence of others arise from the creation of dominant stereotypes in the legal academy and profession.[2] The archetypal law professor is white, male, heterosexual, and older. He channels Professor Kingsfield of *The Paper Chase*, who knows all and represents the quintessential societal image of competence (Osborn 2003).

Yet even with the presence of a presumption of incompetence documented throughout this book, women of all races face skepticism from white male colleagues that this presumption even exists across gender lines. And people of color face skepticism that the presumption exists across racial lines. White male professors may regard the notion that they enjoy a presumption of competence offensive

---

1   The authors thank Ellen Platt, research librarian extrordinaire, and Lea Patricia L. Francisco, superlative research assistant.

2   Lawyers of color report a similar presumption of incompetence. After describing the minuscule numbers of lawyers of color in Massachusetts, the small proportion of women, and the relative youth of attorneys of color, the three Asian American attorneys write, "These demographics reinforce the image—held even by the client community—of the consummate lawyer as an older, white man. Anyone who does not fit this bill is presumed to be less effective" (Lai, Leong, and Wu 2000, 29). One African American female attorney anecdotally told the authors that she had introduced herself by name in a courtroom of plaintiffs and defendants' counsel. After the introductions, one man said, "We are just waiting for the lawyer." He had assumed she was court personnel rather than an attorney present to represent her client. Stereotypes about who could be a lawyer—racing that person white and gendering him male—made her feel like an outsider, even though she belonged in the courtroom.

because they, too, work hard at their jobs (Osborn 2003). Naturally students discount any poor teacher, but these presumptions relating to competence and incompetence operate before anyone says a word. Presumptions can come into play the moment a professor walks to the podium. Any identity category—such as race, age, sexual orientation, nationality, accent, or disability—that varies from the stereotype of competence can trigger the presumption of incompetence.

This presumption of incompetence—faced by many men and women of color—led Jerome Culp's students to ask him every year, "Where did you go to law school?" (1991, 543). Culp, an African American, came to realize that this question really meant, "What qualifies you to teach me?" (1991, 543).[3] Both people of color and white women must prove themselves in the classroom, as well as in other aspects of institutional life. They must overcome the presumption of incompetence that their mere appearance triggers. That classroom reaction to the professor may become a litmus test for retention by the institution. Thus, professors of color (and anyone who triggers the presumption of incompetence) face an added challenge to overcome—not always recognized by their colleagues—in negotiating a retention process that relies heavily on student evaluations.[4]

Although women of color and white women both face a presumption of incompetence, it operates differently across racial lines and other identity categories. Systems of privilege based on race, sexual orientation, economic wealth, and physical ability remain key attributes that crosscut gender, amplifying and affecting the presumption's meaning for all women. For example, the gender presumption of incompetence may mesh with student attitudes about gender roles. Some students expect female professors to be mother, "mammy," or "nanny" figures. Thus, professorial competence becomes entangled in these expectations. A white woman whom students do not perceive as nurturing enough may receive harsh evaluations, even though being maternal is not part of any law professor's job description.

The existence of presumed incompetence that affects both women of color and white women should provide a basis for deeper understanding, sisterhood, and alliance among women and enable work across racial lines to combat the presumption as well as other professional issues. But women can only forge that bond by acknowledging—rather than ignoring—the differences in the presumption's operation. Systems of privilege operate through multiple identity categories and affect a professor's institutional presence and possibilities. Beyond acknowledging difference, white women in particular should be motivated to learn about the impact of race and how it matters (C. West 1993). People of color must not be the only ones to care

---

3   Culp reflects, "I understand that question to be, 'What gives *you* the right to teach this course to *me*?" (1991, 543; emphasis in the original). Who we are matters as much as what we are and what we think. It is important to teach our students that there is a "me" in the law, as well as specific rules that are animated by our experience.

4   "Student prejudices continue to pollute student evaluations, especially when a professor of a different race or culture is involved" (Solender 1995, 255); " . . . the professor might make the pragmatic choice to avoid race, for fear that talking about it would result in his receiving negative evaluations" (Carbado and Gulati, 2000b, 1284). In an extensive study on the way American law schools evaluate their faculty and how these evaluations are used, Richard Abel notes that, because "law faculties have become much more diverse in terms of gender, race, sexual orientation, and political perspective during the last twenty-five years" and "legal education requires students to question their most fundamental values . . . student reactions to teachers will be highly charged and personal" (1990, 451).

about race, nor should they shoulder the primary responsibility for educating white colleagues, who also have a race, about the role of race in society. A commitment to antiracism work is foundational to working across racial lines.

This chapter begins by examining color blindness and the ongoing salience of race. It continues by exploring the significance of the workplace as a site for antiracism work. It next considers ways to work across racial lines by using color insight. Three key aspects of color insight provide tools for working across racial lines to combat the presumption of incompetence: (1) examining systems of privilege, (2) unmasking perspectivelessness, and (3) combating stereotyping and looking for the "me" in each individual. Institutional barriers that support the presumption of incompetence and inhibit work across racial lines in academia remain. Finally, the chapter turns to friendships, coalitions, and working together, suggesting ways to lay the foundation for combating the presumption of incompetence. Interwoven through the chapter appear stories taken from the life of fictitious law professor Teresa Vallero, who has both encountered and observed the dynamics this chapter identifies.

Color Blindness and the Ongoing Importance of Race

Learning about race and understanding the way it operates in society is a key step for whites seeking to work across racial lines. Society purports to prize color blindness, and that goal makes it hard to see race in public spaces. Race is the elephant in the room that everyone tiptoes around (P. Williams 1991, 49). Attorney General Eric Holder has said that the US is a "nation of cowards" when it comes to discussing race with each other (Meyer 2009, 10). A *Newsweek* cover article, provocatively titled "Is Your Baby Racist?" (Bronson and Merryman 2009, 53), points out that the failure to talk about race with children, even when they participate in multiracial educational environments, makes it harder for them to make friends across racial lines. Verbalizing the presence of race can change that dynamic. Failure to talk about race in any sphere—from family life, throughout school, and culminating in the law school classroom—perpetuates racial separation.

As color blindness has emerged as a dominant aspiration in our society, conversation about race has become even more difficult. People of color know that society racializes them into a race other than white. Yet whites often do not think about race, except when they notice people of color as having one. Whites tend not to notice that they, too, have a race. Whites often aspire to color blindness but fail to see the whiteness that privileges them in so many societal interactions.

Whites may fear that talking about race makes them seem racist. It would be more helpful for everyone to notice when race and racism are actually present and think about how to combat the problem. Society cannot battle a phantom that it cannot recognize and name. Whites ignore race at their peril and risk causing unintended harm to colleagues of color as the dynamics of racism grind on their daily lives.

Beyond society's aspiration for color blindness and belief that a color-blind era exists in contemporary US society, the election of President Barack Obama introduced the notion that the United States has entered a postracial era (Wickham 2009, 11A; Harper 2008, A1; Page 2008, 40; Graham 2008, A12; Mitchell 2000, A12). Supporting the wish for color blindness, the idea of a postracial country suggests that race no longer matters because a black man can become president. Ian Haney López (2010) contests this postracial hypothesis in a powerful essay detailing the ongoing racial hierarchy in the United States, using disparities evidenced by the mass incarceration of minorities to illustrate his thesis. Haney López observes, "The nation elected Obama in the midst of profound economic, martial, environmental, and constitutional crises. Perhaps the crises, coupled with Obama's exceptional racial background—combining Kenya and Kansas, an immigrant success story, and the positive exotic of Hawaii—better explain his election than any purported fundamental shift in racial attitudes" (2010, 1024). Beyond the criminal justice system, patterns of wealth and land allocation also show that the structure of ownership has been built on a legacy of racial oppression—favoring whites to the detriment of people of color, particularly blacks (Armstrong 1998; Mahoney 1995; Oliver and Shapiro 1995; Roisman 2002; S. Cashin 2004).

Other examples of the ongoing salience of race abound in the daily press, belying the notion of a postracial reality. Whether a private swim club excludes black children (Urbina 2009, A11), police arrest a prominent African American professor on his own front porch (Goodnough 2009, A13), or a Latina Supreme Court nominee is accused of racial bias (Baker and Lewis 2009), race remains a lens that tempers the lived reality for everyone. Yet legal educational institutions—perhaps more than any others—encourage the acceptance of color blindness as the standard lens for envisioning racial issues in the United States.

*   *   *   *

Teresa Vallero gazed out the window of her office. She was sitting at her desk at Holmes Law School, where she had been hired 15 years earlier (Wildman 1990, 1996). Teresa had graduated Phi Beta Kappa from a prestigious national university, earned membership in Order of the Coif at a top midwestern law school, served as articles editor of its law review, clerked for a federal appellate judge, and published a student note and two articles in peer-reviewed law journals. Those credentials usually opened doors for teaching candidates. Teresa even had prior teaching experience; she had taught at a law school before returning to practice law for several years before considering teaching again. She did not regret the decision to return to the academy. But race played a role in faculty hiring and retention decisions and not the part often assumed—that "less-qualified minorities" snuck in the door. Rather, candidates of color had to prove they were outstanding—better than white candidates—even to have a hiring or tenure committee consider them (Wildman 1990, 1644; 1996, 103).

Teresa proudly told her students that she was an "affirmative-action professor." She used the phrase to emphasize that it had taken a national commitment to integration before white institutions noticed that they remained segregated. Only then did these institutions begin admitting some of the many qualified candidates of color who sought to enter the professoriate. Yet Teresa worried that students might misinterpret her remark. Her colleague Jessica Kearny, a senior white professor, had told Teresa about the unwritten rules that shaped faculty hiring decisions and the institutional struggle that had occurred to enable Teresa being hired (Wildman 1990, 1668–69; 1996, 106–10). Jessica had cared enough to be a moving force in getting Teresa hired. Jessica's behind-the-scenes work was part of the institutional politics conducted in hallways and office meetings that accompanied Teresa's contested hire. That struggle had occurred—even though Teresa possessed stellar credentials of the traditional academic sort—because she was a black Latina, and tall at that.

Although race remains a fixture in the daily news, US culture exhibits little depth of understanding about the topic. The norm of color blindness made it hard even to talk about race, especially in a mixed-race group. Teresa thought to herself how glad she was that she now had other colleagues of color and white colleagues with whom she could raise issues of racial justice without being censored by the color blindness rule. "Talking about race can promote color insight," Teresa thought, "and I could use some insight into the upcoming tenure vote for Karen Romero." Teresa returned to her computer and wrote to Jessica and Constance, one of the first white female law professors, to try to find a time for lunch.

* * * *

The Significance of the Workplace as a Site for Antiracism Work

The importance of working across racial lines within the legal profession becomes urgently clear when you consider current demographic shifts in population. Soon no numerical racial majority will exist in the United States. Yet in law schools and the legal profession, whites remain a substantial majority of the attorneys who provide essential services to every segment of the population. Lawyers and academicians need to be particularly concerned about the declining enrollment of black male students and the continued underrepresentation of other nonwhite communities in the legal profession (Nussbaumer 2006; Koppel 2006; Mustakeem 2007).[5] Studies show that minority students are more likely to return to and work in their communities (Desmond-Harris 2007; Hamlar 1983).[6] Legal professionals should aspire to serve all members of society.

Many states mandate antibias training as part of their continuing legal-education requirements. This commitment to antibias work by the bar reflects its importance in ensuring attorney competence. So even as minority numbers decline in the pipeline of those becoming lawyers, bar organizations recognize that multicultural skills enhance attorney effectiveness.

The workplace is an important site for antiracism work for another reason. Residential housing patterns in the United States remain mostly segregated, as do schools. The workplace has become the location where adults are "most likely to associate regularly with someone of another race" (Estlund 2003, 3). Some scholars have pointed to an erosion of social capital in American society (Estlund 2003, 5). Robert Putnam (2000) captured the image of loss of connection with family, friends, neighbors, and democratic structures with the image of "bowling alone." Putnam observed that more Americans are bowling than ever before, but they are not bowling in leagues. So this phenomenon—bowling alone—refers to the decline in informal socialization that occurs by participating in groups as disparate as the

---

5   John Nussbaumer notes that "the total number of African-Americans enrolled at all ABA-approved law schools peaked in 1994 at 9,681 students, which at that time represented 7.5% of all enrolled students . . . . From 1994-2004 . . . total African American enrollment decreased from 9,681 to 9,488 students (-2%), which represents just 6.8% of all enrolled students" (2006, 167–68). Nathan Koppel cites American Bar Association statistics (1995–2005) that, while the enrollment numbers for white law students increased by 6 percent, the ones for black students decreased by 2 percent).

6   Portia Hamlar discusses the social justifications for having a minority lawyer represent minority clients.

PTA and church groups to professional organizations as well as bowling leagues (Putnam 2000). Participation in those groups had once produced a social capital of norms and trust that created the backbone of democracy (Putnam 2000).

Cynthia Estlund posits that—as people in the US spend less time developing these participatory contacts—the necessity of workplace interactions to sustain democratic practice increases (2003, 6). So the stake in working across racial lines is higher than merely individual on-the-job comfort; it also includes the potential for building the connectedness necessary to make democracy work.

Estlund explains,

> The burden of working under the weight of prejudice and stereotypes is greatest in workplaces that are overwhelmingly white, in which African-American or Latino or Asian workers, or even all of these groups together, make up a relatively small minority of the workforce. Black professional and managerial employees in particular—a comparatively privileged minority within a minority—have recounted experiences of hostility, denigration, and paternalism on the part of white co-workers who assume them to be less able (2003, 82).

The minority professional and managerial experiences of "hostility, denigration, and paternalism" that Estlund describes impact the lives of professors of color who enter the academy with the presumption of incompetence. Law professors serve a role akin to managers, working with the dean and other administrators in a supposed collegial setting to govern the law school.

When the workplace is a law school, institutional barriers may make work across racial lines even more difficult. Law schools are not known for being nurturing environments. Larry Catá Backer writes about law teaching and law schools:

> [Law teaching] is a very conservative profession. Whatever the politics and political ideology of the members of the community of scholars—from hard left to hard right and everything in between, from activist to pacifist—together this community of scholar-teachers is quite conservative in its communal organization. Its mechanics reward and value conformity to communal norms. It highly prizes the reproduction of expectations and the performance of its rituals in the form of scholarship of a certain kind and teaching effected through communally endorsed methods. Like all communities, the community of American legal academics is concerned about the preservation of its norms and cultural boundaries (2009).

The norms and cultural boundaries of legal academics are products of a specific, educationally elite subset of the larger society in which the schools operate.

Reflecting on these societal norms, most law schools would contend that they espouse objectivity and neutral principles. Kimberlé Crenshaw critiques this objectivity/neutrality myth.

> In many instances, minority students' values, beliefs, and experiences clash not only with those of their classmates but also with those of their professors. Yet because of the dominant view in academe that legal analysis can be taught without directly addressing conflicts of individual values, experiences, and world views, these conflicts seldom, if ever, reach the surface of

the classroom discussion. Dominant beliefs in the objectivity of legal discourse serve to suppress the conflict by discounting the relevance of any particular perspective in legal analysis and by positing an analytical stance that has no specific cultural, political, or class characteristics (1994b, 35).

Crenshaw calls this dominant mode *perspectivelessness*. This theoretically neutral lack of perspective perfectly diverts students and professors from examining the way whiteness and many other factors inform law school culture. In spite of the belief in objectivity, subjective components in institutional choices about hiring, retention, and promotion remain inevitable. Furthermore, sometimes a single value can be defined in conflicting ways. For example, congeniality is very subjective, but institutions tout that quality as if it were quantifiable. Institutions apply these subjective criteria inconsistently, so congeniality may be assessed positively in one junior colleague, but not in another. Applying inconsistent standards is often only revealed by who speaks up at a retention meeting.

One of the most crucial times for work across racial lines occurs during the retention and tenure of new law professors. The tenure track is a four- to six-year-long audition for faculty status with aspects of a fraternity initiation ritual mixed in to increase the unpleasantness. Although most schools provide written tenure standards, knowledge of the ways schools actually implement these standards is essential to professional advancement. Each law school has a unique institutional identity. Currently many law schools assign a mentor or mentoring committee to new professors, but it is also necessary to have friends among one's colleagues. And a new appointee must remember that an appointed mentor may not be a friend who can be trusted.

The position of new professors is truly precarious, even when the candidate is hard working, congenial, and a productive, respected scholar. How their mentors interact with them and present a candidate's body of work to the faculty for evaluation may determine the candidate's professional future. This process can be particularly hazardous for faculty of color and women because—in the eyes of some colleagues—any flaw evidences a failure to establish even basic competence. A perceived problem with a new teacher who has been accorded the presumption of competence can potentially be overcome. But without that presumption, assessors may decide a candidate requires improvement to achieve even baseline competence.

Thus, the neophyte professor who is presumed incompetent is at a disadvantage from the start. If an overbearing senior faculty member or a person who sees the new teacher as her acolyte becomes involved, the mentor may inflict great damage when the junior colleague does not follow the senior's advice or directions to his or her satisfaction. Other faculty members will likely view complaints that are based on the candidate's failure to comply with the mentor's directives as a professional failing. A mentor's personal disappointment should not be relevant in judging a candidate. The senior faculty member may have formulated perceptions based on the unmet expectation that the junior faculty member will be appreciative and compliant. The senior colleague's negative comments can become magnified by the bruised ego that results from the candidate's additional failure to appreciate the mentor.

* * * *

Constance greeted Jessica and Teresa as she sat down at the table. Constance had been the first woman hired at her nationally known, private law school. Although she was retired now, she still took an interest in issues relating to women, race, and the academy.

"Thanks for coming, Constance. We really wanted to talk with you because we are worried about Karen's upcoming tenure vote this coming fall," said Jessica.

"We hoped you might have some ideas," added Teresa.

Constance sighed, "I wish we didn't need these conversations anymore. I remember Karen from when she came through our school on the job market. Her presentation to the faculty showed she would be a gifted teacher, and she was very well qualified, but we couldn't get enough votes to hire her. The school already had hired a Latino and a Latina faculty member, so I guess that was the tipping point" (Bell 1986; Olivas 1994).[7]

"Well, that's one reason I came to teach at Holmes," offered Teresa. "They hadn't stopped hiring women when they got to two. They had enough women so there could be some who didn't like me!"

"So what is the issue with Karen?" asked Constance. "She was such a star on the job market."

"It's true," said Jessica. "Karen sailed through the hiring process. We knew other schools wanted her. It's like the worst part of dating: who will the prom queen pick? So she picked us. I think the problem about the way the faculty looks at her goes back to the first meeting when the faculty considered whether to renew her contract. At our school, faculty who are on the tenure track have to apply for retention every year. The candidate works with a mentoring committee that reports to the faculty about progress on the track. Everyone has a chance to review the candidate's classroom teaching and scholarship, but in reality only the committee really does that work.

"So Karen had a rough first year in the classroom. She was the only woman and only person of color (except for legal writing) that the students in her section had. You've seen her; she doesn't have a booming voice, and she is very feminine—nothing like Professor Kingsfield or students' image of a law professor. She didn't get outstanding evaluations. Her evaluations weren't worse than those of a lot of colleagues, but they have tenure, and she was under the microscope.

"Then at the review meeting, when Karen applied for retention, Gladys presented the report for the committee."

Constance groaned.

"Yes," said Teresa, "I guess you know Gladys."

Constance nodded, "We became law professors at about the same time. Not too many women in the academy then, and Gladys thought it was necessary to be as much like the men as possible. In one meeting of that early cadre of women, Gladys opined that she didn't know why we made such a fuss about teaching. 'If you work hard enough, you can be a good teacher,' she said. She wouldn't listen to our protests that just hard work might not be enough to overcome the preformed views that many students brought to our classrooms."

"I knew she was very male identified," said Jessica. "She counseled me not to take a maternity leave because she hadn't done so. She thinks her way is the right way, the only way."

---

7   Michael Olivas compiled the "dirty dozen," a list of law schools located in areas with large number of Latinos that have few or no Latino faculty members.

"Well, poor Karen," Teresa took up the thread. "At this meeting, Gladys relished being the center of attention and the source of all important information. I don't think she realized what she was doing. She underlined the evaluations, in detail, pointing to the negatives. She built herself up, explaining how she had counseled Karen, who just was not, according to Gladys, following her advice."

"I have a friend," interjected Constance, "who calls that behavior 'the white missionary syndrome.'"

"That's a good name for it," said Teresa. "I hadn't heard that before. Is that because the white person tries to colonize the younger colleague and make her feel indebted to the senior professor, who views herself as the savior?"

"Something like that," replied Constance. "It's all done under the guise of trying to help the young colleague and show how liberal minded the savior is. And it may not be guileful. The person may really believe he or she is helping but shares a view of the person of color as presumptively incompetent and needing help."

"Well, in Karen's case," reported Jessica, "the faculty leapt to a conclusion of irredeemable incompetence, so much so that one professor was ready to terminate her on the spot. The negativity of the discussion became so intense that I think it surprised Gladys, who really had considered herself one of Karen's supporters. And now in every discussion since, Karen has faced an attitude that she does not meet expectations. It is as if her candidacy is under a cloud."

"What a shame," said Constance. "It would have been so easy for a mentor to say something like 'Karen's evaluations aren't as high as she would like, and she is working on that.' It would have amounted to the same report but without glorifying Gladys. And Karen wouldn't be in this bind."

"And it snowballs. Now they are complaining about her scholarship, too," added Teresa, "even though at the first review, everyone agreed her scholarship was excellent and her new work promising. Karen published a book chapter that was dismissed as 'descriptive,' rather than normative, even though the work was quite original. She had written more than many of her colleagues, too."

"What does normative mean anyway?" asked Jessica.

"That's the point," answered Teresa. "They are using it as shorthand for 'we don't like it.' They used to say 'not rigorous enough.' But plenty of their work would not withstand their own critical lens."

"It does sound bad," said Constance. "Do you think Gladys would recognize that her behavior started the faculty's view of Karen?"

"I don't know," Jessica and Teresa both murmured at the same time, and then started laughing.

"I guess we haven't been too optimistic about Gladys," said Jessica. "I think I have no credibility with the faculty regarding a candidate of color. I've been on the front line of too many of these hiring-retention battles. They think I have 'no standards.'"

"And she's my friend," said Teresa, "a sure sign that I cannot possibly be objective about any minority faculty member or anything relating to race. And of course my objectivity cannot exist because I'm Latina, too."

"So it might be helpful," said Constance, "to find a conservative white man to speak on her behalf. That's a shame; why should those voices be valued above yours? But I have seen this movie before. I'd like to bring a new colleague to our next lunch; I'll set it up, okay?"

* * * *

Using Color Insight to Work across Racial Lines

Color insight—in contrast to color blindness—provides a tool for work across racial lines. Colleagues can use this tool to combat the presumption of incompetence and overcome the institutional barriers that inhibit cross-racial alliance.

Color Insight

Working across racial lines in the meaningful way that Estlund argues can build democratic connectedness requires color insight, which contrasts with color blindness and offers an alternative that meets the purported goals of color blindness, racial equality, and justice. Color insight recognizes that a racial status quo exists in which society attributes race to each member. While color blindness urges us not to notice, color insight says, "Don't be afraid—notice your race and the race of others around you and learn about what that means." Developing color insight among workers of different races often requires off-site efforts because the workplace itself may not welcome the frank discussion that is essential to cross-racial understanding. A lunch or dinner meeting held away from work, without supervisors or fear of repercussion, may be needed to begin the conversation.

One step to develop color insight is for the parties to the conversation to reflect upon and discuss whether their understanding of race has changed over their lifetimes. Race is a moving target that evolves and is rarely static. Because individuals may come from different regions or have lived through different eras,[8] it is useful to situate and clarify the context of each other's racial understandings. If the parties can understand how their perception of race may have already evolved, they may be more willing to consciously move from favoring the notion of color blindness to supporting color insight.

Color insight promotes equality and emphasizes nondiscrimination among races. Color insight admits that most of us do see race and underlines the need to understand what that racial awareness means. Three key aspects of color insight that provide tools for working across racial lines to combat the presumption of incompetence are (1) examining systems of privilege, (2) unmasking perspectivelessness, and (3) combating stereotyping by looking for the me in each individual.

Examining Systems of Privilege

Working across racial lines takes place against a national backdrop in which race still matters and white privilege continues. Race remains a formative identity category that impacts the lives of both whites and people of color in different ways. So seeing race for whites must mean noticing whiteness, not just noticing race when a person of color is present.

It is not that whiteness simply privileges white people. Whiteness can also negate people of color, who are judged by their conformance to white norms, disparaged by their perceived dependence on whiteness, or silenced by invisible presumptions of nonwhite deviance. Both whites and people of color need to recognize each other's individual privileges. Education, gender, heterosexual orientation, economic

---

8   For example, people who lived in the US throughout the 1940s and 1950s experienced a segregated society, while those who grew up in the 1980s and '90s developed their understanding of race at a time of extensive questioning about its relevance.

wealth, language or accent, and religious privilege continue as societal impediments to equality, a role that race also plays.

Great diversity exists within any given identity group because each individual has many facets. The diversity within racial minority groups keeps expanding as the idea of race evolves in the United States. W. E. B. Dubois's concept of a "talented tenth" is outdated while people who are identified as black in the US broadens to include immigrants of African descent from Africa, the Caribbean, and other parts of Latin America and Europe. A greater percentage of blacks in the US have privileged economic, educational, and parental-achievement backgrounds than at any previous time. It is helpful for people who want to work across racial lines to conduct a self-assessment using Fran Ansley's concept of the power line (Wildman 1996, 29). Power-line self-assessments can point out commonalities, help expose assumptions, and build shared understandings.

By the time a woman becomes a teacher in the legal academy, she is positioned on the dominant side of the power line in at least some respects. Antiracism work has to contend with other forms of injustice and oppression to be effective and not subject to being undermined or sidetracked by claims that racism is less onerous than other types of "isms."

Unmasking Perspectivelessness

Professor Kimberlé Crenshaw's (1994, 35) exposition of perspectivelessness, the fallacy that neutral decision makers create law as the dominant mode of legal discourse, illustrates a key barrier to alliances across racial lines. Perspectivelessness operates through the use of a white norm as the default mode. Whiteness is often the standard of workplace performance (Calmore 2005; Carbado and Gulati 2004, 2000a; powell 2005). The models for most corporate, governmental, and other large-scale employers originated in environments that excluded everyone other than white men from positions of power. The standards that are applied reflect the perspectives and values of their creators and are skewed in their favor. Employees of color and women are often required to meet standards that were not created with their individual qualities in mind. Employers label characteristics that do not conform to white male norms as unprofessional and inappropriate for the worksite.

As with exploring privilege, it may be necessary to examine perspectivelessness somewhere other than work. Conversations at another place may disclose how much of their true selves people sacrifice or suppress to succeed on the job. Examining the personal costs of perspectivelessness may lead to reexamining job-performance standards that unnecessarily make the workplace more oppressive for people of color.

Combating Stereotyping by Finding the Me in Each Individual

Examining race the way color insight requires poses the danger of making false assumptions based on stereotypes. Looking for the person, rather than the stereotype in each individual, helps coworkers appreciate reality from the Other's viewpoint. Telling one's own stories and listening to other people's enable work across racial lines. By fighting the cultural default of whiteness, coworkers can surpass the limits of their individual, personal experience.

When Jerome Culp's students asked him, "Where did you attend law school?" (1991, 543), he told them that he had attended the University of Chicago and

Harvard Law School. Seeking to impact the way they viewed race within his classroom, he also told them he was the son of a coal miner. Culp explained that he wanted to say "to my black students that they too can engage in the struggle to reach a position of power and influence, and to my white students that black people have to struggle" (1991, 539). Yet Culp found that the reaction—from students of both races when he told them his history—was often disbelief. He was facing the students' stereotyping of him and his background.

Culp explained that using autobiography conveyed more than an effort to put his students at ease about his qualifications. He wrote, "My autobiographical statement—I am the son of a poor coal miner—has informational content that has a transformative potential much greater than my curriculum vitae. *Who we are* matters as much as what we are and what we think. It is important to teach our students that there is a 'me' in law, as well as specific rules that are animated by our experiences" (1991, 543; emphasis in original). He was fighting stereotypes by urging students to see the me, the individual who transcends them. Culp's view of the importance of the me in law and his memorable message about where he came from inspires us all to work across racial lines and combat the presumption of incompetence.

Using Color Insight to Overcome the Presumption of Incompetence

Eliminating the operation of the presumption of incompetence in academic institutions requires individual and institutional good faith. A first step is to reflect on past incidents where women or people of color have been subjected to a presumption of incompetence. Consider times when candidates or new teachers have inexplicably struggled at the outset in your school or other workplace. Were these colleagues accorded a presumption of competence? Individuals must honestly assess their own attitudes and perceptions. Ask yourself these questions: Have you ever applied a presumption of incompetence to a member of some group? Reflect on your role in faculty decisions about tenure or hiring. Have you been willing to point out the operation of privilege (for example, when a colleague makes a statement such as "all it takes to be a good teacher is preparation and hard work")?

Institutional good faith requires a diverse faculty and administration as well as an honest and respectful environment in which people of different races, genders, sexual orientation, and politics can disagree without fear of reprisal. Individual and institutional good faith promotes the ability to work across racial lines that is necessary to challenge the presumption of incompetence. To work across racial lines requires recognizing that in the United States, people continue to face racialization in many aspects of their lives.[9] An individual's racial identity or perceived one affects that person's experience and social interactions. In its aspiration to achieve a color-blind society, contemporary culture downplays or even denies this racialized reality. But acknowledging a racialized reality and its impact on perception and reaction is an important element of transracial cooperation.

This requirement must be met by each party regardless of race. People who are not a racial minority may not recognize the importance race can play in daily life or be uncomfortable acknowledging its role because they feel they should be color blind. The pressure to be color blind makes it uncomfortable for many people to

---

9   This racialization is likely true in many countries, but the authors are limiting their discussion to the United States.

consciously notice another person's race.[10] Talking about race with people of other races may be particularly uncomfortable due to fears of saying something offensive. But white persons seeking to work with people of color need to signal openness to talk about race. Of course, it is unnecessary to force the issue if the person of color is not interested in pursuing the discussion. Some people of color do not feel that race is an issue that affects them. But listening, without defensiveness, to a colleague speak about her experience living as a nonwhite person in the US provides a solid foundation for future collaboration (Butler 1998; Wah 1994). Discussions among people of color from different races are similarly important.

People of color must come to the conversation recognizing that privilege is embedded deeply in our society in ways that intentionally make it difficult for the privileged person to recognize its operation. It may open people's eyes to racial privilege if each person recognizes and acknowledges his or her own privileged attributes, such as gender, language, sexual orientation, or educational background.

Institutional Barriers

Law schools may present institutional barriers to working across racial lines. Some of these barriers reinforce the presumption of incompetence and make it more difficult to overcome. Institutional rules can interfere with communication and create situations where lack of transparency fosters betrayals or perceived betrayals. For example, secrecy functions as a shield for presumptions of incompetence. Secret ballots in hiring, retention, or tenure votes and anonymous student evaluations allow unexamined assumptions or presumptions to impact the evaluation process. Where anonymity is necessary, the results must be carefully evaluated for bias. Cultures of secrecy where what happens behind closed meeting doors cannot be discussed (for reasons other than the privacy of the candidate) foster unaccountability. Secrecy also makes junior faculty more vulnerable to false mentors, who can be most treacherous and are easily bred in schools where anonymous voting occurs.

Institutional barriers to working across racial lines should be recognized and discussed. When senior faculty who do work across racial lines receive no credibility for their views about candidates of color, even objective observations lose their effectiveness. When this dynamic occurs, it should be recognized at the very least. The analytical skills that law professors teach their students to help them anticipate what an opponent may argue need to be consciously applied to recognize and object to the operation of institutional barriers that hinder cross-racial work.

The inequality or imbalance of colleagues' reputations within the workplace can prove an additional barrier to collaboration. Regard and respect are necessary ingredients for honest collaborative work. If colleagues seek to work across racial lines in an institutional atmosphere that does not view them both as valuable members, then that dynamic should be discussed. Without some recognition, that institutional context may prove an unspoken barrier to meaningful work together.

* * * *

Teresa was glad it was summer. In addition to the freedom she felt while wearing sandals, summer meant no faculty meetings and therefore the absence of one of the

---

10   Class discussion in the course Race and the Law following an observation assignment asking students to consciously notice race for one day in Santa Clara, California, in August 2009.

places where institutional harm often occurred. Summer also marked a lull in the faculty hiring season.

But summer also meant added duties for her. Holmes Law School's admissions office ran Summer Bridge, a month-long program for college students who were interested in studying law. The program's participants were predominantly minority students who needed encouragement to enter the legal profession. All the teachers in the program volunteered their time. Although the academy rewarded publication, and summer was a prime time to produce legal scholarship because most professors did not have teaching responsibilities unless they chose to teach summer school for extra pay, the professors who taught in this prelaw program gained none of these rewards. Most of the Holmes faculty and staff of color took part. Two white faculty members, including Jessica, also taught these students. Teresa wanted to talk about what had happened in her class. She also looked forward to seeing Constance and her colleague.

Teresa walked toward the restaurant with some trepidation, wondering why Constance had picked it. She hated coming to this neighborhood near Constance's campus. The shopping area that bordered the other side of campus, closer to the working-class part of town, featured student-oriented businesses. She felt more comfortable there. Sure, she was older than most of the crowd, but she wasn't the only person of color around. In this, more upscale neighborhood, her presence still elicited notice and excessive politeness.

She walked into the bistro and asked for the Constance party. The hostess ushered her through the crowded space to an alcove in the back and a beaming Constance, who greeted her with, "Sorry, I know this is the stuffy side of campus, but I thought we needed a quiet place to meet, and I thought of this alcove." Constance nodded toward the woman seated next to her, "This is Lorraine. She clerked for the same judge I clerked for, and she has been teaching at my school for the last year. I thought this might be a good chance for her to meet you both."

Teresa appraised the white woman who had stood up to meet her with a hand extended. She felt slightly annoyed that Constance had brought the woman. Teresa needed some safe space to talk, and a newcomer changed the group dynamic. She extended her hand, however, remembering that she, too, had been a newcomer in the academy. "Hi," she smiled with more enthusiasm than she felt. "So how was your first year teaching?"

"Sorry to interrupt," Constance interjected, "but before we start, I wanted to go back to our last conversation. It reminded me of my own trajectory on the tenure path, something I hadn't thought about in years. One day I had three white, male senior colleagues attend my criminal law class. And their comment after the class? They said, 'You were much better than we thought you'd be!'"

"Wow," said Jessica. "And I bet no one connected that comment to the phrase 'presumption of incompetence.'"

Teresa just shook her head and looked at Lorraine, "See what you've gotten into in this profession?"

Lorraine replied, "So far students are pretty comfortable with me, but I'm worried about how they will react when I don't take a safe path. I understand that whiteness gives me some privilege that counteracts possible gender bias. Students are more used to women law professors in this era than when Constance started. But I'm starting to teach constitutional law this fall. With so much in the news bearing on equality and the Supreme Court, I'm thinking a lot about how to bring up the issues to generate a comfortable discussion. I know from my experience at the law firm and this past year that talking about racial justice is hard to do in public spaces. It helps when the participants have a common text or some mutual basis of understanding."

Teresa listened with a bit more attention. In her experience, it was unusual for white women to raise the topic of racial justice. One exception was Jessica, which was one reason why they had become friends.

The waitress came to take their orders, interrupting the conversation. "So you never did talk about your first year teaching," Teresa said to Lorraine after they had ordered food. "How was it?"

"Intense, but in ways I didn't expect," answered Lorraine. "I took over a property class for a black colleague when she was out for a month for surgery. We had been teaching the same course, working together on class assignments and teaching exercises, as well as quizzes, so our approaches were totally in sync.

"What I couldn't believe was the level of rudeness in the class. Students were talking with each other while I was talking and even when I called on another student. The behavior gave me an insight into the class culture—how they must have behaved when my colleague was teaching. I know that classes presume I am incompetent until I prove myself, but their behavior was at a whole different level of acting out based on that presumption."

"Sounds like a nightmare," offered Jessica. "I would have started calling on those who were talking, giving them grief for not listening."

"But I wonder," said Teresa, "if that tactic would have worked for Lorraine's colleague. Your whiteness, Jessica, might help the effectiveness of that approach."

"You are right," agreed Jessica, "whiteness matters, but race isn't the only identity characteristic in the mix."

Lorraine nodded. "It seems so normal, sitting here with you talking about race. But it is different in the classroom. Many students believe we are in a postracial era with the election of President Obama. How do you think I can engender meaningful discussion about racial justice in constitutional law when the students aspire to color blindness?"

After a moment, Jessica spoke. "Do you think part of whiteness is thinking that race doesn't matter? Or wishing that were so? I know I forget to think about being white all the time. But I'm guessing that Teresa doesn't get to forget she is black and Latina. But Teresa can speak for herself."

Teresa smiled. "It's not that I think about race every second; I can appreciate a beautiful sky as much as the next person. But I do walk through the world seeing it through the lens of race."

"You both seem to get along, as Rodney King would say. Why is that? Are you postracial?" asked Lorraine.

"You mean, how can one of my best friends be white," asked Teresa, "when I think about race?"

"And," chimed in Jessica, "I do think about race and talk about it. I bring the subject up, even though I am white, because we all have a stake in changing the system of privilege based on race."

"It's true," said Teresa, "that I'm glad I'm not always the only one bringing up the subject. It matters to me to have friends who share my concern with the issue, even if they are coming at it from a different perspective."

"You might try an exercise I give my class." Jessica looked toward Lorraine. "I ask them to spend twenty-four hours noticing the race of those around them in daily life. That means noticing whiteness, too."

"Won't some students say it makes them feel racist to be noticing race?" asked Lorraine.

Teresa nodded, "In my experience, many whites feel uncomfortable noticing race or talking about it for fear of appearing racist. But most women of color—people of color, really—live in a racialized reality. Ignoring it—I mean whites ignoring it—denies that reality. But it is true that some students of color coming to law school prefer not to be reminded of race; they just want to blend in and get on with the task at hand—learning law. So there are no easy answers in the classroom. Ignoring race lets white privilege continue unnamed and unnoticed, but talking about race may make some students of color feel as if they are getting more attention than they want, even when I make an effort to keep them out of the spotlight. But some students of color feel relieved to have the subject open to discussion."

"That reminds me of my class yesterday in the Summer Bridge program for those wanting to be lawyers," said Teresa. "My TA is a Japanese American student. She told the class about a case during her first year of law school where an employer had said, 'You're not the only Sony on the shelf' in a staff meeting, speaking to a Japanese American employee. The question was whether that comment alone was extreme and outrageous enough to constitute the intentional infliction of emotional distress under state law.

"No one in the class was willing to make the argument that the comment was outrageous enough. And my TA felt as if she had to do it—but she hated being the one in the spotlight to have to take up the argument. She wished someone else had been willing to speak up."

Constance nodded, "I often tell my students about Sheila O'Rourke's suggestion that they practice on other people's oppressions. She is a white lesbian who says she tries to speak up on racial justice issues; she hopes others will do the same if a classroom or workplace dynamic exhibits homophobia or sexism."

"It's a good idea," agreed Jessica. "But we all choose our battles, and they are often just our own."

"Yes," Constance continued, "that's why O'Rourke's idea is so important. We wouldn't always have to choose our own if our colleagues or allies stepped up."

*   *   *   *

Coworkers, Friends, and Coalitions

When a woman of color works with a white woman, some might think the woman of color needs the association with whiteness to validate her contribution, even if she and the white woman don't feel that way. The person of color may be perceived as less than competent and needing support. This dynamic of invalidation through working together doesn't seem to happen between white faculty members, particularly men. Perhaps male friendship is less demonstrative and therefore more likely to seem neutral.

Even when two individuals of goodwill try to work together, other faculty members can twist that relationship into something else. Close friendships can be viewed with suspicion when the time comes to make decisions about hiring and retention, even though these decisions are supposedly based on objective criteria. A faculty committee's perception that the person being discussed is one professor's friend can undermine any expression of support, even if the friend is simply stating objective facts. A white professor may lose credibility with respect to a coworker who is a person of color; other faculty members may no longer see him or her as objective about the colleague. Although friendship is powerful and essential to fully developed human beings, it seems to be distrusted in law school because objectivity is valued so highly. Nonetheless, new law professors of all races need friends among their colleagues, who in most schools are predominantly white.

Friendship provides a space for speaking the truth about an institution, rather than suppressing or silencing it. Being able to share personal perspectives trusting that they won't be denied, even if the friend has different opinions, is a tremendously important support. Psychiatric health-care providers affirm that having a sounding board is important in times of increased stress or anxiety.

> Although mental health can be maintained by engaging in positive interpersonal communication and using ego defense mechanisms, people may reach out to individuals or groups for support during periods of increased stress or anxiety. Such people are referred to as significant others or support people . . . . Harry Stack Sullivan, an eminent psychiatrist, states that people mistakenly believe that they can solve their own problems and maintain control of their lives without assistance from anyone or anything . . . . Sullivan believed that those who attempt to solve their problems by themselves may become consumed by their problems and suffer some kind of mental disorder or illness (Shives 2007, 9-11).

Friendships are crucial within the stressful environment of the law school.

Race remains a formative identity category that impacts the lives of both whites and people of color in different ways. Working across racial lines in the academy occurs against this national backdrop of race mattering and white privilege continuing. Whiteness does more than simply privilege a certain group of people. Whiteness can also diminish people of color when conformance to white norms becomes the measuring stick for competence. Friendship and coalition create a risk for the person of color, who may be disparaged within the institution by a perceived dependence on whiteness. Invisible assumptions about nonwhite nonconformity may reinforce the presumption of incompetence within the institution and operate to silence a person of color even further. Talking candidly about race entails personal risk for the person of color; at a basic level she exposes herself to the possibility that a would-be ally just won't care.

Friendship and coalition create less risk for whites, who enjoy the benefit of racial privilege. So registering race for whites must mean noticing whiteness, not just being aware of race when a person of color is present. Whites can exhibit support for racial justice, even when they don't have the same personal stake as a person of color. But at a minimum, all whites—indeed all coworkers—have a stake in workplace fairness, antibias, and nondiscrimination: identity categories should not be the basis for hiring, retention, promotion, or a sense of belonging in an institution. All coworkers have an important role to play in trying to ensure a just environment for everyone. Being an observant coworker, speaking out against observed oppression, and seeking to ensure workplace fairness for everyone may lead to friendship.

An individual must consciously choose friendship, a much more personal relationship, to deepen the connection beyond that of coworker. Multiple factors are at work. In her study of friendships between black and white women, Mary McCullough found that the friends "articulated strong commitments to social change" and "to ending racism as a dominant social force" (1998, 161). These relationships were "more than 'just friendships'" (161), although friends did not select each other because of race. But the friendships, combined with the commitment to social change, provided motivation to work through tensions that arose.

Louise Harmon and Deborah Post (1996) explored the beginnings of their friendship that resulted in a collaborative reflection on law teaching. Louise described her nausea—"frequently on the verge of throwing up" (4)—for the first two years of teaching and the surprise of her male colleagues when she confessed that physical reaction. Deborah explained that she was "surprised and pleased" by Louise's fear and anxiety. Deborah elaborated,

> Certain white women—not all, but some—never seemed to have any doubts. Their confidence in their own worth was striking . . . . These white women thought they understood the rules, and generally they were very successful, at least until that day when some man . . . denied them something to which they believed they were entitled. I generally associate this confidence on the part of white women professionals with privilege, with women whose egos have been wrapped in tissue paper and placed in a protective crevice between white privilege and class privilege (Harmon and Post 1996, 11).

For these two friends, the recognition and acknowledgment of performance anxiety, perhaps heightened by the presumption of incompetence that they both faced, became the basis for a bond of friendship and productive collaboration.

Friends do not deny the reality that another experiences; rather, they learn about themselves from their friend's perspective. Color insight provides a tool to deepen the insights that coworkers or friends may gain from each other.

Conclusion

In an equal world, a presumption of competence would be granted to everyone entering the institution. But as this chapter demonstrates, reality based on identity markers creates an unlevel entryway. Within the institution, coworkers, friends, and coalitions all play an important role. For the person of color, they can be a lifeline to validate their own lived reality as well as offer strategic allies. The white person will find his or her life enriched by combating white privilege. Both individuals contribute to a culture of democratic inclusion that has ramifications beyond the personal richness of their relationship.

CHAPTER 16

NATIVE WOMEN MAINTAINING THEIR CULTURE IN THE WHITE ACADEMY

Michelle M. Jacob

Introduction

Issues of women and work are an important part of feminist scholarship, including studies of women's experiences within the academy. However, Native women's experiences are often overlooked, and women working as staff, rather than faculty, are excluded. Drawing from qualitative interviews with five women, as well as personal experience, this chapter discusses the race, class, and gender dilemmas that face Native women working as faculty and staff in the academy. Results indicate that Native women experience the following problems: (1) an extreme sense of isolation, (2) tokenism, and (3) tremendous service burdens. This chapter argues that Native women, as the traditional caretakers of their culture and people, are uniquely burdened with the challenge of maintaining their Indigenous traditions while surviving in a white institution that often pushes them into a dichotomous reality of being viewed as a "friendly squaw" or "hostile Injun." The chapter concludes with institutional recommendations, including revising hiring practices; recruiting and retaining students, staff, and faculty; and building relationships with local tribes and urban Indian populations.

Native peoples face ongoing hostilities within academia. Administrators often want to "have it both ways" by having Natives on staff to count but also denying the importance of the Native voice. To add insult to injury, administrators also publicly voice support for Indigenous initiatives (especially at public gatherings with Indigenous community members) but privately work against supporting them (e.g., cutting or withholding funding, threatening or carrying out sanctions against protest activity, or allowing issues to die in committees and subcommittees that are looking further into the importance of these initiatives). Knowing that the actual numbers of Native peoples (and their dedicated allies) are few, administrators can use these methods to wear down efforts for institutional change. Often Native student activists leave campus (by either dropping out or graduating) before the movement achieves a significant victory. Staff and faculty turnover rates tend to be high as well, so the small number of Native activists—whether intentionally limited by administrators or not—seems guaranteed.

Native peoples who work in academia and their communities perhaps feel an inevitable sense of burnout. Interview data analyzed in this chapter reveal that feelings of burnout are strongly linked to colleges' and universities' inability or refusal to understand and work with Indian communities. Although this chapter raises important questions about tokenism, marginalization, and exclusion, the women I interviewed had a common answer to these problematic questions. By focusing on the future—whether it be Indian youth and generations yet to come, the hopes of more resources for Indian people, better governmental services, or a general sense of more widespread social justice—American Indian women working in academia rely on traditional cultural teachings to fuel their optimism about the change that our struggles can make for the future. Native women are consistent in describing the ways that they exist primarily in the margins of the academy. From low-level student-affairs staff members to tenured professors, the women share stories of the uneasy balance between staying true to their cultural teachings and excelling in their work in academia. Underlying all of the women's stories is a sense that their work to indigenize the academy is part of a larger social and critical critique of racism, classism, and sexism.

Marginalization and the Purpose of Critique

In her article "What Working-Class Intellectuals Claim to Know," Canadian scholar Roxanne Rimstead (1996) critiques the ways that marginalized scholars (such as those with working-class backgrounds) write about their feelings of never being "at home" either in the academy or their home communities. Rimstead acknowledges that people in academia with marginalized backgrounds of race, class, or gender can benefit from a sort of social therapy by writing about their struggles of trying to fit in or never belonging to academia. However, her criticism is that such projects have the tendency to leave current structures of domination unchallenged. Rimstead instead calls for projects that not only describe feelings of marginalization but also go beyond complaining about the academy and focus on challenging current ruling relationships. This chapter attempts to answer Rimstead's call for projects that present a serious cultural critique. Thus, not only do I describe the ways that academia fails to welcome Native peoples in general and Native women in particular, but I also offer an analysis and share suggestions from Native women I interviewed who work in the academy as a cultural critique of the current ruling relationships.

Methods

This chapter analyzes data from qualitative interviews with five Native women who work in the academy in Southern California and Canada. Participants were recruited through a convenience sample and included faculty as well as student-affairs staff. Two participants who spoke of their experiences simultaneously worked in student affairs as students. The interviews were loosely structured with open-ended questions that asked about participants' identities, definitions of community, experiences in the workplace, and pros and cons of working in the academy.

Discussion

Existing in the uneasy space between the dichotomous stereotypes of friendly squaw or hostile Injun means that the women I interviewed rely upon traditional cultural teachings to survive in the academy. A common coping strategy is incorporating Native values into the workplace.

Indigenous scholars write about the importance of leaders caring for the collective good (LaDuke 2005; Alfred 2005). Leaders must put the needs of others before their individual desires or comfort. In academic terms, this can be described as mentoring and service. Care work is central to being a good leader and good person in traditional cultural teachings. This Indigenous cultural logic flies in the face of Western academic views of rugged individualism and careerism. A common result of embracing Native cultural values in academia means Native women become overburdened by carrying heavy service loads (which the academy largely fails to recognize or reward). Native women I interviewed spoke of being overloaded because—in addition to the care work they perform for Native students and communities—they also have their regular duties in the (white) academy. This extra work takes a very personal toll on the women because they are not merely laboring more but are trying to help their culture survive. Underlying all of their extra work is a sense of urgency: if the women do not assume these burdens, then their culture and people will suffer and perhaps die (within the academy).

Whether or not the women do this extra care and service work is not the question in this chapter. Several studies, books, and essays have established that women of color, including Native women, are consistent in providing this extra labor for the academy (e.g., D. Mihesuah 1998; Medicine 2001; Smith 2001). All of the women interviewed discussed their deep desire and motivation to help their communities and Native students in particular. However, navigating that boundary between offering support and being taken advantage of sometimes blurred. In such instances, Native women had to negotiate the tensions of potentially being viewed as hostile Injun or friendly squaw by their communities.

Irene, an administrative analyst within the student-affairs division, discussed the stress from helping students run the annual university powwow. When students were unable to attend all university meetings or file all budgetary paperwork on time, Native students often assumed that Irene would step in and take care of everything. The students, who were frustrated by the increasing amount of red tape that the university was creating, often looked to Irene as their reliable and consistent advocate. This sometimes put Irene's health at risk because she had to work long (sometimes stress-filled) hours and run interference for the students if an administrator did not like the way they were carrying out their event planning. Irene was thus caught in the middle. She had long lists of expectations placed on her by both university administrators and Native students and had to navigate between competing ones. She had to perform in a way that resisted the hostile squaw stereotype but also proved to students that she was not a friendly Injun token of the administration.

Ultimately, Irene felt she was successful at navigating this difficult terrain. However, she also noted that much of the work she did (on behalf of the university and for the Native students) was not related to her job. In short, all of the long hours, stress, meetings, etc. were an optional service that she provided out of the goodness of her heart. It seemed that Irene was consistently putting others' needs before her own as she juggled university administrators' demands and concerns along with the Native students' problems. The care work that Irene provided seemed to be a full-time job by itself. I asked Irene about her motivation to do this care work. In her response, she discussed her feelings of obligation to help Native students: "You know, it's not in my job description to help these students. There's nothing in my job that even sets me up to counsel or to participate in that. But I make it that way. You know, I try to be there for them, no matter how stressful that is at times. And I would not feel good about myself if I didn't do that." Underlying Irene's narrative is the fact that the university gives her no professional reward to help Indian students. Nevertheless, she consistently is a source of support for them, including serving as the advisor to the Native student organization.

Irene's narrative helps illustrate the process of incorporating Native values into the workplace. Her position in the academy has nothing to do with counseling and supporting Native students, yet she chooses to do this work in an official capacity on the campus. She gives us insight into what Native values are being incorporated, stating she would not feel good about herself if she didn't support the students in this way. Irene brings the Native values of collectivism and mutual support into the academy. If Irene had an individualistic or materialistic approach to her work, she would not spend her time and energy helping Native students. This scenario (of women helping students) was repeated across all five interviews.

In Irene's narrative, it is important to highlight that much of her extra work to help the students was due to university administrators creating red tape (bureaucratic barriers) in response to a Native community event, the annual powwow. Making more red tape is historically a classist response to slow down or prevent marginalized groups from gaining legitimate power within the academy. Groups that have greater representation and resources within the institution are more successful in navigating bureaucratic obstacles (and face fewer ones in general due to their privileged status). However, in Irene's case, it was only she and a handful of Native students. Irene, as the only Native staff member at the institution, felt that she had no choice but to support the struggling efforts of the few Native students who wanted to keep the traditional community powwow alive.

How does the academy respond to this exceptional work from Native women like Irene? Colleges and universities are consistent in their message of embracing diversity and fostering cultural competence among their students. It is commonplace for academic institutions to include such claims in their mission statements. But is the academy really responding to the needs of Native peoples? Educational attainment rates continue to be dismal. Recruitment and retention efforts at most institutions are underfunded or nonexistent. In such a climate, it seems that academic institutions are quite content to allow Native women to take on the burdens of being walking Native student-affairs divisions. Allowing Native women to carry the load of an entire division is clearly a form of exploitation. Native women, who are so few within the academy, feel they face a difficult choice: going along with the exploitative conditions and doing what needs to be done, or resisting exploitation and watching Native students and community needs go unmet. As Irene mentioned, she most often pitches in and helps because she has been taught within her traditional culture to support members of her community and put others before herself. Academic institutions are very happy to have such friendly Injuns on staff, but the high burnout rates and staff turnover should be attracting more attention from administrators. Ongoing burnout and turnover continue to be problems within academia and are evidence of institutions continuing to ignore Native peoples' needs.

Isolation, Racism, and Stereotypes

Part of being some of the few Natives at their respective institutions requires these women to serve as sort of cultural ambassadors for their usually white colleagues. Much has been written about the fantasies that nonnatives have about Native peoples (Churchill 1998; D. Mihesuah 2002). Underlying these fantasies are deeply held racial and gender stereotypes of Indigenous peoples like the hostile Injun and friendly squaw discussed in this chapter (Smith 2001; H. Mihesuah 2002; Trask 1999). Such stereotypes, prevalent in Disney movies as well as the American imagination, deny Native women their humanity and tremendous worth as workers in the academy.

Dealing with ignorant stereotypes is part of daily work for Native women. Irene, for instance, discussed that she was expected to represent a fictional, monolithic Native community to nonnatives on campus:

> Oh my God . . . you may be the only Native person they've ever met in their entire life, so they're curious about you and what you do and your customs and you know. So—as annoying as their questions may be and as stupid as some of them may sound—I try to be patient and answer them and let them know that we're all different; we all don't live in teepees, and we don't all speak the same language and, you know, these people are different from my people, and I'm not from this area, so I don't know the customs here. And that sort of thing. It's always, always constantly educating people about what Indians are in this country. It is sad, but this may be their only contact with somebody who's Native.

Irene's narrative reveals the widespread ignorance about Native peoples in the academy. Part of the reason is the lack of Native peoples within the academy. As Irene reveals, she may be the only Native that coworkers and administrators ever meet. When Irene has to take time to answer questions about whether Indians live in teepees, she is expected to become the friendly squaw who exists to please and cater to nonnatives' needs. In this case, she satisfies their ignorance and sense of curiosity about Native peoples. Although Irene shares that it is sad to do this work, she feels she has a responsibility to educate coworkers about Native peoples because there is simply no one else on staff able to do so.

Related to the problem of overall ignorance about Native peoples is a problem that Natalie, a part-time staff member for student affairs, describes—proving to university officials that Native students exist on campus. Native women consistently resist being rendered invisible and silent. Natalie has been involved with the struggle to get resources allocated to Native programs and services. According to her university's records, 1 percent of the students on her campus are Native. Natalie says, "What I don't like is the constant reminders that you have to have just to get recognized on this campus. It just seems like the whole 1 percent thing—that statistic stigmatizes people . . . [the administrators] just feel like 'oh, there's not that many here; why should we do this?' . . . it just seems like that's kind of a struggle: just to get the recognition that you've deserved for a long period of time. So that's always a struggle. I think it's been a struggle for a long time."

In the interviews I conducted, the women all looked to the future and the success of upcoming generations as their hope and motivation for continuing to struggle in the academy. Justine, a director of a student-affairs program, mentioned, "I get to work with the students and help nurture and support them. That's just fabulous. When I see a student sitting in front of me saying that they experience something on a cultural level and they feel their own pride, their own sense of self, that's the gem out of all of it. Certainly there is a paycheck for me once a month, but . . . connection with the students: that to me—that makes me rich." By focusing on a sense of community, rather than her individual needs such as monetary reward or career advancement, Justine can cope with difficulties like struggling to secure resources for programs that serve Native students.

Similarly Marie, a Native faculty member, commented on the racist assumptions of the academy about Indian community members who provide services to the campus. During the interview, Marie shared the pain that she feels when she is placed squarely in the path of colliding value systems:

> People we invite to dance, let's say, or to speak. The university wants [all paperwork completed and filed] several weeks in advance of the event in order to cut a check to get them an honorarium. Well, then they don't, let's say, show. Well, the reason they don't show is because they have family obligations and other things come up that they find are more important than the university. But the university, they see it as being, you know, irresponsible. I see it as they have their priorities in the right place. And so there's a lot of lack of communication or a lack of understanding.

The academy values individualism and a commitment to the institution's inflexible bureaucratic guidelines while Marie and her Native community, including people she invites for campus events, value collectivism and commitment to family. When these two systems collide—such as when a Native community member does not show up for a speaking engagement—Marie is caught in the middle, serving uneasily as a bridge between the two conflicting sets of values. Marie raises a crucial issue for American Indian studies scholars: How can we practically and respectfully serve both our communities and the institutions where we work when their values and ways of doing business are so drastically different?

Lorna, a faculty member, also referred to the conflict in values that Native peoples can experience in the academy. In her interview, she talked about the necessity of having a collective of Native friends and allies in the academy to survive the hostile racist and classist environment. Like the other women, Lorna's narrative speaks to the importance of collectivism and mutual support while they are struggling to succeed in an institution that does not usually acknowledge Native women's tremendous worth as workers:

> Really part of what goes on at the university and why we can't succeed is that there are closed areas that aren't open. It's about power building; you have to really learn how to have a killer instinct to really make it there . . . that's why you have to have collectives. Because developing a killer instinct is not a healthy thing by yourself. You need someone to come around and say to you one day, "Wait a minute, calm down . . . you're getting a little too carried away with that killer instinct business. Let's go see a funny movie, or

you know, let's go to a powwow . . . or let's go see your granddaughter, get a little more balanced here." It's okay to sort of have a warrior aspect to your personality, but when you're in an institution which only supports that one aspect of ourselves, the person is in trouble. And it will start showing up in health, which it did for me. I started getting some very serious symptoms from stress.

Lorna's narrative reveals some of the reasons why more Native peoples don't make it in the academy. As Lorna says, there are closed areas that Natives cannot access because, typically, it is just too much of a conflict in cultural values to claw your way all to the top. Because so many competing and conflicting expectations are placed on Native women (by students, administrators, coworkers, family members, community members), they struggle to be successful in meeting those demands. Ultimately, though, there is a continual danger of being constructed as a hostile Injun or friendly squaw. In Lorna's quote, she refers to that hostile Injun stereo-type of doing whatever it takes to win a battle in the academy. The stress of being a solitary warrior within a highly individualistic institution leads to burnout and poor health. The constant, individualized fighting mentality is unhealthy for Lorna. Other Native scholars have also written about burnout. Alfred (2005) interviewed Native leaders about their experiences and struggles. His interviewees discussed the challenges one faces as a Native leader and admitted that burnout makes it difficult to persist in fighting for one's people.

Lorna commented on the conflict she felt working for an institution that rewarded people on the basis of individual effort and competition, values in contrast to her cultural beliefs: "That system that is built on perks and going up the ladder and all that, that really is completely meaningless to me. All I want to do is to do good for my community—for people like you, the next generation, in particular. I'm an auntie. I have a lot of girls around your age or my daughter's age who have adopted me as their auntie." Lorna, who was working as a tenured professor, expressed her preference for serving the community, including younger Native students, rather than climbing the academic ladder that controls perks and promotions. This is per-haps what Philomena Essed (2000) would call "a dilemma of leadership." Essed has commented on the complications of being a black woman in the academy and the extra, unpaid, activist, mentoring, and tutoring work that women of color are expected to provide.

In her interview, Lorna offered a solution to the burnout syndrome that seems to hit Native academics—building collectives. She said that collectives across institu-tions had served as important sources of social support during times of crisis in her academic career. This issue also underlines the importance of building collectives across generations of Native peoples working in the academy because earlier gen-erations can help teach the next generation to build collectives that will help cope with the bouts of burnout within racist and classist academic institutions.

Importantly, the women I interviewed also shared stories of victories that their collectivities had achieved. One woman was part of a collective that worked with the Indian community to set up an advisory board to the president of the university. Another example was the allocation of a space on the university campus for Native students to use for club meetings and community functions. Also, one woman was successful in communicating the importance of continuing the university's annual powwow during a time of budget cuts for programming. Her lobbying convinced the president of the university to support the powwow—one of the few events that attracts Indian community members onto the campus.

Possibilities for Radical Cultural Critique

The women I interviewed had many stories about facing race, class, and gender bias and exclusion within the academy. While it is important to describe and document that these problems exist, it is also crucial to provide recommendations for academic institutional change. After listening to the stories of the women I interviewed in this small-scale project, my preliminary conclusions are that the academy will be a better, healthier place if we (1) continue to actively build collectives and openly discuss challenges involved with being Native scholars in the academy, (2) continue to be true to our values of honoring the collective above individualism, (3) use our collective strength to communicate and advocate to the academy for community needs, (4) focus on the ways that our struggles will benefit future generations, and, most importantly, (5) continue to raise all of these issues in official capacities inside of the academy to foster progressive change.

By focusing on how we can continue to change the academy in these five main ways, our critique of what's wrong truly becomes radical because serious challenges to the ruling regulations become possible. The women I interviewed all shared the reason why they keep fighting in these institutions of higher education—because they have hope for a better future for the younger generations of Native peoples. And it is this commitment to the traditional cultural value of collectivism that creates the possibility for radical cultural critique—and the possibility for changing the authoritarian hierarchy in the academy.

CHAPTER 17

Dis/Jointed Appointments

Solidarity amidst Inequity, Tokenism, and Marginalization[1]

Michelle A. Holling, May C. Fu, and Roe Bubar

Preface

What follows is our story arranged in multicolored pieces, the remnants of material we imagine was gathered by the brown, worn, and wrinkled hands of grandmothers, tucked away for star quilts in anticipation of upcoming giveaways. Yet none of us have learned to sew. Perhaps like the womyn who have come before us, we honor their wisdom and contributions yet understand that the way we have chosen to walk in the academy is a new path, one that few of our ancestors have traveled, so none of the womyn in our families know how to show us the way.

We have chosen to tell our story as a conversation among three self-identified, womyn of color feminists of working-class backgrounds who are Chicana, Asian American, and Native, respectively. Our story reflects the processual and dialogic nature of our discussions as opposed to the definitive conclusions that are more often emphasized in traditional academic essays. Through this conversation, we expose our individual and collective lives in order to generate "situated knowledges" (Hill Collins 1991). Our discussions took place over a period of five years, and recently, across three different states and time zones, online and on the phone, as we managed shifting personal and professional demands while remaining committed to honoring our resistance and solidarity.

We each accepted joint appointments in ethnic studies and another discipline. Joint appointments were a way to unite theory and praxis, a means of producing and participating in social change through education (Antonio 2002; Freire 1998). Yet the ways in which joint appointments operate and are structured vary across

---

1   We recognize the politics of first, second, and third authorship, so we attempt to expose and disrupt that hierarchy by acknowledging that we contributed equally to the conception, writing, and revising of this article.

institutions nationally (e.g., annual reviews, tenure and promotion, distribution of time to courses and departments, expectations for service and which department it will impact, and workload allocation). At the university where we held/hold joint appointments, the university faculty manual defines them this way:

> Joint appointments . . . should be made only when the professional activities of the individual concerned normally fall, to an appreciable degree, within the purview of two departments. Personal preferences of the individual are not sufficient reasons to justify a joint appointment. Each faculty member with an interdepartmental appointment shall be considered a member of the department contracting for the greater percentage of the time. In the case of a faculty member having equal time in two or more departments, the individual and department heads involved will decide in which department the faculty will be represented; the status of such a member shall remain unchanged unless changes in the academic appointment require a change in departmental representation.

However, our lived experience of joint appointments has differed dramatically from this definition, as this chapter reveals. In our conversations, we explore the benefits and pitfalls of joint appointments and the ways we survived, thrived, and practiced a womyn of color feminist solidarity.

*   *   *

RB: I accepted a tenure-track position in the Ethnic Studies Center with a joint cross-college appointment in the School of Social Work. At forty-three, I was an unlikely candidate for the academy. As a licensed lawyer turned accidental academic, I was largely unaware of the culture in the academy and the implications and complexities of a cross-college joint appointment. The position interested me as a unique opportunity to engage in interdisciplinary research/scholarship with an emphasis in Indigenous studies, social justice, race, gender and gender violence, class, and sexuality. In my second year as an assistant professor, I was chairing critical departmental committees and performing more service than any of my white and/or most of my male colleagues. I was also expected to secure grant monies.

 In this cross-college joint appointment, I was unsure how I would keep up the pace required for early tenure. Three of my womyn of color colleagues were offered similar contract terms to pursue early tenure. None of us had mentors or senior colleagues to advise us on the complexities of early tenure, joint appointments, and, in my case, cross-college issues, double workloads, and succeeding as womyn of color in the academy. In addition, because social work is subject to accreditation standards, I was expected to have a degree in it if I wanted to teach the full array of classes, serve in administrative positions, and pursue other leadership roles within this school. These obligations and challenges never came up as issues in contract negotiations.

MH: My motivations for applying for and taking a joint appointment were a mix of personal and professional. I was living on the East Coast when I was invited to apply. I was far from family, regularly exoticized as a Chicana, and had a not-so-happy partner. I saw the joint appointment as an opportunity to unite all facets of our profession—teaching, research, and service—with my specialization in Chican@ rhetoric. The joint appointment enabled me to teach rhetorical theory and Chican@ experiences, for example, on a regular basis while experiencing an unparalleled synergy in my teaching and research.

MF: My first job out of graduate school was a joint appointment. As a first-generation graduate, I was euphoric about being employed and making more than twelve thousand dollars per year. I viewed the joint appointment as an opportunity to structurally and intellectually bridge an interdisciplinary center with a traditional academic department. I did not anticipate any of the pitfalls and contradictions that I now realize are embedded in joint appointments. Despite amicable relations between the interdisciplinary center and the traditional academic department, lack of coordination between them produced certain structural inequities that had a negative impact on my professional development. For example, the academic department was authorized to evaluate my interdisciplinary research for promotion and tenure without input from the interdisciplinary center. Because I held an appointment in two distinct areas, I was required to attend twice as many faculty meetings, job talks, and events as my non-jointly appointed colleagues. As an assistant professor, I sat on at least eight work-intensive committees while my white peers in traditional departments served on only one or two committees. My experience illustrates the staggering service load that many womyn of color interdisciplinary scholars carry, particularly at predominantly white universities.

RB: I considered the cross-college joint appointment from a strictly utilitarian perspective. It was a career opportunity in Fort Collins. It was also a way to take part in the community and support my partner's choice to live and work here. To consider the advantages and intellectual opportunities posed by the cross-college joint appointment strikes me as a privileged and informed way of understanding the academy. I did not identify myself as an academic. Being an academic meant embracing the institution in ways that positioned me further from working with tribal programs and communities and engaging in front-line work in the field of child maltreatment alongside other professionals. For me, becoming an academic was fraught with class perceptions from childhood of pompousness and elitism as well as layers of contradictions I had to negotiate to locate myself within this space.

I considered what Devon Mihesuah (2003) discusses in her book *American Indigenous Women:* Native peoples have been researched by academics interested in studying them as Other with little interest in what Natives have to say about themselves. As I entered the academy, I witnessed a continuation of research projects being done on Native peoples and about them as Other, and few engaged with them directly. Many of my colleagues were strategically developing their research agendas as I continued to consult with tribal activists and program people about their research needs. I used my one-course buyout and a service-learning grant just before the tenure march to conduct a program evaluation for a tribal child-abuse program because it was needed for continued federal funding.

MH: Being a professor was and remains something I wanted to pursue—an occupational choice motivated by the dearth of Chican@s in the academy. I can recall during my master's program coming across the number of Chican@ professors nationally and experiencing a sense of deflation (and even questioning, "Can I do this?"), simultaneously feeling motivated and determined. At the time—1993 or 1994—there were approximately five hundred Chican@s holding faculty appointments. What I felt then was influenced by being a first-generation student and unaware of all that comes with and confronts me and other womyn of color in the academy. Nonetheless, the professoriate and joint appointment were a way of uniting two worlds—communication and ethnic studies. I did not realize that I would continue to straddle (disciplinary) borders and seek ways of embracing "borderland" spaces (Anzaldúa 1987).

MF: I entered these borderlands with strong lower-class and womyn of color identifications. Being a daughter of Deaf Asian immigrants, translating information in accessible ways made teaching an intuitive vocation for me.[2] Critical ethnic studies, accessible teaching, and student-centered pedagogy became my offerings to my family and communities. I saw the joint appointment as an intellectual and teaching opportunity in an otherwise rigid academic environment, as a structural initiative that joined different intellectual, political, and pedagogical projects—in my case, the study of change over time and the study of race, gender, class, and sexuality. It was a way to engage in the social justice issues that mattered so much to me. It was also a method to sustain myself in academia.

RB: I find it worth noting that each of us punctuates our experiences in the academy with the idea of sustaining ourselves. How come we talk of simply sustaining ourselves whereas our colleagues appear to be well positioned to explore the academy in a multitude of ways that feed them professionally? How come simply sustaining ourselves—surviving versus thriving—becomes the standard for womyn of color in the academy? Each of us grew up in lower-working-class families, where sustaining ourselves and our families was the goal—much more than that was a gift, a good day, and cause for celebration.

MF: I think a lot of us realized how offensive academia could be as graduate students, if not much earlier. On the one hand, I was invigorated by the intense and critical learning environment. On the other, we experienced

---

2   Deaf studies scholars Carol Padden and Tom Humphries explain the significant differences between *Deaf* and *deaf*:

> We use the lowercase *deaf* when referring to the audiological condition of not hearing, and the uppercase *Deaf* when referring to a particular group of deaf people who share a language—American Sign Language (ASL)—and a culture. The members of this group reside in the United States and Canada, have inherited their sign language, use it as a primary means of communication among themselves, and hold a set of beliefs about themselves and their connection to the larger society. We distinguish them from, for example, those who find themselves losing their hearing because of illness, trauma, or age; although these people share the condition of no hearing, they do not have access to the knowledge, beliefs, and practices that make up the culture of Deaf people (1988, 2; emphasis in original).

the elitism, inaccessibility, low minority recruitment and retention, and chauvinism that also marked that space. It was not long before I realized that academia never welcomed all of who I am, that it never truly wanted me to thrive, that it did not affirm my presence, my history, my family, my voice, my body, my memory, or my vision. It is an uphill walk. So I and others formulated ways to keep grounded, healthy, generative, and whole. I thought a joint appointment might be one affirmative, structural response to that reality.

MH: Considering the joint appointment was heavily influenced by my scholarly interests whereas taking it as a career move was impacted by familial relations as well as my ability to obtain credit for prior years of teaching and apply for early tenure. Because I would be moving into my second tenure-track position, claiming service years (and reserving the right to relinquish them) was important professionally and personally so I could communicate to others that my experience, publications, accomplishments, and service mattered. Not taking service years was tantamount to negating these achievements.

However, there were warning signs that the joint appointment was dis/jointed. These signs included two separate interviews (one for each unit), the absence of and inability to receive clarity about the distribution of my time to each unit, explicitly having to negotiate salary with the hiring unit yet ultimately having the nonhiring one play a pivotal role in my determined salary, being accountable to two chairs, performing double service and undergraduate advising, being reviewed annually by two independent units, and being required implicitly to overcome one unit's prior negative experience with joint appointments. I should have realized that I would be compensated as if I were working in one unit while being expected to handle a double workload. In addition, the units' relationship depended on who was in positions of power. Consequently, administrators were not always equipped to devise ways to make the joint appointment healthy and equitable for everyone involved.

RB: Michelle and I negotiated for years of service credit to go up for early tenure. I was encouraged to view service credit as a coveted advantage. Later, I learned that early tenure, on whatever terms, is more often fraught with politics and challenges—especially for womyn of color. The standards for tenure and promotion in a cross-college appointment entailed evaluation of my scholarship, service, and teaching by the tenuring department's committee without the presence/input of any ethnic studies faculty. And while my director could submit a letter evaluating my scholarship, neither she nor any other faculty member from ethnic studies was included during the discussions within the School of Social Work. Meanwhile, the Ethnic Studies Center—because it was situated within a different college—often applied a different tenure-and-promotion standard, thereby producing discrepancies in my annual merit ratings. Evaluations produced a crescendo of stress each year, even though I received consistently high ratings.

In the cross-college joint appointment, I also learned a few lessons about salary negotiations, including how to develop a strategy and how equity issues raised in negotiations can work in favor of an entire group. For example, if a new womyn of color hire is encouraged to ask for a higher salary and shares that fact with her colleagues, and if she later receives it, then other womyn of color can make an equity argument as individuals or a group to increase the salaries of those making less. I eventually figured out that there were equity monies reserved for just this purpose at our university, yet most—if not all—womyn of color faculty were unaware of this possibility.

MF: When I was hired, I had no idea that salaries and contracts could be negotiated, much less that doing so was common—even standard and expected protocol. Womyn of color faculty mentors told me otherwise. Nevertheless, what I did could hardly be called negotiating compared to what some male colleagues did. They not only expected to negotiate but also compiled effective requests for items such as an increased salary, early course releases, additional research funding, a reduced service load, more technical equipment, and so on. When I asked how they knew to negotiate that way, they credited advice passed to them by fathers with professional careers or male mentors. I learned that womyn of color needed to be diligent about seeking and providing mentorship for each other.

It is ironic that as scholars invested in equity issues for disenfranchised groups, we are so poorly valued for our work. We are neither supported nor rewarded for our engaged-activist scholarship, yet the university benefits from our engagement, activism, and scholarship. When we ask that our labor be honored in ways that are reflected in annual evaluations or tenure and promotion, it is telling to observe the strategies the administration uses not only to deny our requests but also to frame their justifications in ways that divide faculty interests and potential solidarities. As much as ethnic studies faculty are praised for their community work, the administration privileges scholarly publications over their efforts and creates a hierarchical divide that strains relationships.

RB: It is also ironic that many of us as womyn of color have strategic, organizing, mediation, and research skills related to equity, allocation of resources, power, and structural racism/sexism; yet seldom do we put those skills into practice in collective ways to address gender inequity and retention of womyn of color within the academy. We create circles of support for students and others, yet our isolation within the academy keeps us from creating that same support for ourselves as a collective. When I first read Michelle's annual merit narrative, I was blown away. I was not mentored to articulate my accomplishments in such a strategic, promoting, and deft manner. Some circles would regard such self-promotion as culturally uncool. Yet I was inspired to compile a list of strategic tips for new faculty but never kept it up due to the press of committee responsibilities, other joint duties, and the demands associated with my bid for early tenure and negotiating the cross-college joint appointment.

MH: Knowing the tips is central to our survival. But let's not forget that putting them into practice is a personal matter. I agree that "a strategic, self-promoting manner" is not rewarded in many cultures, and I remember my discomfort with having to (pro)claim what I had accomplished. I surely wasn't taught to boast about achievements, yet within an academic culture, a very different set of standards exists that necessitates self-promotion, or you risk being overlooked.

MF: I like Roe's suggestion that womyn of color faculty help each other navigate the academy. Those would be very demystifying, empowering conversations that could transform the way we experience these colonial relationships. Both of you guided me through my third-year review in extremely critical ways. You shared your insights about the review, explained its purpose, and recommended ways to gather and organize materials. Michelle even shared a copy of her entire third-year review file for me to review. You both offered and, importantly, modeled a generosity that shaped my experience as a junior faculty member.

MH: Mentoring is crucial to the survival of all of us in the academy and particularly in regard to tenure and promotion. Mentoring is what helps us become aware of any hidden politics (e.g., tenured-faculty opinions about the tenure process, committee composition, etc.), informing the review process as well as simply giving us advice and information about the expectations and/or ways to assemble portfolios and write personal statements. These are just a few suggestions (see Torres-Guzmán 1995; Viernes Turner 2002).

Regrettably, not being mentored or being mentored in disadvantageous ways can produce resentment, which is often provoked, created, and maintained by institutions that as a consequence demoralize faculty and alienate them from one another and impact scholarly and service productivity and teaching effectiveness. One of the ways to minimize resentment is by challenging inequitable arrangements. For example, when I was offered an inadequate salary, I declined the initial offer and devised a counterproposal where I sought other forms of compensation (such as course releases and summer support). I have also learned the importance of understanding the politics of our joint appointments (i.e., who were supporters of faculty who held them and were willing to speak up) as well as practicing womyn of color feminist solidarity. By which I mean an embodied practice that is developmental, contingent, inflected by personal experience, committed to intersectional politics, and informed by other womyn of color's writings about living and surviving within academia that helps ensure that subsequent hires will not be under the same chokehold.

RB: It was particularly difficult to find mentors within the academy, and it took me years to find senior colleagues that I trusted were providing important guidance and sharing their collective wisdom. I find womyn of color feminist solidarity to be the one constant source of meaning that has kept me going in the academy, and as my womyn of color colleagues leave for other positions they believe hold more promise and opportunities for them, the void they leave is profound. The opportunity to engage in solidarity creates a renewed sense of hope, thus taking us from a place of simply sustaining ourselves to a space where our intention to decolonize the academy holds the promise of becoming a reality in some small way.

MF: The experiences that give rise to resentment are also attempts to structurally disempower us. Over time, bitterness and resignation set in, and they can take multiple forms, including forming complicit or pessimistic attitudes about working conditions, not doing the work needed to change things, and, unfortunately, hiding behind heteronormative and/or gender privileges.

MH: I'm struck by your phrase "structurally disempower us." I think it's powerful in capturing the power relationships that are not simply difficult to negotiate but also chip away at our sense of being. As womyn of color in the academy—where clearly we're one of a handful and already confront feelings of marginality[3]—these power relationships wear on our sense of possibilities and erode our desire to continue confronting and challenging inequity.

RB: Listening to both of you reminds me that over time inequity based on race/gender/sexuality can create a level of trauma and, at the very least, a high level of constant stress that is similar (yet in a much less severe and life-threatening way) to trauma experienced over generations by populations that are historically marginalized. Some folks refer to historical trauma as a "soul wound" that then gets stored on a cellular level in our bodies (Duran and Duran 1993; Duran 2006). Others maintain that internalized racism impacts the health of people of color by accumulating over a lifetime (Worcester 2005; Butler et al. 2002).

MF: When we internalize structural disempowerment, it manifests itself through resignation, anger, anxiety, meanness, and so on. It affects our interpersonal relationships. It impacts future generations. Our well-being is not disconnected from the structural reality we inhabit each day.

MH: Structural disempowerment is an integral part of the process we are discussing here. We accepted joint appointments for utilitarian reasons, to achieve synergy in our intellectual interests, and/or to transcend the limitations of disciplinary boundaries. As we recognized their reality, particularly our structural disempowerment as womyn of color, we experienced resentment, discouragement, and resignation.

RB: The discouragement wears us down, and the mulish way that we feel compelled to work then compromises our quality of life. The challenge becomes to recover, replenish, and sustain ourselves.

[We catch ourselves being too critical of joint appointments. We begin asking ourselves and each other whether there were aspects of the arrangement that were more positively sustaining.]

MF: Joint appointments initially appealed to me very much. They were an intellectual opportunity to bridge and transgress disciplinary and methodological boundaries by creating a community of scholars who were invested in interdisciplinary collaboration. This not only generates bodies of interdisciplinary work and dialogue but also creates a culture of working together and camaraderie. We are bound, of course, to face criticism

---

3   In 2001, *The Chronicle of Higher Education Almanac* reported that of 568,719 full time faculty, 204,794 (36 percent) were women. Among the women faculty, 29,546 (14 percent) were women of color, who disproportionately held the rank of assistant professor (cited in Sotello Viernes Turner 2002, 78).

and devaluation by folks entrenched in the philosophies and methods of their field. However, that was part of the understanding—that the work, conversation, and collaboration enabled by the joint appointment would produce this important, if difficult, communication.

RB: The joint appointment offers the opportunity to examine intersections, engage in collaborative projects, and achieve a high level of intellectual fulfillment. My development as a scholar would not have been the same without the cross-college joint appointment.

MH: The joint appointment offered a sense of solidarity and home that felt immediate. These intangibles are conducive to thriving in the academy due to the shared affinities. Absent was the need to explain why race, ethnicity, gender, class, and sexuality must be taken into account in academic work. During the joint appointment, there was also the presence of political praxis that appeared to manifest itself or, at minimum, infuse our teaching, scholarship, and service.

[A week passes. We meet again, simultaneously online and on the phone, for the next part of our conversation. We feel continued excitement and enthusiasm as we work through difficult topics, remaining committed to what may be revealed.]

MH: The question for today is, what are the issues and/or costs of joint appointments? And how do we maintain feminist solidarity?

MF: Also, how did the stress from joint appointments and being womyn of color in academia affect our health?

RB: I experienced health challenges as a consequence of the heightened and sustained stress associated with the cross-college joint appointment. I struggled to remain present in social spaces outside of work while negotiating the expectations that remained constant in my role as mother, sister, daughter, auntie, and partner. In some ways, I see an analogy to former clients that my partner and I represented in Title VII (employment discrimination) cases. In those cases, clients pursing a claim of discrimination in the workplace often had significant health challenges that we, as lawyers, argued were physical manifestations of their discrimination. We now have studies that discuss internalized racism/marginalization and the distinct health implications for children/people of color (Worcester 2005; Butler et al. 2002).

MH/RB/MF: The stresses of the joint appointment exacerbated existing health issues. Collectively, we experienced gallstone attacks followed by surgery; multiple kidney stones (including the mother of all stones—measuring eight millimeters—that required two surgeries); tennis elbow; shoulder problems; perpetual negativity; and weight challenges. We had supportive partners, ones who questioned why we continued to put up with the stress given its impact on family life, and those who considered enforcing a gag order on the joint appointment. We articulated our work-related frustrations to friends and family, who questioned the worth of what we were doing. We found ourselves spending time with family but forced to stay up late to complete other work. Probably if we asked those close to us, they would have additional observations about the impact and cost associated with our positions. Moreover, as womyn of color in joint appointments, we were physically exhausted from regularly working more than twelve hours a day on campus. One of us eventually learned to honor her well-being by developing boundaries and respecting her limits. With little or no mentorship, we were deeply passionate but completely overworked and overcommitted. As obvious as it may seem now, it was harder to balance workload, stress, and self-care than one might think, especially because this schedule seemed to be the norm for most activist professors. Ultimately, the physical toll affected our psychological well-being and interpersonal relationships.

MF: During my first three years in academia, the people closest to me said that I prioritized my work over my relationships with them. At the time, I insisted that this was not the case. It was always a point of contention. It took a postdoctoral fellowship leave to enable me to see that they had been right all along.

RB: When people with past experiences of poverty, marginalization, trauma, and racism subsequently enter very stressful situations (where they are marginalized and experience a sense of being "othered"), these situations can restimulate past wrongs and hurts. The stress of the academic experience can lead to ineffective coping skills that prevent us from naming what is occurring. Personally, I channeled my anxiety into work and ended up working every waking moment. When my partner or children were asleep, that translated into another opportunity to work late into the evening. Work for me was a rhythm I had grown up with; it brought me a sense of accomplishment and relief.

MH: I think I continued out of a sense of obligation, a belief in the value of what we do, and a commitment to the exchange of ideas among ourselves and with students. I was motivated by a belief that ideas matter not only symbolically but also materially. There was also a sense of fulfillment in courses taught, research conducted, and programs built. Why not quit? It crossed my mind near the very end of my tenure, but up until then, I wasn't ready or willing.

MF: Part of why I stayed is because I did not have the privilege of stopping, of not supporting my family financially. Part of it is because the university exploits our hope that people and societies can transform in good ways. Part of it is my belief that nothing will ever change unless we do what we do: critically reflect upon and cocreate new and meaningful ways of being together in the world. And part of it is because I know that knowledge is power, especially when it is generated by communities of color, poor people, queer folks, and other aggrieved groups. I want to put as much knowledge into the hands of young people—our future—as possible.

RB: I believed that what I was and am currently engaged in can make a difference in the lives of other people, particularly Native womyn and children. I continue to work in the field in the county I live in: with tribes and other professionals involved in interventions and investigations of sexual violence. My particular experience and the specialized knowledge others have taught me have accumulated over twenty years. They create what I believe to be a responsibility to promote safety, address health disparities, and advocate for the rights of Native womyn, children, and communities as a scholar and practitioner in the field.

MH: Why not quit? A perceived and/or self-imposed sense of defeatism? This is a possibility in the light of a social mantra that encourages individuals not to give up; to work hard, trudge through, suck it up. Of course, we know such ideologies play into a hierarchical system and maintain hegemony. Conversely, defeat is not an option. I need only consider student demographics and recall my own educational experience, the *testimonios* of Chicanas/Latinas, and the personal narratives of womyn of color in academia to remind me that I can't just quit. There is a younger generation looking for faces and experiences similar to theirs.

RB: I am not so sure I won't quit. I am tired. I started working at thirteen, and I find that the academy will take everything you have and then some. My experience is that womyn—and womyn of color in particular—seem to work harder than others. Many of us grew up working in our homes beside our parents, bringing in additional income, and supporting others in our family who might be struggling. I have always been a worker, and at this point in my life, I need to reconsider what labor I will and will not give so freely.

MF: Roe once said, "Jobs are not supposed to make us sick." If joint appointments and academia are not healthy places—especially for womyn of color—how have we taken care of ourselves? I developed survival strategies and coping mechanisms—some more graceful than others—that allowed me to do important work. I found myself working alongside other womyn of color in unexpected solidarity as we navigated what Roe called the "double duty and double bind."

RB: I thought a university teaching position might be less stressful than the legal field and imagined that I was taking care of myself when I accepted the cross-college joint appointment. I was fortunate my family supported me in this endeavor. And in the sisterhood that developed in the academy, I found a level of unity and sustenance that continues to be irreplaceable in long-distance relationships found on bridge calls, Gmail, and googledocs.com.

MH: I don't know that I took care of myself. Given the stress of being at an R1 [Research One] institution, needing to earn tenure and promotion, and being jointly appointed, I worked a lot, so I have difficulty naming coping mechanisms. Because I grew up working class, I think working is the way you cope: you work to cope and cope by working. Aside from perhaps monthly w(h)ining gatherings with feminist friends and a supportive partner, what comes to mind are my efforts to avoid participating in favoritism.

RB: I found that the academy encourages competition and reinforces favoritism by situating one scholar—for whatever preferred qualities he or she possesses—above others while keeping untenured scholars in a suspended state of stress in their quest for tenure. This dynamic seems to encourage individualism and discourage collective responses.

MH: I have always been cautious—I learned early on that favoritism is exclusionary. At various institutions, I saw favoritism, the divisiveness it created or maintained among colleagues, and the resulting frustration and anger among those who weren't favored.

RB: Favoritism allocates limited resources among a group of people in ways that reinforce behaviors and allegiances that benefit those in power. It sends an important message to workers regarding behavior that will be rewarded and provides those who comply with a continued source of benefits (whether social or material) while disregarding the communal costs to the larger group. Favoritism also has the potential for scapegoating those who don't go along or who challenge the equity issues that are endemic.

MH: Favoritism promotes competition. There's a way that you get seduced by being the favorite at the expense of relationships with Others and womyn of color. *[RB chimes in, "Michelle wasn't seducible."]* This is akin to being male-centered and -identified at the expense of relationships with other womyn.

MF: Living intersectionally should make us more whole, not more splintered. For me joint appointments and academia had the capacity to support intersectionality and solidarity across disciplines, projects, and social identities. In most scenarios, those things were supported in word, but not in action or in, say, tenure and promotion criteria.

RB: It reminds me of the way lateral violence and internalized racism work to sabotage newly formed alliances.

MH: In terms of combating lateral violence and/or internalized racism, we could look back to the writings of early womyn of color, for example, *This Bridge Called My Back* (Moraga and Anzaldúa 1983). Those writers reflected an awareness of the centrality of supporting one another in the presence of hostile climates. Perhaps more fitting was the different position we occupied as untenured womyn of color in contrast to our relationships with other (white) womyn, who occupied positions of power and privilege; these relationships were supportive yet also existed within a context of class and gender politics, where that support felt very different.

RB: I regard working harder and pushing ourselves and students harder as a metaphor for our internal mastery—proving ourselves worthy in a system that defines us as "other." Creating solidarity with one another provides a testament to our collective legitimacy within the academy.

MH: I'm wondering if there are female archetypes from our backgrounds and histories that we can draw upon as a way to think through our feminist solidarity. Womyn's proclivity for self-sacrifice and martyrdom makes me think of La Virgen, but there are other archetypes, such as La Malinche and La Llorona. Working through our complaints, lamenting and crying about the conditions we experience, evokes La Llorona. From a Chicana feminist perspective, La Llorona represents our cries and organizing efforts, including the meetings and other steps we took (or contemplated) to change the structure of joint appointments. However—not wanting to stay in the mode of La Llorona, and not thinking that La Virgen is too applicable here—I'm left with La Malinche. Particularly as her history is revised and (re)imagined by Chicana feminists, Malinche/

Malintzin emerges as a strong, intelligent woman who exercised agency. In many ways, the archetype of La Malinche is consistent with the ways that I/we structured and maintained feminist solidarity by resisting the temptation to be competitive with one another.

[In the background, Roe says La Virgen actually applies since Michelle "reminded us that she was hard to get and thus not vulnerable to favoritism." Michelle replies, "Malinche still applies since I wasn't extended a counteroffer. I guess my resistance worked against me." We all laugh, but the laughter is followed by deafening silence acknowledging the reality that eventually Michelle did quit the joint appointment in the year she would have pursued tenure.]

MH: Who would be the feminist archetypes for each of you?

RB: I would consider the way Native womyn historically have been invisible and underestimated, not acknowledged for their contributions and their wisdom. Native women are often misunderstood and commodified by popular culture. Womyn like Pocahontas, Malinche, and Sacagawea. Each of these women was arguably abducted by white men. Paula Gunn Allen (2003) hypothesizes about these abductions and maintains that Pocahontas, Malinche, and Sacagawea were much more complex than the history books or Disney portrays them. Like other womyn of color, their legacies are undervalued. They are more often represented as mere footnotes to the accomplishments of nonnative men. These womyn are depicted in stereotyped ways in relation to nonnatives without regard to their lives and the roles they maintained within their tribal communities. Gunn Allen (2003) suggests it is the value and contribution of these womyn within their communities that motivated nonnative men to abduct them in the first place.

MF: I think our feminisms are deeply marked by our historical and racialized experiences. I think about how Chicana feminisms are informed by borderland epistemologies, Native feminisms are shaped by Indigenous cosmologies, and Asian American feminisms are influenced by transnational ways of knowing. The Asian archetypes that have personally influenced me are Buddhist and Hindu deities like Avalokiteshvara, Kali, and Durga, who embody the dialectics of wrath and compassion, ferocity and kindness, life and death. Not unlike Coatlicue. Not unlike Mother Earth. Those archetypes profoundly shaped my sense of womynhood. While it may not seem to fit into our discussion about joint appointments, Michelle's inquiry helps us to trace our academic solidarity to our personal and feminist genealogies.

[One week later: we are online chatting and on a conference call. Michelle is working late at her on-campus office in San Marcos, California. Roe has just arrived home in Fort Collins, Colorado. May is at a busy coffee shop in Ann Arbor, Michigan. We greet each other, laughing. Throughout our final conversation, there is much laughter. Perhaps the laughter masks the subtle recognition that this group conversation may be our last. There may not be (and most likely will not be) another gathering when we come together to talk intimately about what we've experienced in our dis/jointed appointments or our jointed dis/appointments. Despite not being together physically throughout the writing of this manuscript, our separation becomes more palpable as we enter the final pages.]

MF: Part of what I love about these conversations is that we are three strong-willed womyn with very different personalities, ancestors, backgrounds, and voices in different places in our lives. The shared acts of listening and writing—and all of the laughter in between—have affirmed and confirmed my sense of feminist solidarity with you. This time together reminds me that feminist solidarities are always in progress, in motion, growing, and unfinished. They are worthy of celebration, laughter, and cultivation.

RB: As I reflect on our coming together for this project and working with one another, there is a sense of authenticity and the unequivocal way we have provided a space to hear one another's voices with no apologies. We honor ourselves and one another in maintaining a space where the experiences of womyn of color in the academy can be heard.

MH: Practicing feminist solidarity encompasses being honest and straightforward with one another, almost unabashedly, unapologetically, yet compassionately. Deepening the practice is leaving open spaces to critique and express disagreement with one another. It also involves feeling comfortable in the company of womyn of color. In many ways, our feminist solidarities have been strengthened in the process of writing this manuscript.

MF: Compassion is so central, because it allows the differences among us to coexist, to exist without negating one another.

RB: In that way, we are able to move beyond class, queerness, age, race/ethnicity, and regional differences that reflect our communities and neighborhoods of origin.

MH: We come from different generations (or decades)—May in her thirties, me in my forties, and Roe in her fifties. The generational span can be an issue and has been used to explain the divergence among feminists. For example, during a feminist scholarship panel at a recent conference, all the womyn of color—straight and queer—called attention to the ways our intellectual and personal concerns and interests had been neglected in published (feminist) scholarship. We did so as a way of emphasizing the importance of intersectionality that contrasted with the group of white feminist scholars also participating in the panel. The feminist solidarity in that context was questionable. Racial/ethnic/class identifications are central to such a connection. A working-class background and continuing to identify with it aids a deepened understanding of economic struggle and its impact on mobility, access, and agency.

RB: I notice that I am present in a different way when Asian/African Americans and Chicanos speak. I buy and read different scholarly articles than I did before my cross-college joint appointment. I know that I listen in a different way to womyn of color scholarship; I have become more informed and involved with womyn of color: their stories, histories, and the challenges within their communities.

MF: Queer womyn of color, especially writers and poets, made clear to me the importance of creating spaces where womyn can love one another. Having that space allows us to bear witness to each other's stories, suffering, strengths, and truths.

RB: The feminists I first read and hung out with were queer, and they inspired much of my radical thinking and catalyzed a sense of resistance and strength within me.

MH: May's reference to sharing spaces with queer womyn of color and bearing witness reminds me of the power of *testimonios* (Latina Feminist Group 2001), the obligations that follow from bearing witness to the experiences of others. Perhaps that is what we have attempted to do with one another throughout these conversations.

[During the revision stage of this manuscript, we recognized that we have an obligation toward other womyn of color to concretize—or attempt to do so—suggestions that support not only surviving but thriving in a joint appointment in the academy.]

MF: I suggest that new womyn of color faculty have a clear understanding of what inequities they will be expected to endure in a joint appointment. Do they have to attend faculty meetings, serve on committees, and advise students from both departments? In other words, will their obligations be doubled because of the joint appointment? Will their tenure file be determined by one or both departments, and how will that affect their research, teaching, and service? How might their department/college address or compensate them for this unwelcome "double duty and double bind"? Are there womyn of color faculty—on and/or off campus—who might support them?

MH: To womyn of color who are contemplating a joint appointment, I would say ascertain specifics about the structure of the assignment being considered, including the expectations of both departments and their past experience and knowledge of what is involved to make the structure work. Also talk with potential non-ethnic studies colleagues across campus to determine the (dis)advantages of having a joint appointment and what responsibilities or commitments they think they have to a jointly appointed faculty member. I would ask colleagues of jointly appointed faculty to familiarize themselves (if they have not already) with the responsibilities and expectations placed upon and assumed by someone with a joint appointment. After they have done that, they need to commit to being an advocate for faculty who undertake joint appointments when circumstances arise where decisions might unduly and inequitably impact them.

RB: Make sure you have in writing all of the benefits from the joint appointment and a clear delineation of the roles and responsibilities expected from the position. Cross-college joint appointments present additional challenges, particularly with tenure and promotion and specific college expectations about teaching loads, grant writing, and service commitments.

RB/MF/MH: Finally, we have struggled with whether we should offer recommendations to administrators (e.g., department chairs, deans, or vice presidents) about ways they can make joint appointments equitable, hospitable, and sustainable. Integral to our dilemma is that there is no singular recommendation to rectify the potential challenges arising from joint appointments, just as there are a myriad of ways to institute them structurally. Consequently, what are needed are dedicated, committed, and attentive administrators who remain mindful that joint appointments are unlike traditional, singularly appointed faculty positions. Ideally, then, administrators need to focus on the ways that institutions benefit from a diverse faculty and carefully examine and seek to implement means to reflect that diversity among jointly appointed faculty. Ideally, compensation for jointly appointed faculty should be commensurate with the double workload that many of us have assumed or continue to carry. Finally, administrators need to undertake—while also soliciting input from faculty who hold these positions—periodic reviews of the way joint appointments are structured and can be improved.

Postscript

Three time zones. Three states. Three weeks later. We are three womyn of color in academia, but not of it. For more than three months, our conversations have brought us closer through our words, laughter, and silences. We experienced familiar dimensions of each other, and we embraced new ones. Our understanding for each other grew from our different ways of sharing, listening, and writing. Our solidarity expanded when one or more of us could talk about feeling excluded from conversations, and it has been nourished by these tentative, hearty, and honest exchanges from the heart. Finally, this contribution is our collective statement, much in the vein of our foremothers' Combahee River Collective Statement (Combahee River Collective 1983). We hope it offers ideas and insight to fellow womyn of color. We recognize the risks inherent in making public those personal conversations that we reserve for private spaces. Those beautiful, trusted spaces. Yet—similar to Gloria Anzaldúa's "Speaking in Tongues: A Letter to Third World Women Writers" (1983)—we intend to blur the lines of not only allegiance and solidarity but also intellectual and disciplinary spheres, so as to expose the un/speakables. May y/our journey be well.

CHAPTER 18

WHAT'S LOVE GOT TO DO WITH IT?

Life Teachings from Multiracial Feminism

Kari Lerum

Who needs a heart when a heart can be broken?

Tina Turner

Meeting Audre

I first "met" Audre Lorde in the late 1980s while attending a midsized liberal arts Lutheran university on the West Coast. Because I grew up in a predominately white working-class town and attended college with mostly white middle-class students and professors, Audre Lorde's work was my introduction to multiracial feminism; she was also one of my first loves. My love for her was abstract because I only knew her through her writing, but she danced into my life at a critical crossroads, sang to me about the "erotic as power," and made me hungry for more. I was a senior in college, writing my thesis on what I called the "evilization of sexuality"— attempting to understand how and why religious and cultural texts so often demonized earthly and bodily matters. Why were the body and sexuality seen as evil? Why were women and people of color so often cast as the source of this evil? Why did religious and cultural texts so consistently associate mind and spirit with maleness and whiteness?

In my own life, I was questioning taken-for-granted knowledge and wondering if anything I had been taught in church was true. As a child and a teenager, my (mostly white, middle-class, college-educated) church had given me a sense of identity and community: one that offered a welcoming space outside of shopping malls and the cliques of my (mostly white, working-class, non-college-bound) high school, a space where I could develop an inner sense of self, mind, and spirit. While I was a basketball and track athlete and a drum major for the school's marching band, I kept myself planted on the sidelines of my high school's social events, playing the role of spectator and social commentator. Tall, shy, and religious as a child, I watched the social/secular world from a distance. I had my small gang of friends—all college-bound white girls like me—but peers also told me regularly that I was too tall. (To which comment I silently wondered, "too tall for what?") Perhaps understandably, I had little desire for dating or taking risks that involved my heart.

But in college—with my expanded intellectual and social repertoire—my church community became increasingly cramped for my growing humanist, pragmatist, and feminist consciousness and my burgeoning sexual appetite for both women and men. Lorde invited me into a fresh intellectual and spiritual space, a way of thinking and living that entailed freedom, creativity, passion, and embodied feminist living. It was a place where the erotic was not a source of shame, isolation, and fear but, rather, a source of power, creativity, community, and an integrated life; a place where hierarchical dichotomies like superior/inferior, good/evil, mind/body, man/woman, and white/black were exposed as man-made justifications for privilege and inequality.

Writing Alone

I went to graduate school for the same reasons many intellectual feminists do: a love of learning and a life of the mind, and a belief in social justice and the radical implications of intellectual thought. I imagined graduate school would bring me closer to purpose, love, and justice politics. My classes would be full of students and professors like Audre Lorde, with whom I would become friends (and maybe lovers), and together we would work for a better world. Since I was going to attend a large, public university in a liberal city, I worried that I would be the most conservative, privileged, and sheltered person in the bunch but hoped that my future intellectual comrades would show me the way toward what Cornell West calls "engaged insurgent praxis" (hooks and West 1991, 144).

Instead, it seemed to me that I was the most radical person in the room. I was surrounded by "cream-of-the-crop" researchers, many from even more privileged class backgrounds than mine. Some of my colleagues were interested in studying social movements but seemed completely disinterested in working for social change. I watched graduate students emulate faculty in public performances of intellectual sophistication and superiority, often, it seemed, at others' expense. My skills in statistics and high theory expanded, but I had to search hard for scraps of radical theory, and even harder for people who were integrating it with action.

It soon became clear that my interests in studying the edges of culture and sexuality through qualitative methods and with a theoretical lens that critiqued structures of power was an awkward fit with my department. I had heard that graduate students were supposed to work with professors, but the process by which faculty chose the students was murky. A couple of male professors took an interest in me but not necessarily in an intellectual way. I became increasingly alienated and deflated. I also became paranoid about the way I was viewed (with my rock-and-roll style and interest in sex workers) by the mostly white male heterosexual faculty. I began to retreat.

Graduate school became an exercise in isolation; my road to a PhD seemed increasingly improbable. My political, social, and intellectual worlds were increasingly fragmented. I seriously considered quitting school to become a documentary film-maker, where I could be free to practice radical social critique.

I did not realize it at the time, but my isolation, fear, and hurt at being excluded from departmental power was not just a result of sexism but also of my race and class privilege. I was well aware of the sexist double standard for appearance: as an unspoken rule, women graduate students and faculty dress and act profession-ally while their male counterparts nonchalantly show up in jeans and T-shirts. I felt angry about this sexist norm and deliberately worked against it. However, due to my own unexamined race and class privileges, I had simply assumed that I could critique social conventions, wear and study whatever I wanted, and still be respected and promoted by senior white male faculty. This was very likely not an assumption shared by my colleagues of color. Additionally, considering an alternative career as a documentary filmmaker also sprang from my class-based security; while nowhere near a trust-fund baby, I knew that my parents would partly protect me from slipping into abject poverty, regardless of my career choice.

Around that time I was encouraged by the faculty hire of an African American woman—the only woman-of-color faculty member in the department at that time. Like me she studied the challenges of oppressed people and worked from a qualita-tive, critical perspective. But in what seemed like the blink of an eye—and before I had even had a chance to take a class from her—she vanished from the department.

I viewed her departure—as did other women in my department—with alarm. The senior-level faculty members were close-lipped about the details of her case, but something bigger than just that was wrong. She was one of three female assistant professors who I had watched just disappear before going up for tenure. Feeling that my position in the department as a graduate student was tenuous, I did not know if I should—or how I could—intervene.

Whereas in the past I had turned to Audre Lorde for guidance on my own and others' sexual and personal freedom, I started to become haunted by the less joyful aspects of her writing: "We have all been programmed to respond to the human differences between us with fear and loathing and to handle that difference in one of three ways: ignore it, and if that is not possible, copy it if we think it is dominant, *or destroy it if we think it is subordinate*" (Lorde [1984] 2000, 605; emphasis added). The real-world implications of racist and sexist systems of oppression, so vividly described by Lorde, were beginning finally to sink in.

Making Connections

> *When we talk about that which will sustain and nurture our spiritual growth as a people, we must once again talk about the importance of com-munity. For one of the most vital ways we can sustain ourselves is by build-ing communities of resistance, places where we know we are not alone.*

> bell hooks, *Breaking Bread: Insurgent Black Intellectual Life*

It was becoming increasingly obvious that junior women faculty were not just falling through the cracks: those cracks were systemic, and women of color were falling through them faster. There were also murmured concerns about potentially exploitative power relationships between faculty and graduate students. This was prior to any formal policy about sexual harassment in the department but was fresh on the heels of the Anita Hill-Clarence Thomas hearings. In response to these galvanizing departmental and cultural/political events, women faculty started to reach out more directly to each other and women graduate students.

Possibly due to this rearticulation of feminist consciousness, some women faculty started to slip me articles or books of interest to my work. I credit two women in particular, one a senior-level professor and one a recent PhD graduate of the department—both queer/lesbian (and white) like me—for getting me back into the game. They invited me to present at conferences and contribute to special edited volumes, connected me to other scholars, served on my dissertation committee, and eventually pulled me through to the dissertation/PhD finish line. Because these two senior women took an interest in not just my work but my welfare, I was able to finish.

The mentoring that I eventually received is the sort that is necessary for graduate students and junior faculty members to succeed. Professional mentoring involves a personal relationship between two people—their shared interests, hobbies, values, and philosophies—in other words, their sense of a shared culture and community, as well as the ways that their social positions of both privilege and oppression matter. This means that newcomers, who have fewer overlapping sociocultural axes of power and privilege with their seniors, simply are not included in as many valued social interactions and networks. Without any formal mechanisms to ensure equal access to mentors, it is easier for those in power to ignore, systematically disadvantage, or destroy the less enfranchised. It is no surprise, then, that mentoring is critical for graduate students and faculty of color in white-dominated departments and disciplines (Stanley and Lincoln 2005).

By the time I finally finished the excruciating task of writing my dissertation and earning my PhD, the tenure-track job market in my field was reportedly more fiercely competitive than ever. But for family reasons (my female partner was in school, and we had a new baby), I focused my job search on positions that were either close to home or in known gay-friendly locations. My upper-class, white, graduate-student colleagues thought I was crazy for limiting my geographical options. In contrast, my friends who were women of color, queer, and/or working class (in other words, those who understood the need for home allies in a hostile world, prioritized their family as much—if not more—than their careers, and did not assume that they could just move anywhere and be accepted by any community) supported me in this decision.

Through one of my mentor's connections, I landed a full-time lecturer position at a local Jesuit university. While I would have to continue to search for a permanent job, this was an important and convenient stepping stone between graduate school and the tenure-track job market. It gave me and my family vastly increased economic stability, a chance to live in subsidized faculty housing in a city and neighborhood where we were already welcome, and the social status of an institutional affiliation.

When the perfect tenure-track job for me opened up within driving distance of home, my same two graduate mentors wrote glowing letters of recommendation. This—in addition to the publications I had then in print, combined with my now-extensive teaching experience—helped me get the job. Upon hearing the news that I had been offered the job, my partner—who was not at all prone to supernatural explanations—tearfully exclaimed, "A miracle has happened!" After so many years of toil, near failure, and being told that I couldn't afford to be picky, I was over the moon with gratitude and glee. It did indeed feel like a miracle. But I also knew that a heavy portion of this miracle had been set up by a lifetime of social connections. And it was with this knowledge that I approached my work as a new faculty member.

Teaching/Learning about Oppression

The teacher, in the flesh, embodies knowledge.

Joanna Frueh, *Erotic Faculties*

As a new assistant professor, I taught classes about a number of socially and politically contentious issues that disproportionately impact oppressed and marginalized populations: sex work, welfare reform, incarceration, teen pregnancy, domestic violence, GLBTQ families, homelessness, and hate crimes. To facilitate productive discussions around these issues, I attempted to create safe and warm classrooms and online discussions. I was consumed with finding and creating assignments to help my students feel connected to both the material and each other. On the eve of every new term, I ritualistically found courage and inspiration in bell hooks's *Teaching to Transgress* (1994). I loved to teach and often felt a deep sense of alliance with and admiration for my students.

My hope in facilitating a warm learning atmosphere was not just for the sake of pleasure and safety (although those are both valuable qualities) but also to help students stretch themselves into new theoretical, empirical, and experiential domains. I hoped that in such an atmosphere, students would examine, rather than defend, their own assumptions and engage in thoughtful dialogue without fear of being attacked. I emphasized to students that they would be graded not on their ultimate position on a topic but on their ability to critically evaluate available evidence, compare and contrast theoretical models, and respond with a comprehensive set of questions and conclusions. I was prepared for conflict and even invited it as a productive process—as long as it did not dehumanize or alienate anyone.

But despite my concern for protecting students and guiding them into discussions that were both rigorous and humane, I neglected to protect myself. Sure, I was aware of the risks of being "out" in the classroom: the national antigay marriage movement was gaining steam, and high-profile hate crimes against the GLBTQ community were on the rise. One of my students brought me a news clipping about a local pastor (whose church was within walking distance of my campus) who was publicly preaching antigay hatred. This student said that she was worried and told me to be careful. However, I assumed that my privileged structural position as a tenure-track faculty member at a top university meant that my subject positions and all that they invoked could stay above the fray, at least in my own classroom.

This false assumption soon rubbed up against my next lesson in intersectional privilege: although I was bolstered by a number of social and institutional factors—including having a position of authority as a faculty member and a reputation for being nice, fair, and attractive (all shaped by gender, race, and class ideologies), and being white with a PhD—this would not spare me from classroom "microaggression" (Pierce 1978) or interactional cruelties inflicted across lines of difference to maintain racist, classist, sexist, heterosexist, and other oppressive social hierarchies.

I will highlight two classroom incidents here. One prolonged situation occurred in a sexuality class that I was coteaching. Midway through the term, someone in the class anonymously posted on our online discussion board an article about the so-called gay agenda that referred to gay people as less than human and responsible for the demise of western civilization. Shortly thereafter another online post specifically named me as a "feminazi." The note was accompanied by an image of a swastika dripping with blood, framed by a pink triangle, and signed by Fred Phelps (the leader of the God Hates Fags movement). The actual author of the second note and image later voluntarily identified himself and said it was meant to be a joke. However, the student who posted the "gay-agenda" article never identified her/himself, and the incident sparked fierce debate among the students. One student (a heterosexual woman with gay friends) threatened to file a lawsuit against the still-unnamed student on the basis of creating a hostile learning environment; she demanded that the student either delete the gay-agenda article or reveal his or her identity. A few others in the class countered with a free-speech tactic, arguing that the student had the right to remain anonymous and the article should remain online. The bulk of the class were silent and/or neutral observers.

As the only acknowledged queer person in the class (of ninety students, two professors, and one teaching assistant), I felt the entire episode was a directly personal and hostile act. And as one of the professors of the class—and an untenured one at that—I also found myself in a very awkward position about how to respond. I shared my sociological analysis of the deleterious impact of hate speech with the class but then ducked and prayed for the term to end. Each remaining moment that I was required to stand in front of that class felt like torture. (After that quarter, I revoked the option of anonymous postings and emphasized the importance of personal accountability for all discussions of course material.)

The second prolonged incident stemmed from a popular course that I taught on social inequality. Using an intersectional framework to discuss a range of social issues, we came to a unit on hate crimes, which included not just violence against GLBTQ populations but also targeted crimes against women and people of color. For this particular class session, I brought in examples of recent local cases of hate crimes and/or discrimination based on sexual or gender orientation and asked for volunteers to read the stories aloud. One story was about a lesbian high school student who had been prohibited from using the girls' locker room. Even though she had no record of causing trouble inside or outside the locker room, some of her classmates and their parents had circulated a petition to ban her from using it; the petition was signed by the principal, and the student was banned.

After hearing this story, a student—a white woman who was approximately my age—raised her hand, looked directly at me, and said, "I sure wouldn't want to get undressed next to a lesbian." I calmly replied that if she was worried about being checked out in the locker room, she could also be concerned about the straight women next to her and that it is possible that those who are most identifiable as lesbians are more likely to keep their eyes cast down, knowing that they are already seen as sexual suspects. Other students in the class (all of whom identified themselves as heterosexual) then jumped in and argued passionately against her position. (Meanwhile, as a lifelong athlete, I silently worried, Does she go to my gym? What if she sees me in the locker room? Will she start a petition to keep me out?)

The next day I received an email from this student requesting a meeting to discuss the "unfair treatment" she felt she was receiving from other students in my class. With extreme trepidation, I set up an appointment for a few days later. My concern was not about meeting with her but about the timing of her request: over the course of the term, she had taken the most extreme position in the class on a number of issues, including affirmative action, corporal punishment in schools, and homelessness. In every case, her discussions with classmates were (in my opinion) vigorous, but civil. Why was it only now that she wanted to complain to me in person? In agreeing to this meeting, I knew that I would be expected to listen compassionately to her desire for locker rooms segregated by sexual orientation (with the subtext that she needed to be protected from people like me). And I knew that if I did not do this, I risked being called biased. I started to become very concerned and wondered, Should I invite another colleague to the meeting? Should I prepare myself for a case of reverse discrimination? Should I hire a lawyer?

This is where the story takes a turn for the worse. Remembering the trauma and isolation of being the only visible gay target in the previous classroom incident, I decided to reach out to my network of feminist academics, a group that was largely dominated by white, nonqueer women with PhDs. I might not always be safe to facilitate critical discussions of homophobia and heterosexism in my classroom, but at least I could do it there, I thought. I sent out a request on the group Listserv for support and advice on the way to approach my upcoming meeting.

Over the next two days, more than a dozen feminist colleagues from around the United States responded to my request. However—to my surprise/shock—most of the advice seemed to lack understanding that this was not just an abstract teachable moment but a live-time, embodied enactment of intersectional systems of power and oppression. A few provided much-appreciated sympathy/empathy. However, the bulk of the responses focused on at least one of the following themes: (1) personal showcasing: using my problem (framed as an individual and classroom-management issue) as an opportunity to showcase their pedagogy and describing ways they (all nonqueer-identified faculty) successfully avoided and/or navigated antigay sentiments in the classroom; (2) gendered instructions: telling me simply to listen and validate the student's concerns, including a suggestion to offer her cookies and tea; (3) blaming me: some questioned why I took this issue personally; others insinuated that I was responsible for the entire incident and had clearly failed to make my class safe for this white heterosexual student. One colleague (whom—prior to this email exchange—I had never met or had any interaction with), scoldingly told me that I was "on the offensive" and had "allowed no room for opinions other than [my] own" in the classroom. This colleague told me to conjure up some sympathy for minority perspectives, saying, "Imagine if it was you—as the only minority view in the classroom."

Such advice tasted like cups of poison disguised as feminist tea. From my perspective, I had spent years bending over backward to make the most conservative of my students comfortable by emphasizing points of common ground, including my love of children, my commitment to parenting, and my recognition of the social function of religious institutions. At the core of my pedagogy was a commitment to ensure that no one ever felt excluded or alienated in my classroom. My teaching evaluations consistently described me as fair, open minded, and supportive of students' opinions and contributions. As a white, middle-class, (former) church girl, I had plenty of experience in playing nice, fair, and sympathetic; what I needed now was a lesson in self-defense. But ultimately what I wanted from my feminist family— my chosen safe community—was an acknowledgment that this was both a personal and political situation; both an act of microaggression against me and a situation that was embedded in a larger system of power and oppression directed at entire categories of people.

The meeting with my student passed without undue pain. Neither of us spoke about locker-room politics; she mostly needed reassurance that I was not going to allow other students to gang up on her. I did not offer her cookies and tea, but I did listen closely, and I empathized with her stress about feeling attacked in the classroom. I carefully assured her that I was committed to making the classroom safe for everyone, both students and faculty. I arranged for a separate meeting with the three other students she named to review expectations of classroom civility.

Ironically, my best self-defense lesson in this case came from my own aggressor; unlike me she felt entitled to speak up for herself when she felt individually targeted. Unlike me, she was confident that structures of power (in this case, me, and if not me, my colleagues and superiors) would protect her. While I understood that a legacy of institutional/cultural protections can create elevated self-confidence, I also reevaluated my own assumptions about what I could and could not say to demand safe spaces for myself and other institutionally and culturally marginalized faculty members. I knew that I needed to become more proactive in my self-protection. I also realized that faculty members who come from the outskirts of dominant power can only be safe from bias-based aggressions if they are embedded within supportive communities.

Shortly thereafter—feeling betrayed and heartbroken—I quietly removed myself from the feminist listserv and distanced myself from that community.

Reassessments

> *Once we realize that there are few pure victims or oppressors, and that each one of us derives varying amounts of penalty and privilege from the multiple systems of oppression that frame our lives, then we will be in a position to see the need for new ways of thought and action.*
>
> Patricia Hill Collins, "Toward a New Vision: Race, Class, and Gender as Categories of Analysis and Connection"

On the heels of these experiences, I felt the air seep from my love of teaching, as well as my overall joie de vivre. I felt traumatized and fearful and realized that maybe I was naïve in believing that I could invite emotion into the classroom, that I could teach about oppression without directly placing my human rights (as well as those of entire categories of people) on trial, and that I could rely on any community to back me up if things got rough. Who was I to think that the classroom, and academia as a whole, could be a safe space for me?

Here was my next embodied lesson in multiracial feminism: faculty of color have a long history of being targets of racial microaggression in their classrooms, disciplines, and universities. Faculty of color are regularly accused of being biased when they teach about inequality and, in particular, racism (Messner 2011), and for that matter are more likely to be presumed incompetent to teach any subject at all (Stanley 2006). Suspicions over their qualifications are often compounded for faculty of color, who may be subjected to assumptions about being token affirmative-action hires (Niemann 2003).

In contrast, many students see white faculty, and in particular white male heterosexuals, as being the pinnacle of individual merit and objectivity (Messner 2011). Faculty in socially privileged categories may be rewarded both with better teaching evaluations and special adoration when they teach about the oppression of others (Peretz 2010). While I am occasionally a gay target in my classroom, faculty of color in white-dominated departments and universities are very often in the spotlight (Stanley 2006). And if those faculty turn to white-dominated networks for support, they may be reminded of their need to be objective and/or be dismissively told that they are taking things too personally.

Such stresses, wounds, and betrayals across lines of privilege were indeed the inspiration for much of the writing I have held so dear to the core of my scholarship, teaching, and life. Scholars such as Audre Lorde, Patricia Hill Collins, bell hooks, Gloria Anzaldúa, Suzanne Pharr, and Shane Phelan have long inspired me; they are the ones who gave me the courage to teach about intersectional oppression to begin with. They also warned me about the dangers of sweeping claims about women, feminists, and lesbians and the need to stay vigilant about multiple and intersecting forms of oppression. Despite the fact that I already knew these things, my personal experiences have made these lessons stick. As hooks writes, "Emphasizing paradigms of domination that call attention to woman's capacity to dominate is one way to deconstruct and challenge the simplistic notion that man is the enemy, woman the victim; the notion that men have always been the oppressors. *Such thinking enables us to examine our role as women in the perpetuation and maintenance of systems of domination*" (hooks 2000, 613; emphasis added).

Academia is a complex, contradictory environment, full of privileges and hierarchies but also potential for transformation. As hooks, Lorde, and other multiracial feminist scholars teach, within this environment (and all others), reflection upon our multiple positions is a necessary and ongoing process. Even those who have been victimized by various oppressions are still quite capable of oppressing others, and "as women, we must root out internalized patterns of oppression within ourselves if we are to move beyond the most superficial aspects of social change" (Lorde [1984] 2000, 610–11).

Integrating Life, Work, and Politics

This has not been an easy chapter for me to write. But I am writing it from my position as a tenured professor, which means that I now have more tools, security, and privilege to both protect myself and instigate institutional and social change.

I now understand from personal experience the complex, paradoxical, precarious, and deeply intersectional experience of attempting to maintain faculty authority while also occupying socially stigmatized and oppressed positions. At the same time, I also know that students find it more palatable when I teach about others' oppression, rather than my own. I am still intimidated by discussions of heterosexism and homophobia (and absolutely need allies when they occur), but I find students receptive to my discussions of racism and have never been accused of having a race agenda. This is part of the reason why I see it as my obligation to speak up for others enduring different types of oppression, but I must do that in a way that explicitly critiques the elevated respect I receive when I teach about people in less-privileged categories. I know that when I witness covert (and overt) racism and classism and see my colleagues and students of color retreating or slipping through the cracks, these things require me to be an active ally, not a neutral bystander (Niemann 2003). I also know that making space for diversity includes cultivating my "decolonized mind" (hooks 1991), as well as creating a welcoming institutional culture, and that diversity thrives when we can encompass complexity, move beyond dichotomies, and honor the expansive creative force of the "borderlands" of identity and culture (Anzaldúa 1987; Keating 2002).

Along with many other faculty who teach from feminist and antioppression frameworks, I share the goals of critical, rigorous, and respectful classroom engagement, combined with a recognition of my position and a commitment to social justice. I do not claim a balanced or neutral view of the social world, particularly about what I consider to be violations of human dignity. (I do not ask my students to be neutral, either; if they insist on striving for this goal, I ask them to recognize that claims of neutrality and objectivity are also social positions—protected by more institutional privilege.) I express my subjective opinions as a starting place, not as a position that rigidly dictates where I stand on any given matter; I see this approach as a way to be honest with students and myself about the production of my knowledge. While I value the criteria for rigorous empirical evidence, gathering that evidence is a political act, full of decisions about what to gather and for what purpose. Through my example, I try to demonstrate that our direct experience mediates the way we construct knowledge (what we know is true), but other sources of information must be considered.

Crucial to this entire learning process is allocating space and legitimacy for personal reflection. All of us—university students, faculty, and staff, and those outside university walls—can benefit from reassessing past assumptions against current evidence and then revaluating future commitments, goals, and strategies. This sort of multilayered reflection facilitates both personal growth and institutional/cultural change. I credit and thank the editors of *Presumed Incompetent,* the book where this chapter is published, for prompting this valuable reflective space in me.

Reflecting on my personal and professional lessons and my approach as a scholar, instructor, activist, and community-based researcher has evolved from assuming that any religious, activist, scholarly environment or classroom is safe (and then feeling shocked when it is not) to understanding that all communities contain multiple visible and invisible subjective ideas and agendas. Given this complexity, my focus has turned to finding and creating workable, pragmatic, conscious coalitions. Shane Phelan (who in turn credits Bernice Johnson Reagon) summarizes coalition strategy as "not about nurturance but . . . about stretching past the limits of comfort and safety to the work that needs to be done" (Phelan 1994, 74).

What would a coalition approach to classroom, departmental, and university-level dynamics look like? As a start, Patricia Hill Collins emphasizes that we need to "recognize that our differing experiences with oppression create problems in the relationships among us" (2003). In response to this recognition, the "work that needs to be done" entails finding common causes and also building empathy (Collins [1993] 2003). An example of a coalition that has been helpful in decreasing the hostile climate of many high schools (and perhaps also universities) is the Gay-Straight Alliance (GSA) (Goodenow, Szalacha, and Westheimer 2006). While each GSA chapter is unique, what unites this movement is a commitment to reflect upon the harmful dynamics of homophobia and heterosexism across multiple lines of institutional and social privilege, including faculty, staff, and students and gay, straight, and other sexual/gender orientations.

In the light of the success of the GSA model, I find it curious why similar models focused on race and class have not emerged on high school and college campuses. (To my knowledge, there are no Black/Brown-White Alliances or Upper Class-Working Class Alliances). I mention this not as a directive that race- and class-based alliances should be organized within this same dichotomous (and potentially essentialist) rubric, but I do think that the pros and cons of employing models like these are worth discussing. This discussion might include questions such as (1) has the GSA model not been applied to race and class issues due to white people's discomfort with acknowledging systemic and unmerited privilege across race and class lines? (2) are GSAs successful partly because their members tend to be homogenous in race and class? (3) is it not still important to name, examine, and critique hierarchical dichotomies like superior/inferior, good/evil, mind/body, man/woman, and white/black and reflect on the work of Audre Lorde stating that these dichotomies are man- and woman-made justifications for privilege and inequality? And (4) after critically examining these socially constructed dichotomies, how can we better facilitate cross-category, empathy-building discussions around common human sources of pain, suffering, hope, and love? I believe that these questions are productive beginnings for coalition and empathy building across lines of social privilege and oppression. They may even help us find personal ways to freedom, creativity, passion, and embodied feminist living.

In her 1984 hit single, "What's Love Got to Do with It?" Tina Turner, the iconic African American singer and survivor of domestic violence, asked, "Who needs a heart when a heart can be broken?" In 1989—in a different modality and across different circumstances—the iconic feminist theorist bell hooks proposed a feminist solution for overcoming betrayal, misunderstanding, and conflict. She calls upon feminists to embrace love as a "mediating force . . . so that we are not broken in this process, so that we do not despair. . . . Embedded in the commitment to feminist revolution is the challenge to love. Love can be and is an important source of empowerment when we struggle to confront issues of sex, race, and class. Working together to identify and face our difference—to face the ways we dominate and are dominated—to change our actions, we need a mediating force that can sustain us so that we are not broken in this process, so that we do not despair" (2000, 618). All of us who are attempting to live our lives based on antioppression principles know that this is a tricky and sometimes treacherous endeavor. But I firmly believe now more than ever that this is something worth pursuing with all our hearts.

CHAPTER 19

SHARING OUR GIFTS

Beth A. Boyd

Presumed incompetent. In thinking about my contribution to this volume, it occurred to me that, in my career, such presumptions have many times come from those around me and, at the worst times, become my presumption about myself. Many people have helped me learn to overcome this way of thinking and discover the gifts I have been given. My hope is that telling this story will pass on that wisdom to someone who needs to find his or her own gifts.

When I was accepted into a graduate clinical psychology program, I automatically assumed that the only reason was because I was an ethnic minority—a Native American woman. This was partly due to my low self-esteem and partly due to knowing I was an alternate choice in the pool of those accepted. Several years later—when we all felt safe enough to really talk to each other—my colleagues and I discovered that, in fact, most of us were alternates, and we all felt that we did not really belong there. But, for me—like many other ethnic minority students—my status led me to buy into the "imposter syndrome" fully and doubt both my abilities and the reasons for my acceptance. I often felt that I had to work extra hard to prove that I deserved to be there and that I could not ask for help because that would only confirm the expectation that I did not have what it took to be successful.

Somewhere in my third year, when I finally began to ask questions about how the psychology we were learning related to ethnic minorities and their communities, I was told that this had nothing to do with psychology, and if I wanted to talk about it, I should seek my own therapy. Thankfully I took this advice and—with the support of a wonderful therapist—learned to believe in myself, build and utilize a support system, and put words to my experiences as a Native American woman. Although my racial/ethnic minority status clearly affected my experience in the academic setting, as a rule these issues were not addressed in a formal way. Diversity and multicultural issues were not yet a required area of focus in clinical psychology. By the time I completed my internship and postdoc just a few years later, they had become much more important. This is not to say that we necessarily understood them any better—we were just required to address them in some formal way.

From the moment I began my job-seeking process, race and ethnicity became the most prominent issues in my decision making. It was the early 1990s, and recruiting faculty of color had become valued—or at least attention to affirmative action and equal opportunity was required. Ethnic minority students, recent graduates, and others who might be job seeking received multiple mass-mailed invitations to apply for positions at very prestigious institutions of higher education. As a person receiving this sudden onslaught of invitations, I could not help but wonder what it all meant. I knew that they did not know me or my work, so the only reason I was being recruited was because I was an ethnic minority. There were some very good opportunities among these—places and positions where I knew I could make a contribution—but I had to wonder if what I could do was as important as who I was as an ethnic minority. Since I was fresh from training, it seemed most important to emphasize my skills, abilities, and knowledge. My clinical, teaching, and research experiences, my publications and presentations—these were the things I expected to showcase.

However, it became clear that, in many cases, my status as a minority was actually more important, and I had to learn how to evaluate this. After all, this status was not something I had achieved, not something I could work harder to enhance, or even something I could lose through total neglect. Furthermore, it was something for which I had often felt punished because it led me to ask questions about difference that seemingly could not be answered, made me feel so different from my peers that I wondered if I really belonged in the academic world, and caused me to think I had to do twice as much just to deserve to be there. But I also had dreams, and my ethnic identity had everything to do with those dreams. As a Native American woman, I wanted to help my people, to make our communities stronger, to fight inequality, and to make a difference in the lives of children.

So I had to decide how important it was that I was being recruited for my ethnic/racial status, rather than my stellar performance as a graduate student and clinical psychology intern. Further complicating things—because I had always imagined myself as a clinician—I had not properly prepared for an academic career. So being recruited for a position in academia did not really fit my expectations. Although it felt good to be recruited, realizing that it was often because I was an ethnic minority took some of the joy out of that experience. A big part of the process was figuring out how much it mattered to me that my ethnic minority status was so important. Did other issues have the same prominence? I wondered what it would mean if I had no interest in working with ethnic minority students, or if I decided to do the research I had been trained to do and not the ethnic minority research academia assumed I would do. (This was not the case, but I wondered if I had a choice.) I wondered if they knew what it would mean if I did do ethnic minority research. And from a personal perspective, I knew I did not have the usual list of publications one expected from a good academic candidate—would coming into this situation less prepared have an impact as I approached promotion and tenure?

I decided to interview at a university that was recruiting me based on the work I had done on a professional organization task force with one of the faculty members. He had been impressed with the contributions I had made to the task force, so it felt as if this recruitment was based on an accomplishment. The program had a strong commitment to building capacity programs to train Native American and nonnative psychologists who would be competent to provide services in Native American communities. Because this was so interesting to me, I challenged myself to consider an academic position after all. As none of the work I had done or showcased in the job talk had anything to do with training Native American students, research in Native American communities, or providing services to Native American people, I felt as if their interest in me was because I was Native American. I had to decide how much that mattered to me and if I thought I had something to contribute regardless. I did not want my most important contribution to be just being there. I decided to accept the position.

As it turned out, just being there became very important in ways I had never imagined. Native American students across campus stopped by my office just to meet me or to visit. They said they had heard there was a new Native American faculty member on campus, and they just wanted to meet me and know it was possible to get through school. Having never experienced a Native American faculty member, I did not understand the power this had and was surprised by how much it meant to Native American students that I was just there. That appreciation also quickly drew me into mentoring Native American and other students of color across campus. It was important to have an open-door policy and be available to students and their needs at any time. My colleagues and supervisors quickly recognized my commitment as an important service, but one that would not receive high priority for promotion and tenure. I was advised to limit this work with students, but this is very difficult for most ethnic minority faculty to do when faced with the overwhelming need of students. Mentoring and supporting also become personally important because you remember what it felt like to be a student and experience similar issues. I quickly had to make a choice about whether to continue doing what I knew students needed versus focusing on what would get rewarded at promotion and tenure time.

As the only ethnic minority faculty member of my department and one of only a handful on campus, it was important to connect to other Native people and create a sense of community for myself and my family. Within the first year, I got involved with the Indian Education Parent Committee of the K–12 public school system. By the end of the next year, I was the president of this group. My supervisor warned me that these activities would be a dangerous drain on my time and not be heavily weighted for promotion and tenure. She expressed surprise that I had so quickly become involved in the Native American community and cautioned that it would not be a good use of my time. However, it was very isolating to have my ethnic minority status be so prominent and then be the only one in my program and department, and one of very few on campus and in the community. It took a great deal of energy, and being involved in my community was actually the lifeblood that sustained me in my professional life. To suggest that I give that up felt even more isolating, but even this was often difficult to explain to my colleagues.

Learning ways to articulate these issues and my feelings about them was also an important task during this time. Having never been mentored by an ethnic minority faculty member or discussed these issues in my training, I had to learn how to talk about them and do it in a way that people could hear what I was saying. I learned that I really needed to engage with my colleagues in creating allies and a supportive environment for myself. If I was going to survive in my position, I needed to not simply react to those things that felt offensive or hurtful.

I am very lucky because I had very good colleagues who wanted to be supportive. They did not always know how to do that, but they were willing, and we were able to stay engaged in meaningful dialogue—often difficult dialogue—long enough to work our way through these issues. I did encounter people on campus who were not so supportive and assumed I was an affirmative-action hire; some felt that the institution was lowering standards—some even said so to my face—but these experiences were tempered by the support of my close colleagues. Even though I hated feeling as if I was always the one bringing up issues of diversity or expressing the ethnic-minority perspective, I now have many allies who are the first to bring up these issues.

Getting involved in my professional association was another important key to survival. I felt that I knew what was valued, and participation provided access to other ethnic-minority professionals and mentors. This occasion was when I learned that I had made all the mistakes that a new faculty member should not make and that this is often the case with ethnic minorities. I learned that becoming too involved in service activities, serving on every committee on campus because it needed an ethnic minority member for EEOC reasons, spending proportionately too much time with students, mentoring an overly broad program of research, and generally getting spread too thin are all traps that ethnic minority faculty members tend to fall into but which will not be rewarded by promotion and tenure.

Sometime in the first several years, I was asked to participate in writing a survival guide for women and ethnic minority faculty members in psychology in my professional association. I helped write this document as someone who did not yet know whether she was going to survive. In the process, I met and was privileged to work with several very senior people in the field, who gently but firmly mentored and helped me become more aware and plan my approach to promotion and tenure. Through writing about what early career ethnic minority faculty should and should not do, I learned what I had done wrong and what I needed to do to change my course. There were times that I found myself becoming angry about feeling tokenized or how easily I had fallen into all the traps that could prevent me from being successful. But becoming angry paralyzed me and kept me from moving forward. Without the intervention of my mentors, I could easily have become lost in the role of the "angry minority." They helped me step back, survey the situation, and make a plan for moving forward. But they also validated my feelings and helped me not get stuck in a role that I was not choosing for myself.

If I had to pick the one thing that helped me to survive in academia, I would have to say that it was learning to ask for help. As a student, I had often "faked it"—pretending I knew what I was doing until I figured out how to do it—and had been reinforced for doing that well. As an ethnic minority student, I had thought that asking for help would just validate opinions that I lacked what I needed to succeed. Unfortunately, what that taught me was not to ask for help when I truly needed it. I am not sure what allowed me to change this, but I am sure it had more to do with the skill of my mentors than anything smart that I did. I was simply very fortunate. I watched as other ethnic minority faculty members on my campus were pushed into the role of being the angry minority. I watched as it damaged them both personally and professionally, and I knew that the same thing could happen to me. I could see how easy that would be because I experienced the same things they did. If I had not learned to ask for help, that person would have been me.

As ethnic minority faculty members, we often get pulled into trying to change the institution to make it a more inclusive environment, more responsive to the needs voiced by ethnic minority students, more aware of inequality in all forms, and generally, more of an antiracist environment. While this may be important work and can initiate meaningful change within the institution, it is not an intellectual issue for minority faculty. It is about our very survival. It is emotional and personal. And it very likely will not help us get promoted or tenured. It takes energy at a level that can deplete, and the change happens at such a slow pace that it is easy to become demoralized.

While we should never stop making this effort, we have to leave space to do the work that will help us stay within the institution. We have to remember that we can do no good for our students if we do not get tenure. We have to learn to choose our battles and that we cannot fight every skirmish that comes our way. We have to learn how to deal with turmoil without getting changed by it. We have to remember why we are doing this work, develop a vision for ourselves. It provides something we are passionate about, something we are moving toward—not just something we are fighting against. By deciding who we are in the face of the reality we are surrounded by and who we want to be, we take ourselves out of a reactive place and into a space that we have designed for ourselves. It is a space that is very much based in reality and focused, a place where we are aware of those things around us we can choose to change. But it is also a space where we balance what we need with what we must do. Just as ethnic minority students are often afraid that they will lose who they really are while they are getting their degrees, ethnic minority professionals may feel equally intimidated. In fact, in the effort to attain promotion and tenure, we can feel that nothing else is as important. It is very easy to lose ourselves in the process. Even once we have become successful and survived promotion and tenure, we can find ourselves waking up one day and realizing how much we have lost of ourselves in the process—and did not even realize that it was happening.

Ethnic minority students often wonder if they can be successful in academia, try their best to be successful, and eventually wonder if they define "successful" the same way the academic world does. We go through the same process as professionals in academia. To many of us, success never had anything to do with things like rich, famous, published, or funded. Success means helping our people, connecting to others, being real, and making things better for our families and communities. It is essential to find a way to integrate that definition into the work that we do— otherwise we do run the risk of losing ourselves in the work for reasons we do not fully understand.

One day I found the personal statement I had written for my graduate-school applications. I realized that the things I was actually doing—the very things I was being told would not help me be successful—were not so far from what I had naïvely written many years before. That forced me to think about the things that had gotten me into this profession in the first place, why I had sacrificed those years of my life to get that degree, and whether I was willing to give up those things to be successful. These questions led me to find the ways to incorporate those important elements into the work that would be valued within the academic world. Once I stopped asking *if* I could include those elements and started asking *how*, the ways presented themselves. The only rule is to make sure that something that gives me joy is always in my schedule. Sometimes that means my schedule for the day, and other times I have to adjust my schedule for the week. But the key is that it is there, and I know it is there because I put it there. I know I cannot wait for it to put itself there.

Nowadays I have survived. On the practical level, I was able—with the help of many mentors—to negotiate my assigned duties to include my work with students, weigh my service activities more heavily, and frame my work in Native communities as theory building. On another level, I have learned so many important things. At this point, I still have many things I need to do, and—as busy and stressful as things can get—I make sure that I am also doing things that I need, things that remind me why I got into this work in the first place—things that I might have said on my personal statement. And sometimes the more naïve they sound, the better! When I always have something on my schedule that gives me joy, I can stay balanced and am able to give my best to those other things that are not as enjoyable.

One day I realized that academia will never give me a neat desk with in and out trays, where—by the end of the day, or week, or semester—I can move everything from one tray to the other and feel that I'm done. When I find myself sitting in line at the drive-up window of a fast-food restaurant and fantasizing about what it would be like to work there (e.g., working my shift, going home, washing off the smell of hamburger, and then not thinking about work again until my next shift), I know that I have let myself get out of balance. I do not define success as never getting out of balance—only that I can recognize it when it happens. And then I turn to my family, friends, mentors, and advisors, because they are the ones who keep me grounded, pick me up when I get down, and generally do not let me take myself too seriously.

One sobering thought that occurred to me recently is that I am approaching senior status in my career. This realization turns my attention to giving back to the generations that will come after me. I have learned so much from the Elders who paved the way; many of them are now guiding us from the Spirit World. My responsibility now is to pass on what I have learned to the next generations. My focus is on learning to become the kind of mentor who made a difference in my life: someone who can show how to care without being reactive, how to share without becoming depleted, and how to give the best I have without giving away myself. The most powerful lesson I have learned came from the first person I really allowed to mentor me. After listening to me fret and worry and go around in circles for quite some time, he said, "It's very simple. It's all about discovering the gifts you have and finding a way to share them with the People." That was nineteen years ago and sounds so simple, but I am still learning what it really means.

Part IV

Social Class in Academia

INTRODUCTION

Samuel H. Smith

This is a remarkable publication that describes the complexity of the internal workings of many of our colleges and universities. Although each institution has its own culture, these descriptive narratives provide real-life examples of the culture and challenges faced by women of color in academia.

Higher education has become a major business in America with annual university budgets often exceeding a billion dollars and employing thousands of individuals. I have been in or around universities for more than fifty years and, on numerous occasions, been asked by nonacademics to describe how they work and how decisions are made. Those asking are often successful individuals wishing either to do business with or to contribute to a university. They recognize that universities contain large numbers of individuals with many advanced degrees. They make the assumption that there is a correlation between advanced degrees, common sense, and logical business practices.

As the individuals asking how universities work are usually successful in their fields and often belong to a variety of private clubs, I point out that—in my opinion—universities have much in common with elite country clubs. The academic credentials are necessary to be invited to join, but like all country clubs, not all members are perceived as equal. The older, usually white males from affluent backgrounds and prestigious universities are traditionally perceived to be the social and academic leaders, as well as the decision makers.

Within academia is a strong history of what is called shared governance: the faculty and staff consider themselves part of the decision-making process. This is fine in theory, but in reality the university administration gives businesslike orders, and the members of the academic community will then decide whether or not to move in the suggested direction.

The perceived social order or structure usually descends from the white males with affluent backgrounds from prestigious universities down through individuals with lesser income or less impressive degrees. Women of all colors are usually considered below men, and their status diminishes more if they are of color, which indicates they may have come from lower-income families and neighborhoods.

The university as a country club has existed for a very long time. It is often unfair and hurtful to those perceived to be of lower status. The narratives in this work speak for themselves, and it took considerable courage for these authors to relate their experiences. Why do I think these authors were courageous in telling of their experiences? Simply stated, universities—like country clubs—do not like to share unfavorable information with those outside their own community.

This work does much more than describe the challenges faced by women of color in academia. The editors and authors do not just describe the problems but thankfully, suggest solutions. Their recommendations should be helpful for all those in academia, enabling them to utilize their skills and talents more fairly, regardless of the way they are currently perceived. This work should be required reading not only for those just entering academia but also for anyone who is considering becoming an academic leader or administrator.

The timing of this work is also excellent. The American National Academy of Sciences has recently released another report comparing our universities and colleges to those in other countries. At one time, we could claim that our system of higher education was the best. We can no longer document such a claim. When compared with universities and colleges in other countries, we are no longer the academic leaders, whether you look at the number of graduates, their research and intellectual achievements, or access to affordable higher education. This is all happening at a time when state support for colleges and universities is being dramatically reduced.

Changing the culture of any university is similar to changing the direction of a very large ship. It is difficult to do and usually takes a very long time. With our perceptions of decreasing quality and increasing financial stress, we have reached a time in our history where it is not only possible but critical for the future of our nation for us to move away from the country-club atmosphere. Yes, I know, every college or university will continue to point out that it is still the best, but few would deny that they could educate more students at a higher-quality level.

The recommendations contained in this work provide thoughtful, logical guidance of what our universities can do to take full advantage of all of their talented individuals, regardless of where they stand on the country-club social scale. We have an opportunity to change the course of these very large ships we call colleges and universities, but we need all hands on deck. It is a matter of both fairness and necessity if we are to survive and flourish.

CHAPTER 20

IGUALADAS

Francisca de la Riva-Holly

Igualada is a condescending term often used by upper-class women who hire domestic workers in Mexico. An *igualada* is a subaltern who wishes to possess the same riches and privileges as her upper-class employer, especially one who hopes to give her children a level of schooling, clothes, and standard of life that she does not possess.

An *igualada* will never receive the respect she longs for from *la patrona* (her boss). She has entered an unequal relationship. The "I" for "*igualada*" inscribed on her forehead for all the acquaintances of the *patrona* to see is indelible. She can never work hard enough or be grateful enough for what the higher class has done for her. The *patrona* who hired her is the smart one, and all the credit for her work, her benefits, and her future success will go to this employer and the people she social-izes with. This is the metaphor that I utilize to describe the social class structure that I entered when I began working in a department where most of the faculty were either privileged white men or privileged Latin Americans.

I pursued a PhD in modern languages from an Ivy League university, hoping to escape the social-class monster that follows the children of working-class immi-grants even after they are successful professionals. What I identify as the social-class monster is a conflation of customs and structures that have prevailed since colonial times and Latin Americans reproduce when they arrive in the United States, thus engendering a legacy duplicated also by immigrant communities. Immigrant chil-dren spiral and reproduce the values with which their parents are judged because of their origin, e.g., rural or urban, upper class or lower class, from a certain region of a Latin American country. In my particular case, my parents' social class dictates my placement in Latin American social circles. I will always be the daughter of the woman who might have cleaned their relatives' homes in Latin America; my creden-tials or skills have been erased by their devaluation of my persona—a phenomenon that has existed for generations, for centuries, and a legacy of their colonized minds.

I also soon realized after I was hired that often women of color in academia are seen as the domestics and scapegoats of their institutions, this of course align-ing with value judgments reinforced by classism and the vision that other Latin

Americans have of Latino/as. This is particularly the case with people who come from very class-conscious backgrounds or countries, often other Latin Americans or diasporic immigrants from Africa and Asia.

Some Latin Americans will never stop seeing a US working-class Latina as the daughter of their maid, someone who has somehow not climbed the same ladder to demand equal privilege with them, and someone who represents the daughter of the rebellious masses in their native country, even though they no longer live there. This was the common belief among the anti-affirmative-action crowd and the privileged Latin Americans—as well as colleagues from other departments—who did not see my value as a Latina, as opposed to any other Latin American, African, or Asian immigrants who might be hired.

Yolanda Flores Niemann synthesizes and contextualizes an understanding of the Chicana experience in *Chicana Leadership* (2002). She writes that "(1) Chicanas are women who function in a patriarchal society, (2) Chicanas are overrepresented in the lower socio-economic and poverty categories in a capitalistic system, (3) Chicanas are racial minorities who lack representative and economic power within the United States, and (4) some Chicanas are lesbians in a predominantly heterosexual society" (viii). This summary is extremely helpful in establishing a foundation where I can begin my analysis of my particular situation. The patriarchal systems of both Latin American and US cultures were very oppressive in my department, where the only people with power were men, and these men could only see my background as unidimensional and, on some level, pathetically inferior.

The Hire

There were many red flags after my interviews at the Modern Language Association conference for a position at what I will call Forward University. I should have listened to the feminist pedestal theories when the Latin American interviewer told me that I was the "best thing" that had ever happened to them. He added that after interviewing two hundred people, he thought I was "the light at the end of the tunnel." As Jo Freeman extensively writes, women who stay within the prescribed roles of their department can remain on their pedestal; those who do not will fall. Better yet, when I visited the school and saw that all the adjuncts and part-timers had been friends for twenty years, I should have known not to accept the position. But coming from a community-centered background and a heartwarming oral culture that appreciates education and believes that it provides people with ethics and good manners, I believed that I was soon to enter paradise. Throughout graduate school, I had been working twenty hours a day, teaching at various universities to pay for day care and an advance on my dissertation to earn both a master's degree and a PhD from an Ivy League university. I hoped that now I had found a community in academia equal to that in societies of the Southwest, and specifically California, where I was from: family centered, offering pride and support for their own from their local community to people with a similar experience or type of work.

In fact, I learned early after I arrived at Forward University that there were—as there are in Latin American dictatorships—several tiers of power. I was both in the bottom tier and in the top one. I was the only tenure-track woman in the department, the only person who had not known and socialized with everybody else for many years, the only one who had not studied at the same state university where they had all received their degrees, and, most importantly, the only Latina born and raised in the United States. I came from the working class, I was the only woman of color from the United States, and I had emerged from poverty, immigration, and economic struggle but had attended privileged universities, received numerous awards and honors, and was a renowned public figure.

After I arrived at the university, one of my initial shocks (knowing that in most companies and private universities, salaries are usually private) was to find out that everybody in my department (including all of the adjuncts and part-timers) knew the details of my salary negotiations. My image was that of a diva with the highest salary in the School of Humanities; I was also the highest-paid junior faculty member at the university. All of this was due, of course, to the two men who had initially interviewed and hired me: the department chair and his friend in charge of the Spanish section. Sometimes—although I realize that this point can be disputed—I imagine in retrospect that maybe my situation would have been much better had I accepted a lower salary and been less infamous, instead of having successfully negotiated with the dean for the good salary that befits an Ivy League graduate. However, my envious colleagues would have had something to say either way: if I had accepted a lower salary, they might have seen it as proof of my lack of qualifications later on, and this would have definitely hurt me financially—as well as psychologically—in the long run for settling for less than what my Ivy league colleagues were receiving from various universities at their first professional assignment. I will never know the other side of this dilemma.

Since I have the skills of an ex-social worker in analyzing problems, I found many of the horrors of dysfunctional families and communities at work in the language department where I had accepted a position. What has been most interesting about my experience at this small private university is that the Latin@s involved (mostly Latin American upper-middle and upper-class people, as well as upper-class Spaniards) turned the stereotypes that had been used against them toward me, validating the voice of mainstream racism and classism, as well as Hollywood portrayals of Chicanos as troublemakers. At my second-year review, where nontenured faculty were asked to comment on my file (without there ever being a precedent), I—who had brought food to meetings and organized parties in my home a number of times—was accused of using food to acquire distinction and many other trivialities. It was obvious at the time that my colleagues had read *Like Water for Chocolate* and subscribed to a simplistic Euro-centered interpretation of the novel and the significance of food and its preparation in Mexico.

On a similar note, Ilan Stavans theorizes about the evolution of Spanish-language departments but also talks about the negative stereotypes about Latino professors and students that institutions have. He establishes the need for a change in the guard that still sees Latinos as the underdog in language studies, including Latino professors: "I sometimes sense that many deans, chancellors, and presidents still harbor a tacit xenophobia, a sense that the rowdy are knocking at the door—they know they need to pay attention to Latino students, but how much do they have to do?" (2005). The cards were shuffled every which way to include affirmations about my profile and persona both from the system and these unprecedented people, and of course—as with many minorities—the halo of affirmative action was placed on my head. As Yolanda Flores Niemann writes, "There is strong documentation for the idea that a stigma of incompetence arises from the affirmative action label, especially when the label carries a negative connotation in the hiring department. Once tagged as an affirmative action hire, colleagues may discount the qualifications of the hire and assume she was selected primarily because of her minority status, thus leading to the presumption and stigma of incompetence" (290, 2002).

I support affirmative action wholeheartedly but denounce the prevailing stereotype that middle- and upper-class people place most often only on African Americans and Latinos: they see minority faculty entering institutions by an unfair miracle since they are undeserving. It becomes a systemic label that sometimes uninformed or unaware academics place in front of our institutional degrees, whether they come from well-reputed universities or Ivy League schools for the highly privileged.

Within the first year, things began to go wrong because I was left in charge of the department while the section director (really the cochair) was abroad. By my second-year review, an entire group in the department, including the administrative assistants and the adjuncts, had made a list of my lack of skills. When my colleagues first accused me of not knowing how to teach, I started laughing. I was the only credentialed professor in the department, one who had spent several years at a four-year institution in pedagogical and methodological classes acquiring a teaching certificate. Not only that, but I had trained teachers (including bilingual ones) in various capacities for many years.

Most of the other language instructors taught in English instead of the target language and were all women who had attempted to get a PhD but had dropped out of their programs. I had been observed as a student teacher in language classes for a year and was extremely proud of my innovative techniques. I had a BA, MA, PhD, and teaching and administrative credentials from Ivy League schools, all in the target language. I had won many awards, including the teacher of the year at the college where I had worked. These accomplishments were essential in my continuing to fight with dignity because the "dimming-the-light" technique did not work in regard to my teaching.

On the other hand, all my colleagues and the institution itself continuously chimed what I call the "social-class bell," including the administrative assistant writing to tell me how I should dress "now that I was a professor" or correcting my pronunciation—and then laughing in front of me at my Chicano accent, which was really just a regional accent from a certain part of México because I spoke impeccable Spanish and had lived and studied in many Latin American countries before I acquired a doctoral degree. I was told later that other professors—historians teaching the classics and, in one particular case, one who was dating one of the Spanish upper-class women, who was an adjunct in the department—wasted his class time discussing my attire and that of another Latina professor on campus and asking the students why on earth we wore Indigenous clothing, such as *huipiles* and *rebozos*, to school. This apparently bothered him tremendously. As Yolanda Flores Niemann writes, a department can care "only about the *appearance* of diversity without actually valuing diversity. In such a manner, people who are well-meaning and unaware of their own racism contribute to a racist climate" (2002, 297; emphasis in original).

Our dean, a minority in mainstream America and an immigrant from Latin America, who very much still wished to be accepted by his upper-class comrades, conducted multiple additional reviews of me, instead of discounting things other faculty members said. Immediately unprecedented events took place during my required third-year review (only I had to have one; no one else in the faculty did), where the adjuncts placed letters against me in my file for the rank-and-tenure committee to see. There were fortunately two wise women on the review committee (both senior faculty members from other departments who had also been mistreated by their respective male department heads), and they were able to delve deeply into the injustices perpetrated by the administration and the department against me.

They concluded that there was definitely a "contagion" against me. Students had commented on confidential information that only hostile colleagues could have disclosed to them. These students should not even have known this information, much less included it in their evaluations. They were attempting to malign me in their class evaluations and through their emails to one another because the department chair was allowing everyone to comment on my faults and even unleashed an international debate presumably discussed openly by instructors inside and outside class. I describe it as international because it included letters against me from people I had not met while I was teaching in a study abroad program in Guadalajara for one semester. (My ex-students later forwarded me an incredible amount of emails, arguing with other students about my teaching skills and coming to my defense, instead of doing their work.) I also later found out that additional, nonofficial evaluations were continuously conducted of my classes and work as a means of acquiring additional ammunition against me. For example, students were asked to write down a list of my negative attributes in the classroom; they were given a blank page where they had to list my negative attributes on one side of the sheet and my positive ones on the other side. The department chair also used these unofficial evaluations in his second-year review letter to evaluate my qualifications and skills.

Falling from the Pedestal

My first sin was to give my honest opinion when I was questioned about a study abroad program in Mexico that I had been part of during the beginning of my second year at the university. As a person who had worked for many years teaching, evaluating, and conducting trainings in study abroad programs, I felt that I should give my honest opinion to the chair of the department. He—Mr. Fremont—and his Latin American friend (and coordinator of the Spanish program), whom we shall call Dr. Carlos Ramírez, had established these two programs abroad. I had also been given the title of codirector of the program. A year later the chair stated in front of the dean that I had never been the codirector of the program; he said, "We only did that on paper to give you a stipend."

They had—in the department—established their own scale of privilege. The chair and Dr. Ramírez had arbitrarily decided to give stipends to certain people to thank them for their services. This song and dance with the rules was common practice: if the chair and/or his friend liked you for some reason, you might get an extra stipend. These events took place at the end of my second academic year. My chair had never met with me individually prior to this. After I constructively criticized the program and recommended changes, he immediately scolded me aggressively, letting me know that I really had no power or say in anything that went on in the department.

There were five other women in the department—all adjuncts or part time lecturers, some of them ex-girlfriends of Dr. Ramírez, and some of them friends or girlfriends of his buddies or friends from graduate school. One other woman was hired at the same time I was; we shall call her Silvia. She was a constant complainer and had primarily been hired because she was the partner of a friend of Dr. Ramírez. The first day I met her she was on the elevator complaining about the administrative assistant she had just met. Silvia had known Dr. Ramírez for many years. This should have also been a red flag for me because they were each other's confidants. Silvia was very upset that her salary—although considered excellent money for a lecturer with a master's degree—was more than ten thousand dollars less than mine. Because she knew my salary to the dollar, Silvia leaked that information and any other discussions about me to the other women adjuncts, including professors in other languages.

The red flags were multiple. They had not tenured a woman in my department in more than a hundred years of the existence of the university. This should have been another of my questions prior to accepting the position: How many tenured women are there in your department?

Collegiality or the "Fourth Bucket"

After my second-year review, when I was described as noncollegial by the five male members (and only senior faculty) of my department, I was overwhelmed with questions nobody at my college was interested in answering or even addressing. I had often hosted department meetings (as well as other social events) at my house at the request of my male colleagues and invited each and all the members of my department to attend all the events for speakers I brought to lecture or read, including dinners with authors. I had fed each and every one of them on different occasions. I did not understand what noncollegial or even collegiality, for that matter, meant in my new world, the hierarchical realm of the institution that would decide my post-PhD future. I was unaware of the secret social norms and behaviors. In one of the meetings after my second-year review, one of the senior faculty members said I was not collegial and he did not know if he wanted to be colleagues with someone like me (again chiming the social class bell) since he and the other senior faculty members all came from a middle- or upper-middle-class background. I had no idea what he meant by that, and he would not explain further.

So I spent the summer after my second-year review researching this subject. In doing so—out of desperation and extreme need for counseling, which I could not afford at the time—I found the Internet, my biggest and best friend through this entire process. I don't say this lightly because I realize that ten or twelve years earlier, when the Internet was not as common, many women must have not had the benefit that I did in contacting others who were suffering from similar situations so we could stop ourselves from falling into absolute loneliness and alienation from the rest of the world. I realize that so many others were tortured and crucified without being able to surf for support or even hear their own voices and those of others articulate and deconstruct this injustice for them. These conversations on the Internet solidified in their minds that they should never have been subjected to extreme and silent suffering in the name of excellence or honor, defined often by unethical social elitism.

Through the Internet, I happened to find the most outstanding women who had been denied tenure because they were characterized as noncollegial as well. This was a wake-up experience for me: most of these women had brought enormous amounts of funding to their universities and were high above their colleagues, dedicated scholars who were conducting cutting-edge research and had been witchhunted at their respective institutions.

This was the first set of women who advised, counseled, and guided me, as well as set me straight about my situation and its nonuniqueness. The president of her college had told one of them that she had not filled "the fourth bucket": collegiality, and as a result, she started a website named The Fourth Bucket. She taught me to subvert acts of aggression directed against me and depersonalize and deeply analyze what had happened to each of us, as well as identify these evils and utilize them to underline my abuse. It was in this manner that I learned to turn things around. I began visualizing myself as a woman warrior, bought myself a plastic figurine in the action figures store when I visited with my daughter, and—instead of crying over what they had said or done to me on a particular day—I wrote it down, began colorful files of my students' emails, and started collecting the job descriptions they sent me or left in my box, thanking all profusely, for thinking of me. As my mother said, I turned the tortilla on the members of my department.

Each of these "noncollegial" women encouraged me to go on, to document everything, to keep publishing, to continue focusing on my teaching, and to not ever feel sorry for myself because we were all in the same boat, and we were by all means a sisterhood of *luchadoras,* resisting victimization. I did not hide under my desk but just continued to do what I had been doing so far that had so aggravated my colleagues, including sending notes to the announcement section of our university newsletter (something chairs normally did) to announce my recent readings, conferences, or accomplishments, including publications. And so I realized that in academia, we were still behind in practicing what we preached about progress and feminism: inclusion, something that women of color feminists had been doing all along. I no longer waited for anyone to include me in events and programs; I did it myself, and in the process, I included everyone I could in my cause.

I still emphasize that some of us are presumed more incompetent than others. None of these Internet women were women of color or working-class women as far as I know; they were just women. I argue this issue with a colleague, Dr. C. C., continually; she says all women academics were/are at one point or another presumed incompetent. I insist that this is true for some of us a little bit more than others, intensified by our race, sexuality, accents, social class, and other markers of difference.

The five brilliant, "noncollegial" research scholars I contacted each wrote or called back after I contacted them and told me that I was in fact not dreaming, although this might be a long nightmare instead. I was so impressed, moved, and deeply touched that they cared about someone on the other side of the United States—the other side of their reality in a totally different discipline, who was surviving similar destructive incidents—simply because of her gender (because we all shared that), and possibly her race and ethnicity, and assuredly her social class background. They, however, never asked whether I was black or Latina, Asian or white; to them (and in the interest of supporting me by listening), that did not matter. They knew that it was just as painful for each of us, but some of us had more obstacles to overcome than others. I was upset that my ethnicity, race, and class were being conflated into one entity: the woman who did not fit in because she was different from the rest of the new faculty and therefore noncollegial to them. Intelligently enough, the term "noncollegial" in this situation became a metaphor for excellence, high achievement, merit, and vision. These Internet colleagues wore the noncollegial badge with pride and taught me to understand that this was just the beginning of a long war of strong women against a fossilized academic environment. One of them asked me several times, "Are you having fun yet?"

There should be a definition of collegiality in the faculty handbook at each university. I wanted to comment on my particular and tumultuous experience with the description and caution women that this is in fact one of the most common terms used when no other accusations can be made about your scholarship, teaching, or service, and you are doing too well in your path toward an assured tenure. So do consult the definition for your particular fourth bucket.

Consejos

Because alienation is easily identified from the top down—since it is those at the top who usually are given the tools to define and isolate us—there should be some type of institutional protection for junior faculty, especially people of color. After my second- and third-year reviews, I could walk around campus and not find a single administrative assistant, colleague, or part-time professor who wanted to truly talk with me. I was a leper—doors were shut as I approached them, secretaries gossiped about me at most events (almost in front of my face), and my colleagues corrected, second-guessed, and excluded me.

One thing that saved me from invisibility was my relationship with my students because they cared deeply for me and were having email conversations wondering why I had been so maligned. These were emails that I later printed as documents proving mistreatment. My students sent many of these emails to me anonymously. They were in fact the most transparent element in my life during this entire period prior to tenure; they sensed my alienation, and—although many stayed away from me—others dropped by; brought me presents, cards, and food; and helped me move my office when I unexpectedly was asked to relocate three times in five years, mostly because no chair wanted me on his or her floor. My students were also the most painful part of the chess game, continuously manipulated by my colleagues into not talking to me or taking my classes. My advisees were taken away from me immediately after my third-year review, I suppose as a technique to alienate and exclude me. Students I had advised, employed, taken to lunch, and mentored often could not even continue saying hi to me after their interaction with other faculty members or their study abroad; instead, they looked at me as the betrayer. Still, it was my students who deeply appreciated my skills, knowledge, and professional work.

Daily Torture

The daily attacks to my image and person were constant and both large and small. I endured job descriptions put in my mailbox and extreme disrespect in misspelling my name (excluding my second to last one, which is my husband's Anglo name) continuously, and there were never any supplies or services available to me. No one ever notified me when the language book was changed so that on one occasion I arrived at class with the wrong one and had to give quite a performance not to let my students know what had really occurred. Students were asked to leave my class to do a presentation in the program director's class, which was held at the same time, without notifying me. Often I was left with two students; the others had been primed to get up at the exact same time and walk out of my class by Dr. Ramírez to show his power over me and my powerlessness. I was constantly excluded from department decisions and meetings, and this was obvious to my students. My advisees were taken away from me; I was not allowed to associate with students professionally as an advisor, only in the classroom.

Aside from all this, I saw the language department faculty eating lunch together, advising other junior faculty from other departments right outside my office, and meeting without me as a matter of usual practice. Something else that was constant was their mantra to all who asked what had happened between us: they replied that I had come and broken up the department. This was particularly important because this was in general a conservative university, where I was accused of allegedly creating divisions in the university's small leftist circles between those who sided with me and those who didn't want me there.

Since two of the senior faculty men were bleeding-heart and armchair liberals, it was difficult for me to construct a relationship with any depth with the people who had already befriended them because I was the home wrecker. I was the one who had broken up the solidarity the department had constructed prior to my arrival. There has always been a "before Francisca" and "after Francisca" attitude on departmental issues, marking my ability to destroy unity as a continually dissatisfied troublemaker.

Tenure

It was through the advice of many wise women, the support of a solid family and partner who enriched my life in other ways when I was being buried at work, the backing of an enormous Chican@ Internet community, and the absolute loss of many nights of sleep while I wrote additional papers and emails, had to prepare my classes, and demanded extreme productivity from myself, that I received tenure. I truly do not know that I would take this road again in life. I cannot say that it is worth having the job that I now have—and profusely enjoy—because chipping away at your soul for six years (more like eight, counting recovery) is not something I recommend to anyone.

Nonetheless, it is extremely important for me to document this territory, the rhetorical geography of this jumbled administrative language: the turns and twists, the stop signs, the obscure hand signals of the country of academia; the rivers of silence and continuation, especially because so few of us are working here, so few members of underrepresented and historically oppressed groups triumphing in these obscene waters of fate through hard work, perseverance, and endurance. There were many obstacles to overcome to earn tenure, which I finally did in 2007. Here are some of the most effective techniques that I utilized—aside from contacting people through the Internet to feel solidarity and sisterhood from others undergoing similar experiences:

Scholarship

I would first like to state that as a member of an underrepresented group and particularly one with a negatively stereotyped characterization, it is important to take the bull by the horns and immediately assume that you will attempt to do at least 50 percent more work than you are asked. Productivity speaks for itself in higher education, and nothing can be left to chance in an institution where we are expected to fail.

I knew that I had to have at least two articles published in peer-reviewed journals to validate my scholarship at this institution. This is never clear at institutions of higher learning because no one wants to delineate the requirements directly; none-theless, if they say they want one article, you attempt to produce two. This was always my mentality in approaching this subject, thus preventing me from feeling cheated. I went in always knowing that the expectations were higher for me than for others. I produced four articles and a published book—as well as multiple research and keynote presentations at prestigious conferences—in five years. I put in the pipeline at least three book manuscripts and continued working until the very last minute, hoping to get more publications and never feeling as if tenure was in the bag.

Teaching

In regard to my students, I left nothing to chance. I got to know most of them and spent a lot of time in my office available to assist them individually if needed, yet continued to teach challenging and demanding courses. Although my requirements represented rigor, I, on the other hand, communicated often with my students and wrote many emails both to individuals and the entire class. I always greeted them with a smile and a proactive and supportive agenda, as well as additional materials. I often invited classes to my house or cooked for an entire class and brought food to the classroom. Most of my evaluations were above 4.0 out of 5.0 and often as high as 4.8.

Service

I never said no to anything I was asked to do: substitute for a colleague, lead a discussion, make a presentation in another teacher's classes, prepare a panel, assist with a translation, share materials when I had anything to give them. I always greeted my colleagues kindly at events without pushing myself on them but attempting to be pleasant. It was not their fault if they had been told negative things about me, and I determined not to act like a criminal—quite the opposite; I constantly allowed them to want to get to know me.

Other Strategies Essential to My Success

Creating Community at the University Level

Although the first warning my senior faculty peers gave me about achieving ten-ure was that I should not socialize with faculty from outside my department, I did. Interacting with that many people continuously was perhaps one of the main things that subverted my situation at work. When I was accused of not being collegial in my second- and third-year reviews, people laughed at the top of their voices at this false accusation because they knew me. I participated in all events at the university—usu-ally as an observer, attended all social gatherings, and introduced myself to every possible professor who would give me the time of day and many who wouldn't. I got to know anybody I could from all other colleges at the university. In sum, I was Ms. Collegiality on campus, knowing that some of these people whom I might talk to once in my pretenure years might be voting on my tenure in the future.

Creating Community among Women

Another of the most salient support systems for me was the women's community that I created. I approached not one or two but several senior faculty women, whom I sought advice from on a continual basis, never being upset if one could not read a letter I needed to respond to, but instead seeking out another mentor. I was also very selective about whom these women were. I chose the hard-working and successful feminists and advisors from my college as my allies and only discussed positive and proactive strategies with them, instead of spending my time complaining about my colleagues. I often asked questions in my sessions with senior faculty mentors. These women are still my prized friends and advisors. They are very proud of me and remain invested in my work and success because they helped me get them.

After I received a horrendous second-year review, I organized a salsa dance at my house, inviting more than forty faculty women to come and socialize and learn salsa from a Cuban *salsero* who taught them a few steps. What I was doing was utilizing a stereotype that people have about Latinas to my advantage, which is that we are all dancing queens. I was also creating community and showing people what dancing is really about, which is talking. With this party as a start, I debunked the notion that I was a victim of the system, society, and my senior faculty because nobody wants to befriend a victim. And a victim does not usually have so much fun in the American imago. I met for lunch with different women chairs and leaders as well as peers as often as I possibly could, attempting to demystify the image my department had created about me as an opportunistic diva. By offering my knowledge, goodwill, and assistance to them if I could help in their programs or departments, I constructed a new persona to replace the ungrateful diva of color.

A Loyal Peer Mentor

Aside from a community of friends and making myself available to all my colleagues as well as the students, whom I served by advising some of their clubs, bringing in interesting speakers, and providing presentations and literary readings to enhance their community on campus, I also had a colleague friend from a different college as a peer mentor. She called me every night without my asking to make sure that I was still alive and hear what atrocities had occurred during that workday. Of all these resistance techniques, I would say this third one was most invaluable because it allowed me to share information and vent anger with someone who did not work at the same school and did not have to socialize or serve on committees with these people, but who was objective in her advice and mentorship of my particular case. She could also understand my particular cultural needs as a woman of color—an Other— as well as follow closely the daily telenovela my life had become and then adequately and objectively advise me. This also saved my marriage and family life because I had someone to talk to without inundating my husband with negative experiences that constantly occurred to me at work and he could often not even fathom.

It is most difficult to find such a person, I understand, but she represented in many ways the renewal of my sense of purpose on a daily basis and the assurance that I was in fact a survivor, a fighter, far beyond the smallness of my colleagues. It was this woman who—when my chair gave me one last set of obstacles (completing three unexpected peer reviews in one week) five days before my tenure file was due—marched into my classroom with a peer reviewer that she had pulled from under her rug overnight. She also stayed in the peer review to make sure everything went as planned and pushed me to secure other reviews for the next two days, thus ensuring that I completed the task in three days, instead of five.

This, of course, I understand is what superwomen do: support each other. I know that you can find a person who can—if not do this—support you in other ways on a daily basis. Sisterhood, if not always global, most often can be local. And our respon-sibility as women and feminist scholars should definitely be acting as this woman for a few of the people climbing up the academic ladder.

Posttenure

Throughout my pretenure years, I was given the lowest-level classes systemati-cally while adjunct men and women were asked to teach the literature and upper-division courses in Spanish. Even after I requested serving on hiring committees for the department, I was again excluded from attending selection-committee meetings for future faculty and openly ignored, even though the adjuncts were included in this process.

I expected that somehow my posttenure situation would improve, but it did not. On the contrary, now I was seen as what I call a "played card." I was no longer the naïve person other professors from inside and outside the department might be able to convince to follow them politically or ideologically, always assuming, of course, that as a new professor, I could navigate the murky waters of academia.

There are still so many areas to write about in educating the established pro-fessors to address the people working-class Chican@s truly are. As a hard-working associate professor who often secures funds to bring writers of color on campus, I am constantly advised by most of my colleagues in a well-meaning tone of voice that I really should slow down. "Take care of yourself" is the most common sen-tence emerging from their emails and mouths about the amount of work I produce. Instead of saying, "I have never met anyone who works as efficiently as you do" or something like that, they continue to ask me to take care of myself, not understand-ing that as a working-class person, putting on events at the university featuring other professors of color, organizing tenure parties to feature their greatness, and bring-ing meals for my students, who have never had decent Mexican food, are part of taking care of myself. This—as a person with a community-centered mentality—is taking care of myself, because the self never exists alone in my reality; I express my inner being by being useful and benefitting others who are climbing the same slip-pery ladder that I recently completed successfully.

As a promoter of diversity, then, I would like to suggest an agenda where we allow members of underrepresented and historically oppressed groups from the United States to act according to their cultural background and not permit people to con-tinue attempting to tell them what to do and when to do it (even after tenure). Too many people assume that the mainstream person knows better and the working-class person needs to have a bell ringing, like an animal, to remind everyone that he or she is not quite done with knowing what is best.

Another issue that I face constantly is having my accomplishments minimized systemically, particularly by my department and the institutional administrators. If I get an award, it is never announced in public; I am never officially congratulated, interviewed for the university newspaper, or invited to lunch by the president or the provost, things that happen when other people—particularly diasporic people of color, white men, and model minorities—receive similar honors. They are hailed publicly and placed in leadership positions almost immediately after their arrival at the university, particularly if they attended Ivy League schools. It is all about the quality of the treatment we accomplished Chicanas and African Americans receive: we are truly never expected to fill the cup with our skills but have been given a cup half full instead, for which we need gratefully to thank the system for the rest of our lives; otherwise, we are considered ingrates of the highest caliber, eternal *igualadas*. I find that this is also an institutional punishment for those who dare speak about what is really going on in our departments. Yolanda Flores Niemann writes that with her department and colleagues constantly questioning her abilities, she, too, began to second-guess her talents and even her decision to become a professor. She refers to this behavior as "self-undermining," and it is a recurring theme in her article (2002, 296).

While I consistently faced similar experiences, I never questioned my abilities, perhaps because I knew I had throughout my education been the star student, the hardworking child of immigrants, the poster child of success from dire poverty in luxurious Ivy leagues. Or maybe it was because I was my courageous mother's daughter, or had received the empowering self-esteem training of many community workers and inner-city after-school programs, the keen advice of my working-class friends who never doubted that they were wrong, not I, because I was their only superstar, and they would not give me up. Or perhaps it was a combination of all these that made me feel that I could always be courageous about continuing the fight.

I believe my insistence on remaining confident helped me get through so much of the undermining feedback thrown in my direction. I urge those in power to recognize the accomplishments of their peers because this should be a common practice but is particularly important for professors of color, who are constantly undermined by most of their colleagues, their institutions, their departments, and sometimes, even their students. Another practice that I continually implement in my job is celebrating the accomplishments of other people of color and all women because this is something that I believe snowballs into creating a healthy environment for all. And I also urge administrators to understand diversity, from which we Latin@s may emerge as a multidimensional group in the United States. Another of my friends, a Latina who left the university where I currently teach because she also began to self-undermine her skills, reminds me that we don't all—nor should we—respond in the same manner to similar situations. Our strength is precisely foundational because of this. And because of our loss of her irreplaceable talents and superior research abilities, I do not wish to forget this particular lesson. Nor should I forget that—in the area of tenure for Latin@s—we are still in diapers in our ability to support or theorize ways to best encourage the minority group we represent, which will soon be the majority minority in the United States.

CHAPTER 21

THE PORT HUENEME OF MY MIND

The Geography of Working-Class Consciousness in One Academic Career

Constance G. Anthony

In a certain respect, being working-class and becoming an academic is an oxymoron. Academics aspire to genteel, professional success; working-class life rejects the genteel for the overt—at times even rude—acknowledgment that life is difficult. Academics revel in a world of carefully chosen words and phrases; subtlety and indirection are prized. A well-delivered, witty repartee at a party is always rewarded. At a working-class party, it would be much safer to say exactly what you mean in a direct way. For example, if you are approached at a bar by someone to whom you do not wish to talk, it may be middle-class polite to say, "I am really not interested," but you might have to say, "Back off!" In political discussion, analysis proceeds often with the appropriate expletive when necessary, not dissimilar to McNulty's or Moreland's assessments of Baltimore city government in *The Wire*. Are these gross stereotypes? Yes, but when you move between two such starkly different social environments, keeping the stereotypes in mind can help you keep your wits. To quote Tracy Strong's political theory article on metatheory, you may need to "hold onto your brains."

In my first year of teaching at Oberlin College, I was in an informal meeting with the chair of my department and two other first-year colleagues. We were in a discussion about football, which at the time—because of a concern for gender balance—Oberlin was considering adding to its athletic department. We were all making fun of this and laughing it up when one of my colleagues, in telling a funny story about an all-Hawaiian football league, used a racial epithet. Without any hesitation, I said, "Hey, that's racist." He laughed and apologized, and in a very friendly, half-joking way, we worked it out between ourselves on the spot. That afternoon, my chair called me at home and told me he was very disappointed in my behavior.

To meet the requirements of collegiality at Oberlin, I needed to apologize formally to my colleague. What to do? Calling a white friend out on something like this was the norm where I grew up. Was this an issue of a meeting with three guys and one women talking about sports? Was it California versus Ohio norms? Had I been rude? I know my comfort in making the comment was rooted in my own, direct, working-class style of talking, and my friend—unlike my chair—totally got it.

I have learned to be not quite so blunt in academic settings, even with friends. With some sympathy for both sides, I watched a similar situation unfold at my university some years ago in which the on-the-street language of one class setting was taken into another. A working-class, faculty friend of mine made a bold, direct, critical comment about national politics with a very mild, little-used expletive attached. The comment was made in a context that, while probably appearing protected to my friend, or at least very limited in its impact, was public. A member of the campus community complained. All sides of the event survived with their integrity intact, but it was clearly one of those circumstances in which class lines came into play. Repeatedly, I have learned that social class structures my view on who the insiders and the outsiders are in the academy.

You can take the woman out of the working class, but you cannot take the working class out of the woman. Sometimes this leads a person to be working-class heroic in ways that make no sense whatsoever in the academy. Don't help a colleague who is up for tenure out of a tough departmental situation when you yourself do not yet have tenure! This is obvious, right? Certainly, Ms. Mentor would agree. But it can be less than obvious early in a career, when the ethics of friends-help-friends in tough situations still prevails in your consciousness. Or growing up working-class can set a foundation that places a greater value on intangibles, rather than professional success. This might lead you to value the richness of ordinary experience, the beauty that daily life offers over middle-class professional success, which beckons you over your shoulder. This can be a problem in a competitive work environment, where others are constantly attentive to moving up the ladder of success. And the material obstacles of limited family resources will not only dog you in graduate school. If you are the only working-class warrior to make it out, they will continue to pose important professional-development challenges throughout your career.

Eventually, after some years of experience in the academy, you will automatically act and in many ways be middle class. However, the claim of your class of origin on your identity never really goes away. This has negative and positive characteristics. You may never make it to the top of your profession and wonder if your class background is the reason. You will stand at conferences and in professional settings where those with much greater family wealth casually refer to a second home, a retirement secured, children sent to excellent, expensive private schools, or another aspect of the good life that eludes you. Unless you develop a very clear, nonmaterial approach to life, this will be a frustrating reminder of informal power in the workplace.

For me, besides the obstacles thrown up at regular intervals on my academic journey, there were also many life-enhancing and, on some occasions, life-saving aspects to growing up working-class in California in the mid-twentieth century. There were very important public goods, like the stunningly beautiful California coast, a historical moment in the 1960s and 1970s when equality of opportunity was celebrated philosophically and generously supported with public tax dollars, and the spirit of the age which encouraged social change and members of my generation to take risks. I was also lucky that while my family was poor and fractured, I had a spirit guide for a life well lived, a role model who taught me the value of persistence and courage, and a romantic adventurer who fed my curiosity about the world. Working-class families can spur the imagination and feed the spirit just as successfully as those with greater resources and education. But the opportunities must be present in society to allow you to light your own fire.

I grew up and was educated in a West Coast world where class was formally dismissed as a relic of the repressed East Coast but was regularly and informally acknowledged in a discussion of geography and neighborhood. In California in the 1950s and '60s, class was certainly rooted in income and employment, but it was visually and experientially all about neighborhood. If you could run your palm down the spine of the California coastal foothills, you would feel the geography of class and race. In the mid-twentieth century, the flatlands of Berkeley or Los Angeles were white working-class neighborhoods that by the 1990s had become Latino or black working- or working-middle-class areas. As both San Francisco and LA were "Manhattanized," neighborhoods which were working class and multiethnic were destroyed by the growth of a freeway system which privileged the white middle- and upper-middle-class areas. When you left the flatlands for a house with a view in Southern or Northern California, this almost always meant a shift upwards in respect to class. More recently, as LA has become increasingly diverse, the foothills have been partially integrated racially but continue to be securely settled by those with much greater wealth and remain class exclusive.

My grandparents left Los Angeles at the end of the Second World War, when there were no more semirural areas to settle, no more living on the margins of the city in neighborhoods that were racially but not class diverse. The Hollywood-by-the-Sea and Silverstrand beach to which they migrated began in the 1930s and 1940s as an outpost for Hollywood hermits, celebrated and otherwise, and those who were escaping the new, almost entirely urban LA for a one hour drive to culturally far-away Oxnard and Hueneme in Ventura County. Many beach communities up and down the coast in the 1940s were still class diverse. My grandparents built an eight-hundred-square-foot cottage with the help of my father and uncle, who were breaking into the construction business after their military service.

I spent the best of my childhood here, first as a visitor when we lived in LA in the 1950s, then as a resident down the block, and finally as part of an extended family household that held most family gatherings at the Beach House. My first memory of the place is standing in the wet sand on the edge of the sea, with hands held on both sides, feeling the intensity of a sunny day. Staring down at my feet, I watched as they disappeared under the very cold, but soft, white foam. As if in a dream, I can hear my grandmother saying, "Look, you are losing your feet." And the miracle of it at the age of two or three took my breath away: "Hey, those are my feet; they are gone, and it feels good!"

The beach became a foundation for my childhood and ultimately a reference point for making important life choices. Until I was well into middle age, I had a recurring, simple, short dream of being in the beach house with a large wave rising out of a deep, dark, stormy sea. The wave was in the shape of a hand ready to knock at a door. An appropriate analytic question would surely be, "what or who is knocking?" The house was a kind of family refuge for my cousins and my brother as well as me, but it was the sea and the character of my grandmother's friendship which helped me figure out what or who was knocking when I confronted challenges in adult life. When my book had been turned down again, it was a long walk, along a very cold, wintry, agitated sea on the coast north of Boston that got me to rewrite it to the reviewer's specifications and successfully resubmit it. When I needed to decide how to deal with a major disappointment in a new professional and per-sonal relationship, an afternoon walking along La Selva Beach, just south of Santa Cruz, put things in perspective. The wisdom of natural environments was deeply engrained in my psyche as a consequence of the days I spent walking the shore, bodysurfing the waves in front of my grandparents' cottage, and crawling across the ice plant that covered the fragile dunes along the sea. The meditative power of the ocean was a public good when my family rooted itself along the Pacific, but in many ways, that has changed.

My grandmother's presence at this place of magic and transcendence crystallized her later importance as someone who helped me imagine a life beyond material and professional success. Raised in Boyle Heights before World War I, and living most of her adult life in on-the-urban-edge neighborhoods in LA, my grandmother experienced considerable hardship during the depression and the war. Her father worked and died in the LA rail yards. Never wealthy and occasionally impoverished, I knew her as someone who relished many things about life. She lived in the pres-ent with an almost Buddhist respect and was the first person to teach me how to be grateful for small pleasures. When I was seven, and my parents were divorcing—both in various states of disarray—my grandmother took care of my brother and me in these new family circumstances. One afternoon, when we were bored out of our minds with playing one too many games of Monopoly, she sent us off to the corner store to buy small, Japanese made paper parachutes. We sat on the walled-in entry to our adobe-like Pasadena rental for hours launching these parachutes out over the crabgrass into the sunny, Southern California afternoon. During my childhood and throughout high school, my grandmother consistently drew my attention to the way life could be enjoyed despite family and economic difficulties. This remained distinctively working-class for me because the experience was connected to a life in which the alternatives were sharply constricted by available resources.

By the end of the century, living at the beach in most of the United States meant owning a second home. By the 1970s and '80s, thanks to an important local devel-oper and the growing wealth and population density of Southern California, owning Hollywood-by-the-Sea beach property became a mark of accomplishment. My blue-collar uncle, who now lived in and owned my grandparents' beach cottage, could not afford the yearly taxes until the property tax revolt in the late 1970s. But in the 1950s, during the years my mother, my brother, and I lived on the beach, there was a cultural and class mix that established a countercultural neighborhood norm for me. Diversity included a gay and lesbian population, working-class evangelicals, Sea-bees, many types of artists, young and old singles, and countercultural types on the right and left who wanted to be near the sea. I went to school with the children of Hawaiian royals, almost-famous artists, Irish blue-collar workers, recent immigrants from Oklahoma and Texas, kids abandoned by beat generation druggies who did not make it in LA, many kids in single-family households, and as many from the kind of working-middle-class families who lived up and down the coast, some of whom like my uncle made their living from the sea. It was a place of marginality for those living there. In our school, we had an almost-openly-gay principal and teachers from all over the country, new to California, who were iconoclastic in their approach to education. Whatever the reasons, we were not socialized to believe in the Cold War, the family with a capital *F*, middle-class virtue, racial hierarchy, or for that matter any status quo norms. Maybe this was because we all knew on an intuitive level that in living on the land's edge we were also on the edge of society.

When my mother briefly remarried and for a time joined a more conventional, though still distinctively working-class culture, we moved to a residential Hueneme neighborhood. The school I went to, the grass, the regularity of the streets, the uniformity of two-parent, mostly two-child households was kind of a shock. When my stepfather left, my mother became the sole breadwinner, and I became her primary assistant. While repressing my feelings, I was very resentful about this. I was proud of my mother's courage, but I was not interested in becoming a full-time household worker. The experience of watching my mother struggle and the desire to escape my responsibilities at home propelled me into a plan to go to college. While some of my friends aspired to go to college, many did not, and there was already a rush to the door at Hueneme High School (HHS) to marry and settle down. I just could not get this picture. While it is difficult to judge in its entirety, the fact that most families did not have the resources and few of us could secure the necessary scholarships drove this worldview. I had already developed a kind of out-of-body sense of myself as different in ways I did not totally understand. This was most certainly part of a very incipient level of awareness that my sexual interests were not like those of my friends, but it was also about where I wanted to go with my life professionally.

While in this respect I was trying to avoid my high school's mostly bourgeois values of heterosexual marriage and having children, there was another way that despite the uniformity of the neighborhood and the homogeneity of its family structure, this part of adolescent life gave me an experience of close-in racial diversity. HHS in the mid-1960s was a place that aspired to be a genuine multicultural and multiracial society. I certainly had no intellectual tools to critique my own experience or understand how extensive my white privilege was, but in an era in which the battle for black civil rights in the South was broadcast nightly, it seemed that while we were watching history being made, we were also making it. Oxnard, the immediate neighbor to Hueneme, elected a Chinese American mayor, and its Colonia was home to César Chávez for part of his childhood. The homecoming queen in my junior year was African American, the best woman athlete in my graduating class was a Chicana, and the valedictorian in the class immediately before me was Japanese American. While white students were still in the majority, a growing percentage of HHS was working-class Asian and Latino. When the first boy I wanted to date was Japanese American, my mother hesitantly agreed, but my grandmother helped me make it happen by enthusiastically supporting my choice. The fact that I had been part of a world where my peers and I dated across racial lines, argued with our parents about it, and made this a part of our early adult lives introduced me to working across cultural and racial lines, though primarily in the safety of working-class society and white privilege.

While I was a student in Hueneme, you could pretty much assume everyone was working or working-middle class. There were some middle-class families, but they were few. Once I had gone to college, graduate school, and then begun to teach as a professional, the most striking characteristic of class for me became its invisibility. Very similar to gay and lesbian life in earlier decades, social class is still something that remains so invisible that working-class academics can choose whether and when to reveal it. Even if you hide it, unlike your middle-class and upper-middle-class peers, you will see the ghost of class which haunts the academy. Its eerie presence is there when you are up late grading papers, paying careful attention to the ones from students who are new to academic life. We do this the same way our professors worked to redefine and refine our street smarts into intellectual savvy.

Or the ghost of class identity can show up in a hallway conference conversation with new colleagues. You mispronounce an ordinary, but little-used, word; it's a legacy of your underfunded, public school education. No one says anything, but in a split second, you have identified yourself as a member of the unwashed to those who prize the well-chosen word or phrase above all else. The ghost of class reappears as well when you feel free to talk to staff employees in your department or some other part of the university like genuine friends, exchanging information about family and work life with knowledge of their experience. For you, staff may share an ordinary life appreciation for work at the university that other peers do not. If you treat them as friends, some of your colleagues will see you as having bad professional boundaries.

Perhaps most frustrating of all, the markers of your identity will be misinterpreted or, in many cases, completely invisible to your colleagues. When I went to college in the late 1960s, when asked where I was from at the early freshmen gatherings, I discovered that my neighborhood was invisible. When I replied, "Port Hueneme," most people instantly assumed I was from out of state. If you came to college from Hollywood, Newport, Sausalito, or San Mateo, your neighborhood identification met with instant recognition. As a graduate student, even at a public institution like Berkeley, my class identity was not something that peers or faculty noticed. In the 1970s, while there was rage in the streets, there was a fair degree of complacency in the academy. There were no need-based fellowships or work, and it was not cool to mention that you often were on the margins of economic life. And although in political science some limited professional consciousness raising eventually took place on gender and race, I really have never seen anything similar in respect to class. When I went out on the job market, one mentor I had at the University of California, Santa Cruz, who had grown up working class, addressed the challenging nature of my family background in her reference letter. As a consequence, in a couple of instances, institutions interested in my application assumed that because my research had been done in part in Africa, this family background information meant that I was African American. Invisibility and lack of recognizable status went hand in hand, and it worked both ways. You can be working class and be asked to pass as middle or upper class, or if your class background is identified as an obstacle to success, class is reduced to another category of exclusion like race, which is both classist and racist.

The invisibility of class identity is not primarily about passing or staying in the closet, though certainly there is plenty of that going on. It is about a class-phobic professional environment in a society which only recently, in the face of catastrophic economic collapse, has acknowledged the concept itself. Given the marginality of class in the academy, you may very well be tempted to remain closeted. Not only can you easily hide it, but indeed you are often strongly encouraged to do so. In graduate school—after I explained to a mentor that I was the first person to go to college in my family—he gamely insisted that "really you are middle class."

Even when you make a choice about whether and when to come out, most people simply ignore your self-identification as unimportant, or as in the case of this Berkeley mentor, do not accept it. Once a working-class colleague and I participated in a summer faculty seminar at Seattle University designed to foster interdisciplinary intellectual conversation on the university core. When we read a book on urban America that explained in what ways aspects of publicly supported housing in the United States were like apartheid, some members of the group did not understand the character of the evidence. To elaborate their analysis, my friend identified themselves as someone who had firsthand experience with such settings. Her comment was met with silence. No matter how awkward or uncomfortable, these kind of personal rejections have never happened when I have made a decision to explain to a friend, colleague, or group that I am gay.

While there is still plenty of homophobia in the academy and the larger society, being gay is not considered out of the realm of probability, and no matter the level of acceptance I have received after such a proclamation, I have never been met with silence or told, "But you are really straight, right?" When I recently explained to a member of the upper administration that there were settings on a Jesuit campus where gay faculty and staff felt safe and others that were not as welcoming, while surprised, they accepted what I said. In contrast, when attempting to explain to peers that working-class faculty, who have no professional family members or early role models, find it more difficult to network in professional settings where their class background is underrepresented, I was met with incomprehension.

The frozen smile, deer-in-headlights stare at professional conferences should be universally recognizable as a class-based, "what am I doing here?" stance. Instead, some see such shock as the evidence of those who really "aren't that good." If you grew up in a working-class family, even as you learn a new set of class behaviors and can pass, you will never quite connect with an insider sense of comfort and entitlement. And unless you have particularly insightful and politically aware working-class colleagues, no one will really acknowledge your distinctive experience. They may even deny it. And this will happen in the face of the fact that many understand it very well analytically!

That a successful or newly middle-class professional might choose to hide their class identity and that of their families of origin is not limited to those who work at colleges and universities. It is so socially unacceptable to be working-class in American society that many people I have known over the years, who grew up in poor, even desperately impoverished neighborhoods, either work hard to maintain the invisibility of class identity or actually see themselves, if they make it out, as middle class. One friend who grew up in a part of St. Bernard Parish in New Orleans, steadfastly maintained a middle-class identity, until we visited the old neighborhood and drove past the levees, the red brick of Our Lady, the local joints, and then deep into the white equivalent of the Ninth Ward. We both had to acknowledge what was plain to the eye. Unlike the evolution of gay identity in American society, there are no cool T-shirts, no exciting revelations, no working-class pride day, and really no recognizably celebrated culture. And in a university setting in particular, as you make it into the middle class as a consequence of your PhD and climb the ranks of academic accomplishment, there is no one at the end to congratulate you for scaling Everest. Rather, the academy encourages you to see yourself in every way as part of the privileged world that you have now joined. My journey through the academy as a gay, working-class woman in an overwhelmingly straight, middle- and upper-middle-class male field, has been constrained by each of these social states, but despite the intersectionality of these pieces of identity, class is the least socially recognized and perhaps for that reason, the most corrosive.

When I went to college and graduate school in California in the late 1960s to late 1970s, you could indicate class by talking a language of geography and neighbor-hood. In a society that does not want to see it, class can masquerade as many things, and in my native state, it traveled up and down the El Camino Real, made itself known in the distinctions between the flatlands and the foothills, and showed up in frequent and passionate discussions of cities and neighborhoods and their lifestyles. Even in a city like New Orleans, where many historical and cultural affiliations are celebrated, and there is a party when more than nine people stand in line for the bus, the floats at Mardi Gras are rooted in neighborhood, which is an indirect, geo-graphical way to indicate class as well as racial hierarchy.

Of course, in the past half century, many physical features of California have changed. This is especially pronounced for me in respect to the gradual, but terribly definitive redefinition of the California coast. In the face of this change, a certain nostalgia colors this discussion of neighborhood. Was the city more beautiful in the 1960s before its skyline was completely redefined? Remember how lovely the old Catalyst in Santa Cruz was before the earthquake? Wasn't it nice when you could see the foothills of Santa Barbara without the hundreds of homes scattered across their fawn and grey color? These kinds of discussions include social and class content, if not entirely acknowledged, as well as a kind of contemporary mourning for a more equitable and available world.

And the world of mid-twentieth-century California *was* more equitable. Pat Brown put a public education system in place which took me and other working-class friends to very fine, highly accessible, public universities that were virtually free for both undergraduate and graduate education. It is possible that I would not have been an academic if I had been raised in another state or historical era. The Univer-sity of California, Santa Cruz (UCSC), had genuinely small classes and a residential college system which committed its faculty to undergraduate education. While I had many excellent teachers in high school, I left HHS less prepared for college than my peers at UCSC, who went to very competitive public high schools in places like Palo Alto, Marin, and Brentwood. Many of my educational gaps were addressed by the Stevenson College core and a major in government. Reading Wittgenstein, Freud, and Marx in the first quarter of my freshman year began my academic transition. My professors fostered a deep intellectual hunger, which I ultimately acknowledged. As one mentor pointed out, Santa Cruz "ruined me" for any life other than that of an academic.

Thus, leaving Hueneme for college education in Santa Cruz was life transform-ing. However, there were ways that I was unable to ride that wave past the class undertow that followed me. I had done well in high school, but I had worked very hard to do so. I could say that was because I was given so many responsibilities at home, but this was true for other friends as well. While only a very small percentage of Hueneme graduating seniors went to a four-year college, some of my best friends for whom school was not as much of a challenge had impressive opportunities. One of them, who graduated at the top of our class, went off to Pitzer, only to return to Port Hueneme after a few months of rooming with a surgeon's daughter. She missed her boyfriend and a more familiar life. When she got married in my sophomore year at UCSC, I was the only bridesmaid who was not eager to be there. This might in part be attributed to my basic tomboy approach to life, but equally as important was the fact that I was going through my own class shock at Santa Cruz. I was going to classes with new friends whose parents were paying for their education, who did not have to work, who expected to go on to graduate school, and who were making plans to travel to Europe, the prime student destination in the 1960s and 1970s.

I wanted to beg the bride to go back to LA and finish college. As someone who had known me since the sixth grade, she was intent on convincing me that I should "get into" what it meant to be a member of the wedding party. From my perspective, she had been accepted at an elite private school with a free ride, and she was retreating into a world that seemed to be uniform and unchanging. This was of course wrong, an invention of my late adolescence, but I wanted some fellow travelers, and was finding it difficult to find them in the redwood forest that was now my home.

One initially casual way I eventually was able to bridge the class differences between myself and my new friends was to get comfortable with the popular language of class that leveled distinctions and at the same time acknowledge them. When I was in college, if California students did not arrive with skis, which in the mid-1960s to mid-1970s was a social faux pas, they were nonetheless smoking the "high" life, eating macrobiotically, making regular trips to Big Sur, and scheduling visits to their therapists during academic breaks. UCSC was the alternative to a Stanford education for many of my peers.

However, the ability to partake of this life came with a language of what life was like in Russian Hill or Malibu, which everyone shared on the level of natural beauty, public space, and lifestyle. These places were accessible to all Californians. You could drive through Malibu Canyon, hike there, and walk on the nearby beach to partake of a common California lifestyle of sun and a spectacular natural environment. In the 1960s and '70s, you could even afford to eat at local beach cafés and restaurants. Thus, the privilege could be popularized in a language of regional culture, but the view from a home in Russian Hill and Malibu came with an income and life possibilities that were not shared. This blurring of class lines could lead you to believe that such a lifestyle was within reach.

There are many ways you can resolve these expectations of the good life and the blurring of class lines. For some, academic accomplishment and success might do it, but for me, it did not. The direction I took was to become politically active. This began with two friends whose families by the 1960s were middle or upper-middle class, but who embraced a working-class identity because of a family history of political and/or racial exclusion. We were able, as a consequence, to talk the same language of social exclusion and political change.

One of the first people I met when I moved into the dorms at Stevenson College was the child of Chicago Communists, whose family had helped hide an important party leader on the edge of a remote part of the Great Lakes in the midst of the Red Scare of the 1950s. This meant that her parents were blacklisted, and because they were politically marginalized, they lived in largely working-class communities. As my friend pointed out, "What did our neighbors care if we were being investigated by the men in suits who wanted to know if we had ever said anything that was not patriotic?" While her parents were both successful professionals and by the mid-1960s were doing fairly well economically, she carried that earlier experience close to her heart at the age of eighteen. Another friend's family had been interned during the Second World War, and the memory of that internment and its material impact on their lives during the 1950s was so searing in respect to class and racial status that he openly identified himself as working class in an intellectual and activist respect. In fact, all three of us protested the war; helped plan and execute the invasion of the UCSC administration building; pushed for an ethnic studies, Malcolm X College; and were members of the steering committees for campus strikes and shutdowns.

The political awakening of my college years helped me integrate my family and childhood class experiences with my college education. I read Marx in four different class settings, and while I was never a doctrinaire Marxist, the macro-theory of revolution, class, the state, and the political economy of historical change stayed with me throughout my academic career. In my junior and senior years in college, I sought out opportunities for work in the local community. As a summer research assistant for Bill Domhoff, a social psychologist whose study of power challenged the pluralist theories so dominant in the study of politics, I was influenced to study local power relations in Watsonville from the standpoint of community power theory. My thesis supervisor, one of the first tenured Chicano political scientists in the country, had no difficulty with this, but the department did not buy it. Ultimately, I am sure my thesis was improved by incorporating a carefully fleshed-out liberal perspective from thinkers such as Robert Dahl, but other opportunities for community work led me to remain convinced that my first inclinations had probably been right.

In my junior year, I had volunteered at the Legal Aid Society and became a regular in the county tax assessor's office, researching rural property relations to assist the lawyers in their work with the farm workers. This job and the summer one that followed in New York City opened me up to the intersections linking class, race, and the need for political change. I lived that summer in what is now called Alphabet City, before the neighborhood was in any way gentrified. One of my roommates, Jerry Rivera, was the lawyer for the Brown Berets. I watched one afternoon as Herman Badillo walked Bella Abzug down Avenue C, and thus through his neighborhood, to assist her in her bid for Congress. The optimism and activism of the 1960s and early '70s made my working-class identity seem to be on the cusp of an impending world-historical change. How wrong could one young student of politics be?

While my undergraduate political life at Santa Cruz mirrored the actions taken by many at the time all over the country, it was almost impossible for me to translate it for my family and friends in Hueneme. When I graduated from college, with some ambivalence about whether I should try for graduate school or law school, my mother, worried about my direction, encouraged me to come home and "take a job as a waitress for a while." My mother was trying to help me get comfortable in the adult world, and she was right that I was a bit lost, but I was not ready to return to the culture of my youth or my family. While I had considerable sympathy for friends in Port Hueneme who had not left, my college years and my summer in New York City had left an indelible impact on my politics, my tastes, my desires, my aspirations, and my identity. When I went home for a visit one summer, walking through my neighborhood, a group of kids hanging out of a passing pickup truck, seeing me in my blue jeans and work shirt hollered out, "Hey hippie," and I wanted to call back,

"No guys, it's 'hey, rad.'" While fairly clear about the intersection of class and politics in my own identity, nothing about my work at Santa Cruz had prepared me for how challenging this would be in graduate school.

Class is a huge material obstacle to success for working-class academics in graduate school and beyond. It denies you the material opportunities that might assist in your career and professional development and, as a consequence, makes you more dependent on your mentors and professors, who are the purveyors of jobs, grants, and fellowships. At Berkeley, while I certainly envied the ability of some of my peers to access their parents' income, I came of age before upper-middle-class became the new middle class and parents were economically responsible for their twenty-something-year-old children. I was historically lucky in this respect. My peers in graduate school, though much wealthier, were often expected to support themselves. It also helped that I was educated at both the graduate and undergraduate level within the University of California system, which, at the time, had very minimal fees of a few hundred dollars a year. While this was an age of relatively more economic equity among students, it preceded a period when only upper-middle-class individuals could afford to go to graduate school without another form of income or economic support.

Because of this, class distinctions became more important in the later stages of my academic career. Class position follows you throughout adult life, unless your family of origin also moves up to the middle class or the earning power of your spouse surpasses that of the average academic. Working-class adults are not going to inherit income from their families, and, as a consequence, retirement savings are much more important. Academic careers and income are a problem for everyone who is not independently wealthy, but for the working-class academic, being a faculty member is a lifelong material challenge.

While the material disadvantages are an important impediment to the development of an academic career, the asset which was not so obviously a consequence of the market, but that many of my peers in graduate school had in spades, was their sense of entitlement. I think this might be even more important over the length of your professional development than material resources. While the academy was a new place for some, it was not a foreign country. In most cases, both of their parents were professionals, their siblings were all college graduates, and they occasionally had family members who were already members of university communities. In contrast, I wanted to quit graduate school every year, because I did not connect with so many aspects of the experience. The class distinctions were certainly accentuated by the fact that less than a quarter of my peers were women. I was literally one of two to three women in courses of twenty or more students. The class shyness that seemed to characterize my early graduate school years made it difficult for me to fight my way into classroom debates and discussions, which were often all-male experiences. There were days when I seriously wondered what I was doing in a PhD program in political science at the University of California, Berkeley.

Ultimately, Berkeley marked me in several respects, and one was class-based. As I entered my thesis work, I realized that despite the international backgrounds and educational polish of my primary mentors, they were all working class. And in fact, in the 1970s in the political science department, there was a kind of working-class, in-your-face quality to the faculty culture. However, while there was a certain comfort in this, I never really embraced the competitive drive for success and status.

By the time I left graduate school, I could make a presentation at a conference with authority and field dismissive or very critical commentary on my work without crawling under the table. But this toughness has always been a cultural overlay, not something that I really admire about myself. Even though working-class environments are not genteel, there is a way that they can be more humane than the petit bourgeois culture. I remember that first summer I spent in New York City, and how surprising it was that some small, street merchants yelled at their customers, "Hey, girlie, ya want that cantaloupe?" However, once you began the conversation, they were actually very interested in you and what you wanted! I loved this about New York, especially the Lower East Side and West Village of the 1970s.

Competitive, pushy, or aggressive worlds that value the individual are very different from those that value winning first, success always, and status for sure. Are ideas really the most important aspect of academic life? I am not saying that it is all a sham, just that there is something traditional about some aspects of working-class culture that are not part of American academic culture, and for me that is a loss. I recently participated in a weeklong, collective research seminar that grew out of LatCrit, and most of the participants came from Latin America, representing many different countries. The discussions at the end of a day of collective fieldwork and intercity travel were extremely lively, intellectually challenging, and exciting. But at the same time, they were amazingly humane, without anyone trying to establish a status hierarchy.

When I taught at Oberlin College, my students were impressed with the fact that my degree was from Berkeley, which to them meant that I had received a left-of-center education. I found this quite humorous and never really succeeded in finding a way to explain to them that the local culture of progressive politics did not really characterize my graduate student experience. Their excitement about this was the flip side of my own inability to integrate my politics with my work theoretically. The age of identity politics was just beginning, and political economy was being sanitized of its political bite. I had found an intellectual home in two different, but not competitive, areas of political science, the study of world order and of comparative development. I tried to meld these in my thesis, which integrated a comparative development analysis with the study of international development. My goal was to expose the way economic constraints determine political relations. This was a personal, rather than theoretical, class analysis, because no real class analysis existed in political science at the time. I was privileged to work with two early and famous international relations constructivists and two really excellent Third World development scholars.

I went to Europe and Africa to do the field research for my thesis, which became a book several years later. Africa was important to me, and still is, because of its historical location in the development of the global economy. The development professionals I met, who were attempting to change the environment of international assistance, were appealing policy revolutionaries who were unassuming and cautious about what could be done about global poverty. Because I learned from them and also saw many counterexamples, both international and national, that lacked vision and reflected a distorted understanding, I had an early education in the limits of international aid as tool for changing the world.

Despite encouragement along the way to turn my intellectual work in a policy direction, I have always found the political foundations of the work of international agencies, states, and other actors involved in the problem of global poverty, as well as other areas of north-south policy making, to more clearly identify the truth of the matter. While it may not be heartening to confront the fact that well-intentioned international agencies with resources available for development assistance do no good unless they collaborate on the ground in the implementation, it is the truth. As I moved further away from my graduate training, my interest in the concepts of imperialism and hegemony and the role of US foreign policy in setting the foundations of North-South global relations were further articulated. The work I began in graduate school concerning the role that state building and political institutions play in national and international development continues to matter to me. These commitments have most recently led me to a concern about the absence of serious debate in political science about north-south global justice. And for me, North-South Relations has become a way to see how societies across the developed, developing world divide share many similar factors, for example, hierarchies of ethnicity and race, in their own political and economic development.

My biggest disappointment about my field has been the pursuit of a moderate or conservative political agenda in the name of an apolitical, scientific study of politics. This idea has been worked and re-worked by a variety of political theorists, including most impressively, by Sheldon Wolin, but it has made little impact on the field as a whole. I have been fairly consistently at odds with this, and until recently with the opening of a more interdisciplinary approach to both international relations and comparative development, it made my work somewhat iconoclastic. At the same time, I remain committed to practical as well as intellectual work in the pursuit of a more inclusive and just society and have spent considerable professional resources in teaching and administration to that end.

If you do not reject your working-class origins, changing the world will be as, if not more, important than becoming a success in your field. The three phases of my work life—research, teaching, and administration—have all kept my attention for as long as this has been the case. Personal and institutional life and distractions have prevented me in some instances from going the distance, but to the best of my ability, I have avoided one of the costs Marx identified as part of the proletarian life: alienation from one's own identity. This is a real danger, when you substitute success at all costs for genuine integration of your working-class identity in a bourgeois world. The academy's siren call, as you repeatedly pass the rocky shoals of professional choice, will take you to a seemingly safe harbor. However, it is my experience that the call is not addressed to your authentic self, which includes a much wider array of life's objectives—personal, spiritual, familial, communitarian, and political—and which ultimately allows you to love your "pilgrim soul," as well as the moments of "glad grace."

CHAPTER 22

ON COMMUNITY IN THE MIDST OF HIERARCHY (AND HIERARCHY IN THE MIDST OF COMMUNITY)

Ruth Gordon

When I began teaching, I attended the Association of American Law Schools' (AALS) Workshop for New Law School Teachers, as did most of my colleagues. We received much good counsel, were advised on potential pitfalls and problems, and, if lucky, formed bonds with our fellow new law teachers. I still vividly recall one of the presenters stating with a big grin, "Welcome to the goose that lays the golden egg."

He was candidly informing us that when all is said and done, we were about to enter an exceptionally satisfying profession, and I have found that he could not have been more right. Our vocation is fulfilling and flexible in a way that most employment is not, and, if we so desire, we can carve out time with family and friends, as well as for travel and community. In short, it is what labor and life should be: a deeply satisfying balance of work and play (McGinley 2009).[1] It is also a passage to status and privilege because professors may be greatly admired and can achieve prominence and access to the upper reaches of the American power structure—or, at the very least, the upper echelons of their local fiefdoms (Merritt and Reskin 1997, 199). Considering that so many people outside of academia toil at tedious jobs for low pay while countless others are struggling to find any work at all, I feel fortunate that my profession has provided me with an extraordinary forum to

---

[1] Some disagree, however. Ann McGinley argues that the tenure process usually takes place during a woman's primary child-bearing years, thus disadvantaging women professors. I have seen women colleagues successfully navigate this morass, however, including obtaining tenure and then taking time to have children while they were young, returning to write full force once their children were in school. Of course, my colleagues were not trying to thrive at one of the country's top-ranking schools.

exercise my mind, heart, and spirit. As a scholar who hails from modest beginnings and who now studies and writes about the most economically, socially, and politically downtrodden people on earth, it is vital to keep in mind the very real struggles of millions and have a sense of humility as I voice what in comparison are rather unimportant grievances.

I began teaching law in 1990, and it has and continues to be a fascinating journey; I am usually quite content with my work, albeit not with the distressing world I write about. I did wonder—when asked to contribute to this volume—if there was anything I could add to the brilliance that fills these pages. Ultimately, I concluded that the invitation to participate in this project afforded a rare opportunity to reflect on a life within an academy that has been welcoming and hostile; hierarchical and communal; and also sexist, racist, and homophobic, although not to the extent found in the world where most of America, including my family, resides. Not being a product of privilege, yet now being rather firmly enveloped in it, I have had a foothold in several worlds and, like many black people, have been aware of the world from multiple locations and within varied spheres. What follows are my particular observations on the role of gender, race, and class in my personal journey and the way these multiple locations subsist and flourish within the larger legal academy and, at times, even among people of color.[2] These musings flow from being a black, female, heterosexual law professor at a middle-ranked law school for a little more than twenty years (Gilmore 1990–91, 74).[3] I do not purport to represent anyone's experiences beyond my individual and specific universe, for black women law professors are multifaceted and multiexperienced, having suffered multiple and varied injuries, pains, and both micro- and macroaggressions and transgressions. Thus, while these words may sometimes speak for others, they are not intended to do so; mine is only one voice, and in this particular academic space a somewhat uneducated one. Nonetheless, I hope this chapter adds to the discussion.

Part I depicts my private narrative, although it is etched with the trepidation of exposing the personal in a very public place (A. Harris 1990–91, 107; Jordan 1990–91b, 113). It is the story of a working-class girl who made out very well and happened upon a particularly satisfying career in an era when black women, other people of color, and white women were finally joining the legal academy in more significant numbers. My journey, at least in part, speaks to the respective roles of race, class, and gender in obtaining a teaching position and the way these identities serve as obstacles to some communities while benefitting others.

Part II explores the community I encountered when I finally became a member of the legal academy. As might be expected, the doors to legal academia did not

2   We all have complaints—indeed perhaps countless grievances—about sexism and racism that result in offense, both intended and unintentional; powerlessness and marginalization; tenure battles and silencing. Airing such matters in public is not only difficult but may accomplish little, because those who perpetrate and sustain this discord are often unaware of their transgressions or alternatively are pleased with them. Although many drafts of this piece began with such rants and raves, they will not be part of this essay even if they are very real and, at times, extraordinarily painful.

3   I recognize that I have benefited from my heterosexual orientation throughout my career. For example, I was hired by a Catholic law school in 1990. Villanova University School of Law has not hired an openly gay, lesbian, bisexual, or transgendered faculty member during my twenty years on the faculty, although there have been recent attempts to correct this state of affairs. Angela Gilmore discusses the challenge of being a black lesbian in the academy.

fling open, and I did not simply stroll in. I was the beneficiary of the efforts of fearless pioneers who braved the full wrath and loathing of both students and colleagues who doubted their competence. By the time I arrived, a group of outstanding black women law professors were already in place to welcome me with open arms into an inclusive, safe space where they helped me excel and provided wise guidance and advice. The Northeast Corridor Collective was a refuge in the midst of this black woman's sea of uncertainty. It was a nurturing community, and you only needed to be female and black to be a member; hierarchy was imperceptible within this cocoon. Moreover, it was a community that presaged others that law professors of color would create to support and develop their own.

Part III turns to the other side: the persistence of hierarchy in legal academia. I have encountered, and continue to confront, racist and sexist conduct, but it has not been particularly horrific and certainly pales in comparison to the battles waged by others. Moreover, while we often discuss gender and race, we do not much discuss class and hierarchy within our ranks. In some respects, class is connected to race and gender, but in other ways, it transcends these categories. There seem to be few class distinctions among tenure-track faculty members, perhaps due to the nature of the qualifications to be hired. Rather, hierarchy and other distinctions in the legal academy take a different form and instead seem to be situated in the differences between tenure-track professors and everyone else, and between professors teaching at higher-ranked schools and the rest of us. Within the more circumscribed community of black women, these distinctions have not been as stark, perhaps because we have faced so many kinds of discrimination or because within our ranks, we have greater numbers of "everyone else"—namely clinicians, librarians, and legal writing instructors. Still, it is worth exploring the reality of these distinctions and our seeming belief in rankings and hierarchy within academia, even as we eschew it elsewhere.

Part I: Entering the Academy via the Very Long, Very Winding Road

My roots are firmly and proudly planted in the working class. We were not poor—just working folks living in a small house in Jamaica, Queens, New York. While we would probably now be called middle class, that is only because this term has become ubiquitous since no one wants to be considered poor or working class these days.[4] In my day (now the olden days), working-class kids seeking to join the middle class often gravitated toward the most obvious professions, basically the

---

4   One of the great dividing class lines is education, which is often desired but can be elusive for working-class families. I am the first member of my immediate family to graduate from college; in regard to my extended family, my uncle is a physician. The divisions this difference in social status caused during my childhood were readily apparent. Moreover, my shift from working class to middle class sometimes caused resentment and tensions in my nuclear and extended family. Nonetheless, in recent years, a college education has essentially become the norm for the younger generation in my whole family. At first it was simply attending college without necessarily graduating; now graduation is expected, and even older family members have returned to earlier studies. I fully expect graduate school soon to be the new norm, having just heard that a great-niece will be pursuing a PhD. I have tried to play a significant role in fostering these expectations and serving as a source of information and guidance; indeed, I would like to take some credit for this turn of events.

only ones we knew—teacher, doctor, or lawyer.[5] Since I loved school and all of my teachers, I initially wanted to be a teacher. But then my world began to expand. Being very black and very proud, I expertly debated my high school teachers, and thus my career goals morphed into wanting to be a lawyer, a profession that everyone seemed to believe matched my skill set. Moreover, being a lawyer meant I could help people and perhaps save the world—an important purpose in the 1970s and a fundamental aspiration for me personally. In fact, while recently moving my office, I actually unearthed my application to law school. It seems I really did want to save the world and thought I could do so with a law degree (and that Afro was too cute!).

Being an excellent student from the beginning—despite being discouraged by white teachers at various points along the way[6]—I managed to attend very good to excellent schools, eventually ending up at New York University School of Law, where I did well and planned to be a civil rights lawyer (what else?)—a goal I achieved. Fighting for the rights of the oppressed both here and abroad was satisfying in many ways, but being an attorney was not quite right for me. Thus, off I went to London and the London School of Economics and Political Science to study international law and retune my career as that type of lawyer.

To be honest, my plans were not exactly a model of clarity. Nonetheless, I reset my life in this rather muddled progression, for the kind of exposure you gain from studying abroad for fifteen months as a black American with an open heart and left politics is unfathomable. The teachers and coursework were illuminating, my classmates came from all over the world (and were the type who in the 1980s chose to study somewhere other than the United States), and the range of opinions was diverse and encyclopedic. I learned that America is one place in a very big world and that people live, work, and think in ways we know little about.

As a black American, I could straddle several worlds and was able to befriend African students, who helped me understand just how American I am and that American views of race and more particularly blackness were quite distinct and not universally shared. My housemates were a native Brit and an Australian, both progressive women, but with politics that were still quite different from my American brand. I also befriended students from the Middle East, the Caribbean, Australia—quite rich people and some not so privileged—and I left a very different person from the

---

5   It is, after all, impossible to reach for what you do not know exists. Anita Allen (1990–91) discusses being a role model.

6   In my experience, black students—regardless of how smart they are—may be discouraged by white teachers from reaching their full potential. My favorite junior-high teacher advised me not to attend Stuyvesant High School, which is one of the best public high schools in the United States and a guaranteed ticket to college. This was after I passed the entrance exam, sans affirmative action, and beat out white classmates (who, by the way, thereafter hated me). My teacher's rationale was that the commute would be too long. In high school, my advisor informed me that I could not get into Columbia or other Ivy League schools, and while in college, I was counseled that I would not like Yale or Harvard Law School. When I applied to Yale because I was invited, I later discovered that a professor who had given me an A in two of his classes wrote a poor recommendation, and I then learned that he could not believe I had been accepted by any law school.

   I have heard similar stories from my peers of being discouraged by their teachers. I had hoped this practice had abated until I learned that my nephew's favorite teacher told him he should go to a lesser college because he would probably not make it at the better and more challenging school that had, in fact, accepted him. This occurred in 2008. My nephew believed her and was crushed. However, despite this "advice," I talked him into attending the better university, where he has thrived.

woman who had arrived. I gained a much keener sense of myself and America in the world at large; that experience was an eye-opener. Moreover, I was happy again, and it slowly (ever so slowly) dawned on me that being in a university setting was my personal nirvana. Within a few years, and with the help of my alma mater NYU, I was contemplating a career teaching law.

Let me quickly and emphatically say that this is not the way to enter the legal academy. I did not begin preparing for a career in legal education before attending law school, as did many of my white (and a few of my black) peers (Allen 1990–91, 22; Greene 1990–91, 81; Guinier 1990–91, 93). As the child of a working-class mom, I simply did not know the blueprint—despite attending perhaps the best public high school in the nation, Stuyvesant High School, and then a first-rate university.[7] Yet one cannot underestimate the value of mentors—those wise individuals who pluck a student out of the group and point him or her in a different direction.

Nor can one take role models lightly. In junior high, I was fortunate enough to become best friends with a classmate whose family was African American and solidly middle class—her dad was an engineer and her mom a special education teacher. In retrospect, they lived modestly but still better than my family, and the exposure was invaluable—I discovered very concretely that there was more beyond my world, which—while not impoverished—was more circumscribed. Perhaps most importantly, my friend's brothers had attended Stuyvesant, and since Stuyvesant had just been forced to admit girls, she would, too, if she could pass the test. Since I was her best friend, I went along with this program, and we studied our hearts out, passed the test, and went off to Stuyvesant, where my life changed forever. Stuyvesant grads go to college; it is simply assumed. There were no proms, no caps and gowns (those came in college)—just the Westinghouse Science Talent Search and letters to our parents encouraging us to take more advanced math courses. We correctly eschew and question being role models and the manner that this idea is used to belittle us as academics. Yet sometimes having mentors and role models may be invaluable because they alert us to unimagined possibilities (Allen 1990–91; Greene 1990–91; Guinier 1990–91).

I entered academia before entrée became so heavily weighted against practice and so extensively tilted toward scholarship and managed to obtain a teaching position after having been out of law school for ten years. Currently this agenda would be highly improbable because—although obtaining an LL.M. is acceptable—practice is frequently penalized (Merritt and Reskin 1991, 2299).[8] I also happened to

---

7   One very important thing my mom did for me was to work at New York University Hospital. She worked in medical records, where—over a more than twenty-year career—she rose to the position of assistant supervisor. My mother made it possible for me to attend New York University as an undergraduate free of charge. There are many individuals toiling in the kitchens, mailrooms, and offices; cleaning classrooms and toilets, mowing lawns, engaging in maintenance, and doing the other countless jobs that keep the university humming with the hope that their children will benefit by tuition remission. Of course, there are restrictions, including having the grades to be admitted, but I know this was part of my mother's rationale for working at NYU, and I have heard the same sentiments expressed by Villanova employees.

8   Obtaining an LL.M. is one avenue to law teaching, especially if a candidate does not know how crucial it is to attend a top law school. An LL.M. from one of the higher-ranked schools can then be quite helpful. Deborah Merritt and Barbara Reskin (1991) explain the importance of the law school you attend and discuss the election to the Order of the Coif during law school, law review membership and the type of editorial position, the possession of a master's degree in law (LL.M.) or a doctoral degree in another field of law, and the number

attend one of the fifteen or so feeder schools chosen by approximately 48 percent of the members of legal academia (Neumann 2000, 313, 319), and I clerked for a federal judge.[9]

Although I ended up at one of the feeder schools, I did not know at the time that it was one. I only knew that it was free (due to a very generous scholarship) and that the University of Pennsylvania School of Law, my other top choice, was not. Although Penn was then ranked slightly higher than NYU, the difference was not great enough to outweigh the free tuition. Of course, either school would have been acceptable—but most students do not come to law school with a career in academia in mind; they are already at a disadvantage unless they happen to attend one of the few schools that can open the door to law teaching. Here class and class privilege are important: those students whose parents are professionals and who are already firmly planted in the middle class (a goal toward which I was lurching) are much more likely to be aware of and contemplate varied careers, including teaching law.

Hence, in my case, none of my credentials were deliberately acquired because they were not chosen with a law-teaching career in mind. I attended NYU because it was the best school that seemed to work for me. I clerked because a good friend had told me how enjoyable and useful federal internships could be—and he was right. I attended the London School of Economics and Political Science because I desired a career in international law and had not really practiced in that area; teaching law was not part of my thought process. Although the degree was practically worthless for entering an international legal practice at that stage of my career, it was still pivotal because I was back in an intellectually challenging—indeed remarkable— academic environment. In truth, I was overjoyed to be in school again—it was better than practicing law—at least for me, and within the next three years, I began slowly moving into law teaching.

Throughout these meanderings, however, no one ever mentioned teaching law. Indeed no one raised the idea of a career in legal academia while I was in law school in the late 1970s—neither professors nor colleagues, and certainly not family or friends. When I received my LL.M and finally applied, I was not accepted for any of the distinguished programs that have helped African Americans gain traction on the arduous path to a teaching position. They are few in number, and they simply did not accept me.[10] Thus, I entered the job market without published articles, and although this was before producing several publications virtually became a hiring prerequisite (Angel 2006, 173–74, 177), not having a publishing record created lingering doubts about whether I would or could write. Today I would be practically unemployable in the legal academic market because the system is now highly structured toward those actually seeking a career in legal education, conceivably before they even begin law school (Angel 2006, 173–4, 177).[11]

---

and type of judicial clerkships that are available.

9   According to a consensus derived largely, but not entirely based, on the *AALS Directory of Law Teachers,* so-called feeder schools include Yale, Harvard, the University of Chicago, NYU, Columbia, Stanford, Berkeley, Michigan, Duke, Georgetown, the University of Virginia, and the University of Pennsylvania (Neumann 2000).

10   Examples include the William H. Hastie Fellowship Program at the University of Wisconsin, the Reginald F. Lewis Fellowship for Law Teaching at Harvard University, and the Abraham L. Freedman Teaching Fellowship at Temple University.

11   While a law degree with honors and a clerkship used to be the ticket to a teaching career,

Of course, some of this chronicle is about a youthful and naïve me, someone a bit clueless and bereft of adequate self-confidence. But it is also about race, gender, and class. If you are from the working class, teaching law is not likely to be within your realm of possibilities or an objective to work toward. If friends and relatives are lawyers, the prospect seems closer to your consciousness and thus more within your knowledge and grasp. If you do not travel in such circles, someone must pluck out the future professor, tell her that the academy is an option, and school her in all that must be achieved to realize that ambition: attending the right schools, being on the law review, publishing an article, not practicing law for too long.[12]

If you make it to the right school and the professors are white—possibly harboring doubts about whether a black student should even be in law school, or at least in their law school—such mentoring is highly unlikely. The ranks of professors of color were extremely thin in the late 1970s, as they remain today at many schools. Ambivalence about role modeling and mentoring aside (Allen 1990–91, 22), it is also quite difficult to be a mentor to everyone, is it not? Because women were also excluded from the tenure-track ranks of legal academia, at least in the late 1970s, the professors choosing mentees were less likely to be women or pick women. And what of the students who were the potential mentees? Standing before them were professors who were white men who did not seem to be like them in any shape or form. Neither black nor women (and the few women were more likely to be catching hell from the students anyway), they certainly and most definitely were not black women.

Part II: Finding Community

> *When we take the podium we threaten the legitimacy of an academic world*
> *in which males, primarily white males . . . are hegemonic.*
>
> Linda Greene, "Tokens, Role Models, and
> Pedagogical Politics"

In 1990—ten years after completing law school and after two years and two trips to the AALS "meet market" (a.k.a., the "meat market"), I was finally offered a teaching position.[13] Indeed I had four offers (practice does make perfect) and finally settled on Villanova University School of Law, which is near a major city and also

---

the rules of the game have changed. One or two law review publications are now a requirement to be hired as an assistant professor at many schools—implying that candidates must find time during their short period of employment between law school and teaching in a law school to write articles. This tends to favor men, who are less likely to have responsibilities outside of their job while women may have both work and family responsibilities. Professor Angel maintains that discrimination against women is systemic because the overall perception is that it is almost impossible for women to achieve.

12   Many law professors have not engaged in practicing law for more than a few years, suggesting that nominal lawyers are training future ones. At this juncture, legal academia seems almost to disdain the practicing members of the very profession that we are training our students to join. Our practical skill set, or lack thereof, is surely affecting efforts to change both the hundred-year-old methods we use to teach as well as reform our curricula.

13   The AALS holds a sizeable recruitment conference in the fall each year. It can seem like an endless marathon for both interviewers and interviewees. I had a full schedule of interviews on both outings , although by the second time, I realized it helps immensely to take time for lunch.

happens to be where the northern contingent of my extended family resides. I was still in New York preparing to move to Philadelphia and feeling a bit anxious and green but also very excited. Continuing to rely on NYU amenities, I ran into Professor Paulette Caldwell, who had begun teaching at the law school in 1980—unfortunately for me, the year I graduated. I had many questions, several that I could only ask another sister. Could I wear braids? Would it hurt my chances for tenure, alienate my colleagues or students? How do you command respect in the classroom, especially when teaching outside your area of expertise and feeling rather nervous? Paulette was all knowing and all wise and shared much good advice about being a law teacher[14]—advice that the AALS Workshop for New Law School Teachers, as good as it is, could not begin to provide. She also told me about the Northeast Corridor Collective of Black Women Law Professors, better known as the Northeast Corridor Collective, and invited me to the next meeting.

I immediately understood that I was following in the glorious footsteps of others. By the time I entered academia, a remarkable cadre of black women was already teaching at both majority-white and historically-black institutions (Jordan 1990–91a, 1; Cahn 1972).[15] These women had borne the brunt of breaking barriers in a racist and sexist milieu, where they faced hostility regarding their very legitimacy as law professors as both students and colleagues questioned their credentials and qualifications. Some were "shouted down in the classroom by white males, shunned by colleagues, had their teaching credentials openly challenged in the classroom, received anonymous and detailed hate notes critical of their teaching style, syntax and appearance and discovered colleagues had encouraged students to act disrespectfully" (Greene 1990–91, 81). Professor Linda Greene, who began teaching in 1978, described her early experiences as "an intellectual version of a nighttime ride through the deep south countryside . . . [with] a constant awareness of racist and sexist danger, both real and imagined (1990–91, 81)."[16]

I cannot say that these conditions had abated by the time I entered legal academia because for many black women, they had not (Russell 1997, 110). Still for me, the situation was not quite so terrible, even if I had my moments. The most dreadful aspect of my first semester was having to teach two three-credit courses,

---

14   Paulette Caldwell is the author of a brilliant, groundbreaking article on black women's hair (1991), and after much discussion, we decided that I could keep the braids.

15   The first black woman to teach full time and attain tenure at an American law school was Sybil Jones Dedmond, who began teaching in the fall of 1951 at North Carolina Central University School of Law; the first black woman law school dean was Patricia Roberts Harris, who was appointed dean of Howard University School of Law in 1969. Harris held this position for only thirty days, however (Jordan 1991). For a detailed history of these women, as well as an account of the founding of Antioch School of Law by Jean and Edgar Cahn in 1972, see Broderick (2009).

16   Professor Linda Greene was a mentor extraordinaire during my early career. She encouraged me at every turn, answered my every question, and gave the best down-to-earth advice imaginable. She was and still is amazing. In the early 1980s, Greene was one of about a dozen African American women law professors in the United States; of this time, she recounts, "Having begun with verve and confidence, self doubt grew with negative experiences. The indulgent reactions of faculty 'colleagues' to the virulent criticism of students, the readiness of students to judge and dismiss my decisions in the classroom, the insistence of alumnae that I must be a student after I had been introduced as Professor, as well as hundreds of other experiences, suggested to me that my modest aspirations to teach threatened deeply-held notions about who ought to exercise this authority" (1990–91, 81–2).

something almost unheard of these days. I only worked, ate, slept, and struggled to hang on. On the surface, it seems that this was an attempt to sabotage a young-ish, inexperienced, African American, female professor. But in retrospect, I believe it was more that an older faculty had forgotten what it was like to prepare a new course in combination with acting as a substitute to teach an established course for a professor on sabbatical. Not surprisingly, my teaching got off to a very bad start, and then race and gender reared their ugly heads as they often do in these circum-stances. My student evaluations did not simply say I was a poor teacher; instead, they degenerated into derogatory comments about my intellect, my hair, and my body—in other words, about my race and gender.

When I arrived at Villanova, there was only one black member of the faculty, and he was an associate dean (albeit with tenure), who did not spend much time in the classroom. Today there are still two of us: the school added one black woman, who will soon be up for tenure, and the associate dean has departed. At the time, the entire staff was white—from the dean to the cleaning personnel; of course, students, alumni, and the entire staff had to be informed I was a professor—it was clear that no one assumed it, even though I was in my midthirties. Although it is true that black women do age well and I was not that much older than my students, I still wondered how much this misperception was based on my race and gender and the virtual absence of people of color. Over the ensuing years as faculty and legal-writing hires of color seemed increasingly unlikely, I finally convinced the dean to employ more people of color on the support staff, telling him how demoralizing it was to never see "myself" coming down the hall. This seemed even more significant at an institution that is only five miles from Philadelphia, which has a large black popula-tion. I can recall attending a Christmas party where there was finally an entire table of black people who worked at the law school. That was in 2007. In sum, there were and still are racist and sexist comments, but mostly by folks who would be absolutely and genuinely shocked to be told just how racist and/or sexist they sound.

Besides, in the early years, perhaps it was the sexism that was worse among an aging faculty that was unaccustomed to having women professors among their ranks. For example, despite the presence of five women on the faculty (including me) when I began teaching at Villanova—two of whom were on my floor—we did not have a restroom on our wing. The restroom was marked "faculty," and faculty members had always been male; obviously, the needs of the two faculty members and three female administrative assistants were not considered significant. Embar-rassed at going to the restroom with the students I was about to teach and tired of the blatant gender discrimination, I finally insisted that we share the restroom by posting a sign on the door indicating the gender of the occupant. It was not until my sixth year at Villanova, however, that the large men's room was split and a women's restroom constructed.

Nonetheless, I was treated reasonably well by my colleagues and eventually by my students. Two master teachers—one a female colleague at Villanova, the other a black male at another institution—helped me correct my teaching deficiencies. A yearlong fellowship at a top ten law school interrupted the negative advance press about my teaching that invariably follows first-year professors and gave me a new standing upon my return. I soon became a much better teacher and rather popular with most of my students. I was also a darling of the administration—at least during the tenure of the dean who had hired me. I was visible in segments of the broader

academic community and was bringing newfound attention and a modicum of prestige to the school in the form of fellowships at prominent schools, faculty workshops, book projects for African law schools, and all kinds of high-quality "stuff," for
which the dean was most appreciative, even if all of my colleagues were not (Young
1996, 270, 279).[17]

Obtaining tenure was not a problem; I had done the work and had a great internal advocate and mentor who was and is very prominent in my field. There also
seemed to be a bit of controversy regarding the only other person of color who had
ever come up for tenure, although thankfully, it was not enough controversy to deny
him tenure. Nonetheless, I thought there could not possibly be problems regarding both of our tenure votes, so I was not overly worried about what can be quite a
grueling process. Yet the law school has thus far stopped with me when it comes to
granting tenure to African Americans. In its fifty-five-year existence, Villanova has
given tenure to only one black professor—namely me, although I hope that by the
time this chapter is in print, the law school will have corrected this blemish.

Besides, when I began my teaching career, I felt that I possessed a secret weapon,
a safety net, a connection with a much wider community. There was always the
Northeast Corridor Collective, whose members I could count on to help with gen-
der- and race-based slights, to assist in navigating tenure, to read and critique my
article drafts, and to assure me that I could keep my braids and the rest of myself.
The collective was pure bliss at the outset of my teaching career, for not only was
I entering an exciting intellectual community, but I was immediately invited to be
part of a gathering of the most dynamic black women I could imagine who were
welcoming me—indeed welcoming all newcomers—into their ranks simply because
I was an African American woman teaching at a US law school.[18] It was community
writ large.

The Northeast Corridor Collective of Black Women Law Professors was a "group
of black women law professors who met each quarter in each others' homes to discuss works-in-progress and to exchange ideas, including thoughts on the development of black feminist theory and practice," which culminated in a groundbreaking

17   Professor Michael Mulroney (one of my colleagues at Villanova, it turns out), at a discus-
      sion at a 1994 AALS meeting, said "that as an older faculty member [sixty-two] and as a tax
      professor, he can call himself a minority, too. 'I can retreat to that,' he said. 'I can use that
      as an excuse for mediocrity.'" Statements such as these reflect the presumption that women
      and minorities may be mediocre professors (Young 1996). At least this colleague seemed
      to equate minority with mediocrity. One wonders if he believed my presence on the Villa-
      nova faculty indicated mediocrity. This would be almost laughable because my credentials
      more closely matched contemporary hiring criteria than did those of a number of Villanova
      faculty members during the early 1990s. This was not unusual at middle-ranked schools: as
      hiring standards became increasingly rigorous, newer faculty members were more heavily
      credentialed than their senior counterparts.

18   Because I was teaching six credit hours, I barely had time to live, much less be fully cogni-
      zant of some of the discussion taking place around me. In the spring, I came up for a bit of
      air but was almost immediately struck by personal tragedy. I was aware of the controversy
      surrounding black women in the academy as Professor Derrick Bell left Harvard Law School
      because of its failure to employ even one black women law professor. I knew, I listened, but
      I did not really participate in this discussion. I did not have the history, I already had a full
      plate, and when I did research, it was on the United Nations Security Council and the use of
      force. Many of my colleagues in the collective, however, were discussing this controversy in
      depth, and I could at least listen in on the conversation.

series of essays in the *Berkeley Women's Law Journal*.[19] The collective began modestly as an informal discussion group among black women law professors who lived and taught in the cities between Boston and Washington, D.C. The first meeting was held in March 1988 in Washington, and over the next decade, the group continued to expand its numbers as well as its geographic coverage (Watson 2008, 7).[20] It created a safe place for black, female members of a profession that did not mean to include them. Because Villanova is just outside Philadelphia, I was immediately welcomed into the fold—and what a fold it was! One particular hierarchy that prevails in the legal academy (namely, the top schools versus the want-to-be-top schools versus the rest of us) seemed to be nonexistent in this group. Instead, this safe place allowed each of us to work through our ideas, including presenting written drafts to the best and brightest, who read them and gave them a careful review as we helped each other make our work the best it could be. The first article I submitted for publication was accepted by numerous international law journals and barely edited—and I am certain this was in part because of the generous input I had received from members of the collective.

People of color within the academy have continued to create safe places to nurture each other and ensure survival of the tenure process and beyond. At annual people of color conferences, young and not-so-young legal scholars can present their works in progress and receive feedback and assistance. Workshops for young scholars abound as senior members of the academy support their younger colleagues with writing, teaching, obtaining tenure, and other facets of being a successful law professor. Conferences on critical theory or LatCrit include subconferences devoted to assisting younger colleagues, who are also invited to participate fully in the larger proceedings. Black women have also continued to organize, with the Lutie A. Lytle Black Women Faculty Writing Workshop being the most recent example. This contemporary group is much larger and surely more sophisticated than our humble beginnings, but that is, after all, as it should be. We are building upon our foundations and expanding our achievements. Indeed it is gratifying to see how much we have grown and progressed.

Part III: The Persistence of Hierarchy

Once you are established in the legal academy, race, gender, and class emerge along different boundaries. At the very top of the law school hierarchy are deans, who are the head administrators and members of the tenured faculty. Law school deans have traditionally been white men; only recently have men of other races, women, and finally black women been admitted to their ranks in perceptible numbers (McGinley 2009).[21] At the next stratum are tenured full professors, closely fol-

---

19   This history is taken from the papers collected in volume six of the *Berkeley Women's Law Journal*. Organized by Professor Emma Coleman Jordan, this series of essays is stunning in its breadth and depth. I read them almost in their entirety in writing this essay and would advise us all to visit or revisit them.

20   The first meeting was attended by sixteen black women; within three years, the gathering had grown to encompass participation by up to ninety-one black women (Watson 2008). Watson also notes that the collective was begun by Emma Coleman Jordan, who does not take credit for that in her article that recounts the collective's beginnings. Moreover, while the name of the group suggests a criterion of geographic eligibility, participants have ranged from as far west as California and as far south as Florida.

21   Professor McGinley notes that from academic year 1998–99 to 2008–9, the percentage of

lowed by tenure-track faculty members, who together are near the top of the peck-ing order within both the law school and the larger culture. In the legal community and perhaps the world at large, a professor of law is well respected, even if black women must often struggle to establish their membership within this group (Moran 1990–91, 118; Wing 1990–91, 181; Merritt and Reskin 1997, 199). Issues of gender and race continue to play out within this small privileged group, including who becomes a professor, at what rank you are hired, how you obtain tenure and thus remain within this circumscribed circle, and how you address—much less endure—diverse and distinct expectations from colleagues and students (Merritt and Reskin 1991–92, 2299; McGinley 2009; Chused 1988–89, 537).

Nevertheless, these particular status games are being reproduced within law schools at the top of the institutional hierarchy. Professors are still "the professor" after all, and with that title, we can choose how to interact with other law school employees. For example, almost everyone knows and is friendly with the men and women who keep the building clean; they are usually nice people who are quite easy to get along with. But we could just as easily decide to be unfriendly or rude—it is our choice and an option not readily available to the cleaning staff. However, the people who currently maintain our building look like folks in my family, so it is natu-ral for me to be gracious and pleasant; indeed my grandmother cleaned elementary school classrooms, and I still have relatives who work on university cleaning staffs. When I see the custodial staff, I see part of me, and we share something—a cul-tural identity or our blackness; to be honest, I am not precisely sure what it is, but I know it is there, and we acknowledge it implicitly and sometimes explicitly. Recent examples of sharing include Michael Jackson's untimely death and our pride in the election of President Obama. I talked, cried, and lamented with the custodial and kitchen staff, the secretarial staff—indeed everyone with a black face; there was a connection: shared memories and pride, regardless of our job descriptions. Yet professors—whether they are of color or not—decide to be friendly or unfriendly from their perch at the apex of the law school social order. Indeed—for women and people of color of either gender—the goal is to make colleagues, students, and administrators respect our status and grant us the same deference, esteem, and respect that are bestowed upon our white male colleagues (Guinier 1994; Bartow, Fine, and Guinier 1994; McGinley 2009).[22]

Beyond professors and deans, there is a broader community where race and especially gender loom large. Law schools need administrators, most have legal writ-ing staffs, and many have clinics where students engage in the supervised practice of law. Legal writing positions are seldom tenure-track while those of clinical profes-sors may or may not be. Nor are all administrators created equal. Some are associate deans who teach and are tenured faculty members. Others, usually assistant deans, are part of the administration but are not members of the faculty. Nonteaching administrators have proliferated, and assistant deans tend to be heavily represented by white women and, to a lesser extent, women of color. A disproportionate num-ber of legal writing instructors are also women, unless they have one of the rare tenure-track jobs or serve as a director of legal writing; they are also paid less and do

female law-school deans rose from 10.4 to 19.8 percent.

22   Of course, my personal experiences are an oversimplification. Black and white women have written about how problematic this structure is, including its racial and gendered aspects.

not have voting privileges, even when given such titles as professor of legal writing (Merritt and Reskin 1990–91, 199; Liemer and Temple 2007–8, 383). Clinical positions are often devalued, although many clinicians do triple duty—handling cases, teaching, and writing articles. Yet the legal academy tends to undervalue practice, especially when it comes to filling the ranks, and thus—not surprisingly—it also undervalues clinicians (Seibel 1996). Although diversity has increased within the law school hierarchy, white men still disproportionately occupy positions at the top while women overwhelmingly fill the lower ranks.

Is this hierarchy? Undoubtedly yes, for within law schools, some are clearly more privileged and powerful than others in status, pay, working conditions, and other areas (Merritt and Reskin 1990–91, 199).[23] Is it a class-based hierarchy? If class is evidenced by "similar economic and social position, and thus a sharing of political attitudes, lifestyles, consumption patterns, cultural interests and opportunities to advance" (Scott and Leonhardt 2005, 2), then it seems doubtful. Clinicians and legal writing professors are attorneys who have attended college and graduate school, even if the schools that dominate professorial hiring are not as prevalent (Liemer and Temple 2007–8, 383). If my institution is any guide, many associate deans are also attorneys who have forsaken practice and—like many of their colleagues—are married to attorneys or other professionals. On some level, then, all of the characters in this production are solid members of the middle—if not upper-middle—class, and the divisions and demarcations fall within a somewhat privileged group.

Class distinctions within the ranks of tenured and tenure-track professors are even more partial; in fact, in many respects, broader class distinctions seem almost nonexistent. Even if class influences whether or not you become a law professor, many remnants of class—besides being part of the middle class—have been wrung out of an individual by the time that goal is achieved. I believe it is part of qualifying for the job, which requires attending highly ranked schools, writing law-review articles, and working in high-status jobs, which all indicate an upper-class existence. It seems working-class markers must be almost expunged and you must struggle to retain this vestige of yourself. Some of my colleagues within the legal academy, however, have proudly and defiantly managed to do so. At any rate, I cannot tell or guess the background of most of my colleagues. I know some are the descendants of generations of professors and scholars, and many more share at least parts of my history, but I generally know this because they have chosen to declare or share it (Banks 1990–91, 46; Jordan 1990–91b, 113). I personally relish seeing with multiple eyes and having, in fact, lived in the communities we theorize, ponder, and write about; I take pride in my origins. Perhaps my peers with upper-middle-class genealogies have additional insights and may be able to detect the origins of their colleagues who emerge from working- and lower-middle-class backgrounds, whether declared or not. I do not know this and thus cannot speak about it.

Although tenured and tenure-track professors are at the apex of the hierarchy within their respective institutions, when they step into the broader milieu of legal academia, that is, circulate among their peers in the wider academic community, they may or may not be at the top, for within this setting, where one teaches also

---

23   Deborah Merritt and Barbara Reskin (1990–91) note that law schools are particularly structured, making them easier to study.

becomes important. Perhaps these are not primarily class distinctions, for we are all middle class; rather it is due to, as Deborah Ware Post opines, our obsession with rankings. As Professors Merritt and Reskin note,

> Most faculty members, in law as well as in other disciplines, seek appointment at the most prestigious institutions within their fields. Elite schools tend to offer higher salaries, lighter teaching loads and more successful students than do less prestigious schools. Professors at highly regarded schools also have more direct access to the networks of academic and political power that produce invitations to deliver prestigious lectures, publish in top-ranked journals, or assume influential government positions. Institutional prestige thus is an important factor affecting both the quality of a faculty member's initial appointment and his or her career advancement (1990–91, 199).

We seem almost to be obsessed with this particular hierarchy. If you are not so advantaged as to be hired at an elite school, then you attempt to climb the law school pecking order and obtain a lateral hire at a better-ranked school, even if not the most elite. Those who are not so ambitious at the very least trade up their articles in an effort to publish in the most prestigious law journals, which means at the most elite institution possible. As Professor Deborah Ware Post states,

> Our preoccupation with hierarchy is reflected in our obsession with rankings, the periodic publication of lists in the national press which rank law firms and law schools and the protests which are published in response. . . . Even though we condemn rankings, ranking plays a very important role in law school teaching. It is used in evaluating those who wish to enter law school teaching. Top tier schools overvalue their own graduates, creating a kind of inbreeding while mid and lower tier schools undervalue their own graduates. Scholarship has become the most important factor in deciding who gets tenure and often the quality of a publication is measured by the rank of the law review in which it is published. . . . We also refer regularly to these rankings in making career choices. Law teachers, all teachers are pretty mobile and . . . visitorship is used to trade up in much the same way we trade up our consideration of offers from law reviews. There are some people who make decisions on some other basis, but this is considered irrational (1994, 69 n39).[24]

It is not surprising that legal academia, which is constructed on hierarchical grounds within a larger class-based society, would be fixated upon rankings and standings. What is more interesting is that many of us spend our professional lives

---

24   Professor Post cites her move from the University of Houston to Touro, which entailed rejecting a higher-ranked school in favor of a lower-ranked one. Her colleagues warned her it was a bad move. When I weighed those four teaching offers my second time on the hiring circuit, several colleagues told me to go to a school that was ranked higher than Villanova and cautioned that it would be difficult to trade up. I am certain it was good advice, although like Deborah, I took into account other considerations such as being relatively young and single and wanting to be near a city with a large black population, where my extended family resided. I often note to my colleagues that candidates for faculty positions may consider such factors as quality of life in deciding whether to accept a position and that school rank is not the only relevant factor; however, many remain skeptical.

contesting hierarchy and exclusion—whether on the basis of race, gender, or class—but when it comes to academia—and I would suggest especially legal academia—we appear to have finally found a hierarchy we can believe in. It not only goes unquestioned but is often at the core of our complaint. Thus, Professors Merritt and Reskin's excellent study focuses on access by white women and people of color of both genders to the sixteen most prestigious law schools. But most of us, regardless of gender, race, or class, do not teach at those schools, nor do most of the law students in this country attend them.

While it is incontestable that many rewards and accolades result from being on the faculty of an elite school, it is mystifying that we do not question the assumptions and beliefs that have created this situation. Instead, we readily acquiesce and participate to the point that colleagues at elite schools often feel they do not even have to listen to the rest of us speak, nor read what we write. As Professor Post notes, "Those of us at mid or lower tier schools often attend conferences only to discover that the only representatives from the top tier schools present are the speakers. I think it is safe to say that there is a perception among those of us who teach in the lower tier schools that this limited form of participation is considered uncollegial, and well, in a word, snobbery. When no one from Harvard or Yale shows up as a member of the audience at the meetings of the professional association you have to ask, have we all been dissed?" (1994, 69 n39).

I suspect this is not only true but probably even more common when it comes to majority professors. For example, I can recall being almost invisible during a fellowship at a top-ten law school. For many (with the exception of most of the few people of color, my international law host, and a sprinkling of very welcoming and gracious people), I seemed not to exist—except for the moment I received word that my first article had been accepted to numerous journals and would be published in the *Michigan Journal of International Law.* I gained some legitimacy but only for a few days. I believe that this was the result of a variety of factors, but perhaps the major one was that I did not teach at another top-ten school and thus lacked a certain measure of legitimacy, despite attending one of those schools.[25]

Still, are people of color more inclusive and less hierarchical? In many ways I think we are, especially when it comes to fellow teachers—whether they teach legal writing or work in clinical programs—and perhaps even when it comes to assistant deans. I have not observed these distinctions being reinforced at gatherings of people of color. Yet, in my very humble opinion, I believe that we black women law professors, like most others, protect and take pleasure in our privilege; I am quite certain that I do. While we may have less privilege than others because we are often penalized for our race and gender, within the academy, we are still at the top of the hierarchy and own a privilege we may not even be fully aware of (Angel 2000, 1; Angel 2004–5, 789; Grillo and Wildman 1991, 397; Flagg 1993, 953, 969).[26]

25   Over the course of this appointment, I also realized that I did not want to teach at a top-ten school (a wise decision since none have come calling). Still, the fellowship was exceptionally good for me and my career. I taught one class (not course!), attended many classes, joined in campus events, held great conversations and received input on my work from most of the international law scholars, participated in faculty colloquia, and made several very good friends. In other words, I gained much from the experience and found time to write what would eventually be some of my most influential articles. Clearly being at a top-tier school has its benefits, or perhaps it also had something to do with just having a year to reflect.

26   We tend not to be as aware of what privileges us. Barbara Flagg (1993) implies that whites,

But are we really that different from each other? Do we so believe in the hierarchy that envelops us that we judge some are not worth listening to and their work—even significant bodies of it—is not deemed noteworthy enough to know or cite because the author does not teach at a top-fifteen school?[27] I have observed the frustration and pain of those who believe their articles and books are ignored by colleagues at elite schools, and others who desperately seek to move up the law school hierarchy and just be acknowledged by those residing within those rarefied circles. I understand that most of us want to move up the ladder, even if only to trade up our articles to more elite journals. Nearly all feel validated by tenure, even as we disdain the racism, sexism, and arbitrariness that is part of this pursuit, for once it has been attained, work becomes a vocation, and our profession feels and perhaps is different. We want the chairs, money, benefits, and accolades that can come with tenure, and I am no different, although I decided long ago that I was not interested in elite schools, which, incidentally, have also never been interested in me.

Yet I believe we who eschew hierarchy in so many quarters can perhaps do better than our majority counterparts and definitely better than we have been doing. We, meaning people of color, hold multiple annual conferences to help all of our colleagues attain tenure, not just those at elite schools. The Northeast Corridor Collective was open to all comers, and my paper was read by everyone, regardless of institutional affiliation. In general we are more inclusive and open and do not make as many distinctions as seem to prevail in academia at large. But we also do not seem to question the structure where we exist. Instead, we simply try to succeed within it and criticize our exclusion. It is fitting to contest racism and sexism and attempt to neutralize class barriers, but this battle is at the margins, and it is somewhat puzzling

---

for example, are unaware of their race and the privileges associated with their whiteness. For example, my heterosexuality privileges me, and I can choose when or if to focus on it. I usually think about it most when I am with my friends and colleagues who are members of the lesbian, gay, bisexual, and transgendered (LGBT) community, and even then only when the conversation or discussion turns to issues confronting them. Thus, even when we are together, I still do not think about it for very long because usually we are not pontificating on these issues, but rather simply enjoying each other's company. However, the point is that I can consider these issues at my discretion because they usually do not affect my day-to-day life. The same cannot be said for problems of gender and race, which for me are omnipresent even when they do not seem to be there at all.

27   Many law schools are aggressively trying to join the ranks of the top twenty-five—or at least the top fifty—in *US News and World Report* law-school rankings. But how different are law schools, especially within their respective tiers? In my opinion, not very, at least if we omit schools that are strapped for funds and thus cannot or will not support research, or schools that cripple faculty who want to write with untenable teaching loads, or schools that essentially do not value scholarship or high-quality service—which I believe are our windows to the outside world, whether that is the realm of practicing attorneys, our fellow law teachers, or the policy makers that we hope embrace our work to make the world more tolerable.

Schools that discourage or make engaging in scholarship or very high-level service difficult for their faculties actually are different. Scholarship allows us to remain current and intellectually alive, as does writing important briefs in crucial cases, consulting for government agencies, or running groundbreaking clinics such as the Innocence Project (http://www.innocenceproject.org/). Teaching is also another crucial way to change the world—by impacting students. But, in my opinion, teaching without scholarship or some other form of community engagement means atrophy over time. It is hard to stay fresh for students without having other interests besides teaching. If an institution supports research, travel, and publication without burdening its faculty with untenable teaching loads, is that not enough to achieve the ultimate goal of all faculties and perhaps of all people in their own way—to have some impact upon the world?

to me why the system as a whole remains unchallenged. Surely we can listen to each other even more at conferences and workshops, read each other's work without the blinders of institutional affiliation, and try to open ourselves to each other. We can chip away at hierarchy within our ranks. We know how to do it and are often quite good at it. What we must still nurture is a greater consciousness of our common goal of community and the need to challenge hierarchy, not only when it is unjust but even when it may benefit us.

Part V

Tenure and Promotion

Introduction

Deena J. González

The essays in this volume drove me back to one of my favorite books, Spivak's *Outside in the Teaching Machine*. As I move ever closer to the "inside"—training as I am for a position as a higher education administrator—I see far more clearly the sheer, utter necessity of testimony, of analysis, of wit, and more, of wisdom from classroom practitioners, from researchers and scholars, wherever we locate ourselves along the spectrum of academic positions. Women of color—guest workers, as so many conceptualize their positions and work—offer a unique and daring perspective. We watch as Sonia Sotomayor must "regret" her wise, womanly remark, feeling aghast as well at what it takes to get the job. We've all done it ourselves—in small, less-public forums, or in loud, recorded moments where the only outcome is vilification, misunderstanding, and migration (to another institution). From the congressional chambers through the corridors of the academy, the hallway is lined with regret, horror, and the agonizing need to "set the record straight," "get this just right," "fix this race/ethnic/gender/sexuality problem." We all try to advance or move the dialogue along, knowing what we know, and, for the effort, we often are left with only the reward of internal, organic, empathetic understanding of what it took for Justice Sotomayor to get there.

This volume was being compiled as Shirley Sherrod made her way across our screens in July 2010, a woman whose great sin appears to be that she was intelligent.[1] Occupying a position in what even the mildly liberal reporters call "the most racist or prejudiced agency" in the US government, the USDA, evidences how eminently qualified she is for a post even higher than the one she held; you wonder how many women endure Sherrod moments. The authors in *Presumed Incompetent* reveal many such moments—moments of grief, anger, despair—and, as with Sherrod, advance the will to continue to change institutions of higher learning from the inside out. This is the challenge of the twenty-first century: the race for equity, equality, and commensurate wages as each struggle faces an ever-expanding, larger battle—as Spivak noted in her book on the university—because

---

1   Sherrod was the Georgia state director of rural development for the United States Department of Agriculture; a blogger captured a segment of her remarks before the NAACP, not their full context, and posted them as evidence of racism, when in fact the opposite was the case. She had attempted to use her consciousness about the impact of racialism in her position working with white farmers as well as those of color. She was forced to resign, although subsequently the Obama administration offered her a post in the USDA, which she declined.

the goal or aim of guest workers is to confound and debunk Eurocentricism, in other words, not simply to teach the students but to teach the institution. The challenge is mighty and all encompassing, and it can endanger health and sanity.

These articles suggest what it takes to survive, thrive, and stay until retirement: many began as interlopers and critics, moved closer to an understanding of the difference they could make, sought alliances and vowed not to stand alone, or engaged the blunt instruments of power in its various forms, including racism, sexism, heterosexism, and classism. Some entered fields that by definition were founded on the idea of criticism and conscience or consciousness. Others entered mainstream disciplines determined to make them better, seeking out the humanism that many of us believed was the watchword of so many areas of study. The cumulative effects, the destructive power of unaltered structures, of traditional bases of privilege and identity, eroded the confidence many had at the beginning of their careers to be able to reach students, who in turn could indeed embody better ways of thinking or change the world as we knew it through practice. Students also respond slowly—like people in positions of power—to problems or issues.

I admire the work ethic and brilliance these essays advance; none of the authors are offering retreat or planning to leave academia, although all of them seem to have considered it from time to time. From the struggles to make institutions more humane or responsive to basic and expanding human needs, the lessons accumulate. We are richer for hearing these lessons told in the words of those who have seen, heard, and spoken "truth to power." If we watched apartheid crumble (ostensibly), walls come tumbling down, the end of a half century's Cold War, and the election of an African American man to the highest office in this country, we can certainly believe that the hope we embody by detailing our academic lives will have resounding impact—if not today—then when the first woman of color is elected president, when many more take their place as university presidents, as school superintendents, as heads of city councils, as mayors and governors.

The strand unifying these articles is the message that we remain wary of tokenism and will not forsake one another as we advance through the academic ranks. Tenure and promotion review remain mysteries for many outsiders, from first generation scholars to those with working-class origins, where the tone, values, or ideals of the academy were initially learned in a formal university setting, not at home or by visiting the institutions throughout one's early life. Additionally, the tenure process differs by institution, making mentoring place specific. Some institutions have few mentoring programs while others rely on traditional evaluative criteria or rarely consider service activities relevant to promotion. The sum of these barriers to advancement—at any stage in one's career—can derail research agendas, create an air of incompetence (or failure), and dog even the most dedicated scholar across the various arenas related to academic rewards or recognition of achievement.

As some authors note in this volume, the authenticity of the self is sorely tested under these conditions. The advice and message are sound because—as the coeditors note in their introduction—power is concentrated in the hands of a few, and elbowing our way to the table requires many allies, including white men and others already there who believe in the diversity of our perspectives. Our hope—as these essays attest—is that we can offer a method grounded in justice, reconciliation, and faith in a future guided less by rhetoric and promise and measured more by realistic goals and our true achievements. These contributors have delivered on the promise of making things better for the next wave and deserve our attention to their inventive ways, accrued wisdom, and strategic analysis.

CHAPTER 23

THE MAKING OF A TOKEN

A Case Study of Stereotype Threat, Stigma, Racism, and Tokenism in Academe[1]

Yolanda Flores Niemann

Ethnic/racial-minority faculty continue to be underrepresented in the US professoriate, representing only about 6 percent of all professors in the academy (Garza 1993). Obstacles to reaching the academy abound, including institutional racism, socioeconomic barriers, and, for Latinas, traditional gender-role expectations (Martinez Aleman 1995; Gandara 1995; Niemann, Romero, and Arbona 2000). Once Latinas overcome these obstacles and make it into the academy, they—like other faculty of color—face yet another set of obstacles, including experiences of racial tokenism, overt and covert racism, and stigmatization. These experiences are generally grounded in the undermining attitudes and behavior of people within the institution.

Largely as a result of these experiences, faculty of color may also undermine their own competence. They may fall victim to *stereotype threat,* which is defined as being vulnerable to internalizing the negative stereotypes about your own group in a given situation, even when you do not accept these stereotypes (Steele 1997). A prevalent stereotype about Latinos/as and African Americans is lack of competence in academic domains, making faculty from these groups particularly vulnerable to the self-undermining effects of stereotype threat (Niemann et al. 1994). This situation reflects vulnerability independent of the behavior and attitudes of colleagues. As a result, the obstacles faced by faculty of color involve interactive forces of two types of undermining of competence—that done by others, and self-undermining.

Such was the case with my first faculty experience. I went from having strong feelings of self-efficacy in the academy to wondering why I had the arrogance to

---

1   I wish to thank the persons who provided guidance and comments on previous drafts of this paper, especially John Dovidio, Pamela Cole, Kelly Ervin, and Tatcho Mindiola.

think I could succeed in an academic career. Only distance from that experience has enabled me to analyze the processes that occurred during those first four shaky years as an assistant professor. Based on a daily journal I kept during that time period, the following is an analysis of that situation illustrating the way the insidious, psychologically damaging processes of stereotype threat, tokenism, stigma, and related racism may occur. While publishing this personal essay represents a certain amount of personal risk, I believe it is important to discuss openly the effects of what is a reality for many people of color in academia. It is my hope that this chapter will help illuminate these processes so that others either just entering academia or struggling to survive there may benefit from enhanced awareness of pitfalls associated with being a scholar of color. Awareness can lead to prevention and facilitate coping. Institutions attempting to recruit and retain minority scholars may also gain insight on the undermining processes that may jeopardize faculty of color at various levels in the institution.

The Recruitment Process

Until I was offered a tenure-track position, my graduate experience in the rigorous social science program of a large, predominantly white, urban university was relatively uneventful. I was a very successful graduate student, having defended my master's thesis, sailed through most of my course work, completed my doctoral minor, successfully finished my comprehensive exams, and moved my way toward defending my dissertation proposal—all within a three-year period. I had also lobbied for—and been allowed to develop and teach—the first course on ethnic/cultural issues in the department. My advisors referred to me as a star student. Then, in my third year of the program and two weeks before my dissertation pre-orals, the chair of the department (who was also my principal advisor, chair of my dissertation committee, and director of the program) called me into his office, and everything about my experience at the university began to change—from very good to very bad. Yet the day began with seemingly good news for me.

The chair informed me that a junior faculty member had just tendered her resignation (she left for a more prestigious university). He further stated that the dean had given the department permission to replace that faculty member but with the very strong encouragement to hire a Mexican American or African American. At that time, there were about thirty tenure-stream faculty in the department—all white—and only a handful of women. The department had been under fire from the faculty-of-color associations on campus for this lack of representation. The chair enthusiastically reported that the faculty wanted me to apply for the tenure-track position and believed I could be successful in achieving tenure at the institution. He elaborated that under no circumstances should I think I was getting the opportunity because I was Mexican American; it was just a coincidence that my ethnicity coincided with the dean's preference. I asked the chair about the extent of the search, and he replied that the department had other applications on file to consider and would be working hard to put out feelers for others, but I was considered the leading candidate.

I was surprised because the university was not known to hire its own students, and I was quite flattered by what I then interpreted as my faculty's faith in my competence and their eagerness to keep me around. In terms of the ethnicity requirement, I reasoned that because affirmative action was still a viable hiring tool in most universities, my ethnicity would likely have been a factor at any institution. I was then too naïve to realize that the dean's ethnicity preference was undermining me before I even interviewed, especially given the anti-affirmative-action sentiment in that department.

There is strong documentation for the idea that a stigma of incompetence arises from the affirmative-action association (Heilman, Block, and Lucas 1992), especially when it carries a negative connotation in the hiring department. Once tagged as an affirmative-action hire, colleagues may discount the qualifications of the applicant and assume she was selected primarily because of her minority status (Heilman, Block, and Lucas 1992; Dovidio and Gaertner 1996), thus leading to the presumption and stigma of incompetence. Beginning with recruitment and hiring, academics of color may be vulnerable to stereotype threat and begin consciously or unconsciously to internalize stigmatizing myths and stereotypes relative to academia (Pratkanis and Turner 1996). In my case, the stigma of incompetence and my tokenization began almost immediately with the dean's strong request that the new faculty member be African American or Mexican American. However, I was then unaware of the events taking place that would undermine my competence and my colleagues' perception of me. Unawareness equaled blindness and exacerbated my vulnerability.

In retrospect the signs of my harsh future in the department were glaring. For instance, a white, female, junior faculty member spent the entire interview with me repeating how much she was against affirmative action. I dismissed her behavior by convincing myself that if she knew how competent I was, she would not think of me as an affirmative-action hire. Another sign of future trouble was that an unusually small number of the faculty showed up for my colloquium. This was particularly unsettling because—in this rigorous research department—the faculty generally wanted to know if potential members could conduct and discuss research. They couldn't evaluate me as a scholar if they were not present to assess my performance in the colloquium.

I learned later that the program's faculty had been "explaining the situation" to those in other department programs and lobbying them to vote for me. In essence, then, the decision to hire me was made before my colloquium. Still, I could not bring myself to think that this lack of interest in my research skills meant they didn't see me as a scholar. I convinced myself that many of the department faculty already knew me and respected my ability.

At about that same time, the director of an ethnic studies program asked me to apply for his program's postdoctoral fellowship. We both reasoned that the postdoc would allow me a year of distance from my advisors before becoming their colleague. New PhDs often covet postdoc positions as a way of moving toward independence from training professors and getting their research off the ground before fully engaging in a tenure-track position. This turn of events seemed fortuitous. I informed my department chair that I was also applying for the ethnic studies position and—since he was my principal advisor—I would need a letter of recommendation from him. He said he would write one, but reluctantly because my program was counting on me.

Shortly after my colloquium, I was offered both positions. My department's vote had been unanimous, with one abstention. I was later told by a voting faculty member that someone at that meeting had asked about my possible postdoc and the chair had immediately said the department wasn't interested in that for me and would not discuss it. Still, I convinced myself that the department was just afraid to lose me.

The day after the department's vote, I received anonymous racist hate mail in my department mailbox. I immediately took the letter to the department chair, who stated that he was horrified at the content but took no action. He advised me to ignore it, saying it could happen anywhere. He said he wanted to keep the letter, and I naïvely gave it to him. Incredibly, I felt ashamed and somehow responsible for having received hate mail, a symptom of stereotype threat.

I was so embarrassed that I didn't even tell the dean about the hate mail. I did tell him that I wanted the year of postdoc, followed by the tenure-track position in my department. He told me that such an arrangement was not unusual and universities often waited for a new faculty member who had a fellowship and/or was on leave. He agreed that the extra year to get my research off the ground would give me an edge, especially since I was completing graduate school so quickly. The dean further said that he could arrange it so that my tenure clock would not begin until after the year of postdoc and, as far as the college was concerned, I would be a department faculty member on a year's leave of absence so that my faculty position would be secure. I was excited; things seemed to be taking a turn for the better.

This excitement was replaced with the foreboding of coming trouble when I subsequently met with the department chair. He told me in no uncertain terms that the department's wishes were that I accept only its position. He further stated that I should consider that memories die hard and the department could hold it against me on my future tenure vote. He explained that I should keep in mind that the current dean might or might not have the power to help me in the future. He also stated that a senior program faculty member, who was quite powerful because he brought in extensive grants (let me call him Dr. Grant), had lobbied the department heavily for me, and I should be grateful.

My reaction—kept to myself—was that I would have preferred it if the faculty had voted for me because they had been impressed with my colloquium and competence, not due to political lobbying. I felt stigmatized to learn that someone had had to lobby department faculty to vote for me. Was I a charity case? Now my ego was beginning to feel the blow. I slowly started to question my own competence. After all, these were smart people with experience in academia. Did they know something I did not? Besides affecting me personally, the stigma of incompetence, facilitated by the lobbying, consciously or unconsciously allowed my future colleagues to begin thinking of me as a token minority, rather than a fellow scholar.

The prospect of staying at that university now seemed unappealing. I dearly wished I had immediately said no to the chair when he had first made the offer and that I had never mentioned it to my family or the ethnic studies director. At the time of the offer, however, the temptation to stay in that department was great for several reasons. For instance, I would not have to endure the stress of going out on the job market the following year as I had anticipated. Job hunting is an anxiety-provoking experience for most graduate students, and I was no exception.

However, my most compelling reason to stay was my family. My husband had a well-paying job, and our children—then fourteen and eleven—were happy and settled and had established long-term friendships. When I told them about the offer to stay in my current department, they were thrilled. They would get to stay in school with their friends and continue with their sports teams. They were so relieved not to have to move out of town. My husband had faithfully supported me—economically and emotionally—throughout graduate school. After my announcement of the job opportunity, we started talking about the way—with both of us employed—we could finally pay our debts and save some money for our children's college education.

I had dealt with role strain as a graduate student, making sure that I attended all of my children's extracurricular activities. Consistent with Latino/a values, my family had always come first. As I began to see ominous signs of trouble for me in the department, I was put to the test: should I do what was in my professional interest, or what seemed best for my family's interest? From the time I told my family about the job opportunity and heard their reaction, I really did not believe I had the option of applying for a job in another city.

Other role strain also affected my decision, especially my position as a student with strong ties to the chair of the department, who had been my principal advisor for three years. Until this situation, he had treated me respectfully and had spoken highly of my course work and research. The ties between graduate students and advisors are strong, but the power is always with the professor. His authority in that role was still very evident when he asked me to apply for the job. However, his ability to advise me was now diminished. He was chair of the department and director of the program at the same time, so he acted on behalf of both interests. A lesson here for future job candidates is that—when the offer is in your department—your advisor may find it difficult to be loyal both to the department and to you.

In terms of deciding which position to accept, the pull involved personal and political loyalty to the ethnic studies program, which had been very generous in supporting me. I wanted the postdoc year to get my research started without the ticking of the tenure clock. On the other hand, I still wanted eventually to be successful in the social science tenure-track position. I remembered the chair's threat—what if the faculty made me pay by denying me tenure?

It seemed to be widely known in the department that I was strongly considering the ethnic studies position. A senior faculty member called me into his office and said I needed to answer one question: "What are you, a scholar or a Mexican American?" He said that if I answered Mexican American, I should take the postdoc but not follow it with the department position because "the department is only interested in scholars, not Mexican Americans." I replied that I hadn't ceased to be Mexican American by becoming a scholar any more than he had stopped being a man when he had gotten his PhD. He retorted that it wasn't the same thing and I should give the matter serious thought. He also said that other faculty members shared his views.

It had never occurred to me to choose between my ethnicity and my identity as a scholar—it was neither possible nor logical. Before this experience, my holistic identity included being mother, wife, scholar, social scientist, friend, Mexican American, and woman. Separating them would be like expecting my major organs to work independently of each other in my body. I was bewildered.

This struggle to separate aspects of themselves likely affects other ethnic/racial minorities applying for academic jobs. It is critical for ethnic/racial minorities to understand that the forced duality (scholar or Mexican American) is a façade. For women, in particular, identity includes, at a minimum, issues of being female in a male-empowered academic workplace and personal (e.g., mother and wife) and professional role definitions, as well as ethnicity. Nevertheless, the forced duality reinforced my feelings of tokenism and, by extension, stigmatization and stereotype threat. The professor had made it seem as if being Mexican American was a disease.

The duality further played out in the tug-of-war for me between the social science department and ethnic studies program. The pull was so great that the department chair asked a respected Mexican American tenured professor to arbitrate between the department and the ethnic studies program and convince the program director to persuade me to accept only the department position. I now felt guilty because there was disagreement among campus Mexican American faculty about my situation. I felt as if everyone was talking about me. This sense of extreme visibility is consistent with the experience of tokenism (Kanter 1977; Niemann and Dovidio 1998a; Pollack and Niemann 1998). My identity as Mexican American was more salient to me than ever before in my life, and my holistic sense of self was being shattered.

I began to have trouble sleeping and focusing on my classes (I was still a third-year graduate student). My close friends, most of whom were also students in the department, were greatly concerned about me. The stress showed so much that the professor of the department's ethics course—the only female full professor in the department—approached me to discuss my options. She was quite fair and said she believed the postdoc would give me the needed distance from my advisors before I became a member of the department faculty. She also thought the year would give me more respectability (someone else valued my work) and diffuse the perception that the department was being strong-armed into hiring me without a search. I had not yet even gotten the job and already I was stigmatized and tokenized by the perception that the department was being forced to hire me. The reality was that the department faculty did not take the time and effort to widely solicit other candidates for the position. I was the one paying the price for their reliance on convenience.

The ethics professor was so concerned about the political ramifications of my accepting the postdoc that she made arrangements to become my dissertation chair (replace my current chair) if I took the position. That might minimize reprisals from the faculty. She had reason to be concerned about my future as a student. I had rapidly gone from being a star in my program to being thought of as a potential problem. She explained that the department faculty felt a sense of benevolence for having offered me the tenure-track position. She told me that they were incredulous that I would consider postponing working with them to become involved with the ethnic studies program for one year.

My Experience as a Faculty Member

I accepted the social science department position and turned down the postdoc. I convinced myself I could make this situation work in spite of my newfound awareness of the racism of some members of the department. As a Mexican American woman raised in economic poverty and the daughter of two people with third- and seventh-grade formal educations, I had overcome obstacles before. Although my identity was in turmoil, and I felt stigmatized by the hiring process, I had retained substantial confidence in my ability to achieve tenure and believed things would be different after I was "one of them." It didn't occur to me that I would never feel as if I belonged there.

My competence had not yet been completely undermined. I defended my dissertation in July (having collected all the data, analyzed it, and written the results and discussion since my pre-orals in April). One month later—after only three years as a social science graduate student—the tenure clock started ticking, and my life in the department went from a bad hiring experience to an even worse faculty situation. I was about to feel the interactive, psychologically damaging effects of others' and my internalized racism.

Stigmatization

The social science department's failure to conduct a national search for my position had created legal problems for the university administration, which had received complaints about my hiring process. One of the Mexican American faculty members from the law school had to present legal precedents to the administration for my hiring to be approved. It seemed that the circumstances surrounding my appointment had become common knowledge in the university. I thought that when people saw me, they believed, "She's the one the dean forced the social science department to hire." I felt lonely and stigmatized.

I also believed I had alienated the ethnic studies faculty, who might now see me as a traitor for not taking their postdoc. In the social science department, except for some polite greetings, I had little or no conversation with colleagues. The faculty distanced themselves from me and made no attempt to mentor me or facilitate my road toward tenure. As for the ethics professor, I was not sure whether she had the interests of the department, rather than mine, foremost in her mind, so I did not trust her. I did not trust the department. I did not know whom or what to trust!

This inability to trust is debilitating for junior faculty who are still in the early stages of their professional development. Generally feedback allows us to improve, but in situations where colleagues may be two-faced and/or racist, it becomes meaningless. Improvement thus happens much more slowly because we have less feedback to work with. This situation is exacerbated for faculty of color and can permeate all professional interactions, in and out of the institution. Research indicates that due largely to the societal prevalence of racism, people of color often make attributions about race when considering feedback or reactions of others to them, whether the feedback is positive or negative (Crocker et al. 1991). Once the boundary of distrust has been crossed, we cannot will ourselves into believing again in that environment. The cycle of not trusting any feedback continues, even when it is self-defeating.

For instance, I received fairly positive reviews with a request for a revision of a paper I had submitted to one of the top journals in my field of social science. However, that feedback was inconsistent with the racism and stigmatization I felt from the department. The positive reaction was therefore disorienting. I did not know what to believe. I had begun undermining my belief in competence and did not have the confidence to submit a revision. I later learned that the editor had put that paper in a file indicating the revision had a 70 percent chance of acceptance, but he never got my rewritten paper, an example of self-undermining behavior.

Tokenism and Covert Racism

During my first year, I was the only faculty of color in the entire department. My colleagues seemed content with that situation and oblivious to its effects on me. I was told, "Now that we have you, we don't need to worry about hiring another minority member." This sentiment is an example of covert racism in academia, which includes the "one-minority-per-pot syndrome" (de la Luz Reyes and Halcon 1997). This tokenism also occurred with social science graduate students. For instance, in my first year as faculty, I argued to bring in two Latina graduate students with excellent credentials, though other program faculty disagreed with me. After I persuaded faculty to conduct a person-to-person interview with these women, both were judged acceptable, but I recall Dr. Grant arguing that "one minority is enough." I accused him of tokenism and insisted that both women get into the program. The faculty reluctantly agreed.

One of the effects of tokenism is what is known as the pressure of a double-edged sword: "simultaneously, a perverse visibility and a convenient invisibility" (Tierney and Rhoades 1993). I was inordinately visible as a minority female in a predominantly white, male department. I was also visible when it was in the department's best interest to have an ethnic scholar, so my name, teaching, and research were brought up during visits of the national program-accrediting association, international scholars, and elected officials of color. Even some of the well-meaning faculty seemed oblivious to this tokenism. For instance, after one of these visits, one of my senior colleagues pulled me aside and excitedly said, "We told them all about your class and your research! They were really impressed with our diversity." I believe this colleague was well intentioned and that his comment was meant to be encouraging and supportive. However, the statement made me feel tokenized and devalued as a scholar. I felt representative of all ethnic/racial minorities and believed that the department cared only about the appearance of diversity without actually valuing it. In such a manner, people who are well meaning and unaware of their own racism contribute to a racist climate.

In my second year as faculty, an African American woman was hired in another department program. Her presence helped diffuse some of the attention from me. However, her research and teaching were considered mainstream while I was considered the ethnic researcher. This label also meant that my research was undervalued and not considered scholarly, an experience consistent with that of other faculty of color who believe that they, and their research, are underrated and seen primarily as affirmative-action appointments and only secondarily as scholars in their own right (Garza 1993).

My increasingly salient ethnic identity continued to play a role in my relationships with colleagues. In program faculty meetings, I was the only person who openly argued in favor of admitting minority graduate students. The other faculty members wanted to "be objective" and "color blind." One of the biggest ironies of this whole situation was that the department party line was that the faculty were oblivious to color and saw only people. This attitude, in conjunction with racist behavior, is consistent with what has been called *aversive racism*. Aversive racists are people who outwardly proclaim egalitarian values but express racism in subtle, easily rationalized ways, such as unfair hiring procedures for nonwhite group members (Dovidio and Gaertner 1996). It was hypocritical, then, that the department paid attention to race/ethnicity when it was in their interest.

For instance, one of the Latinas whom I was successful in getting admitted into the program had worked with me as an undergraduate and wanted me to be assigned as her advisor. However, Dr. Grant argued that he needed minorities on his team to help get grants and had her assigned to him. In a related occurrence, I learned that Dr. Grant had listed me as an unpaid consultant for a grant where the agency required ethnic/racial expertise—without ever asking my permission or discussing this grant with me.

I was also told that Dr. Grant routinely made negative, cutting remarks about me personally, about my teaching, and about my research. I learned about many of these remarks from the people who worked for him because he did not seem to have any qualms about openly disparaging me. As one of my colleagues told me, "Dr. Grant is not your friend. Watch your back." When I discussed Dr. Grant's behavior toward me with the department chair, he advised me just to dismiss the remarks and not take him seriously. He argued that, after all, no one would really listen to such comments from Dr. Grant. The chair was wrong, as became clear later in my third-year review.

I was furious with the chair's response but did nothing. I didn't have the courage or know-how to file a claim with the university center for human rights. This lack of action went against my sense of personal integrity, and, consequently, my self-esteem plummeted further. I contained my anger and gained forty pounds, most of it within my first year as an assistant professor. I began to question why I had ever thought I would do well in academia. If I was struggling, I reasoned, it must be due to my lack of competence. Of course, I also blamed the program faculty for not supporting me. However, I reasoned that if I were really good enough, I wouldn't need their support. In the midst of this experience, I could not see what external forces in my situation were doing to me, even though my academic training had prepared me to do so.

This lack of awareness is particularly ironic because the hallmark credo of my field of study is that behavior is a function of the person and the environment and that—when it comes to explaining behavior and attitudes—the situation matters. Still, the effects of stereotype threat, stigmatization, tokenism, and racism are so insidious that I couldn't see how they related to me at that time. That I undermined my sense of competence is particularly indicative of the power of the situation because by then I had begun studying the psychological effects of tokenism. Though I was well versed in the scientific literature, I was nevertheless too immersed in the situation to apply that knowledge to my situation.

Evidence of Tokenism and Racism—Undermining by Workload

My teaching and advising load was unprecedented for recently hired junior members of the department. In the four years I was a member of that department, I taught four different graduate seminars and three different undergraduate courses. From my discussions with colleagues, I learned that most new professors in the department taught only one or two graduate seminars in their area of specialty, which they continued for the first few years before they added others. Included in my teaching load were both of the core graduate courses in my field. My experience was consistent with documented disparities in the teaching load assigned to women as compared to men (Johnsrud 1993). These disparities—evidence that your scholarship is not valued—are exacerbated for women of color.

I was also the principal advisor for eight graduate students as well as chair of their thesis and/or dissertation committees. Two of the students assigned to me had been considered problem students previous to my becoming faculty. Two of the other program faculty, both full professors, had only two graduate students each, and one of them later transferred to me. I also supervised and advised approximately fifteen undergraduate students as members of my research team.

This workload contrasts sharply with that of the faculty member I replaced. She was white, a graduate of an elite university who was hired after an extensive national search, and the department had high expectations of her. Although she taught two critical graduate courses, she had been sheltered from extensive advising responsibilities. After three years in the department, she was formally advising only one student, a workload consistent with department standards for junior professors. The difference in the department's perception of us was obvious from the disparities in our workloads.

I was assigned complex and time-consuming administrative tasks necessary for the program. What this workload meant was that there was little time for research. I was working every day and late hours at home every night to try to complete manuscripts, prepare classes, grade papers, and do program administration. I wanted so very badly to succeed. The more overwhelmed I became with nonresearch responsibilities, the more incompetent I felt.

The assigned teaching and administrative load became significantly heavier because of unassigned responsibilities and obligations. As a woman of color, I felt duty-bound to respond to students who felt marginalized in the institution, especially ethnic/racial minorities. These students often sought me out to advise their campus organizations and listen to their experiences of racism, sexism, or homophobia in the university. Sometimes they asked me to help them take action about their discriminatory experiences. For instance, I assisted a white female student who was being sexually harassed by a professor. Several Latino/a students sought guidance as they experienced conflict between their academic goals and their families' financial needs.

Of course, at one level, I did have the choice of turning these students away. Emotionally, however, I felt pulled to respond to them. I believed that if I did not, no one else would listen to their issues. Furthermore, I would not have been able to face myself if I had turned my back on these students, especially knowing about the difficulties for students of color in predominantly white institutions. This work was necessary and important—and even fulfilling—because I knew my response to them, at the very least, validated their needs and concerns. Nevertheless, it was emotionally draining to hear constantly about students' experiences with discrimination, especially because I was also experiencing the effects of racism.

When I discussed the overwhelming teaching/advising/administrative load with the chair, he explained that the social science faculty were very busy with administrative duties so I had to carry the load. He said he wanted me to know that the faculty appreciated my service to the department. I only knew that my assigned duties and unassigned obligations as a woman of color were draining my time and energy. It was a situation I felt powerless to change, and it made me feel increasingly incompetent as a faculty member.

Overt Racism and Isolation

I endured overtly racist comments from a few department faculty members. For instance, one senior faculty member stopped me in the hall one day and asked—regarding a graduate student fellowship the ethnic studies program was offering—"If one of our students accepts that fellowship, will they have to do Mexican shit, or can they do real research?" I replied that research on Mexican Americans was real—period! Then I simply turned and walked away. These types of incidents happened to me regularly. I wished I had had the courage to say more. What had become of the feisty and confident person I had been only recently? I would often sit in my office and think about things I could have—and wished I had—said in response to racist statements. Of course, I knew this was not a productive use of time. The more I ruminated about racist comments, the more incompetent I felt.

Another example of departmental racism occurred when I was serving on a thesis committee for a student working on depression. During his defense, I pointed out that he had not conducted any analyses by gender or race/ethnicity. Although it was typically considered disrespectful to contradict other faculty member during student defenses, one of the other committee members replied, "Why in the world would gender or race make any difference? A brain is a brain!" This devaluing of the central importance of ethnicity in the human psyche, a role now recognized by the American Psychological Association, appeared to me to be another example of aversive racism in the department: prejudice disguised as color blindness.

In my third year, I applied for and received a one-semester fellowship from the university ethnic studies program. As protocol required, I asked the department chair's permission to go on a one-semester leave. He replied that I was valuable to the department and he would approve the leave as long as I continued to advise my many students during the semester. He also said that—unlike other fellowships—this one would not be considered prestigious for me because it was assumed I had attained it only by being Mexican American, not due to my accomplishments. What an ironic twist. I believed he had hired me, in part, because I was Mexican American. Now he seemed to be telling me that an otherwise-prestigious fellowship was meaningless for my evaluation because it was intended for Mexican Americans. Nevertheless, I took the leave and continued to meet with my graduate and undergraduate students throughout that semester. I did not know that it was not necessary, nor was it the norm, for faculty to continue meeting with and advising students while on leave.

I must point out here that the overt racism I experienced came from a relatively small portion of the department members: a few powerful full professors who created a hostile department climate for minorities. While the more junior faculty did not seem to agree with these attitudes, they were not in positions of power to confront the full professors. It also did not seem to me that the fair-minded, nonracist full professors in the department attempted to keep their racist colleagues in check, nor did they create a support system for those affected by the hostile climate. It seemed impossible that they could be unaware because some racist statements were made during faculty meetings. Thus, racists and nonracists contributed directly and/or indirectly to the negative department climate.

Some Companionship and Support

I eventually sought out and found companionship and mentoring among the Mexican American, African American, and Puerto Rican campus faculty members. Whatever feelings there may have been among the ethnic studies faculty because I had not accepted the postdoc were now replaced with an expressed desire for me to succeed. These groups of faculty members supported me emotionally and offered professional opportunities, such as speaking engagements, collaborative research, small grants, and a fellowship. Within my social science department, one white, male full professor befriended me and seemed to have my interest, rather than that of the department, at heart. He listened and offered to prereview my manuscripts, which I did not give him. I still could not bring myself to trust anyone on the department faculty. Fortunately I did rely on my close friends from graduate school. Having trusted friends listen and validate my reality helped me maintain a sense of sanity.

Stereotype Threat

In spite of this support, I quickly became resistant to positive feedback as my negative self-perception increased. For instance, over the course of my four years at this institution, I became well acquainted with three highly esteemed, internationally known and respected, widely published scholars in my discipline, each of whom worked at different institutions. Each one gave me positive feedback regarding my research ideas, writing, and potential. I even began publishing with two of them and planned collaborative research with the third. Each of these professors was more highly esteemed in the discipline than any of my faculty colleagues. Even so, when they praised my work, I reasoned that they were good, generous men who just felt sorry for me but didn't really believe I was competent. This is another example of the disorienting effects of feedback when you do not know whom to trust. An esteemed woman faculty member from another university in a closely related field also stayed in contact with me and practically pleaded for me to leave my university. She argued that I could not possibly flourish under these conditions. I reasoned that she liked me enough not to care whether or not I was competent. By discounting this feedback from people who were trying to help me, I undermined myself in several ways. Most especially, I slowed my professional development by not trusting their input.

In retrospect discounting the input these esteemed, decent scholars gave me about my work and potential was one of the most obvious symptoms that my self-esteem and sense of self-efficacy in the academy had suffered great harm. I no longer recognized the person in the mirror. The energetic, healthy, enthusiastic person I had been up until the time I had become a faculty member seemed to have disappeared. I wondered what I had done to destroy her. This self-blaming is a mark of the effects of stereotype threat, stigmatization, racism, and tokenism. Yet, at the time—even with my social science professional training—I could not account for what was happening to me.

Third-Year Review—Oops! We Forgot!

The worst of my experiences, but the one that finally sent me on the road to physical and psychological health, centered on my third-year review. My department forgot to administer the review, an unprecedented occurrence. That my review was forgotten indicated that the department had never acknowledged my identity as a scholar. The third-year review was a university requirement designed to facilitate faculty's successful movement toward tenure. I was told that this forgetfulness had occurred because of transitions in the department. By the end of my third year, the dean who had insisted on hiring me had been fired and transferred (I don't know if there was a connection between my hiring and his dismissal), and the department chair, my former advisor, was named dean. Therefore, my third-year review was administered during my fourth year.

From all accounts by other department faculty, my review was conducted like none other. The established general procedure was for the review committee to meet individually with faculty members in the reviewee's program and then deter-mine where there was consensus. The committee was also supposed to read the person's published work, third-year review statement, and teaching evaluations and ascertain the probability of success should he or she continue on the current track. It was generally considered a helpful—though stressful—process, expected to guide the reviewee toward tenure. In my case, however, the committee met with the entire department faculty at one time, including the very powerful, very vocal Dr. Grant, who everyone knew had made disparaging remarks about me since I had been hired. Immediately after the review committee met with my program faculty, it was my turn to meet with them.

The first question they asked me was, "What do you have to say about your poor teaching evaluations?" I was astounded. I knew from the department data that my teaching evaluations were not only outstanding but were among the highest in the department. I had also been nominated as an outstanding teaching fellow in the university. My teaching evaluations had been so high that during the previous fall, they were more than one standard deviation above the department norm and had thus prompted a raise in salary. I asked if the committee had read my teaching evalu-ations. The committee chair—the same person who had earlier said "a brain is a brain"—pulled out what may have been the only two negative evaluations in the stack (I had taught hundreds of undergraduate students and about forty graduate ones). As I made this known to the committee, the chair stated that my faculty mem-bers had indicated that people had complained about my teaching. I was later told that Dr. Grant had made a negative statement about my teaching of the only course on ethnicity and race conducted by a tenure-stream department faculty member; my more mainstream courses were not mentioned. Also although I had a couple of pub-lications in top-refereed disciplinary journals, a chapter in press, and several other manuscripts under review (all in mainstream, peer-reviewed journals), I was told that my faculty colleagues had questioned the quantity and quality of my research.

Later that evening, two of the persons present at the meeting told me that most of the talking had been done by one person—Dr. Grant—and I learned most of what he had said. Among his statements was "she'll never be a superstar. She doesn't fit in this department." Let me point out that in this department—as in most others in public universities—the majority of the faculty members were not superstars, so I was being judged by unique and stringent standards. They also said that—because of political ramifications—with the exception of one retired professor, the other full professors, who were my former advisors, did not speak up to contradict Dr. Grant or defend me.

The day after my meeting with the review committee I placed a call to the chair and told her that it seemed to me that the review had been extremely negatively biased. She agreed and told me that in her opinion I would never be able to shake the circumstances surrounding my hire and the department resentment was still deep. She stated that Dr. Grant would never evaluate me fairly and the commit-tee had no choice but to listen to his opinion because he was now director of the program. She further stated that my case would be better if I agreed to disassociate myself from any ethnically/culturally related research and teaching.

I needed help. Still in shock from the unfair review, that weekend I met with my former advisor, then dean of the college, who was among the faculty with whom the committee had met. I told him that I had heard what had transpired in the meeting and I was not receiving a fair evaluation. I also told him I had been extremely disappointed and hurt to learn that he had not spoken on my behalf and against Dr. Grant. He replied that he had been embarrassed to hear Dr. Grant go on but when Grant was in the room, it was pointless to try to get a word in. He explained that the committee had made a big mistake by meeting with the entire faculty at one time. However, he also stated that the review committee had the final word, and he really had no say in their conclusions. He had no response to my argument that the committee's conclusions had to be biased by what had been said—and not said—by my colleagues during the review meeting.

The following week I met with the new department chair and told him what had transpired in the review and about my other negative department experiences, including the hiring process. The new chair seemed genuinely surprised and unaware of my situation and expressed anger over the way the review had been handled. He, too, stated that the faculty should have been interviewed separately because they do not usually contradict each other in meetings of this nature. However, to my knowledge, there was no subsequent attempt to reinterview faculty individually.

In retrospect the way my work was evaluated is consistent with literature that indicates that stigmatization results in negative expectations. Heilman, Block, and Lucas (1992) found that negative expectations of individuals spawned by a stigma of incompetence could cause distorted perceptions of their behavior and work performance. This situation demonstrates one of the perils of being a Latina faculty member, 80 percent of whom teach courses and conduct research related to their specific ethnic group (Garza 1993). Although 90 percent of Latino scholars consider themselves intellectuals and 85 percent are committed to the rules and standards for scientific pursuits, most also believe that their research is seen as academically inferior and illegitimate (Garza 1993). They cite the taboo of "brown-on-brown" research as one of the top reasons why they are denied tenure (Major, Feinstein, and Crocker 1994).

Also, in retrospect, for my colleagues to have spoken up about my extensive advising and service would have admitted the way they were using me to fulfill program needs while pursuing their own agendas. It would also have meant defending me before faculty who knew they had pushed for my hire in spite of department resentment. I came to believe that my faculty colleagues would only have felt redeemed in the eyes of the department if I had achieved superstar status in only three years.

My Decision to Leave and Return to Identity Integration

I was devastated by the events of the third-year review. Throughout my time teaching, I had increasingly lost self-confidence because my research was constantly described as "ethnic stuff" and not real science. The publication of my articles in prestigious journals indicated that several reviewers and editors did consider my work good. However, I did not think about that positive feedback. I had begun to have difficulty focusing on my writing, something that had previously come easily to me. My lack of confidence had become such a problem that—in a couple of cases where editors had recommended that I revise and resubmit a manuscript—I convinced myself that the quality of my work was not good enough to rewrite. All of this was symptomatic of the effects of tokenism, stigmatization, racism, and stereotype threat. It was also an example of the way attributed ambiguity made me question whether I had ever deserved to be hired or published (Niemann and Dovidio

1998a). Thus, my state of mind resulted from the negative attitudes and beliefs I had internalized as well as the behavior and attitudes of others.

After the review, I began to believe that the department had used me with no intention of keeping me on as a tenured faculty member. I conferred with friends and scholars from other universities who had become aware of and come to be concerned about my life in that department. They all agreed that—because of the way it had been handled—the review could not be considered valid. However, there was also consensus that the review was evidence of my department's perception of me—I would always be regarded not as a scholar, but as the token minority the department had had to hire. I started to understand that in this department, I would likely continue to be overwhelmed with advising responsibilities and trivial, nonprestigious administrative duties, leaving little time for my research. I came to the difficult and painful conclusion that I had to leave to regain my holistic identity. That week I sent out job applications.

Transition from Mexican American to Chicana

The Mexican American faculty reacted negatively to my intention to leave the university. They wanted me to stay and legally fight what seemed an inevitable negative tenure decision in a couple of years. Their contention was that if I left, the department would win. The department would have used me to appease temporarily those who had demanded racial/ethnic representation and then discarded me. The department would claim that it had hired a Mexican American, and she had chosen to leave. Better to stay—some Mexican American faculty argued—and make the department own up to its members' behavior toward me, especially since I had documented their treatment in my journal. The ethnic studies program was even supportive to the extent of offering me another fully funded, one-year fellowship. The director of that program argued that with the fellowship year, I could get more publications in press, and he would fight to keep that year off the tenure clock, thus buying me one additional year before my final review.

His argument strongly appealed to my political identity. After the "third year" I had made the transition in identity from Mexican American to Chicana, the description used by politically conscious Mexican Americans. My university experiences had changed me from a naïve, politically insulated, and unaware Mexican American to a person whose consciousness about racism and its effects had been raised to heights I had not previously imagined.

I met with the university provost, who had already heard about my situation from Mexican American faculty on campus. She seemed embarrassed about and apologized for the delay in my third-year review. She offered to extend my tenure clock by one year to make up for that mistake. However, she did not agree to stop the tenure clock for the one-year fellowship from ethnic studies. Additionally, when I told her about Dr. Grant's role in my bad experience, she avoided the subject by discussing how important grants were to the university.

I was now convinced more than ever that if I stayed, my shattered sense of competence and identity might not recover. I believed that it was in my best personal and professional interest—and, by extension, my family's interest—for me to leave. At the time, I needed badly to win for myself; then later—through my future success—I could make contributions to my ethnic community. I no longer wanted just to survive; I wanted to thrive—a sign that I was recovering.

That spring I made the short list for positions at two university social science departments and one ethnic studies department. I accepted the latter. My writing is once again focused and consistent. I have published about a dozen articles—most of them in mainstream, refereed journals—and have obtained roughly seventy-five thousand dollars in grants in the two years since I left the first institution. I feel respected and valued. I am productive and once again ambitious and motivated. My identity seems integrated. I once again recognize and like the person I see in the mirror. I feel personal peace.

Recommendations

Several recommendations for faculty of color and institutions hiring them are already evident in this chapter. In addition, I offer the following:

Faculty of color must be aware of the consequences of putting themselves in a situation where they become vulnerable to the effects of tokenism, racism, stigmatization, and stereotype threat—all related concepts. These effects can be psychologically, physically, and professionally damaging. If you do want to continue working where you were trained, I recommend insisting on two things. First, temporarily leave your training institution for at least a one-year postdoc to gain distance from your advisors. Leaving for a period of time also lets your faculty know that your work is valued elsewhere. Second, to keep from having your sense of competence undermined, insist on an extensive, national search. When you come out on top, your own sense of worth will be heightened, as will your colleagues' perception of you. Contentment as an academic does not depend upon your working in an ethnic studies department. It relies on working in an accepting and validating climate.

I recommend accepting a position in a department where you are not the only minority member and not the only faculty person conducting research and/or teaching on ethnic/racial issues. My research on tokenism indicates that solo minorities are less satisfied with their jobs than those who have colleagues (Kanter 1977). People who feel like tokens tend to believe they are always representatives of their ethnic groups—constantly in the spotlight and living in a glass house—and they often have reason to think that their white colleagues are threatened by their accomplishments (Dovidio and Gaertner 1996).

It is also important to look for signs of overt, covert, and unconscious racism among potential colleagues; racists cannot evaluate ethnic/racial minorities fairly. For instance, do comments indicate an assumption that minorities are not as qualified as whites? Does the department undervalue publications in ethnic studies journals? Is the department under pressure to hire a minority person? Does the department showcase its only minority faculty members? These are signs you may become a department token with detrimental psychological consequences. Inquire about the reactions of faculty when a colleague makes a racist or sexist statement. Do others just stand by and say and do nothing, or do they take action. Remember that those who just stand by help maintain a negative climate.

Institutions can infer that this chapter suggests that affirmative action is inherently detrimental. I do not believe that is the case. Research indicates that when affirmative-action policies are framed in a positive manner (e.g., increasing our diversity will contribute different, valued perspectives to the discipline), the potentially stigmatizing effects of the policies may be avoided (Dovidio and Gaertner 1996). Additionally, because departments often do contain racist members, "good intentions are not sufficient to guarantee that equal opportunity will insure equal treatment" (Dovidio and Gaertner 1996), thus rendering affirmative-action policies necessary. Therefore, the university administration must encourage departments to frame affirmative-action hiring in a positive, nondetrimental fashion. It is important for nonracist members of departments—especially the more senior, powerful ones—to be aware of the pitfalls that faculty of color face and ensure support and mentorship for them. It is not acceptable to rationalize that if someone is not personally racist or unfair, then the behavior of others is not his or her business. It is incumbent on the powerful members of departments to use their influence to develop a positive working climate for faculty of color and, by extension, all faculty.

It is also important to recognize the detrimental effects of covert racism, such as tokenism, which often occurs concurrently with denial of the importance of race/ethnicity (for example, color blindness). Denying the role of race/ethnicity for members of socially oppressed groups is negating their realities. This denial may be especially harmful for Latinos/as and African Americans, who are particularly stigmatized in the realm of academia.

It is critical for administrators and colleagues to understand that faculty of color have responsibilities and obligations to respond to students who seek them out precisely because they are faculty of color. This situation is exacerbated for women of color, who are also befriended by white women in predominantly male departments. Due to gender-role expectations, women often do not feel the freedom to maintain distance from students. Latinas, in particular, often feel that to be successful they may have to behave in a manner contradictory to their cultural values. The extant feminist literature indicates that women who behave in a culturally consistent feminine are considered unprofessional. To be successful women faculty must conform to, and accommodate, cultural values outside of their gender role (Aleman 1995).

Keeping in mind these added obligations, easing the assigned load for these faculty is not a sign of favoritism or lowered expectations. It is a recognition of their additional responsibilities, especially to communities of color. It is also critical during evaluations to emphasize that these interactions enhance the reputation of the department. Additionally, administrators and faculty must understand that department and institutional climate can affect individual performance.

Finally, it is absolutely critical for faculty of color to understand their role in undermining their competence. This self-undermining is often a result of others' racism or at least interacts with the behavior and attitudes of others. However, awareness of your attitudes and behavior in these situations can empower you to diffuse self-undermining behavior.

Concluding Comments

In my view, no one was blameless for the negative department climate and my resulting harsh experience, including me. Five interactive forces contributed to the generation and maintenance of racism, stigmatization, tokenization, and stereotype threat: (1) the negative connotations of hiring associated with affirmative action that set the stage for tokenization and stigmatization; (2) the overtly biased persons who created adverse effects; (3) those faculty members who didn't recognize their negative biases and whose manner of encouragement indicated racist attitudes and was therefore undermining; (4) those people who were not biased but stood by and let racist behavior occur without intervening; (5) my undermining of my competence. My credentials as a scholar who knew about these attitudes and behavior did not prevent my succumbing to the effects of stereotype threat. Being vigilant of these effects on you in these situations and adhering to your sense of competence are necessary to overcome these potentially psychologically damaging situations.

In conclusion, people of color who pursue an academic career and conduct ethical, culturally-sensitive research contribute admirably to their ethnic communities and universities in many ways. They are role models and mentors for other students, faculty, and community members. Through their research, they can facilitate understanding of and improvements in their communities and more trust in academic institutions, which are often perceived as ivory towers with nothing in common with surrounding communities. The case study in this article is not intended to scare Latinas or other people of color away from academia. Quite the contrary, if we are aware of the processes that can undermine our competence and physical and psychological health, we can coopt those oppressive forces in our interest and that of our communities. As Paulo Freire concludes, our perception of ourselves as oppressed is impaired by our submersion in the reality of oppression (Freire 1970). With awareness comes power.

I hope the description and analysis of this case study have been helpful. I equally hope that this narrative facilitates better mentorship of and appreciation for the needs and situations of faculty of color from their colleagues and administrators.

Epilogue, July 2011

In 1996, I joined the Department of Comparative Ethnic Studies at Washington State University (WSU) as an assistant professor. At WSU I was afforded the opportunity to develop my scholarship and teaching, as well as my leadership skills. My numerous professional accomplishments have been validated by publications in refereed journals and books and more than twenty-five million dollars in federal grants. I achieved the rank of tenured full professor and have served in various administrative roles, including: vice provost; dean of the College of Humanities, Arts, and Social Sciences; special assistant to the dean for assessment and accreditation; special assistant to the provost for diversity and faculty affairs; head of the Department of Comparative Ethnic Studies; and director of Latino/a outreach. I also had the privilege of being an American Council on Education (ACE) Fellow.

Although I am widely published on the subjects of stereotypes and tokenism, none of my work has received as much attention as the account of my first assistant-professor experience, "The Making of a Token: A Case Study of Stereotype Threat, Stigma, Racism, and Tokenism in Academe." I am humbled by the way this narrative has resonated with so many people. For instance, I have been informed that at various times it has been required reading in some psychology departments. I have received emails from people I don't know who thanked me for informing them they were not alone and survival was possible. After sharing this story at conferences, a group of people invariably want to speak with me to tell me that they are experiencing some of the same challenges and ask for further advice and guidance. Some of these conversations have resulted in ongoing friendships. The response to this work has been overwhelmingly validating and gratifying.

On the other hand, I have also been informed that I was not considered a candidate for positions in some universities because search-committee members did not appreciate the message in "The Making of a Token," and/or they feared that I would write about them some day. So be it. I am relieved that I did not have to learn what it was they feared I would write about. This article has thus served as a mutual "screen test" for me and for those interested in my skills and talents.

Serving in administrative positions has given me an intimate view of the best and worst of the university. The best includes ethical, caring, hardworking, generous, and visionary administrative leaders—men and women across race/ethnicity and gender/sexual identities. The best also includes the large number of dedicated faculty and eager, energetic students who make me smile and remind me why I chose an academic career. I believe that the vast majority of persons in the academic world fit this description.

The worst—those representing a relatively few, but very influential and powerful, minority—include those who can be described as unethical, unprofessional, narcissistic, abusive, and/or bullying people whose words and behavior can sometimes be categorized as psychologically violent assaults. These toxic people use their positions to ensure that they get their way—by any means necessary. They abuse their role by taking advantage of students and engage in vindictive behavior toward faculty, staff, and anyone who is less powerful and does not support their agenda. It is this minority, I believe, that shapes the often-horrific experiences of less-powerful members of historically underrepresented groups in academia.

But this minority cannot stand alone in blame or guilt. Its members would not get away with their unprofessional behavior were it not for the good people who stand by and remain silent. It is only through the silence of the majority that abusive persons can get their way, wreak havoc, and/or destroy careers. In some cases, persons who are very powerful in their own right also remain silent or choose not to take action, thereby keeping their own roads as smooth as possible. These failures to do what is right allow the least powerful within the academic world to be harmed.

I have recently returned to the faculty as a professor of psychology after serving in several administrative positions. Although I continue to be honored by nominations for interesting positions in highly regarded institutions, this time has been a respite from the very political administrative world of academia. I am reflecting on the lessons learned from my experiences and solidifying connections with faculty, students, my scholarship, and the ideals that drew me to higher education. If I return to administration, I will be a better servant for having taken this time to think about how I want to contribute to the mission of institutions of higher education.

My experiences in the administrative world have provided many lessons that are too detailed to be shared in this article. The most important outcome is that I know myself better than ever, resulting is greater self-confidence, a stronger center, and enhanced appreciation for and understanding of my values. I am considerably less naïve about the breath of moral codes represented in the academic world across rank and file. I am more secure about the kind of people with whom I will chose to associate and work. In the future, I will endeavor to serve on leadership teams with people who share my ideals.

I have had the privilege of knowing such leaders. These men and women have been models of the ethical and empowering way to treat others when serving in relatively powerful positions. My role models include faculty colleagues who are welcoming and strive to be helpful to all their peers and students. My heroes include those who have survived extremely challenging situations and, indeed, whose resilience has allowed them to thrive in harsh academic climates. They give me courage and energy to continue to advocate for access and equitable treatment for all persons.

I continue to be blessed by a loving and supportive husband and our two grown children, a close extended family, and treasured friends and mentors. All of these people facilitate my ongoing idealistic view that, collectively, we can do much better and, individually, we can each make a difference in moving toward a more positive cultural shift in the academic world.

Chapter 24

Lessons from a Portrait

Keep Calm and Carry On

Adrien Katherine Wing

In 1990 the *Berkeley Women's Law Journal* asked me to write an article for a special issue on the lives of black female law professors.[1] I was a young pre-tenure professor learning to juggle all the responsibilities of teaching, research, and service, and I was very excited that the journal had invited me to participate. Even though I was a very junior faculty member, someone thought I might have something to say and was willing to give me the space to say it.

I was inclined to accept, but where would I find the time to do it? The pressures on me as the first black female law professor at the University of Iowa College of Law were enormous. I knew if I failed in my quest to get tenure, it would not be regarded as just a personal failure. It is the plight of minorities to know that their whole subgroups may be judged by their individual behavior. If I failed, it might mean that no other black woman would be hired in the future. "We tried a black woman once. It didn't work out" might be the refrain. Yet the administration would never say that the failure of one white male meant that another should never be hired again.

I *was* having trouble drafting my articles for tenure. Although I had written a small coauthored article with my law-firm mentor, Manuel Angulo, while still in legal practice, creating a hundred-page, double-spaced publication with many hundreds of footnotes was proving difficult. Students in my required course, Constitutional Law I, did not seem to relate to me as well as those in my elective classes, where they could choose me as an instructor. Some of their comments on the evaluations could be interpreted as racist and/or sexist. I remember some comments: "I know we have to have affirmative action, but do we have to have her?" "I'll never give a dime if we have professors like that around!" "I came to class every day because I wanted to see what she would wear." How much was due to the fact that I did not look like any law

---

1   I would like to thank my research assistants Brooke Amos, Benjamin Carter, Atanna Essama, Peter Nadimi, and Kapri Saunders for their help with this chapter.

professor that they had ever seen? How much was due to the fact that maybe I was new and not as good a teacher as some of my colleagues?

I remember having a chat with my wonderful and truly supportive dean, Bill Hines, after a very bad set of evaluations. To try to provide more context to review the situation, I remember invoking former Harvard professor Derrick Bell and that he had had first-year students at Stanford literally create a separate set of lectures because they did not feel he was teaching constitutional law correctly. If such an affront could happen to the great Bell, a very senior scholar and former dean, I could receive bad reviews, especially when complicated by the gender issue. I feared that privileged white men would not be able to relate to my scores other than as an individual failure.

The service component was proving the most overwhelming. It seemed as if everyone wanted me to do everything. I was inundated with requests for assistance from black law graduate and undergraduate students, as well as other black professors and staff on campus, not to mention other students and faculty who had heard that I was someone who would listen to their concerns. While Dean Hines protected me from onerous law-school committees, I was asked to serve on several time-consuming campuswide committees and invited to make presentations at numerous national and international venues. Various groups like the American Bar Association (ABA), Association of American Law Schools (AALS), Society of American Law Teachers (SALT), and American Society of International Law (ASIL) all wanted me to get involved with their committees or activities.

If I complained about my workload, well-meaning colleagues said that I should just close my door. With the demand so great and coming from a personal background where my family was committed to service, I could not just do as my colleagues suggested. I could not wall myself up in an ivory tower writing my articles and wait to get involved in the world until after tenure.

On the personal side, the pressure was just as relentless. I had become pregnant and had a second child during this period while my marriage was disintegrating. Going to soccer games and traveling to conferences were mixed in with visiting a husband who was in Alaska, Atlanta, and then Baltimore. Moreover, I was paying one-third of my take-home pay to a devoted live-in nanny, Yan Lin, and still having to bring my kids into the office late at night while I worked. After all, I could not exploit another woman of color by having her work around the clock. There were no other faculty members in a similar situation to whom I could turn. My family back East was so proud of me because of my status as a professor that I did not feel that I could burden them with these problems.

So when the request came from the journal to write a short narrative piece, many advised me against it: "This will not help your tenure file." "This narrative stuff is not law." "It is a distraction." "You will seem like you have a chip on your shoulder." "It will be political suicide." Yet something compelled me to accept when every other source said to say no. I sat down tentatively to write, and the entire essay flowed out of me in a few sittings. I called it "Brief Reflections Toward a Multiplicative Theory and Praxis of Being." I noted the dual discriminations I felt as a black female. To me that discrimination was multiplicative, not additive. In other words, I was black times a woman every day, not black plus a woman, which implies you may be able to subtract an identity. The discrimination I felt was against me as a holistic *black woman*.

On the other hand, I noted in the article that I could also experience privileging. As a law professor, I had class privilege that sometimes entitled me to many benefits. Even though my salary would never be that of a Wall Street businessman, I could travel around the country to conferences with my way paid, even upgrading to first class for free based on miles accumulated. If I got tenure, I would have that incredibly rare thing—a job for life, barring some illegal activity. I would be paid to think, write, and teach for the rest of my days with time off in the summer.

When I wrote my article, I did not know if anyone else felt the same way about the burdens and benefits of academia, but it was cathartic for me to write it. I submitted it, and then I forgot about the essay and went back to grapple with my international law pieces. When the issue came out with my first reprints as a law professor, I was so excited. I decided to read the journal from cover to cover. I cried and cried—big heaving sobs—as I poured through each page and discovered that other black women law professors felt just like me. We were caught between race and gender discrimination, doubted by some of our students and colleagues, and considered not good enough, despite our stellar academic and professional credentials and the multiple burdens that we were juggling. I was affirmed. I was not alone. Many people might not understand our situation, but we were not isolated.

Inspired in part by this Berkeley issue, a few years later, I decided to edit a collection of stories and other articles that focused on the legal standing of women of color. *Critical Race Feminism* had two editions, and I put together *Global Critical Race Feminism* a few years later. I became very well known in this jurisprudential area, authoring more pieces and doing countless panels and speeches around the world. It is hard to believe that this immersion in what became known as CRF started twenty years ago.

When asked to contribute to this anthology, I thought, What could I say now—two decades later? What had changed and what was the same? While the number of women of color professors has grown, black women are still a minuscule part of the legal academy at 3 percent (AALS). In reviewing the Berkeley issue, as well as my own anthologies, I see, sadly, that not much has changed. All of the narratives that talk of pain, isolation, and discrimination are still relevant. They are not merely historically interesting even in this day when we have a former black male law professor as president and a black female lawyer as first lady.

So I decided to think back to my beginnings as a law professor. I remember the first day I entered the University of Iowa College of Law in 1987. I had been asked to present a lecture by the head of the international law program, Burns Weston. Burns and I knew each other from ASIL, the premier international law organization. As a young black female international lawyer, I was a rare commodity on the basis of either my race or gender, much less the combination. Burns knew that I specialized in African issues, including a stint at the United Nations Council for Namibia. He thought the topic of Namibia's continued occupation by the apartheid South African regime would be a good one for Iowa's program. His letter inviting me to lecture lay on my desk many months. As a New York–based attorney who had primarily grown up on the East Coast, was originally from California, and had gone to UCLA graduate school and Stanford Law School, I regarded Iowa as the end of the universe. It was certainly not a priority destination. I was one of those East Coast folks who thought like that famous poster—civilization stopped at the Hudson River, skipping over what lay between to include California.

Two things changed my mind about ignoring the letter. First, Burns was very persistent. He followed up politely but doggedly when I did not respond. Second, my New York–based life was going into a tailspin, and Iowa was potentially involved. My husband, Enrico Melson, owed time to the Public Health Service for receiving government aid to go to medical school. President Reagan decided that doctors needed to go to remote places like Appalachia, the Bureau of Prisons, or Indian reservations. Communities like the Bronx, where we lived, were no longer acceptable. Iowa was a possibility since it had an Indian settlement for the Mesquakie tribe in Tama—a place that lacked a doctor.

I entered the Boyd Law Building on a cold February day. The law school was in its first year of use—shiny silver on the outside, gleaming in the winter sun. On the inside, I was struck by its traditional look. Throughout the main-floor lobby and hallways were many oil portraits—dead white males and some living ones. Their eyes stared out, emanating gravitas—wisdom and power. The colors in the paintings were somber, and the same artist appeared to have painted most of them. The portraits seemed to say, "We are important. We are the law. This is our world." I was told that these men were all faculty who had taught law for twenty-five years or longer. Some were still there, but a number had passed away. Even if the faculty member had subsequently left the school, the portrait stayed. Of course, I had seen such pictures before—at Princeton especially—my undergraduate alma mater. Never had I seen such a large collection with the pictures placed so closely together outside of a museum, however. Every day all the Iowa faculty and students walked by them.

I learned that placing the portraits in the new building had not been without controversy. To counteract the overwhelming sense of white male privilege, a metal plaque had been placed in the lobby as well. It had the images of the first female graduate, Mary B. Hickey Wilkinson, class of 1873, and the first black graduate, Alexander G. Clark Jr., class of 1879. Yet even on this plaque, the white male presence dominated. Above the black and female graduates appeared the image of a member of the first graduating class from 1865—Charles Wright—a white male.

In my tour around the building, I was shown the lower-level hallway, where photographs of all the graduating classes back to the beginning were kept. I was impressed when I saw the occasional female or minority face over the hundred-plus years. I learned that the father of the first black alum, Alexander G. Clark Sr., had graduated as well and became the US envoy to Liberia in 1890. One graduate, Fred "Duke" Slater, an All-American football player who became a judge, had a campus dormitory named after him. I was impressed to learn that Iowa had been a place to educate blacks from southern states because they did not educate black lawyers during the separate-but-equal days of Jim Crow segregation.

These photos of the graduates also included the faculty for each year. I noticed the two black faculty members—Greg Williams and Joe Knight—as well as a Japanese American professor, Barry Matsumoto. In my tour of the library, I saw an oil portrait of a black man, George Strait, the former librarian who had recently retired.

My talk on Namibia went well. The room was full of many friendly faces. I was impressed that the minority faculty came, and there were even some minority students. A number of female faculty members were there, as well as other international-program faculty besides Burns. Everyone was very friendly. I began to think that maybe there was some civilization in the state. I mentioned to Burns that I might have to move to Iowa due to the Public Health Service fiasco. "Do you have any idea what I might do in this state as an international lawyer?" I asked plaintively. I thought he would know about all the international practice going on in such a small state. With less than three million people, there could not be that many international lawyers. "Have you ever thought about teaching?" he queried.

Well, I come from three generations of college-educated black people on my mother's side. When I student-taught social studies at Princeton High School during my senior year of college, I became a third-generation teacher. While no one back at Stanford had advised me to consider teaching, I had thought about it occasionally and had had some tentative discussions. It just seemed so far-fetched—if there were few black students in that era and even fewer black lawyers, the possibilities for black law professors seemed very slim. At Stanford there had been one black professor, but almost no one identified him as a black man. Bill Gould had a Jewish name and was very light skinned, so undoubtedly many people thought he was Jewish. When I visited in 2009, I was amazed that the black law students still did not realize that Gould was black.

Apparently the Iowa law school faculty was so impressed by my talk and credentials that they were willing to consider me for an open position, but it would mean coming back to do a full set of interviews, a job talk, etc. I came back within a couple of weeks and presented that article I had recently written on the act of state doctrine and foreign-sovereign immunity. On this visit, the oil portraits did not surprise me. I swept past them. I wondered what they would think of a black female joining the ranks of the faculty. Soon I found out because some of those portraits were living voters.

Before I knew it, I had an offer. Rico nailed down the Mesquakie job, and I accepted the teaching post. I later found out that the faculty had been trying to diversify that year. Their offers to other blacks had fallen through. They had given up at the point when I walked through the door—with the proper credentials from a top school. Plus I was open to coming to Iowa with a husband that might actually need to work there! It had been perfect for them.

Rico and I thought that maybe we would be around for a few years—long enough for him to finish his legal obligation and perhaps for me to get tenure, and then we would move back to a city on one of the coasts. Little did I know that he would only stay around a year until the government shipped him to Alaska to direct a hospital, and our marriage would ultimately implode during my journey toward tenure.

I remember entering the building for the first time as a new faculty member in July 1987. Now the portraits seemed to be silently screaming—intruder alert. Who is this woman?! I am pleased to say that over the years, the law school has done things to make the front entrance more inclusive. George Strait's portrait was moved from the library to the hallway. The front hallway near the administrative suite contained display cases with all the faculty publications, and 5-by-7 photos of each author accompanied them. It made me proud to see the pictures diversify. Now we have close to twenty women and seven people of color represented, including two Asians and one Latino.

Amazingly, I am the senior black faculty member now. Greg Williams, who chaired my tenure committee, left to become dean of Moritz College of Law at Ohio State University, and he is now a college president at the University of Cincinnati. Joe Knight left to become the dean of the University of Washington Law School. We have four black women, all of whom have been deeply involved in all aspects of the institution. Marcella David has been associate provost for diversity, associate dean for admissions, and is now associate dean for international programs. Peggie Smith has chaired the Appointments Committee and served on the Dean's Search Committee. Our youthful colleague, Angela Onwuachi-Willig, is a force of nature: having a third child, cranking out publications, organizing two outside conferences in one semester, and turning down an offer from Duke Law School. There is also a collage mural in the front hall depicting a diverse array of distinguished alums.

On the fourth floor, which contains faculty offices, we have display cases as well. When I became associate dean for faculty development, I decided to provide another opportunity for diversity in images. I collected and displayed recently published faculty books to inspire and acknowledge all colleagues. We took the Web site photos of those who were featured and touched them up a bit to make them look more painterly in the 8½-by-11 format. We had several women featured in that case, including some who did not have an oil portrait or were too junior to have received one. The women included Lea Vandervelde, Josie Gittler, Hillary Sale, Ann Estin, Margaret Raymond, and me.

Finally, a few years ago, the faculty oil portraits diversified on the basis of gender. Lea became the first woman to have her portrait done. Clinical professors Patricia Acton and Bobbi Schwartz soon followed.

How has the time passed so quickly? It seems like yesterday that I was that young woman fresh from New York City, who looked barely older than the students. Now only my youngest son is younger than my students.

Now I am the next tenure-track woman to have her portrait done. I have finished nearly twenty-five years teaching. 2012 is my year for a picture. There is only one person whom I would permit to paint my portrait. My current partner, James Sommerville, is an artist, and he has known me for thirty years since our Stanford days. I dated him before I met Rico, and we have been a recycled couple since 1996. Only James will I trust to paint me for eternity.

How shall I appear to make such a statement? How will my pose convey that I, too, belong—not only now but forever? I am currently directing our semester-abroad program in London. One of the joys of living there is that there are so many fascinating museums. The National Portrait Gallery has thousands of oil paintings dating back centuries. I have slowly walked the massive galleries studying the giant canvases. Some are mundane or merely acceptable, but some are literally breathtaking. Will I have such a portrait? I have confidence in James, who will paint with love, not merely technique.

What is the significance of the fact that now I, too, will have a portrait? Twenty years ago, Lani Guinier, the first black female tenured professor at Harvard Law School, wrote about the oil portraits at her alma mater, Yale, when she went there to give a speech. I do not know of any other school that has an oil portrait of a black female faculty member.

Thus, I decided to write this chapter to reflect upon the status of women of color as professors from a position of seniority—someone who will soon have that oil portrait. For most of my career, I have been part of the few black women in the academy, and now I am among the most senior. What lessons can I give to those behind me, to those considering such a career, to those who cannot dream of the pressures we face as pioneers?

My thoughts can be summarized using another great statement that I found in a London museum. I visited the Winston Churchill Centre and Museum at the Churchill War Rooms, the underground World War II headquarters. I was impressed that the country's leadership, including Prime Minister Churchill and his staff, had stayed underground in the city to direct the war efforts. King George and Queen Mary had stayed as well, endearing them to their citizens. In the gift shop, I was struck by a poster that was issued during the war—when bombs were falling daily and it was unclear if the country would survive Hitler's wrath—"Keep calm and carry on."

My advice to my sisters when they are under attack, when the bombs are dropping—literally or figuratively—is to keep calm and carry on. I have unknowingly tried to pursue this motto over the years in all the areas that affect us as teachers, scholars, and service providers, as well as on the personal level. Here are seven lessons that I have learned.

Lesson One: Do More Than the Minimum

Despite the professional and personal difficulties along the way, I persevered, received tenure, and became a full professor in 1993. It was not easy, as I have mentioned, and it was not quick. I was the first female faculty member to have a baby while on the tenure track. So the dean gave me a maternity leave. Then I was still not finished with my publications after that extra year because my long-distance marriage finally fell apart, and I went through a grueling divorce. So I invoked my right to an extension.

The question about how many articles were necessary for tenure came up. The rules stated that two major pieces were required, so some people thought I just needed two. Others thought I needed three since I had had the extension. Some even thought I needed four since I had had the maternity leave and should have been able to write during that time as well. As any mother knows, maternity leave is not the equivalent of a sabbatical. Years later, I became the chair of the university's Gender Equity Task Force, where we suggested tenure rules that made it clear that childcare leaves did not necessitate extra scholarship.

What to do about my articles? I decided to submit four, one being the Berkeley essay. I counted the pages that those tenured in the five years before me had done. I noted the journals. I decided to exceed the page number and make sure my articles appeared in equivalent journals. To cover my bases, I submitted Derrick Bell's name as one of my reviewers for that Berkeley piece. He was a founder of critical race theory and its narrative technique. A strong reference from him supporting my article would carry weight with those colleagues who doubted whether such an article should count.

Aiming for the top was a more successful approach than merely fulfilling the minimum. After all, in our academic careers, we had always aimed for an A, not just to pass.

Lesson Two: Tenure Is Only the End of the Beginning

After I received tenure, I had some colleagues who thought that I had finished writing, that I would just coast now that I had a job for life. After all, it had taken me six years to get tenure. To me tenure represented the moment of freedom. I could continue to even higher levels. I really started cranking. My active participation in groups like AALS, SALT, and ASIL got me known in various scholarly circles. Because of my publications, including my specialty in critical race feminism, I was invited to give many presentations at these group's meetings and other scholarly conferences. Law journals published the results.

In 2001, I gained a very meaningful scholarly honor when I replaced my retiring mentor, Burns, as the Bessie Dutton Murray distinguished professor of law. He is Bessie Dutton Murray professor emeritus. We are now Bessie Sr. and Jr. I skipped over nine more-senior colleagues to receive this honor. I do not know how many black female professors there are in the country who have an endowed chair or distinguished professorship—probably less than a percentage point. At Iowa, of the two-hundred-plus chaired professors, I was the first black female, and now there is one other—also from the law school.

Now I have more than a hundred scholarly publications, including peer-reviewed articles published in both the US and abroad. I have long surpassed almost all my colleagues in productivity. University of Chicago Law School professor Brian Leiter compiles various statistics involving law schools and has listed me in the top-ten cited University of Iowa professors for a number of years. No one dares say now that I am not a scholar. My accomplishments led me to receive an offer to teach at the University of Michigan Law School for a semester, which I accepted. I have turned down a number of very attractive offers along the way as well. My family and I have become Iowans. I would not leave the state easily, not even for much more money, not even for big-city life.

Additionally, I spent three years as associate dean for faculty development. I wonder how many black women have held an administrative post of this nature—the intellectual heart of the law school.

Lesson Three: Keep Teaching the Teacher and Teach on a Grand Scale

Everyone knows of professors who zone out and just teach the same courses in the same way from the same materials year after year. While this can be deadly for any professor, black women must be even more careful of not taking such an approach since many people already do not perceive us as acceptable professors. So I decided to keep innovating in my courses. I added Race, Racism, and American Law, a course initiated by Derrick Bell, to the Iowa curriculum. I designed Law in Radically Different Cultures, a course I took as a law student at Stanford. Because AIDS was a new disease, I designed a seminar called the International and National Legal Aspects of AIDS. As you may expect, I developed critical race theory for my institution. Ever since the semester after September 11, 2001, I have taught Law in the Muslim World. Even for traditional courses, such as Comparative Constitutional Law and International Human Rights, I often compile my own materials. As any professor knows, developing class materials from scratch is time consuming. Yet I have always felt that it was worth the effort.

I have also always felt that innovating my techniques is important as well. When I earned my high school social-studies teaching credential at Princeton, I had to take a number of courses on educational theory. I was amazed that there was no equivalent requirement to teach on the university level. It is just assumed that if you are smart enough to be a professor, you can teach. In the law school, we have used the Socratic method as a predominant approach for more than a hundred years. I know that I disliked the method as a student, especially the idea of possibly intimidating adult students into learning. I felt that students might resist and resent minority women using this approach as well. I also didn't like having a single examination as the sole source to evaluate students.

Consequently, I developed a variety of techniques in each course, especially my electives. I value students being able to participate actively, so I have them do class presentations and grade them for class participation as well. I often do simulations that involve them going another step beyond the usual legal synthesis. It works for me and the students.

I also decided that teaching on a grand scale was useful, so I have taught in Howard University School of Law's study abroad program in South Africa and directed Iowa's summer program in France and now our London program. I have found that taking students outside their comfort zone and getting them to interact on a more intimate basis with their peers and professors in an alien environment enhances their learning potential both inside and outside the classroom.

Additionally, I discovered that the study abroad programs attract a higher percentage of ethnically and geographically diverse students than ordinarily attend Iowa. Also having students from more than one school is great for the students as well. In the programs, the students are often attracted to the place more than the particular curriculum. Thus, it is great to be able to teach students who might not have taken my courses at home. They get exposed to the content and often to the first black female teacher of their entire lives. I have innovated even further in recent years by designing an additional component to my France-based summer Law in the Muslim World course. I take most of the students to Egypt, where they can live what they have just been taught. Instead of just reading about the call to prayer, they hear it every day. They observe that women can effortlessly wear the black *niqab* headpieces and robes with only their eyes showing in the hundred-degree heat.

Lesson Four: Service Is the Rent We Pay for Living on the Planet

This phrase, which I adopted from Children's Defense Fund Director Marian Wright Edelman, has been one of my mantras for a long time. I have already mentioned that I have done a lot of service. Posttenure, this has been a joy as well as a very serious responsibility for someone with the global privilege of a job for life. I feel that it is essential to write tenure letters for other people of color. If I skim their materials and realize that I cannot be sufficiently positive, I decline to write the letter. I do not want to be the source of such a serious loss in their careers. I also feel, as one of the few black women to hold an endowed professorship, that I must write letters for other scholars as well. These can be even more time consuming than tenure letters because they require commenting on the overall corpus of a career. When requested to write letters for someone seeking a lateral-hire position with tenure, I also cooperate, even though it may require commenting on a large cluster of articles.

At this stage of my career, I am often asked to do blind reviews of book manuscripts. As long as the book is in my area of expertise, I get involved since I will learn a lot from the manuscript. Likewise, when colleagues ask me to review their book manuscripts, I also agree. Occasionally I have reread books of more than a thousand pages more than once.

On the student end, giving references for former students, especially those of color, is part of my service obligation. Often I have gotten to know students beyond the class context. Writing a reference for a student who was not at the top of the class but has the qualities to succeed is even more important than giving one to an A student.

Those early efforts to involve me in various professional organizations have deepened as I have matured. The governor appointed me to a commission to examine the overrepresentation of blacks in the Iowa prisons. I became a consultant for the Amer-I-Can Program, owned by Jim Brown, the former football player, actor, and activist. I brought this self-esteem curriculum to Iowa and New Orleans. I am proud to have served as the chair of the thousand-person-strong AALS Minority Groups Section. Receiving the Clyde Ferguson Award for service from the section was very moving. I became an ABA site inspector, even chairing some of the teams that gather information about educational standards. I even recently served as vice president of the ASIL, the first black woman since the early 1980s. Maybe one day I will be the first black female ASIL president.

Lesson Five: We Have to Be Involved in *Othermothering*

There is a mammy stereotype about black women, and rather than reject that image, I have embraced the concept of nurturing and extended it. I am a firm believer that everyone needs mothering throughout his or her life, and I think that anyone can mother anyone else.

On the professional level, this may be classified as mentoring. I could not have excelled in my career if I had not had the mentoring of many people, none of them black women. They did not exist in the relevant positions when I was coming through the system. My mentors include the previously mentioned Burns Weston, Greg Williams, Joe Knight, and Dean Bill Hines. Outside my own law school, mentors like Derrick Bell, Richard Delgado, and Hank Richardson have been tremendous. Prior to becoming a lawyer, I was fortunate to have Bill Gould and while I was at Princeton, Mike Mitchell and Howard Taylor. Way back in high school, Joe Borlo helped perfect my French and English skills. I was incredibly pleased when he sat at my table when I was honored at my thirtieth high school reunion with the Newark Academy Distinguished Alumni award.

I felt that all these men treated me as a daughter or little sister. In some cases, though, I had to handle the situation of what to do when bounds were crossed—when I was treated as an intimate confidante. I am sure this has happened in many mentor/mentee relationships. The race/gender factors complicate that situation. Hearing about sexual behavior was TMI (too much information). In one case, a partner in my former law firm, who had had too much to drink, ended up slobbering over me in a cab as he wept about his sexual and personal problems. I was trapped on a highway with nowhere to go. The next day he seemed to have forgotten the incident.

When such TMI situations have occurred, I have never known if the senior male has regarded me in some kind of mammy role—a black woman servant whom you can confide in. Or did he view me as a Sally Hemings, Thomas Jefferson's mulatto mistress, who was younger, sexual, and also subservient? Were these examples of courting behavior or sexual bragging, hoping to attract me, or was it just treating me as one of the boys with whom someone could brag about his activities? Perhaps each situation was different.

If there are other people of color at your school or certainly in your field, you must be very careful not to assume they want to mentor you. In other words, do not assume that someone will be your mentor or even your confidante just because he or she is the same race, gender, or race/gender as you. I know of horror stories where senior people of color have stabbed junior colleagues in the front and back in the workplace. Issues can spill out into the blogosphere or other media in ways that cast a very bad light on the institution. You may become known as a trouble-maker and be unable to move to a more congenial environment.

There are senior people who resent a young person who is a rising star. She may remind them of what they will never be. She may have superior paper credentials or pretenure publications. The senior person may resent no longer being the sole or dominant voice on minority issues—being the only woman of color. These senior people may even be unconscious about what they are doing.

The senior person may initially even have been a mentor of sorts but then backed away when the person being mentored did not stay in her place. If the tables flip, and the junior person is now in a superior position as a committee chair or adminis-trator, for example, the senior person of color may be her biggest nightmare.

Another problem can be that the whites on the faculty may not realize how com-pletely they have ceded a gatekeeping responsibility to the original or more senior persons of color. A thousand small belittling statements over the whole pretenure period may undermine the rising star's candidacy as what the senior person says assumes disproportionate weight.

I have seen where a senior person of color is not appropriate as a mentor. I invested a lot of time and energy and poured my heart out to a person outside my school, and he swore that he would help me with some issues. Then nothing hap-pened. I never knew if the mentor ever followed through. It may be that he was well meaning but too scattered to follow up in a timely manner. It may be that this person had no clout with or respect from the folks he was attempting to influence. For better or worse, maybe he had become marginalized, and it actually harmed me to be seen as his protégée or even someone taking his advice. Maybe he tried, but others were not persuaded.

What are the solutions to these mentor problems that can derail a woman of color's career? I think my approach of having a wide variety of mentors from various professional and personal backgrounds has been a lifesaver. I never put all my eggs in one basket. If one mentor did not work out, that was fine because there were oth-ers. People can mentor in many different ways and with various levels of intensity at different times. That is to be expected.

As I have become more senior, it has become my turn to other mother. Mentor-ing potential professors of color has been a joy. We used to have a faculty-fellow pro-gram at Iowa that brought in aspiring law professors of color for one to two years. I was always delighted to develop special relationships with the fellows. Most of these professors have far surpassed me, and I am so joyful to see their success. They include UCLA Vice Dean Devon Carbado, former University of Arkansas School of Law Dean Cynthia Nance, Michigan Professor Laura Beny, DePaul Professor Sumi Cho, Ohio State Professor Creola Johnson, and North Carolina Central University Professor Angela Gilmore.

I have also enjoyed mentoring faculty of color at my own institution, includ-ing the other three black women, one former Asian colleague, one current Asian professor, and one Latino colleague. I feel the dynamic is much more fluid than the traditional mentoring one, where the senior white male mentor is all knowing, and the junior person just absorbs the wisdom. I feel that we can learn much from junior colleagues and should be humble enough to be open to that possibility. What I have enjoyed is that each of these junior professors has become a superstar in his or her own right. Also their existence on the faculty has relieved the pressure of being called upon to be the minority person in every context. The whites realize that we cannot be lumped together and thought to have one view on any issue.

Also service burdens can be shared. I was delighted when another person of color was put on the hiring committee after I had been on it for ten years. I had replaced another black person. I was intrigued to learn that some people thought I would resent being yanked off the committee, yet no one asked me how I felt.

When I became associate dean, I was able to mentor colleagues of color on another level. I could help run interference when they lacked mentors or experienced inappropriate mentoring. I could connect them to folks outside the institution for mentoring in their fields or the wider community of color. Of course, I mentored white professors, too, but I felt particularly protective of young people of color.

Many times I have met students at speeches I give, and they express the desire to teach. I keep in touch. I may meet people at the AALS hiring conference even though they are not interviewing with our school. I definitely keep in touch with people we do interview, even if we cannot hire them, or they refuse our offer.

I also think it is important to mentor research assistants (RAs). At Iowa we are lucky because we can have many RAs; I often have six or more. I know that some faculty only want to hire one RA, and definitely from the very top of the class. They may not be concerned with diversity at all. I do not maintain such criteria to ensure that I have as diverse a group as possible. One of my current RAs, a black female, has just been named the editor-in-chief of our *Journal of Gender, Race & Justice.* Another former RA from Turkey became editor-in-chief of the *Iowa Law Review.* I have enjoyed having leaders of various minority student groups as my RAs as well. I can get insight into what these groups are thinking and provide informal assistance to their leaders.

Additionally, I have given RAs the opportunity to coauthor an article with me if the person has the skill level and we can come up with a mutually interesting topic. Of my more than one hundred publications, about fifteen were coauthored with students. As I mentioned at the beginning of this chapter, Manuel Angulo, a partner at my former law firm of Curtis, Mallet-Prevost, Colt & Mosle, coauthored an article with me, and it was a great experience. It ended up being critical to my getting a job at Iowa just a year later. One RA who wrote with me is going on the teaching market himself now. Our coauthored piece is one of which I am especially proud.

I like to stay in touch with my former RAs as well. One RA coauthor named her child for me, and another visited me in London.

When I became the associate dean for faculty development, I viewed the job as a form of othermothering. Supporting colleagues in their scholarly and teaching missions was a joy. Recognizing the accomplishments of many people—whether through the display case or the newsletter I created—was a concrete way to acknowledge the often-unsung efforts of so many colleagues.

A number of law schools have approached me about becoming the dean. I have even been a finalist in some searches. I view a deanship as the ultimate type of othermothering—for an entire institution, including faculty, students, staff, alumni, and quite possibly a local or statewide legal and public constituency as well.

I have not ultimately decided if becoming a dean will be the best way for me to do my othermothering. For many years, there were no black female deans at any predominantly white law schools. Marilyn Yarbrough was the dean at the University of Tennessee College of Law in the 1990s. Even though deanships have been turning over every three to five years, once again black women have not been perceived in that role of father figure, chief intellectual, and visionary leader. I am delighted that my former student Cynthia Nance is a dean already, one of fewer than ten black females. So our time for this job is beginning to come.

I had a very interesting experience when I was a dean finalist at a private southern law school. In a town that was predominantly black—with black colleges even—this law school did not have any black female faculty or administrators—not in admissions, financial aid, student services, or the library! There were a few black males on the faculty. I will always remember that a secretary made sure to introduce me to Beulah, one of the long-term janitors, in a school where all the janitors were black. I was delighted to meet Beulah, and I thought of her when I made my presentation on the vision of the law school to a group that included no one of my race or gender. I wondered what Beulah thought of someone of her race and gender as a possible dean. It was clear to me that the school was not ready to jump from black women as janitors to black women as not even a colleague but the BOSS.

I have othermothered on the international level as well. I assisted with the constitutions of three places: postapartheid South Africa, the Palestine Authority, and postgenocide Rwanda. It was truly momentous to be involved with the founding mothers and fathers of such places. Meeting people who had put their lives on the line for justice for their people helped keep the various issues in US academia in perspective. It was most rewarding to be able to grapple with equality clauses that include gender and other identities—something not likely to happen in the United States for the indefinite future.

For example, article nine of the South African Constitution covers antidiscrimination, affirmative action, and equal protection, stating that neither the state, nor any person, may "unfairly discriminate directly or indirectly against anyone on one or more grounds, including race, gender, sex, pregnancy, marital status, ethnic or social origin, colour, sexual orientation, age, disability, religion, conscience, belief, culture, language and birth."[2] The article makes clear that discriminatory or disparate impact, as well as intent, is actionable under the constitution.

The South African Constitution permits a much more complex approach to equality, one related to critical race feminism. In South Africa, the justices are particularly attuned to the plight of black women. Imagine an America where a justice would note—as Justice O'Regan of South Africa did in *Brink v. Kitshoff*—that black women face "particularly acute" disadvantage. In *Nat'l Coal. for Gay & Lesbian Equal. v. Minister of Justice,* a judge mentioned that discriminatory categories may intersect, and thus their impact cannot be evaluated on one basis only. For example, African widows have suffered as "blacks, as Africans, as women, as African women, as widows and usually, as older people, intensified by the fact that they are frequently amongst the lowest paid workers"[3].

---

2   South African Constitution Article 9 (1996).

3   *See Nat'l Coal. for Gay & Lesbian Equal. v Minister of Justice,* 1998 (12) BCLR 1517 (CC) at ¶

Othermothering is particularly important on the personal level. Many black female professors may never get married but want children. I have urged many colleagues not to wait for Prince Charming to become a parent—to get involved with children, whether through a big-sister program or taking in a nephew or niece. They have the financial ability to be foster parents or adopt as well.

I became the surrogate mom to three young men almost twenty years ago. One of them, Dr. Willie Barney, has earned his doctorate and is a high school principal. He has been together with his wife Jody since college days. They have six children, including two they adopted. I have a seventh grandchild from the second son, Brooks. I am delighted that this summer I can continue my global interests with another generation by bringing two of my grandchildren, as well as Willie and Jody, to France for the first time.

Lesson Six: Take Care of Yourself

If everyone tried to do all the things I have mentioned in this essay all of the time—as well as juggle the pressures of being the first or only or one of the few black female professors—they would have a stroke. I realized a few years ago that I was prioritizing everything and everybody except myself. Thus, my health was not good, and my spirit was in pain. I ate for comfort and—like most black women—was considerably overweight. My back hurt a lot. I thought that I did not have any time for exercise.

One day I just decided I had had enough. I became a vegetarian and started exercising at the beginning of my day. I put healthy food and exercise at the center of my life, instead of at the margins. I ended up losing more than forty pounds and got more energy than I had had when I was in my twenties. In addition, I have regular facials, pedicures, and massages.

Even when busy at a conference, I take the time to go to the weight room or have some aromatherapy or just explore something about the city where I am by walking around or taking a short tour. Recently I attended the Critical Race Studies conference at the UCLA School of Law. After listening to an energizing panel that warmed my spirit, I took a brisk walk on the campus that is my graduate school alma mater. I lay down on the grass beside students who were studying or sleeping and thought about how my father would have felt when he was an undergrad in the class of 1948. There were almost no blacks then, and he had told tales of having to run off the campus when taunted by whites. My UCLA in the late 1970s had many blacks, and it was delightful. Now I was on the ground on a campus that more resembled that of my father. There is only 2 percent black enrollment in the post-Proposition 209 era. Despite the injury to my spirit that thinking of this UCLA caused me, I drew strength from the ground and thought that one day, this must change. Eventually UCLA will reflect a diversity that includes African Americans once again in more than token numbers—maybe by the time my grandchildren enroll—which is less than ten years!

When I pay attention to my own physical and mental engine, I find that I can help others more effectively than if I neglect myself. Despite the various trials and tribulations, I want to stay in great shape in all ways. The portrait should radiate

---

113, 1998 SACLR LEXIS 36 at *141-42 (S. Afr.), *available at* http://www.constitutionalcourt. org.za/uhtbin/cgisirsi/20080302190747/SIRSI/0/520/S-CCT11-98.

and reflect my light, not the darkness. Part of taking care of yourself involves giving yourself a break. No one is perfect. You will make mistakes. Even those who look as if they have it all together, really do not. Oprah Winfrey may be the first black woman billionaire, but she has clearly struggled with issues about self-esteem—her weight, her personal life. The most beautiful talented black women in the world—like Halle Berry—can win an Oscar and still have a husband who cheats on them and humiliates them publicly.

Lesson Seven: Give Credit Where Credit Is Due

For me this means that I submit myself to the will of God. I believe that things happen for a reason. I have a divine purpose, and I must fulfill it. This does not mean that I make excuses and just assume certain things are overwhelming. Instead, I aim to maximize my contributions on the personal and professional level because that is part of God's plan for me. In my case, being grateful also means that I must credit those who help me, whether it is my hardworking assistant Kelley, or my RAs, or my family members, especially my mother and wonderful children.

At the center of all my credit, I must put James, my partner. I know and frequently state that I could not be where I have been for the past fourteen years if not for him. We met at Stanford in 1980, where he was called the Black Prince, and we only dated one year. We broke up and ultimately married and divorced other people. We kept in touch over the years, however. When we recycled, he came to Iowa from California and became a father figure for five sons. That first winter—when he had to learn to use the snowblower—was fun. Of course, he did the so-called male chores, such as shoveling snow, raking leaves, fixing various things, and managing the car. Trained as an engineer, he loves to handle all the computer and other technical matters.

What was also great was that he did the so-called female things, too. He became the family cook, did the laundry, and drove the kids to their activities. My youngest son, Nolan, would not have been able to become a collegiate gymnast today at West Point if James had not started driving him to his practices five days a week when he was seven. James taught Nolan and Che how to drive. James was a football player at Stanford, so he could talk to all five young men about football—a subject where my eyes glaze over. All of these sons played high school football, and three of them played on the line for the University of Northern Iowa. James designed the T-shirts that twenty-one of us wore to drive down to Chattanooga, Tennessee, to watch Charles play for the 1AA collegiate football championship. James goes to watch Charles play professional-arena football and also went to see thirty-five-year-old Willie in the national Tae Kwan Do championship in Austin, Texas.

As an artist, James redesigned our home—painting and wall papering, even redoing fixtures. The intricate murals he created on each child's bedroom wall are still there—incredible works of art. With his wonderful eye for color, he can even pick out accessories for me to wear to work or take on a big trip. If I need him to, he even comes on my trips, providing invaluable support and companionship.

You may ask what exactly do I do with a man like that around. All of his contributions enable me to efficiently handle being the primary breadwinner, including traveling a lot to paid speaking engagements. I handle the finances, trip planning, and arranging social engagements. Many, many women have asked if James has a clone they can have. Alas, no.

Now what is the catch here? In my twenties, if someone had said that I would be the primary breadwinner I would have thought they were crazy. I thought I needed a man who had as many degrees as I did and made more money—ideally a doctor. I then married that man, but it did not work out. In my forties, I realized that a nontraditional relationship could really work, and I encourage other young black women lawyers and law professors to think out of the box as well. If women think that they must wait for a man like Barack Obama to come calling, they will remain alone.

One of my favorite gifts to James was taking him outside the US for the first time when he was forty. When we dated back in 1980, we used to chat in French, which he had studied for two years and I had studied for six. He loved French and France but could not imagine actually going there because he came from a poor family of nine children. In 1997 James went with me to France for the first time—it was magic! We were young again—1980 all over but better. Then we went to South Africa, where I was teaching, and he had his first birthday party—in Cape Town. As part of a large family, he had not had that birthday party experience that many of us take for granted.

My other favorite gift was when I arranged for James to visit his dad, James Sr., in California and take a trip to the Grand Canyon together. Coming from such a large family, the two men had NEVER had a trip together. For those of us from smaller families or middle-class backgrounds, it is inconceivable to think about being fifty years old and having never traveled with your parent. It was a trip they both treasure and that brought them closer together than they had ever been. I truly envied them this special time together because my father died when I was nine. Yet I remember trips we took together as if they happened yesterday.

The Future

The portrait looms in my dreams. I hope that my mother—who is in the early stages of Alzheimer's—will live long enough and be sufficiently coherent to make the trip from New Jersey to Iowa to see it. Many of my colleagues have continued teaching for twenty or more years after their portraits were done. Will I have such a luxury? What would I write twenty years from now? I hope that we will have advanced by then in terms of our presence in the academy—that the tales that have been written over the past twenty years by women of color professors will be of only historical interest. Perhaps one of my granddaughters will be a law professor, too, by then, and what inspired her as a child will have been the experience of observing her grandmother's portrait being hung at the University of Iowa College of Law.

CHAPTER 25

"NO HAY MAL QUE POR BIEN NO VENGA"

A Journey to Healing as a Latina, Lesbian Law Professor

Elvia R. Arriola

Part I: Surviving or Thriving?

Blessing in disguise: I often heard my *abuelita* say, *"No hay mal que por bien no venga,"* or "You can find something good coming out of something bad—eventually."

This has not been an easy project for me to undertake. I knew I would have to revisit painful memories. Even though I have told and published the stories about my experiences of being presumed incompetent a few times now (Arriola 1997, 2005), I wanted this rendition to be different because time has allowed me to heal from the emotional wounds, and I am in a very different place. I am comfortably now not only tenured but also a full professor. From the outside, all is good. The past is over. The battle scars from a rough beginning are mostly memories. Except that now and then I get a strong reminder of old hurts, and I find myself reeling from feelings of self-doubt about the choices and decisions I made about what to do and where to go after I resigned from my tenure-track position.

In the bitterly cold winter of 2008, as the community of my workplace, Northern Illinois University, reeled in shock and pain from a tragic campus shooting that left five students dead and sixteen wounded, I, too, questioned my role and place as a teacher, survivor, fellow potential victim. I wondered often, "What am I doing here?" And although I am grateful for my job, now and then resentment rears its ugly head, especially when my body rebels against this midwestern climate that is too uncomfortably cold and far from my southwestern Mexican roots. Repressed feelings of resentment are not good. They disturb the most benign moments or conversations, as when I am in the middle of explaining to someone why I have a job in northern Illinois and still have a home and a life partner in central Texas and no intentions of living permanently in the Midwest. Yes, the journey to healing from being presumed incompetent by the first school—where I started as an assistant professor—has been at times confusing, and the painful parts of the story are indeed over, part of the past, the experiences memorialized here and there in an essay or one of several poems that helped me survive.

My contribution to this brave collection of stories will try to explain the process of healing from the emotional wounds that came from my battle to keep my job as a law teacher and a feminist Latina, lesbian scholar. As I said, I have described in earlier articles many of the details of what happened and some of the lessons that others can use to create a strategic path toward success in the chosen profession of law teaching as an outsider (Arriola 2003). Here I hope to do two things—reflect on the past through a few memories of what it felt like to be presumed incompetent and unable to qualify for a tenured post at a flagship state-university law school, and secondly, describe the way I internalized just enough of the unfair attitudes held by a few former colleagues to delay my career progress as a law professor.

However, I did survive by engaging with communities and projects that countered the negative messages that had been directed at me (bad scholarship, bad teaching) by individuals heavily invested in an image of the law school as too good or mainstream to tenure a professor committed to writing and teaching on marginalized topics like feminism or lesbian and gay rights.[1] But the most important part of my healing transcended the drive to get involved in new research projects or professional communities focused on the production of critical, cutting-edge scholarship on questions of race, feminism, or sexuality. The most profound aspect of my healing has been an inward spiritual journey to a place of self-realization, a process that took many forms and years and forced me to look at law and my role in the legal academy from the inside out.[2]

Survival from a trauma or tragedy can take many forms for a person who is not in touch with her pain. There can be anger and violence or passive victimization. In between, however, for most people, there is a process of grieving the loss of something precious and important that—as Elizabeth Kubler-Ross wrote wisely (1973, 2005)—is a delicate journey with many stages before you arrive at the place of acceptance. I could not succeed as a teacher, a scholar, an activist, a writer, a mentor until I accepted the reality and consequences of having been rejected as a qualified

---

1   I was coming onto the faculty with two major articles, which have been reprinted several times in books and anthologies (Arriola 1988, 1990). The latter had grown out of my master's thesis in history at New York University, which I officially earned the year I was hired as an assistant professor.

2   I have gathered some of my most personal thoughts and feelings about the transition I made from law student to attorney, to yoga practitioner, and to law professor in an unpublished manuscript I titled "Law from the Inside Out" and drafted the summer after my first year as an assistant professor. It is a body of work that mostly poses questions about the relationship between intellect and emotion and the balance that you can strike through the ancient philosophy of yoga, which means "union." The student of yoga and meditation—like the practitioner of any art that uses disciplined physical exercise to improve the self, seeks union of body, mind, and spirit. In Eastern philosophy, the goal is enlightenment, which in Western ways of thinking is simply practicing the tools of a science that produces positive mental health by regularly engaging in rigorous physical practices. Through the discipline of a practice requiring mental focus, a positive by-product strengthens the body and immune system, including relief from negative, obsessive thinking patterns, thus leading to a greater sense of personal wholeness, freedom, and well-being (Weintraub 2004, 9–10).

tenure candidate and—despite that rejection—accepted and learned to love deeply myself and the work I do as a law teacher and scholar.

Part II, titled *"La Quemada,"* focuses very briefly on the "what happened" at my first place of employment as an assistant professor through just a few selected bad memories. *Quemar* means "to burn." Many details are covered in previous articles, so there will be more of a focus in this essay on the emotional experience that illustrates being burned.

Part III is an effort to describe the objective process of recovering from the burning that resulted from moving on as an academic, an activist, and a candidate again for hire at a university that was happy to employ someone who was well published. Woven throughout this narrative is the story of the healing processes that were critical to my ability to move on and away from the notion that I was incompetent.

Part IV is the conclusion and contains samples of the poetry that emerged from an exercise for healing depression called the "morning pages" that I have used for many years and that was critical to my overcoming the loss of my first job as an assistant professor of law (Cameron 1995). These poems were part of my journey through the stages of grief and loss to acceptance. I offer them as a gesture of hope to others. They are the only way that I can explain the part of my healing that totally came from the inside out.

Part II: *La Quemada:* The Burning

I am an overachiever. Guided by ambition, inherited smarts, a sense of perfectionism, and childhood values instilled in me always to do my best, I worked my way up from a humble working-class background in the Los Angeles metropolitan area of Southern California. I was the child of immigrants who had come north for adventure in the 1940s and '50s; the elders in my family were not unlike many who came to the United States to better their lives. My ancestors range from people who had money, education, and property to *campesinos*[3] who worked on haciendas[3] or as nannies and maids in the homes of the wealthy. Between the Rivas-Arriolas and the Garcias-Rosales, then, my siblings and I got very strong messages about the importance of hard work and education, even if our parents never went as far in their educational pursuits as they would have liked. As a young adult, I was able to work and attend college at night and managed to promote myself into increasingly better jobs. And thanks to the policies of affirmative action still in existence in California in the late 1970s and '80s, the doors of the University of California, Berkeley Law School were open to a young former legal secretary with a high GPA from a state university who was passionate about learning. My resume marks a steady progress to better placements, but nothing in it indicates the ways in which I was never prepared emotionally or politically for my advancements.

When I arrived at my first place of university employment as an assistant professor, I learned even before starting the job that my appointment had caused some furor on the campus. I found out from two professors who were about to become my colleagues that a public talk had taken place among the dean, faculty, and students shortly after I accepted the offer of employment. The dialogue had produced a divided camp—those who were excited that I had been hired as the first-ever Latino/a, and those who felt the law school had lowered its standards and resorted

---

3   In Mexico the hacienda was similar to the plantation system of agricultural labor and production, except that the haciendas were massive land grants that had originated during Spanish colonialism.

to an unqualified affirmative-action choice. I barely realized that I was being introduced to the intense politics surrounding hiring and diversity at a prestigious law
school. Only later did I understand that even though more than 90 percent of the
faculty had voted to hire me, the few who strongly opposed my appointment had
already helped create an environment that made me feel a lot less welcome than the
other new professors who had been hired that year and apparently were thought to
have more prestigious credentials.

I was hired by a school ranking in at least the second tier—to some in the first
tier—of the silliest measure of quality ever swallowed whole by law schools across the
country. Of course, the *US News and World Report*'s tier system is completely arbitrary,
and many people know this. But it is an effective marketing device and has created
a vast culture of false superiority and inferiority among schools across the nation.
Based on the statements I heard in our faculty meetings, I cynically said to people:
"I work for one of twenty-five schools that all believe they are in the top fifteen at
one time or another." Though arbitrary, however, committed belief in the rankings
impacts hiring and tenure decisions, in some places more subtly than others. In my
own workplace, the influence was blatant, obvious, and loud.

Eighteen years later, I can look back and say that I was in fact qualified for the
position I had been hired to fill. And I was qualified for tenure, and it was taken away
from me. I came into the position with two lengthy articles published in national
law journals. I had a writing agenda. I knew what I wanted to do. I was excited about
becoming a law professor. But my excitement soon turned into dread and fear.
This is where my lack of experience in politics and my poor self-confidence became
important. I have no words to describe the way it felt when little by little I sensed that
someone was trying to pull away the welcome mat as I stepped through the door-
ways of my first workplace as an assistant professor. I still remember, however, the
words of a senior female colleague, who did try to warn me: "Elvia, remember this:
all tenure battles are political. It's not a question about your abilities because you
would not even have been hired if your qualifications were in doubt." My response?
"I hate politics."

One who has been burned and survives is *la quemada*. In modern society, witch hunts
and burnings do not take the medieval European form, when thousands of women who
defied male supremacist systems of power were burned or hanged.[4] However, they still
take place. Anyone who has been involved in or witnessed the politics of tenure at a university understands well that metaphoric burnings at the stake are common. Women of
color are frequent outsiders whose identities have been brightly burned at the stake of
academic politics. Burnings destroy and cleanse simultaneously. The old is covered with
the new. The scar holds the memory. In this part of my chapter, I hope to infuse my
description of my engagement with the legal academy from the inside out with the awareness that my healing journey and place of acceptance today were hard earned and have
left scars that no longer hurt, yet do teach.

---

4   The infamous *Malleus Maleficarum,* published in 1487, instructed magistrates about ways to
      discover, interrogate, and convict witches. It has been described as one of the most misogy-
      nistic texts that ever indoctrinated the world about the dangers of "free-thinking women."
      Allegedly the millions (although historically accurate figures are unknown) of women who
      were burned as witches in medieval Europe included female scholars, mystics, herb gather-
      ers, midwives, and nature lovers. See http:www.malleusmaleficarum.org; Laura Miller, *Who
      Burned the Witches?*, available online at http:www.Salon.com, reviewing Lyndal Roper, *Witch
      Craze.*

When I fell in love with learning about the law, I didn't have Latina professors who could serve as guides for me as kind of *curanderas*[5] along the desert paths of a professional journey. I did have a few caring and supportive white men in positions of influence and power in the places where I was a student from undergraduate days to law school, and to them and their willingness to put their progressive politics to work on my behalf, I say thank you. Beyond that, I had only the strength that was part of my lineage as the daughter and granddaughter of women who had migrated to California from Mexico. From my Abuelita Petra and Mama Lucy, I did learn the values of hard work and compassion in action. But I also naïvely believed that hard work would earn me credit, recognition, and acceptance. So the core values that had taken me from worker to labor activist, law student, civil rights lawyer, and finally law professor were only partially helpful when the more I achieved, the harder it became to get to my next goal. These are the lessons that we don't find in a textbook. They come from the experiences in life we have little power over, except the way we react to them.

Early in my teaching career, I struggled to find a balance between my love of ideas in the law and my newfound love of ancient philosophies like Kripalu yoga. The latter evoked a desire to live more in the present, to nurture the spirit and body as well as the mind. I understood on some level that all of life's experiences can be used to help you learn and grow and become stronger and better able to be of service in the world. In fact, as a survivor of sexual abuse and rape, the grounding practices of yoga and meditation have done wonders for my sense of wholeness and ability to develop personally and professionally.

But no amount of meditation or yoga in that early period of my career taught me how to handle being one of the first women of color ever hired on that faculty. I was just so afraid most of the time. One time at the end of my first semester of teaching—on a visit to the ashram where I trained in yoga and meditation—I told Guru Amrit Desai that I was entertaining the idea of applying to live and work in the ashram because the new law-teaching career didn't seem to be going well. He responded, "Leaving may not be the answer; often if we leave before the lesson is learned, we just find the problem arising in a different form in the new place." I stayed. And learned. Here are some of the select memories from that burning time.

Memory Number One

Memory number one is forever etched in my head, and it is not at the beginning of my years on the tenure-track faculty but, rather, on the day I realized that there was no future for me at the law school. I was in my fourth year of employment. My school had a very short promotion track—three years. Two articles were required in those three years. I had about five the first time around. Now it was another year later; I had been encouraged the year before to delay my application because my teaching scores were not great. So I worked on my teaching, and this was the second go around.

Memory number one is a mental picture of me sitting on my bed at home next to the telephone. I am in my beautiful old home built in the 1930s, and the window looks out on a tall, southern pecan tree. I am wondering who I can call. I feel an incredible sense of emptiness in the middle of my body. I pick up the phone to call my oldest friend in California and then put it down. Instead, I grab a pillow and put

---

5   In Mexico, a *curandera (o)* is a traditional folk healer or shaman who may use herbs and rituals, probably rooted in ancient Indigenous culture, to bring about healing.

it over my stomach and begin to cry my guts out. I am crying because less than hour before I had walked out of the dean's office after a bizarre meeting with him and a few members of the promotion and tenure committee, who had tried to talk me out of proceeding with my application for tenure.

It was the second time. I now had six articles in my folder. And everything was still "not enough." My work was not enough, and my teaching scores were mixed, and therefore I was not good enough. And like the victim of abuse who disassociates from her body to survive trauma, I remember the implosion, the fading of their voices, and the awkward posture of everyone on the dean's leather couch as they executed their act of rejection. And before too much more could be said, I barely uttered, "I don't have to listen to this . . . ," and I walked out. And the next day I met with a lawyer.

The lawyer and I talked for hours. What I mainly remember are her words: "Think about the people who will be on the jury; they're graduates of this university . . . your case has to be perfect." And I thought about it and—because I didn't feel confident and didn't believe in myself, and instead believed just enough of their opposition to hurt myself—I resigned with a formal letter to the dean two weeks letter. I laid down the sword. For weeks I had hardly slept; I'd lost weight from the anxiety, and I was simply tired of the fighting. I felt I had been in a battle for survival from the moment I had stepped onto the campus. And I was all alone.

With the lawyer's help, I negotiated a renewable contract for at least two years. At the time, this seemed best: continue doing my job, be stripped of the title "assistant professor," and be called a senior lecturer. When it was all over and the letter was signed, I moved like a person in shock. An automaton. Once exams had been graded, I turned to mundane tasks that required no thinking, like repainting my home office. I accepted an invitation from Frank Valdes, whom I had just met at the 1995 Lavender Law conference a few weeks earlier, to attend a first-ever Latina/Latino critical legal theory conference that would take place the following spring in La Jolla, California.

The only plan I had now was to get back to the business of writing law review articles and at some point find a new job. For the next few years, I would have a paycheck and an office but no substantial emotional connection to my work environment. I taught, I supported student activism surrounding *Hopwood v. University of Texas*,[6] I began to get involved in Society of American Law Teachers (SALT) activities. I failed to see that the window of opportunity for moving on to another university was slipping away. This was my denial.

In her book *On Death and Dying* (1973), Elisabeth Kubler-Ross describes the five discrete stages of the process that people go through to deal with grief and tragedy from events such as getting a terminal illness diagnosis or experiencing a loss. Although her work was written as a prescription for better treatment of persons facing terminal illness, the analysis has helped people deal with other forms of loss (e.g., divorce, death of a loved one, addiction). Grief over the loss ultimately leads to acceptance, but not before the person experiences the varied stages of denial, anger, bargaining, and depression, not necessarily in any particular order. Inevitably acceptance comes, although it may be slow, painful, and without a clear sense that you are changing.

---

6   *Hopwood v. University of Texas* held unconstitutional the admissions policies of the university, ruling that they were racially discriminatory against nonminority applicants and a violation of the fourteenth amendment equal protection clause.

Not getting tenure at the place where I had worked so hard and produced enough to be qualified was a profound loss. And during the academic year (1997–98) when I finally left the university, I also had to face my mother's terminal illness with cancer. I stayed an additional year because I could not handle looking for work and taking care of my mother, I told the dean. This may have been the stage Kubler-Ross refers to as bargaining, which accompanies denial: the person confronting the loss tries to postpone or delay the inevitable. In my case, the inevitable was that my career at this school was over, and I had to move on. The dean begrudgingly renewed my contract.

When I reentered the teaching market, I had put a total of nine years into my career, and I was still untenured. I was exhausted from my mother's yearlong illness and her death. No longer able to bargain for another year of employment, I left my job, went on unemployment, and struggled with depression. But I was also in another phase of loss—a different manifestation of denial where you vacillate between "being OK" and not willing to understand or accept what is happening. I did not comprehend how precarious and tentative my position had always been in the academy as a woman of color. A mentor had told me I would have no problem making a lateral transfer to another school because of the university's prestigious status. He spoke from the perspective of a white male, someone who cared but could not strip from me the denial over how deep the institutional resistance is to the hybrid identity that is the woman of color law professor. I went to the teaching market. And it should have gone better. I was befuddled. I had more publications than ever and few interviews. I understand now that the stigma of being presumed incompetent was slapped like a badge on my suit lapel, and I could do nothing about it. Much of the writing I did during this period was about the struggle for reemployment.

Memory Number Two

I am sitting in my office at the law school, and a female colleague walks in to ask, "What are you working on?" She is young herself, already tenured. She and her husband are prolific writers. Both Yale graduates. This story is probably unfair to her. She perhaps meant well. She certainly understood better than I the resistance I was facing from many colleagues on the faculty. I only remember the sense of betrayal when she actively discouraged me from continuing with a writing project that was "too feminist, too lesbian, too controversial" for a pretenure candidate. In an earlier article, I had indeed warned junior colleagues that if they were going to write about the cutting edge, or feminist issues, or critical race, or LatCrit, they needed to know that there were consequences. I was at a school that had written off feminism and narratives in legal scholarship long before.

Memory number two is that moment of disconnect between me and my former colleague, who has since moved on to an even-more-prestigious law school. This is the memory of my profound sense of disconnection at the university, even from those with whom I supposedly shared gender and progressive politics. Except in the politics of the workplace, where she was an accommodator and I was closer to either a lost child or a rebel.

Memory Number Three

In this memory, I have just arrived in town to start my new job. I traveled in a beat-up Volvo for four days, leaving behind a career in New York City following law school that had included an ACLU fellowship, law practice with the Civil Rights Bureau for the New York attorney general, two jobs as a writing instructor at local law schools, and a return to graduate school to earn a master's degree in American history. After unpacking my stuff in my home, I headed to campus to move files and books into my new office. In this memory, I have found the faculty mailroom, and the box with my name on it is chock full of the standard voluminous stacks of university mailings. Snuck in between a few sheets is the copy of a magazine article with a yellow sticky note, unsigned, that simply says, "Thought you would find it interesting."

The article, written by two law students, contained a virulent attack on affirmative action by a conservative magazine and the decision of the law school to hire me. Details had been lifted from my resume to ridicule and compare me as far inferior to the white male candidate who had just finished clerking for Justice Clarence Thomas on the Supreme Court. Later, I learned that the way the authors of the article had acquired those details was that a copy of my resume had been given to them by a vocal opponent of my appointment, who was noted in the legal academy for outrageous expressions of hostility to the policy and practice of affirmative action. In the slow-motion version of this memory, I am initially reading with interest until I realize that the article is about me, and then I feel embarrassed, naked, vulnerable. In the memory, I hurriedly bury the article under the stack of papers along with my feelings of hurt and rejection.

Memory Number Four

This one takes place a few months after the encounter with the cowardly, anonymous, yellow sticky note. It is now October, and I have ended another class hour. I have been struggling for weeks to keep up with the pace of reading, absorbing, and preparing for a class while simultaneously trying to find my style and voice for the demanding task of teaching the law. A student has come to complain that I am not giving the class enough "black-letter law." I have been teaching employment discrimination, and because I had recently been trained as an historian, I assigned readings in history and literature to contextualize the twentieth-century emergence of civil rights legislation.

Memory number four is so much like memory number one. I am crying hard, and thoughts of just running away and escaping back to New York City fill my mind. It's just a few months into this new job, and mixed with my tears of frustration is an overwhelming desire to return to the status of an unknown graduate student, simple government attorney, or maybe even just legal-writing instructor. I regret ever wanting to teach no matter how much I love learning, ideas, history, and writing. But at the end of crying for two hours or so, I have calmed down with a phone conversation to old friends in New York. I am reminded that I do have a reserve of inner strength and the power that comes with accepting what is and my feelings. The next day I tape the article that was placed in my mailbox to the front of my office door along with a little poem I wrote at the end of the crying jag (Arriola 1997).

Part III: New Skin

When I was young and growing up in Southern California, I occasionally went to the beach, fell asleep on the sand face down, and got a sunburn. The next few days I examined my reddened-brown skin, peeled the burnt skin off, and enjoyed the smoothness of the emerging new tissue. I committed to this writing project by saying that I wanted to focus on the journey of healing that allowed me to shed old, burnt skin and embrace a new vision of myself. Survivors of abuse, for example, know that key to the process of integration and becoming whole is acknowledging the past and the traumas that changed us.

I have sat in women's support groups for survivors of rape and incest on and off for many years. In these safe settings, we talk about surviving by learning to love ourselves, learning to embrace and identify the coping symptoms that have both served us well but also hurt us. Denial is one of those aspects of survival that helps you move on, but it can also impede progress. Take, for example, the ways that a survivor of rape, like me, who grew up in a cultural setting that demands silence and obedience on matters of sexuality and gender expectations, must learn to cope. Survivors have to unlearn patterns that invite revictimization or encourage silence in the face of personal boundaries being violated.[7] When I learned about feminism, I also saw that my abuse survivor patterns of response had let old bosses sexually harass me and get away with it.

I sometimes wonder how things might have turned out if I'd been in touch with my anger about the way I was being treated from the moment I arrived at my old workplace. Instead, I was in so much denial and shock that I was being subtly undermined that it was easier to feel the hurt and want to run back to a simpler career as a lawyer in New York City, rather than confront the attackers. I wonder how many stories of past abuse underlie the experiences of institutional harassment or rejection of women of color in the legal academy, especially among those who simply did not survive and went back into law practice.

Therefore, to talk about survival means to get very personal about the ways that we understand how we are seen, how we see ourselves, and how we respond to abuse. Only later did I learn from people I met through LatCrit conferences that in the period when I was feeling rejection at my first job, other women of color were having similar experiences at their own schools. But we didn't know each other or often didn't have communities outside of work that could offer us support or understanding when we had experiences that made us feel isolated, alone, and unwelcome. Some of the women of color I met who had struggles similar to mine are no longer in law teaching today, and that is an unfair institutional loss that repeats itself and must be changed.

What does it take to be one of the survivors? And what can we say to those coming behind us that prepares them for teaching beyond their brilliant careers as graduates of top-notch law schools, judicial clerks, and/or lawyers with major firms or important public agencies? What is survival, and what does it look like? Here are some of the things I did to survive and move on.

Daily Journaling

Writing certainly helped me recover. I have kept a daily journal for many years. The inspirational writer Julia Cameron, author of *The Artist's Way* (1995) and dozens of other books on writing and journaling for personal change, invented the "morning pages" experience. Wake up, get the first cup of coffee, find a quiet space, and begin to write at least three longhand pages without stopping. It is like emptying your mental trash can. It is a dumping of raw emotion. Writing to heal creates change. It opens the mental and spiritual channels for creativity. It may turn into a creative work or the beginning of one.

---

7   I found support for my healing process from Ellen Bass and Laura Davis book *The Courage to Heal: A Guide for Women Survivors of Child Sexual Abuse.*

When we honor our pain, our feelings, our life's experience, we are in touch with the spiritual part of our lives whether as academics or students, which can be defined as the capacity to live in the present moment, to lose oneself in tasks and projects without an attachment to the outcome for the sheer love of the work (Militz-Frielink 2009).[8] Writing has literally saved my sanity. I have written myself out of depression, anger, and denial over the years.

But there was a time when I had to be taught how to feel before I could write honestly and from the gut. Sometime after my mother's death and on the eve of my leaving my old workplace, I attended a workshop for people at Kripalu Center on ways to grieve.[9] For one week, our group of sixteen in the class talked about the psychology of grief and used physical exercise, yoga, and dance to learn how to embrace changes ranging from the sale of an old home to dramatic body alterations from accidents and/or illness, divorce, or the death of a loved one. We embraced the idea of yoga postures as a metaphor for holding our place in the world with a sense of purpose, balance, and self-acceptance despite the feelings of resistance. We talked, cried, laughed, shared stories, and unloaded the burdens of secret fears and worries in a safe setting.

During that week, I engaged in a role play, a fictional confrontation with the dean of the law school who had actively undermined my success for attaining tenure. I accessed fully my anger and my fears of ever getting over the loss and returning to a productive life in law teaching. And several hours after that role-play session, I wrote a poem that embraced both my anger and the humor that I needed to move on as a survivor of male supremacist politics in law teaching. I have included this poem with this chapter.

Creating/Finding Community

That fortuitous meeting with Frank Valdes at Lavender Law in 1995 changed my life.[10] I said yes to attending what became LatCrit I.[11] Even though I felt like an outsider at first because of my lesbian identity and articles (Arriola 1997), it did not take long for me to know that I had found the community I had sorely needed during my early years of teaching. Staying connected to this critical scholarship community was essential to my continued healing and to my decision to stay in law teaching and continue developing as a serious scholar and teacher.

Activism

In the academy, my involvement with SALT was tremendously helpful.[12] My tenure battle happened at the height of the post-civil rights resistance movement to affirmative action. I was working at the very institution that had given birth to the shocking decision in *Hopwood v. University of Texas* (1996), which had ruled that affirmative-action policies at the law school violated the fourteenth amendment to

8   I have borrowed this definition of the spiritual in education from Sarah Militz-Frielink's insightful graduate thesis.

9   The Kripalu Center for Yoga & Health is located in Lenox, Massachusetts. See http://www.kripalu.org.

10   See http:www/lavenderlaw.org The conference gathers attorneys and scholars for workshops on developments in the law for gay, lesbian, and transgender peoples and communities.

11   http://www.latcrig.org (Latino/Latina critical legal theory, a.k.a. LatCrit).

12   See http:www.saltlaw.org.

the US Constitution. Diversity was questioned. SALT took on the battle, and I can say that the years I was on the Board of Directors working on the resistance movement to post-*Hopwood* policies were exciting and filled with purpose.

New Research Projects

My involvement with LatCrit was the most crucial experience for personal and professional healing. Because I found a professional community, I no longer felt alone. Because I understood that every part of my identity had been attacked by the colleagues who undermined my tenure candidacy—Latina, lesbian, feminist— I knew it was important to honor every part of me in my quest for new scholarly projects. Today I am considered something of an expert on the subject of women in the global economy under NAFTA at the Mexican border. I owe the inspiration to get involved in this work to the first yes I said to Frank Valdes to attend a little conference in Southern California, where other progressive/critical scholars posed questions about Latino/as and the law.

Ultimately, there were three phases to my journey since I started out as an assistant law professor. The first was indeed the painful part that taught me several things: a female senior colleague's words to me about the resistance I felt to my presence at this historically white and male-dominated law school were right: "It's all politics," she said. "If your qualifications were ever in doubt, you never would have been hired." But I refused to take in the words and didn't learn the lessons about how to pick your battles in a struggle with the white male supremacy that infiltrates so many a good law school and that Pat Williams brilliantly referred to as the White Polar Bear (1991). In phase one, I was too often naïve, afraid, or in utter denial. In phase two, I understood and worked toward healing by getting in touch with my pain and my anger. I put the anger to work in activism surrounding the post-civil rights agenda of the Right to undo affirmative action in higher education. I did that with on-campus politics, even though I was now only a senior lecturer, and I did it through the activism of SALT.

Through my tentative involvement in the burgeoning LatCrit movement, I began to embrace the part of my professional identity that had been so troublesome for some of my colleagues—the fact that I came from a working-class background and immigrant parents from Mexico. In this period, I almost left law teaching and formed a nonprofit organization[13] to advance awareness about the conditions for women working in the factories spawned near the Mexican border under NAFTA.[14] In between all these periods, I was always doing yoga, meditating, writing morning pages, creating poems, and trying to shape a professional identity I could be comfortable with. I told people that I was actually more authentic in my writing on the subject of discrimination after my resignation. I had tasted blood. Continuing to write and become more activist in my scholarly work helped me get over the harder part of having been forced to leave my old institution.

Finally, in phase three, I found a new institutional home and focused on my professional development. In this phase, I have come to a deeper understanding about the importance of nurturing your sense of self while balancing the demands of professional work. This last phase is ongoing, and in recent months, I have

---

13   See Women on the Border, Inc. at http:www.womenontheborder.org.

14   The North American Free Trade Agreement.

come full circle to a quiet place of introspection that is telling me to be careful and beware—that if I want to live a full and good life, I must reassess the ways I have traveled to the place of personal and professional success using such familiar coping skills in the academy as workaholism, perfectionism, and people pleasing. All of them work together to deny our fundamental human nature and our need for balance.

At one time, working very hard had served me well. And at one time, perfectionism probably had also done right by me. But often the motivation to work beyond our capacity, to burn ourselves out to the point of serious illness, stems from deeply rooted insecurities. And therefore it is a coping skill that must be thrown out. And when we do that and embrace a life of balance and working to serve and have joy, we become better people, better teachers. We become more serene and, in this way, probably more helpful to our students. My own serenity has been the product of hard-earned lessons and the willingness to change myself because I couldn't change others. Acceptance came for me without research or intellectual rigor or politics. It came from learning to love all over again, starting with loving myself.

Part IV: A Poetic Unfolding of a Healing Process

The emotional work was constant in the years after I resigned from the tenure-track position and eventually reentered the teaching market. I attended various personal development workshops that introduced me to the healing balm of witnessing through the word to my own spiritual condition. In 1998—right after my mother passed away and I closed up her tiny apartment—I took a physical journey to the Berkshire Mountains to heal from the loss of her being in my life as a parent, friend, and mentor. I enrolled at the Kripalu Center for Yoga & Health's workshop for people wanting to embrace grief so as to move into a happier state of existence, free from depression and the sense of defeat that accompany dramatic change in your life (e.g., death, illness, divorce).

I hope these words or maybe these poems can help someone heal further, or can guide someday the person who hasn't even considered yet that she will become a law professor. The woman who may one day read this anthology and think to herself, "I know it may be hard, but I think I want to teach." May she be happy. May she know the limits of becoming too driven with ambition. May she learn to build bridges. May she embrace the feminine side of the Buddha/God/love. May she write a lot and teach a lot and be surrounded by love, joy, and prosperity.

Introductory Note on the Poems

The stages of grief identified by Elisabeth Kubler-Ross were applied first to people struggling with terminal illness. The model, however, has been extended to describe the process of acceptance of any dramatic change in life through catastrophe, illness, or tragedy. There is no linear order in which the stages appear, nor does any one person necessarily experience them all. I have tried to label each poem for an aspect of my stages of recovery leading to acceptance of who I am and where I am today: much more at peace and confident that some very good things can come out of something bad. *No hay mal que por bien no venga. Gracias, abuelita.*

* * * *

Anger

Weenie Power

What would it be like
to really tell you to your face
how enraged I finally am at you
and your fellow weenies
but especially you
in your representative capacity
as the head of this
institution
of petrified attitudes
for all the ways in which
you contributed to
the devastating loss
of my academic dreams?

What would you say if
I suddenly appeared
out of nowhere
minutes after you'd just
finished brushing your teeth
and were still adjusting
the collar of your shirt
and pulling on your tie
my presence seeming like
the fulfillment
of a nightmare
of meeting up with
a VERY ANGRY WOMAN
who with raging fire
spewing from my eyes
my pores
my hands like
laser swords
aimed at your
groin and shouting
"You !
Hey, you!"
wearing that
cloth of power
"Yeah, you!"
with the
stinking cigar
and the
vest decorated
with the nails
left over from

sealing my
professional coffin?

Yes, what would
you do if
you understood
that you'd buried
my spirit alive
and that
I've come back
from the land of
those presumed
a fatality
under one of the
rails of the tenure track
and that it is burning
a set of footprints
on your doormat
as I await the
moment of
seeing you
buckle
just for a second
and reach for your
weenie whistle
and the aid of
your subjects
those marzipan soldiers
who confused
the Tin Man
for a leader
and like frightened roaches
are scurrying off
to other corners
under the
flashing lights
of the public's scrutiny?

What would you do
oh, gracious leader
with your Cheshire-cat smile?
What would you do
if you understood
finally
that sandwiched between
my rage and my anger
there is an old wound
now covered up with scars
and that

I've just come back
to caution you to
stay out of the way
of the healed warrior
who has reclaimed her power?

I tell you what
don't tell me what you'd do
I don't really care
What's more important
is that in this mind's eye
I've got a six shooter
on my hip
We're on a dirt street
in front of that shameful parlor
they call a learned hall of legal education
and you've got one, too,
but it's me and my target-practiced
fury against you
and your
little weenie
power

Denial

TELEPHONE MESSAGE FROM A DEAN

Well
I made the phone call
and I still feel
phoney baloney
This thing called
the hiring process
of looking for a new job
stinks to high heaven
as bad as when my
dogs need a visit
to the groomers
Nothing ZEN about
my attitudes is there?
but wait
Enlightenment is NOW
This is my fucking ZEN
moment
this chaos
this pissed offness
about the stupidity of
that phone call

with a dean who
doesn't know me
doesn't care to know me
sees me as all of a resume
a CV and some syrupy
fake interest I conjured
up for that stupid phone call
"Oh yes, I'd love to be
on your f———faculty
Those brilliant
idiots savant
annoy the hell
out of your students
or your resident
bigot or arch defender
against the invasion
of the feminazis."

Good thing I
got to an AA mee . . .
Ah, shit
the truth is I would love to
get rid of this
feeling
A wodka would be vewwy
vewwy nice wight now

Hey, remember
when you were
surviving in NYC?
Things were not easy then
and there's no reason
for them to be easy now

Ahhh, so sleepy
very sleepy
from fear
Turn me into
a magicube
and tuck me in your pocket
roll me down a
bowling alley
away from
these deans
I'm supposed to
talk to about
getting a job
these guys who have this uncanny
knack for making me

waste all this time
wondering
"did he like me?"

Physical Release of My Anger

IT'S A SCREAM

Bounce bounce
thump thump
wave your arms in the air
arch ch ch ch ch ch
your back
now send those arms
forward in a lunge
and punch punch punch
and SCREEEAAMMMM!!!!
AARRRRRGGHHHH!!!
YES, THAT IS THE DEPTH
of AAARRRRRGGHHH!!!!!
gaaasssssppp! for AAARRRGGGHHHH!
thump
thump
lunge, punch, jump
wave and
arch and
lunge and
oh, my God, I am
S CREeeammmming out my
FFRRUUSTRATIION!!!!!!!!!
WHO DO YOU SEE?
THEM, HIM, THEM, HIM
The ones who have
who have
who have
who have
AAARRRGGGGGHHHHH!

bounce bounce
thump thump
lunge lunge
air
lung
breathe
it's OK
they are not here
and they are
all I have to do is

SCREAM
think of a word
of a word that
makes you want to
SCREEAAMMMM!!!
It's, it's
the university's
GoddammmmNNNN
tenure system
AAARRRRRGHGHHHH
bounce
bounce
thump thitty thump
lunge
wave
slump
thump
wave
bounce
step
lie down and
feel the thump thitty thump
of my heart
wave
in whhhish
out whooosh
MMMMmmmmmm!!!
How good
I feel

Nearing Acceptance

SWEATING *SUDASINI*?

I don't feel like the
"sweet goddess"
That's what *sudasini* means in Sanskrit
sounds of honey water
dulce diosita

I am filled with self-condemnation
because
the worries have taken over again
like soldiers marching
on the Red Square of my heart

No renter therefore no income
No prospects of a job to move to
No job here at all

I can't even finish
this poem
because I feel
so draggy
tail not waggy
eyes are baggy
and I can't pretend
a smile

Shit . . . .
A mere chat yesterday
with Mr. Mediocrity
who got tenure because
he's white and has a penis
and I don't

I want out of this net
tangled web of deception
and lies
especially
the ones I tell myself

When Mom was alive
she would have said
"Rezale a San Antonio"
"Pidele a Dios"
light a candle
I do
and I sit
and I wonder how
Buddha learned to smile
through pain and hardship

My wonderful ideas for
a book
have their bags packed
and are walking out
the door
No, wait!
Come back!
I don't mean
to let you go
I'm just stuck right
now
Wait, really . . .

Curtain down
on the drama in
my own mind
wondering

as audience
and director both
where this play will end
and where I'll be
one year from now
and how impatient
I'll be then
and for what

So will I make it to
three pages?
Maybe . . .

I wander back
to the little worries
getting the apartment rented
for God's sake
getting it rented
and moving on
to the next task
and the last page
and the last line
of this poem***

Acceptance (with Some Humor)

Ex-lax-legis-Fear

Well
so this is what I did
finally talked about the fear
that I'm not going to
get a job
that it's looking very
tight on the job market
that pigs don't fly
that pigs who sit in deans' offices
wearing ties and trousers
assassinated my professional identity
two in particular
the Dean of Popsicle Land
formerly of the University of
High Tech Cowboys
who was such a wimp
no different from the
one who took over his seat
a pig
oink oink
That's about as mad

as I can get
and I don't really hate him
I pity him
It's too hard to get really angry
when I'm this
shitting-in-my-pants-
afraid
that I'll never get a job as a
law professor again. ***

CHAPTER 26

La Lucha

Latinas Surviving Political Science

Jessica Lavariega Monforti

As a little girl growing up in New York, I was one of three girls in a sea of boys in my close-knit family.[1] I learned that—to survive among my cousins—I had to play rough and not be thin-skinned. I never thought those childhood lessons would be relevant to my professional life as an adult. However, today I find myself in an academic field dominated by men and Anglos;[2] clearly my ethnicity and my gender (in addition to the fact that I am married to a Spanish-speaking foreign national) place me outside the mainstream. At times I have questioned whether I made the right choice in pursuing this career, knowing that I would have to struggle against preconceived notions about who I am and what my capabilities and beliefs are.

In casual conversations with friends and colleagues—many of whom are also women of color in academia—we share stories about our experiences, about the uphill battles we face in our profession. Often there are expressions of frustration, anger, stress, injustice, and worry, and on relatively fewer occasions, we celebrate each others' victories. This research is the result of those conversations because it occurred to me that while anecdotal stories about our experiences as women of color in political science are good to share, ours is a data-driven field of study. To my knowledge, no one has ever undertaken a systematic study of the experiences of Latinas in political science. Therefore, this is an effort to document—using scientific inquiry—*la lucha que enfrentamos*.[3]

In recent years, the number of women who have earned advanced degrees in the United States has increased. In political science, for example, in 2006 women comprised 26 percent of the US professoriate (Sedowski and Brintnall 2007). While this figure represents a 7 percentage-point increase since 1991, women

---

1   I would like to thank all of the Latina respondents who chose to take part in this research for allowing me to tell their collective story. I would also like to thank my family, friends, and supportive colleagues for their encouragement in writing this chapter.

2   Anglos refers to non-Hispanic whites.

3   Translated, "the fight we face."

are still underrepresented in the field, and women's advancement in political science as a discipline has been studied far less than in economics, sociology, and a number of the hard sciences (APSA 2004). To complicate matters, racial and ethnic minority groups, even among women, are also underrepresented in the discipline. According to Hall (2000), 85 percent of the women in the political science professoriate are Anglos while only 6.9 percent are black and 3.4 percent are Asian. Despite comprising a large and increasing proportion of the United States population—about 15 percent, according to March 2006 Bureau of the Census estimates—Latinos continue to be severely underrepresented in political science and today comprise less than 2 percent of the academy (U. S. Bureau of the Census 2006; Michelson 2006).

While there is some data that indicate that the majority of Latinos in the professorate, generally speaking, come from upper-class South American families, that does not seem to be the case in political science and other social sciences. Compared to US citizens who receive doctorates, fewer temporary residents who earn PhDs (typically this is the way international students are classified on visas) are female. In 2007 more than half (52 percent) of all US citizens who were awarded research doctorates were female, compared to about a third of temporary residents (34 percent). US citizens were more likely than non-US citizens on temporary visas to receive a doctorate in the social sciences (18 percent) (National Science Foundation 2007). Increased recent attention to recruitment and retention of Latino political scientists by professional associations such as the American Political Science Association (APSA) notwithstanding, the number of Latino scholars in the field continues to lag behind that of other racial and ethnic groups and severely behind Latino population growth in the United States. We see this trend in the face of higher-than-average interest in the field of political science by undergraduates (Lavariega Monforti and Michelson 2008).

The barriers Hispanics face to attain a postgraduate education are substantial; they include low high school and college graduation rates and lack of finances, among others (Quaid 2009). The focus of this research, however, is on the experiences of those Hispanic women who are successful in negotiating these barriers and enter graduate school in the field of political science. Latinas in political science as graduate students and faculty members have beaten the odds and statistics that indicate that they should not be where they are. To bring a fresh perspective to the limited body of research on women and minorities in political science, my investigation asks several important questions. Do the barriers that Latino populations face continue to be a problem once they have been accepted into a graduate program? After joining the academy? My research provides an analysis of the potential barriers, such as lack of mentorship and financial resources and the mounting familial responsibilities Latinas face in their pursuit of higher education in political science, which is one of the most male- and Anglo-dominated fields of study in the social sciences. Once they have earned a PhD in the field, what kind of situations do Latina faculty members experience? How are they treated by their colleagues, department chairs, and students? These are the questions that drive this investigation.

Rudder (1990) noted the need to recruit more minorities into graduate school and the political science professoriate; Garcia and Smith (1990) argued that this required not only effort on the part of professional organizations but also direct mentoring by faculty and graduate students. Avalos (1991) noted that Latinas were particularly underrepresented in political science, with few women entering or completing PhD programs. In an effort to increase diversity in the field, APSA continues to maintain a list of mentoring resources on its Web site, including a service that matches individuals seeking help with those registered as potential mentors. Since 1969 the organization has actively sought to provide institutional mentoring for minorities through the APSA Minority Fellows Program. While these services are certainly a step forward, survey results from Lavariega Monforti and Michelson (2008) reveal that poor or absent mentoring continues to contribute to the leaky pipeline, even among those associated with APSA.

In their research, Lavariega Monforti and Michelson (2008) conducted the second wave of a panel study of Latino graduate and undergraduate students known to the APSA in 2000. Respondents to the original survey were asked for updates about their educational and professional situations, as well as their reflections on monetary and other types of support and challenges they faced during their education and careers. The authors found that Latino and Latina respondents had very different perceptions about the "quality and quantity of mentoring available to Latino scholars, and of the challenges they face in the profession. Latinas were more likely to cite family concerns, such as needing to work near a spouse or take time away from their careers for children; were less likely to believe that they had received good mentoring, particularly from Latino and non-Latino senior male colleagues; and were more likely to believe they had been hindered by sexism and racism" (2008, 165).

To illustrate, Lavariega Monforti and Michelson reported that "one Latina was very specific about how her faculty mentoring fell short: 'It would have been helpful to have more professors invite me to gather and interpret their research data and publish papers with them. Only one professor gave me such an opportunity'" (2008, 164). The authors also noted that Latinas were more likely than Latinos to cite family concerns as barriers in their postgraduate education and employment pursuits. Another Latina respondent, who had completed her PhD, is a mother of two preschool children, and holds a tenure-track position, stated, "Hindrances include . . . most importantly the lack of support for being the primary caregiver in the family . . . . When I brought my son home I was told by my department chair that I couldn't have course releases without taking FMLA—meaning no pay! and that I wouldn't be eligible for a year extension on my tenure clock" (2008, 164).

Finally, these authors reported that Latinas also were more likely to mention service demands. One tenured Latina respondent in their study stated, "Since there are not as many women in the profession we often end up on more committees than the average male because committees typically need to be diverse. The same is true with being Latino. For a Latina the combination can mean extra work that may or may not be rewarded" (2008, 165). Another Latina respondent who was in a tenure-track position in their study noted, "I think one of the biggest issues is being given the time to do research and not get your energy sucked away with teaching and service. The college tends to assign women of color a great deal of committee work, not to mention asking us to attend various diversity functions on campus" (2008, 164). The data in this study demonstrated that significant issues of mentoring young Latinas in the profession exist and pointed to the additional burdens of financial concerns and family responsibility, sexism, and increased service demands as hindrances to Latinas' professional success.

The results of previous research, therefore, have indicated some substantial issues of concern for Latinas in political science. However, to date there is no systematic analysis of the experiences of Latina graduate students and faculty members. Using the results of an original data collection, I relate the stories of these Latinas in their own words in this chapter. This research is essential as we see significant increases in the number of Latinas entering and successfully matriculating through their undergraduate and postgraduate programs. Data for this investigation come from interviews with seventy-three Latina graduate students and faculty members who were registered with APSA in 2009 or known by the author.

In total, 193 individuals self-identified as Latinas were asked to complete a brief survey; 73 finished the survey for a response rate of about 38 percent. In addition to some demographic information, this survey asked respondents about their mentoring experiences in graduate school and the academy, experiences of discrimination and/or oppression in the workplace and graduate school, and the way—if at all—their gender and ethnicity have impacted their teaching experiences and interactions with students, as well as if their familial responsibilities have slowed or interrupted their careers. The final question of the survey asked respondents for their suggestions about ways to deal with the problems they may have faced.

Early in 2009, 193 Latina political science graduate students and faculty members in the United States were contacted via email and asked to participate in this project. Each respondent was given the option of completing her survey via email, telephone, or regular mail. Furthermore, each respondent was guaranteed confidentiality and anonymity if she chose to participate. Interestingly I received several answers from potential respondents with myriad questions and concerns about the consequences of their participation in this study. Many were worried that they would be identified and that, as a result, their careers would be negatively impacted. I continued to reassure these concerned Latinas that I would not include identifiable data in the final manuscript. Other respondents thanked me for taking on such an important—and potentially explosive—topic, and a few even expressed concern about the impact such a study might have on my career. These comments reveal the significance and seriousness of the subject of this research.

The Respondents

Of those Latinas who chose to participate, about 25 percent were graduate students; 11 percent identified themselves as lecturers, visiting professors, or adjunct instructors; 2.7 percent said they were currently on a postdoc; 31.5 percent said they were assistant professors on tenure track, 16.4 percent indicated that they were associate professors, and only 1.4 percent said they were full professors (see table 1). These findings are not much different than what Collins, Chrisler, and Nand Quina found in 1998, eleven years earlier. She concluded that "despite the increasing number of women who have earned advanced degrees, women faculty remain clustered in the lower ranks—the three A's: adjunct instructors, assistant professors, and associate professors" (1998, xvi).

For a little perspective on this topic, it is important to remember that the first woman to earn a PhD in political science was Sophonisba Preston Breckinridge in 1901 from the University of Chicago. The first African American woman to earn a PhD in political science, Jewel L. Prestage, did so in 1954 from the University of Iowa, and in 1971, a full seventy years after Breckinridge's degree, the University of

Table 1: Demographics Characteristics of the Sample[1]

	All Respondents		All Respondents		All Respondents
Not in POLS field	9.6%	US Politics	45.2%	In POLS Dept	80.8%
Grad student	24.7	Comparative	48	Term MA	4.1
Lecturer	11	International Relations	30	PhD since '91	82.2
Postdoc	2.7	Theory	12.3	Teach REG	60.3
Assistant	31.5	Methods	8.2	N	73
Associate	16.4	Public Ad/Policy	9.2		
Full	1.4	Ethnic/Gender/ American Studies	12.3		
Total	100%	N	73		
N	73				

---

1   It is important to note that the percentages in this column do not add to 100% because respondents often chose multiple fields of study.

California, Riverside granted a PhD to Adaljiza Sosa-Riddell, the first Latina to earn one (Telgen and Kamp 1993). As table 1 demonstrates, the earliest PhD earned in political science in this study was in 1991. Given this history, perhaps we should expect to find few Latinas at the highest rank in the field.

There are a few other fascinating patterns in the demographic information about the sample of respondents. For example, 48 percent focused on comparative politics, 45.2 percent focused on US politics, about 30 percent concentrated on international relations (including international political economy and international law/ human rights), about 12.3 percent were also in ethnic or gender studies or American studies, about 12 percent were in political theory, just under 10 percent claimed to be in public administration and/or policy, and just over 8 percent said they were in research methods. This pattern is interesting because of the perception that Hispanics are focused on the politics of Latin America and therefore unable to become part of the larger sociopolitical landscape in the United States (Huntington 2004). These data seem to squarely contradict these ideas.

Furthermore, about 81 percent of the Latinas who responded said they were currently members of a political science department while 19 percent were not. Of these 19 percent, some had left academia to work in the corporate world or for nonprofit agencies or transferred to some other field in academia (one was retired). Finally, when asked if they taught courses or did research in the areas of race, gender, or ethnicity, about 60.3 percent said that they did. It is intriguing to discover that more Latinas in this sample taught minority politics that in any of the traditional subfields, such as political institutions or public policy, in the discipline.

Now that we have an understanding about who these women are, it is essential to examine their experiences with mentoring while in graduate school. Respondents

Table 2: Types of Mentoring Received in Graduate School

When in grad school	All Respondents	By Subfield		By Status			Teach REG	
		US Politics	Non-US Politics	Graduate Students	Faculty	Left academia	Yes	No
Mentor – guide	46%	66.7% (22)	60% (24)	66.7% (12)	56.3% (27)	71.4 (5)	59.1% (26)	71.4% (20)
Mentor – publish	27	42.4 (14)	32.5 (13)	44.4 (8)	31.3 (15)	57.1 (4)	31.8 (14)	46.4 (13)
Mentor – research support	41	63.6 (21)	50 (20)	66.7 (12)	50 (24)	71.4 (5)	50 (22)	67.9 (19)
Mentor - networking	36	51.5 (17)	47.5 (19)	66.7 (12)	43.8 (21)	42.9 (3)	47.7 (21)	53.6 (15)
N	73	33	40	18	48	7	44	28

were asked, "During your time in graduate school, did you have a mentor to help (1) guide you through your studies, (2) publish research with, (3) support your research interests, or (4) help you build professional networks?" The answers to these four questions appear in table 2. While it is necessary to look at the sample as a whole, previous research has shown that differences within groups can be missed if cleavages within communities are ignored (García Bedolla, Lavariega Monforti, and Pantoja 2007). Therefore, the data has been broken down three different ways: by subfield, by status within the profession, and by whether the respondent researches or teaches in the area of race, ethnicity, and/or gender politics.

In terms of the type of mentoring, Latinas seem to have received more guidance in their coursework than any of the other areas. This is followed by support for their research interests, then help in building professional networks, and finally, only about 27 percent said they had published with a mentor. The data in table 2 show that Latinas in US politics have a higher frequency of being mentored. Also, students currently in graduate school report a significantly higher frequency of being mentored across the board than their faculty counterparts. Perhaps this gap in mentoring is a demonstration of progress over time.

However, many of these Latinas spoke very specifically about who was mentoring them and said that they had to be persistent to receive assistance. They also pointed out that more minority and women colleagues and professors, or those who were clearly dedicated to diversifying political science, were mentoring them. For example, one respondent wrote, "Initially it was hard to find mentorship in graduate school. The faculty members that were closest in research interests were junior faculty and were limited in their ability to help. But they did help introduce me to larger communities outside of my graduate department that have been extremely helpful. While I have not had one mentor, I feel that I have had a lot of mentorship (it takes a community). Some of that mentorship has been through membership in the Latino and Women's Caucuses." Other respondents talked about being assigned an advisor, rather than a mentor, while they were in graduate school; several pointed out that mentoring them was not seen as a priority by faculty members in their departments (many said, "He or she had no time for me").

One Latina respondent in international relations said, "During graduate school I had an advisor, not a mentor. He was too busy with his own research and traveling to South America, that he was never available. I had taken some electives in the field of Latino/a Culture where there was one professor, who guided me somewhat on my research. She was not in my field . . . . I feel that responsibility should have lied with someone in my field department." Another very interesting conclusion from the data in table 2 is that across all four areas of mentorship, Latinas who did *not* teach or research in the areas of race, ethnicity, and/or gender reported substantially higher frequencies of being mentored than those who did. It is also worth noting that Latina faculty members were asked whether they were mentored once they graduated and entered the professoriate. Only 34.7 percent of the respondents answered affirmatively. Therefore, mentoring experiences at the graduate and professoriate levels do not seem to be connected. Even faculty members who claimed that they had received some type of mentoring while they were students generally did not continue to receive it after graduation.

While all aspects of mentoring are important, in a field that increasingly demands publications, it seems strange that publishing with a mentor occurs the least frequently. Even among those most likely to be mentored—Latinas who do not teach or research minority and/or gender politics and those currently in graduate school—only 46.4 percent and 44.4 percent, respectively, had published with a mentor. To examine this factor a bit further, I investigated whether the respondents felt their mentoring experiences (or lack thereof) were affected by their gender and ethnicity and perceptions about their interests and abilities.

Respondents were asked, "Do you think your ethnicity or gender impacted the level or quality of mentoring you received? If so, how?" The responses to this question were coded into three categories for both ethnicity and gender: (1) yes, negatively; (2) no, no impact; (3) yes, positively. Overall, about 16.4 percent of the respondents said that being a woman and about 15.1 percent said being Hispanic positively impacted the level or quality of mentoring they received (see table 3). Even larger portions 37 percent for gender and 46.6 percent for ethnicity—indicated that the mentoring they received was not impacted at all by their characteristics. Respectively, 31.5 percent and 22 percent said that gender and ethnicity had a negative impact on the level or quality of mentoring they received. Again if we look across the various breakdowns in table 3, some interesting patterns emerge.

Latinas in US politics and those who teach minority and/or gender politics were the most positively impacted by mentoring and also had the highest percentage of negatively impacted mentoring relationships as a result of gender. As a matter of fact, almost across all groups, gender appears to have a more negative impact than ethnicity. On the positive impact of her gender and ethnicity, one associate professor remarked, "Yes, I think [mentor's name] was more receptive to mentor a Latina. He felt strongly that there should be greater diversity in our field. He might not have made time for me if I was not Latina." This statement is fairly representative of the respondents who reported a positive impact. Similarly another respondent wrote, "Actually I think my grad[uate] school mentors took an interest in mentoring me partly because I am Latina (as they understand the historical structures of

Table 3: Gender, Ethnicity, Discrimination, Intellect, and Mentoring

	All Respondents	By Subfield		By Status			Teach REG	
		US Politics	Non-US Politics	Graduate Students	Faculty	Left academia	Yes	No
Gender & mentoring positive	16.4 (12)	27.3 (9)	7.5 (3)	5.6 (1)	17.8 (8)	14.3 (1)	20.5 (9)	11.1 (3)
Gender no impact	37 (27)	33.3 (10)	42.6 (17)	55.6 (10)	33.3 (15)	28.6 (2)	31.8 (14)	48.1 (13)
Gender & mentoring negative	31.5 (23)	36.4 (12)	27.5 (11)	27.8 (5)	31.1 (14)	57.1 (4)	36.4 (16)	11.1 (3)
Ethnicity & mentoring positive	15.1 (11)	24.2 (8)	7.5 (3)	16.7 (3)	15.6 (7)	14.3 (1)	18.2 (8)	22.2 (6)
Ethnicity no impact	46.6 (34)	42.4 (14)	50 (20)	50 (9)	46.7 (21)	57.1 (4)	45.5 (20)	51.9 (14)
Ethnicity & mentoring negative	22 (16)	24.7 (8)	20 (8)	22.2 (4)	22.2 (10)	28.6 (2)	22.7 (10)	11.1 (3)
Expert on LA and Latino Politics	58.9 (43)	69.7 (23)	50 (20)	38.9 (5)	64.4 (29)	71.4 (5)	59.1 (26)	63 (17)
Discrimination – overt	24.3 (17)	36.4 (12)	15 (6)	5.6 (1)	26.7 (12)	57.1 (4)	31.8 (14)	11.1 (3)
Discrimination – subtle	27 (19)	33.3 (11)	17.5 (7)	11.1 (2)	35.6 (16)	14.3 (1)	34.1 (15)	14.8 (4)
Discrimination – none	48.6 (34)	33.3 (10)	60 (24)	83.3 (15)	33.3 (15)	28.6 (2)	31.8 (14)	74.1 (20)
Intellect questioned	41.1 (30)	57.6 (19)	32.5 (13)	33.3 (6)	44.4 (20)	57.1 (4)	45.5 (20)	37 (10)

discrimination and believe deliberate efforts must be made to reverse them), but also because I demonstrated intellectual promise and other positive character traits that facilitated my academic success."

On the negative side, there were references to the "good-ol'-boys' network," as well as the limitations of those who are not female minorities in the field to help, despite good intentions. As one respondent noted, "I think there are limits to what white men and women can offer in terms of advice; our experiences will not parallel—even if I structured my every move just like theirs, it is just different. Yet, I think they have a great deal of insight and wisdom to impart (and some have been eager to do so) since this remains their profession in terms of the composition of the discipline." Another Latina remarked, "I feel that gender has impacted my mentoring experience. I think males would rather work with males. This applies to all races and ethnicities." Similarly, another respondent said, "As a graduate student, I had one professor (who was the only Mexican American male professor in the department) who I expected to receive mentoring [from], and did not. I felt, at the time, it had to do with the fact that I was female."

It is also essential to investigate the assumptions that others made about the intellectual abilities and interests of Latinas in political science. It is logical that if senior faculty members believe that Latinas, who are junior to them, are intellectually weak and/or can only be experts in Latin American or Latino politics, they will not mentor them. Also, certain perceptions about Latinas may lead to discriminatory or oppressive interactions. To ascertain whether issues exist here, respondents were asked three questions. First, they were asked, "Have you had an experience of overt discrimination and/or oppression in the workplace or in graduate school? Please explain." Later, they were asked, "Do you feel that you are expected to be an expert in Latin American politics, Latino/a politics in the US, and/or gender politics, regardless of your graduate school training, because you are Latina?" And finally, respondents were asked, "Has your intellectual ability been questioned by students or colleagues because of your gender and/or ethnicity or the intersection of these identities? Please elaborate." The answers to these questions appear in table 3.

Overall, about 59 percent of the Latinas in this survey said that they were expected to be experts in Latin American and ethnic and/or gender politics—regardless of their training—because they are Latinas. Three notable patterns become apparent from the written comments. The first trend is summarized by one respondent who said, "Yes—there are incidences in seminars where faculty will ask me questions regarding anything regarding race or Latin American politics." Similarly another woman said, "Yes, all the time. However, I know this kind of thing happens to other minority faculty members too. I know of one instance where an African American male was applying for a comparativist position and during the job interview many comments were made about the fact that he could also teach black politics. An assumption was made by the interviewing institution that because he was an African American he had been trained in black politics." There were many references to these kinds of experiences.

Next, a group of women said that the people in their departments who know them did not make this kind of assumption. A representative comment was, "Colleagues know better, but outsiders including media, vendors, faculty from other schools met in different settings, seem to expect both an ability and desire to speak Spanish and to deal with both substantive areas mentioned." A final, smaller group of respondents said that they were not considered experts in anything, so by default they weren't given any credence in these areas, either. This is directly linked to the fact that 41.1 percent of the respondents said that students or colleagues had questioned their intellectual ability; these occurrences were more frequent for those in US politics (57.6 percent) and those who teach minority or women's politics (45.5 percent).

Respondents commented at length about intellect. One wrote, "My ability to be 'objective' as a scholar has been questioned most often, which I think is the same thing. I've never heard a white man who studies American politics accused of lacking objectivity." Another wrote, "I don't have actual proof of this, but when colleagues roll their eyes when one is speaking or change the topic and even walk away while one is speaking it is quite evident that one's intelligence is looked upon as inferior." Another respondent commented, "Yes. I always have to remind them what my training is in. And then they ask for your contribution on committees, and then ignore you or continue on as if you don't exist." Along the same lines, another stated, "My ability to teach and do sophisticated research methods is constantly being questioned, despite the fact that I went to one of the most rigorous graduate programs in the country." Yet another wrote,

> White senior faculty members have said that because I am Latina I cannot be credible teaching Latino politics. They don't see my research as intellectually challenging. When I tried to create curricula to suit our largely Latino student body, I was told that I was ghettoizing the department. Therefore only we had one Latino politics course offered in our department. They (white faculty members) re-wrote the course description for the Latino politics course to be ethnic neutral—so now it is a course about ethnic politics rather than one looking at the political and socio-economic challenges that Latinos face. In other words, coding was used and despite the fact that I am qualified to teach this course it has been given to a professor with no formal training in this area.

While these quotations are representative of many respondents' comments, it is important to point out that at least 50 percent of the respondents in the sample (across all groups) reported that their intellectual abilities had not been questioned; most of the respondents did not elaborate about their experiences.

The answers to the open-ended discrimination questions were coded into three categories based on the respondents' comments: (1) no discrimination or oppression; (2) subtle, but not overt, discrimination or oppression; (3) overt discrimination or oppression. Overall, about 48.6 percent of the respondents reported no incidents of discrimination or oppression, while about 27 percent said they had experienced subtle discrimination, and another 24.3 percent reported experiences of overt discrimination or oppression. Taken together, slightly more than half of the Latinas in this study reported negative experiences; some respondents even made references to ongoing investigations and legal matters. Comments by those who said that they had not had such experiences were rare; a hopeful finding in the data from table 3 is that more than 80 percent of Latina graduate students fall into this group.

Most respondents who reported having discriminatory experiences talked about being an outsider, missing out on informal mentoring networks, being ignored/marginalized, and having assumptions made that their employment or admission to graduate school was based on affirmative action, rather than their intellectual abilities. One associate professor gave a typical response: "inappropriate comments regarding my work, my desire to have a family, the time off I got during maternity leave, my emotional position on issues. All difficult to pinpoint, but a general environment that makes very clear you don't belong." Others reported more serious problems like sexual harassment, questions about immigration status, and inappropriate comments that undermined them in public, professional spaces. One respondent said, "One of my colleagues (my chair, actually), in elaborating about his theory of education, said that he doesn't want our graduates to be delivering pizza. He continued, 'Sure, that person can deliver pizza, but so can the Mexican down the street.' I said, 'What?' He said, 'I mean, not to denigrate Mexicans!' But clearly he had meant to imply that our students should be better than Mexicans. (My dad is Mexican.)" Another respondent recounted her experience:

> The [C]hair of my department was present at a talk I was asked to give by the Chicano Studies department (there is no joint research or regular interaction between the two departments) on the 2000 Mexican elections. After the talk, the Department Chair (who has since then been replaced) commented to another graduate student that my "Mexican-ness" was clearly evident in my presentation. When a graduate student asked the Chair to clarify, she (the Chair) responded that I spoke with [a] distinct accent, and that my body movements and viewpoints were indicative of a Chicano scholar. The graduate student, who also happens to be one of my closest friends, responded that that was a rather odd observation due to the fact that my first language is English (and I did not grow up in an ethnic enclave) and she didn't note any differences from my normal mannerisms. Nonetheless, the Chair remarked, she had seen my ethnicity come through (as if I had been previously hiding my ethnicity in the department).

Respondents were also asked if students react to them differently (either positively or negatively) because of their gender and/or ethnicity or the intersection of these identities. Overall, 48.5 percent said that students reacted to them negatively, 25.8 percent said students did not react at all, and 15.2 percent said students reacted positively to them. A similar question was asked about peer reactions. The results here are bit more positive: 29.4 percent indicated negative treatment, 45.6 percent said no reactions, and 16.2 percent said they received positive reactions from their peers.

One assistant professor summed up many answers when she responded to the questions about negative student reactions:

> Do they ever! How could they not? They, too, are socialized in this sexist and racist society and so are unaccustomed to seeing women of color in positions of authority. During my first academic job one of the older undergraduate students wanted to date me and when I rejected him he got angry and dismissive of me as his professor. Other students have questioned my grading publicly in class in disrespectful ways that I doubt my white male colleagues would receive. One student actually said I speak English the way I speak Spanish: "too fast." He'd never heard me speak Spanish. Just made his racist comment about the cadence of my speech blaming my speed for his lack of understanding of the material.

She went on to say, "The problem with being a female faculty of color is that you get it from all sides—from your colleagues AND from your students. Eventually you get exhausted with dealing with them. After a while you have to pick your battles and decide what to focus on or you're going to be caught up in the struggle for legitimacy and not have the energy you need to do what you really need to do to get tenure. You can't let it consume you, but it is still draining and demoralizing."

Another assistant professor wrote, "Gender plays a big role in the classroom. Students half expect me to be their mother, while others tend to start off challenging my ability to teach or know anything mathematical (I assume that is gender not race but hard to tell)." On the positive side of things, a newly hired assistant professor expressed a fairly representative sentiment: "I think for Latino students it provides a sense of comfort, common bond, and inspiration to have a shared ethnicity. In particular, I think my Latina students respond well to me on both gender and ethnicity levels . . . "

To deal with issues of socioeconomic status in this research, respondents were also asked if their progress as a student or faculty member had been delayed because of financial burdens. More than a quarter of the respondents indicated that financial burdens have slowed them down. About 64 percent of respondents talked about receiving adequate funding, applying for receiving scholarships, having a spouse/partner with stable financial resources, and possessing familial resources. For instance, one comment was, "My family and friends pitched in financially when needed. I chose not to get married or have children until well after I had completed graduate school. Thus, while I had minimal material resources while I was in graduate school, I also had minimal financial obligations."

Other respondents referred to the lack of funding during their graduate training, as well as low wages offered in some postdoctoral and faculty positions. For example, one respondent wrote, "Absolutely. University of_____, while prestigious, is one of the worst places to go for financial support. There is no summer funding, stipends are low, and not everyone has health insurance. I have worked several jobs throughout grad[uate] school, many simultaneously. I think I only had one year in which I did not work, and that was the first 3 quarters of grad[uate] school." Another Latina responded, "Through most of grad[uate] school I had scholarships. But when I had to depend only on teaching it was a terrible financial burden. However, with my current job I've been able to meet my financial goals." And finally, another respondent explained,

> Financial—yes in grad[uate] school. This was a major concern. In grad[uate] school, family ties were not understood by faculty and colleagues. I am a primary caregiver and that makes things hard financially, and in terms of needing time. I found out that I was given a lower salary than whites who were hired at the same time as me, they had no publications. My chair said that even though I was being paid less, that that salary was "okay for me." It is very hard to get leave, but it is done for other white faculty without any sort of explanation.

Finally, respondents were asked if their progress as a student or faculty member had been slowed because of family responsibilities. Overall, 55.6 percent said yes. Generally respondents' written comments focused on their roles as primary caregivers of young children, the lack or unavailability of maternity leave, and the length of their tenure clock, as well as having/wanting to care for parents, having to convince parents about the value of postgraduate education, and having to leave academic positions to support a spouse's job move. One graduate student wrote, "School was not something they [my parents] promoted in their children. Instead, they wanted us to join the labor force from the age of 16 and just work like everyone else. Bringing the money in now and not later was their priority. . . . I feel like this affected the quality of my school work." One respondent who left academia said, "I did have to fight my father to go to grad[uate] school; he did not understand why I needed to keep going to school. He actually accused me of trying to be better than the rest of the family. It took me sitting him down and explaining why going on to grad[uate] school was important and he finally relented. Now, he's the main person who wants me to get my PhD."

Along a different vein, the comments of one assistant professor summed up many others when she wrote,

> Yes. Family responsibilities have most definitely slowed my progress in academe. When I went on extended maternity leave I was encouraged to give back two years towards my tenure clock rather than one by a provost who does not have children. I refused and will go up for tenure after returning for one year. I'm sure it will all work out but the pressure is definitely there. I feel that there are unspoken pressures in academic life about not having a family. If you decide to be a professor you practically have to take a vow of "no family" and instead adopt a model where your commitment is first and foremost to the profession and institution. I was even told not to have children until I was tenured, which would have put me beyond child-bearing years. It wasn't until another female professor (with two children) told me not to ever give an institution that much power did I realize how wrong that advice was.

One visiting lecturer commented,

> My familial responsibilities (that include financial responsibilities to help support family members who are currently unemployed as well as aging parents) have required me to take on any and all temporary teaching opportunities that present themselves. As a result I now teach a very wide diversity of classes, many that are outside my research interests and training, at the expense of publication and greater specialization. I have become a "jack of all trades" when it comes to teaching but an expert in nothing because my teaching responsibilities take so much time away from research and publication.

Finally one assistant professor noted, "This is not a child friendly profession, I have learned. I suppose that is fine—few industries really care at all about helping parents work out their family and work needs. I just wish people were more candid about the fact that the professoriate is not particularly well suited for parents after all. There is a lot of hostility toward parents from both men and women without kids in this discipline, really harsh."

Discussion and Conclusion

The focus of this research was on the experiences of Latinas in political science as graduate students and faculty members. Using their own words, this chapter provided a systematic evaluation of their experiences in graduate school and in the profession. The results offer a serious wake-up call for those who laud the increasing numbers of Latinos in political science without recognizing the often harsh reality Latinas face in the profession. Administrators are failing to take personal action to recruit, mentor, and work alongside Latinas in the field; this situation is unacceptable and should not be tolerated. There is considerable room for improvement in political science, and the academy in general, in relation to the representation, mentoring, and treatment of Latinas. It is essential, therefore, to make suggestions for improving the experiences and environment in political science and academia as a whole. Some respondents, when prompted, mentioned possibilities for improvement. The suggestions included these:

- Continuing to diversify the academy;
- Mentoring those who follow them;
- Speaking about these issues and finding allies;
- Educating others; educating themselves better to support graduate programs and departments;
- Preparing those who are coming in about the battles they may face;
- Getting more support from Hispanic males;
- Working harder and not taking a defensive posture;
- Funding formal mentoring programs and rewarding mentoring by professors.

Most of these suggestions have been talked about in previous studies, but few have actually been put into practice (Ng 1993). Some of the respondents were doubtful that the field will change because of the institutional nature of some of the problems discussed in this chapter. Furthermore, many times these types of suggestions are lost on those who most need to hear them, and we end up "preaching to the choir"; those who are aware of and sensitive to the issues surveyed in this research are already engaged in mentoring, recruiting, and nurturing well-prepared Latina political scientists. The data show that as more women and minorities become part of the professoriate, they are sometimes effective in positively impacting the lives of those who enter political science after them.

Given this reality, what can students of color do? First, prepare yourself to handle the issues that are discussed in this chapter. Talk to colleagues you can trust, even if they are outside your field of study or at a different institution. If possible, use instances of discrimination as opportunities to educate. Get everything in writing (including funding offers, workload issues, information on salary and benefits, and tenure and promotion expectations) and document everything if something does not feel right. However, it is also important to realize that these are survival strategies, *not solutions*. Students are not responsible for bringing about the changes that are needed in academia. That responsibility lies directly on the shoulders of institutions, administrators, department chairs, and faculty. Anglo administrators and faculty, who clearly comprise the largest portion of those working in political science, need to make an investment of time, energy, knowledge, and funding in women of color as students and faculty.

On many occasions, I have heard—directly or indirectly—that Latinas are not chosen because "none applied for the job/funding/position" when what is beneath these kinds of comments is that these people believe that none are *qualified* for the job/funding/position. Thus, what is needed is a shift in thinking as well as action on the part of decision makers in the academy. Perhaps more aggressive suggestions should be implemented. One assistant professor suggested that (1) close public and private auditing of the workplace and educational institutions should be conducted to find any violations, (2) victim protection programs should be created to encourage denouncement of violations, and (3) rewards should be given to the institutions that do outstanding work to prevent and correct violations from taking place, including research funding assistance for "best practice" implementation and training for other institutions that need to meet higher standards.

Another respondent said that institutions, programs, and faculty who discriminate against—as well as those who encourage the development of—Latinas should be publicly acknowledged.

It is also important not to ignore the role that racism/ethnocentrism and sexism play in political science. Latinas are marginalized because of their ethnicity, and they are further marginalized as women by their male coethnics. This marginalization clearly impacts their development and progress in the field. The lack of personal effort on the part of male coethnics and non-Latina women and men is obvious from the responses of many of the Latinas in this study. Questions that they can ask themselves include, Is there a pattern in the students I choose to work with, share data with, publish with, write the best letters of recommendation for, train as researchers and/or teaching assistants, and/or fund? Am I—consciously or not— excluding Latinas and other women of color? If the answer is yes, what changes in their personal behavior are they willing to make? The future, perhaps, is a hopeful one as graduate students report more positive experiences than their predecessors. However, as a colleague recently pointed out, it is also possible that graduate students are too new and have too few experiences in comparison with Latina faculty members. I question if, with time, their responses will fall more in line with those of the veterans of *la lucha*.

CHAPTER 27

FREE AT LAST! NO MORE PERFORMANCE ANXIETIES IN THE ACADEMY 'CAUSE STEPIN FETCHIT HAS LEFT THE BUILDING

Mary-Antoinette Smith

> *Free at last! Free at last! . . . I have a dream that . . . [I] . . . will one day [work in academia and] not be judged by the color of [my] skin but by the content of [my] character.*
>
> Martin Luther King Jr., adapted from
"I Have a Dream" (1963)

> *Stepin Fetchit . . . his is a "mean, hurtful, dirty name," says New York stage director Dr. Bill Lathan. . . . Black to black it is a curse of condemnation, ostracism and betrayal meant to wound and stigmatize, leaving a mark not easily to be erased. For the white, it is a coded way of saying "n——r," all the while safe in the knowledge that he or she has never used the N word.*
>
> Champ Clark, *Shuffling to Ignominy: The Tragedy*
of Stepin Fetchit (2005)

Introduction: Facing Hard Truths and Fostering High Hopes

The following discussion is a long-overdue narrative analysis of the challenges and rewards I have faced as an African American woman pursuing a meaningful and comfortable fit in the academy. It was a struggle to write this chapter, in part, because its anomalous content is peculiar to my personal and professional journey as a black woman in higher education and, in part, because it forced me to reflect back upon situations that either I had convinced myself no longer mattered, or had denied into dormant nonexistence. However reluctant my reminiscent journey, the profound truth I have embraced in the process is that these events did happen, and they do matter, even if since then I have overcome any latent trauma and moved into a more positive outlook about their occurrence. I also have come to terms with the honest appraisal that—even though incidents in my narrative may be characterized as mild when compared with those of my fellow faculty members of color—they have made an indelible mark on the ways that—and the reasons why—I still feel I have to "perform" as a dark-skinned university professor, colleague, and conference presenter.

As the following discussion reveals in greater detail, my testimonial comes from a relatively fortunate African American academic woman, but even though it is embedded within a woven fabric of more challenging and less grace-filled narratives of a wide range of women of color in the academy, I know it is an important and intriguing, bittersweet memoir that begs to be told. Certain parts of my story are not the norm, and my overall success and perspective indicate what is possible, rather than hopelessly grim, for faculty women of color in the academy. Consequently—in spite of the occasional difficulties that have surfaced throughout my journey to professional success in the ivory tower—I maintain a positive and hopeful outlook for myself and other faculty of color in our pursuits of achievements within the academy.

Finally—and perhaps most importantly—I am realistic and sensitive to the reality that my positive perspective is juxtaposed against troubling and pervasive statistics on the possibility that faculty of color, particularly women, can integrate affirmatively, substantially, and successfully into a congenial, scholarly, working environment in the academy. For example, within the past decade, a report titled "The (Un)Changing Face of the Ivy League" cited that minority "women have made little progress in breaking into the faculty ranks of the Ivy League . . . . In 2003 Ivy League campuses hired 433 new professors in tenure-track jobs, but only 14 were black and 8 were Hispanic, and of the overall total only 150 were women. These figures show the slow progress such highly visible universities as Harvard, Yale, and Princeton are making in diversifying their faculty" ("Media Resources," *New York Times*, March 1, 2005).

Given these realities, how can I not be concerned about my fellow faculty women of color, not only on my own campus but on other campuses nationwide as well? There are dark days in the ivory tower when my sensibilities weep for the pain-filled experiences endured by faculty women of color who combat covertly and overtly hostile campus environments that are unwelcoming and downright exclusionary. Some of their narratives are found in this current volume, as well as in comparable works, such as *Black Women in the Academy: Promises and Perils*; *Race, Class and Gender: Black Women in Academia*; *Spirit, Space and Survival: African American Women in (White) Academe*; *The Leaning Ivory Tower: Latino Professors in American Universities*; *From Oppression to Grace: Women of Color and Their Dilemmas within the Academy*; *Faculty of Color: Teaching in Predominantly White Colleges and Universities*; and *Indigenizing the Academy: Transforming Scholarship and Empowering Communities*, among others. The stories of abuse and discontent among faculty of color are riveting, heart-wrenching, and true. They also are dismayingly representative, percentage-wise, of the norm.

Nevertheless, hopeful and positive anecdotes are emerging daily that witness what is possible for faculty women of color in academia as we strive to keep our eyes on the prize of full and congenial integration in higher education. My narrative is one such story, and the catharsis I have experienced while writing this memoir has been invaluable in my evolution as a teacher and scholar. In the end—however labored the revelatory process—I am grateful for this opportunity to help vent the discordant and valorize the victorious academic anecdotes that follow.

Racism Lite, the "They" Philosophy, and Performing for the Professoriate

Although some may consider my academic memoir "racism lite" by comparison to those of other faculty women of color, it is rooted within a framework of the various kinds of performance anxieties that I have experienced throughout my academic career as an African American university student, professor, and scholar. I have had to negotiate and interrogate real and perceived difficulties in my professional interactions with colleagues and students while also trying to eradicate perceptions about my performance as a college professor of color in the classroom.

As is typical in the life of an academic of color, I have weathered my fair share of racist, classist, sexist, and misogynistic hardships and pitfalls along my journeying through higher education. From my undergraduate days as an English literature major to my time as a graduate student who earned a master's degree in Victorian literature before leaving academia for a career in public relations and advertising because of parental pressures, I have experienced and overcome trials and tribulations that threatened my academic achievements. I am a firm believer that someone has to lead the way, and—even though it was not my conscious intent at the time—I realize in retrospect that when I made the choice to leave a lucrative career in the business world to pursue my doctorate in eighteenth-century literature, I was on the road to becoming a leader as a faculty woman of color.

In the mid-1970s, I was one of very few African Americans to pursue English literature as a major, and even though my parents were fearful that I ultimately would be unemployable, reading, writing, researching, and the ideal of teaching were like life's breath for me, so I stuck with my selected major. I was fortunate that my undergraduate professors at the University of Southern California (USC) were astute and aware of my earnest interest in English literary studies, and one of them was instrumental in arranging for me to complete my BA during a senior year abroad at St. Mary's University College at the University of London. This experience proved to be an extraordinary formative educational and cultural opportunity for me as a black student, and it spawned my desire to return to the United States to earn my master's degree in Victorian literature from Loyola Marymount University. Completely anxiety-ridden by where I seemed to be misdirecting my career goals, my parents convinced me to abandon my dreams of becoming an English professor and find a well-paying job in the business world, and that is how I ended up working for eight years in public relations and advertising.

I managed to maintain my dignity and a moderate level of success in the business world, but it was not enough to sustain me. I began to act out of character by pretending to be a happy and well-paid real-world professional when, in fact, I was quite miserable. Acting this role for superiors at work and my parents in private was unnatural for me and ultimately gave birth to the first kind of performance anxiety that began to pepper my career life. The strain took its toll and manifested itself in challenging work and personal complications that led me to reevaluate my career choices, options, and desires.

Leaving public relations and advertising was not a difficult decision for me, but I had a hard time explaining my choice to my nay-saying parents. They could not understand why I would abandon a corporate career with an attractive salary for the risky prospect of earning a PhD in a discipline with few guarantees for an African American woman. I explained to them that I was not happy in the fast-paced business world, and for eight long years, I had been nurturing a deep longing to be a college professor. Further incentive came with a fortuitous invitation from a former professor, who knew of my discontent, to return to USC to earn my doctorate. Needless to say, I jumped at this opportunity. Soon thereafter, however, I began to learn that all would not be bliss, for the challenges in being a person of color who pursues a career from undergraduate to graduate student to joining the professoriate in the ivory tower are controversial and complex.

Surprisingly, the first challenge came from off campus, rather than on, and it was from my father, who was inordinately nervous and ambivalent about his thirty-something daughter being a doctoral candidate—by invitation no less! His skeptical queries included, "Why did 'they' ask you to come back to USC? Why would you want to do this? What do 'they' want from you? What future can you possibly have as a black college professor? Don't you know that 'they' will never let you do this?"

I was all too familiar with my father's "they" philosophy, although I never actually knew who they were. They seemed to be perfectly real to him, but I never saw them. So they remained the nameless, nebulous, yet powerful, members of the dominant white American culture that he was convinced took concerted efforts to put obstructions in the way of progressive and talented blacks all across this country. My father's life was ruled by the "theys" in ways that mine was not. Consequently, I developed a lifelong habit of choosing to do what I wanted to do, led largely by a sure vision of what I was put on earth to accomplish, rather than being directed by the "theys" who might actually be very real but had little power over my goals. In spite of my father's nay-saying, I reentered the ivory tower as a doctoral candidate, and, to his surprise, the "theys" offered me full tuition remission as a complement to a graduate student teaching assistantship. Although this remuneration was substantially less than my professional salary, it was sufficient to cover my rent, utilities, other monthly bills, and more.

During my six years as a grad student at USC, my father watched my progress, and he seemed particularly challenged by my lively love of teaching in my Freshman Writing 101 and 102 courses. His apprehensions led to a second kind of performance anxiety that began to surface in two ways. First, I performed well as a knowledgeable and engaging teaching assistant, and my students loved my courses. I began to emerge as a natural-born teacher, one who was content and confident in her profession. Second, I performed excitedly for my father, with whom I frequently shared my pedagogical strategies and successes in getting students actively involved in the enjoyment to be found in writing college compositions. I also worked with them in elevating their academic discussions to the college level in fun and informative ways. I was aware at the time that there were elements of performance in what I was doing, but I also knew from my educational experience that my best teachers and professors were those who acted and performed in interesting and innovative ways. So I easily adopted a very effective—perhaps somewhat postured—teaching style that proved very successful.

Doubtful as ever, my father listened to my delightful anecdotes about my classroom successes with cynical reserve, and he was absolutely flabbergasted that I received the Outstanding Graduate Teaching Award several years in a row. This was an extraordinarily affirming testament to my abilities as an instructor, particularly given my status as the lone African American graduate student in USC's Department of English at the time. I simply could not understand why my father could not seem to endorse and validate my developing success as a college-level instructor. Clarity came to me unexpectedly, however, when my mother inadvertently revealed that my father was afraid that—instead of me actually being a gifted and talented professor-in-training for entering my perfect-fit profession—I was perceived as a Stepin Fetchit–type figure who was earning my success through clowning and buffoonery. With illumination came more explicit stories from my father's past, which revealed his core concerns about any African American actions that could be misconstrued as shucking and jiving. To have his daughter associated with such attitudes was fearful and shameful for him, and even though this concept was completely foreign to me since I had no such performance anxieties, they were very raw and vivid to my father.

At first I was offended that my father held these beliefs or at least that he could not see the difference between his perceptions of what had once been an authentic step 'n' fetchit phenomenon that was truly demeaning to blacks and what was actually occurring with my success as a college teacher. Over time I became more forgiving once I realized that his viewpoint came from something deeply rooted in his personal background as a black man who had endured far more overt racism during his lifetime than I had. He and my mother, in fact, had devised a plan to protect their children from experiencing as much direct racism as they could. They also structured our upbringing so that we had every advantage they could provide to ensure our success as people of color in the United States. Paradoxically—and in spite of his anxieties about my performance as a graduate student and teaching assistant—my doctoral experience was precisely what my father would have hoped for me in theory, but he was deeply troubled and mistrustful of it in practice. While his concerns never had the power to steer me off course in my goals, they did cause me to develop peripheral performance anxieties that I would not likely have had to overcome if he had not been so suspicious of my graduate student experience.

While many doctoral programs can be fraught with difficulties and pitfalls, I can honestly say that mine was a comparatively painless—though not effortless—experience. There were challenges along the way, but periodic hardships never diverted me from successfully completing my doctoral program. On occasion—as the lone black graduate student in the department—I had to contend with racist and competitive graduate student peers. There were also isolated incidents with professors, such as the Victorianist who believed I did not have graduate-level potential (which is why I ultimately chose eighteenth-century literature as my doctoral-research area), as well as an anomalous, but revealing, episode where one of the graduate professors mentioned to me in passing one day, "You know, Mary-Antoinette, I am really sorry for all of the doors that have been closed to you during your doctoral process." Puzzled, I replied, "What are you talking about? No doors have been closed to me." To which he proclaimed, "Oh, yes, they have. I've been in faculty meetings, in fact, where doors have been deliberately closed on you." Aghast, I said, "What doors have been closed? I never knew anything about them!" And he said, "Well, that's because the amazing thing about you is that when a door is closed on you over here, you have the remarkable ability to have already opened a door for yourself somewhere else . . . "

At first I was angry about this revelation—in addition to being somewhat resentful of the messenger—but I soon came to treasure the information that he had imparted. What a testament to a young black woman's tenacity and capabilities to be able to work her way through a doctoral program with relative comfort and ease in spite of pitfalls along her way about which she is utterly unaware!

When I mentioned this incident to my dubious they-philosophy-adhering father, he came close to an "I told you so" moment until I reassured him that this was an isolated incident and in no way threatened to obstruct me from pursuing my goal. My father remained apprehensive, but I think he started moving toward a moderate appreciation of the way I could perform tasks in covert Machiavellian ways that might actually facilitate my getting a doctorate, rather than reflecting the negative step 'n' fetchit, shucking-and-jiving behaviors that he had originally suspected might underlie academic careers. And—as it turned out—he need not have worried because I was always very much in command of my situation, and, ultimately, the "theys" never materialized to prohibit me from becoming Dr. Mary-Antoinette Smith. Nor did "they" obstruct me from being hired directly into a tenure-track position as an assistant professor in the Department of English at Seattle University (SU) in the fall of 1994.

Still somewhat stunned at the ease with which my professional academic career seemed to be progressing, my father persisted in retaining his skeptical "they" philosophy for my future in the ivory tower. He next believed that they would use me for six to seven years before denying me tenure, and then I would be out of SU in a flash and probably unemployable since I would be in my early forties with no remaining career options. To lend credence to my father's concerns—at least about not being accepted on a predominantly white college campus—I have to admit that the initial adjustment was strained in spite of my good-natured outlook. And even though, overall, I had a reasonably congenial reception from faculty colleagues and administrators at SU, it is common for faculty of color to encounter cool receptions when they come to campus.

The actual degree to which my fellow faculty members of color have been discomforted on our campus became evident when I led a Justice Faculty Fellows Seminar titled Having a Say and Leading the Way: Narratives of Distress and Visions for Success from Faculty of Color in the Academy, which I advertised as follows:

> The experience of immigrants coming to America for all that it represents in terms of the "land of opportunity" serves as a useful metaphor for the challenging and disorienting experience that faculty members of color often undergo as new arrivals onto the "landscape of academic opportunity" at universities across the US and, most importantly, at Seattle University. What makes the arrival of faculty of color onto the academic scene akin to the "immigrant" experience is that the terrain of the ivory tower frequently is uncharted by forerunner academics of color who have paved the way in integrating the hallowed halls of traditionally Anglo academe. Whether one is Native-American, African-American, Latino/a, Chinese-American, Japanese-American, of another Asian-American culture, or an ethnic academic from abroad, the transitional commonalities are often

parallel, and they can be fraught with difficulties that are rarely understood or even noticed by the dominant academic culture.

In addition to the intellectual and emotional traumas of this metaphorical, faculty of color, "immigrant" experience onto college campuses, there is a psychic one that reflects the "double consciousness" that W. E. B. DuBois describes in *The Souls of Black Folk*, particularly when adapted as follows:

> [The faculty member of color] is gifted with second-sight in this American [university] world—a world which yields [her/]him no true self-consciousness, but only lets [her/]him see [herself/]himself through the revelation of the other world. It is a peculiar sensation, this double-consciousness, this sense of always looking at one's self through the eyes of others, of measuring one's soul by the tape of a world that looks on in amused contempt and pity. One ever feels [her/]his two-ness—an American [academic], a [faculty member of color]; two souls, two thoughts, two unreconciled strivings; two warring ideals in one [ethnic-other] body, whose dogged strength alone keeps it from being torn asunder ([1903] 2007, 8).

Dr. Ana M. Martínez Alemán of Boston College wrote a statement with a similar double-consciousness slant describing her plight as an emergent Latina academic: "I am struck by my lived contradiction: To be a professor is to be an Anglo; to be a Latina is not to be an Anglo. So how can I be both a Latina and a professor? To be a Latina professor, I conclude, means to be unlike and like me. *Que locura!* What madness! . . . As Latina professors, we are newcomers to a world defined and controlled by discourses that do not address our realities, that do not affirm our intellectual contributions, that do not seriously examine our worlds. Can I be both Latina and professor without compromise?" (1995, 74) In both statements, the gender and ethnicity of the authors can be interchanged with female and male academics from a diverse range of cultural and racial backgrounds: Native American, African American, Chinese American, Japanese American, Latino, LGBTQ, and others, while the self-doubting queries: "Am I welcome in this bastion of traditional Anglo values, and will I survive this daunting challenge?" and the perpetually perplexing quandaries: "Where/how do I fit into this academic schemata as a proud, productive, and contributing faculty member of color (or difference)?" are pervasively the same.

As previously stated, my entry as a faculty woman of color into our SU community was not as strained as that of many of my fellow colleagues of color, but I still have a huge awareness of and sensitivity for the challenges they face on a day-to-day basis, and I have become an increasingly outspoken advocate on their behalf. I also treasure the fact that—although my father had deep concerns about my tenure-track process—the "theys" did not deny my tenure or concurrent promotion to associate professor. The only downside to this uplifting news that came in spring 2000 is that my father had died two years earlier, so he never knew I had succeeded in making my academic career dreams come true. I believe, now, that it might have been the one occurrence that caused him to abandon his "they" philosophy and, possibly, even begin to believe that—although there may be malignant "theys" in the world—there are also benign ones who are able to look beyond race, class, and gender to true persons and innate talents and then support those individuals in becoming their best selves and achieving their desired goals.

Emergent Performance Anxieties in the Classroom

When I began teaching at SU, I was eager to claim my career as an African American teacher and scholar of eighteenth- and nineteenth-century British literature. Though I may have been an anomaly in my choice of literary and cultural time periods, I was exactly what my department had been looking for in their efforts to become more ethnically diverse. I was also a perfect fit in reflecting the goals of our Jesuit mission, particularly with my religious background as a cradle and actively practicing Catholic. At the time, I could not have been happier with my choice to make SU my academic home community, and I have never once regretted my decision to join our Department of English faculty.

Over the past fifteen years, admittedly, my integration into the SU academic setting has been far less challenging than some of the rockier roads traveled by fellow faculty members of color, both at SU and at colleges and universities throughout the United States. So I won't promote the illusion that there have not been difficulties along the way. However, I now offer several anecdotes that indicate the ways that my career as a professor has been peppered with both overt and covert racist undertones that are all too common for faculty members of color.

For the most part, I have always been congenially received on SU's campus—at least by those who recognize me as a professor. There are days, however, when the general campus population perceives me as either a nontraditional coed or a department administrative assistant. This is why I insist that my students call me Dr. Smith, both in the classroom and, most especially, outside. And believe me, there is the occasional astonished whiplash/gasp from overhearers and onlookers across campus when I encounter one of my students out in the quad or in a building hallway, and that person greets me as Dr. Smith. Will there ever come a time when folks are not surprised to learn that there are African American, Native American, Latino/a, Japanese American, Chinese American, and a huge range more of people of color who are college and university professors? And will there ever come a time when I can rest from wearing the proverbial mask so splendidly described by Paul Laurence Dunbar in "We Wear the Mask"?

We wear the mask that grins and lies,
It hides our cheeks and shades our eyes,—
This debt we pay to human guile;
With torn and bleeding hearts we smile,
And mouth with myriad subtleties.

Why should the world be over-wise,
In counting all our tears and sighs?
Nay, let them only see us, while
We wear the mask!

We smile, but, O great Christ, our cries
To thee from tortured souls arise.
We sing, but oh the clay is vile
Beneath our feet, and long the mile;
But let the world dream otherwise,
We wear the mask! ([1896] 1993, 71)

I have been wearing this mask since day one of entering my first class at SU back in 1994. I was very excited to begin teaching that fall quarter, particularly because I enjoy teaching freshmen. At SU we have core curriculum classes upon which we structure our students' educational formation, as well as their development as whole persons committed to achieving equity and diversity for a just and humane world. As a faculty member of color, I take this aim seriously because I have an affinity for shaping young minds from the moment they enter the halls of higher education. Syllabi for my Freshman English 110 and my Masterpieces of Literature 120 courses have always been a pedagogical joy to develop, and the classes are rewarding to teach. This is not always, true, however, with my English major courses, which tend to be more challenging, not because of the content, but rather because students often have a difficult time reconciling their notions of what an English professor looks like with what I look like, i.e., black female teaching canonical British literature of the eighteenth and nineteenth century, rather than black female teaching African American literature and/or ethnic studies.

Over the years, such responses thankfully have become attenuated, particularly as my presence on campus has become better known, but for the first several years, I had to learn to overlook the coolness I experienced from English majors, as well as their lower student evaluations of my classes. This is why I elected to earn tenure on the strength of the easy rapport I was able to establish with my non-English major freshmen-core students, who were more open and accepting of my role as a learned and competent professor of composition and literary analysis. And they also gave me very high student evaluations. So all was bliss with teaching first-year students, at least for the most part.

There came a time, however, when my ivory-tower, rose-colored glasses no longer concealed subliminal undercurrents that were pervading even my freshman classrooms, and layers of denial began to deconstruct into crystal clarity that pervasive elements of cognitive and visual dissonance were working while I taught at the helm of my classes—even with my seemingly more receptive and accepting freshmen. Illumination dawned soon after I gave an explication quiz in a Masterpieces of Literature class during spring quarter of my first year at SU. The poem was William Blake's "The Chimney Sweeper" (1789):

> When my mother died, I was very young,
> And my father sold me while yet my tongue
> Could scarcely cry 'weep! 'weep! 'weep! 'weep!
> So your chimneys I sweep, and in soot I sleep.
>
> There's little Tom Dacre, who cried when his head
> That curled like a lamb's back was shaved: so I said,
> "Hush, Tom! never mind it, for when your head's bare,
> You know that the soot cannot spoil your white hair."
>
> And so he was quiet; and that very night,
> As Tom was a-sleeping, he had such a sight,—
> That thousands of sweepers, Dick, Joe, Ned, and Jack,
> Were all of them locked up in coffins of black.
>
> And by came an angel who had a bright key,
> And he opened the coffins and set them all free;

Then down a green plain leaping, laughing, they run,
And wash in a river, and shine in the sun.

Then naked and white, all their bags left behind,
They rise upon clouds and sport in the wind;
And the angel told Tom, if he'd be a good boy,
He'd have God for his father, and never want joy.

And so Tom awoke; and we rose in the dark,
And got with our bags and our brushes to work.
Though the morning was cold, Tom was happy and warm;
So if all do their duty, they need not fear harm. (2002, 10)

This poem is a straightforward one about exploitative child labor in late-eighteenth-century England, and I was certain my students would have no problems passing the quiz by executing well-crafted line-by-line analyses. That evening I was struck dumb, however, to discover that nearly 75 percent of the students had completely misread the poem. Their explications described a sad situation where a black father had sold his child into slavery, and the child's life ended up in total misery. Hope was offered the child, though, in the form of sage advice from the speaker, who encouraged "little Tom Dacre" not to cry and coaxed him into slumber, during which Tom dreamed of an angel who encouraged him to look to the future rewards of heaven as a means of blocking out the horror of his enslavement. Tom awakened to a new vision for his future and faced his duties as a slave filled with hope, tossing fear to the wind. My mouth agape, I read explication after explication using the same misguided analysis.

Perplexed at the discrepancy between the content of the poem and the distortions present in the students' papers, I sat there utterly baffled, believing myself to be a complete failure as a teacher. The next class period I decided to confront this problematic situation head-on, and began class with a probing query of my students about their analyses of "The Chimney Sweeper." I mentioned that their quizzes revealed "slight" misreadings of the poem, and most of them looked as perplexed as I had the evening before while marking their papers. What was interesting about the interplay between me and the students was the earnestness with which we presented our interpretations of Blake's poem, and my students taught me a lot that day.

Most of them had surmised that since the poem was published in 1789 and mentioned a father selling a child that, of course, it related to Negro slavery; and since the poem intriguingly contrasts black and white and light and dark imagery, that was further evidence that slavery was the theme of the poem. Also—as is well known—it is common to steer all victims of abuse and oppression toward heavenly visions and promises for improved circumstances in the afterlife as a means of providing hope for better times to come. As we continued to discuss their "perceptive" analyses of the poem, I was poised to ferret out elements of racism in their comments but found none. What I discovered, instead, was eagerness on their part for me to answer the question, "If we aren't accurate in our explications, then WHAT IS the poem really about?" I then explained the historical period, context, and location of the poem (late eighteenth century, child labor/exploitation, England). It began to dawn on my thunderstruck students that the poem was not set in America, nor was it about Negro slavery.

I carefully went through the poem line by line, stanza by stanza, and students were well satisfied with the "final analysis" and pleased with their newly acquired "expertise" in poetry explication (at least until the next poem). I was pleased, too, with their receptive interest in learning the art of literary explication and analysis. This situation served as an excellent teachable moment in a safe, nurturing classroom environment, but I was not done with seeking the cause of the original discrepancy regarding the theme and content of the poem we had so successfully managed to understand and analyze. I wanted to ask my students directly, "What in the world made you go so far astray in your perception of what this poem is about?" But I chose not to do so. I decided, instead, to work it through for myself.

Fortunately, within a week, I attended a session at a conference on diversity at the Seattle Convention Center during which some remarks by Dr. Tanya Pettiford-Wates, formerly of Seattle Central Community College, helped shed light on this situation. Her paper commented on the concepts of cognitive and visual dissonance in the faculty member of color's classroom, and I started to understand why my students had mistakenly thought "The Chimney Sweeper" was about Negro slavery in America. Dr. Pettiford-Wates explained that *cognitive dissonance* is a psychological conflict resulting from incongruous beliefs and attitudes held simultaneously, so students—when they see a faculty member of color at the head of the classroom—find all of their preconceived notions interacting with what they observe in the professor's teaching style and subject matter. This is when *visual dissonance,* defined as a lack of agreement or an inconsistency among the beliefs you hold or between your actions and your beliefs, kicks in. As she explained these two concepts through her personal and professional anecdotes as a faculty woman of color, I began to compare her experiences in the classroom with my own, and I was suddenly illuminated about my "The Chimney Sweeper" explication assignment.

The students in my class saw a black woman who was teaching them how to analyze a variety of literary works from several genres, including poetry, short stories, novels, and drama. Through syllogistic reasoning, I ultimately deduced that—although my Masterpieces of Literature syllabus focused largely on canonical works, my students' assumption, based on cognitive and visual dissonance, was that since their teacher was black, then the literature she was teaching must be black literature; therefore, William Blake's "The Chimney Sweeper" was, of course, about Negro slavery. Rather than presume that this situation emanated from my students being innately racist, I convinced myself that the culprits were cognitive and visual dissonance and the students were not responsible for the dominant-culture indoctrination with which they had been reared. This viewpoint reaffirmed my good relationship with my freshman-level students, and my course evaluations remained high in those courses, so it was not difficult to maintain a positive outlook regarding the cause of a subtly pervasive disconnect between me and my students in general.

It took some time, in fact, for me to realize the degree to which another kind of performance anxiety was surfacing for me in the classroom. I began to become increasingly more concerned about consciously performing to maintain my acceptably high student evaluations and what the cost might be to my self-esteem and fulfilling my responsibilities as a teacher. Aside from the time and effort involved, I found myself concentrating more on earning high evaluations and less on the pedagogical goals of my courses. This behavior stemmed from a need to compete with my white faculty colleagues, whose course evaluations continually raised the bar, even though they did not seem to have to work as hard to earn them. This was a frustrating twist along my professional career path since I had not encountered these difficulties at USC; they were becoming more pervasive at SU, and it seemed that I was losing ground, rather than advancing.

Conclusion: From Performance Anxiety to Performance Empowerment

To process and understand what was occurring, ultimately I concluded that it had to do with regional and institutional differences rooted in the type and caliber of students in the Pacific Northwest versus Southern California, and an urban-teaching versus urban-research university. Also the reality was that at USC I was not as much of an institutional anomaly as I turned out to be at SU. Perhaps this is because I was a fully acculturated, born-and-reared Los Angeleno back home in California, whereas in Seattle I am a nonnative who still has not completely understood, adopted, and adapted to the cultural codes and mores of the less ethnically diverse and individual-affirming Pacific Northwest. So, while I believe that in some cases—perhaps in the better part of them—embedded racism and sexism are at the root of the problem, I also think other factors are involved as well.

What I can say for certain, in conclusion, is that over the course of my sixteen years at SU, I have fought covertly and competitively to set myself back on the road to success as a professor and scholar. It took some time, but I have recovered my stride and assumed visible roles as a faculty member of color who is an excellent educator, a collegial colleague, the director of women studies, and more. Presently I find that with increasing promise, I am becoming a better-respected black woman academic and campus presence, but I also understand realistically that my status will never be the same as that of my white academic colleagues. On occasion—during dark days in the academy and the classroom—my performance anxieties revisit me but never to the degree that they once did; they cannot alter my perception of my value as a faculty woman in higher education.

Overall, I would say that at this stage of my academic career, I am flourishing and very much in command of all areas of my career responsibilities. It has been a long time coming, but now I have moved permanently from those perpetual and pervasive performance anxieties to a level of performance empowerment in all areas of the academy, including the classroom, the conference room, and the conference circuit. My long-range hope is to be a source of inspiration to future scholars of color who may worry that the intellectual talents and abilities they bring to higher education as students and potential leaders in the professoriate will neither be welcome nor cultivated. What I say to them is that we need you here as representatives of the virtues of faculty members of color in the ivory tower, and however fearsome or difficult the challenges, I believe in Eleanor Roosevelt's wise observation in "You Learn by Living: Eleven Keys for a More Successful Life" that "You gain strength, courage, and confidence by every experience in which you really stop to look fear in the face . . . You must do the thing you think you cannot do" (2009, 29).

Therefore, do not despair at any point along the journey to achieving your academic goals as persons of color; and if at any point, you should find yourselves concerned—as I have been—with performance anxieties that distort your image of yourself as a important contributor to the academy, do not perform like Stepin Fetchit because he has at last left the building. Perform, rather, in the spirit of Martin Luther King Jr.'s credo of being "free at last" and feeling fully liberated to perform according to your best intellectual and professional talents as faculty members of color in the academy.

CHAPTER 28

AFRICAN AMERICAN WOMEN IN THE ACADEMY

Quelling the Myth of Presumed Incompetence

Sherri L. Wallace, Sharon E. Moore,
Linda L. Wilson, and Brenda G. Hart

Introduction

African Americans have consistently been at the heart of education.[1] Upon emancipation from human bondage, Reconstruction governments led by African American legislators instituted free public schools for all citizens along with other forms of democratic government and social legislation. In fact, for many years, education was the only respectable profession that was open to African Americans before and after emancipation (McKay 1997). Many black educators played prominent roles in the struggle for social justice for not only African Americans but America as a whole. Similar to these early pioneers, African American women continue the struggle for racial enrichment and advancement through higher education.

African American female faculty constitute a numerical minority at institutions of higher learning. Their presence on these campuses is critical, however: they serve as mentors and role models for colleagues and students, particularly those who share

---

1   We honor the late Dr. Veronica D. Hinton-Hudson, who contributed to early versions of this chapter. She was an assistant professor in computer information systems in the College of Business at the University of Louisville in Kentucky. She earned her PhD in industrial engineering at the J.B. Speed School of Engineering at the University of Louisville in 2002. She received her MSISyE and CIMS certificate in industrial engineering from the Georgia Institute of Technology in 1991 and her BSIE from Purdue University in 1982, where she was an avid supporter of the Purdue University Minority Engineering Program and the Purdue chapter of the National Society of Black Engineers. Her research interests were statistical analysis; mathematical modeling of systems; mentoring; and the design, implementation, and improvement of precollege programs for underrepresented students in engineering. She published coauthored, refereed articles in a variety of research journals. She passed away on February 27, 2011.

the same characteristics; they dispel untruths and false characterizations held by students, especially those who have had little experience with cultural diversity; and they challenge the negative and low expectations of students, staff, colleagues, and administrators, who may question their competence. Their overall experiences can be characterized as both positive and exigent opportunities, manifested in a variety of ways and producing myriad consequences. Often these women—not being privy to mentoring, informal networks, and information—work in isolation which can have detrimental effects on morale and may cause them to leave the academy altogether (Fries-Britt and Kelly 2005; Alex-Assensoh et al. 2005; Jayakumar et al. 2009). In addition, these women are subject to both racial and gender devaluation (Alexander and Moore 2008; Fries-Britt and Kelly 2005), a process where the status and power of an authoritative position are downplayed when a woman holds it and penalized for those agitating for change (Monroe et al. 2008, 216).

The purpose of this chapter is to use personal narratives, situated within the context of extant literature, as an analytical framework to provide coping strategies for women to conquer the presumption of incompetence. Rather than a definitive study, this chapter seeks to heighten awareness of African American women who are surviving and thriving in the academy. Emerging themes are identified and discussed. This work entails not so much a shift as a widening of the gender/racial equity debates to incorporate and understand the impact and uniqueness of African American women in higher education.

African American Women in Academia: A Review

African American women faculty share some common characteristics. Often these women earn doctorates at rates higher than their African American male counterparts but still tend to be older than the average student and take longer to obtain their degrees. Also they are usually single and have never married, raising children as single parents, and have parents with limited education. They are most likely to earn their doctorates in education, the social sciences, and the professions (Moses 1997). Nevertheless, African American women employed in higher education have to spend a good deal of their time and creative energy planning for and countering the expectations others hold for them. Thus, the intersections of race, gender, and sometimes class are always present as multiple levels of oppression that can and do inhibit their emotional, psychological, physical, legal, social, and even spiritual well-being (Alexander and Moore 2008) as they struggle to balance teaching, research/publishing, and community service obligations for promotion and tenure.

We know that race- and gender-based discrimination—whether overt, subtle, or institutional—continue to permeate the academy. Despite decades of efforts on the part of institutions of higher education to diversify their faculties, men and women from historically marginalized groups continue to face challenges and difficulties because they are unlike their majority counterparts—white males. In a recent unpublished report titled the "Task Force on Political Science for the 21st Century" (Fraga, Givens, and Pinderhughes 2011), the authors aptly summarized the current state of women faculty of color on issues ranging from campus climate to professional expectations and obligations.

African American women faculty often work in isolation at their institutions. In a recent national study of campus climate, retention, and satisfaction, Jayakumar et al. (2009) found that 75 percent of faculty of underrepresented backgrounds described their campus climates as moderate to highly negative, and low job satisfaction and an increased desire to leave the academy were associated with perceptions of high racial hostility on campus. Interestingly, these authors also noted that institutions where these faculty members perceived hostility was highest also had the largest retention rates for white/Caucasian faculty (Jayakumar, Howard, Allen and Han 2009).

These feelings of isolation and perceptions of hostility by African American women faculty are often associated with research interests as well. When underrepresented faculty study issues of race/ethnicity, gender, or poverty, they realize that their work may be undervalued and their chances at promotion and tenure smaller because their research may be construed as too narrow (Fraga, Givens, and Pinderhughes 2011). In fact, Thomas and Hollenshead (2001) report that women faculty of color, in particular, are most likely to feel scrutinized by their colleagues and report great concerns that their research is not valued.

Because research interests are often associated with what you teach, studies have also shown that faculty of color, especially African American women, can face unique obstacles in the classroom. Thomas and Hollenshead (2001) observed that these faculty are more likely to face challenges to their authority in the classroom on subject matter. In addition, several studies have shown that they must be especially careful about tone of voice, facial expressions, body language, and dress in the classroom because these choices can have direct consequences on their perceived level of competence, which also can negatively impact student evaluations (hooks 1981; Collins 2001; Weitz and Gordon 1993; Gregory 2001; Jackson and Crawley 2003).

Pyke's discipline-focused study found that that women, especially women of color, "perform a disproportionate share of care labor and 'institutional housekeeping,'" and such labor is "not optional, nonessential, unskilled labor; rather, it is vital to the day to day and long term operation of the university" (2010, 86–87). These numerous service obligations of African American women faculty are a barrier to successful career advancement in the academy. For example, African American women—like other faculty from underrepresented backgrounds—are often expected to mentor students from similar backgrounds, which can contribute to their stereotypical perception as nurturing, maternal figures rather than rigorous academics (Fraga, Givens, and Pinderhughes 2011). Rockquemore and Laszloffy (2008) argue that faculty of color often pay a cultural or race tax when they are asked to serve on committees largely because of their race, ethnicity, and/or gender. This not only slows progress toward promotion and tenure but can lead to feelings of tokenism, based upon signals that the primary reason they were asked was because of their background, instead of competence or expertise (Fraga, Givens, and Pinderhughes 2011).

Learning to balance research, teaching, and service obligations is also related to mentoring, which is often cited in the literature of higher education as one of the few common characteristics of a successful career, particularly for faculty of color and women (Van Emmerick 2004; Alex-Assensoh et al. 2005; Michelson 2006; Sorcinelli and Yun 2007; Yun and Sorcinelli 2008; Monroe et al. 2008; Jayakumar et al. 2009). Mentoring can be formal or informal. Monroe et al. define formal or institutional mentoring as "formal structures, universally defined goals, and relationships developed with some form of assistance or intervention from the organization, which carries more egalitarian implications," whereas informal mentoring "evokes . . . the image of an unskilled junior who requires the protection and assistance of a more professional colleague" (2008, 224). Demonstrated benefits to those mentored include the development of skills and intellectual abilities; engagement in meaningful, substantive tasks; entry into the world of career advancement opportunities; and access to advice, encouragement, and feedback (Sorcinelli and Yun 2007). Two studies report that faculty of color and women experience a number of significant challenges that are roadblocks to productivity and career advancement, such as getting oriented to the institution and its culture; getting access to informal networks and information, monetary resources, and collegial feedback in research and teaching endeavors; managing expectations for performance, particularly the tenure process; finding collegiality; and creating a balance between professional roles and family life (Sorcinelli and Yun 2007; Yun and Sorcinelli 2008).

In surveying gender equity issues and the reasons for so few female faculty, Monroe et al. (2008) found in their study "Gender Equality in Academia" that statistical research using employment and salary figures to measure gender discrimination suggests that academia is no different from the rest of society. It bears repeating that even though both men and women are hired at roughly the same rates in academia, generally men continue to outnumber women in academic positions in all types of higher education institutions by a ratio of at least two to one (National Center for Education 2006). This disparity is most prevalent in institutions that are comprehensive, doctorate-granting, and research-intensive (Nelson 2004). However, while graduate enrollment at degree-conferring institutions has increased to more than 50 percent, women account for only 44–45 percent of the recent doctorates awarded, 38 percent of full time faculty in all institutions of higher education, and slightly more than 15 percent of the tenured and tenure-track faculty in top departments (Monroe et al. 2008, 216).

US Department of Education statistics compiled for the fall of 2005 (see table 1) show that African American (non-Hispanic) women represent 2.7 percent (18,429) of the total (675,624) full-time teaching faculty employed by all institutions of higher education. Contrast this with 2.7 percent African American female representation to 31.7 percent (214,215) for white women and 46 percent (313,685) for white men. These race/ethnic- and gender-targeted data are disaggregated further by academic ranks, such as full professor, associate professor, and assistant professor, as well as tenure- and nontenure-track positions. The comparisons indicate that African American women are underrepresented at specific academic ranks as well. Full professors constitute 24 percent (165,697) of the total (675,624) tenured, full-time faculty in academe as of fall 2005; in this time period, African American women represent 1.2 percent (1,986) of the total tenured, full-time professors (165,697), while white women account for 22.2 percent (36,808) and white men make up 65.8 percent (109,128)—a decline of 1 percent since fall 2003.

Additionally, African American women constitute 2.5 percent (3,455) of the total tenured, full-time associate positions and 3.5 percent (5,438) of the total tenure-track, full-time assistant positions, with the largest concentration of 3.7 percent (7,550) in lower, nontenure-track positions. This differs significantly from white women, who hold 32.8 percent (44,124) of the tenured, full-time associate positions, 34.9 percent (54,226) of the tenure-track, full-time assistant positions, and 38.9 percent (79, 057) of the lower, nontenure-track positions. Interestingly enough, both African American and white women have the same distribution: faculty are

Table 1: Comparison of Academic Faculty by Rank, Sex, and Racial/Ethnic Characteristics, Fall 2005

	Total	U.S. citizens and resident aliens			
		Black women	White women	White men	Other[1]
Total full-time faculty	675,624	18,429	214,215	313,685	112,266
Total percentages*	97.45%	2.72%	31.70%	46.42%	16.61%
By rank					
Full professor	165,697	1,986	36,808	109,128	17,772
Percentages*	99.92%	1.19%	22.21%	65.8%	10.72%
Associate professor	134,497	3,455	44,124	68,383	18,535
Percentages*	99.98%	2.56%	32.80%	50.84%	13.78%
Assistant professor	155,230	5,438	54,226	60,244	35,322
Percentages*	99.98%	3.50%	34.93%	38.80%	22.75%
All other ranks[2]	203,174	7,550	79,057	75,930	40,637
Total percentages*	99.99%	3.71%	38.91%	37.37%	20.0%

SOURCE: U.S. Department of Education, National Center for Education Statistics, 2005 Integrated Postsecondary Education Data System (IPEDS) (2006).

* Percentages do not add to 100.

1 This category includes Black males, Native American, Asian (American), Latino/a (American), and other racial/ethnic groups, both male and female.

2 This category includes instructor, lecturer, and other unknown ranks.

concentrated heavily in the lower, nontenure-track ranks, as revealed in the subsequent study by Monroe et al. (2008). White men hold the lion's share of tenured, full-time positions, with a larger concentration in the higher ranks at 50.8 percent (68,383) for tenured, full time associate positions, 38.8 percent (60,244) for tenure-track, full-time assistant positions, and less concentration of 37.4 percent (75,930) in the lower, nontenure-track ranks.

If you compare the percentage of African American and white women who are full professors with white men, gender inequities explain why there is such a significant difference. Some evidence suggests a generational effect. Professors holding doctorates for less than ten years match the gender distribution in employment (predominantly male) while those who have had their doctorates for more than ten years are almost all male (Monroe et al. 2008, 217). These series of studies have documented disparities in male and female wages, career-path decisions related to family (marriage and children), scholarly achievements, and perceptions of the job environment as common reasons for gender inequity and fewer female faculty (Monroe et al. 2008; Monroe and Chiu 2010).

More importantly, Monroe and Chiu (2010) reported that gender discrimination is certainly still occurring and the theory that gender inequality is a result of insufficient numbers of women in the hiring pool is not the case. All these studies conclude that merely increasing the pool of qualified women has not led to women rising to the top in academia. Women still find themselves in lower-paying jobs and continue to earn less than men in comparable positions (Monroe et al. 2008; Monroe and Chiu 2010). In addition, when women faculty are separated (i.e., African American and white women), research suggests that other factors, such as race privilege historically rooted in racial discrimination and prevailing attitudes regarding the social-class status of African Americans, may further explain these inequities within the academy.

Race- and gender-based disparities are still prominent in institutions that are considered less prestigious (e.g., K–12 schools, two-year colleges, and technical schools), where women outnumber men. The downside is that these institutions tend to pay lower salaries. Although academia is slightly more equitable than society in general, the average salary for female faculty is roughly 80 percent of that of their male counterparts, as opposed to 76 percent for society as a whole (National Center for Education 2006). Overall "women are still underrepresented in almost all disciplines, and men are more likely than women to hold tenure-track positions, be promoted to tenure, achieve full professorship, and be paid more than women of equal rank" (Monroe et al. 2008, 217).

However, with the exception of historically black colleges and universities (HBCUs), the data continue to reveal the underrepresentation and low academic status of African American female faculty at institutions of higher learning. The evidence exposes the sad reality of "a rigid system of rewards that makes scant allowance for deviation from the traditional male model, high levels of isolation, stress and fatigue among female faculty, continuing unconscious and deep-seated discrimination and stereotyping by male colleagues, and a remarkably unbreakable glass ceiling" (Monroe et al. 2008, 217), which strongly impacts the presence and success of African American women in the academy.

Two broad theories have been posited to explain the disparities for African American women in higher education. The first emanates from the historical legacy of race. Like most African Americans, these women must deal with the "double consciousness" of being both American and African American (Du Bois [1903] 2007). The second stems from gender: African American women must deal also with the dual burdens of being both African American and female in academic environments that place little value on either trait (Singh, Robinson, and Williams-Green 1995, 401), thereby compounding the unique oppression that emerges from the intersection among race, gender, and class.

As a result of the negativity imposed upon them based on their racial/ethnic and gender identification, coupled with class and sexual orientation, many African American female faculty encounter acts of race and sex discrimination in hiring practices, as well as ill treatment from other members of the academic community (Burgess 1997, 227–234). Because they are viewed as the product of targeted initiatives, which generate unworthy, handout attitudes, they fall victim to societal perceptions that they are incompetent—defined as lacking ability, unskilled, amateurish, and/or inept—by students, staff, colleagues, and administrators in the academy. These women are continually challenged to prove that they do not have their job—or will be kept in their job—because of affirmative action, opportunity hiring, and/or tokenism (Harley 2008; Niemann 1999). Finally, duality is also rooted in role perception and expected professional performance, leaving African American women faculty to maneuver the academic terrain fully aware that their professional achievements may either not be rewarded like those of their nonblack colleagues and/or can be held against them as signs that they may be stepping out of place or benefiting undeservedly from good fortune or affirmative action (Weitz and Gordon 1993, 32).

In describing the uniqueness of African American female academicians, Nellie McKay surmises, "Blackness and femaleness ensure that we can never be them . . . [and] experience tells us we occupy our own space . . . sometimes at the margins of all that go[es] on around us" (1997, 13). We now survey the personal survival testimonies of five African American women faculty who are at various stages in their careers and share similar challenges and ordeals relating to their competence and worth because they are underrepresented faculty, specifically African American women.

Methodology

This study is comprised of five African American women faculty, whose positions range from part-time/adjunct instructor to full professor, at a doctoral/research-extensive university in the South. The study began as a response to a "call for papers" for a project focusing on women in the academy and their presumed incompetence. The authors met informally to discuss the project, then decided that to best illustrate the women's individual, yet common, experiences, personal narratives or testimonials would make the most suitable analytical tool. Oral narrative research methods better highlight individual and collective experiences because they "provide a means of enfranchising and empowering people whose lives have previously been shaped by 'colonized history' written from the standpoint of outsider" (Etter-Lewis 1997, 83). In addition, these narratives offer an insider's view, as well as culturally determined interpretations and values of intimate and unique life circumstances (Collins 2001; Etter-Lewis 1997).

Thus, the narrative approach is a way by which human existence becomes meaningful. Following this logic, this approach allows a more in-depth examination of people in cultured spaces while taking into consideration both internal and external influences that construct and shape their experiences. In regard to African American women on the margins in the academy, Patricia Hill Collins (2001), one of the primary originators of black feminist thought, argues for the usefulness of identifying and using your own point of view in conducting research because the ideas expressed best clarify the position of the individual, especially people in touch with their marginality in academic settings. This approach produces distinctive analyses of race, class, and gender that render them very real.

Over the course of her career, each author has had experiences where she felt she was marginalized and/or presumed incompetent by those around her. These personal testimonials, situated within the context of extant literature, are used to highlight strategies to combat the unconstructiveness of each experience. The predominant themes are then discussed. Although the authors' names are on this chapter, they remain unidentified in the testimonials to preserve anonymity. Each narrative is written in the author's individual voice, and they are not in any particular order.

Testimonial Number One—When Lack of Mentoring Leads to
Presumed Incompetence

When I first accepted my position at the university, I was a young married woman who had relocated to the South from the East Coast. My father had been a professor and coach at a HBCU, so I naïvely thought I was prepared for a life in academia. I was oblivious to all the minefields that lay in my path. I came from a professional background onto the faculty of a Research-One university at the very bottom of the totem pole in the rank of instructor on tenure track. I quickly learned that I was the first African American hired within my college, just on the heels of the civil rights movement when universities began to open doors more widely to people like me. Also, there were only two other white females on the faculty in this college.

To complicate matters even more, I was joining the faculty of a highly specialized technical discipline with a nontechnical background but with expertise in student affairs—not exactly a field embraced or valued by 95 percent of the professionals with whom I'd be working. Truly these were grounds for a presumption of incompetence! However, I adjusted as much as I could to this nontraditional, white-male-dominated environment. My job was to work with undergraduate students, teach three sections of technical writing, serve on committees, and interact with my faculty colleagues, even though most had limited contact with me.

After three years of doing my job in semi-isolation, someone suggested that I deserved a raise and promotion to the rank of assistant professor on tenure track. In retrospect, it was probably someone not even connected to the academy who made the suggestion. I had been receiving solid teaching and annual evaluations, so I thought this sounded like a good idea. I had absolutely no idea what it really meant or how to prepare an academic-promotion dossier properly. Someone from the dean's office simply handed me a red folder that had three sections in it to hold my documents and gave me a sheet of basic written guidelines of what was required for review. I was told to update my curriculum vitae and solicit some general letters of support. I thought that I knew how to resend the required material and was confident that I would get the promotion that I felt I deserved.

Needless to say, a few months later I learned that my request for promotion had been denied. My feelings were hurt, of course, but in retrospect, I am more embarrassed than hurt. Now—having served several terms on my department's Promotion and Tenure Committee—I have learned how to prepare a dossier for promotion and obtain letters of support and how much research needs to be published in which "proper" journals. But back then I was a naïve junior faculty member with no mentor to guide or encourage me in the ways of the academy; no one instructed me on the proper way to undertake and the timing for such an action, and no one told me (and I believe there were no formal written procedures at that time) that I had not done what was needed before having my credentials reviewed by our school's Promotion and Tenure Committee. No wonder I was being judged incompetent!

I swallowed my pride and sought help and guidance. An African American male faculty member from outside my college knew that I had not received any support or mentoring from faculty within my unit. He had known about me for several years prior to this and realized that what I needed was help from someone who had successfully climbed the academic ladder. He invited me to work with him on manuscripts we submitted for publication, thus enabling me to become published in peer-reviewed journals. He suggested that I assume a leadership role on a few key committees within my college and also on the broader main campus (so that others would recognize my competence and value to the academy), and he also constantly reminded me not to allow service and mentoring of students to prevent me from my research and publications, which were crucial to my survival in academia. The mentoring, support, and encouragement I received from him were terribly important. This colleague (now deceased) helped me regain my confidence so that when I applied for promotion two years later, I was well prepared and successful.

Having received recognition for having served more than thirty-five years on the faculty at this institution, I am one of a very few female African Americans who have achieved the rank of full professor. Although I was on an academic road far less traveled by those before and after me—given my unconventional and unique entry into the academy—it has not been easy. I am certain there are still some at this institution who question my competence, tenure, and longevity, but I hold my head high. My credentials for my particular position—earned and gained via "stick-to-it-tive-ness," are comparable to those of my colleagues.

I now understand how important it is to know your strengths and the way the academic promotion and tenure game is played. Often the formal, written procedures are unclear or interpreted differently while the unwritten rules are hidden from those who "aren't a good fit." This causes African American women and other marginalized groups to stumble and appear incompetent when that is not the case. I have learned that it is imperative that we receive or seek out the information and support we deserve for success in the academy. As I reflect back on my particular experience, I find that I survived by putting two recommendations for women on how to play by the political rules of the academy to good use: (1) find out what is going on around you, and (2) sharpen your political skills by such activities as volunteering, managing people, running meetings, and making effective presentations (Aisenberg and Harrington 1988).

Testimonial Number Two—When Determination and Persistence Challenge Presumed Incompetence

When I decided to make the career change from industry into higher education, I was not prepared emotionally and psychologically—I was simply naïve. Despite having more than fifteen years of pragmatic industry experience and successful matriculation and graduation from two premier research-extensive universities, I was totally ignorant of the racial and political landscape that fostered tokenism, isolation from social and information networks, and the presumption of incompetence I encountered. Additionally, I noticed that while many of my male peers had an inherent support system through a supportive or trailing wife, as a woman I was significantly disadvantaged by being a divorced single parent raising two children. These combined variables tainted my efforts in attaining a tenure-track position.

My initial shock during the transition from a career in private industry to a non-tenure-track assistant professorship involved receiving a much lower salary, which in turn significantly affected my standard of living. While adjunct instructors, or executives-in-residence, are valued for the specialized knowledge and real-world experiences they bring to the classroom, I realized that they are also an economic benefit to the university because they are paid lower than an assistant professor. Such information was not shared during my conversations with friends and colleagues who had taken the plunge from much-higher-paying jobs to pursue doctoral degrees and careers in higher education. However, a longtime colleague and hiring administrator assured me that—given the "nontangible freedoms" of higher education—I would welcome the change of pace and adjust to the salary difference—of course, this advice came from a male who had a working wife to support his salary reduction.

As I adapted to this newly acquired family-friendly career, I worked with colleagues who not only respected my academic credentials but also expressed appreciation for my industry experiences and skills. I was encouraged to bring my knowledge and abilities into the classroom to allow students to be exposed to this invaluable combination of an academically and professionally qualified person who was an African American female, which also made it highly probable that I would be a first for many students, staff members, and colleagues in my school.

After my first year in the position, my discussions with the department chair and dean focused on strategies for my move into a tenure-track job. One option presented to me was to transition into a part-faculty/part-staff position. I quickly rejected this idea after a colleague advised that you should "always have a home"—meaning to get tenure in an academic department before considering administrative appointments. This meant that I would have to go back to graduate school for my passport into higher education: a terminal degree in the discipline or department where I had been hired. My professional technical degrees allowed me to teach in business industry but limited my scope and usefulness. Thus, in the middle of my three-year academic contract, I left my position to pursue my doctoral degree full time.

I anticipated funding my graduate education with a part-time, adjunct-faculty position, but I had no idea that my particular college was under governmental and institutional pressure to recruit and hire underrepresented faculty. Because the college had recently hired a white female, I was therefore offered an instructorship in a nontenure-track position—instead of the part-time adjunct position—to comply with government mandates, contingent upon my pursuing a doctorate in that department. I believe the offer was made simply because of my race and gender.

It is widely known that the perceptions of preferential selection based on gender and/or race are stigmatizing, particularly in higher education. While it is not uncommon for African American women and others to complete their doctorates while teaching full time, I was not only concerned about the stigma associated with my target-hire status but also worried about faculty perceptions of my competency. Even though my job opportunity grew out of meeting state-mandated affirmative-action goals, I entered the position as a competent, well-prepared professional person. My concerns became apparent in conversations with colleagues, such as when one stated, "We are happy to have you and may as well get all we can out of you." I could hear the unspoken "as long as you are here" added at the end, which meant that I was not being considered for a tenure-track position.

The dean voiced a similarly patronizing, yet demeaning, comment when I requested financial support to attend a professional conference on mentoring and teaching for prospective graduate students. His answer was "we really do not want you to go to such conferences because others may steal you from us"—as if I were chattel that existed only for affirmative-action purposes! It became apparent that I was marginalized and isolated from my colleagues. Eventually even graduate students in the program questioned my competency.

One white male doctoral candidate who had been teaching part-time in the department for a few years asserted, "I'm really upset because you got the position that I wanted." In another conversation, he added, "You only got the position because you are a black female and the department gets to count you twice." I was stunned that he was so audacious! Was I perceived as incompetent? Were they not aware of my credentials? Did it even matter?

These examples of covert racism that I experienced in academia demonstrate the way African American female faculty have to prove their competence continually among students, staff, faculty, and administrators, many of whom are oblivious to their plight. This often results in the white majority ignoring the multiple levels of oppression and discrimination that increase our vulnerability to such hostile acts (Niemann 1999). The intersections of race, sex, and class are openly discussed and acknowledged in the academy, and celebratory lip service is paid to them; however, there is little oversight to identify and combat reoccurring allusive actions that result from them. When I chose to share these comments and my reactions to other colleagues with the executive administration—particularly when I was probed about conditions in my department—apparently I spoke too candidly because I was informed shortly afterward that the dean was no longer funding my position. Did sharing the enslaving comments he had made during one of our meetings contribute to his decision to terminate me?

By the time my job ended, I had completed all my doctoral work except for the dissertation. I received no explanation for my termination. My performance reviews were stellar, progress toward the doctorate was steady and progressive, I had received significant funding from the National Science Foundation, and yet I was terminated! Despite this action, I stayed focused on my goals and completed my doctorate. Regardless of this particular outcome, now I know my lack of knowledge and understanding about promotion and tenure at the start of my probationary period cost me greatly. I learned the hard way that, generally, institutions do not hire their own graduates for faculty positions directly out of graduate school. It was my prior professional experience in the discipline area, coupled with my track record in the department as an instructor and the lack of available affirmative-action candidates, that resulted in my getting the job—no more, no less.

Additionally, not having a mentor and advocate crippled my progress. Yet—however unfair the decision—I refused to allow anyone to determine or control my destiny. Keeping a positive attitude and my strong faith and prayer life are my defense strategies against obstacles that arise in my academic career.

Testimonial Number Three—When Early Success Dispels Presumed Incompetence

In my last year of graduate school while pursuing my PhD, I took a course within my program on research methodology from a professor who was nationally and internationally recognized for his expertise. After our major assignment for that class had been submitted and graded, my professor/mentor encouraged and offered to assist any students in the course who wanted to submit their work for possible publication in a peer-reviewed professional journal. His invitation included reviewing the paper from the perspective of a peer and giving recommendations for submission.

I was thrilled at the offer and took him up on it. The prospect of having an article published prior to or soon after graduation was appealing because it would (1) teach me the way to write for peer-reviewed publications; (2) demonstrate to prospective employers within institutions of higher education that I had the skills to publish in peer-reviewed journals—a major requirement for tenure; and (3) allow me to have a publication that could be counted toward tenure before I left my graduate program.

The focus of my paper was adolescent African American males. After revising the paper per his suggestions, I submitted it, and indeed a well-respected journal in my discipline area accepted the article. I was elated, and my professor/mentor was proud of my accomplishment. I notified the dean of the school, who congratulated me and informed faculty and students within the program of my achievement. One day shortly after, I was passing by the office of a white senior faculty member within the program. She and another white female faculty member were discussing my recent notification that my article had been accepted. To my surprise, they revealed their amazement that I had been able to accomplish such a feat. When I looked into the office and directly into their eyes, I could see that they were embarrassed that I had overheard them. Their nonverbal behavior reminded me of the way children often respond when caught with their hands in an off-limits cookie jar.

At that moment, I felt immensely disappointed about their low appraisal of my ability to write and get published in a quality journal within our field. After all, I had taken courses from both of them and demonstrated my writing ability by doing well in assignments. Additionally, they were part of the cadre of faculty who were preparing me for professional writing and the rigor of the professoriate. Their reaction raised a number of questions that demanded answers: What contributed to their surprise that I could have written an article accepted for publication? White students in my class and others I knew had been similarly successful. Were these two faculty members stunned by my white peers' accomplishments? What opinion did they have about the overall writing ability of the other students of African descent who were matriculating through the program, most of whom had not yet published (Mukherjee 2001)? Was their reaction an invalidation and racial devaluation of diversity-focused research, which is often common among white faculty but frowned upon when produced by nonwhites (Alfred 2001)? Or could it be that they presumed that I was incompetent to publish? I shudder to think so because then it would follow that—even with my proven track record as a successful doctoral student—they perhaps had no confidence in my ability to be a successful academic. While some may point to other reasons, I was almost certain that the answer was related to race and gender stratification.

Upon graduation I secured a tenure-track position. Seventeen years after graduation, I am now a full professor at a predominately white university—described as a Research-One institution. Having coauthored a text that has been adopted for courses by several social work programs throughout the United States and written numerous peer-reviewed articles, essays, book chapters and reviews, an invited paper, an instructor's manual, and reviews of journal manuscripts, I have more than demonstrated my ability to publish quality work across broad venues.

I was able to cope with the disappointment of this experience through my belief in my divinely created potential for greatness, self-affirmation, high self-esteem, and the support that I received from family and significant others (Alexander and Moore 2008). I believe that God has created every individual for a purpose and, furthermore, that each person has been given talents and attributes to carry out that purpose. Self-affirmation is extremely important because it helps to mitigate the myriad negative messages and circumstances that we receive daily from our environment, such as racist and sexist comments from colleagues and students, social isolation on campuses where there are few African Americans, and various manifestations of social and economic injustice. At predominately white institutions, research has proven that social support is a significant coping aid for historically underrepresented scholars (Gilbert and Tatum 1999). It is crucial to recognize your strengths, particularly when placed in an environment like postsecondary institutions, where Eurocentric paternalism, sexism, racism, and devaluation of African culture are virulent (Hamilton 2002).

Testimonial Number Four—When Teaching Defies Presumed Incompetence

As an associate professor with tenure, my story is somewhat atypical. Unlike many of my African American female peers, I went straight from kindergarten to a doctorate without life's interruptions like marriage, motherhood, and/or multiple careers; but like many African American academics, I was the first in my immediate family to earn my college degree from an Ivy League institution in my midtwenties. Thus, I share the same struggle with my counterparts who are working and living in majority-white-cultured spaces.

As Toni Morrison aptly surmised, "[The black woman] had nothing to fall back on; not maleness, not whiteness, not ladyhood, not anything. And out of the profound desolation of her reality, she may well have invented herself" (Giddings 1984, 15). Becoming a successful African American scholar requires the innate ability to (re)invent yourself time and time again. As Barnes observed, "One black woman might enter the system with a clear, well-founded belief that this parochial, chauvinistic, traditional system has worked hard to keep her out or to limit her involvement and advancement . . . [while] [a]nother might come without such preconceived notions and learn to maneuver the uncertain academic course by trial and error" (1986, 66). I learned by trial and error.

Time and space do not permit me to share all of my professional experiences, but suffice it to say that I had to learn to challenge and counter unspoken, yet pervasive, racism and sexism, most often in the classroom. I view myself as a facilitator engaging students in active and participatory learning. The African proverb "she who learns must also teach" best characterizes my approach (Gregory 2001, 124). My pedagogy is similar to that of many of my peers because it often has a decidedly political mission: to foster responsibility, respect, and commitment to social justice. My progressive delivery openly and critically analyzes conventional norms and/or traditions to reach a deeper understanding.

Many students need time to adjust to an approach that seems diametrically opposed to their social reality. Even though I take time to prepare students and communicate my expectations in detail on the course syllabus and through readings, films, and active in-class exercises to lessen fears and tension and create a safe, inclusive environment, each semester has its challenges. For example, male students have sometimes intentionally defied my presence and authority. In addition, students often question my knowledge about subject matter, and many expect me to be less stringent or more laid back about their meeting course requirements.

Often I find I must battle against the negative, historical images shaped by American popular culture that many people in society hold about African American women, such as the "mammy, Jemima, Sapphire, matriarch, and welfare mother" (Collins 2001; hooks 1981); and less-positive—even ominous—contemporary impressions that white students have of African American women as "loud, aggressive, argumentative, stubborn, and bitchy" as compared to the "sensitive, attractive, sophisticated, career-oriented, and independent" traits for American women in general (Weitz and Gordon 1993, 26–27). This is similar to what our African American male colleagues experience, as Jackson and Crawley observed:

> Race is a powerful preverbal communicative cue that may shift students' perceptions of an otherwise qualified and credible black male instructor, because with it comes certain presumptions about what it means to be black and male in the United States. For example . . . there are several popular and public projections about black males including, but not limited to, *black masculine persons as violent, criminal, non-intellectual, and lazy/inferior.* These popular cultural projections serve as the basis from which prejudices may be formed when individuals do not have direct contact and/or relational experiences with black males. *Consequently, when a white student who grows up in a racially homogenous environment meets a black person for the first time face-to-face, it can be shocking. Moreover, when the black person is the white student's professor, racial projections about that professor may become exacerbated by issues of power, authority, and credibility* (2003, 26; emphasis added).

When determining perceptions of power, authority, and competence in the classroom, written comments on course evaluations clarified them: they made scant reference to my scholarship and course content but focused mostly on how I interacted with the students or what my attitude toward them was. Disillusioned in the past, I began to research ways to combat these perceptions and found evidence that an interaction effect appears to exist between students' characteristics and the instructor's race, sex, and sexual orientation and must be considered when interpreting and understanding student evaluations (Gregory 2001).

I realized that my physical presence in the classroom, in conjunction with course's subject matter, could be perceived as marginal and a challenge to the mainstream. Even though my teaching evaluations—both statistical and written—as well as personal notes from students approved and supported my teaching style, I began to see that generally—aside from the impact of class size and type and subject matter on student evaluations (Hobson and Talbot, 26–31), an additional causal relationship linked my expectations and the students' reaction to the complexity of the course material. You must also factor in their preparation for the course. The result is that students who performed well gave more positive evaluations, and vice versa (Gregory 2001; Rama and Rahgunandan 2001; Worthington 2002).

Armed with this scholarly research on teaching evaluations and to offset potentially negative comments on future ones, my survival strategy has been to use student information slips at the beginning of the semester or midterm evaluations to gauge the evident unevenness among the students. This tool helps me identify problems and create solutions; more importantly, it allows me to document students' progress and comments about the course. I realize that students can use teaching evaluations to commend or retaliate. I have learned that unwritten codes and customs can weigh as heavily as written policies and procedures for African American women faculty. As Burgess has observed, "even in the face of an irrefutably excellent record in grantsmanship and publishing, 'poor teaching' is sometimes cited as a reason for denying tenure and promotion of women" (1997, 232).

As one who personifies and embodies diversity, I bring a unique perspective to academia. This will not change. Seeking to find that right balance in the classroom where I can teach effectively, as well as maintain a level of respect among my students, is a continuous work in process, and I had to "age to perfection" much sooner than my colleagues; yet it is up to me to determine the way I want to be judged. It is also up to me to "weigh the cost of [my] choices against the balance of energy, will, and the determination to survive with human dignity" (McKay 1997, 15). Survival for me means I must seek out mentors inside and outside of my department, university, and professional discipline. Having faculty mentors—through a variety of professional connections—opens up informational networks, resources, and promotional opportunities. More importantly, they are advocates who can watch my back as I progress in my career. As a beneficiary of effective mentoring, I have the same obligation to give back—as I do graciously and humbly—being grateful for those who took the time to do the same for me.

Testimonial Number Five—When Promotions Become Presumed Incompetence

Although I teach part time in adjunct positions at the university level, my story stems from my full-time administrative staff career. As an expert in student affairs and development, I attended administrator-focused conferences and listened to the stories shared by chief administrative professionals from historically underrepresented groups of highly qualified and credentialed colleagues who had been removed from their positions without explanation or due process. The stories were similar: when a new (often white) administrator took the helm, these former leaders were stripped of their formal responsibilities and left only with their titles, salaries, and offices (if they were fortunate). I often pondered what preventive measures could have been taken to avoid such atrocities. Since I had witnessed a similar incident, I knew that there was no incompetence involved, only administrative politics. Yet this individual suffered the same outcome as the others: a tarnished reputation, a damaged career, and minimal, if any, possibility for legal recourse.

Years later, as I continued to climb the administrative ladder, little did I know I was destined to join this group. I recall walking into the office of the president of my institution one August morning only to be told that my position had been given to someone else. One of his newly hired white female administrators stated matter-of-factly, "I'm going to say that you *requested* to be moved to another affiliated position—off campus—and that it was a promotion." Standing there with more than ten years of exemplary performance appraisals and instructional responsibilities that had produced superior teaching evaluations, I was devastated and felt violated! It wasn't clear to me whether I was being demoted or actually dismissed, thus ending my career—which had spanned more than twenty years— in student affairs. More importantly, others would presume my transfer was due to incompetence.

To make matters worse, I came under constant scrutiny in the new off-campus office where I had been banished. The mounting anxieties from ostracism, isolation, stress, and the loss of professional support and interaction made me feel like a pariah. The sanctions and actions connected to this traumatic experience created a lot of emotional distress. I felt the situation was literally eating me alive and I was totally alone. No support came from the staff in student affairs, including my African American peers. However, I did receive support from former students, who refused to accept my replacement and actively sought me out.

Encouragement from other administrative staff, faculty, and friends was invaluable as I persisted through the ordeal. A small group of African American and Latino male faculty kept me grounded and wrote letters of support for my personnel file, though surprisingly no African American female faculty offered assistance. However, having completed a dissertation in education through sheer determination, I successfully rebuilt my career in the area of diversity both as administrative staff and part-time adjunct faculty.

As I reflect back on my experience that may have resulted from possibly unforeseen administrative politics to personal intimidation from the newly hired white female administrator, I realize that the presumption of professional incompetence often manifested by white, economically privileged women toward their African American female peers emanates from and mirrors the same systemic forms of oppression in this society. Historically, there have been tensions between nonwhite and white women due to the latter attempting to define other women based upon their status of privilege (Moraga and Anzaldúa 1983), thereby shattering the notion of a universal sisterhood that views the politics of gender as an ongoing struggle for all professional women. The evident strain caused by such political and social stratification, unfortunately, inhibits opportunities for women in the academy to take collective action to mitigate and eliminate oppression in higher education. What happened to me certainly caused me to feel devalued for a time, but I was ultimately undefeated because, internally, I knew I was a competent and capable African American professional woman who had much to offer academia.

Discussion and Conclusion

The research described in this chapter provides empirical evidence to show that despite obstacles, African American female faculty are successful at institutions of higher learning—demonstrated not only by promotion and tenure but also by their tenaciousness. Specifically, our narratives defined three distinct strategies for combating institutional and cultural biases in academe: mentoring, individual coping, and righteous indignation. Each one embodied different political and social responses for dealing with the complexities of racial and gender biases in professional academic life.

Unfortunately, empirical data on African American female faculty across the academy and their mentoring experiences at various points in their careers are alarming, regardless of what they encountered prior to becoming faculty members. Similarly to Monroe et al. and previous studies, we found that mentoring was "the most uniform and enthusiastic recommendation" from these women (2008, 223). When Holmes, Land, and Hinton-Hudson (2007) investigated the experiences of black women faculty employed in higher education at various stages in their careers, they found that being a targeted hire and having mentoring support are quite different in industry from the academy for minority racial/ethnic groups. In higher education, black female affirmative-action candidates are sometimes perceived as less qualified than their white counterparts because race is viewed as more central in their hiring than their skills, knowledge, and expertise. In industry, however, the opposite is true: these applicants are viewed favorably because their skills, knowledge, and expertise are believed to enhance the organization (Holmes 2003; Holmes, Land, and Hinton-Hudson 2007). Thus in industry, mentoring an affirmative-action candidate is a commitment to bolster this person's success within the organization. Because the academy is structured around the traditional, white, male, good-ol'-boy network with its self-serving nature, new teachers or junior faculty "are [often] regarded by administrators and full-time [tenured] faculty alike as 'second-class' citizens" (Wallin 2004, 373) or outsiders who must fend for themselves. Nevertheless, each author identified mentoring as integral to her progress, from publishing in graduate school to promotion and tenure.

This mentoring took place formally and informally. One author benefited from formal mentoring by her professor, who recognized her potential and encouraged her to publish. Another author had someone who witnessed her unfair treatment and sought to protect and assist her while she learned how the system worked. One author actively sought out colleagues to establish both formal and informal relationships, benefiting most often through the informal ones with other senior women faculty. Although two authors received neither formal nor informal mentoring to mitigate their situations, both realized its intrinsic value and that not having it intensified their dilemmas. One author did note the support she received from African American and Latino male faculty. Surprisingly, her comments reveal the opposite of what most women in the academy have discovered: "women have shared experiences that heighten sensitivity to the plight of other women . . . [which] aids professional success by providing general encouragement and direction in areas that are new, puzzling, and unanticipated, a role filled by traditional mentoring" (Monroe et al. 2008, 224). Although it is not clear whether the author, an administrative staff employee, reached out to African American female faculty for support or these women were even aware of her plight, the lack of mentoring and connection increased her feelings of isolation and desertion.

Individual coping determines how well you can effectively balance the inconsistencies among actions that confirm your professional (academic) identity and your gender (Wiley and Crittenden 1992). Strong ties of nuclear and extended families, flexible gender roles, and a strong sense of obligation, support, and interdependence among family members traditionally characterize African American culture. Family, marriage, procreation, and commitment to the community are revered as a means for survival and protection from institutional systems of discrimination and oppression (Calhoun-Brown 2000). African American women faculty must juggle their careers while acting as parents to their children and sometimes caretakers to other siblings and/or parents.

Studies show that religious and spiritual beliefs are at the basis of African American culture and heritage, provide continuity within the family, and support the struggle to survive (Kort 2002). Scholars of religion and African American culture have argued that blacks bring a historically unique perspective to the Christian faith. Kort explains that when oppressed and denigrated African Americans read and interpreted the Bible during slavery, their actions were not so much a cultural exit and self-abjection as social construction, world reconstruction, liberation from theological domination, and elevating messages of hope revealing "that the physical and the spiritual, the internal and external, and the individual and community" are interconnected (Kort 2002, 267).

African Americans do not separate their faith from their culture. What makes the African American dependence on faith so vital is that it liberates the individual to affirm her or his potential in a hostile culture or environment. Thus, individual coping via strong religious beliefs is symbiotic to the African American struggle, for the two are integrally connected. Although only two authors made specific references to their reliance on faith, based on its centrality in African American culture, its importance may be shared by other authors as well.

Finally, some righteous indignation was detected in the authors' stories of continually battling racial, gender, and cultural biases without institutional intervention. This is probably due to the fact that African American women have never been able to afford the politics of disinterestedness and the "luxury of obliviousness" as the way the beneficiaries of white privilege can (Johnson 2001). Unlike their white female counterparts, African American women often internalize responsibility for balancing family and career as a fact of life and are less willing to raise their "voices of struggle, denial, helplessness, and [are] ultimately lacking the empowering strategies to handle or change their seemingly intractable circumstances" because they know that such "political demands are doomed to fail in eliciting a positive institutional response" (Monroe et al. 2008, 225). For black women faculty, survival hinges on openly confronting oppression if necessary.

In the light of the duality of their experiences in academia, African American female faculty can choose to become victims or survivors. In her book *Feminist Theory from Margin to Center,* bell hooks noted that "being in the margin is to be a part of the whole but outside the whole. The sense of wholeness, impressed upon our consciousness by the structure of our daily lives, provided us with an oppositional world view—a mode of seeing, unknown to most of our oppressors, that sustained us, aided us in our struggle to transcend poverty and despair, strengthened our sense of self and our solidarity" (1984, ii). The women in this particular study chose to survive with dignity born from self-affirmation.

These experiences have implications for colleges and universities that wish to attract and retain black female faculty and provide the necessary environment for their success. The academic environment, which includes the overall treatment of and regard for faculty candidates and their scholarship, is a significant consideration when new faculty are considering employment offers (Gilbert and Tatum 1999; Marbley 2007). Isolation, hostility, indifference, and invisibility, as well as a lack of understanding of the experiences of African American women faculty, are too often part of the daily climate where this group must seek to thrive and survive. Given the ascendance of a new generation of African American women faculty, our institutions of higher education will be better served if they take note of our findings.

CHAPTER 29

THE EXPERIENCES OF AN ACADEMIC "MISFIT"

Kelly Ervin

As I reflected on my past and present academic career, I wondered if there was anything specific about my journey that would be of any value to a discussion of the experiences of women of color in academia, for I no longer work full time in the academy. I am currently a public servant in federal service with the Department of Defense (DoD), and I have built a career as a senior research psychologist with the United States Army Research Institute for the Behavioral and Social Sciences (ARI). In addition, I am an adjunct, full professor with the University of Maryland University College (UMUC).

I did not leave full-time academia because of any negative experiences due to my being African American and an assistant professor. My decision to depart from full-time teaching and abandon my academic research program was in part based on the desire to return to my home state and the need to earn a larger salary. I struggled with this decision, but it was made much easier by some of the frustrating experiences that I did have as an assistant professor. The value of my story is that it is less about trauma than it is about triumph. I feel triumphant in that I have always had a dual career in public service and academia; I always moved forward, and I did not allow any negative experiences as a full-time assistant professor keep me from one aspect of what I consider my academic calling: teaching. My dual career began after my graduation from Michigan State University with a PhD in social psychology in 1993.

Public Service Versus Academia: Why Not Both?

I come from a family of public servants. My father served twenty years in the United States Air Force (USAF) and after his retirement, he embarked on a new twenty-year career with another agency within the Department of Defense (DoD). My mother also enjoyed a twenty-year career with the DoD, and my brother also served in the USAF. After graduating from Michigan State University, I made the decision to accept a position as a social science analyst with the General Accounting Office (GAO).[1] The decision to jump into public service, to the chagrin of my professors, rather than seek a full-time academic position, was due mostly to the fact that my father was terminally ill, and I was motivated to return to Maryland—regardless of the job. I applied for a few academic positions in the Maryland/D.C./Virginia area, and GAO provided the first offer of employment. I accepted that offer, and I have never regretted this decision because I was able to spend the remainder of my father's life with him.

While working at GAO, I also learned the valuable lesson that there are a multitude of nonacademic career opportunities for social psychologists—this is a lesson that I never received in graduate school, where nonacademic work was seen as less prestigious than tenure-track positions at Research-One institutions. My work at GAO was very satisfying and lasted five years. During this time, I was also working part time as an adjunct assistant professor in the psychology department at George Washington University (GWU) in Washington, D.C., where I taught undergraduate and graduate courses but did not conduct research.

During my fifth year at GAO, I began to get the academic itch because I began to miss the academic lifestyle and the ability to pursue my own research interests. Teaching at GWU satisfied my craving to teach, but I missed conducting independent research. I applied for, and was offered, a tenure-track assistant professor position at Washington State University (WSU) in Pullman in the Department of Comparative Ethnic Studies (CES). This career move marked my first and last journey as a full-time academic, and my experiences in the CES department solidified my decision to return to a full-time federal service and part-time academic career.

As an assistant professor, I experienced some pretty stressful situations and events. I would like to share two of them in this chapter, but before I do, I want to acknowledge that during my brief time at WSU, I received tremendous support and friendship from the other women of color in the department—they made life in Pullman quite enjoyable. First, I believed, and still do, that the majority of my stress as an assistant professor was the result of being an academic misfit in the CES department. This lack of fit was less about being a woman of color and more about being an experimental social psychologist in an ethnic studies department. Second, I had agreed to take charge of the *Western Journal of Black Studies (WJBS)*, an international, multidisciplinary periodical, as editor-in-chief. In doing so, I learned—in a very agonizing manner—that editor-in-chief of an academic journal is a politically charged leadership position that no new assistant professor should ever undertake.

An Academic Misfit

Although I do not believe that my experience in the academy as a woman who happens to be African American was unique, I do believe that my education and training as an experimental social psychologist who was teaching and conducting research in an ethnic studies department created an unusual, frustrating dilemma. I loved teaching in the CES department, and I taught and developed several courses that combined African American issues and the tenets of social psychology. For example, I taught African American Studies, African American Women in US Society, African American Cinema, Black Social Psychology, Critical Cultural Studies, Cross-Cultural Psychology, and the Social Psychology of Prejudice.

---

1   In 2004 the name of the GAO changed to the Government Accountability Office.

My research interests and accomplishments revolved around the social psychology of African Americans, and I was able to publish quite extensively in a number of peer-reviewed journals, such as *Personality and Social Psychology Bulletin, Sex Roles: A Journal of Research, Journal of Applied Social Psychology,* and the *Journal of Black Studies.* I always respected and nurtured the relationship between empiricism and relevance, and I took special care to design and report my work so that the theoretical foundations applied to the practical manifestations in society. I was very enthusiastic about the marriage of ideas and methods between social psychology and African American studies. My research program, I felt, was distinct because I used the theoretical foundations of social psychology to guide my quantitative-research projects, and then I always provided a discussion of the social applicability of the empirical results. I made it a practice to engage in an analysis of what my research meant, not only to the African American community, but also to researchers, practitioners, and educators who are interested in African American psychology. I believed that I could make significant contributions to the fields of African American studies, ethnic studies, and social psychology.

Alas, the senior CES faculty were less enthused about my research program, and I was informed time and time again that my projects were too social psychological in nature and too quantitative. I kept finding myself in the position of having to defend the value of combining African American studies with the empirical foundations of social psychology. The fact that I could not, would not, give up my social-psychological foundation put me in a difficult position and caused me to suspect that I would not earn a favorable vote during my third-year tenure review.

I wrote about this dilemma years ago, and my ruminations were published in the *Psych Discourse* (the official journal of the Association of Black Psychologists) in October 2000. I am including portions of that article because I believe that the sentiment is timeless for anyone who is trained in empiricism, yet finds him or herself working in an academic department that does not value empirically-based scholarship. The article was entitled "An African American Psychologist's Response to 'The SPSSI Bridge'" and was written in response to a commentary that was published in the Society for the Psychological Study of Social Issues (SPSSI) newsletter. The SPSSI president, John F. Dovidio, wrote an interesting editorial in which he lamented the poor working relationship between the discipline of psychology and other fields of inquiry (2000). This text is a portion of my response to his plea:

Dear Dr. Dovidio,

I am a quantitative social psychologist who is currently an assistant professor in an Ethnic Studies department. My research, the methods I use to implement my research, and the perspective from which I teach my classes are all grounded in social psychology. Specifically, my interests revolve around the social psychology of African Americans. My work concentrates on social identity, racial self-esteem, stigma, racial attitudes, and intra-/inter-group relations. I am very much a social psychologist. However, at the same time, it has always been my goal to situate myself in an academic environment in which I could combine my training as a social psychologist and apply it to the study of African Americans, which is more commonly referred to as "Black or African American Studies."

Based on your argument presented in the "The SPSSI Bridge" article, if you were to assess the location of my academic employment (i.e., in an Ethnic Studies department) you would conclude that it makes intuitive and practical sense. . . . The need for research psychologists, especially social psychologists, to partake in an intellectual partnership with other disciplines is critical if we are to continue to contribute useful and practical knowledge. . . . I argue that the SPSSI Bridge, an inter-connection with other pursuits of knowledge, already exists. However, what we need is to get scholars to not only use the bridge but to also have respect and value for it. The problem is, those of us who attempt to traverse this bridge are sometimes discouraged and often penalized from doing so. Allow me to illustrate my case in point.

Among many Ethnic Studies scholars, there is a lack of value and understanding for the scientific method and an inability to evaluate statistical segments of a body of work . . . and in general, there is difficulty in being able to form mentoring relationships with senior faculty who understand and appreciate one's work.

Because of this lack of value for the scientific method and data driven work, I am being asked to make a choice between social psychology and ethnic studies. If I want to possibly get tenure in my current department I have been told that I must focus less on data driven, social psychological work and more on qualitative ethnic studies work. Herein lies my personal dilemma. If I continue to use the scientific method to pursue my research interests and if I continue to follow the guidelines of my discipline the intellectual bridge in which I am attempting to traverse back and forth from social psychology to Black/African American Studies will crumble and I will end up in the waters of the non-tenured and out of a job.

This all amounts to a situation in which I fear that I am guaranteed to fail. If I stay immersed in social psychology and continue to publish in psychology journals, I will not get tenure because my work will be too data driven. If I concentrate solely on Black/African American studies, I will not be able to publish my work in most psychology journals and I will not be working within the "standards" of my discipline. Therefore, in 2½ years, when I come up for tenure review, I believe that I will have a most difficult time in securing external reviewers of my work. I will not be able to secure social psychologists to review my work if it is too ethnic studies oriented and I will not be able to secure ethnic studies scholars to review my work if it is too data-driven and social psychological in nature. Alas, I am in pretenure purgatory.

I am on that SPSSI Bridge, Dr. Dovidio, but the intellectual factions on opposite ends of the bridge have me placed in the middle and have pressured me to "choose sides." Ideally, I would like to be able to traverse this bridge while contributing to the knowledge of the social psychology of African Americans. Ideally, I would like to earn tenure. Unfortunately, I feel that these ideals are incompatible.

If scholars of social psychology learn to respect and value the issues and methods of ethnic studies and if ethnic studies scholars learn to respect and value the issues and methods of social psychology, I believe that the intellectual pursuit of the psychological study of social issues will become a bigger package with a brighter bow.[2]

The *Psych Discourse* article captures the frustration I felt as an academic misfit who was trying to carve out a research program built on two disciplines, and it summed up my experiences as a social psychologist working in an ethnic studies department. I never felt as if I fit, and therefore I did not remain in the CES department long enough to go through the official tenure review. At this point in my story, you may be wondering if I then attempted to secure a tenure-track position in a psychology department. When I made the final decision to develop a strategy to leave the CES department, I did interview for a few tenure-track positions in psychology departments. However, most were not interested in hiring me because I was now eight years out of graduate school, and I had not spent these years conducting experimental research. The five years working at GAO and the four at WSU meant that I had gotten far removed from working and conducting research in social psychology, and I had also experienced skill degradation in the areas of experimental design and advanced statistics. This worked against any chance I had to secure a tenure-track position in a psychology department.

Editor-in-Chief of the *WJBS:* Too Much, Too Soon

During my second year in the CES department, a tenured, full professor, who happened to be a male of color, asked me to take over the editorship of the *WJBS*. The current editor had recently retired, and this full professor did not have the time to take on the task. The journal was floundering in a number of areas. I was young, I was cocky, and I was ambitious, and so I thought, "I can do this!" I did not know it at the time, but I was about to be thrown under the proverbial bus.

Prior to my editorship, the *WJBS* was a journal that had a 100 percent acceptance rate, and there was a multiyear backlog of manuscripts that needed to be reviewed. The journal already had an editorial board, but it was not being used as efficiently as it should have been. One of the first changes I made as editor-in-chief was to implement a peer-review process of all manuscript submissions. I felt strongly that—as with any peer-reviewed journal—all manuscripts should be evaluated by the authors' peers, and judgment of acceptance (or not) should be by those who were experts in the subject matter of the manuscript. I began to use the editorial board as the gatekeepers and judges of which manuscripts would be reviewed, accepted, and subsequently published in the *WJBS*. A consequence of using this peer-reviewed process was that many manuscripts were now being rejected—including those from full professors who had enjoyed many years of publishing in the *WJBS*.

Many of the senior academics who received rejection letters were quite angry and even more livid once they learned that the editor-in-chief, whose name was on the rejection letters, was a lowly assistant professor. A few of these professors began a smear campaign in which they demanded that I be removed as editor-in-chief. They wrote numerous letters to the professor who had asked me to take over the helm,

---

2   Dr. Dovidio's response to me was open and welcoming. We met during an SPSSI conference in Minneapolis in June 2000, and we discussed the possibility of an American Psychological Association convention program that would focus on and address these issues. Unfortunately, this program never materialized.

and they also wrote many letters and made repeated telephone calls to the dean, provost, and president of WSU.

I was mortified. I had never experienced such vitriol, and I did not know how to handle such an attack. I was astounded that a group of scholars could and would act in such an immature way. I had studied and trained in social psychology, a field where the rejection rates of the top-tier journals hovered around 99 percent. I naïvely thought that rejection of a manuscript was part of academic life. What I failed to realize was that rejection of full professors' work by an assistant professor was too much for them to bear.

As a consequence of this smear campaign, I found myself—along with the full professor who had asked me to take over—in a very uncomfortable meeting with the dean of the College of Liberal Arts at WSU. In this meeting, the full professor concluded that the best action to diffuse the situation was to remove me as editor-in-chief and ignore the letters and phone calls. The dean supported his decision. I countered that if he took this course of action, he would be agreeing with the instigators and supporting their criticisms, even though I was not actually reviewing and evaluating the manuscripts. He knew that I was farming the manuscripts out to the experts on the editorial board, and I wanted the rejected professors to know this as well. I felt strongly that it was important for them to know that I—as an assistant professor—was not personally rejecting their work—their academic peers were.

This fact fell on deaf ears, and although I had assumed that this professor would come to my defense, he did not. Consequently, I was removed as editor-in-chief, and I assume—for I have never checked—that the *WJBS* returned to a periodical with a 100 percent acceptance rate, regardless of quality. Never again did I speak to the professor who, up to this point, I had considered a mentor. Several years later, he tried to apologize to me, and he acknowledged that he should have supported me and probably should not have installed a nontenured, assistant professor as editor-in-chief. I did not accept his apology. This experience—along with the frustration I was feeling as a misfit in the CES department—contributed greatly to my decision to depart from full-time, tenure-track teaching and research and move to full-time federal service and part-time teaching.

As I think about the comparison between my experience in the academy as a full time assistant professor and my current situation as a civilian in a military environment, I've come to the conclusion that there is no comparison (a good analogy is trying to compare apples with Volkswagens). The work culture of the federal government is very different from an academic environment. It has been my experience that my treatment as a woman of color, working as an army civilian, is a nonissue because those of us who work for the army benefit from advances that the government has made in workforce diversity and establishing an environment where rank, command experience, and the ability to complete a mission are what is respected and valued, regardless of your ethnicity.

Today, I am very satisfied with my full-time federal career as a senior research psychologist and part-time teaching for UMUC. I truly believe that I have found my niche. I enjoy working for the US Army because it gives me a feeling that I am part of something that is very important and much bigger than I am. ARI's mission is to improve soldier, leader, and unit performance through advances in the behavioral and social sciences. ARI's research areas are personnel, organizations, training, and leader development, and its findings provide innovative behavioral and social science solutions that enable the US Army senior leadership to supply prepared forces and capabilities.

Working in the area of military psychology is a homecoming for me. I fit—at last. As you finish reading my story, you may be thinking that I am/was conflicted in some way. I am! I was! However, I see internal conflict as beneficial—a catalyst for moving away from or toward something that is new, challenging, and advantageous to personal and professional growth. Human emotions are complex, and life decisions are all rooted in some level of internal conflict. I have always lived by the mantra that—every now and then—I need to reinvent myself by understanding and knowing when I am bored and not learning anything new and then having the power, strength, and courage to make a change.

CHAPTER 30

LESSONS FROM THE EXPERIENCES OF WOMEN OF COLOR WORKING IN ACADEMIA

Yolanda Flores Niemann

> . . . they [senior colleagues of color] refused to engage in unforgivable silences that would have perpetuated a presumption that the average white male professor's experiences are the same as those of women of color. They exposed for their dean the reality that we—female faculty of color—do not function in a color- and gender-blind profession and that we who are female and colored are never presumed competent.
>
> Angela Onwuachi-Willig, "Silence of the Lambs"[1]

Women of color face harsh realities in their professional lives as university faculty members. At the same time, even within the walls of these often-pernicious academic environments, women of color can assert their voices, effect change, find allies, and not only survive, but thrive. These are the courageous truths revealed by this book's authors. They tell us that women of color are the canaries in the academic coal mine (Guinier and Torres 2002) and warn us of the toxic nature of academic workplaces for members of historically underrepresented groups. The challenges these authors have faced are grounded largely in the quadruple threat of racism, sexism, homophobia, and class-based subordination. This combination of "isms" can be lethal to their careers, bodies, and spirits in the culture of the predominantly white, male, heterosexual, and upper-middle-/upper-class academy. These authors' firsthand knowledge and observations take place in diverse types of institutions—from private schools to land-grant state universities, Hispanic-serving institutions, and community colleges—and across academic disciplines.

---

1   All italic quotations in the present chapter are taken from previous chapters in this book.

The psychological evidence suggests that readers—both women and men—will be inclined to dismiss the events described as exaggerations or illustrations of "oversensitivity." Others will believe the incidents are real and accurately portrayed but will attribute the problem to rare and unusual "bad actors." However, the examples the authors describe, which may startle those of us who live a different social existence, typify life for a woman of color in academia.

John F. Dovidio, "Introduction," Part II

A summary chapter cannot take the place of the transformative understanding that results from absorbing the emotional content of each of the experiences shared in this volume. These narratives evoke a wide range of emotions and responses—from sadness, frustration, anger, and tears to contentment, validation, and laughter. They plant the seeds of change so that future generations of women of color and members of other historically underrepresented groups may have more fulfilling, respectful, and dignified experiences as faculty in the academic realm. Readers are encouraged to take the time to absorb and truly understand the narratives.

They [the narratives in this book] expose problems related to being "outsiders" within that reveal the ubiquitous power of numerous dominant ideologies in US society, including white supremacy, patriarchy, heteronormativity, classism, ethnocentrism, and rationality. Their combined narratives illustrate ways that members of the academy routinely and robotically rely on these prevailing belief systems as they indoctrinate one another into specific roles.

Brenda J. Allen, "Introduction," Part I

The authors of this collection, and the countless untold stories they represent, deserve a theoretical discussion and analysis of how and why group-based discriminatory practices are still occurring in today's academic world. They merit and demand a comprehensive theory of the foundations of tokenism and related damaging experiences too often sustained by members of underrepresented groups in these places that are supposed to be bastions of knowledge and enlightenment. A viable theory must include scrutiny of the roles of institutionalized power and privilege and societal mores, history, and values in generating and exacerbating the realities these women have lived. A theory that can serve as a foundation for change must reflect lessons from the extensive social science research on racism, sexism, classism, heterosexism, stereotypes, group dynamics, cognitive distortions, and the role of socioecological forces in individual and group behavior toward members of historically underrepresented groups. In addition, illuminating constructs that have been developed and documented in the field of law—e.g., critical race theory—and other academic disciplines will help formulate such a theory. It is a daunting and complex task but one that I hope talented scholars will be moved to develop and disseminate upon reading this collection. However, that much-needed thesis is not provided in the present concluding chapter. The intent in this chapter is to formulate more immediate, concrete, and applicable recommendations that may help circumvent and/or diffuse the conditions described in this anthology.

The goals of this chapter are fourfold. The first is to help readers understand the ways existing structures create the hostile environments that these women describe. These structures include formal and informal practices, processes, and policies that create barriers against job satisfaction and tenure and promotion. Tenure is the coin of the realm for faculty (Seldin and Miller 2009). Increasingly, however, institutional preferences for contractual faculty (MLA Task Force 2007), coupled with biases against women of color, are contributing to their overrepresentation in adjunct roles (Ryu 2010). This state of affairs is increasing the number of under-represented group members who are especially vulnerable to inequitable practices and hostile climates.

Existing academic structures facilitate different realities and rules of the game for members of historically underrepresented groups as compared to those of their white, heterosexual colleagues. These disparate realities create shaky ground for women of color and provide evidence that no matter how hard they work, how many degrees they possess, what titles they earn, or what levels and/or positions they acquire, they are still vulnerable to malevolent experiences as faculty members. The more -isms associated with their identities, the more personally directed is the antagonism and the more oppressive is the unchallenged, status-quo environment.

> *I now understand how important it is to know your strengths and the way the academic promotion and tenure game is played. Often the formal, unwritten rules are hidden from those who "aren't a good fit." This causes African American women and other marginalized groups to stumble and appear incompetent when that is not the case.*
>
> Sherri L. Wallace, Sharon E. Moore, Linda L. Wilson,
> and Brenda G. Hart, "African American Women
> in the Academy: Quelling the Myth of
> Presumed Incompetence"

Existing structures also affect misinformation about federal affirmative action policies, contributing to the stereotypical idea that persons of color enter faculty ranks not because of their high qualifications and competence, but rather due to a policy perceived as "reverse discrimination" against white males (Rai and Critzer 2000). Practices generated by this misinformation produce biased search processes that prevent equal access to members of underrepresented groups. As Derrick Bell (1980) and others postulate, and research demonstrates (Kinder and Sears 1985; Lipsitz 1998; Niemann and Dovidio 1998b), the will of the majority is almost always informed by their self-interest. The academic majority consists of white males, who typically see affirmative action as a zero-sum game that disadvantages them, thereby fueling resentment toward persons of color and, to a lesser extent, toward white females (Lipsitz 1998; Rai and Critzer 2000). In stark contrast to the reverse dis-crimination argument, however, are the data—white men and white women consti-tute 45 percent and 32 percent of the full-time faculty, respectively, while US men and women of color combined account for only 17 percent of the total distribution of full-time faculty (African American—5.4 percent, Hispanic—3.6 percent, Asian American—7.6 percent, and American Indian—0.5 percent; these totals include only known race/ethnicity) (Ryu 2010). Foreign nationals constitute 4.4 percent of the total full-time faculty (Ryu 2010).

. . . it is stunning to read the essays in this volume showing the repeated efforts by contemporary white academics, lawyers, and politicians to manipulate statistics and feign liberal intentions while denouncing affirmative action, claiming "reverse discrimination"—as if there even were such a thing—and blaming students of color and women for their presumed "failures." . . . America's public discourse on race often remains entrenched in fear, self-delusion, denial, and co-optation, including the presentations, papers, and essays by some very powerful academics and politicians. Some, who even declare themselves liberals or feminists, continue to deny every statistical, sociological, and political study of actual, verifiable discrimination based on race and/or gender. It is truly mind-boggling arrogance and ignorance.

Bettina Aptheker, "Foreword"

To build diversity and inclusion in our institutions and disciplines . . . , we need more than numbers. . . . we must create a healthy climate. This requires a culture of collaboration where issues of intersectionality can be addressed. Inclusion requires justice and due process. It also needs the give and take of social support, of flexibility of models and respect for individual and group differences, and, perhaps most daringly, of risk taking where leaders and others are free to make mistakes and change course. . . . We have an opportunity to create a "new normal," to establish policies and foster practices that will become second nature in the culture of departments and units because they truly expand the possibilities of excellence for everyone.

Nancy Cantor, "Introduction," Part III

The second goal of this chapter is to help members of historically underrepresented groups understand that their challenging experiences are grounded in their situation, not in their competencies. For example, women of color experience the psychological and career consequences of tokenism, which is defined as "the policy of making only a perfunctory effort or symbolic gesture toward the accomplishment of a goal, such as racial integration; . . . the practice of hiring or appointing a token number of people from underrepresented groups in order to deflect criticism or comply with affirmative action rules" *(American Heritage Dictionary* 2000, "Tokenism"); ". . . the practice of making only a token effort or doing no more than the minimum, especially in order to comply with a law" *(Collins English Dictionary,* 2003, "Tokenism"). Tokenism is most likely to occur when members of the minority group in any situation account for fewer than 15 percent of the total (Kanter 1977; Niemann 2003; Pollak and Niemann 1998; Yoder 1985). Since women of color represent only 7.5 percent of all full-time faculty (Ryu 2010), they are highly vulnerable to being tokenized with the harmful consequences that are shared in this collection of narratives and explored in this chapter. The recommendations provided to administrators and to women of color and their allies in this chapter address the challenges of tokenization in a predominantly white institution of higher education.

The strand unifying these articles is the message that we remain wary of tokenism and will not forsake one another as we advance through the academic ranks.

Deena J. González, "Introduction," Part V

The third goal of the chapter is to provide a road map by which women of color may navigate the difficult terrain chronicled in this volume and gain a sense of belonging. Lacking genuine acceptance from students, colleagues, administrators, and staff, women of color often feel like outsiders in the academic world. They must consider a multitude of perspectives when they determine whether the academy is their right career choice. They reflect on ways they can help pave the road for all students and faculty who follow. They heed their years of preparing for an academic career, including the accumulated fiscal debt resulting from their commitment to earn a PhD. Due in large part to cultural expectations and values, they must also weigh the impact of their decisions on their families.

Belonging, then, becomes a complex reality in this context. But serving in predominantly white academic institutions (which describes almost all research universities) often comes at a high price. When women of color gauge their fit, they must also ask, "How much of a price can I afford to pay at this time?" "What are the costs to my physical and psychological health?" And they must walk into these positions with eyes wide open, without naïveté, and with a positive outlook, but also with a realistic understanding of the world they are about to enter. As someone with considerable administrative experience, I can attest that the price that women of color pay may get heavier with increasing visibility, authority, and power within the institution.

As the individuals asking how universities work are usually successful in their fields and often belong to a variety of private clubs, I point out that—in my opinion—universities have much in common with elite country clubs. The academic credentials are necessary to be invited to join, but like all country clubs, not all members are perceived as equal. The older, usually white males from affluent backgrounds and prestigious universities are traditionally perceived to be the social and academic leaders, as well as the decision makers . . . The perceived social order or structure usually descends from the white males with affluent backgrounds from prestigious universities down through individuals with lesser income or less-impressive degrees. Women of all colors are usually considered below men, and their status diminishes more if they are of color, which indicates they may have come from lower-income families and neighborhoods. The university as a country club has existed for a very long time. It is often unfair and hurtful to those perceived to be of lower status. The narratives in this work speak for themselves, and it took considerable courage for these authors to relate their experiences. Why do I think these authors were courageous in telling of their experiences? Simply stated, universities—like country clubs—do not like to share unfavorable information with those outside their own community.

Samuel H. Smith, "Introduction," Part IV

Change may be on the horizon as the *zeitgeist* presently surrounding academia may be compelling transformation to this elitist world. US demographics are compelling some state legislatures, regents, and trustees to begin to see their universities through lenses of members of underrepresented groups, even if only out of concern for financial implications of lowered enrollment numbers. Legislative demands increasingly focus on accountability with a greater emphasis on the needs and expectations of the greatest number of consumers. The very existence of tenure is being challenged by some legislative bodies (Arum and Roksa 2011; Bok 2006; Spellings 2006).

Allies of historically underrepresented groups are slowly gaining power to facilitate change. A few white male university leaders and faculty are increasingly taking a public role in advocating and developing opportunities for members of underrepresented groups (e.g., Bowen and Bok 1998; articles by Samuel Smith, John Dovidio, and Dean Spade in this volume). White women with the courage to challenge the status quo, like Syracuse Chancellor Nancy Cantor, who also contributed to this volume, are succeeding in the highest-level university positions. Slowly, a very small number of men and women of color are being appointed president at research universities; Elson Floyd (Washington State University), Ruth Simmons (Brown University), Frances Córdova (Purdue University), and Mildred Garcia (California State University, Dominguez Hills) are recent examples. These persons have broken through barriers into leadership positions dominated by white men, and are slowly, but effectively challenging the elitist culture in the universities they lead. Others will follow. Their leadership may inspire a cultural shift, even as they carefully pace their actions to ensure their own survival in their roles in predominantly white institutions. In particular—as the group that has the most in common with white men—white women have the greatest potential to be allies of women of color and lynchpins of cultural change in the university. However, to do so they must acknowledge and understand the privilege generated by their whiteness and its benefits.

> *Was I aware of my privilege as a white woman? I am not sure, but I believe I did not fully consider the racial privilege that bolstered my position. I believe my lack of consciousness did not arise from an exclusionary impulse but from a limited experiential horizon, a lack of consciousness that contributed to a false sense of normalcy . . . . I didn't notice anyone missing as I moved from one environment to the next. This, of course, is the essence of privilege.*

> Stephanie A. Shields, "Waking Up to Privilege:
> Intersectionality and Opportunity"

> *My years in grassroots activism provide an anchor for the values I want to bring to this work, just as the example of radical academics intervening on these issues supplies inspiration.*

> Dean Spade, "Notes toward Racial and Gender Justice
> Ally Practice in Legal Academia"

A fourth goal of this chapter is to remind women of color of their resilience and ability to overcome the very challenging realities described in this anthology's narratives. These essays illuminate some of the various strategies utilized by women faculty of color and their allies to subvert entrenched hierarchies and maintain their physical and psychological health. The recommendations they provide inspire women of color to thrive and to become leaders across rank, position, and role within the academy.

> *Regardless of all the things I have discussed and the complicated interactions I may have with my students, I love being a college professor. I see it as a contribution to improving this most incomprehensible society. I also see it as my way of helping leave this place in a better condition than I found it.*
>
> Carmen R. Lugo-Lugo, "A Prostitute, a Servant, and a
Customer-Service Representative: A
Latina in Academia"

Outline of Recommendations and Lessons from Narratives

> *Changing the culture of any university is similar to changing the direction of a very large ship. It is difficult to do and usually takes a very long time. With our perceptions of decreasing quality and increasing financial stress, we have reached a time in our history where it is not only possible but critical for the future of our nation for us to move away from the country-club atmosphere.*
>
> Samuel H. Smith, "Introduction," Part IV

In this chapter, I provide timely, specific actions that academic leaders may take to effect impending change and develop a climate where all faculty members have opportunities for a successful career in higher education (Bok 2006; Hurtado 2007). The overarching goals of the recommendations that follow are to: (1) provide administrators the tools to effectively facilitate climate and cultural change in their institutions and eliminate and/or diffuse the effects of tokenism; and (2) empower women of color and women from gender and sexual identity minority groups to succeed in these environments while retaining their dignity, integrity, and self-efficacy. Recommendations focus primarily on faculty members who are navigating challenging university climates and the tenure and promotion process. These suggestions are written from my perspective as a heterosexual Mexican American woman who comes from a very humble socioeconomic background, has achieved tenure and the rank of full professor in a research university, and has served in various university administrative roles. Recommendations are guided by the general structure of the book and are organized as follows:

1. General Campus Climate
2. Faculty/Student Relations
3. Social Class, Tokenism, and the Search Process
4. Tenure and Promotion
5. Networks of Allies and Mentors

As indicated in this flowchart, the recommendations overlap and feed into each other.

General Campus Climate

Recommendations for Administrators

1.   Model a culture of respect

Campus climate is created from the top down. Teaching does not only happen in front of the classroom. The campus leadership team models the way to treat all members of the community and must be strongly encouraged to behave accordingly. Persons with the greatest formal power and authority have an ethical obligation and moral responsibility to be particularly sensitive to their treatment of persons with less power.

> *His yelling at me in a mailroom that at the time was full of white faculty and students felt as if my fate had been sealed—I wasn't as smart as everyone else. I couldn't cut it, and now it seemed everyone knew it. My face began to get hot, tears began to form, and I watched the white faculty and staff make a hasty exit from the mailroom so they did not have to witness any more of my humiliation.*

Serena Easton, "On Being Special"

2.   Be color conscious, not color-blind

From the time that faculty of color are recruited, publicly convey your understanding that they bring added value to the university community through their diverse perspectives in addition to their disciplinary expertise and scholarly accomplishments and potential. In a meaningful way, reward faculty of color for their engagement with the community of color within and surrounding the university. Color blindness is a façade. Adherence to color blindness as an expected outcome or goal is not only unrealistic; it denies the experiential realities of people of color and stymies productive discussions about how persons can genuinely get to know one another across racial/ethnic/national group identities.

> *Society purports to prize color blindness, and that goal makes it hard to see race in public spaces. Race is the elephant in the room that everyone tiptoes around . . . Whites may fear that talking about race makes them seem racist. It would be more helpful for everyone to notice when race and racism are actually present and think about how to combat the problem. Society cannot battle a phantom that it cannot recognize and name. Whites ignore race at their peril and risk causing unintended harm to colleagues of color as the dynamics of racism grind on their daily lives.*

Margalynne J. Armstrong and Stephanie M. Wildman,
"Working across Racial Lines in a
Not-So-Postracial World"

> *. . . She observes that most white women are extremely uncomfortable distinguishing between the realities of their lives and those of women of color. White women become angry when they use the word "woman," and she interjects, "You mean white women."*

Stephanie A. Shields, "Waking Up to Privilege:
Intersectionality and Opportunity"

3.   Model your value of campus diversity by including members of
      underrepresented groups in your leadership team and engage
      your team in color insight groups

Be sure that some of the persons of color across gender and sexual identities on your team have line authority and power and are not just in associate or assistant positions. Engage your leadership team in color-insight discussions to model healthy and productive attitudes and discussions about race/ethnicity, stereotypes, and biases. To admit these prejudices, however, can arouse defense mechanisms that protect one's sense of self, making honest conversations on this topic very difficult. These discussions, therefore, require facilitation by persons skilled and trained in diversity matters. The first step toward changing group perception is acknowledgment of biases. Toward that end, advise your leadership team to take the Implicit Association Test, which confidentially helps participants discover what stereotypes they hold about different groups. The test may be found at https://implicit.harvard.edu/implicit/demo/s.

> *Color insight . . . contrasts with color blindness and offers an alternative that meets the purported goals of color blindness, racial equality, and justice. Color insight recognizes that a racial status quo exists where society attributes race to each member. While color blindness urges us not to notice, color insight says, "Don't be afraid—notice your race and the race of others around you and learn about what that means."*

Margalynne J. Armstrong and Stephanie M. Wildman,
"Working across Racial Lines in a
Not-So-Postracial World"

4.   Incorporate a dean of the faculty into your university
      administrative structure

Through a dual reporting structure to both the university president and provost, empower the dean of the faculty to have oversight of faculty-specific equity, equality, recruitment, and retention issues. This position is important because faculty do not typically have a trusted person or advocate in a position of authority outside of persons who are in their supervisory chain of command. Diversity offices typically do not have power over academic affairs. Faculty must often file an official complaint to receive intervention from offices of human resources or affirmative action/equal opportunity. As such, faculty are usually left on their own to face challenging and institutionalized matters that impact their success and job satisfaction, e.g., unequal salary between men and women in a given unit, and inequitable work distribution. The dean of the faculty can also address issues of recruitment and retention of members of historically underrepresented groups, and do so with the power and authority of an academic dean. As such, the dean of the faculty can be a critical link for faculty success, faculty morale, and for positively impacting climate and cultural change in the institution.

> *The cumulative effects, the destructive power of unaltered structures, of traditional bases of privilege and identity, eroded the confidence many [women of color] had at the beginning of their careers to be able to reach students, who in turn could indeed embody better ways of thinking or change the world as we knew it through practice. . . . . From the struggles to make institutions more humane or responsive to basic and expanding human needs, the lessons accumulate. We are richer for hearing these lessons told in the words of those who have seen, heard, and spoken "truth to power."*

Deena J. González, "Introduction," Part V

5.   Develop an action- and outcome-based diversity plan that focuses
       on the most underrepresented group members of your campus

Develop a well-documented, very-public statement of the university's goals for a climate of inclusion and mutual respect for all persons. Establish a campus representative task force to develop a strategic plan to meet these goals. To be taken seriously, the committee must be outcome- and action-oriented and have financial and personnel resources to accomplish goals. The committee should have dual reporting lines to the president and provost, and/or dean of the faculty, indicating top-down support. Committee members should include the most senior, productive, and powerful faculty on campus, representing faculty campus leadership that will influence the attitudes of their colleagues. It should also include sub-groups of student and community members that report to the committee, reflecting grass roots and town-gown support for the initiative. If you make this matter the sole purview of select units, such as offices of diversity or equal opportunity, you will be sending the wrong message and will symbolically—if not actually—marginalize this important initiative.

> *It has been my experience that my treatment as a woman of color, working as an army civilian, is a nonissue because those of us who work for the army benefit from advances that the government has made in workforce diversity and establishing an environment where rank, command experience, and the ability to complete a mission are what is respected and valued, regardless of your ethnicity.*

Kelly Ervin, "The Experiences of an Academic 'Misfit'"

6.   Issues related to discrimination and prejudice can change the
       tenor and interpretation of a discussion and/or situation

Perceptions of what happened and ways to interpret behavior may vary dramatically when a situation becomes charged with anxiety about race, gender, and/or gender and sexual identity (Sue 2010). Remember that we see what we expect to see (Fiske and Taylor 1984). You may be surprised by the degree to which seemingly small issues can be blown out of proportion when race, gender, and gender and sexual identity are involved. Ordinarily calm and trustworthy colleagues can suddenly turn irrational when their unconsciously held expectations and stereo-types about others are openly challenged. Fair-minded people often do not want to acknowledge the -isms of their community members and colleagues.

You may not understand how a colleague who treats you with respect can treat others so abominably. You may be blind to discrimination if you deny the existence of aversive, covert/subtle, and overt racism. But women of color do not have the option of not seeing racism and sexism. They are targets of the -isms and experience them in their professional lives in the academy. Sexist attitudes are also a reality in the academy, in some disciplines more than in others. If men of color have been accepted into the department, do not assume that women of color will be accepted as well. Remember, also, that racism and sexism are not only a matter of intentions. Even if you believe a colleague genuinely said or did something without any malevolent intent, if others perceived the comment or action as racist or sexist, harm has been done, and you should act accordingly and appropriately in the interest of all parties concerned, especially those with the least formal power and authority.

> . . . it's okay to sort of have a warrior aspect to your personality, but when you're in an institution which only supports that one aspect of ourselves, the person is in trouble. And it will start showing up in health, which it did for me. I started getting some very serious symptoms from stress.
>
> Michelle M. Jacob, "Native Women Maintaining Their
> Culture in the White Academy"

7.   Do not let people get away with vague, unsubstantiated
      accusations

Be an active, careful listener when members of historically underrepresented groups are accused of misconduct. Insist on verifying accounts of their alleged behavior. It is especially critical that you hear the perspective of the victim of the accusations when that person is a member of an underrepresented group. As a result of racist and sexist agendas, people are sometimes willing to perpetrate and believe outright lies and distortions about people of color in their workplace. To the best of your ability, ascertain the veracity of allegations. People will learn to stop irresponsibly complaining about faculty from historically underrepresented groups if you ask detailed questions and insist on evidence. It is critical that you ask the persons of colors being accused how they recall the event. If accusers do not want to confront the person of color, why not? Understand that white anger about any-thing—low wages, changes in rigor or expectations—often results in lashing out at people of color, especially women.

When a woman of color makes an accusation, the same rules apply. Understand that her attributional ambiguity (Crocker et al. 1991), or not knowing whether or not behavior toward her is grounded in bias, may lead her to interpret acts as racist, sexist, or homophobic. At the same time, it may be difficult for her to describe how she knows that someone is biased. Many clues about how people perceive us are unconsciously understood after years of experience interacting with members of the dominant group, e.g., eye movement and other body language, patronization, and general discomfort. For people of color, knowledge of people's biases often becomes instinctive.

> *I feel an incredible sense of emptiness in the middle of my body. I pick up the phone to call my oldest friend in California and then put it down. Instead, I grab a pillow and put it over my stomach and begin to cry my guts out. I am crying because less than an hour before I had walked out of the dean's office after a bizarre meeting with him and a few members of the promotion and tenure committee, who had tried to talk me out of proceeding with my application for tenure. . . . And like the victim of abuse who dissociates from her body to survive trauma, I remember the implosion, the fading of their voices, and the awkward posture of everyone on the dean's leather couch as they executed their act of rejection. And before too much more could be said, I barely uttered, "I don't have to listen to this . . . ," and I walked out. And the next day I met with a lawyer.*

Elvia R. Arriola, "'No hay mal que por bien no venga': A
Journey to Healing as a Latina, Lesbian Law Professor"

8.　Understand why people are leaving the university

Conduct exit interviews of faculty; analyze the data for patterns, correlations, and causality; take action accordingly. The interviews should be conducted by persons in human resources, or other appropriate units, who may be trusted with confidential information. Identifying information should be removed from the interview before the data are passed along for analyses.

> *Standing there with more than ten years of exemplary performance appraisals and . . . superior teaching evaluations, I was devastated and felt violated! More importantly, others would presume my transfer was due to incompetence. The mounting anxieties from ostracism, isolation, stress, and the loss of professional support and interaction made me feel like a pariah. . . . I felt the situation was literally eating me alive and I was totally alone. . . . I did receive support from former students, who refused to accept my replacement and actively sought me out.*

Sherri L. Wallace, Sharon E. Moore, Linda J. Wilson,
and Brenda G. Hart, "African American Women
in the Academy: Quelling the Myth
of Presumed Incompetence"

9.　Develop an "equity scorecard" to determine how faculty members
　　fare by gender and race/ethnicity by department and college

This "scorecard" (Bensimon, Hao, and Bustillos 2006; Bensimon 2005) should include data on retention, tenure and promotion across ranks, numbers of courses and students taught, and documentation of service responsibilities. Your institutional research office can readily collect and analyze these data. You want information to determine if race/ethnicity and/or gender impact faculty success within a given unit.

> *I began to realize that their stories [those of white colleagues] sounded very different from mine. In my sections, everything I said was questioned, scrutinized, and cross-examined. Fully expecting my compatriots to complain about the same problems, I was stunned when they began looking at*

me as if I had just grown an eyeball on my forehead. They weren't having these difficulties in their sections—it was just me . . . Only I was forced to pull up statistics, photos, theories, graphs, and charts constantly as evidence that what I was saying was true. I would bear witness to their privilege over and over again, only reinforcing my loneliness in that six-year period and reinforcing my race as a master status in a way it hadn't been before. For most of my life, race was there and was a reality but not one that necessarily confronted me every day.

Serena Easton, "On Being Special"

10. Examine salaries by rank, race/ethnicity, and gender to ensure equity within departments and disciplines

Salaries may be inequitable because women often lack the mentoring to know how to negotiate their initial salaries and increases. But they may also be inequitable due to racism and sexism. Higher salaries for men than for women may reflect the sexist biases of the appointing supervisor and the value they place on appointees. The biases must be challenged up the supervisory chain, and the inequitable salaries must be corrected.

When I asked how they knew to negotiate that way, they credited advice passed to them by fathers with professional careers or male mentors. I learned that womyn of color needed to be diligent about seeking and providing mentorship for each other.

Michelle A. Holling, May Fu, and Roe Bubar, "Dis/ Jointed Appointments: Solidarity amidst Inequality, Tokenism, and Marginalization"

11. Use resources as a carrot to shape campus diversity and climate

The most powerful accountability measure you have is allocation of resources. Make the bases of college, unit, department resources, evaluations, and faculty salary increases, in part, dependent on their successes with increasing diversity and enhancing collegiality, mentorship, and retention in their units.

. . . when you are fighting for your life within a context of inequality, you can become so busy trying to survive that you have no time to reflect on the system that is putting you in that position in the first place. I was in the trenches of the academic jungle, taking grenades. When you are fighting a war like that, you don't have time to think about the structure of the war, whether or not it should be happening in the first place, or what has put you in the midst of it. No matter how much you may know in your head that you and your people are victims of a system that you didn't create, it doesn't really matter when you're taking grenades. You must react to stay alive.

Serena Easton, "On Being Special"

12.   Language matters

Do not use the word "tolerance," which implies a forced attitude. People of color want to be accepted, respected, and valued for who we are, not tolerated. The phrase "members of historically underrepresented groups" is now more commonly accepted than the word "minorities." Use group-specific terms, e.g., African American/black; Latino/Latina (but use the actual group identifier when known, e.g., Mexican American, Puerto Rican); Asian American (again, use specific group names when known, e.g., Vietnamese American, Japanese American); American Indian or Native American. Use the description "persons across gender and sexual identities" for members of non-heterosexual groups.

> *Or they'll tell you about how their momma and poppa and uncle and everyone else in their family hates niggers, but they don't—that's a quote.*

Sherée Wilson, "They Forgot Mammy Had a Brain"

13.   Do Not Define white Women as the De Facto Norm for All
       Women by Using the Phrase "Women and People of Color" or
       "Women and Minorities"

Women of color are women; they are also people of color; they are also minorities. The use of the phrases "women and people of color" and "women and minorities" makes women of color invisible while defining white women as the de facto norm. The use of these phrases minimizes the intersectional realities that both link and separate white women, men of color, and women of color and that the essays in this collection reflect.

> *. . . third-wave feminism steers clear of essentialist notions of femininity to embrace the experiences of all women, rather than only those of a particular race and class. . . .*

Kimberly R. Moffitt, Heather E. Harris, and Diane A.
Forbes Berthoud, "Present and Unequal: A Third-Wave
Approach to Voice Parallel Experiences in Managing
Oppressions and Bias in the Academy"

> *Probably the most blatant example of blindness to white privilege was lurking at the heart of my own research. . . . Unthinkingly I began the way that most gender-stereotype researchers did—by using descriptions of a generic woman and generic man to explore the stereotypes. And—as research has shown time and time again—generic in the US academic world signals white . . . Interestingly none of the probably all-white audience of editors, conference attendees, or other colleagues who assessed my work stopped to ask "which woman? which man?"*

Stephanie A. Shields, "Waking Up to Privilege:
Intersectionality and Opportunity"

14.   Learn how to supervise women of color

Supervising women of color is a new experience for most white men and women in academia, as well as for most men and women of color. Supervisors may not be aware that—although they are looking at a woman of color—*they often do not really see her.* They see what they expect to see, and often that expectation is based on racist, sexist, homophobic, and classist ideology (Jones 1997; Allport 1954). When persons do not fit a group stereotype, they often arouse anxiety and anger in the perceiver (Fiske and Taylor 1984). This response is true especially when the person is exceptionally competent, which arouses conscious and unconscious biases and resentments regarding who deserves to have power over whom (Dovidio and Gaertner 2010). In addition, stereotypical expectations often lead supervisors to assign women of color to teaching and service related to diversity issues, responsibilities for which they may not have been trained nor have vested interest.

> . . . *(a) no matter how we frame our research agenda, prospective employers think our work will be connected to African American women; (b) we are eager to nurture and mentor other students of color, regardless of their majors or career interests; (c) we will incorporate race and gender into the courses we teach (despite the fact that many of us have no coursework on our transcripts related to these issues); (d) we will enthusiastically serve on any committee with the word "diversity" in the title; and (e) we are well equipped to "deal with" students from underprivileged backgrounds who are not as well prepared for college as they should be.*

Cerise L. Glenn, "Stepping in and Stepping out:
Examining the Way Anticipatory Career Socialization
Impacts Identity Negotiation of African American
Women in Academia"

15.   Avoid knee-jerk reactions to accusations of racism

Inevitably, a student, faculty member, or administrator will accuse someone in your university community of engaging in racist, sexist, or homophobic behavior. It is very important to be proactive, rather than reactive. Be prepared with processes in place that thoughtfully investigate the claim, and then publicly report the findings, thereby identifying unfounded claims as well as verified incidents. Ensure that complaints provide as much specific information about persons, times, and places as possible. Be clear that unfounded accusations of racism, sexism, and anti-homosexual behavior, if not clearly refuted, weaken the response to the actual experiences of discrimination on your campus. Have the courage to stand your ground when the accusation is clearly false but also be aware that it can be difficult for a grievant to prove that an action was grounded on bias. Use the entire context of the situation, including the culture and demographic makeup of your campus and community, to inform your judgment.

> *So seeing race for whites must mean noticing whiteness, not just noticing race when a person of color is present. . . . It is not that whiteness simply privileges white people. Whiteness can also negate people of color, who are judged by their conformance to white norms, disparaged by their perceived dependence on whiteness, or silenced by invisible presumptions of non-white deviance.*

Margalynne J. Armstrong and Stephanie M. Wildman,
"Working across Racial Lines in a
Not-So-Postracial World"

16.   If you celebrate Martin Luther King Jr. Day, make it meaningful

This celebration is at once an experience of pride for African Americans and a time that many dread. Most women and men of color dislike being asked to engage in ethnic celebrations that lack any real meaning or significance, and are implemented for the university's ability to engage in an empty public-relations gesture. Do not use these occasions to put people of color on display or tokenize them. Rather, ask for volunteers to participate in the events of the day. Plan activities that involve all university constituents. For instance, Martin Luther King Jr. Day celebrations might be a time to award service-related achievements to the university community-at-large. Solicit awards and nominations from different sectors of the university community, including tenure-track faculty, lecturers, students, fraternities, sororities, staff, and student affairs, research, and development departments. The more inclusive the events of the day, the more meaningful the commemoration of the work of Dr. Martin Luther King, Jr.

> *They are going to trot you out and trot you around as their African American person, but that's not considered in terms of your workload. It doesn't count. They are going to expect you to mentor and take care of students of color, but you're not going to get credit for that, either. I learned a lot. They wanted our visibility in the service arena, but they didn't want to reward you for it. . . . It was almost like the mammy syndrome.*
>
> Sherée Wilson, "They Forgot Mammy Had a Brain"

17.   Provide a parent-friendly environment

Lactation rooms are absolutely critical for women who do not have a private office, e.g., students, lecturers, adjuncts. Provide day care as much as possible; infant care is especially challenging for working parents. Offer nonpunitive leaves of absence for pregnancy and/or new parents. The climate in the university should support all prospective new parents in stopping their tenure clock for a designated period of time.

> *. . . when I organized a campus-wide workshop on family-friendly policies targeted to educate junior faculty on their options . . . , few people attended. I learned that some were afraid to attend: they did not want their colleagues to know they were planning to have children, instead of focusing on their publications.*
>
> Linda Trinh Võ, "Navigating the Academic Terrain:
> The Racial and Gender Politics of Elusive Belonging"

> *I just wish people were more candid about the fact that the professoriate is not particularly well suited for parents after all. There is a lot of hostility toward parents from both men and women without kids in this discipline, really harsh.*
>
> Jessica Lavariega Monforti, "*La Lucha:* Latinas
> Surviving Political Science"

18. Mandate meaningful sexual-harassment-prevention training and
    address complaints immediately

An expert in the area of sexual harassment prevention and consequences should oversee this training. Have policies in place to address sexual harassment and, through policy, mandate consequences to faculty who have sexual contact with students and /or with employees they supervise. Understand that some persons stereotype women of color as sexually exotic, docile, permissive, and available to them. Social-class issues may also become important in these situations because the culturally based friendliness and generosity of women of color, especially from lower socioeconomic backgrounds, may be misinterpreted as willingness or availability (Dews and Law 1995). Provide good training to help all members of the campus community understand what constitutes sexual harassment and other inappropriate behavior with sexual undertones. Complaints in this domain must be addressed immediately. The victims of these situations may be in both psychological and physical danger, and the perpetrators are often people who have formal authority and power over their victims. It is also likely that if perpetrators get away with victimizing one person, they will continue to perpetrate against others.

> *I have had male graduate students and faculty make inappropriate sexual statements and advances toward me, and I know I am not alone. . . . Ideally we should not have to worry about being harassed in the workplace by our colleagues or forced to take action, but the reality is that gender and sexual harassment in both mild and severe forms occurs much more often than is officially reported. . . . it is not the sexual orientation or gender that matters as much as the power relationship: those who are harassed usually have less power in these situations. . . . The preponderance of sexualized and racialized stereotypes about Asian Americans and other women of color can make us vulnerable targets. The converging perceptions of Asian American women as exotic and docile "model minorities," who are less likely to file a complaint, increases the chances of us becoming victims of "racialized sexual harassment."*

> Linda Trinh Võ, "Navigating the Academic Terrain:
> The Racial and Gender Politics of Elusive Belonging"

> *Magazine covers are full of phrases like "sizzling hot" and "hot tamales"*
> *or the word "sexy" when describing Latinos/as.*

> Carmen R. Lugo-Lugo, "A Prostitute, a Servant, and a
> Customer-Service Representative: A
> Latina in Academia"

19. National and state leaders can effect change

Changes in the status quo for women of color advocated by this collection of narratives can be facilitated by Congress, the US Secretary of Education, governors, and/or state legislatures through allocation of grant money, which is critical to most universities. Require that institutions provide evidence of real equity and equality in treatment of all their students, faculty, and staff to be qualified to obtain grants and other resources.

20. Boards of trustees, boards of regents, and chancellors can effect change

One way to facilitate change is to hire university leaders with a demonstrated knowledge of underrepresented communities and a commitment to enhancing the diversity of institutions. Currently, relatively few administrators of color serve in academia. In 2003, only 10.39 percent of administrators, including those with academic and student-affairs appointments, were people of color (McCurtis, Jackson, and O'Callaghan 2009). Charge university presidents with creating a respectful cultural climate for all constituents and proving they have done so by recruiting and retaining members of underrepresented groups.

Recommendations for Women of Color and Allies

1. Model appropriate behavior for students and colleagues

By virtue of your position and accomplishments, you are a role model whether or not you want to be seen as such. Students, faculty, staff, administrators, and community members learn from your behavior and attitudes, for better or worse.

2. Know how merit and qualifications are defined

When you serve on student-admission, faculty, or administrator search committees, ensure that the group is looking beyond candidate test scores and schools where degrees were received. Do your best to steer the discussion away from pedigree or elitist backgrounds. Speak up when people are judged negatively on the basis of perceived lower-social-class background. When you have the opportunity, make extra efforts to include people of color across gender and sexual identities on your own staff and/or research teams.

3. When meeting with administrators, present specific solutions to your concerns

Due to their personal ethics and values, and in the interest of the university's reputation, most leaders genuinely want to do the right thing by all members of their academic community. However, they often lack the experience and expertise to develop solutions to your concerns. So let them know what you are experiencing, but go to them with a recommendation or solution. When possible, go to the president's office as part of a collective; it is more time-effective for the president and more powerful for you. Focus on change, on solutions, rather than critiquing what is wrong. University administrators cannot change people's attitudes, but they can model diversity-related values and address issues through policy, code, and process.

4. Document events and interactions that make you uncomfortable; you may have to provide evidence later

Keeping a journal is useful for healing and stress relief, as well as providing evidence that may be needed at a later time. Your detailed journaling will bolster your memory when you complain about an experience or observation. Journal about disrespectful treatment and misinterpretation of statements or actions, especially if you are accused of behavior that may impact your evaluations. Document all agreements regarding assignments and rewards. Also journal about positive experiences;

these will lift your spirits. Do not use nonconfidential venues such as e-mail or Face-book for your journaling.

5.   If you are asked to participate in Martin Luther King Jr. Day
     celebrations, make sure the event is meaningful to you

Be prepared to respond to requests to be a visible participant in Martin Luther King, Jr. commemoration events. If the event is superficial, politely decline. Some faculty of color make a point of being out of town on this day to ensure they have a legitimate excuse not to participate in events they believe are a deceptive depiction of university attitudes. Understand that you have a right not to engage in meaning-less gestures, but be wary of repercussions of saying no to administrative requests to participate. You need to determine the best way to handle these situations in your academic environment.

6.   Follow the process

Bring to the attention of administrators any failure to follow due process with respect to your evaluations, tenure, and promotion process. At the same time, do not expect or ask to be the exception to the rule. Follow protocol and move through the chain of command—department chair, dean, provost, and president—progress-ing through the hierarchy only when a previous level fails to address the matter. Diversity officers typically do not have the authority, funding, or power to address faculty matters, so stay within the academic chain of command. A dean of the faculty can be a good resource for you. You may also need to report your experience to the human-resources division of the university; action from these units may require that you file a formal complaint.

7.   Practice color consciousness

Help your supervisors understand the distinction between color blindness and color consciousness. Practice color consciousness. Do not try to be a "white woman of color." That is, do not attempt to be just like the majority but with a different skin tone; you will not succeed. Use your difference to your advantage. Your uniqueness allows you to see what others cannot because they are surrounded by realities similar to their own. Your level of consciousness is different from that of the homogenous majority. You are at once an outsider with the experiences of being on the inside. This complex and broader perception can make you an excellent leader.

8.   Do not use the phrases "women and people of color" or "women
     and minorities"

When you hear others use these phrases, rephrase by saying, "You mean white women and men and women of color" or "white women, women of color, and men of color." Point out that the realities of women of color are distinct from those of white women and men of color.

9.   Report Any Instances of Sexual Harassment Immediately

If people make inappropriate statements and/or advances toward you, report them. If someone misinterprets your friendliness or generosity as a sexual invitation, immediately correct them. Tell them that in your culture, warmth, friendliness, and sharing are normal and have no bearing whatsoever on more intimate relationships or your professional skills. If harassment persists, file a formal complaint. It is likely that you are not the perpetrator's only victim. Keep doors open when meeting with persons whom you suspect may behave inappropriately toward you. When possible, meet in public places, e.g., the student commons, library, university café.

10. Reflect on whether academia is the right place for your
professional contributions

Determining whether to enter into or remain in academia requires reflective analysis of the gains and losses—to your mind, body, family, finances, and your impact on your discipline, institution, and students. Those in administrative positions, in particular, must also take time to heal from wounds that multiply, one upon the other, taking a tremendous physical and psychological toll on their bodies and minds. Not taking the time to heal risks paying the ultimate and inconceivable price—losing your life and/or mental health. Not taking the time to heal also risks internalizing oppressive behaviors and then becoming the oppressor.

Faculty/Student Relations

Recommendations for Administrators

1. Students carry overt and covert racist attitudes and biases
(Stanley 2006).

We are not living in a postracial society. We are all products of our socialization in what is still a racially segregated country and where the majority of the national, state, and corporate leaders are white men. All persons, including university students, have overt biases and stereotypical attitudes, as well as unconscious ones. In addition, foreign students bring with them racial, religious, sexual-orientation, and patriarchal biases from their respective cultures. Remember that these prejudices impact the way students perceive, respond to, and evaluate women of color faculty.

> *I contend that the white student's revulsion toward me was transformed into my so-called hatred of "them."*

> Delia D. Douglas, "Black/Out: The White Face of
> Multiculturalism and the Violence of the Canadian
> Academic Imperial Agenda"

2. When women of color teach topics related to social justice—
especially about racially and sexually underrepresented groups in
the US—Some, if not most, white students will meet their message
with resentment

> *So when I actually tell them . . . that racism and racial inequalities are alive and well, their understanding of the world where they live is threatened. By me. A woman. Of color.*

> Carmen R. Lugo-Lugo, "A Prostitute, a Servant, and a
> Customer-Service Representative: A
> Latina in Academia"

Until they reach the university, many students have not received an accurate account of the histories of historically underrepresented groups in the United States. When they hear this information for the first time, they react with surprise, anger, and/or resentment. Some of these feelings arise from the white guilt persons feel upon learning of atrocities committed against persons of color in the United States. Women of color may be the first professors—even first persons—to challenge students' preexisting ideas about race, sexuality, social class, and the role of the United States government in creating and supporting group-based hierarchies and discriminatory practices. Readings and discussions that confront these assumptions may evoke cognitive dissonance, resulting in anxiety and/or anger. Additionally, the very fact that a woman of color is standing in front of the class and exercising authority may cause students discomfort and resentment. When information about group-based discrimination is provided by women of color and/or persons from underrepresented gender and sexual identities, these feelings intensify. If a white, heterosexual male teaches the material, his privileged positionality in the United States makes it more likely that his teaching will be accepted as factual. When a woman of color presents the same material she may be perceived as acting like a victim or having a chip on her shoulder (Vargas 2002). Complaints about women of color's teaching must be considered in this context.

> White senior faculty members have said that because I am Latina I cannot be credible teaching Latino politics.

> Jessica Lavariega Monforti, "*La Lucha:* Latinas Surviving Political Science"

3.   Keep in mind that students' teaching evaluations may reflect their biases more than the competencies of their instructor

Women of color can be very vulnerable to students' verbal violence toward them, including constant and unwarranted criticism of their teaching. Students harbor stereotyped expectations of women of color. They may be less accepting of poor grades from a person of color, especially a woman, than from a white professor. They may not be aware of what are often unconscious biases about which groups are superior and deserve authority over others. Because students may not be equipped to handle their anxiety, discomfort, and resentment—conscious and unconscious— they may discharge their feelings in generalized complaints about and unjust teaching evaluations of women of color. The latter are frequently bimodal, reflecting both intensely positive and negative comments. As with the investigation of campus and workplace conflicts, administrators must gather specifics, rather than rely on generalized criticism. Candidly discuss different interpretations of these evaluations at departmental and college levels.

> If student evaluations are subjective, are they then also subjective about the race and gender of the instructor? To what extent will a student's reaction to a professor's gender and race influence his or her evaluation? . . . Whites and men start from a presumption of competence; minorities and women do not and have to deal with a multitude of unconscious biases that put them at a disadvantage. The playing field is not level . . . If decision

*makers do not take the time or care to fully understand the candidate's
teaching file, including evaluations, and permit important personnel decisions to proceed on the basis of potentially misleading or biased data, then
they ethically fail the professoriate, students, and the institution.*

> Sylvia R. Lazos, "Are Student Teaching Evaluations
> Holding Back Women and Minorities?: The Perils of
> 'Doing' Gender and Race in the Classroom"

4.   Use teaching portfolios to evaluate faculty, rather than relying
     solely on end-of-course teaching evaluations

Evaluating teaching effectiveness solely on the bases of subjective end-of-course
student evaluations is a mistake. This practice is often unfair and harmful to women
of color and members of underrepresented gender and sexual-identity groups. Help
faculty develop well-prepared teaching portfolios that include a comprehensive
understanding of each individual's engagement in the teaching process, broadly
defined (e.g., including student advising, consulting with the community) as well as
information related to student learning outcomes (Seldin 2004, 2009).

> *I began to become increasingly more concerned about consciously perform-
> ing to maintain my acceptably high student evaluations and what the cost
> might be to my self-esteem and fulfilling my responsibilities as a teacher.
> Aside from the time and effort involved, I found myself concentrating
> more on earning high evaluations and less on the pedagogical goals of
> my courses.*

> Marie-Antoinette Smith, "Free at Last! No More
> Performance Anxieties in the Academy 'Cause Stepin
> Fetchit Has Left the Building"

5.   Lesbian, bisexual, transgender, and transsexual women of color
     are particularly vulnerable to student violence and harassment

Women of color who are also members of underrepresented gender and sexual-
identity groups are particularly vulnerable to being challenged, getting hate mail,
and receiving negative evaluations. This situation may be most pervasive in more
conservative areas of the country. Have processes and practices in place to protect
faculty from racist, sexist, and homophobic actions of students and peers. Develop
support mechanisms for these faculty members.

> *. . . although I was bolstered by a number of social and institutional fac-
> tors—including having a position of authority as a faculty member and a
> reputation for being nice, fair, and attractive (all shaped by gender, race,
> and class ideologies), and being white with a PhD—this would not spare
> me from classroom "microaggression" or interactional cruelties inflicted
> across lines of difference to maintain racist, classist, sexist, heterosexist,
> and other oppressive social hierarchies. . . . Midway through the term,
> someone in the class anonymously posted on our online discussion board
> an article about the so-called gay agenda that referred to gay people as less
> than human and responsible for the demise of western civilization. Shortly*

thereafter another online post specifically named me as a "feminazi." The note was accompanied by an image of a swastika dripping with blood, framed by a pink triangle, and signed by Fred Phelps (the leader of the God Hates Fags movement).

Kari Lerum, "'What's Love Got to Do with It?': Life
Teachings from Multiracial Feminism"

6.   Male students may be especially likely to challenge the authority
      of women of color

Patriarchal attitudes, grounded in cultural, religious, and historical norms, make some males resentful that women have power and authority over them. These challenges are heightened when students do not receive the grade they want or think they have earned, or when their special requests, e.g., to take an exam on a different date and time, are not accommodated. These students sometimes react with overt hostility when they do not get their way with women of color faculty. Their biases do not allow them to accept that these faculty members should have any authority or power over them. When students come to you with complaints about women of color faculty members, buttress their authority. Be clear that you have complete confidence in her intelligence, competence, and authority. Do not promise to fix the problem for the student; that action sends the message that the faculty member is in error. Develop a process to address students' disrespect for faculty in the classroom. Let students know what you expect of their behavior in the classroom and the kind of learning campus climate you are attempting to create, e.g., through university mission and/or value statements, and in your oral and written communications. Let faculty know their options. Address and challenge—through public institutional values—the consumer mentality that allows students to believe that by virtue of paying tuition, they control the professor and the curriculum. Your institution's professional development staff may be able to assist you with this process.

White students in particular feel entitled to be discourteous, arrogant, and abrasive. They feel very comfortable lashing out. There have been many days when I feel incompetent, disconsolate, and enraged, and in those moments, I simply want to give up.

Delia D. Douglas, "Black/Out: The White Face of
Multiculturalism and the Violence of the Canadian
Academic Imperial Agenda"

7.   Attitudes about affirmative impact behavior toward women
      of color

Students, faculty, administrators, and staff often assume that women of color were hired due to affirmative action requirements and not because of their competencies (Rai and Critzer 2000). This assumption is often coupled with the belief that qualified white men are not being hired due to affirmative action policy (Niemann and Dovidio 1998; 2005; Rai and Critzer 2000). As indicated earlier, the data belie these attitudes and beliefs. Nevertheless, attitudes about affirmative action manifest in overt and in subtle and sometimes unconscious judgments, such as the presumption of incompetence. This bias is exacerbated when women of color teach issues related to social justice to predominantly white classes of students. Take these biases into consideration when you interpret end-of-course evaluations and complaints against faculty. Make public the demographic make-up of the faculty and point to the data that clearly indicates that affirmative action policies are not keeping white males from being hired and promoted to the highest levels of the institution, especially relative to white women and men and women of color.

> *Given the white student's racial pronouncement, the director's failure to consider the complexities involved when a black woman teaches a course that focuses on race and its connection to gender and power indicates a lack of awareness (or denial?) of white resentment and resistance, as well as this student's categorization of me as the racial other.*

Delia D. Douglas, "Black/Out: The White Face of
Multiculturalism and the Violence of the Canadian
Academic Imperial Agenda"

8.   Due to perceptions of socioeconomic status, students of color may not support women of color faculty

Due to internalized racial stereotypes, students of color from low socioeconomic status backgrounds often believe that faculty of color must have grown up in upper socioeconomic status backgrounds. They may resent these perceived differences between themselves and the faculty of color (Niemann, et al. 1994). In addition, they may expect these faculty members to be lenient in grading them. Students from highly patriarchal and hierarchical communities and cultures may be particularly resentful of women of color in positions of authority who may hold different values and/or will not lower their academic expectations. Do not assume that a complaint about a woman of color is legitimate because it comes from a student of color.

> *These standards included things like writing using proper grammar, spelling, and paragraph structure. . . . And so, inevitably, what my black students saw was a young black girl who talked like a white girl, had been given privileges that they could only dream about, and thus thought she was better than her students, even though that couldn't be further from the truth. Essentially the intersections of race, class, and age conspired to make my life rather difficult at my first job.*

Serena Easton, "On Being Special"

9.   Students and faculty may have adverse reactions toward women of color who are not perceived as adequately nurturing

Faculty, staff, and students may have particularly adverse reactions—conscious and unconscious—toward women of color who are not perceived as adequately nurturing or feminine. The stereotype of the mammy and the motherly Latina are particularly strong. Women who do not meet stereotypical expectations that they will nurture students arouse anger, distrust, and feelings of betrayal. Be aware of these different expectations—not only from students but often from faculty colleagues— and their harmful impact on evaluating women faculty members.

> *You're supposed to always be chuckling and nurturing no matter what*
> *they do. You're not supposed to demand the same level of performance.*
> *'You's the mammy.'*

Sherée Wilson, "They Forgot Mammy Had a Brain"

10. Value and expect scholarship and teaching on social justice and
     emancipative social thought

It is very important that people of color are not the only members of the faculty
teaching these often-controversial and emotionally charged topics. Encourage all
department faculty to incorporate information about these issues into their course
content. In some disciplines, such as the humanities, social sciences, and education,
all faculty members should be expected to cover this curricular content, which can
make courses transformative for students and enrich the experience of the faculty
members teaching the courses. Encourage deans to assess learning related to race/
ethnicity, sexual identity, social class, and gender, as appropriate for the discipline.
Afford faculty members the opportunity to develop new courses that explore these
topics and reward them for doing so. Send a message about the importance of this
curricular content by providing a small summer stipend, e.g., $1000, as incentive for
faculty to update their course materials and content. When only women and men
of color explore these issues, the message students receive is that this content is not
valid or important enough to be taught by white faculty. You also send a message
about the value and legitimacy of faculty of color. At the same time, when faculty of
color have expertise in these areas, tangibly value their competence and willingness
to teach these topics.

> *I do gain affirmation from many of my varied teaching experiences and*
> *from students of color, queer students, and white and working-class stu-*
> *dents who express their appreciation for my work in real, tangible ways. I*
> *also take great pride in the possibility that I am challenging those students*
> *suffering from white, upper-class, and heterosexual privilege.*

Grace Chang, "Where's the Violence? The Promise and
Perils of Teaching Women of Color Studies"

Recommendations for Women of Color and Allies

1. There is no reason for you to be the only person whose course
    content includes issues of social justice and/or the intersections
    of race, ethnicity, socioeconomic status, and sexuality

Being the only person who teaches these issues may set you up to receive poor
teaching evaluations because of students' unwillingness to have their existing views
challenged, especially their beliefs about the racial history of the United States. It will
also send a message to students that this content is not important or valid enough
for white faculty to include it and that you teach these topics because you have a
chip on your shoulder. In the disciplines within the social sciences, humanities, and
education, in particular, there is no excuse for any faculty member to lack expertise
on these issues. If your department head assigns only you to teach these emotion-
ally-charged topics, then respectfully challenge the assignment and explain that you

are concerned about critical teaching evaluations that may be related more to the course content than to your competence. This situation is particularly anxiety producing if you are not yet tenured. Seek support from your dean if your department head is not supportive. When possible, take a break from teaching topics related to discrimination and prejudice. You might alternate semesters when you teach these topics, focusing on more emotionally neutral areas of your discipline during the other semesters. This practice will give you a much-needed respite from the physically and psychologically draining impacts of teaching the more controversial topics.

 2. Do not use the classroom as a pulpit.

Do not abuse your privilege as a professor to pursue your personal and/or political agenda in the classroom and/or solicit student advocacy for your cries of racism or other -isms. It is unethical for you to expect or ask students to advocate for your personal views, especially when there may be negative consequences to them for doing so. Furthermore, when students lead a protest group and/or engage in discussions for change from a grass-roots level, they are much more powerful than when a faculty member is engaged with them in these efforts. Teaching means exposing students to critical examinations of diverse perspectives, not preaching your politically charged agenda. At the same time, however, it is appropriate to inform students of factual issues, histories, and/or situations that they may find challenging and/or anxiety-provoking in the context of a course that encompasses these topics. Let your ethical teaching and the information you present, relative to the appropriate course, be students' motivation for their actions.

 3. Establish and assess learning outcomes for each of your courses

Course goals and expected learning outcomes should be clearly outlined in your course syllabus and in your teaching portfolio. Develop exams that correlate to expected learning outcomes for the course. Analyze your exam results with respect to these expectancies. In that manner, you will have data and evidence other than end-of-year teaching evaluations to attest to your success and competence in the classroom.

 4. Develop a clear and detailed syllabus

The syllabus is your contract with students and your best protection from those who claim biased grading. Detail the manner in which students will be graded, the dates of exams, your expectations, and the university policies that are to be followed in the classroom, e.g., regarding plagiarism and accommodating students with disabilities. A word of caution—if you deviate from policies outlined in your syllabus on behalf of one student, you may be accused of discrimination by other students.

 5. Immediately report abusive students to your department head
  and/or dean

If their responses are not helpful, seek help from your university human-resources and/or student-affairs offices. Document these situations in writing and retain the documentation. Seek support and advice from allies. If appropriate, seek guidance from the university attorney's office. Let the university police know what you are experiencing and, if appropriate, ask for their protection. If the university does not act, you may have to seek counsel and intervention from a private attorney and local or federal law enforcement agencies.

6.   Conduct midsemester course evaluations

This process gives students the message that you care that they are learning the course content. It also affords you an opportunity to make a midcourse correction, if appropriate.

Social Class, Tokenism, and the Search Process

Recommendations for Administrators

1.   Social-class challenges include those related to the hierarchical structure within the university as well as cultural differences between groups

Faculty in non-tenure-track positions, whose numbers are increasing, may be particularly vulnerable to bullying and other harmful treatment. They do not have the protection of tenure. They are often perceived as second- or third-class members of the faculty. You need to have policies in place to protect these members of the academy from the oppression of more powerful members.

> *Rather, hierarchy and other distinctions in the legal academy take a different form and instead seem to be situated in the difference between tenure-track professors and everyone else, and between professors teaching at higher-ranked schools and the rest of us.*

> Ruth Gordon, "On Community in the Midst of
> Hierarchy (and Hierarchy in the Midst of Community)"

Social-class differences may include family expectations, patterns of speech, emotional expression, responsibilities to communities, cultural mores, ways of expressing friendliness and warmth, music, and dress. Women of color cannot—and should not—reasonably be expected to change their culture because they have entered a white academic world. However, cultural differences may be misperceived, misinterpreted, and/or translated as not belonging to academia or noncollegial by their white colleagues and/or students. As much as possible, ensure that negative evaluations are not grounded in cultural differences.

> *Unlike the evolution of gay identity in American society, there are no cool T-shirts, no exciting revelations, no working-class pride day, and really no recognizably celebrated culture . . . You can take the woman out of the working class, but you cannot take the working class out of the woman . . . My journey through the academy as a gay, working-class woman in an overwhelmingly straight, middle- and upper-middle-class male field, has been constrained by each of these social factors, but despite the intersectionality of these facets of identity, class is the least socially recognized and—perhaps for that reason—the most corrosive.*

> Constance G. Anthony, "The Port Hueneme of My
> Mind: The Geography of Working-Class Consciousness
> in One Academic Career"

2. Be aware of the psychosocial consequences of tokenism and establish structures to minimize these effects

The effects of tokenism include high visibility, distinctiveness, loneliness, attributional ambiguity, stereotyping and racism, representativeness, and role encapsulation (Dovidio et al. 2001; Niemann 2011; Pollak and Niemann 1998; also see Niemann 2003 for a more thorough discussion of these effects). Tokens are highly visible, living in a glass house; their actions, words, demeanor, dress—virtually everything about them—is noticed in these environments. Memories about persons of color are often stereotype-consistent and have no basis in actual occurrences. Whether or not they wish to be, tokenized persons are seen as representatives of members of their distinctive group in their environment (Fiske and Taylor 1984; Steele 1997, 2010). Their failures, in particular, are seen as reflective of their demographic group, while their successes are considered exceptions to the rule or stereotype about their group.

> *I knew if I failed in my quest to get tenure, it would be regarded as not just a personal failure. It is the plight of minorities to know that their whole subgroups may be judged by their individual behavior. If I failed, it might mean that no other black woman would be hired in the future. "We tried a black woman once. It didn't work out" might be the refrain. Yet the administration would never say that the failure of one white male meant that another should never be hired again.*

Adrien Katherine Wing, "Lessons from a Portrait: Keep Calm and Carry On"

Tokens are seen stereotypically. For people of color, the stereotypes are largely negative, racist, and sexist, and there are damaging consequences of these perceptions. Tokenized persons feel isolated and lonely, not only on the campus, but sometimes in their predominantly white communities-at-large. Tokens experience attributional ambiguity; they do not know whom to trust. They do not know whether feedback they receive is valid, or if it is the result of biases, racism, sexism, or other -isms. Not to be able to trust feedback is not to know how to improve. They experience role encapsulation—assignments to projects associated with teaching topics related to historically underrepresented group and/or to the university's diversity goals- as unpaid grant consultants, as university spokespersons, and as mascots for diversity (for a more detailed discussion of the effects of tokenism, see Niemann 2003; Niemann and Dovidio 1998a).

> *Overall about 59 percent of the Latinas in this survey said that they were expected to be experts in Latin American and ethnic and/or gender politics—regardless of their training—because they are Latinas.*

Jessica Lavariega Monforti, "*La Lucha:* Latinas Surviving Political Science"

You will minimize or eliminate tokenization of faculty when you increase the numbers of historically underrepresented groups on your campus. The minimal point is for these persons to represent at least 15% of nonwhite, US-born, or domestic members in any given unit/department. In predominantly male fields, e.g., engineering, females need to represent at least 15 percent of the total department members in tenure-track positions. Members of historically underrepresented groups will begin to achieve feelings of belonging and safety when their numbers reach a critical mass. In the meantime, following recommendations in this chapter will help diffuse or minimize the negative impacts of tokenism.

3.   Do not turn people of color into mascots

As institutional leaders, be particularly sensitive to the possibility of turning people of color into mascots to demonstrate your institution's diversity to internal or external constituents. Do not assume that women of color will understand or accept your expectations for them in relation to the university's diversity efforts. Not all women of color want to participate in these efforts, especially prior to earning tenure. Be aware that you are placing faculty of color in an extremely uncomfortable position when you—as a person with authority and power—ask them to represent the school's diversity by appearing at on-campus or off-campus events designed to celebrate ethnic or racial holidays—particularly if there are very few faculty of color at the university. If they say no, do not retaliate against them for not being team players. Rather, respect their values and try to understand that they do not wish to be tokenized or they are simply too busy with academic responsibilities to engage in these activities. If women of color are expected, or agree, to contribute actively to the campus diversity mission, they should be rewarded in currency that is valued in the institution, such as teaching relief, increased salary, and/or positive impact on their evaluations.

> *Then he said that I was spending too much of my time with people of color. He wanted to show me off more to white people. He tried to assure me that black people would love me, even if I did nothing for or with them. He laughed eerily as he explained that he wanted me to shun black folks and focus on white folks to help my image and that of the school. Oh no, I was staring in the face of the "just be our Negro" ghost.*
>
> Angela Mae Kupenda, "Facing Down the Spooks"

Be aware that white curiosity about people of color may be based on stereotypes or the desire to seem "cool" or nonracist by befriending a person with a seemingly exotic background. The social lives of women of color are often very different from their professional ones. They often have to negotiate completely different identities and values, and their friends from home may be a completely different group from their professional colleagues. Therefore—even if you are genuinely curious—be respectful of people's privacy and do not intrude on the personal lives of faculty of color with probing questions. These more personal dialogues can occur after trust has been established between individuals.

> *The problem he stated was that I did not tell him and my colleagues enough about my personal life. He said I was beginning to be much too private, just like the other woman of color on the faculty. . . . He wanted me to trust them more with the intimate details of my life. I explained that they already knew those details: I was single, had no children, was close to my family and friends, lived a quiet life, was active in my community, attended church, and enjoyed travel, my books, and the arts . . . Growing*

*increasingly frustrated, he leaned forward in his chair, looked me straight
in the eye, and with his ordinarily pale face turning red, he yelled, "You
must trust us more if you want to succeed here; there are no spooks behind
the door!"*

Angela Mae Kupenda, "Facing Down the Spooks"

4. Do not ask students or faculty of color to share their painful
    experiences to arouse white guilt or white empathy under the
    auspices of diversity training

This model of diversity training may be well intentioned, but it revictimizes persons of color, who do not typically believe they have an option when asked to participate in these training sessions. Be careful about mandating any type of diversity training across the entire faculty and/or student body. Such an order may generate resentment and/or retaliation toward people of color and result in little genuine learning. Instead, encourage training led by professionals in the area and ask for volunteer participants. You can also encourage small group discussions on topics of different experiential group realties on campus, led by students, faculty, and/or community members at grass roots levels.

*Administrators often want to "have it both ways" by having Natives on
staff to count but also denying the importance of the Native voice. To add
insult to injury, administrators also publicly voice support for Indigenous
initiatives (especially at public gatherings with Indigenous community
members) but privately work against supporting them (e.g., cutting or
withholding funding, threatening or carrying out sanctions against protest activity, or allowing issues to die in committees and subcommittees that
are looking further into the importance of these initiatives).*

Michelle M. Jacob, "Native Women Maintaining Their
Culture in the White Academy"

5. Conduct searches that will yield a pool of faculty of color

If 90 percent of your workforce is white, or if almost all of your faculty of color are foreign nationals, there is a good chance that your university hiring process has a virus of overt and/or covert racism. In most academic fields, the availability of PhDs of color exceeds 10 percent, in some cases, significantly so (Ryu 2010). Add to that fact the ready availability of foreign nationals of color, and there is simply no excuse today for an all-white department or for a unit that has only one token faculty member of color. Encourage heads of search committees and all department heads and members of your leadership team to receive training from a professional who can help them understand the conscious and unconscious biases evoked during a search process. A competent and well-trained EEOC office and/or well-charged diversity office should participate in all faculty searches. These offices can provide lists of publications that target persons of color. Many of these outlets are online (e.g., *Hispanic Outlook* and *Diverse Issues in Higher Education*), and some of them are on free listservs. Advertisements in these outlets send a different message about your institution than do position announcements placed only in *The Chronicle of Higher Education*.

Deans may need to examine the entire pool of candidates, even before the final-ists are selected. Ask the Affirmative Action/Equal Opportunity office to provide you with a list of candidates sorted by demographic category. Examine the candidacy materials of members of historically underrepresented groups. Add them to the pool of final candidates, if you deem them qualified. Inform department members and search committees that you will be more than glad to turn over this practice to them, but must be assured that every candidate from a historically underrepresented group is given strong, intentional consideration for the position. As an added measure, academic deans may need to interview each candidate of color personally, especially if a department has an all-white faculty. If you are a leader at a historically black college or university (HBCU), Hispanic-serving institution (HSI), or tribal college, is your faculty representative of the community you serve? If not, address the situation. In some HSIs, in particular, the majority of faculty are typically white, while most of the students are Latino/a.

> I sometimes feel like they [faculty] automatically assume I cannot possibly be here on my own merit. They just look right through me because someone in the admissions office made a mistake. Girls don't do science, but black girls especially don't.

Deirdre M. Bowen, "Visibly Invisible: The Burden of Race and Gender for Female Students of Color Striving for an Academic Career in the Sciences"

Reward women of color for serving as consultants on a search, but remember that there is a fine line between being consulted and being held responsible. Beware of the pitfall of expecting people of color to know and to find all the other people of color who may be qualified for the job. It is not their job to diversify the department or campus, and you should not expect them to be the primary salespersons for the job. If the university or community cultural climate is hostile to members of historically underrepresented groups, it may be very difficult for members of these groups to recommend that faculty work at their campus.

> But then the department head said, "Well, I'm just going to be honest with you. You're going to get this job because you're black and a woman. So we're going to give you this job. But we're going to hire someone else for the job we advertised."

Serena Easton, "On Being Special"

6.   Word your job ads in a way that lets faculty of color know that their unique skills and experiences are particularly welcome

Your posted job qualifications should communicate that you value unique contributions of members of underrepresented groups. State that you require or strongly prefer significant experience with diverse communities. Go beyond the typically used, but meaningless phrases, "University XXX is an affirmative action employer," or "Women and minorities are encouraged to apply." Remember that students of color, in particular, often find role models and community among faculty of color, which facilitates student retention for students and faculty.

Native American students across campus stopped by my office just to meet me or to visit. They said they had heard there was a new Native American faculty member on campus and they just wanted to meet me and know it was possible to get through school. Having never experienced a Native American faculty member, I did not understand the power this had and was surprised by how much it meant to Native American students that I was just there.

Beth A. Boyd, "Sharing Our Gifts"

7. How is merit is defined across campus?

Does merit mean the candidate graduated from an elite institution or comes with a "pedigree?" Does it mean upper social class? Due to the racism and discriminatory history of people of color in the United States, members of historically underrepresented groups are less likely than their white counterparts to have attended an elite institution. What is the role of standardized tests in your admission process for undergraduate and graduate students? Given the strong correlation between socioeconomic status and test scores (Sacks 2007), as well as the research findings that standardized college entrance exams do not predict college success more significantly than does high-school grade-point average, why does your school use them? What is the empirically demonstrated value of graduate school screening exams, e.g., the GRE, MCAT, . . . ? Understand that the presence of students of color attracts faculty and administrators of color, and vice versa.

Our hope—as these essays attest—is that we can offer a method grounded in justice, reconciliation, and faith in a future guided less by rhetoric and promise and measured more by realistic goals and our true achievements.

Deena J. González, "Introduction," Part V

8. Avoid sham searches

Particularly for high-level, visible positions, searches are often conducted as a façade. A typical situation for a sham search occurs when an interim or internal candidate, or a personal acquaintance of the department head, dean, or president, is the preferred and preordained choice. Nevertheless, the university must put up a front of fairness and equal opportunity for legal, funding, reputation, and policy reasons. Consequently, the search proceeds with several candidates who in reality have no chance of obtaining the position. People of color are especially vulnerable in these façade searches because they are often included in campus interviews so that the search committee and university can claim they considered a diverse pool of candidates. Avoid these games. Not only are they unethical, but word of the dishonesty gets around quickly, impacting your university's reputation and the willingness of women of color to work there. Avoid appointing interim candidates who are interested in the permanent position, and you will increase the likelihood of a meaningful external search. For administrative positions, it is especially important that the hiring administrator review the applicant pool for qualified members of historically underrepresented groups who may be overlooked by a biased search committee.

For years women of color have been an extremely attractive group to administrators in academia. Besides the ideological benefit of providing female and minority students with successful role models, they have had the practical advantage of counting as a "twofer" in affirmative-action accounting. However, once they have been brought through the doors of the university, their experiences belie their value to the academy, as reflected in the essays in this book.

John F. Dovidio, "Introduction," Part II

9.   Require understanding and implications of state and federal affirmative-action policies and consider the pros and cons of opportunity hires

Even in states where consideration of a candidate's race and gender for hiring is illegal, federal affirmative action is still the law (Rai and Critzer 2000). Affirmative action to create a diverse candidate pool is not illegal—anywhere in the United States. Ensure that your search committees understand this distinction. The history of racism and discrimination in the United States has resulted in *de facto* preference for white men and women in the academy (Katznelson 2005). As evidenced by the very low numbers of people of color in the academy relative to their availability, this white preference continues to be very strong today. Acknowledge the negative impact of historical and ongoing white preferences as you make a case for recruitment, hiring, and retention of faculty of color. Point out the existing demographic data on your campus faculty, which privileges white males. Help students and faculty understand the value of a heterogeneous faculty for preparing students for today's world.

Because of the negative biases associated with affirmative action (Heilman 1996; Heilman, Block, and Lucas 1992; Heilman, Block, and Stathatos 1997), reconsider the pros and cons of *opportunity hires*, or employment that takes place outside of the typical searches conducted in compliance with standard university hiring procedures. Despite the good intentions of such policies, an opportunity-hire policy can work against the diversity goals of the institution. For instance, a department may select a white candidate for a position—although a woman of color was also an excellent candidate—with the justification that "the provost can pay for the diversity hire; we don't have to use our department funds for her." This practice can result in the ghettoization of candidates of color. In most cases, it is better to have a good, broad, inclusive search—led by a person trained to avert racist, classist, homophobic, and sexist biases—through job ads placed in publications that target people of color than it is to have an opportunity-hire policy.

But something bizarre did happen. . . . I got to the teaching demonstration, and no faculty . . . were present. . . . I was their affirmative-action hire, and they were going to give me special treatment by gifting me with the position. . . . It's not that we don't know that we may be beneficiaries of affirmative action. Of course we know. But no candidate or faculty member wants to feel patronized, humiliated, or treated with condescension as if they are wholly unqualified for the position they are seeking. They particularly don't want this kind of treatment after they have fought tooth

and nail within a context of inequality to get where they are. And yet this
department head had gone out of his way to treat me this way.

Serena Easton, "On Being Special"

Recommendations for Women of Color and Allies

1. People of color who are tokenized experience personal and career-damaging impacts of this context

It is critical that you remember that the psychological experiences associated with tokenism, described earlier in this chapter (see also Niemann 2003; Niemann 2011; Niemann and Dovidio, 1998a) are about the situation, not about you. You will need mentors, friends, family, and allies to help you negotiate these experiences that may be harmful to your career and your mental and physical health.

2. Try not to allow yourself to be tokenized or showcased as an example of diversity in a predominantly white institution

You may have to explain to administrators, in a professional manner, why you cannot maintain your integrity and dignity while being put on display. Try not to succumb to pressure to perform. Until you have developed trust with colleagues, maintain your privacy when intrusive colleagues attempt to question you about your life outside the workplace. Tactfully make clear that you value your privacy. Try not to feel pressured to socialize with people you do not want to be with. Stay away from diversity-training models that use the pain of participants of color as their major teaching tools for white members of the institution. Do not dumb down to be liked or seen as nonthreatening but try to be aware of the way your actions, speech, and achievements are being perceived.

3. Numbers matter

Remember that the challenges you are experiencing are not about you; they are about the situation, especially relative to the very small numbers of members of historically underrepresented groups at your university. The research on the psychology of token status documents its negative impacts. Help change the situation by becoming engaged—informally and formally—in faculty searches when possible, but only if you can do so without jeopardizing your successful tenure trajectory. Send job ads to various networks in and out of the discipline in question. Ask people to spread the word about the job announcement. At the same time, understand that you are not responsible for changing the diversity of the campus. If you are asked to participate in a number of search committees beyond that expected of your colleagues, request a reduced teaching load to compensate for the time spent. You must remember that excellent teaching and scholarly productivity, not service, are almost always the areas considered for tenure, promotion, and salary increases. If you work at an HBCU, HSI, or tribal college, understand that you may still experience the issues addressed in the narratives in this volume. It is not a given that the majority of faculty in these institutions are faculty of color or that they will treat you better than do your white colleagues.

4. Try to avoid being a sham or token candidate for an
    advertised position

Reconsider being a candidate for a position if an interim appointee is also among the candidates; your candidacy in this search could be a no-win situation for you. It may be that you are being used to create a diverse pool for the position and will be wasting your time. When administrators are serious about external searches, they will not appoint interims who want the position permanently. Even if the upper administration wants an outsider, in all likelihood the faculty will press for the internal or interim candidate, especially when the alternative is an unknown person of color. Do not assume that the presence of an external search firm mitigates the likelihood of a sham search. Make inquiries; ask colleagues in your discipline and mentors questions about the standing of the internal candidate.

5. Remember that every university has had—and most still have—*de
    facto* preferences for white males and females (Katznelson 2005;
    Rai and Critzer 2000)

Your understanding of academia's long-standing historical preferences for white members will help you personally manage and respond to others' assumptions and overtly racist accusations that you were only hired due to affirmative action or community pressure. A look at the data is all you need to confirm the dominance of white faculty and administrators in the academy (for detailed data, see Ryu 2010). The data for your institution are generally posted on your institutional research website. However, you do not need to spend your time convincing others of this status quo. Just know it. In addition, be aware of what state and federal laws permit and require; you may need to correct misinformation on these matters, especially if you serve on search committees. Furthermore, be aware of the racist baggage sometimes associated with being an opportunity hire. When opportunity hires are white—as with accommodating spouses or particular expertise—these situations are received much more positively with attitudes that consider them good fortune. In contrast, when this hiring occurs in efforts to increase campus racial/ethnic diversity, it tends to be received with resentment.

Tenure and Promotion

Recommendations for Administrators

1. Make tenure and promotion policies as transparent as possible

Probably nothing creates as much angst for faculty as the tenure and promotion process. Good, well-meaning administrators can fall into the landmine of not providing adequate, transparent information about what it takes to earn tenure at their institutions. Many administrators make assumptions that the quality of mentorship across the campus is good and expect that faculty members know the rules of the game for success. They underestimate the level of isolation of faculty caught within the intersections of race/ethnicity/class and gender and sexual identities.

Send your faculty copies of tenure and promotion policies along with their letter of offer, accompanied by a signature page to be returned to you that acknowledges that they have received and read the policies. Develop workshops for junior faculty on the expectations of an excellent tenure and promotion binder. Provide concrete guidance on what to include in a good self-assessment letter: what information do your committees look for and need to know to evaluate the candidate? Let faculty know the makeup of the tenure and promotion committees and how you select external reviewers. Train department heads to mentor their faculty through this process, including beginning the development of the portfolio from the first day on the job. Develop workshops for tenured associate professors and encourage their transition to full professor. Many women of color get stuck at the associate-professor level, especially those with service responsibilities, thereby limiting their options for administrative advancement.

> *I learned that becoming too involved in service activities, serving on every committee on campus because it needed an ethnic-minority member for EEOC reasons, spending proportionately too much time with students, mentoring an overly broad program of research, and generally getting spread too thin are all traps that ethnic-minority faculty members tend to fall into but which will not be rewarded by promotion and tenure.*

Beth A. Boyd, "Sharing Our Gifts"

2.   Be careful of assignments that will prevent women of color from engaging in their required research scholarly productivity

These assignments include excess advising, using the justification that "students are attracted to her because she is a woman of color." They include service on department, college, university, or community committees that is out of proportion to that expected of white male faculty. Such assignments are often unfairly rationalized due to the need to "diversify" a committee. These assignments also include teaching overload courses and/or preparation for new courses that is not expected of white male faculty. In general, assignments to and responsibilities of members of historically underrepresented groups should be equal or equitable to those of white male faculty. Department heads have a particular responsibility to protect junior faculty from service and/or teaching and student advising, including chairing thesis and dissertation committees, that will detract from research/creative scholarly expectations. Outstanding assignments beyond the scope of reasonable expectations must be compensated in a meaningful manner.

> *"We know you are concerned about becoming a scholar and getting tenure, but we can't afford for you to work on your research this summer. . . . We need you to teach in the summer program because you are black, you are a woman, you are a great teacher, and you nurture, mother, feed, and nurse all the students."*

Angela Mae Kupenda, "Facing Down the Spooks"

3.   Address the culture of privilege and entitlement

Every university has a significant number—some far greater than others—of persons with tenure who have ceased to be productive. These persons have essentially retired in place. Due to historical conditions of access to the university, most of these persons are white males, followed by white females. The problems with this situation are beyond the scope of this chapter, but a few are particularly relevant to the experiences of women of color. First, these tenured, non-active faculty members are holding positions that could be opened up for searches to bring in fresh perspectives and diversity and open doors to women of color. Secondly, these persons are the most likely to be insecure about their lack of productivity, most resistant to concepts and arguments about historical white male privilege, and most threatened and/or intimated by successful women of color (Sue 2010; Wise 2010). Conscious and unconscious racist attitudes underlie and exacerbate the matter. Third, senior faculty with attitudes of self-entitlement and privilege may be the ones most likely to engage in bullying and coercion of junior faculty, especially women of color (Cavaiola and Lavender 2000). You can challenge this situation without threatening tenure by insisting on meaningful, outcome-oriented yearly post-tenure reviews that challenge the culture of privilege and entitlement.

> *"We had a faculty member who really should have been asked to retire some time ago, and we were in a committee meeting . . . He went totally off on me. Stood up, started spitting in my face, talking about 'you people.': 'What's wrong with you people?' . . . My white colleagues left the room— ran out. Yes, they did. Debra, bless her heart, she stayed and tried to defend me, but then he started attacking her. . . . This faculty member had just been bizarre, just had done awful things, and it was tolerated."*

Sherée Wilson, "They Forgot Mammy Had a Brain"

4. Faculty members perceive women of color through their own biased lenses

Unconscious bias is likely to be exacerbated when the number of people of color in a department is relatively small; the women of color in a department are objectively more competent, successful, and/or productive than their white counterparts; and/or women of color have authority and/or power over whites, such as when they are department heads, deans, provosts, or presidents (Dovidio and Gaertner 2010). In these situations, familiar stereotypes are likely to converge with garden-variety resentment and insecurity to create an atmosphere of hostility toward the women. As is the case with students, male and female faculty across race/ethnicity may resent the authority and power of women of color. The perceivers' biases affect evaluations and perceptions of collegiality. Color-insight discussion groups with small groups of faculty who volunteer to participate will slowly facilitate a cultural shift away from these harmful biases.

> *For example, our research and the work of others show that blacks, Asians, and white women who have impeccable qualifications may be hired or promoted at rates comparable to those of white men, but when their record is anything short of perfect, they are victimized by discrimination. In these cases, decision makers weigh the strongest credentials of white men most heavily while they systemically shift their standards and focus on the weakest aspects of racial minorities. The process often occurs unconsciously, even among people who believe that they are not racist or sexist. Moreover, because people justify their decisions on the basis of something other than race or sex—how a particular aspect of the record falls short of the standards, for example—they fail to understand the way racism or sexism*

operated indirectly to shape the qualities they valued or devalued and, ultimately, what they decided.

John F. Dovidio, "Introduction," Part II

5.   Ensure due process throughout the institution and remember
      that equity is sometimes more important than equality

The best protection against discrimination by and toward any members of the institution is insistence that administrators follow the same policies and evaluative structure for every member of the academy. Department heads are key points of connection and relationship building between faculty and the university. It is, therefore, especially important to conduct department-head training that emphasizes due process for all. Department heads must also understand the difference between equality and equity. An example of inequitable evaluation is demanding differential contributions to service, and then expecting those with the higher service expectations to have the same number of publications as those who do minimal service for the institution and community at large. Another example of inequity is expecting a woman who was on family-related leave for one year and stopped the tenure clock during that time, to have more publications/creative productivity than a person who went through the tenure process in the standard time period. That practice may be unconscious as evaluators count the number of publications per year, without taking into consideration the meaning and significance of an approved leave of absence. Policies should be put in place to avoid this practice.

> *The service component was proving the most overwhelming. . . . I was inundated with requests for assistance from black law graduate and undergraduate students, as well as other black professors and staff on campus, not to mention other students and faculty who had heard that I was someone who would listen to their concerns. . . . I was asked to serve on several time-consuming campus wide committees and invited to make presentations at numerous national and international venues. Various groups . . . all wanted me to get involved with their committees or activities. . . . I could not wall myself up in an ivory tower writing my articles and wait to get involved in the world until after tenure.*

Adrien Katherine Wing, "Lessons from a Portrait: Keep
Calm and Carry On"

6.   Define and describe the role of collegiality

Most tenure and promotion policies stipulate requirements for research, service, and teaching. However, underlying the interpretation of these accomplishments is the issue of collegiality. Part of knowing the rules of the game is understanding the role that perceived collegiality plays in faculty success and even the definition of collegiality within a given context. For instance, persons who refuse to be treated as mascots may be deemed poor team players by their peers and/or supervisors. Policies and practices regarding the definition of collegiality should be apparent.

> *I did not understand what noncollegial or even collegiality, for that matter, meant in my new world, the hierarchical realm of the institution that*

would decide my post-PhD future. I was unaware of the secret social norms and behaviors.

Francisca de la Riva-Holly, *"Igualadas"*

7.   Respect the significance of group-based research and teaching
     contributions by members of underrepresented groups

The university decides the way to define "merit." Therefore, there is simply no reason for group-based research and/or teaching related to prejudice and discrimination to be devalued in any discipline. This work adds richness and depth to students' understanding of their world and the scholarship of their disciplines. Yet, these negative judgments are often made, derailing the tenure and promotion process for members of underrepresented groups.

> *For instance, one senior faculty member stopped me in the hall one day and asked—regarding a graduate-student fellowship the ethnic-studies program was offering—"If one of our students accepts that fellowship, will they have to do Mexican shit, or can they do real research?"*

Yolanda Flores Niemann, "The Making of a Token: A Case Study of Stereotype Threat, Stigma, Racism, and Tokenism in Academe"

> *"When I tried to create curricula to suit our largely Latino student body, I was told that I was ghettoizing the department."*

Jessica Lavariega Monforti, *"La Lucha:* Latinas Surviving Political Science"

8.   Take community service into account when you consider tenure,
     promotion, and compensation

Every university needs to carefully review practice and policies regarding the way faculty are rewarded for service work on and off campus. This examination should ideally include empirical evidence of either similarities or disparities between the service of women of color and other faculty with appropriate follow-up. Women of color often struggle with conflicting demands. They may feel value driven to support other people of color in their academic and geographic community. Students often ask for their advice and guidance on personal, as well as academic, matters. Faculty of color are often treated as family representatives for and by students of color, especially those whose home is a significant distance from the campus. This mentorship takes much time and energy and may conflict with institutional priorities that are part of the faculty member's evaluations. Deans and department heads can help diffuse their responsibilities by providing diversity training to all faculty members and assigning community service tasks that relate to race/ethnic/sexual-orientation groups and student advising to all trained faculty.

Deans can support the collective cultural/racial projects of their faculty in other ways as well. For example, if American Indian/Native American faculty are leading projects on reservations, can their teaching load be reduced? Sometimes equity makes more sense than equality. When performing an equity review, look at advising loads and service to community. Just counting numbers of courses, students in courses, and publications and grants is not enough. What else is the person doing that is valued by the university? How is the university demonstrating in significant ways the value of this work? If you do not value the work enough to reward it, be direct and forthright with faculty of color about this attitude. That information is critical for the faculty member to make an informed decision about the consequences of proceeding with the service work.

> *The academy values individualism and a commitment to the institution's inflexible bureaucratic guidelines while Marie and her Native community, including people she invites for campus events, value collectivism and commitment to family.*

Michelle M. Jacob, "Native Women Maintaining Their
Culture in the White Academy"

9. Establish a mentoring training program and assign
   trained mentors

Effective mentorship is critical to the success of women of color. Before you assign mentors, however, develop and implement training on how to be an effective mentor. Most people are not experienced in mentoring, in general, and especially not across demographic lines of ethnicity/race, social class, or sexual orientation; they may not know what it means to be a good mentor in these contexts. Some persons do not understand that mentorship is something more than writing letters of recommendation. What are the expectations? How do good mentors go about advancing the development of advisees? Do they understand the difference between mentoring and patronizing, and know that the latter is demeaning and insulting?

Mentors are generally full professors and/or administrators who know the rules of the academic game. They can teach mentees ways to navigate the academic culture, which tends to incorporate upper-middle-class behavioral norms, including communication styles. For instance, people who are raised in working-class families, including many people of color, are more likely to speak in more direct, forthright ways. Directness can be intimidating, however, to people reared in white upper-middle to upper-class families. Mentors must also help women of color navigate inappropriate expectations, e.g., teaching diversity-related courses for which they have no training or interest. Mentors need to understand the psychological struggle of being the first member of a group in an environment. Mentors must also help women of color transcend cultural values of humility as they develop self-assessment letters for tenure and/or promotion portfolios. For instance, many American Indian women struggle with what they perceive as bragging when they put together their portfolios. The value of humility is paramount in American Indian cultures, as well as other cultures of color.

White men and women who acknowledge their white privilege and value intersectionalities can be excellent mentors to women of color. They are most likely to know the rules of the game and can provide outstanding guidance, support, and advocacy. At the same time, it is crucial that some white faculty who exhibit a missionary and/or patronizing attitude *never* serve as mentors to women of color. Department chairs should speak to both faculty mentors and mentees before determining assignments, rather than making assumptions about faculty wishes or just following a rotation schedule. Mentors from within and outside of the faculty members' departments, and even from outside the university, can be helpful. Upper-level administrators can engage in very powerful mentoring; this modeling sends a message about the importance of the process.

> *We women of color have to learn the skill of self-promotion and also become comfortable with being boastful, flaunting our accomplishments, and ensuring we receive due credit for our work.*
>
> Linda Trinh Võ, "Navigating the Academic Terrain: The Racial and Gender Politics of Elusive Belonging"

10. Develop a formal grievance process that affords the grievant a realistic and fair opportunity to win his or her case

Most grievance-related policies are written in a way that the university can almost never lose, except in the cases of flagrant disregard of policy. The latter is relatively rare because university administrators frame most situations as different interpretations of policy (e.g., perceived value of research and teaching), rather than disregard. Develop a faculty review team to evaluate complaints and make recommendations to administrative decision makers.

> *A few of these professors began a smear campaign in which they demanded that I be removed as editor-in-chief. They wrote numerous letters to the professor who had asked me to take over the helm, and they also wrote many letters and made repeated telephone calls to the dean, provost, and president of WSU [Washington State University]. I was mortified. I had never experienced such vitriol, and I did not know how to handle such an attack.*
>
> Kelly Ervin, "The Experiences of an Academic 'Misfit'"

11. Framing matters

Keep in mind that tenure and promotion committees, department heads, and other administrators—depending on their motivation—may frame a faculty's member's portfolio so that even the most accomplished person looks like a failure and the most unaccomplished one looks like a success. For example, expectations that women—especially women of color—should be nurturing may undermine the success of someone whose nurturing parallels that of most men whose evaluations are not harmed if they do not nurture students. Expect upper-level tenure and promotion committees to evaluate the entire portfolio for themselves, and not just read the recommendations of decision makers, some of whom might have interpreted the file with a negative bias.

> *Ultimately, though, there is a continual danger of being constructed as a hostile Injun or friendly squaw.*
>
> Michelle M. Jacob, "Native Women Maintaining Their Culture in the White Academy"

12. Caution women about the challenges and risks associated with
     joint appointments

Given the preexisting pressure and demand on women of color, joint or split
appointments may be disastrous for women of color unless you ensure that they
are supported. Remember that there is really no such thing as a fifty-fifty time commitment. The department heads involved will place competing teaching, research,
advising, and other service demands on jointly appointed faculty. Ideally, appoint a
faculty member to one section of the university with a buyout possibility for teaching
and/or research in others.

> To womyn of color who are contemplating a joint appointment, I would
> say ascertain specifics about the structure of the assignment being con-
> sidered, including the expectations of both departments and their past
> experience and knowledge of what is involved to make the structure
> work. . . . Make sure you have in writing all of the benefits from the
> joint appointment and a clear delineation of the roles and responsibilities
> expected from the position.

Michelle A Holling, May Fu, and Roe Bubar, "Dis/
Jointed Appointments: Solidarity amidst Inequality,
Tokenism, and Marginalization"

13. Persons in token situations expend much energy spent on
     impression management

Understand that—due to the consequences of tokenism and their small numbers in the institution—women of color typically expend much energy on efforts
to manage the impressions they make on others. They live in a glass house. Their
uniqueness in the white academic environment attracts attention to every aspect of
the communication and behavior. You can minimize the need for excessive impression management efforts by providing concrete, constructive feedback and guidance, which will lead to increased self-confidence and less need for energy spent on
impression management. A trusted mentor is invaluable in this regard.

> The simultaneity of being invisible and hypervisible has meant that I cus-
> tomarily operate in a state of alertness. I watch/observe while I am being
> watched/observed. In the classroom, I am mindful of every look or stare,
> of every whisper, and I am cognizant of the ever-present undercurrent of
> white allegiances/alliances that often commence partway through a course
> and continue until the end.

Delia D. Douglas, "Black/Out: The White Face of
Multiculturalism and the Violence of the Canadian
Academic Imperial Agenda"

14. Department heads make a difference

In almost all universities, the department head/chair is the main lifeline for
women of color, indeed for all faculty. The faculty's relationship with you is often
reflected in their feelings about the university. You are their primary administrator,
protector, and professional-development mentor. To the extent of your power, you

need to protect women of color from excess service, unwanted summer teaching, and paid and unpaid overloads. But you also need to understand that their cultural values prompt people of color to engage in serving the community-at-large and advising individuals and student groups. If the university values this work, you can release women of color from other responsibilities to ensure equitable time for them to attend to their scholarship and teaching. On the other hand, be forthright about which of their contributions will be considered for tenure, promotion, and/ or yearly evaluation and salary increases.

You also need to protect women of color from senior faculty, some of whom may engage in harassment, bullying, and/or coercive behavior, especially when junior faculty do not support their causes and/or agenda. Be aware that women of color are sometimes named on grants as consultants, especially when the agency values a diverse research or creative team. In these cases, ensure that the women of color are named as co-PIs (principal investigators) and not just consultants. Do not be bashful about seeking advice from administrators and/or faculty within and outside your institution about supervising women of color.

Women from minority gender and sexual identity groups may be most vulnerable to harassment and violence—from students, faculty, staff, and community members. Connect these women to support groups and pay particular attention to ways in which students and faculty may impart their contempt for these group members via their end-of-course and yearly evaluations.

> . . . when I finally began to ask questions about how the psychology we were learning related to ethnic minorities and their communities, I was told that this had nothing to do with psychology.

Beth A. Boyd, "Sharing Our Gifts"

Recommendations for Women of Color and Allies

1.   Study the tenure and promotion materials of your university

Speak with recently promoted faculty about the expectations; ask to see copies of their portfolios. Learn how to develop a good self-assessment letter; this letter should include information about the quality of the venues where your works are published, displayed, performed, etc. What is the significance of those sites? Why are these bragging points for you and the university? Begin developing your tenure portfolio on your first day on the job. Obtain the binder where your work will be submitted and begin filling it as you complete your scholarly projects (your department staff can provide guidance). Remember that until a work is published or "in press" (with documentation), it is not complete and does not count toward your achievements. Your third-year review will come more quickly than you expect, so you do not have time to waste. Do not sit on revise-and-resubmit opportunities; complete the work. When you give conference presentations, turn those into publications—immediately. You must be a productive scholar to be successful at research universities. Mentors can be invaluable throughout this process. If you are tenured, continue your productivity until you reach full professor. You must have this rank if you want a reasonable chance to attain and succeed in administrative positions.

Place boundaries on your service commitments. In most universities, service above and beyond the nominal work expected of a good department and university citizen is not rewarded. Understand that excess service does not take the place of expected scholarly productivity for your review. Use your time wisely and effectively. Structure your time that is not allocated to classroom teaching. If you manage your schedule well, you can still have a balanced life that includes teaching, scholarship, service, family, and personal time. Time management is one of the most essential components of a successful career and gratifying personal life.

If the president develops a task force to address faculty diversity, provide your concrete, solution-oriented input. However, if the committee is not action- and/or outcome-oriented, politely decline or serve with an understanding that your responsibilities will be appropriately lightened. You must be realistic about what changes you have the power to produce.

2. Women of color often invest much energy in impression management

You are living in a glass house when you work for a predominantly white institution. People comment on things about you that they do not notice about your white colleagues. These things include your dress, opinions and contributions during meetings or events on or off campus, food and music preferences, etc. You will face negative reactions for not meeting stereotypical expectations, which can also result in severe stress. At the same time, you become very aware that—to the majority of persons in your academic environment—you represent members of your underrepresented group, thereby increasing the pressure you feel about the way you are perceived.

Share your feelings and reactions with other people of color. Find a trusted friend and/or mentor who will give you honest feedback about how you are perceived by others. If you want to make a different impression and it is in your power to do so, obtain guidance on strategies to achieve the outcome you desire. Persons in public relations, life coaching, and acting fields may be helpful. You might also consider hiring a professional consultant in this area. Remember that you still have to produce excellent scholarship and teaching, no matter how much energy you are expending on other matters.

3. Women of color are especially subject to negative consequences of attributional ambiguity

Attributional ambiguity means that you may not know whether the treatment you receive is due to biases about your race/ethnicity, culture, sexual identity, or gender, or whether it is good, unbiased, and informed feedback. Not knowing whom you can trust negatively impacts your advancement. You need reliable feedback, and a trusted and competent mentor is invaluable in this area. Mentors can help you understand the rules of the game at your institution. Let the mentor know what you need and want. Communications between mentor and mentee are not the time to be bashful. Ask about language, communication styles, clothing, even office decorations—whatever you think sends messages about you. At the same time, you want to maintain your personal integrity and identity, so make informed decisions about what you do and do not want to change. Ask mentors about valued venues for your work. They may be able to review your work and advise you how to respond to invitations to revise and resubmit journal articles. Follow their informed advice; target those journals, presses, galleries, and other venues appropriate for your discipline.

Alternately, let mentors help you educate your department chair about the prestige of other venues for your work.

Develop your own network of mentors. They do not have to be people of color, and they do not have to be women. Due to their entrenchment and privilege in the academy, white men tend to know the playing rules better than members of any other group. Some of these white men will genuinely care about you and make efforts to promote your development and advance your successes. Recognize, however, that what works for white men may not work for you. At the same, beware of the missionary instincts of some white faculty, who need to believe that they are more talented than people of color; this attitude results in patronizing, which you will sense and resent. If this happens to you, or you do not agree with an assigned mentor, speak with your department head about changing your assignment. When possible, ask the department head to consult with you before appointing a new mentor.

4.   When addressing change, pick your battles

Focus on what is in your power to challenge, change, or address. You will have to learn to put aside hurt feelings, humiliation, and rumination about poor treatment. Fight for fairness but be ready to let go when it becomes clear that it is a losing battle, or you may be the main casualty. Try not to be the only person out on a limb on any given issue. You need support. Be aware of and challenge—through your department head—unequal treatment, such as unequal distributions of labor that some senior professors may attempt to justify. Most of all, remember that people's attitudes toward you often say a lot more about them than about you. As a person inside the academy, you will see poor treatment and misjudgment of colleagues of color from the inside (Turner and Myers 2000), which will create stress for you as you vicariously experience these situations. When possible, take a break from emotionally charged assignments and service. Although it is very difficult, try not to take racist, sexist, homophobic, and/or classist treatment personally. Find support; learn what you can live with. When necessary, seek a different university environment in which to work. Just because some of your colleagues do not acknowledge your value does not mean you are not exceptionally important to the academic world. Remember that you have to focus on your work to be successful.

5.   Do not assume that the university will reward you for community service and engagement

Along with others, you can work toward making this reward system happen, but until it does, understand that you may be sacrificing your career by fulfilling community service. Guest lectures, consulting work in the community, and advising student groups may mean extra, noncompensated, and unvalued work for you. Understand that nonacademics in your community may not recognize how much time you must devote to your job to be successful. Consider telling people who make these requests that you can participate in larger, time-consuming community projects after you have earned tenure and/or full professor status. Explain that you want to be at the university long enough to have the privilege of serving your community and that—if you do not progress through the academic ranks and achieve tenure— your time at the institution may be very short, and you may never have the freedom to work on their projects. In the meantime, refer them to appropriate people who can help. Develop trusted faculty networks that can advise students of color and work on various community-service projects. Be selective serving on graduate theses and dissertation committees, which are very time-consuming, especially if you are the chair. Before agreeing to serve as an advisor to student groups, learn what the group expects of you; do not accept the invitation unless you have the time to complete your scholarly expectations.

6.   Work away from your office

Consider working away from your office at least one or two days or afternoons per week and use this time to produce the scholarly/creative work upon which you will be evaluated. You need to develop a plan where you can work in an uninterrupted environment. You must be a productive scholar as defined by your discipline.

7.   Regarding performance evaluation, learn to make a case for
      equity, not just equality

For instance, if you can document extraordinary advising compared to your colleagues, you may have a good case for a reduced teaching load. Documentation is the operative word here. You may also have a good reason for teaching to count more than publications in your annual reviews. However, you must not make presumptions. Discuss the matter at length and in concrete terms with your department head. Document in writing, with appropriate signatures, any agreements that you make with supervisors and/or evaluation committees. Unless any deviations from standard expectations have been documented as approved, expect to be evaluated using the same standards as your colleagues who have not performed extraordinary service or had higher teaching loads.

8.   Your success can be intimidating and threatening, not only to
      insecure white colleagues but also to some colleagues of color
      who have internalized racist, homophobic, and sexist ideologies

Women of color are often criticized by colleagues across rank, race/ethnicity, and gender and sexual identities. Some faculty-of-color colleagues seek external excuses for their shortcomings or lack of success. Some of these persons use racism and other -isms as reasons for their failures and discontent. As such, your success undermines their excuses. They may also be accustomed to being the only member of their group and feel displaced and insecure when you reduce their authority to deliver the minority perspective. As a professor, you may find that the students of color who flock to your classes are the same ones who most test your authority. They may see you as an outsider because they perceive your social class is higher and/or because you do not advocate their political ideology or cause. If you advance to administrative positions, be prepared for comparatively unsuccessful faculty of color to call you a traitor, "oreo," and/or other demeaning and racist terms.

Some men of color—especially those from highly patriarchal cultures—will challenge your authority to evaluate them, particularly when the appraisal is negative. These insecure people will like and accept you only as long as you cater to their wishes, advocate their causes, and subscribe to their views of themselves. Reject their attempts to race-bait, belittle, or guilt-trip you. Do not engage in rank-ordering oppression. Continue being successful and maintain your integrity. Do your best in whatever position you hold.

9.   Do not assume that every negative experience or action toward
     you is grounded in racial, gender, or sexual-identity bias

When you believe that you have experienced or observed an injustice, try to produce compelling evidence to support the charge. Remember that not every negative
experience or evaluation is about your race/ethnicity/gender/gender or sexual
identity. In some cases, rude behavior toward you is not about you at all; the perpetrator may behave in that manner toward all persons. Be careful not to allege racism
without foundation. If you do so, you will be dismissed as a whiner and someone
who is angry, lacks personal responsibility and accountability, and blames everything
in life on your race/ethnicity and/or sex. Most importantly, your empty cries of
racism will undermine the validity of legitimate complaints by yourself and others.

10.   Develop teaching portfolios

These are the equivalent of tenure portfolios but are dedicated to teaching. They
include a statement of your teaching philosophy, documentation of your assessment
of what was learned in all your courses, syllabi, intermittent student feedback, and
your response to that feedback (see Seldin 2004 and Seldin and Miller 2009 for a
thorough explanation and samples). They also include examples of your teaching
outside the classroom, e.g., at conferences, as a consultant, and in the community-
at-large. Well-prepared teaching portfolios are good protection against retaliatory
course evaluations and negative evaluations by students who do not want to hear
about issues of race/ethnicity. You must be proactive, or administrators may just use
standard end-of-year student evaluations to assess your teaching.

Ask experienced senior teachers to sit in on your classes and write an assessment
to include in your tenure and promotion portfolio. Preferably they will visit your
classroom more than once so they can get an accurate sense of your relationship
with students. This observation is particularly important if you begin to experience
hostility from your students. A mentor or trusted friend can help you remedy the
situation and also attest to inappropriate student comments and behavior so that
you are not caught in a he said/she said argument about your classroom behavior. Developing an excellent teaching portfolio is an excellent preemptive defense
against negative teaching evaluations.

11.   Be wary of joint appointments

Do not accept joint appointments unless you can be reasonably assured, via
written expectations, that the faculty and administration in both departments will
support you. Be wary of competing teaching and service assignments in different
departments. There is no such thing as a fifty-fifty time commitment; joint appointments often add up to two 100 percent jobs.

12.   Learn how to interview

Practice your formal presentation in front of trusted colleagues who will provide
constructive feedback. Practice your research presentation, teaching/lecture, and
question/answer session. Ask trusted colleagues to help you learn how to address
questions from students, faculty, and administrators. When interviewing for administrative positions, practice with supporters in higher positions than those you want
to obtain. Dress professionally and conservatively for all interviews. Promptly write
concise thank-you letters or e-mails to persons who interviewed you.

13.   Your department head is your main lifeline in the academy

Good department heads take their role with respect to faculty development very seriously. Candidly discuss expectations with your head/chair, especially relative to scholarly productivity, teaching, service, leaves of absence, office hours, and anything else that reflects upon or impacts your success. Let them know your goals. If you are interested in administration, ask your department head to nominate or appoint you to lead committees involved in important service to your department, college, or university. However, it is best to wait until after you have achieved tenure to volunteer for time-consuming service activities. Discuss problematic relationships with colleagues. The department head should be the first person to know if you are bullied or harassed in any way. If your head is the perpetrator of this oppression, immediately go to your dean; proceed up the hierarchy of supervisors if necessary. If you have difficulty relating to your department head, a mentor from outside your department may be particularly helpful in facilitating communications and guiding you. Meet with your dean and ask for the support you need, but remember that as the administrative chain of command rises, the responsibilities and number of faculty under the guidance of these people increases substantially. Be succinct with your concerns and requests and arrive at meetings with possible solutions.

Networks of Allies and Mentors

Recommendations for Administrators

1.   Understand the different types of experiences and needs of members of United States underrepresented groups and foreign-born nationals on your campus

Although these groups may be lumped together as people of color, they typically have very different ideals, values, expectations, and needs (Ogbu, 1998). It is not the case that all groups identified within the United States as people of color support or understand one another. For instance, foreign nationals may need assistance with immigration issues. Have an office with expertise on these matters that can provide assistance and advice. Foreign nationals may not see themselves as people of color nor believe that others see them as people of color. They may not even know what it implies to be perceived as a member of a historically underrepresented group. Quite to the contrary, having come to the US from places where they were part of the majority group, they may reject an identity as people of color and/or as a minority. They may also share common prejudices against people of color born in the United States. Foreign nationals—especially those who were able to leave their countries for education in the United States—often come from upper-class backgrounds in their home countries. In contrast, members of domestic minority groups are over-represented in the lower socioeconomic ranks. These differences in social class may adversely impact relationships between foreign nationals and domestic faculty of color.

Finally, do not assume that the presence of several foreign-born people of color in an academic area precludes racism in that field. Some white people may be more likely to accept foreign-born nationals than native-born people of color. The difference reflects the domestic person of color's knowledge of the way racism functions within the United States, and the guilt and/or denial that some whites feel about historical and current racism. The foreign-born and -raised typically do not know US racial history the way natives do. In addition, members of US historically under-represented groups often have reputations as activists and troublemakers who do not remain passive when their civil rights are violated. That makes them a threat to some people's perception of collegiality.

> *Some Asian American women from low-income immigrant families financially support their parents and, at an early age, assumed adult responsibilities because their parents spoke limited English, and they continue to shoulder these burdens as graduate students and faculty . . . . strong cultural expectations dictate that we must defer to and respect our elders. . . . Being nurturing and humble does not translate well into the competitive academic cultural environment, so adapting mandates some cultural retooling for many of us.*

Linda Trinh Võ, "Navigating the Academic Terrain:
The Racial and Gender Politics of Elusive Belonging"

2.   Address intersectionality

Race, class-based subordination, and gender and sexual identities do not act inde-pendently. Hostility against lesbian, gay, bisexual and transgender (LGBT) people is still overtly and publically sanctioned. Because homosexuality is often associated with white men and women, they may dominate support groups for LGBT people, and these student support groups may not be accepting of people of color. As a result, queer, black, and female students, once admitted to the university, are often left to deal with campus hostilities on their own. All persons—especially university leaders—need to embrace this battle to respect persons across gender and sexual-identity boundaries. It is imperative that social-sciences and humanities courses address intersectionality.

> *We have both a moral and a practical obligation to recognize—not deny— that other group-based markings—race, sexual orientation, class, and dis-ability—are at work among women. It's both difficult and important that women who are white—the relatively privileged ones who have been the primary beneficiaries of feminism—perceive, acknowledge, and then act against the additional forms of discrimination experienced by women of color without feeling defensive.*

Nancy Cantor, "Introduction," Part III

3.   Do not assume that people of color support other people of color

Crab mentality—the desire to bring down other people in your subordinated group who are getting ahead of you—affects some individuals. In addition, men of color—especially those from patriarchal backgrounds—may be disrespectful to women of color. Older faculty may be intimidated by or hostile toward younger faculty who manifest their identity differently or seem insufficiently deferential. Be aware that successful women of color may refute those who want to use race, sex, sexual identity, and social class and their intersectionalities as excuses for their lack of achievement, which arouses anger and resentment. Avoid using one senior person of color as the gatekeeper or official spokesperson on race. You do not want someone in authority to subtly undermine the varied perspectives of others of color in your community. Consult with faculty from across ranks and disciplines. Do not let one person's attitudes—especially toward other people of color—devalue the contributions of their colleagues. Racial/ethnic groups have different experiences, shaped by their history in the United States. Those histories have implications for life today. You must ascertain the needs of each group. Do not assume that the expectations, needs, and values of one group of color speak for all.

> *"A troubling pattern that plagues many educational institutions is the tendency of faculty and administrators to adopt a faculty member of color as the official pet or mascot. The pet may be a key administrator's personal favorite, who serves as the official spokesperson for all faculty of color. She may be the 'exceptional' woman of color whose accomplishments (real or imagined) or compliant attitude put other faculty of color in a negative light. In public the pet makes a dramatic display of her selfless efforts to support colleagues of color. In private the pet is harshly critical of the teaching and scholarship of these same colleagues, thereby reinforcing the race- and gender-based presumption of incompetence."*

Angela P. Harris and Carmen G. González,
"Introduction"

4.   Facilitate development of social networks to counter isolation and create circles of safety and camaraderie

Such networks increase faculty retention and facilitate interdisciplinary work, valued by most institutions and funding agencies. Additionally, when women of color cannot find support in their own departments, they will know other faculty to whom they can turn for support (Padilla and Chávez, 1993; see chapters in Turner and Myers 2000). You can facilitate networks by sponsoring breakfasts, lunches, or dinners that provide an opportunity for persons of color to gather and meet each other. Commit resources for community building.

> *. . . I was fortunate to have the chance to participate in a support group for junior women of color faculty. We just gathered over delicious meals (you are compelled to learn how to make your favorite ethnic foods in these locations) and shared stories about overcoming isolation. We shared advice on campus policies, networking opportunities, and contending with the promotion process. . . . I have also been at institutions with white women presidents, one who sponsored informal gatherings at her residence for women faculty of color to network and to provide input on how to make the campus culture more supportive of their needs.*

Linda Trinh Võ, "Navigating the Academic Terrain:
The Racial and Gender Politics of Elusive Belonging"

5.   Establish leadership-development paths and opportunities

Women of color are frequently not groomed for management and administrative positions (Valverde 2003). To increase the pool of qualified women of color

candidates, especially for upper administrative positions, develop internal internships—such as special assistant to the president—which typically last one year. Create a meaningful, visible, significant task and appoint a woman of color to chair the
committee. Appoint presidential commissions to resolve campus-wide issues and
place women of color in charge of them. However, make sure that these appointments do not deal only with issues of race, ethnicity, sexual identity, and gender.
If you assign women of color exclusively to positions involving these marginalized
problems, you are guilty of stereotyping and tokenizing them and you may also be
ensuring that their work is ghettoized. Nominate women of color for institutional
leadership-development programs, such as the American Council on Education Fellows Program.

Pay particular attention to the mentoring needs of women of color in positions
of power and authority. Remember that, because of racist and sexist biases held by
persons from all groups, people will be especially resentful that these women are
in powerful positions. It is also important not to keep department heads for long
terms, e.g., more than eight to ten years. This longevity deprives women of color of
the opportunity to develop key administrative leadership skills that prepare them
for further advancement.

> *Leadership roles can be treacherous for women of color since their author-
> ity is often challenged more than that of white males or females. . . . Asian
> American women still have to work against the prevalent stereotypes of
> them as submissive and subservient, which can undermine their author-
> ity and prevent them from being considered for leadership positions I
> am still taken aback by the level of incivility and disrespect female admin-
> istrators experience, behavior that male colleagues would not direct at
> male administrators.*

Linda Trinh Võ, "Navigating the Academic Terrain:
The Racial and Gender Politics of Elusive Belonging"

Recommendations for Women of Color and Allies

1.   Establish informal, grassroots organizations for men and women
     of color

These can be social- and/or task-oriented. Examples of task-oriented groups
are ones that organize for collective meetings with the administration or reading
groups that create safe places to provide and receive feedback. Social gatherings,
such as potlucks at alternating homes, provide a connection with faculty across campus, as well as a feeling of family in the community. These networks facilitate collective action and maintain positive subgroup identity (Wright 1997; Wright, Taylor,
and Moghaddam 1990). Developing informal and/or formal social networks facilitates a sense of belonging and hence encourages retention. Some of these groups
may be focused on developing race consciousness and navigating discriminatory
experiences and environments. Invite the president to some of your events. The
presence of the president or other high-ranking administrators helps legitimize the
importance of the group to the campus. Find solidarity; go to conferences and find
allies as you listen to presentations. While these networks support your feelings of

belonging and safety, it is important also to seek out white colleagues and allies who can mentor you and whom you can learn to trust.

2.   Seek out alliances with productive faculty across race/ethnicity, socioeconomic status, and gender and sexual identities

Productive faculty are less likely to be threatened by your successes than are those whose scholarship is stagnant. Form relationships with persons across disciplines whose research/creativity has commonalities with yours. These can lead to greater scholarly productivity and enhanced grant writing successes for you and them. These alliances reduce feelings of alienation and loneliness. They may also become persons whose feedback you learn to trust.

3.   Take advantage of multiple identities

No one is free from realities associated with intersectionality. Intersections can place you at the margins, or they can situate you in a unique place to form bridges. If you are from a lower socioeconomic background, you can learn a great deal about the academic rules of the game from members with upper-class roots. The rules of academia were created for white, upper-class men. However, do not automatically stereotype white men and women as coming exclusively from the upper class.

5.   Be proactive and cautious in choosing formal mentors, rather than relying on a first-come rotation of the department's available senior faculty

In general you will find that productive faculty members are the most welcoming because they are the least likely to be threatened by your success. However, you must be careful. The most alienated people—often out of desperation—are quick to recruit allies, some of whom may give them bad advice.

6.   Build relationships and alliances with foreign nationals

Foreign nationals often lack knowledge of United States history and its racist foundation and ongoing racial struggles. You may need to educate them about past and present discrimination. Foreign nationals may also not identify as people of color or understand that some white people may lump them together with US racial minorities. They may not understand that other white people often prefer them to people of color born in the United States or the resentments that this discrimination may generate. Do not assume that all foreign nationals had upper-social-class upbringings. At the same time, however, after you have formed relationships with members of this group, you may discuss the topic of social class and learn what it means in their culture. You can help them understand how it functions in the United States. Bring foreign nationals into your reading or social group. The alliance will benefit them as well as the members of US historically underrepresented groups.

7.   Form alliances with white men and women who value intersectionalities and acknowledge their white privilege

To be allies, white women must avoid the urge to lecture women of color on feminism or try to bond as sisters without acknowledging the significance and consequences of intersectionality. They must be fully cognizant that many women and men of color have different priorities, such as challenging racism, class-based subordination, and/or homophobia. White women must take to heart the lesson of intersectionality: women of color face the challenge of overcoming not only the presumed incompetence of race, but due to racist and sexist stereotypes, that of their gender. Regarding white men, remember that they may know the rules of the game better than any other persons on campus. Supportive white men will co-opt the privileged status of their group by using their expertise to guide you through what would otherwise be a foreign cultural maze.

8. If you are interested in an administrative career, seek out and accept leadership-development opportunities by serving on committees and task forces and successfully chairing these groups

The more significant the task is for the campus community at large, the more visible will be your contributions. Let your upper-level administrators know if you are interested in administrative development. Do not, however, allow yourself to be appointed only to committees and task forces concerned exclusively with diversity. In addition, do not assume that this committee service takes precedence over excellent teaching and scholarly productivity when it comes to tenure, promotion, evaluation, and compensation consideration. If you want these development opportunities—which will give you administrative experience—be selective and understand that you have increased your workload. It is best to achieve tenure and the rank of full professor before adding service work that will not be considered for promotion. An added word of caution—when you serve in leadership positions, remember to pace yourself. Faculty are often resistant to change. Keep in mind that small wins matter, and enough small wins can change a culture over time.

9. The silence of reasonable and fair-minded members of the academy allows the unethical treatment of their colleagues to continue

Dr. Martin Luther King Jr. cautioned that we remember the silence of our friends more than the words of our enemies. In the case of academia, the silence of the supposed friends of those who are being unjustly treated is deafening. These persons who witness and/or are aware of miscarriages of justice often sacrifice their integrity to ensure their own success by accepting the status quo.

10. Do not adopt victim status and/or make an identity for yourself out of the pain you have experienced

Such status robs you of your positive identity and cheats your spirit. Remember that you are a survivor and a person who can thrive in any situation. As Eckhart Tolle (1999) and other spiritual writers have noted, the pain is part of you, but it is not you. Do not create drama; others will create enough without your adding to it. Accepting a situation does not mean that you like it or agree with it. You may need to find internal peace to remain healthy. To the extent you are subordinated in some way (race, class, gender, sexual identity), use that subordination as a means of empathizing with others, rather than simply favoring the group you come from. Recognize the similarities and differences in the various forms of subordination that we face. Do not rank the severity of oppressions. Try to foster an atmosphere of solidarity, mutual respect, and support with other subordinated groups. Be alert to efforts to divide and conquer.

11.   Be conscious of other ways that we are privileged

These ways include race, sexuality, social class, mental and physical health, and nationality, among unlimited others. Use your privilege to benefit others. We are privileged to have our degrees and work in educational environments that can positively affect people's lives. One of the most important ways we are privileged is reflected in our circle of relationships and love. Nurture those relationships.

12.   Understand that there is a price to pay for not remaining silent
      and for remaining silent

The first price may affect your career; the second may impact your spirit. Your academic self may be inconsistent with your authentic nature. As you determine how to respond to uncomfortable situations, keep your long-term goals in mind and let them inform your response. Find a way to hang onto your authentic self—through mentors, friends, family, and social networks. Understand what it means to maintain your integrity. You must know yourself and know your boundaries.

Final Words to Women of Color

Nurture personal relationships with those who love you and listen when they express concern. Sometimes loved ones know better than we do what is best for us. Be aware that, when psychologically injured at work, you may experience the stages of grief identified by Elisabeth Kubler-Ross (1973)—denial, anger, bargaining, depression, and acceptance. Awareness and understanding of these stages facilitates your healing. Remember, also, that when you are in psychological pain you may not be able to focus on producing your best work. Receive support from a counselor or psychologist, especially when trusted friends are not physically accessible in your current location. Try not to take things personally. Try to maintain hope and faith that difficult situations will pass. Life goes on. Finally, remember to laugh. Be sure to take care of your body and your spirit. Enjoy the moments that make an academic's life worthwhile and gratifying. Remember that—even under the most challenging circumstance—ours is a noble and privileged profession; we can transform minds and lives. We can make a positive difference for someone every day.

> *We have to learn how to deal with turmoil without getting changed by it. We have to remember why we are doing this work, develop a vision for ourselves . . . By deciding who we are in the face of the reality we are surrounded by and who we want to be, we take ourselves out of a reactive place and into a space that we have designed for ourselves. It is a space that is very much based in reality and focused, and a place where we are aware of those things around us we can choose to change. But it is also a space where we balance what we need with what we must do. . . . Success means helping our people, connecting to others, being real, and making things better for our families and communities. It is essential to find a way to integrate that definition into the work that we do—otherwise we do run the risk of losing ourselves in the work for reasons we do not fully understand.*

Beth A. Boyd, "Sharing Our Gifts"

AFTERWORD

Gabriella Gutiérrez y Muhs

> *Much has changed since I was involved in women's studies there [Stanford University] and elsewhere. What I've seen of the materials you sent looks like a developed and cogent indictment of institutional biases and assumptions which have lived on despite token "diversity." With respect for the project and the goal of intellectual justice it pursues, and with my best personal regards to you, sincerely, Adrienne Rich.*
>
> Adrienne Rich, letter to the editors of *Presumed Incompetent,* January 7, 2010

As a twenty-first-century Latina, I came across many obstacles in my quest for tenure and particularly an epistemological gap in academia: an emptiness in the journey from graduate school to an assistant professor to full professor. To my knowledge, there was no one document readily available for new PhDs that defined, deconstructed, described, or clarified the evolution of terminology in academic settings about acquiring tenure. Although these documents perhaps exist in some institutions, they are purposefully written to possess certain levels of mystery, obscurity, and avoidance, depending on the university. Seemingly faculty handbooks often delineate issues peripherally but not in detail, the way that particular populations— new to these professions—need these unknown and unfamiliar, as well as evolving, rules spelled out. Hence, there was no manual that made the difficult experience of the tenure process clearer to me, or many of the women with whom I work or attended graduate school.

In 2004—after four years of working at my current university—through reading about Cecilia Burciaga's concept-metaphor of the dense, impenetrable "adobe ceiling" in academia for Latinas (as opposed to a more penetrable, see-through "glass ceiling" encountered by white women), I became more aware that in fact there was a difference in the way that the intersection of gender, race, and class came together in our professions. As a minority and a working-class feminist, I observed that most of the women I knew were forced—if they wished to become part of the academy— to blindly follow a yellow brick road without road signs, an imaginary and supposedly ethical yellow brick road, at best only described peripherally by others. This interminable road was supposed to lead us into a permanent position in an institution that was part of the American academy. I felt that academia's bedside manner was lacking, to put it mildly, in providing a manual for new users, particularly for those who had invested deeply with high stakes, especially if they were women or came from the working class. Often new professors from the working class did not have the hidden agendas that other professors (a majority of them coming from the middle class and university-educated parents) possessed or could rely on for advice.

Also, amazingly enough, most of the tenured women I met—especially if they were working class or were unmistakably identified by others as women of color—had walked a treacherous road that was never discussed post-tenure or even spoken about along the way. Most had had a tumultuous and even surrealistic journey—which a couple of them described to me as "hazing"—seen as part of entering the fraternal and paternalistic institutions that they had chosen to join. Many women professors on my voyage dropped out of the process, precisely because acquiring tenure became an obscure procedure; they were often described by colleagues as the casualties of an intellectual war, or was it a quest?

As the daughter of migrant/immigrant farm-working parents, who lived their lives in fear of their *patrones* firing them—or of someone else at the migrant camps making up something about them to steal their highly desired manual-labor position—I identified similar patterns of external and internalized oppression and undermining feelings of paranoia in academia. I recognized this as unsettling, particularly coming from the educated and privileged lot that ran these institutions. I had practice with difficult situations; I also had been forced to redefine high school and college for my population of children of farmworkers who attended major universities, only to become the Other, not unlike the role of an assistant professor of color or from a background of poverty, who now holds a position romanticized by the outside world but one that becomes, at times, impossible to navigate without support and instruction.

Thus, from all of this emerged the idea of *Presumed Incompetent,* which my friend and colleague Carmen G. González and I diligently proposed as a possibility for a book that administrators and professors of color could use to understand the complexity of the particular situation in this historical moment of women of color and those emerging from the working class not merely as tokens. Carmen and I were able to recruit two outstanding colleagues to join us in this task—Angela P. Harris, a very well-known scholar who has published extensively on race, gender, and class; and Yolanda Flores Niemann, an expert in tokenism in academia, who also possesses extensive experience in administration. Together we collected a series of papers that exposed the current situation of women faculty struggling in institutions of higher learning, survivors succeeding against enormous odds. As editors, we received hundreds of papers from which we selected the ones in this volume.

For the past six years that I have had the task of managing this project, I have responded to numerous people and read their work. Through this process—in a climate of increasing anti-immigrant hostility and ongoing war against the poor—I have become even more determined to underscore the often-tokenized and overlooked experiences of women in academia who have emerged from poverty, in many cases from immigrant families and other non-privileged backgrounds.

As a young woman, I was raised in the Bay Area by feminists and very strong women. My mother was a cannery worker and a resistance leader among those in her cannery. Seeing her exit the workforce because of the incredible 1985–1987 Teamsters' strike in Watsonville, California, I knew that the best way to resist is to put all your chips on the table. At the time of the strike, I watched as supporters donated canned goods, which the leaders distributed openly and evenly among the strikers, instead of secretly bestowing more on some than others to gain a political or social advantage. In this case, it is only by including all the voices of women emerging from various experiences in academia, including the positive ones, that we can comprehensively analyze and correct the institutional process. As a junior faculty member, I knew very well that victimization and acting like a victim did not work. Those behaviors and mental pathologies only make the oppressor stronger. I did not want to reproduce that way of acting, even in my own struggle for tenure. The goal of this text is to encourage positive behavior in academia, to assist others to prevail and succeed.

This anthology will empower and instruct new and established academics and administrators into professionalizing a process that includes the voices of working-class women and women of color in academia, who are heroic not merely for creating a personal and unique path of triumph to acquire tenure but also for knowing that their experiences have been important as historical markers. The voices in this anthology speak often from a perspective limited by obstacles, yet they have firmly resisted injustice through a feminist agenda. Their essays are analytical, delineating and theorizing their journeys to help women of color succeed with dignity in academia.

Most of the women who wrote essays for this anthology did so out of the need to document their experiences as tools for others to examine and utilize so they could prevent a negative outcome at their home institutions. By inscribing their process, these women are attempting to diminish the litany of unexpected, mostly unpleasant, and difficult experiences facing new assistant professors of color, in particular, but also those encountered by women professors emerging from the working class. Some of these women survive the tenure process by the skin of their teeth and come out very wounded and demeaned on the other side, yet they are never asked to analyze this process during their academic lives. In addition, the people who demean them and slander their image during their tenure process seldom apologize to them. Our book also expects to contribute to the prevention of anxiety that assistant professors undergo and to assist in the healing of those who came before us in the academy.

Nonetheless, *Presumed Incompetent* is about more than obtaining tenure. The essays presented here are about surviving and even thriving in what are often foreign and hostile environments, no matter what rank these working-class women and women of color have achieved. Most of the women represented in this collection have, in fact, soared, thrived, and succeeded with very few resources and courageously wanted to make the process of navigating the academic world democratically transparent, not only so that others might succeed but to reveal that other women who did or did not triumph in academia were part of some negative force that was national and existed in most institutions of higher learning, even in the twenty-first century.

The purpose of this anthology is also to ensure that even those women who survived and soared realize that they are part of a greater phenomenon that relates more to power and gender relations than their particular stories, to social class at times more than racist attitudes. In *Presumed Incompetent,* we chiefly attempt to situate working-class women and women of color in a transparent and proactive light that does not exist at the margins but is clearly central to the academy of the twenty-first century. Through this invaluable collection of academic and personal essays, we aim to contribute to cultivating humane, positive experiences for women of color and working-class women in academia, as well as their allies, their institutions, their colleagues, and especially, their families.

References

Abel, R. 1990. Evaluating evaluations: How should law schools judge teaching? *Journal of Legal Education* 40, no. 4 (December): 407–65.

Abrami, P., S. d'Apollonia, and P. Cohen. 1990. Validity of student ratings of instruction: What we know and what we do not. *Journal of Educational Psychology*, 82: 219-31.

Abrami, P.C., S. d'Apollonia, and S. Rosenfield. 1997. The dimensionality of student ratings of instruction: What we know and what we do not. In *Effective teaching in higher education: Research and practice* eds. R. P. Perry and J. C. Smart. Bronx, N.Y.: Agathon Press. 321-67.

Abrami, P.C., L. Leventhal, R. Perry. 1982. *Review of Educational Research* 52, no. 3 (Autumn).

Abu-Lughod, L. 2002. Do Muslim women really need saving? Anthropological reflections on cultural relativism and its others. *American Anthropologist* 104, no. 3: 783–90.

Aguirre, A., Jr. 2000. *Women and minority faculty in the academic workplace: Recruitment, retention, and academic culture.* ASHE-ERIC Higher Education Rep. no. 27-6. San Francisco: Jossey-Bass.

Ahmed, L. 1992. *Women and gender in Islam.* New Haven: Yale University Press.

Aisenberg, N., and M. Harrington. 1988. *Women of academe: Outsiders in the sacred grove.* Amherst: University of Massachusetts Press.

Alemán, A. M. M. 1995. Actuando. In *The leaning ivory tower: Latino professors in American universities,* ed. R. V. Padilla and R. Chavez, 67–76. Albany: State University of New York Press.

Alexander, C., and C. Knowles. 2005. Introduction to *Making race matter: Bodies, space & identity,* ed. C. Alexander and C. Knowles, 1–16. New York: Palgrave Macmillan.

Alexander, R., and S. E. Moore. 2008. The benefits, challenges, and strategies of African American faculty teaching at predominantly white institutions. *The Journal of African American Studies* 12, no. 1: 4–18.

Alex-Assensoh, Y., T. Givens, K. Golden, V. L. Hutchings, S. L. Wallace, and K. J. Whitby. 2005. Mentoring and African American political scientists. *PS: Political Science and Politics* 38, no. 2: 284–85.

Alfred, M. V. 2001. Reconceptualizing marginality from the margins: Perspectives of African American tenured female faculty at a white research university. *Western Journal of Black Studies* 25, no. 1: 1–11. Alfred, T. 2005. *Wasase: indigenous pathways of action and freedom.* Peterborough, Ontario: Broadview Press. Allen, A. L. 1990–91. On being a role model. *Berkeley Women's Law Journal* 6: 22.

Allen, B.J. 1996. Feminism and organizational communication: A Black woman's (re) view of organizational socialization, *Communication Studies*, 47: 257-71.

———. 2000. Learning the ropes: A black feminist critique. In *Rethinking organizational & managerial communication from feminist perspectives.* ed. P. Buzzanell. Thousands Oaks, CA: Sage: 177-208.

———. 2011. *Difference matters: Communicating social identity.* Long Grove, IL: Waveland Press. 2nd Ed.

Allen, W. R., A. Haddad, and M. Kirkland. 1984. *1982 Graduate professional survey, national study of black college students.* Ann Arbor: University of Michigan Center for Afro-American and African Studies.

Alper, J. 1993. The pipeline is leaking women all the way along. *Science* 260: 409–11.

Ambady, N., F. J. Bernieri and J. A. Richeson. 2000. Toward a histology of social behavior: Judgmental accuracy from thin slices of the behavioral stream. *Advances in Experimental Social Psychology* 32: 201–71.

Ambady, N. and H. Gray. 2002. On being sad and mistaken: Mood effects on the accuracy of thin slice judgments. *Journal of Personality and Social Psychology* 83: 947-61.

Ambady, N., J. Koo, F. Lee, and R. Rosenthal. 1996. More than words: Linguistic and nonlinguistic politeness in two cultures. *Journal of Personality and Social Psychology* 5: 996-1011.

Ambady, N. and R. Rosenthal. 1993. Half a minute: Predicting teacher evaluations from thin slices of behavior and physical attractiveness. *Journal of Personality and Social Psychology* 64: 431-41.

American Association of University Professors (AAUP). 2010–11. *Report on the economic status of the profession.* Available online at http://www.aaup.org/AAUP/comm/ rep/Z/ecstatreport10-11/default.htm.

American Association of University Women (AAUP). 2004. *Under the microscope: A decade of gender equity projects in the sciences.* Washington, DC: AAUW Educational Foundation. Available online at http://www.aauw.org/research/upload/underthemicroscope.pdf.

American Council on Education. 2001. *Facts in brief: Percentage of women and minority faculty grew between 1987 and 1999.* Available online at http://www.acenet. edu/AM/Template.cfm?Section=Home&TEMPLATE=/CM/ContentDisplay. cfm&CONTENTID=6388.

American Political Science Association (APSA). 1971. Women in political science: Studies and reports of the APSA committee on the status of women in the profession, 1969–71. Washington, DC: American Political Science Association.

American Political Science Foundation. 2004. *Advancement in political science: A report of the APSA workshop on the advancement of women in academic political science in the United States.* Available online at http://www.apsanet.org/imgtest/womeninpoliticalscience.pdf.

Anderson, K. J., and G. Smith. 2005. Students' preconceptions of professors: Benefits and barriers according to ethnicity and gender. *Hispanic Journal of Behavioral Sciences* 27, no. 2: 184–201.

Angulo, M., and A. K. Wing. 1986. Proposed amendments to the foreign sovereign immunities act of 1976: The act of state doctrine. *Denver Journal of International Law* 14: 299–316.

Anthias, F., and N. Yval-Davis. 1983. Contextualising feminism: Gender, ethnic and class divisions. *Feminist Review* 15: 62–75.

Anzaldúa, G. 1983. Speaking in tongues: A letter to Third World women writers. In *This bridge called my back: Writings by radical women of color,* ed. C. Moraga and G. Anzaldúa, 165–74. 2nd ed. New York: Kitchen Table.

———. 1987. Borderlands/*la frontera:* The new *mestiza.* San Francisco: Aunt Lute Books.

Armstrong, M. J. 1998. Race and property values in entrenched segregation. *University of Miami Law Review* 52: 1051–65.

———. 2003. Meditations on being good. In *Critical race feminism: A reader,* ed. A. K. Wing, 107–9. 2nd ed. New York: New York University Press.

Arreola, R. A. 2000. *Developing a comprehensive faculty evaluation system.* 2nd ed. Bolton, MA: Anker Publishing.

Arriola, E. 1988. Sexual identity and the Constitution: Homosexual persons as a discrete and insular minority. *Women's Rights Law Reporter* 10, no. 1 (winter): 143–76.

———. 1990. "What's the big deal?": Women in the New York City construction industry and sexual harassment law, 1970–1985. *Columbia Human Rights Law Review* 22: 21–71.

———. 1997. Welcoming the outsider to an outsider conference: Law and the multiplicities of self. *Harvard Latino Law Review* 2: 397–410.

———. 2003. Tenure politics and the feminist scholar. *Columbia Journal of Gender and Law* 12: 532.

———. 2005. *Encuentro en el ambiente de la teoria:* Latina lesbians and Ruthann Robson's lesbian legal theory. *New York City Law Review* 8, no. 1 (fall): 519–41.

Arum, R., and J. Roksa. 2011. *Academically adrift: Limited learning on college campuses.* Chicago: University of Chicago Press.

Ashcraft, Karen L. and Brenda. J. Allen. 2003. The racial foundation of organizational communication. *Communication Theory* 13: 5-38.

Askmen.com. Angelina Jolie. Available online at http://www.askmen.com/celebs/women/actress/8_angelina_jolie.html.

———. Penélope Cruz. Available online at http://www.askmen.com/celebs/women/actress/56_penelope_cruz.html.

Association of American Colleges and Universities (AACUA). 2005. *Liberal education outcomes and student achievement of educational excellence: A preliminary report on student achievement in college.* Available online at http://www.aacu.org/advocacy/pdfs/leap_report_final.pdf.

Association of American Law Schools (AALS). 2005. *The racial gap in the promotion to tenure of law professors: Report to the committee on the recruitment and retention of minority law teachers.* Available online at http://www.aals.org/documents/racialgap.pdf.

———. Statistics for the academic year 2007–8. 2008. Available online at http://www.aals.org/statistics/2008dlt/gender.html.

Astin, H., C. M. Cress, and C. W. Astin. *Race and ethnicity in the American professorate, 1995–96.* 1997. Los Angeles: Higher Education Research Institute, Graduate School of Education and Information Studies, UCLA.

Attewell, P., D. Lavin, T. Domina, and T. Levey. 2004. The black middle class: Progress, prospects, and puzzles. *Journal of African American Studies* 8, no. 1 and 2: 6-19.

Avalos, M. 1991. The status of Latinos in the profession: Problems in recruitment and retention. *PS: Political Science and Politics* 24, no. 2 (June): 241–46.

Babad, A., D. Avni-Babad and R. Rosenthal. 2004. Prediction of students' evaluation from brief instances of professors' nonverbal behavior in defined instruction situations. *Social Psychology of Education* 7, no. 1: 3-33.

Baca Zinn, M. 1979. Field research in minority communities: Ethical, methodological and political observations by an insider. *Social Problems* 27, no. 2 (December): 209–19.

Baca Zinn, M., and B. T. Dill. 1996. Theorizing difference from multiracial feminism. *Feminist Studies* 22, no. 2: 321–31.

———. 1999. Theorizing difference from multiracial feminism. In *Race, identity and citizenship: A reader,* ed. R. D. Torres, L. F. Miron, and J. X. Inda, Cambridge, MA: Blackwell Publishers. 103–11.

Back, L. 2004. Ivory towers? The academy and racism. In *Institutional racism in higher education,* ed. I. Law, D. Phillips, and L. Turney, 1–6. Sterling, VA: Trentham Books.

Backer, L. C. 2009. Tenure and the minority law professor in the United States: Teaching against the demons. *Law at the end of the day,* June 20. Available online at http://lcbackerblog.blogspot.com/2009/06/tenure-and-minority-law-professor-in.html.

Bain, K. 2004. What the best college teachers do. Cambridge and London: Harvard University Press.

Baker, P., and N. A. Lewis. 2009. Republicans press judge about bias and activism. *New York Times,* July 15, A1.

Banks, T. L. 1990–91. Two life stories: Reflections of one black woman law professor. *Berkeley Women's Law Journal* 6: 46.

———. 1997. Two life stories: Reflections of one black woman law professor. In *Critical race feminism: A reader,* ed. A. K. Wing, 96–100.

Bannerji, H. 1996. On the dark side of the nation: Politics of multiculturalism and the state of "Canada." *Journal of Canadian Studies* 31, no. 3 (fall): 103–28.

Barnes, D. 1986. Transitions and stresses for black female scholars. In *Career guide for women scholars,* ed. S. Rose, 66–77. Springer Series vol. 8: Focus on Women. New York: Springer Publishing Co.

Bartow, A., M. Fine, and L. Guinier. 1994. Becoming gentlemen: Women's experiences at one Ivy League law school. *University of Pennsylvania Law Review* 143, no. 1 (November): 1.

Basow, S. A. 1986. Gender and stereotypes: Traditions and Alternatives. Brooks/Cole.

———. 1994a. Student ratings of professors are not gender blind. *AWM Newsletter* 24, no. 5 (Sept-Oct). Available online at http://www.awm-math.org/newsletter/199409/basow.html.

———. 1995. Student evaluations of college professors: When gender matters. *Journal of Educational Psychology* 87: 656-64.

———. 1998. Student evaluations: The role of gender bias and teaching styles. In *Career Strategies for Women in Academe: Arming Athena.* Eds. L. H. Collins et al.

Basow, S. A., and N. T. Silberg. 1987. Student evaluation of college professors: Are female and male professors rated differently? *Journal of Educational Psychology* 79, no. 3: 308–14.

Bass, E., and L. Davis. 1988. *The courage to heal: A guide for women survivors of child sexual abuse.* New York: Harper & Row, Publishers.

Bell, D. A., Jr. 1980. *Brown v board of education* and the interest convergence dilemma. *Harvard Law Review* 93: 518.

———. 1986. Application of the "tipping point" principle to law faculty hiring policies. *Nova Law Journal* 10: 319.

Benjamin, L., ed. 1997. *Black women in the academy: Promises and perils.* Gainesville: University Press of Florida.

Bennett, S.K. 1982. Student perceptions of and expectations for male and female instructors: Evidence relating to the question of gender bias in teaching evaluation. *Journal of Educational Psychology* 74: 170-9.

Bennett, S. M. 1998. Self-Segregation: An oxymoron in black and white. In *African American culture and heritage in higher education research and practice,* ed. K. Freeman, 121–31. Westport, CT: Praeger Publishers.

Bensimon, E. M. 2005. *Equality as a fact, equality as a result: A matter of institutional accountability.* Washington, DC: American Council on Education.

Bensimon, E. M., L. Hao, and L. T. Bustillos. 2006. Measuring the state of equity in public higher education. In *Expanding opportunity in higher education: Leveraging promise,* ed. P. Gándara, G. Orfield, and C. Horn, 143–66. Albany: State University of New York Press.

Berk, R. 2006. *Thirteen strategies to measure college.* San Francisco: Jossey-Bass.

Berry, T. R., and N. D. Mizelle, eds. 2006. *From oppression to grace: Women of color and their dilemmas within the academy.* Sterling, VA: Stylus Publishing, LLC.

Bernieri F. J., J. S. Gillis, J. M. Davis, J.E. Grahe. 1996. Dyad rapport and the accuracy of its judgment across situations: A lens model analysis. *Journal of Personality and Social Psychology* 71: 110.

Bernstein, B., S. L. Blaisdell, M. J. Perez, C. J. St. Peter, A. J. Sumner, and L. Burke.1995. *Faculty gender, effort, style and rigor: Relative contributions to student evaluations.* Paper presented at the meeting of the American psychological Association in New York.

Bertrand, M. and S. Mullaithan, 2004, Are Emily and Greg more employable than Lakisha and Jamal? A field experiment on labor market discrimination. *American Economic Review* 94: 991-1013.

Bérubé, A. [2001], 2003. How gay stays white and what kind of white it stays. In *Privilege: A reader,* ed. M. S. Kimmel and A. L. Ferber, 253–83. Boulder, CO: Westview Press.

Bierra, A., S. Griffin, and M. Liebenthal. 2007. To render ourselves visible: Women of color organizing and Hurricane Katrina. In *What lies beneath: Katrina, race, and the state of the nation.* Cambridge, MA: South End Press.

Blackburn, R. T., and R. J. Bentley. 1993. Faculty research productivity: Some moderators of associated stress. *Research in Higher Education* 34, no. 6: 725–45.

Blackburn, S. 2005. *Truth: A guide.* New York: Oxford University Press.

Blair, I. V., C. M. Judd, M. S. Sadler, and C. Jenkins. 2002. The role of Afrocentric features in person perception: Judging by features and categories. *Psychological Science* 15, no. 10: 674-9.

Blake, W. 2002. The chimney sweeper. In *The complete poetry and prose of William Blake,* ed. Harold Bloom, Berkeley: University of California Press.

Bok, D. 2003. *Universities in the marketplace: The commercialization of higher education.* Princeton, NJ: Princeton University Press.

———. 2006. *Our underachieving colleges.* Princeton, NJ: Princeton University Press.

Bonilla-Silva, E. 2009. *Racism without racists: Color-blind racism and the persistence of racial inequality in the United States.* Lanham, MD: Rowman & Littlefield Publishers, Inc.

Bonner, F., II. 2004. Black professors: On the track but out of the loop. *The Chronicle Review, Chronicle of Higher Education,* June 11. Available online at http://chronicle. com/weekly/v50/i40/40b01101.htm.

Bonner, Florence. 2001. Addressing gender issues in the historically Black college and university. *The Journal of Negro Education,* 70: 176-191.

Bowen, D. 2010. Brilliant disguise: An empirical analysis of a social experiment banning affirmative action. *Indiana Law Journal* 85: 1197–254.

Bowleg, L. 2008. When black + lesbian + woman? ≠ black lesbian woman: The methodological challenges of qualitative and quantitative intersectionality research. *Sex Roles: A Journal of Research* 59, nos. 5–6: 312–25.

Brand, D. 1998. *Bread out of stone: Recollections on sex, recognitions, race, dreaming and politics.* Toronto: Vintage Canada.

Braskamp, L. A., and J. C. Ory. 1994. Assessing faculty work: Enhancing individual and institutional performance. San Francisco: Jossey-Bass.

Brockway, L. H. 2002. *Science and colonial expansion.* New Haven, CT: Yale University Press.

Broderick, K. S. 2009. Nation's urban land-grant law school: Ensuring justice in the 21st century. *University of Toledo Law Review* 40, no. 2 (winter): 305–26.

Brodoff, L. 2008. Lifting burdens, proof, social justice, and public assistance administrative hearings. *N.Y.U. Review of Law and Social Change* 32, no.2: 131–89.

Bronson, P., and A. Merryman. 2009. See baby discriminate. *Newsweek,* September 14, 53.

Brown, L. A. 2003. Ask and you shall receive?: Gender differences in negotiator's beliefs about requests for a higher salary. *Human Relations* 56, no. 6 (June): 635–62.

Brownmiller, S. 1975. A question of race. In *Against our will: Men, women and rape.* New York: Bantam Books.

Brubacher, J. S., and W. Rudy. 1997. *Higher education in transition: A history of American colleges and universities.* Piscataway, NJ: Transaction Publishers.

Buchanan, N. T., and T. A. Bruce. 2004–5. Contrapower harassment and the professorial archetype: Gender, race, and authority in the classroom. *On Campus with Women* (Association of American Colleges and Universities) 34, nos. 1–2 (fall–winter). Available online at http://www.aacu.org/ocww/volume34_1/feature.cfm?section=2.

Burack, C., and S. E. Franks. 2004. Telling stories about engineering: Group dynamics and resistance to diversity. *NWSA Journal* 16, no. 1: 79–95.

Burgess, N. J. 1997. Tenure and promotion among African-American women in the academy. In *Black women in the academy: Promises and perils,* ed. L. Benjamin, 227–34.

Butler, C., E. S. Tull, E.C. Chambers, and J. Taylor. 2002. Internalized racism, body fat distribution, and abnormal among African-Caribbean women in the Dominica, West Indies. *Journal of National Medical Association* 94 (3): 143-148.

Butler, S. 1998. *The way home: Women talk about race in America.* DVD. World Trust Educational Services, Inc.

Caldwell, P. M. 1991. A hair piece: Perspectives on the intersection of race and gender. *Duke Law Journal* 41, no. 2 (April): 365.

Calhoun-Brown, A. 2000. Upon this rock: The black church, nonviolence, and the civil rights movement. *PS: Political Science and Politics* 33, no. 2: 168–74.

California Legislature. 1973. *Report of the joint committee on the master plan for higher education.* Available online at http://sunsite.berkeley.edu/~ucalhist/archives_exhibits/masterplan/post1960.html.

Calmore, J. O. 2005. Whiteness as audition and blackness as performance: Status protest from the margin. *Washington University Journal of Law and Policy* 18: 99–128.

Cameron, J. 1995. *The artist's way.* New York: Penguin Putnam.

Camper, C. 2004. Into the mix. In *"Mixed race" studies: A reader,* ed. Jayne O., A. Ifekwunigwe, 176–82. New York: Routledge.

Canada Task Force on the Participation of Visible Minorities in the Federal Public Service. 2000.

Embracing change: Report of the task force on the participation of visible minorities in the federal public service. Ottawa, ON: Treasury Board Secretariat.

Canadian Association of University Teachers (CAUT). 2007. A partial picture: The representation of equity-seeking groups in Canada's universities and colleges. *Equity Review,* November. Available online at http://www.caut.ca/uploads/EquityReview1-en.pdf.

Carbado, D. W., and M. Gulati. 2000a. Conversations at work. *Oregon Law Review* 79: 103–45.

———.2000b. Working identity. *Cornell Law Review* 85: 1259–308.

———. 2003a. The law and economics of critical race theory. *Yale Law Journal* 112: 1757–828.

———. 2003b. Tenure. *Journal of Legal Education* 53: 157–73.

———. 2004. Race to the top of the corporate ladder: What minorities do when they get there. *Washington and Lee Law Review* 61, no. 4: 1643–91.

Carby, H. 1992. The multicultural wars. In *Black popular culture,* ed. Gina Dent, 187—99. Seattle: Bay Press.

Carrell, S. E. and J. E. West. 2010. Does professor quality matter? Evidence from random assignment of students to professors. *Journal of Political Economy* 118, no. 3: 409-432.

Carrell, S. E., M. E. Page, and J. E. West. 2009. Sex and science: How professor gender perpetuates the gender gap. *Quarterly Journal of Economics* 125, no. 3 (August): 1101–44. Available online at http://www.nber.org/papers/w14959 Carter, D., C. Pearson, and D. Shavlik. 1987–88. Double jeopardy: Women of color in higher education. *Educational Record* 68–69 (fall–winter): 98–103.

Cashin, S. 2004. *The failures of integration: How race and class are undermining the American dream.* New York: Public Affairs.

Cashin, W. E. 1995. Student ratings of teaching: The research revisited. IDEA paper 32, September. Center for Faculty Evaluation and Development, Kansas State University, Manhattan.

Castilla, E. 2008. Gender, race, and meritocracy in organizational careers. *American Journal of Sociology* 113: 1479–526.

Cavaiola, A. A., and N. J. Lavender. 2000. *Toxic coworkers.* Oakland, CA: New Harbinger Publications, Inc.

Centra, J. A. 1979. *Determining faculty effectiveness: Assessing teaching, research, and science for personnel decisions and improvement.* San Francisco: Jossey-Bass.

———. 1993. *Reflective faculty evaluation.* San Francisco, CA: Jossey-Bass.

Centra, J. A., and N. B. Gaubatz. 2000. Is there gender bias in student evaluations of teaching? *Journal of Higher Education* 71, no. 1: 17–33.

Chan, S. 2005. *In defense of Asian American studies: The politics of teaching and program building.* Urbana: University of Illinois Press.

Chang, G. 2000. Disposable domestics: Immigrant women workers in the global economy.

Cambridge, MA: South End Press.

Chang, R. S., and A. Davis. 2010. An epistolary exchange: Making up is hard to do: Race/gender/sexual orientation in the law school classroom. *Harvard Journal of Law & Gender* 33: 1–57.

Chin, G. J. 2002. Regulating race: Asian exclusion and the administrative state. *Harvard Civil Rights–Civil Liberties Review* 37: 1–64.

Chinen, Mark. 2010. Teaching as a Form of Love. *Seattle Journal of Social Justice 9* Seattle J. for Soc. Just. 221. citing P. Freire, *Pedagogy of the Oppressed*, (Translated by M. B. Ramos. New York: Continuum, 1970): 46.

Ching Louie, M., with Linda Burnham. 2000. *WEdGE: Women's education in the global economy*. Berkeley: Women of Color Resource Center.

Cho, S. K. 1997. Asian Pacific American women and racialized sexual harassment. In *Making more waves: New writing by Asian American women*, ed. E. H. Kim, L. V. Villanueva, and Asian Women United of California, 164–73. Boston: Beacon Press.

Churchill, W. 1998. *Fantasies of the Master Race: Literature, Cinema and the Colonization of American Indians*. San Francisco: City Lights Books.

Chused, R. H. 1988–89. The hiring and retention of minorities and women on American law school faculties. *University of Pennsylvania Law Review* 137: 537.

Clark, C. 2005. *Shuffling to Ignominy: The Tragedy of Stepin Fetchit*. Lincoln, NE: iUniverse.

Clarke, G. E. 2006. Foreword to *The hanging of Angélique: The untold story of Canadian slavery and the burning of old Montreal*, by A. Cooper, xi–xvii. Toronto: HarperCollins Publishers.

Clarke, K. M., and D. A. Thomas, eds. 2006. *Globalization and race: Transformations in the cultural production of blackness.*. Durham: Duke University Press.

Clayson, D. E., and D. A. Haley. 1990. Student evaluations in marketing: What is actually being measured? *Journal of Marketing Education* 12, no. 3: 9–17.

Clayson, D. E. and M. J. Sheffet. 2006. Personality and the student evaluation of teaching, *J. Marketing Education* 28: 149–58.

Cohen, P. A. 1981. Student ratings of instruction and student achievement: A meta-analysis of multisection validity studies. *Review of Educational Research* 51 (fall): 281–309.

Cole, E. R. and S. Omari. 2003. Race, class and the dilemmas of upward mobility for African Americans. *Journal of Social Issues* 59, 4: 785-802.

Collins, L., J. Chrisler, and K. Quina. 1998. *Career Strategies for Women in Academia: Arming Athena*. New York: Sage Publications, Inc.

Collins, P. H. 1998. *Fighting words: Black women and the search for justice*. Minneapolis: University of Minnesota Press.

———. [1993] 2000. Toward a new vision: Race, class, and gender as categories of analysis and connection. In *The Social Construction of Difference and Inequality: Race, Class, Gender, and Sexuality*, ed. T. E. Ore, Mountain View, CA: Mayfield Publishing Company. (Originally published in 1993 in *Race, Sex, and Class* 1, no. 1: 25–45.

———. 2001. *Black feminist thought: Knowledge, consciousness, and the politics of empowerment*. New York: Routledge.

———. [1993] 2003. Toward a new vision: Race, class, and gender as categories of analysis and connection. In *Privilege: A reader*, ed. M. S. Kimmel and A. L. Ferber, 331–48.

Collins, Patricia Hill. 2000a. *Black feminist thought: Knowledge, consciousness, and the politics of empowerment*. New York: Routledge.

Collins, Patricia Hill. 2000b. The social construction of Black feminist thought. In *The Black feminist reader*, ed. Joy James and T. Denean Sharpley-Whiting, 183-207. Malden: Blackwell Publishers Ltd.

Collins, Patricia Hill. 1986. Learning from the outsider within: The sociological significance of Black feminist thought. *Social Problems* 33: 14-23.

Combahee River Collective. 1986. Combahee River Collective statement: Black feminist organizing in the seventies and eighties. New York: Kitchen Table/Women of Color Press.

Costanzo M. and D. Archer. 1989. Interpreting the expressive behavior of others: The interpersonal perception. Task Journal of Nonverbial Behavior 13, no. 4: 225-45.

Cooper, A. 2000. Constructing black women's historical knowledge. *Atlantis: A Women's Studies Journal* 25: 39–50.

———. 2006. *The hanging of Angélique: The untold story of Canadian slavery and the burning of old Montreal.* Toronto: HarperCollins Publishers.

Cooper, A. J. 1892. *Voice from the South.* Xenia, OH: Aldine Printing House.

Cooper, J. E., and D. D. Stevens, eds. 2002. *Tenure in the sacred grove: Issues and strategies for women and minority faculty.* Albany: State University of New York Press.

Cooper, T. L. 2006. *The sista' network: African-American women faculty successfully negotiating the road to tenure.* Bolton, MA: Anker Publishing.

Corkorinos, L. 2003. *The assault on diversity: An organized challenge to racial and gender justice.* New York: Rowman & Littlefield Publishers, Inc.

Correll J., B. Park, C. M. Judd, B. Wittenbrink, M. S. Sadler, and T. Keesee. 2007. Across the thin blue line: Police officers and racial bias in the decision to shoot. Journal of Personality and Social Psychology 92: 1006-23.

Costin, F., W. Greenough, and R. Menges. 1971. Student ratings of college teaching: Reliability, validity, and usefulness. *Review of Educational Research* 41 (December): 511–35.

Cox, T., R. Dicker, and A. Piepmeier. 2000. Introduction to *Catching a wave: Reclaiming feminism for the 21st century,* ed. R. Dicker and A. Piepmeier, 3–28. Boston: Northeastern University Press.

Crenshaw, K. W. 1991. Mapping the margins: Intersectionality, identity politics, and violence against women of color. *Stanford Law Review* 43, no. 6: 1241–99.

———. 1994a. Foreword: Toward a race-conscious pedagogy in legal education. *Southern California Review of Law and Women's Studies* 4 (fall): 33.

———. 1994b. Mapping the margins: Intersectionality, identity politics, and violence against women of color. In *The public nature of private violence: The discovery of domestic abuse,* ed. M. A. Fineman and R. Mykitiuk, 93–118. New York: Routledge.

———. 1997. Color-blind dreams and racial nightmares: Reconfiguring racism in the post-civil rights era. In *Birth of a nation'hood: Gaze, script, and spectacle in the O. J. Simpson trial,* ed. T. Morrison and C. B. LaCour, 97–168. New York: Pantheon Books.

Critical Resistance and INCITE! Women of Color against Violence. 2006. "Gender violence and the prison-industrial complex. In *Color of violence,* ed. INCITE!, 223–26. Cambridge, MA: South End Press Crocker, J., K. Voelkl, M. Testa, and B. Major. 1991. Social stigma: The affective consequences of attributional ambiguity. *Journal of Personality and Social Psychology* 60: 218–28.

Culp, J. M., Jr. 1991. Autobiography and legal scholarship and teaching: Finding the me in the legal academy. *Virginia Law Review* 77: 539.

Curtis, J. W. 2005. *Inequities persist for women and non-tenure-track faculty: The annual report on the economic status of the profession 2004–05,* 28. Washington, D.C., American Association of University Professors (AAUP). Available online at http://www.aaup.org/NR/rdonlyres/0A98969B-FA6C-40F5-8880-5E5DC3B7C36D/0/05z.pdf.

Cynkar, A. 2007. The changing gender composition of psychology. *APA Monitor* 38, no. 6: 46–47.

Dasgupta, N., D. E. McGhee, A. G. Greenwald, and M. R. Banaji. 2000. Automatic preference for white Americans: Eliminating the familiarity explanation. *Journal of Experimental Social Psychology* 36: 316-28.

Daufin, E. K. 1995. Confessions of a womanist professor. *Black Issues in Higher Education* 21, no. 1 (March 9): 34–35.

Davis, A. Y. March. 2008. Women of color in the academic industrial complex. Paper presented at Campus Lockdown: Women of Color Negotiating the Academic Industrial Complex, Ann Arbor, MI, March 14–15.

Davis, P. 1989. Law as microaggression. *Yale Law Journal* 98: 1559–77.   de la Luz Reyes, M., and J. J. Halcon. 1997. Racism in academia: The old wolf revisited? In *Latinos and education: A critical reader,* ed. A. Darder, R. D. Torres, and H. Gutiérrez, 423–38. New York: Routledge.

Delany, S. L., and A. E. Delany, with A. H. Hearth. 1997. *Having our say: The Delany sisters' first 100 years.* New York: Dell Publishing.

Delgado, R. 1989. Storytelling for oppositionists and others: A plea for narrative. *Michigan Law Review* 87: 2411–41.

———. 1999. Making pets: Social workers, "problem groups," and the role of the SPCA—Getting a little more precise about racialized narratives. *Texas Law Review* 77: 1571–84.

———. 2007. The myth of upward mobility. *University of Pittsburgh Law Review* 68: 835–913.

Delgado, R. and D. Bell. 1989. Minority law professors' lives: The Bell-Delgado survey. *Harvard. Civil Rights-Civil Liberties Law Revision* 24: 349.

Desmond-Harris, J. 2007. "Public interest drift" revisited: Tracing the sources of social change commitment among black Harvard law students. *Hastings Race & Poverty Law Journal* 4 (spring): 335.

Dews, B. C. L., and C. L. Law. 1995. *This fine place so far from home: Voices of academics from the working class.* Philadelphia: Temple University Press.

Diaz, A. 2003. Postcolonial theory and the third wave agenda. *Women and Language* 26: 1, 10-7.

Diggs, G. A., D. F. Garrison-Wade, D. Estrada, and R. Galindo. 2009. *Smiling faces and colored spaces: The experiences of faculty of color pursuing tenure in the academy. Urban Review.*

Dill, B. T. 1983. Race, class and gender: Prospects for an inclusive sisterhood. *Feminist Studies* 9: 131–50.

Discover the Networks. 2011. Indoctrination Studies. Available online at http://discoverthenetworks.org/viewSubCategory.asp?id=522.

Domestic Workers United and DataCenter. 2006. *Home is where the work is: Inside New York's domestic work industry.* July 14. Available online at http://www.datacenter.org/reports/homeiswheretheworkis.pdf.

Dovidio, J. F. 2000. The SPSSI bridge. Editorial in the *SPSSI Newsletter* 211, April.

Dovidio, J. F., and S. L. Gaertner. 1996. Affirmative action, unintentional racial biases, and intergroup relations. *Journal of Social Issues* 52, no. 4: 51–76.

———. 2010. Intergroup bias. In *Handbook of social psychology,* ed. S. T. Fiske, D. Gilbert, and G. Lindzey, 2:1084–1121. 2 vols, 5th ed. New York: John Wiley & Sons, Inc.

Dovidio, J. F., S. L. Gaertner, Y. F. Niemann, and K. Snider. 2001. Racial, ethnic, and cultural differences in responding to distinctiveness and discrimination on campus: Stigma and common group identity. *Journal of Social Issues* 57: 167–88.

Drakich, J., and P. Stewart. 2007. After 40 years of feminism, how are university women doing? *Journal of Higher Education: Academic Matters,* February, 6–9.

Drayton, R. 2000. *Nature's government.* New Haven, CT: Yale University Press.

Du Bois, W. E. B. [1903] 2007. *The souls of black folk.* New York: Oxford University Press.

———. [1935] 1998. *Black reconstruction in America, 1860–1880.* New York: Free Press.

Dulin, B. 1993. Founding project challenges young feminists. *New Directions for Women* 21, no. 1: 33.

Dunbar, P. L. [1896] 1993. We wear the mask." *The collected poetry of Paul Laurence Dunbar.* Ed. J. M. Braxton, 71. Charlottesville: University of Virginia Press.

Duran, Eduardo. 2006. *Healing the soul wound: Counseling with American Indians and other Native peoples.* New York: Teachers College Press.

Duran, E., and B. Duran. 1995. *Native American postcolonial psychology.* Albany: State University of New York Press.

Eagly, A. 1987. *Sex differences in social behavior: A social-role interpretation.* Psychology Press.

Eagly, A. H., M. G. Makhijani and B. G. Klonsky. 1992. Gender and the evaluation of leaders: A meta-analysis. *Psychological Bulletin* 111, no. 1: 3-22.

Ellis, E. M. 2001. The impact of race and gender on graduate school socialization, satisfaction with doctoral study, and commitment to degree completion. *Western Journal of Black Studies* 25, no. 1: 30–45.

Eng, Phoebe. 1999. *Warrior lessons: An Asian American woman's journey into power.* New York: Pocket Books.

Ensler, E. 2001. *The Vagina Monologues.* New York: Villard Books Erdle, S., H. G. Murray, and J. P. Rushton. 1985. Personality, classroom behavior and student ratings of college teaching effectiveness: A path analysis. *Journal of Educational Psychology* 77, no. 4: 394–407.

Errante, A. 2000. But sometimes you're not part of the story: Oral histories and ways of remembering and telling. *Educational Researcher* 29, no. 6: 16–27.

Essed, P. 2000. Dilemmas in leadership: Women of color in the academy. *Ethnic and Racial Studies* 23, no. 5: 888–904.

———. 2002. Everyday racism. In *A companion to racial and ethnic studies,* ed. D. T. Goldberg and J. Solomos, 202–16. Malden, MA: Blackwell Publishers.

Estlund, C. 2003. *Working together: How workplace bonds strengthen a diverse democracy.* New York: Oxford University Press.

Etter-Lewis, G. 1997. Black women in academe: Teaching/administrating inside the sacred grove. In *Black women in the academy: Promises and perils,* ed. L. Benjamin, 81–90.

Fanon, F. 1967. *Black skin, white masks.* New York: Grove Press.

Farber, D. A., and S. Sherry. 1993. Telling stories out of school: An essay on legal narratives. *Stanford Law Review* 45: 807–55.

Farley, C. H. 1996. Confronting expectations: Women in the legal academy. *Yale Journal of Law and Feminism* 8: 333-6.

Feagin, J.R., H. Vera, and N. Imani. 1996. *The agony of education: Black students at white colleges and universities.* New York: Routledge.

Feldman, K. A. 1986. The perceived instructional effectiveness of college teachers as related to their personality and attitudinal characteristics: A review and synthesis. *Research in Higher Education* 24, no. 2: 139–213.

———. 1989a. The association between student ratings of specific instructional dimensions and student achievement: Refining and extending the synthesis of data from multisection validity studies. *Research in Higher Education.* 30: 564-83.

———. 1989b. Instructional effectiveness of college teachers as judged by teachers themselves, current and former students, colleagues, and administrators, and external (Neutral) Observers. *Research in Higher Education* 30: 137-94.

———. 1992. College students' views of male and female college teachers: Part I—Evidence from the social laboratory and experiments. *Research in Higher Education* 33: 17-75.

———. 1993. College students' views of male and female faculty college teachers: Part II—Evidence from students' evaluations of their classroom teachers. *Research in Higher Education* 34, no. 2: 151–211.

Fish, S. 2010. Deep in the Heart of Texas. *Opinionator.* (New York Times on Line) Jun 21. Available online at http://opinionator.blogs.nytimes.com/2010/06/21/deep-in-the-heart-of-texas/.

Fiske, S. T., and S. E. Taylor, 1984. *Social cognition.* Reading, MA: Addison-Wesley.

Flagg, B. J. 1993. "Was blind but now I see": White race consciousness and the requirement of discriminatory intent. *Michigan Law Review* 91: 953–1017.

Fleming, J. 1984. *Blacks in college: A comparative study of students, success, in black and in white institutions.* San Francisco: Jossey-Bass.

Forgas, J. P. 1992a. Affect in social judgments and decisions: A multi-process model. *Advances in Experimental Social Psychology* 25: 227.

———. 1992b. On mood and peculiar people: Affect and person typicality in impression formation. *Journal of Personality and Social Psychology* 62: 863–75.

Fraga, L. R., T. E. Givens, and D. Pinderhughes. 2011. Task force on political science for the 21st century. Unpublished manuscript.

Freire, Paulo. 1998. *Pedagogy of freedom: Ethics, democracy and civic courage.* Lanham, MD: Rowman & Littlefield.

———. [1970] 1999. *Pedagogy of the oppressed.* Trans. Myra Bergman Ramos. New York: Herder and Herder.

Fries-Britt, S., and B. T. Kelly. 2005. Retaining each other: Narratives of two African American women in the academy. *Urban Review* 37, no. 3 (September): 221–42.

Frueh, J. 1996. *Erotic faculties.* Berkeley: University of California Press.

Frye, M. [1992] 1996. Getting it right. In *The second signs reader: Feminist scholarship, 1983–1996,* Ed. R.-E. B. Joeres and B. Laslett, . Chicago: University of Chicago Press.

Gage, A. 2003. "The great American pastime" is shopping, says history professor in new book. *St. Olaf College News,* December 5. Available online at http://www.stolaf.edu/news/index.cfm?fuseaction=NewsDetails&id=1871.

Gandara, P. C. 1995. *Over the ivy walls: The educational mobility of low-income Chicanos.* Albany: State University of New York Press.

García Bedolla, L., J. L. Monforti, and A. Pantoja. 2007. A Second Look: The Latina/o Gap. *Journal of Women, Politics, & Policy.* 28, nos 3/4: 147-71.

Garcia, J. A., and R. C. Smith. 1990. Meeting the national need for minority scholars and scholarship: What professional associations might do. *PS: Political Science and Politics* 23, no. 1 (March): 62–3.

Garcia, M(arisa). 2006. The brown diamond: A Latina in the sciences." In *The Latina/o pathway to the Ph.D.,* ed. J. Castellanaos, A. M. Gloria, and M. Kamimura, 243–54. Sterling, VA: Stylus Publishing, LLC.

Garcia, M(ildred). 2000. *Succeeding in an academic career: A guide for faculty of color.* Westport, CT: Greenwood Press.

Garza, H. 1993. "Second-class academics: Chicano/Latino faculty in U. S. universities." In *Building a diverse faculty*, ed. J. Gainen and R. Boice, 33–42. San Francisco: Jossey-Bass.

Gates Foundation. 2010. Postsecondary education overview. Available online at http://www.gatesfoundation.org/postsecondaryeducation/Pages/overview.aspx.

Geoghegan, M. 2008. Managing dissent through legal aid: Assessing the history and legacy of restrictions on grassroots organizing in the legal services corporation act of 1974. Unpublished manuscript in possession of Dean Spade.

Giddings, P. 1984. *When and where I enter: The impact of black women on race and sex in America.* New York: Bantam Books.

Gilbert, E., and B. L. Tatum. 1999. African American women in the Criminal Justice Academy: Characteristics, perceptions, and coping strategies. *Journal of Criminal Justice Education* 10, no. 2 : 231–46.

Gilmore, A. D. 1990–91. It is better to speak. *Berkeley Women's Law Journal* 6: 74.

Giroux, H. A. 2009. Democracy's Nemesis: The Rise of the Corporate University. *Cultural Studies ó Critical Methodologies* 9, no. 5: 669–95.

Gladwell, G. 2005. Blink: The Power of Thinking Without Thinking. New York: Back Bay Books, Little, Bay and Company. 21-39.

Goff, P. A., M. A. Thomas, and M. C. Jackson. 2008. "Ain't I a woman?": Towards an intersectional approach to person perception and group-based harms. *Sex Roles: A Journal of Research* 59, nos. 5–6: 392–403.

Goffman, I. 1963. *Stigma: Notes on the Management of Spoiled Identity.* New York: Prentice Hall.

Goldberg, D. T. 2005. Afterwards. Afterword to *Making Race Matter: Bodies, space & identity*, ed. C. Alexander and C. Knowles, 218–23.

Golde, C. M. 2000. Should I stay or should I go? Student descriptions of the doctoral attrition process. *Review of Higher Education* 23, no. 2: 199–227.

González, K., P. Marin, M. A. Figueroa, J. F. Moreno, and C. N. Navia. 2002. Inside doctoral education in America: Voices of Latina/os in pursuit of the Ph.D. *Journal of College Student Development* 43, no. 4 (July–August): 540–57.

Goodall, Jr., H.L. and Sandra Goodall. 2002. *Communicating in professional contexts: Skills, ethics, and technologies.* Belmont, CA: Wadsworth/Thomson Learning.

Goodenow, C., L. Szalacha, and K. Westheimer. 2006. School support groups, other school factors, and the safety of sexual minority adolescents. *Psychology in the Schools* 43, no. 5: 573–89.

Goodnough, A. 2009. Harvard professor jailed: Officer is accused of bias. *New York Times,* July 21, A13.

Gordon, B. M. 1992. The marginalized discourse of minority intellectual thought. In *Research and multicultural education: From the margins to the mainstreams*, ed. C.A. Grant, 19–31. Washington, DC: Falmer Press.

Gould, S. J. 1981. *The mismeasure of man.* New York: W. W. Norton & Co.

Graham, R. B. 2008. Obama's story is writ larger than himself. *Wilmington (DE) News Journal,* November 13, A12.

Grassroots Organizing for Welfare Leadership (GROWL). 2000. Welfare reform as we know it. Oakland: Applied Research Center (ARC).

Green, C. E., and V. G. King. 2001. Sisters mentoring sisters: Africentric leadership development for black women in the academy. *Journal of Negro Education* 70: 156–65.

Greenhouse, Steven. 2004. Abercrombie & Fitch Bias Case Is Settled. *New York Times*, November 17.

Greene, L. S. 1990–91. Tokens, role models, and pedagogical politics: Lamentations of an African American female law professor. *Berkeley Women's Law Journal* 6: 81.

———. 2003. Tokens, role models, and pedagogical politics: Lamentations of an African American female law professor. In *Critical race feminism: A reader*, ed. A. K. Wing, 89. 2nd ed.

Greenwald, D., E. McGhee, L. Jordan L., and K. Schwartz. 1998. Measuring individual differences in implicit cognition: The implicit association test. *Journal of Personality and Social Psychology* 74, no. 6: 1464-80.

Gregory, S. T. 1995. *Black women in the academy: the secrets to success and achievement.* New York: University Press of America.

———. 2001. Black faculty women in the academy: History, status and future. *Journal of Negro Education* 70, no. 3: 124–38.

Grillo, T. 1997. Tenure and minority women law professors: Separating the strands. *United States Federal Law Review* 31: 747–54.

Grillo, T., and S. Wildman. 1991. Obscuring the importance of race: The implication of making comparisons between racism and sexism (or other –isms). *Duke Law Journal* 41: 397–412.

Guiffrida, Douglas. 2005. Othermothering as a framework for understanding African American students' definition of student-centered faculty. *The Journal of Higher Education* 76: 701-23.

Guinier, L. 1990–91. Of gentlemen and role models." *Berkeley Women's Law Journal* 6: 93–106.

———. 2003. Of gentlemen and role models. In *Critical race feminism: A reader*, ed. A. K. Wing, 106–14. 2nd ed.

———. 2005. The miner's canary. *Liberal Education* 91, no. 2: 26–31.

Guinier, L., and G. Torres. 2003. *The miner's canary: Enlisting race, resisting power, transforming democracy.* Cambridge, MA: Harvard University Press.

Gunn Allen, P. 2003. *Pocahontas: Medicine woman, spy, entrepreneur, diplomat.* New York: HarperCollins Publishers.

Hall, J., J. Carter, and T. Horgan. 2000. Gender Difference in nonverbal communication of emotion. *Gender and Emotion: Social Psychological Perspectives.*

Hall, S. 1996. *Race, the floating signifier.* Northampton, MA: Media Education Foundation. Videotape.

Hall, S. T. 2000. Political Science/Government Doctorates Awarded by Gender and Ethnicity 1981–1998. Arlington, VA: National Science Foundation, Division of Science Resources Study.

Hamermesh, D. S., and A. M. Parker. 2005. Beauty in the classroom: Instructors' pulchritude and putative pedagogical productivity. *Economics of Education Review* 24, no. 4: 369–76.

Hamilton, K. 2002. Dual dilemma. *Black Issues in Higher Education* 19, no. 18: 40–43.

Hamlar, P. Y. T. 1983. Minority tokenism in American law schools. *Howard Law Journal* 26: 443.

Hancock, G., D. Shannon, and L. Trentham. 1993. Student and teacher gender in ratings of university faculty: Results from five colleges of study. *Journal of Personnel Evaluation in Education* 6: 235.

Haney López, I. F. 2010. Post-racial racism: Racial stratification and mass incarceration in the age of Obama. *California Law Review* 98, no. 3 (June): 1023–74.

Harding, S. 1998. *Is science multi-cultural?* Bloomington: Indiana University Press.

Harley, D. A. 2008. Maids of Academe: African American Women Faculty at Predominately White Institutions. *Journal of African American Studies* 12, no. 1: 19–36.

Harlow, R. 2003. Race Doesn't Matter, but . . . : The effect of race on professors' experiences and emotion management in the undergraduate college classroom. *Social Psychology Quarterly* 66: 348-63. Harmon, L., and D. W. Post. 1996. *Cultivating intelligence: Power, law, and the politics of teaching.* New York: New York University Press.

Harper, T. 2008. A dream fulfilled: Obama victory forged on promise of change. *Toronto Star,* November 5, 40.

Harris, A. P. 1990–91. Women of color in legal education: Representing *la mestiza.* *Berkeley Women's Law Journal* 6: 107.

———. 2006. From Stonewall to the suburbs?: Toward a political economy of sexuality. *William and Mary Bill of Rights Journal* 14, no. 4 (April): 1539–82.

Harris, A. P. and M. M. Shultz. 1993. "A(nother) critique of pure reason": Toward civic virtue in legal education. *Stanford Law Review* 45: 1773–805.

Harris, T. M. 2007. Black feminist thought and cultural contracts/Understanding the intersection and negotiations of racial, gendered, and professional identities in the academy. *New Directions for Teaching and Learning* 110: 55–64.

Harvey, W. B. 1994. African American faculty in community colleges: Why they aren't there. *New Directions for Community Colleges: Creating and Maintaining a Diverse Faculty* 22, no. 3: 19–25.

Hecht, M. L., R. L. Jackson II, and S. A. Ribeau. 2003. *African American communication: Exploring identity and culture.* 2nd ed. Mahwah, NJ: Lawrence Erlbaum Associates, Inc.

Hecht, Michael L. 1993. A research odyssey: Towards the development of a communication theory of identity. *Communication Monographs* 60: 76-82.

Hecht, Michael L., Ronald L. Jackson II, and Sidney A. Ribeau. 2003. *African American communication: Exploring identity and culture* (2nd ed.). Mahwah, NJ: Lawrence Erlbaum.

Heilman, M. E. 1983. Sex bias in work settings: The lack of fit model. In *Research in organizational behavior* V Eds. B. Staw and L. Cummings: 269–98.

———. 1996. Affirmative action's contradictory consequences. *Journal of Social Issues* 52, no. 4: 105–9.

Heilman, M. E, C. J. Block, and J. A. Lucas. 1992. Presumed incompetent? Stigmatization and affirmative action efforts. *Journal of Applied Psychology* 77, no. 4: 536–44.

Heilman, M. E., C. J. Block, and P. Stathatos. 1997. The affirmative action stigma of incompetence: Effects of performance information ambiguity. *Academy of Management Journal* 40, no. 3: 603–25. Hekman, D. R., K. A. Aquino, B. Owens, T. R. Mitchell, P. Schilpzand, and K. Leavitt. 2010. An examination of whether and how racial and gender biases influence customer satisfaction. *Academy of Management Journal* 53, no. 2: 238–64.

Henry, F. and C. Tator. 1994. Racism and the university. *Canadian Ethnic Studies* 26: 74–90.

———. 2007. The rightness of whiteness: Enduring racism in the Canadian academy. Paper presented at the biennial meeting of the Canadian.

———. Through a looking glass: Enduring racism on the university campus. *Journal of Higher Education: Academic Matters,* February, 24–5.

Hernández-Truyol, B., A. Harris, and F. Valdés. 2006. Beyond the first decade: A forward-looking history of LatCrit theory, community and praxis. *Berkeley La Raza Law Journal* 17: 169.

Herzig, A. 2004. Becoming mathematicians: Women and students of color choosing and leaving doctoral mathematics. *Review of Educational Research* 74, no. 2: 171–214.

Heywood, L., and J. Drake. 1997. Introduction to *Third wave agenda: Being feminist, doing feminism*, ed. L. Heywood and J. Drake, 1–20. Minneapolis: University of Minnesota Press.

Hill, A. F. 2002. Insider women with outsider values. *New York Times*, June 6, A31.

Hine, D. C. 1997. The future of black women in the academy: Reflections on struggle. In *Black women in the academy: Promises and perils*, ed. L. Benjamin, 327–39.

Hobson, S. M., and D. M. Talbot. Understanding student evaluations: What all faculty should know. *College Teaching* 49, no. 1: 26–31.

Hochschild, J. 2006. *Facing up to the American dream: Race, class and the soul of a nation*. Princeton: Princeton University Press.

Holmes, S. L. 2003. Black female administrators speak out: Narratives on race and gender in higher education. *National Association of Student Affairs Professionals* 6: 45–63.

Holmes, S. L., L. D. Land, and V. D. Hinton-Hudson. 2007. Race still matters: Considerations for mentoring black women in academe. *Negro Educational Review* 58, nos. 1–2: 105–29. hooks, b. 1981. *Ain't I a woman: Black women and feminism*. Cambridge, MA: South End Press.

———. 1984. *Feminist theory from margin to center*. Cambridge, MA: South End Press.

———. [1989] 2000. Feminism: A transformational politic. In *The social construction of difference and inequality: Race, class, gender, and sexuality*, ed. T. E. Ore, (Originally published in *Talking back, thinking feminist, thinking black*. Cambridge, MA: South End Press.) ———. 1994. *Teaching to transgress: Education as the practice of freedom*. New York: Routledge.

———. 1997. *Wounds of passion: A writing life*. New York: Henry Holt and Company.

hooks, b, and C. West. 1991. *Breaking bread: Insurgent black intellectual life*. Cambridge, MA: South End Press. 1991.*Hopwood v. University of Texas*. 1996. 78 F.3d 932 (5th Cir.) Houh, E. M. S. 2006. Toward praxis. *U.C. Davis Law Review* 39: 905–38.

Houston, Marsha. 1988. What makes scholarship about Black women and feminist communication scholarship? *Women's Studies in Communication* 10: 78-88.

Hu-DeHart, E. 1993. The history, development, and future of ethnic studies. *The Phi Delta Kappan* 75: 50–4.

———. 2000. Office politics and departmental culture. In *Succeeding in an academic career: A guide for faculty of color*, ed. M. Garcia, 27–38.

Humes, E. 2006. *Over here: How the G. I. Bill transformed the American dream*. New York: Houghton Mifflin Harcourt.

Hune, S. 1998. *Asian Pacific American women in higher education: Claiming visibility and voice*. Washington, DC: Association of American Colleges and Universities.

Hurtado, A., and M. Sinha. 2006. Differences and similarities: Latina and Latino doctoral students navigating the gender divide. In *The Latina/o pathway to the Ph.D.*, ed. J. Castellanaos, A. M. Gloria, and M. Kamimura, 149–68.

Hurtado, S. 2007. ASHE presidential address: Linking diversity with the educational and civic missions of higher education. *Review of Higher Education* 30, no. 2: 185–96. Hurtado, S., D. F. Carter, and D. Kardia. 1998. The climate for diversity: Key issues for institutional self-study. *New Directions for Institutional Research* 98: 53–63.

Hutchinson, E. O. 2006. Discrimination, not illegal immigrants, fuels black job crisis. New America Media. Available online at http://news.newamericamedia.org/news/view_article.html?article_id620a7a4dc8b8f2319c0f74fa1f746a0c April 24.

Ihnatowycz, Mark. 2007. Historic society and owner feud over "nigger rock." *The McGill Daily.*

INCITE! Women of Color against Violence, ed. 2007. *The revolution will not be funded: Beyond the nonprofit industrial complex.* Cambridge, MA: South End Press.

Iton, R. 2008. In search of the black fantastic: Politics and popular culture in the post-civil rights era. New York: Oxford University Press.

Jablin, Frederic M. 1987. Organizational entry, assimilation, and exit. In *Handbook of organizational communication,* eds. Frederic M. Jablin, Linda L. Putnam, Karlene H. Roberts, and Lyman W. Porter, 680-740. Beverly Hills, CA: Sage.

Jablin, Frederic. M. 2001. Organizational entry, assimilation, and disengagement/exit. In *The new handbook of organizational communication: Advances in theory,   research and methods,* eds., Frederic M. Jablin and Linda. L. Putnam , 732-819. Thousand Oaks, CA: Sage.

Jackson, J. 2004. The story is not in the numbers: Academic socialization and diversifying the faculty. *NWSA Journal* 16, no. 1: 172–85.

Jackson, L. R. 1998. The influence of both race and gender on the experiences of African American college women. In *Review of Higher Education* 21, no. 4: 359–75.

Jackson, R. L., II, and R. L. Crawley. 2003. What student confessions say about a black male professor: A cultural contracts theory approach to intimate conversations about race and worldview. *Journal of Men's Studies* 12, no. 1: 25–42.

James, C. E. 2007. It will happen without putting in place the measures: Racially diversifying universities. Paper presented at the biennial meeting of the Canadian Ethnic Studies Association, Winnipeg, MB, September 27–30.

James, Joy. 1998. *In resisting state violence: Radicalism, gender, and race in U.S culture.* Minneapolis: University of Minnesota Press.

Jayakumar, U. M., T. C. Howard, W. R. Allen, and J. C. Han. 2009. Racial privilege in the professoriate: An exploration of campus climate, retention, and satisfaction. *Journal of Higher Education* 80, no. 5: 538–63.

Johnson, A. G. 2001. *Privilege, power and difference.* Mountain View, CA: Mayfield Publishing Company.

Johnson, B., P. Kavanagh, and K. Mattson, eds. 2003. *Steal this university: The rise of the corporate university and the academic labor movement.* New York: Routledge.

Johnson, V. E. 2003. Grade inflation: A crisis in college education. Springer.

Johnsrud, L. K. 1993. Women and minority faculty experiences: Defining and responding to diverse realities. In *Building a diverse faculty,* ed. J. Gainen and R. Boice, 3–16.

Johnsrud, L. K., and K. C. Sadao. 1998. The common experience of "otherness": Ethnic and racial minority faculty. *Review of Higher Education* 21, no. 4 (summer): 315–42.

———. 2002. The common experience of "otherness": Ethnic and racial minority faculty. In *Racial and ethnic diversity in higher education,* ed. C. S. V. Turner, A. L. Antonio, M. García, B. V. Laden, A. Nora, and C. L. Presley, 137–50. ASHE Reader Series. 2nd ed, Boston: Pearson.

Jordan, E. C. 1990–91a. Black women in the legal academy. *Berkeley Women's Law Journal* 6: 1.

———. 1990–91b. Nepenthe. *Berkeley Women's Law Journal* 6: 113.

Jung, Eura and Michael L. Hecht. 2004. Elaborating the communication theory of identity: Identity gaps and communication outcomes. *Communication Quarterly* 52: 265-283.

Kanter, R. M. 1977. *Men and women of the corporation.* New York: Basic Books.

Karabel, J. 2006. *The chosen: The hidden history of admission and exclusion at Harvard, Yale, and Princeton.* New York: Houghton Mifflin Harcourt.

Katznelson, I. 2005. *When affirmative action was white: An untold history of racial inequality in twentieth-century America.* New York: W. W. Norton & Co.

Keating, A. L. 2002. Writing, politics, and *las lesberadas: Platicando con* Gloria Anzaldúa. In *Chicano leadership: The frontiers reader,* ed. Y. F. Niemann, with S. H. Armitage, P. Hart, and K. Weathermon. Lincoln: University of Nebraska Press.

Keep calm and carry on. Poster history. Available online at http://www.keepcalmand-carryon.com/pages/history.

Keister, L. A. 2000. *Wealth in America: Trends in wealth inequality.* Cambridge: Cambridge University Press.

Keller, E. F. 1983. *A feeling for the organism.* New York: W.H. Freeman & Co.

Kerber, L. 2005. We must make the academic workplace more humane and equitable. *Chronicle of Higher Education* 51, March 18, B-6.

Kierstead, D., P. D'Agostino, and H. Drill H. 1988. Sex role stereotyping of college professors: Bias in students' ratings of instructors. *Journal of Education Psychology* 80: 342-4.

Kimmel, M. S. 2003. Toward a pedagogy of the oppressor. Introduction to *Privilege: A reader,* ed. M. S. Kimmel and A. L. Ferber, 1–10.

Kinder, D. R. and D. O. Sears. 1985. Public opinion and political action. In *Handbook of Social Psychology,* ed. G. Lindzey and E. Aronson, 659–741. 3rd ed. New York : Random House.

King, J. E. 2008. Too many rungs on the ladder? Faculty demographics and the future leadership of higher education. Center for Policy Analysis, American Council on Education.

King, M. L., Jr. 1965. Our God is marching on. March 25. Available online at http://www.mlkonline.net/ourgod.html.

———. 1992. I have a dream. In *I have a dream: Writings and speeches that changed the world.* San Francisco: HarperOne.

Kinser, A. 2004. Negotiating spaces for/through third-wave feminism. *NWSA Journal* 16, no. 3: 124–53. Kobayashi, A. 2006. Why women of colour in geography? *Gender, Place and Culture* 13: 33–8.

———. 2007a. Making the visible count: Difference and embodied knowledge in the academy. Paper presented at the annual meeting of the Canadian Federation for the Humanities and Social Sciences, Saskatoon, SK, May 30–June 2.

———. 2007b. More than representation: Faculty of colour and student mentoring. Paper presented at the biennial meeting of the Canadian Ethnic Studies Association, Winnipeg, MB, September 27–30.

Koppel, N. 2006. Fewer blacks enter law school, prompting plan for monitoring. *Wall Street Journal,* February 14, B6.

Kort, W. A. 2002. African Americans reading scripture: Freeing/revealing/creating. A review essay. *Christianity and Literature* 51, no. 2: 263–72.

Krieger, L. H. 1998. Civil rights perestroika: Intergroup relations after affirmative action. *California Law Review* 86: 1251–333.

Kubler-Ross, E. 1973. On death and dying. 2nd ed. New York: Tavistock/Routledge.

———. 2005. *On grief and grieving: Finding the meaning of grief through the five stages of loss.* New York: Scribner.

Kvale, S. 1995. The social construction of validity. *Qualitative Research* 1: 19–40.

Lacy, K. R. 2007. *Blue chip black: race, class and status in the new black middle class.* Berkeley: University of California Press.

Laden, B.V., and L. S. Hagedorn. 2000. Job satisfaction among faculty of color in academe: Individual survivors or institutional transformers? In *New Directions for Institutional Research.* no. 105, ed. L. S. Hagedorn. San Francisco: Jossey-Bass.): 57-66.

LaDuke, W. 2005. *Recovering the Sacred: The Power of Naming and Claiming.* Cambridge, MA: South End Press.

Ladson-Billings, G. 1997. For colored girls who have considered suicide when the academy's not enough: Reflections on an African American woman scholar. In *Learning from our lives: Women, research, and autobiography in education,* ed. A. Neumann and P. Peterson, 52–70. New York: Teachers College, Columbia University.

Ladson-Billings, G., and Tate, B. 1995. Toward a critical race theory of education. *Teachers College Record* 97, no. 1: 47–67.

Lai, Z., A. Leong, and C. C. Wu. 2000. The lessons of the Parcel C struggle: Reflections on community layering. *Asian Pacific American Law Journal* 6 (spring): 1.

Lane, K., A., Mahzarin, R. Banaji, B. A. Nosek, and A. G. Greenwald. 2007. Understanding and using the implicit association test: IV what we know (so far) about the method. In *Implicit Measures of Attitudes.* Eds. B. Wittenbrink and N. Schwarz. New York: Guilford Press, 59-102.

Lavariega Monforti, J. and M. Michelson. 2008. Diagnosing the leaky pipeline: continuing barriers to the retention of Latinas and Latinos in political science. PS: Political Science and Politics 41, 1 (Jan.): 161-6.

Lepore, S. J. 2006. Effects of social stressors on cardiovascular reactivity in black and white women. *Annals of Behavioral Medicine* 31, no. 2: 120–7.

Lewin, T. 2010a. Law school admissions lag among minorities. *New York Times,* January 6. Available online at http://www.nytimes.com/2010.01.07/education/07law.html.

———. 2010b. Once a leader, US lags in college degrees. *New York Times,* July 23.

Lewis, T. T. 2006. Chronic exposure to everyday discrimination and coronary artery calcification in African-American women: The SWAN heart study. *Psychosomatic Medicine* 68: 362–8.

Liemer, S. P., and H. S. Temple. 2007–8. Did your legal writing professor go to Harvard? The credentials of legal writing faculty at hiring time. *University of Louisville Law Review* 46: 383–436.

Lincoln, Y. S. 1995. Emerging criteria for quality in qualitative and interpretative research. *Qualitative Inquiry* 1: 275–89.

Lipsitz, George. 1998. *The possessive investment in whiteness: How white people profit from identity politics.* Philadelphia: Temple University Press.

Little, R. G. 2002. Rage before race. *Village Voice,* October 16–22. Available online at http://www.villagevoice.com/news/0242,little,39205,1.html.

Locke, M. E. 1997. Striking the delicate balances: The future of African American women in the academy. In *Black women in the academy: Promises and perils,* ed. L. Benjamin, 340–6.

Lorde, Audre. 1984. *Sister outsider: Essays & speeches by Audre Lorde.* Berkeley: Crossing Press.

————. [1984] 2000. Age, race, class, and sex: Women redefining difference." In *The social construction of difference and inequality: Race, class, gender, and sexuality*, ed. T. Ore,.

Lotz, A. D. (2003). Communicating third-wave feminism and new social movements: Challenges for the next century of feminist endeavor. *Women & Language*, 26: 2-9.

Ludwig, J. and J. Meacham. 1997. Teaching controversial courses: Student evaluations of instructors and content. *Educational Research Quarterly* 21: 27.

Lustbader, P. 2006. Walk the talk: Creating learning communities to promote a pedagogy of justice. *Seattle Journal for Social Justice* 4, no. 2 (spring/summer): 613.

Luther, R, M. Whitmore, and B. Moreau, eds. 2003. *Seen but not heard: Aboriginal women and women of colour in the academy*. Feminist Voices 14. 2nd ed. Ottawa: Canadian Research Institute for the Advancement of Women.

Mabokela, R.O., and A. L. Green. 2001. *Sisters of the academy: Emergent black women scholars in higher education*. Sterling, VA: Stylus Publishing, LLC.

Mackenzie, S. 1991. *Remember Africville*. National Film Board of Canada. Documentary film.

Mackey, E. 1999. *The house of difference: Cultural politics and national identity in Canada*. London: Routledge.

Mahoney, M. R. 1995. Segregation, whiteness, and transformation. *University of Pennsylvania Law Review* 143: 1659.

Mahtani, M. 2002. Interrogating the hyphen-nation: Canadian multicultural policy and "mixed race" identities. *Social Identities* 8: 67–90.

Major, B., J. Feinstein, and J. Crocker. 1994. Attributional ambiguity of affirmative action? *Basic and Applied Social Psychology* 112: 113–41.

Mananzala, R., and D. Spade. 2008. The nonprofit industrial complex and trans resistance, sexuality research and social policy. *Sexuality Research and Social Policy* 5, no. 1 (March): 53–71.

Maranville, D. 2006. Classroom incivilities, gender, authenticity and orthodoxy, and the limits of hard work: Four lenses for interpreting a "failed" teaching experience. *William & Mary Journal of Women and the Law* 12: 699, 716-21.

Marbley, A. F. 2007. Finding my voice: An African-American female professor at a predominantly white university. *Advancing Women in Leadership Online Journal* 22 (winter). Available online at http://www.advancingwomen.com/awl/winter2007/finding_my_voice.htm.

Margolis, E., and M. Romero. 1998. "The department is very male, very white, very old, and very conservative": The functioning of the hidden curriculum in graduate sociology departments. *Harvard Educational Review* 68: 1–32.

Marsh, H.W. 1987. Students' evaluations of university teaching: Research findings, methodological issues, and directions for future research. *International Journal of Educational Research* 11, no. 3: 253–388.

Marsh, H. W. and M. Dunkin. 1992. *Students evaluations of university teaching: A multidimensional perspective*. In *Higher Education: Handbook of Theory and Research*, ed. J. C. Smart.

Martinez Aleman, A. M. 1995. *Actuando*. In *The Leaning Ivory Tower: Latino Professors in American Universities*, ed. R. V. Padilla and R. C. Chavez, 67–76.

Mason, M. A., and M. Goulden. 2002. Do babies matter?: The effect of family formation on the lifelong careers of academic men and women. *Academe* 88, no. 6 (November–December): 21–7.

Massey, Douglas S. 2008. *Categorically unequal: The American stratification system.* New York: Russell Sage Foundation Publications.

Matthews, J. 1997. In Response to Williams and Ceci. *Change* 29: 17.

Mattis, J. S., N. A. Grayman, S. A. Cowie, C. Winston, C. Watson, and D. Jackson. 2008. Intersectional identities and the politics of altruistic care in a low-income, urban community. *Sex Roles: A Journal of Research* 59, 5–6: 418–28.

McClellan, J. E. 2010. *Colonialism and science: Saint Domingue in the old regime.* Chicago: University of Chicago Press.

McClelland, K. 2003. How race matters: The integration of immigrant and involuntary minorities on a predominantly white college campus" Paper presented at the annual meeting of the American Sociological Association, Atlanta, GA.

McCloskey, D. 1998. *The rhetoric of economics.* Madison: University of Wisconsin Press.

McCroskey, J. C., K. M. Valencic and V. P. Richmond. 2004. Toward a general model of instructional communication. *COMM. Q.* 52: 197.

McCullough, M. W. 1998. *Black and white women as friends: Building cross-race friendships.* New York: Hampton Press, Inc.

McCurtis, B. R., J. F. L. Jackson, and E. M. O'Callaghan. 2009. Developing leaders of color in higher education: Can contemporary programs address historical employment trends? In *Rethinking leadership in a complex, multicultural and global environment,* ed. A. Kezar, 65–92. Sterling, VA: Stylus Publishing, LLC.

McGinley, A. C. 2009. Reproducing gender on law school faculties. *Brigham Young University Law Review:* 99–155.

McKay, N. Y. 1995. Minority faculty in [mainstream white] academia. In *The Academic's Handbook,* ed. A. L. Deneef and C. D. Goodwin. 2nd ed. Durham, NC: Duke University Press, 1995.

———. 1997. A troubled peace: Black women in the halls of the white academy. In *Black Women in the Academy: Promises and Perils,* ed. L. Benjamin, 11–22.

McKeachie, W. J. and M. Kaplan. 1996. Persistent problems in evaluating college teaching.

AAHE Bulletin, (February): 5-9.

McKinney, K. D. 2005. *Being white: Stories of race and racism.* New York: Routledge.

McKittrick, K. 2002. "Their blood is there, and they can't throw it out": Honouring black Canadian geographies. *Topia* 7: 27–36.

———. 2006. *Demonic grounds: Black women and the cartographies of struggle.* Minneapolis: University of Minnesota Press.

McNeill, J. R. 2010. Mosquito empires: Ecology and war in the greater Caribbean, 1620–1914. Cambridge: Cambridge University Press.

Medicine, B. 2001. *Learning to Be an Anthropologist & Remaining "Native:" Selected Writings.* Champaign: University of Illinois Press.

Merrit, D. J. 2008. Bias the brain and student evaluations of teaching. *82 St. John's Law Review* 235: 251-2.

———. 2010. Piercing the brilliant veil: Two stories of American racism. *Indiana Law Journal* 85: 1255–59.

Merritt, D. J., and B. F. Reskin. 1991. The double minority: Empirical evidence of a double standard in law school hiring of minority women. *Southern California Law Review* 65: 2299–359.

———. 1997. Sex, race, and credentials: The truth about affirmative action in law faculty hiring. *Columbia Law Review* 97: 199–311.

Messner, M. A. 2000. White guy habits in the classroom. *Men and Masculinities* 2: 457–69.

———. 2011. The privilege of teaching about privilege. *Sociological Perspectives* 54, no. 1: 3–13.

Meyer, J. 2009. "Nation of cowards" on race, 1st black attorney general says. *Chicago Tribune,* February 19, 10.

Michelson, M. R. 2006. APSA fund successfully mentoring Latino scholars. *PS: Political Science and Politics* 39, no. 4 (October): 949–51.

Mies, M. 1983. Towards a methodology for feminist research. In *Theories of women's studies,* G. Bowles and R. D. Klein, 117–39. Boston: Routledge & Kegan Paul. 1983.

Mihesuah, D.A. 1998. *Natives and academics: Research and writing about American Indians.* Lincoln: University of Nebraska Press.

Mihesuah, D. A. 2002. *American Indians: Stereotypes & realities.* Atlanta: Clarity Press.

Mihesuah, D. A. 2003. *Indigenous American women: Decolonization, empowerment, activism.* Lincoln: University of Nebraska Press.

Mihesuah, D. A., and A. C. Wilson. 2006. *Indigenizing the academy: Transforming scholarship and empowering communities.* Lincoln, NE: Bison Books.

Mihesuah, H. 2002, *First to fight.* Ed. D. A. Mihesuah. Lincoln: University of Nebraska Press.

Militz-Frielink, S. 2009. Spirituality and education: An inquiry into definitions and practices taking shape in charter schools.

Miller, L. 2005. Who burned the witches? February 1. Available online at http://www.salon.com/2005/02/01/witch_craze/.

Mitchell Dean. 2010. *Governmentality: Power and Rule in Modern Society.* London: SAGE Publications. 2nd ed.

Mitchell, M. 2009. Why we still need black history month. *Chicago Sun Times,* February 15, A12.

Modern Language Association (MLA). 2007. *Report of the MLA Task Force on Evaluating Scholarship for Tenure and Promotion.* Available online at http://www.mla.org/pdf/task-forcereport0608.pdf.

Moghissi, H. 1994. Racism and sexism in academic practice: A case study. In *The dynamics of "race" and gender: Some feminist interventions,* ed. H. Afshar and M. Maynard, 222–34. London: Taylor & Francis Ltd.

Mohanty, C. 1984. Under Western eyes: Feminist scholarship and colonial discourses. *Boundary 2* 12, no. 3/13, no. 1 (spring/fall): 338–58.

———. 2003. "Under Western eyes" revisited: Feminist solidarity through anti-capitalist struggles. *Signs* 28: 499–535.

Monroe, K. R. 2003. Mentoring in Political Science. *PS: Political Science and Politics* 36, no. 1 (January): 93–96.

Monroe, K. R., S. Ozyurt, T. Wrigley, and A. Alexander. 2008. Gender equality in academia: Bad news from the trenches, and some possible solutions. *Perspectives in Politics* 6, no. 2: 215–33.

Monroe, K. R., and W. F. Chiu. 2010. Gender equality in the academy: The pipeline problem. *PS: Political Science and Politics* 43, no. 2: 303–8.

Montoya, M. 1994. *Máscaras, trenzas y greñas:* Un/Masking the self while un/braiding Latina stories and legal discourse. *Harvard Journal of Law & Gender* 17: 185–220.

———. 2000. Silence and silencing: Their centripetal and centrifugal forces in legal communication, pedagogy, and discourse. *Michigan Journal of Race & Law* 5 (summer): 847.

Monture-Angus, P. 2003. "In the way of peace": Confronting "whiteness" in the university. In *Seen but not heard: Aboriginal women and women of colour in the academy,* ed. R. Luther, E. Whitmore, and B. Moreau, 33–54. Feminist Voices 14. 2nd ed.

———. 2007. Racing and erasing: Law and gender in white settler societies. In *Race and racism in 21st-century Canada: Continuity, complexity, and change,* ed. S. P. Hier and B. S. Bolaria, 197–216. Peterborough, ON: Broadview Press.

Moody, J. 2004. *Faculty Diversity: Problems and Solutions.* New York: Routledge Falmer.

Moore, M. and R. Trahan. 1997. Biased and political: Student perceptions of females teaching about gender. *College Student Journal* 31: 434.

Moore, V. A. 1996. Inappropriate challenges to professorial authority. *Teaching Sociology* 24: 202-6. Moraga, C. L. 1983. *La guera.* In *This bridge called my back: Writings by radical women of color,* ed. C. Moraga and G. Anzaldúa, 27–34.

Moraga, C. L. 2000. *Loving in the war years.* Classics series. 2nd ed. Cambridge, MA: South End Press.

Moraga, C., and G. Anzaldúa, eds. 1983. *This bridge called my back: Writings by radical women of color.* New York: Kitchen Table.

Moran, B. I. 1990–91. Quantum leap: A black woman uses legal education to obtain her honorary white pass. *Berkeley Women's Law Journal* 6: 118–21.

Moreno, J. F., D. G. Smith, A. R. Clayton-Pedersen, S. Parker, and D. H. Teraguchi. 2006. The revolving door: Underrepresented minority faculty in higher education. *Insight,* April, 1–19.

Moses, Y. T. 1989. *Black women in academe: Issues and strategies.* Project on the Status and Education of Women. Washington, DC: Association of American Colleges and Universities.

———. 1997a. Black women in academe: Issues and strategies. In *Black women in the academy: Promises and perils,* ed. L. Benjamin, 23–37.

———.. 1997b. Salaries in academe: The gender gap persists. *Chronicle of Higher Education,* December 12, A60.

Moulton, R. G. ed. 1918. *The modern reader's Bible.* New York: Macmillan.

Moya, P. M. L. 1997. Postmodernism, "realisms," and the politics of identity: Cherríe Moraga and Chicana feminism. In *Feminist genealogies, colonial legacies, democratic futures,* ed. M. J. Alexander and C. T. Mohanty, 125–50. New York: Routledge.

Mukherjee, A.P. 2001a. In but not at home: Women of colour in the academy. *Resources for Feminist research* 29, nos. 1–2: 125–35.

———. 2001b. The "race consciousness" of a South Asian (Canadian, of course) female academic. In *Talking about identity,* ed. C. E. James and A. Shadd, 212–18. Toronto: Between the Lines.

Munshi, S. 2009. Exceptional victims and unruly others: Violence against South Asian immigrant women and biopolitical citizenship. Paper presented at the annual conference of the American Sociological Association, San Francisco.

Murray, H. G., J. P. Rushton, and S. V. Paunonen. 1990. Teacher personality traits and student instructional ratings in six types of university courses. *Journal of Educational Psychology* 82, no. 2: 250–61.

Muscatine Arts Center acquires prize possession. 2005. *Muscatine Journal,* May 20. Available online at http://www.muscatinejournal.com/news/local/article_50b51e8d-1c8a-599d-a251-46a9ad0cd7b5.html.

Mustakeem, A. 2007. The challenge to diversify begins with law school: The profession could do more to end the decline in minority enrollment. *National Law Journal,* October 8, S3.

Myers, K. A. 2005. *Race talk: Racism hiding in plain sight.* New York: Routledge.

Nader, L. 1989. Orientalism, occidentalism and the control of women. *Cultural Dynamics* 11, no. 3: 323–35.

Naftulin, D.H., J.E. Ware, and F.A.Donnelly. 1973. The Doctor Fox lecture: A paradigm of educational effectiveness. *Journal of Medical Education* 48: 630-635.

Nakanishi, D. T. 1993. Asian Pacific Americans in higher education: Faculty and administrative representation and tenure. *New Directions for Teaching and Learning* 53 (spring): 51–59.

Nakano, G. E. 1999. The social construction and institutionalization of gender and race: An integrative framework. In *Revisioning gender,* ed. M. M. Ferree, J. Lorber, and B. B. Hess, 3–43. Thousand Oaks, CA: Sage Publications.

National Academy of Sciences, National Academy of Engineering, and Institute of Medicine of the National Academies. 2006. *Beyond bias and barriers: Fulfilling the potential of women in academic science and engineering.* Washington, DC: National Academies Press.

National Center for Education Statistics, US Department of Education. 2005. Digest of education statistics. Institute of Education Sciences. Available online at http://nces.ed.gov/programs/digest/d07/tables/dt07_239.asp.

———. 2006 Integrated Postsecondary Education Data System (IPEDS), Winter 2005–06.

———. 2007. Integrated Postsecondary Education Data System (IPEDS) Completions Survey, 1995–2005. Available online at http://caspar.nsf.gov.

———. 2009. 2009 Digest of education statistics. Institute of Education Sciences. Available online at http://nces.ed.gov/programs/digest/d09/tables/dt09_254.asp.

———. 2010. Fast facts. Available online at http://nces.ed.gov/fastfacts/display.asp?id=40.

Nat'l Coal. for Gay & Lesbian Equal. v. Minister of Justice. 1998. (12) BCLR 1517 (CC) at ¶113, 1998 SACLR LEXIS 36. at *141 (South Africa). Available online at http://www.constitutionalcourt.org.za/uhtbin/cgisirsi/20080302190747/SIRSI/0/520/S-CCT11-98.

———. 2007. Survey of Earned Doctorates Fact Sheet, 2007 Available online at http://norc.org/Research/Projects/Pages/survey-of-earned-doctorates-(sed).aspx.

———. 2008. Doctorate recipients from US universities: Summary report 2007–08. Available online at http://www.nsf.gov/statistics/nsf10309/content.cfm?pub_id=3996&id=8.

Nelson, C. 2010. No university is an island: Saving academic freedom. New York: New York University Press.

Nelson, C., and S. Watt. 2004. Office hours: Activism and change in the academy. New York: Routledge.

Nelson, C. A., and C. A. Nelson. 2004. Introduction to *Racism, eh? A critical interdisciplinary anthology of race and racism in Canada,* ed. C. A. Nelson and C. A. Nelson, 1–29. Concord, ON: Captus Press.

Nelson, D. J. 2004. *Nelson diversity surveys: A national analysis of minorities in science and engineering faculties at research universities.* Norman, OK: Diversity in Science Association. Available online at http://faculty-staff.ou.edu/N/Donna.J.Nelson-1/diversity/top50.htm.

———. 2005. *A national analysis of diversity in science and engineering facilities at research universities.* Available online at http://faculty-staff.ou.edu/N/Donna.J.Nelson-1/diversity/top50.htm.

Nelson, J. 2008. *Razing Africville: A geography of racism.* Toronto: University of Toronto Press.

Nerad, M., and D. S. Miller. 1996. Increasing student retention in graduate and professional programs. *New Directions in Institutional Research* 92 (winter):61–76.

Nettles, M. 1990. Success in doctoral programs: Experiences of minority and white students. *American Journal of Education* 98: 494–522.

Neumann, R. K., Jr. 2000. Women in legal education: What the statistics show. *Journal of Legal Education* 50, no. 3: 313–57.

New York Times. 1995. Rediscovering cornrows. July 30. Available online at http://www.nytimes.com/1995/07/30/style/noticed-rediscovered-cornrows.html.

Ng, R. 1993. "A woman out of control": Deconstructing sexism and racism at the university. *Canadian Journal of Education* 18: 189–205.

———. 1997. A woman out of control: Deconstructing sexism and racism in the university. In *Women in higher education: A feminist perspective,* ed. J. Glazer-Raymo, B. Townsend, and B. Ropers-Huliman, 360–70. Boston: Pearson.

Niemann, Y. F. 1999. The making of a token: A case study of stereotype threat, stigma, racism, and tokenism in academe. *Frontiers: A journal of women's studies* 20, no. 1: 111–34.

———. 2002. Chicana leadership: The frontiers reader. Lincoln: University of Nebraska Press.

———. 2003. The psychology of tokenism: Psychosocial reality of faculty of color. In *The handbook of racial and ethnic minority psychology,* ed. G. Bernal, J. E. Trimble, A. K. Burlew, and F. T. L. Leong, 100–118. Thousand Oaks, CA: Sage Publications.

Niemann, Y. F., and J. F. Dovidio. 1998a. Relationship of solo status, academic rank, and perceived distinctiveness to job satisfaction of racial/ethnic minorities. *Journal of Applied Psychology* 83, no. 1: 55–71. ———. 1998b. Tenure, Race/ethnicity and attitudes toward affirmative action: A matter of self-interest. *Sociological Perspectives* 41: 783–96.

Niemann, Y.F., L. Jennings, R.M. Rozelle, J.C. Baxter, and E. Sullivan, 1994. Use of free response and cluster analysis to determine stereotypes of eight groups. *Personality and Social Psychology Bulletin, 20*(4): 379-90.

Niemann, Y.F., A. Romero, and C. Arbona, 2000. Effects of cultural orientation on the perception of conflict between relationship and education goals for Mexican American college students, *Hispanic Journal of Behavioral Sciences*: 46-63.

Nolan, R.E. 1999. Helping the doctoral students navigate the maze form beginning to end. *Journal of Continuing Higher Education* 48, no. 3 (fall): 27–32.

North American Free Trade Agreement (NAFTA) 1993. US-Can.-Mex., December 17, 1992, 32 I.L.M. 289.

Nussbaum, M. C. 2010. Not for profit: Why democracy needs the humanities. Princeton: Princeton University Press. 2010.

Nussbaumer, J. 2006. Misuse of the law school admissions test, racial discrimination, and the de facto quota system for restricting African-American access to the legal profession. *St. John's Law Review* 80, no. 1 (January): 167–81.

Ogbu, J. 1978. *Minority Education and Caste: The American System in Cross Cultural Perspective.* New York: Academic Press.

O'Laughlin, E. M., and L. G. Bischoff. 2005. Balancing parenthood and academia: Work/family stress as influenced by gender and tenure status. *Journal of Family Issues* 26, no. 1 (January): 79–106.

Oliver, M. L., and T. M. Shapiro, eds. 1995. *Black wealth/white wealth: A new perspective on racial inequality.* New York: Routledge.

Olivas, M. A. 1994. The education of Latino lawyers: An essay on crop cultivation. *Chicano-Latino Law Review* 14: 117.

Olsson, J. 1997. Detour—Spotting for white anti-racists. Available online at http://www.racialequitytools.org/resourcefiles/olson.pdf.

Onwuachi-Willig, A. 2006. Undercover other. *California Law Review* 94, no. 3: 873–906.

———. 2007. Volunteer discrimination. *UC Davis Law Review* 40: 1895–1932.

Oppenheimer, M. 2008. Judgment day. *New York Times Mag.* (Sept. 19): 24.

Orr. C. 1997. Charting the currents of the third wave. *Hypatia* 12, no. 3, 29–45.

Ortega, M. 2006. Being Lovingly, Knowingly Ignorant: White Feminism and Women of Color. *Hypatia,* 21 (Summer): 56-74.

Osborn, J. J., Jr. 2003. *The paper chase.* Spec. ed. Albany, NY: Whitston Publishing Co. Inc.

Pabst, N. 2006. Mama I'm walking to Canada: Black geopolitics and invisible empires. In *Globalization and race: Transformation in the cultural production of blackness,* ed. K. M. Clarke and D. A. Thomas, 112–32.

Padden, C., and T. Humphries. 1998. *Deaf in America: Voices from a culture.* Cambridge, MA: Harvard University Press.

Padilla, A.M. 1994. Ethnic minority scholars, research, and mentoring: Current and future issues. *Educational Researcher* 23, no. 4: 24–27.

Padilla, R. V. and R. Chàvez. 1995. *The leaning ivory tower: Latino professors in American universities.* New York: State University of New York Press.

Page, C. 2008. Jackson's eloquent tears. *Chicago Tribune,* November 9, 40.

Pager, D., and H. Shepherd. 2008. The sociology of discrimination: Racial discrimination in employment, housing, credit, and consumer markets. *Annual Review of Sociology* 34: 181–209.

Patai, D. 1991. US academics and Third World women: Is ethical research possible? In *Women's words: The feminist practice of oral history,* ed. S. Gluck and D. Patai, 137–53. New York: Routledge.

Patterson, Orlando. 1972. Toward a future that has no past—reflections on the fate of blacks in the Americas. *Public Interest* 27: 25-62.

Peake, L., and B. Ray. 2001. Racializing the Canadian landscape: Whiteness, uneven geographies and social justice. *Canadian Geographer* 45: 180–86.

Pearson, A. R., J. F. Dovidio, and S. L. Gaertner. 2009. The nature of contemporary prejudice: Insights from aversive racism. *Social and Personality Psychology Compass* 3: 314–38.

Pender, P. 2004. Kicking ass is comfort food: Buffy as third wave feminist icon. In *Third wave feminism: A critical exploration,* ed. S. Gillis, G. Howie, and R. Munford, 164–74. New York: Palgrave Macmillan.

Peretz, T. 2010. No more Mr. Goodguy? Stepping off the pedestal of male privilege. *Voice-Male: Changing Men in Changing Times,* winter, 10–13.

Peters, R. M. 2006. The relationship of racism, chronic stress emotions, and blood pressure. *Journal of Nursing Scholarship* 38, no. 3: 234–40.

Peterson-Lewis, S. and L. Bratton. 2004. Perceptions of 'acting black' among African American teens: implications of racial dramaturgy for academic and social achievement. *The Urban Review* 36, 2: 81-100.

Phelan, S. 1994. *Getting specific: Postmodern lesbian politics.* Minneapolis: University of Minnesota Press.

Pierce, C. M., J. Carew, D. Pierce-Gonzalez, and D. Willis. 1978. An experiment in racism: TV commercials. In *Television and Education,* ed. C. M. Pierce, 62–88. Beverly Hills, CA: Sage Publications.

Pierson, R. R. 2004. White academic women and imperialist and racist knowledge production. *Atlantis: A Women's Studies Journal,* special issue 2: 90–102.

Pinar, William F. 1993. Notes on understanding curriculum as a racial text. In *Race identity and representation in education,* C. McCarthy and W. Crichlow, 60–70. New York: Routledge.

Pinkney, Alphonso. 2000. *Black Americans.* Upper Saddle River, NJ: Prentice-Hall.

Piven, F. F., and R. Cloward. 1993. *Regulating the poor: The functions of public welfare.* 2nd ed. New York: Vintage Books.

Pleck, E. 1990. The Unfulfilled Promise: Women and Academe. *Sociological Forum* 5: 517–24.

Pollak, K., and Y. F. Niemann. 1998. Black and white tokens in academia: A difference of chronic versus acute distinctiveness. *Journal of Applied Social Psychology* 28, no. 11: 954–72.

Post, D. W. 1994. Critical thoughts about race, exclusion, oppression, and tenure. *Pace Law Review* 15, no. 1 (fall): 69–110.

Powell, J. A. 2005. Dreaming of a self beyond whiteness and isolation. *Washington University Journal of Law and Policy* 18: 13–46.

Pratkanis, A. R., and M. E. Turner. 1996. The proactive removal of discriminatory barriers: affirmative action as effective help. *Journal of Social Issues* 52, no. 4: 111–32.

Putnam, R. D. 2000. *Bowling alone: The collapse and renewal of American community.* New York: Simon & Schuster.

Pyke, K. 2010. Service and gender inequity among faculty. *PS: Political Science and Politics* 44, no. 1 (January): 85–87.

Quaid, L. 2009. Hispanic enrollment rising in US schools, colleges. *International Herald Tribune.* Available online at http://www.iht.com/articles/ap/2009/03/05/america/NA-US-Schools-Changing-Demographics.php.

Raffaelli, M., and L. Ontai. 2004. Gender socialization in Latino/a families: Results from two retrospective studies. *Sex Roles: A Journal of Research* 50, nos. 5–6 (March): 287–99.

Rai, K. B., and J. W. Critzer. 2000. *Affirmative action and the university: Race, ethnicity, and gender in higher education employment.* Lincoln: University of Nebraska Press.

Rains, F. V. 1999. Dancing on the sharp edge of the sword: Women faculty of color in white academe. In *Everyday Knowledge and Uncommon Truths: Women of the academy,* ed. L. Christian-Smith and K. Kellor, 147–74. Boulder, CO: Westview Press.

Razack, S. H. 2000. *Looking white people in the eye: Gender, race, and culture in courtrooms and Classrooms.* Toronto: University of Toronto Press.

———. 2002. When place becomes race. Introduction to *Race, space, and the law,* ed. S. H. Razack, 1–20. Toronto: Between the Lines.

———. 2008. *Casting out: The eviction of Muslims from Western law and politics.* Toronto: University of Toronto Press.

Reid, P. T., and E. Kelly. 1994. Research on women of color: From ignorance to awareness. *Psychology of Women Quarterly* 18: 477–86.

Rendon, L. I. 1992. Eyes on the Prize: Students of color and the bachelor's degree. *Community College Review* 21, no. 2: 3–13.

Resnik, J. 1989–90. Housekeeping: The nature and allocation of work in federal trial courts. *Georgia Law Review* 24: 909–64.

Rimstead, R. 1996. What working-class intellectuals claim to know. *Race, Gender & Class* 4, no. 1: 119–41.

Roberts, D. 1999. *Killing the black body: Race, reproduction, and the meaning of liberty.* New York: Vintage Books.

———. 2000. The paradox of silence: Some questions about silence as resistance. *Michigan Journal of Race & Law* 5: 927.

Rockquemore, K. A., and T. Laszloffy. 2008. *The black academic's guide to winning tenure— without losing your soul.* Boulder, CO: Lynne Rienner Publishers.

Rogers v. American Airlines. 1981. 527 F. Supp.229 (S.D.N.Y.).

Roisman, F. W. 2002. Teaching important property concepts: Teaching about inequality, race, and property. *St. Louis University Law Journal* 46, no. 3 (summer): 665–90.

Roosevelt, E. 2009. You learn by living: eleven keys for a more fulfilling life. Louisville: Westminster John Knox Press. 29.

Roth, B. 2004. *Separate roads to feminism: Black, Chicana, and white feminist movements in America's Second Wave.* New York: Cambridge University Press.

Rudder, C. 1990. APSA minority programs addressing the pipeline problem. *PS: Political Science and Politics* 23, no. 2 (June): 229–32.

Russell, J. M. 1997. On being a gorilla in your midst, or the life of one blackwoman in the legal academy. In *Critical Race Feminism: A Reader,* ed. A. K. Wing, 110–12.

Ryu, M. 2010. *Minorities in higher education: Twenty-fourth status report.* Washington, DC: American Council on Education.

Sacks, Peter. 2007. *Tearing down the gates: confronting the class divide in American education.* Berkeley: University of California Press.

Samuel, E., and N. Wane. 2005. "Unsettling relations": Racism and sexism experiences by faculty of color in a predominantly white Canadian university. *Journal of Negro Education* 74, no. 1: 76–87.

Sandler, B. R., L. A. Silverberg, and R. M. Hall. 1996. *The chilly classroom climate: A guide to improve the education of women.* Washington, DC: National Association for Women in Education.

Sandoval, Chela. 2000. *Methodology of the oppressed.* Minneapolis: University of Minnesota Press.

Saunders, D. 2010. Neoliberal ideology and public higher education in the United States. *Journal for Critical Education Policy Studies* 8, no. 1: 42–77. Available online at http://www.jceps.com/?pageID=article&articleID=176.

Schick, C., and V. St. Denis. 2005. Troubling national discourses in anti-racist curricular planning. *Canadian Journal of Education* 28: 295–317.

Schor, J. 1992. *The overworked American.* New York: Basic Books.

Schwitzer, A. M., O. T. Griffin, J. R. Ancis, and C. R. Thomas. 1999. Social adjustment experiences of African American college students. *Journal of Counseling and Development* 77: 189–97.

Scott, J., and D. Leonhardt. 2005. Shadowy lines that still divide. *New York Times,* May 15. Available online at http://www.nytimes.com/2005/05/15/national/class/OVERVIEW-FINAL.html?pagewanted=28incamp=article_popular_1.

Scott, J. C. 1998. *Seeing like a state: How certain schemes to improve the human condition have failed*. New Haven, CT: Yale University Press.

Scully, J. M. 2000. Cracking open CRACK: Unethical sterilization movement gains momentum. In *Defending reproductive rights: An activist resource kit*, 101–4. Somerville, MA: Political Research Associates (PRA).

Sedowski, L., and M. Brintnall. 2007. Data snapshot: The proportion of women in the political science profession. American Political Science Association. Available online at http://www.apsanet.org/imgtest/Website%20brief%20on%20 women%20in%20PS%20v2%201%202007.pdf.

Segura, D. 2003. Navigating between two worlds: The labyrinth of Chicana intellectual production in the academy." *Journal of Black Studies* 34, no. 1: 28–51.

Seibel, R. F. 1996. Do deans discriminate? An examination of lower salaries paid to women clinical teachers. *UCLA Women's Law Journal* 6: 541–61.

Seldin, P. 1993. The use and abuse of student ratings of professors. *The Chronicle of Higher Ed.*, 39 Jul. 21: 40.

———. 1999. *Changing practices in faculty evaluation*. Bolton, MA: Anker Publications.

———. 2004. *The teaching portfolio: A practical guide to improved performance and promotion/tenure decisions*. 3rd ed. San Francisco: Jossey-Bass.

Seldin, P., and E. Miller. 2009. *The academic portfolio*. San Francisco: Jossey-Bass.

Sherif, C. W. 1983. Carolyn Wood Sherif. In *Models of achievement: Reflections of eminent women in psychology*, ed. A. N. O'Connell and N. F. Russo, 279–93. New York: Columbia University Press.

Sherif, S. A. 2008. Gender: An intersectionality perspective. *Sex Roles: A Journal of Research* 59, nos. 5–6: 301–11. Introduction to the special issue Intersectionality of social identities: A gender perspective.

Shevlin, M., P. Banyard, M. Davies and M. Griffiths. 2000. The validity of student evaluation of teaching in higher education: Love me, love my lectures? *Assessment & Evaluation in Higher Education* 25, no. 4, 397–405.

Shields, S. A., and S. Bhatia. 2009. Darwin and race, gender, and culture. *American Psychologist* 64: 111–19.

Shives, L. R. 2008. *Basic concepts of psychiatric–mental health nursing*. 7th ed. Philadelphia: Lippincott Williams & Wilkins.

Shriver, M., and the Center for American Progress. 2009. *The Shriver report: A woman's nation changes everything*. October 16. Available online at http://www.americanprogress.org/issues/2009/10/womans_nation.html.

Shugart, H. 2001. Isn't it ironic? The intersection of third-wave feminism and Generation X. *Women's Studies in Communication* 24, no. 2: 131–68.

Siegel, R. B. 1996. "The rule of love": Wife beating as prerogative and privacy. *Yale Law Journal* 105 (June): 2117–2207.

Sinclair, L. and Z. Kunda. 2000. Motivated stereotyping of women: She's fine if she praised me, but incompetent if she criticized me. *Personality and Social Psychology Bulletin* 26: 1329–42.

Singh, K., A. Robinson, and J. Williams-Green. 1995. Differences in perceptions of African American women and men faculty and administrators. *Journal of Negro Education* 64, no. 4: 401–8.

Slaughter, S., and G. Rhoades. 2004. Academic capitalism and the new economy: Markets, state, and higher education. Baltimore: Johns Hopkins University Press.

Smith, B. 1998. Doing it from scratch: The Challenge of Black Lesbian Organizing. In The truth that never hurts: Writings on race, gender and freedom. New Piscataway, NJ: Rutgers University Press.

Smith, D. G. 2000. How to diversify the faculty. *Academe* 86, no. 5: 48–52.

———. 2009. *Diversity's promise for higher education: Making it work.* Baltimore: Johns Hopkins University Press.

Smith, D. G., C. S. V. Turner, N. Osei-Kofi, and S. Richards. 2004. Interrupting the usual: Successful strategies for hiring diverse faculty." *Journal of Higher Education* 75: 133–60.

Smith, G., and K. J. Anderson. 2005. Students' ratings of professors: The teaching style contingency for Latino/a professors. *Journal of Latinos and Education* 4, no. 2: 115–36.

Smith, L. T. 1990. *Decolonizing methodologies: Research and indigenous peoples.* New York: Zed Books.

Smith, M. S. 2007. Telling tales on white li(v)es, diversity-talk, and the ivory tower. Paper presented at the annual meeting of the Canadian Federation for the Humanities and Social Sciences, Saskatoon, SK, May 30–June 2.

Smith, P. 2001. Tyrannies of silence of the untenured professors of color. *UC Davis Law Review* 33, no. 4: 1105–34.

Smith, P. J. 1999. Teaching the retrenchment generation: When Sapphire meets Socrates at the intersection of race, gender, and authority. *William and Mary Journal of Women and Law* 6, no. 53: 162–3 (1999).

Smith, W.A. 2004. Black faculty coping with racial battle fatigue: The campus racial climate in a post-civil rights era. In *A long way to go: Conversations about race by African American faculty and graduate students,* ed. D. Cleveland, 171–90. New York: Peter Lang.

Smith, W.A., T. J. Yosso, and D. G. Solórzano. 2007. Racial primes and black misandry on historically white campuses: Toward critical race accountability in educational administration. *Educational Administration Quarterly* 43, no. 5: 559–85.

Smitherman, Geneva. 1986. *Talkin' and Testifyin': The language of Black America.* Detroit: Wayne State University Press.

Solender, E. K. 1995. The story of a self-effacing feminist law professor. *American University Journal of Gender, Social Policy & the Law* 4, no. 1: 249–64.

Solórzano, D., M. Ceja, and T. Yosso. 2000. Critical Race Theory, Racial Microaggressions, and Campus Racial Climate: The Experiences of African American College Students. *Journal of Negro Education* 69, nos. 1–2 (winter–spring): 60–73.

Sorcinelli, M. D., and J. H. Yun. 2007. From mentors to mentoring networks: Mentoring in the new academy. *Change: The Magazine of Higher Learning* 39, no. 6: 58–61.

Sotello Viernes Turner, C. 2002. Women of color in academe: Living with multiple marginality. *Journal of Higher Education,* 73 (1), 74-93.

Spade, D. 2006. Compliance is gendered: Struggling for gender self-determination in a hostile economy. In *Transgender rights: History, politics and law,* ed. P. Currah, S. Minter, and R. Juang, 217–41. Minneapolis: University of Minnesota Press.

———. 2008. Documenting gender: Incoherence and rulemaking. *Hastings Law Journal* 59: 731–841.

———. 2010. Making the classroom welcoming for trans students. Available online at http://cruciferous.livejournal.com/15984.html.

Spellings, Margaret. 2006. *Commission report. A test of leadership; Charting the future of US higher education.* A report of the commission appointed by Secretary of Education Margaret Spellings. Washington, DC: US Department of Education.

Spivak, G. C. 1988. Can the subaltern speak? In *Marxism and the interpretation of culture,* C. Nelson and L. Grossberg. Chicago: University of Illinois Press: 271-313.

Sprague, J., and K. Massoni. 2005. Student evaluations and gendered expectations: What we can't count can hurt us. *Sex Roles* 53:779-93.

Springer, K. 2002. Third wave black feminism?. *Signs,* 27: 1059-1082.

Stanley, C. A. 2006a. Coloring the academic landscape: Faculty of color breaking the silence in predominantly white colleges and universities. *American Educational Research Journal* 43, no. 4: 701–36.

———, ed. 2006b. *Faculty of color: Teaching in predominantly white colleges and universities.* Bolton, MA: Anker Publishing.

Stanley, C. A., and Y. S. Lincoln. 2005. "Cross-race faculty mentoring." *Change: The Magazine of Higher Learning* 37, no. 2: 44–50.

Starr, P. 2000. *Speakers for the dead.* National Film Board of Canada. Documentary film.

Statham, A. et al. 1991. Gender and university teaching: A negotiated difference 123-41.

Statistics Canada. 2007. *2006 Census: Immigration, citizenship, language, mobility and migration.* Available online at http://www.statcan.gc.ca/daily-quotidien/071204/dq071204a-eng.htm.

———. 2008. *2006 Census: Aboriginal peoples in Canada in 2006: Inuit, Métis and First Nations, 2006 census: Findings.* Available online at http://www12.statcan.ca/english/censUS06/analysis/aboriginal/surpass.cfm.

Stavans, Ilan. 2005. The challenges facing Spanish language departments. *The chronicle of higher education.* Available online at http://chronicle.com/weekly/v51/i47/47b006 01.htm(n.d.).

Steele, Claude M. 1997. A threat in the air: How stereotypes shape intellectual identity and performance. *American Psychologist* 52, no. 6: 613–29.

———. 2010. *Whistling Vivaldi: And other clues to how stereotypes affect us.* New York: W. W. Norton & Co.

Steinpreis, R., K. A. Anders, and D. Ritzke. 1999. The impact of gender on the review of the curricula vitae of job applicants and tenure candidates: A national empirical study. *Sex Roles* 41: 509-28.

Stevenson, B. E. 1993. "Rich tokens": The recruitment and retention of women-of-color historians. *Journal of Women's History* 4, no. 3: 152–57.

Steward, R., M. Gimenez, and J. Jackson. 1995. A study of personal preferences of successful university students as related to race/ethnicity and sex: Implications and recommendations for training, practice, and future research. *Journal of College Student Development* 36, no. 2: 123–31.

Stewart, A. 2004. Penn and Teller magic: Self, racial devaluation and the Canadian academy. In *Racism, eh? A critical interdisciplinary anthology of race and racism in Canada,* ed. C. A. Nelson and C. A. Nelson, 33–40.

St. Jean, Y., and J. R. Feagin. 1998. *Double burden: Black women and everyday racism.* Armonk, NY: M. E. Sharp.

St. Lewis, J. 2007. Getting radical: Racism, complacency and self-deception in academic culture. Paper presented at the annual meeting of the Canadian Federation for the Humanities and Social Sciences, Saskatoon, SK, May 30–June 2.

Stout, P.A., J. Staiger, and N. A. Jennings. 2007. Affective stories: Understanding the lack of progress of women faculty. *NWSA Journal* 19: 124–44.

Sturm, S. 2006. The architecture of inclusion: Interdisciplinary insights on pursuing institutional citizenship. *Harvard Journal of Law & Gender* 29, no. 2 (summer): 247–334.

Sue, D. W. 2010. *Microaggressions in everyday life: Race, gender, and sexual orientation.* Hoboken, NJ: John Wiley & Sons, Inc.

Tagomori, H. T., L. A. Bishop. 1995. Student evaluation of teaching: Flaws in the instruments. *The NEA Higher Education Journal* 11: 63-78.

Takagi, D. 1992. *The retreat from race: Asian-American admissions and racial politics.* Piscataway, NJ: Rutgers University Press.

Tapia, R. 2007. True diversity doesn't come from abroad. *Chronicle of Higher Education,* September 28, B34.

———. 2009. Minority students and research universities: How to overcome the "mismatch." *Chronicle of Higher Education,* March 27, A72.

Task Force on Faculty Diversity. 2006. *The representation of minorities among regular rank faculty: Report of the UC president's Task Force on Faculty Diversity.* May.

Tate, W. F. 1997. Critical race theory and education: History, theory, and implications. *Review of Research in Education* 22: 201–47.

Telgen, D. and J. Kamp. 1993. *Notable Hispanic American Women.* Detroit: Gale Research Inc. Huntington, Samuel. 2004. "The Hispanic Challenge" *Foreign Policy.* March/April. Available online at http://cyber.law.harvard.edu/blogs/gems/culturalagency1/SamuelHuntingtonTheHispanicC.pdf. Accessed 5 July 2010.

Terenzini, P. T., A. F. Cabrera, and E. M. Bernal. 2001. Swimming against the tide: The poor in American higher education. Research report 2001-1. New York: The College Board.

Theall, M. and J. Franklin. 1991. Using student ratings for teaching improvement. *Effective Practices for Improving Teaching.* San Francisco: Jossey-Bass. 83-96.

Thomas, G., and C. Hollenshead. 2001. Resisting from the margins: The coping strategies of black women and other women of color faculty members at a research university. *Journal of Negro Education* 70, no. 3: 166–75.

Thompson, G., and A. Louque. 2005. *Exposing the culture of arrogance in the academy: A blueprint for increasing black faculty satisfaction.* Sterling, VA: Stylus Publishing, LLC.

Thornhill, E. M. A. 2008. So seldom for us, so often against us: Blacks and law in Canada. *Journal of Black Studies* 38: 321–37.

Thurgood, L., M. J. Golladay, and S. T. Hill. 2006. *US Doctorates in the 20th century.* National Science Foundation. Available online at http://www.nsf.gov/statistics/nsf06319/pdf/nsf06319.pdf.

Tierney, W. G., and R. A. Rhoades. 1993. *Enhancing promotion, tenure, and beyond: Faculty socialization as a cultural process.* ERIC Clearinghouse on Higher Education Report no. 6. Washington, DC: School of Education and Human Development, George Washington University.

Tillman, L. C. 2001. Mentoring African American faculty in predominantly white institutions. *Research in Higher Education* 42: 295–325.

Tokarczyk, M. M., and E. A. Fay, eds. 1993. *Working-class women in the academy: Laborers in the knowledge factory.* Amherst: University of Massachusetts Press.

Tolle, E. 1999. The Power of now: A guide to spiritual enlightenment. Novato, CA: Namaste Publishing.

Torres, V. 2006. Bridging two worlds: Academia and Latina/o identity. In *The Latina/o Pathway to the Ph.D.*, ed. J. Castellanaos, A. M. Gloria, and M. Kamimura, 135–48.

Torres-Guzmán, M. E. 1995. Surviving the journey. In *The leaning ivory tower: Latino professor in American universities.* Albany: State University of New York Press. eds. R.V. Padilla and R. Chávez. 53-65.

TransJustice. 2006. Trans day of action for social and economic justice. In *Color of Violence*, ed. INCITE! Women of Color against Violence, 227–30.

Trask, H. 1999. *From a Native daughter: Colonialism and sovereignty in Hawai'i.* Honolulu: University of Hawai'i Press.

Tsang, C. W., and T. L. Dietz. 2001. The unrelenting significance of minority statuses: gender, ethnicity, and economic attainment since affirmative action. *Sociological Spectrum* 21: 61–80.

Turner, C. S. V. 2002a. *Diversifying the faculty: A guidebook for search committees.* Washington, DC: American Association of Colleges and Universities.

———. 2002b. Women of color in academe: Living with multiple marginality. *Journal of Higher Education* 73, no. 1 (January/February): 74–93.

Turner, C. S. V., J. C. Gonzaléz, and J. L. Wood. 2008. Faculty of color in academe: What 20 years of literature tells us." *Journal of Diversity in Higher Education* 1, no. 3: 139–68.

Turner, C. S. V., and S. L. Myers Jr. 2000. *Faculty of color in academe: Bittersweet success.* Boston: Allyn and Bacon.

UCI advance program for faculty equity and diversity. Available online at http://advance.uci.edu/media/brochures/Brochure_FWLB5508_Statement.pdf.

Uh Huh; But How Do It Free Us?, first produced in Chicago, IL, at Northwestern University Theater. 1975 (included in The New Lafayette Theatre Presents: Plays with Aesthetic Comments by Six Black Playwrights, Ed Bullins, J. E. Gaines, Clay Gross, Oyamo, Sonia Sanchez, Richard Wesley. Ed. Bullins, Anchor Press [Garden City, NY], 1974).

Unger, R. K. 1998. *Resisting gender: Twenty-five years of feminist psychology.* Thousand Oaks, CA: Sage Publications, 1998.

University of California Berkeley Campus News. 2002. Chang-Lin Tien, UC Berkeley chancellor from 1990–97 and an internationally known engineering scholar, dies at age 67. October 30. Available online at http://berkeley.edu/news/media/releases/2002/10/tien.html University of Michigan Center for the Education of Women. 1999. *Through my Lens: A video project about women of color faculty at the University of Michigan.* Ann Arbor: University of Michigan Center for the Education of Women.

Urbina, I. 2009. Club in Philadelphia suburb faces accusations of racism. *New York Times,* July 11, A11.

US Census Bureau. 2008. *Racial and Ethnic Residential Segregation in the United States: 1980–2000.* Housing and Household Economic Statistics Division. Available online at http://www.census.gov/hhes/www/housing/housing_patterns/pdftoc.html.

US Census Bureau. Fact Sheet 2006 American Community Survey. Available online at http://factfinder.census.gov/servlet/ACSSAFFFacts?_event=&geo_id=01000US&_geoContext=01000US%7C04000US48&_street=&_county=&_cityTown=&_state=04000US48&_zip=&_lang=en&_sse=on&ActiveGeoDiv=geoSelect&_useEV=&pctxt=fph&pgsl=040&_submenuId=factsheet_1&ds_name=ACS_2006_SAFF&_ci_nbr=null&qr_name=null&reg=null%3Anull&_keyword=&_industry=.

Valian, V. 1998. *Why so slow? The advancement of women.* Cambridge: M.I.T. Press.

Valverde, L. A. 2003. *Leaders of color in higher education: Unrecognized triumphs in harsh institutions.* Walnut Creek, CA: AltaMira Press.

Vargas, L. 1999. When the "other" is the teacher: Implications of teacher diversity in higher education. *Urban Review* 31: 359–83.

———. 2002. Women faculty of color in the white classroom. New York: Peter Lang.

Vedder, R. 2010. Student evaluations, grade inflation, and declining student effort. *The Chronicle of Higher Education.* Jun 19.

Vikesland, G. 1998. Communication 101: Supervising men.

Available online at http://www.employer-employee.com/comm101.htm.

Viernes Turner, C. S. 2002. Women of color in academe: Living with multiple marginality. *The Journal of Higher Education* 73 (1): 74-93.

Wah, L. M. 1994. *The color of fear.* StirFry Seminars. DVD.

Waheed, S., N. Ly-huong, and A. Couey. 2005. Decolonizing research. DataCenter: Research for Justice newsletter, issue 27 (spring–summer). Available online at http://www.datacenter.org.

Walcott, R., ed. 2000. *Rude: Contemporary black Canadian cultural criticism.* Toronto: Insomniac Press.

———. 2003. *Black like who? Writing black Canada.* Toronto: Insomniac Press.

Walker, J. W. St. G. 1997. *"Race," rights and the law in the supreme court of Canada: Historical case studies.* Waterloo, ON: Wilfrid Laurier University Press.

Wallin, D. L. 2004. Valuing professional colleagues: Adjunct faculty in community and technical colleges. *Community College Journal of Research and Practice* 28: 373–91.

Walsh, S. 2002. Study finds significant increase in number of part-time and non-tenure-track professors. *Chronicle of Higher Education,* October 29.

Ware, J. E. and R.G. Williams. 1975. The Dr. Fox effect: a study of lecturer effectiveness and ratings of instruction. *Journal of Medical Education* 50, no. 2: 149-156.

Washburn, J. 2006. University Inc.: The corporate corruption of higher education. New York: Basic Books.

Waterhouse v. Hopkins. 1988. Brief for amicus curiae American psychological association in support of respondent. Supreme Court of the United States.

Waters, M. et al. 1988. High and low faculty evaluations: Descriptions by students. *15 Teaching Psychology* 15: 203–04.

Watson, E. D. 2008. *Outsiders within: Black women in the legal academy after* Brown v. Board. New York: Rowman & Littlefield Publishers, Inc.

Waxer, P. H. 1976. Nonverbal cues for depth of depression: set versus no set. *J. Consult. Clin. Psychology.* 44: 493.

———. 1977. Nonverbal cues for anxiety: An examination of emotional leakage. *Journal of Abnormal Psychology* 86, no. 3. (Jun): 306-14.

Weick, K.E., and D. K. Meader. 1995. *Sensemaking in Organizations.* Thousand Oaks, CA: Sage Publications.

Weintraub, A. 2004. *Yoga for depression: A compassionate guide to relieve suffering through yoga.* New York: Broadway Books.

Weitz, R., and L. Gordon. 1993. Images of black women among Anglo college students. *Sex Roles: A Journal of Research* 27: 19–35.

Wenneras, C. and A. Wold. 1997. Nepotism and sexism in peer-review. In *Women, science, and technology: a reader in feminist science studies.* Ed. M. Wyer. Routledge, NY.

West. C. 1993. *Race matters.* Boston: Beacon Press West, M. S. 2000. Faculty women's struggle for equality at UC Davis. *UCLA Women's Law Journal* 10: 1–259.

———. 2007. Unprecedented urgency: Gender discrimination in faculty hiring at the University of California. *Feminist Formations* 19: 199–211.

White, S. B. 2005. Releasing the pursuit of bouncin' and behavin' hair: Natural hair as an Afrocentric feminist aesthetic for beauty. *International Journal of Media and Cultural Politics* 1, no. 3: 295–308.

White, R. A. 2004. *The promotion, retention, and tenuring of law school faculty: Comparing faculty hired in 1990 and 1991 to faculty hired in 1996 and 1997.* December 14. Available online at http://www.aals.org/documents/2005recruitmentreport.pdf.

Whittier, N. 2006. From the second to the third wave: Continuity and change in grass-roots feminism. In *The US women's movement in global perspective,* ed. L. Banaszak, 48–68. New York: Rowman & Littlefield Publishers, Inc.

Wickham, D. 2009. How Obama can bridge nation's racial divide. *USA Today,* October 28, 11A.

Wildman, S. M. 1990. Integration in the 1980s: The dream of diversity and the cycle of exclusion. *Tulane Law Review* 64: 1625–76.

Wildman, S. M., with M. Armstrong, A. D. Davis, and T. Grillo. 1996. *Privilege revealed: How invisible preference undermines America.* New York: New York University Press.

Wiley, M. G. and K. Crittenden. 1992. By your attributions you shall be known: Consequences of attributional accounts for professional and gender identities. *Sex Roles: A Journal of Research* 27: 259–77.

Williams, B.N., and S. M. Williams. 2006. Perceptions of African male junior faculty on promotion and tenure: Implications for community building and social capital. *Teachers College Record* 108, no. 2: 287–315.

Williams, P. J. 1991. *The alchemy of race and rights: Diary of a law professor.* Cambridge, MA: Harvard University Press.

———. 1997a. *Seeing a color-blind future: The paradox of race.* New York: Noonday Press.

———. 1997b. Spirit-murdering the messenger: The discourse of fingerpointing as the law's response to racism. In *Critical race feminism: A reader,* ed. A. K. Wing, 229–36.

Williams, W. M. and S. J. Ceci. 1997. How'm I doing?: Problems with the use of student ratings of instructors and courses. *Change* 29, no. 5: 12-23.

Wilson, R. 2006. At Central Florida, Hispanic women give each other advice and a sympathetic ear. *Chronicle of Higher Education,* 53: 5.

Wing, A. K. 1990–91. Brief reflections toward a multiplicative theory and praxis of being. *Berkeley Women's Law Journal* 6: 181–201.

———. 1993a. Communitarianism v. individualism: Constitutionalism in Namibia and South Africa. *Wisconsin International Law Journal* 11: 295–379.

———. 1993b. Legal Decision-making during the Intifada: Embryonic self rule. *Yale Journal of International Law* 18: 95–153.

———. 1994. Custom, religion and rights: The future legal status of Palestinian women. *Harvard Journal of International Law* 35: 149–200.

———, ed. [1997] 2003. *Critical Race Feminism: A Reader.* New York: New York University Press.

———, ed. 2000. *Global Critical Race Feminism: An International Reader.* New York: New York University Press.

Wing, A. K., and L. Weselmann. 1999. Transcending traditional notions of mothering: The need for critical race feminist praxis. *Journal of Gender, Race and Justice* 3: 257–81.

Winkler, J. A. 2000. The faculty reappointment, tenure, and promotion: Barriers for women. *Professional Geographer* 52, no. 4: 737–50.

Wise, T. 2005. *White like me: Reflections on race from a privileged son.* Brooklyn: Soft Skull Press.

———. 2010. Colorblind: The rise of post-racial politics and the retreat from racial equity. San Francisco: City Lights Books/Open Media Series.

Wisniewski, R., E. R. Ducharme, and R. M. Agne. 1989. *The professors of teaching: An inquiry.* Albany: State University of New York Press.

Woessner, M. and A. Kelly-Woessner. 2006. My professor is a partisan hack: How perceptions of a professor's political views affect student course evaluations. *PS: Political Science & Politics* (Apr): 495-501.

Woods, R.L. 2001. Invisible women. In *Sisters of the academy: Emergent black women scholars in higher education,* ed. E.O. Mabokela and A.L. Green, 105–15.

Worcester, S. 2005. Internalized racism may affect adolescents' metabolic health. *Pediatric News.* 39 (3): 31.

Wright, S. C. 1997. Ambiguity, social influence, and collective action: Generating collective protest in response to tokenism. *Personality and Social Psychology Bulletin* 23: 1277–290.

Wright, S. C., and J. Dinkha. 2002. Gendered reality: The experiences of women faculty of color. Concurrent session paper presented at the 2002 Keeping Our Faculties Conference, Minneapolis, MN, April 21–23.

Wright, S. C., D. M. Taylor, and F. M. Moghaddam. 1990. Responding to membership in a disadvantaged group: From acceptance to collective protest. *Journal of Personality and Social Psychology* 58: 994–1003.

Yoder, J. D. 1985. An academic woman as a token: A case study. *Journal of Social Issues* 41: 61–72.

———. 2002. Division 35 presidential address: Context matters: Understanding tokenism processes and their impact on women's work. *Psychology of Women Quarterly* 26: 1–8.

Yokomizo Akindes, F. 2002. The pacific Asianized other: Teaching unlearning among Midwestern students. In *Women faculty of color in the white classroom.* New York: Peter Lang. ed. L. Vargas: 163-81.

Yoshinaga-Itano. 2006. Institutional barriers and myths to recruitment and retention of faculty of color: An administrator's perspective. In *Faculty of color: Teaching in predominantly white colleges and universities,* ed. C. Stanley, 344–60. Bolton, MA: Anker Publishing.

Yoshino, Kenji. 2006. *Covering.* New York: Random House.

Youmans, R. J. and B. D. Jee. 2007. Fudging the numbers: Distributing chocolate influences student evaluations of an undergraduate course. *Teaching of Psychology* 34, no. 4 (Dec): 245-247.

Young, D. C. 1996. Two steps removed: The paradox of diversity discourse for women of color in law teaching. *Berkeley Women's Law Journal* 11: 270.

Yun, J. H. and M. D. Sorcinelli. 2008. When Mentoring is the Medium: Lessons Learned from Mutual Mentoring as a Faculty Development Initiative. *To Improve the Academy* 27: 365-384.

Yuracko, K. A. 2006. Trait discrimination as race discrimination: An argument about assimilation. *George Washington Law Review* 74: 365.

Contributors

Editors and Foreword Authors

Gabriella Gutiérrez y Muhs holds an MA and PhD from Stanford University and is an associate professor at Seattle University in modern languages and women's studies. She held the Wismer Professorship for Gender and Diversity from 2007 to 2009 and is the current Latin American studies program director. Gutiérrez y Muhs has also been the director of the Diversity, Citizenship, and Social Justice Core Track at the university for several years. She works in transnational feminism and has presented her research on Latina identity and subjectivity both in Chile and Colombia. Her writing appears regularly in national newspapers and journals, including *Border-Lines, Commonweal, Ventana Abierta, Puentes, Chicana/Latina Studies: The Journal of MALCS, Hispanic Outlook,* and the *National Catholic Reporter.* She is the author of a book of interviews with Chilean and Chicana authors, *Communal Feminisms: Chicanas, Chilenas and Cultural Exile,* a poetry collection, *A Most Improbable Life,* and a forthcoming novel, *Fresh as a Lettuce: Malgré Tout,* as well as the editor of the forthcoming *Rebozos de Palabras: An Helena María Viramontes Critical Reader.* In 2011 Gutiérrez y Muhs represented the United States in India as one of the featured poets at the Kritya International Poetry Festival. Her latest collection of poetry *¿How Many Indians Can We Be?* addresses issues of colonization, im/migration, indigeneity, post-colonialism, and identity from a transnational feminist perspective.

Yolanda Flores Niemann earned her PhD in psychology from the University of Houston and is senior vice provost and professor of psychology at the University of North Texas. Previously she served in administrative roles as vice provost and dean of the College of Humanities, Arts, and Social Sciences at Utah State University. At Washington State University, she held administrative roles as chair of the Department of Comparative Ethnic Studies, director of Latina/o outreach, assistant to the provost for faculty morale and outreach, and special assistant to the dean of the College of Liberal Arts for accreditation and distance degrees. She has held faculty positions in the Psychology Department and Mexican American and African American Studies programs at the University of Houston, and as professor of ethnic studies, affiliate faculty in women's studies, American studies, and speech and hearing studies at Washington State University. Niemann also served on the Washington State Commission on Hispanic Affairs and on committees for the division of the study of ethnic minority issues for the American Psychological Association. Her research interests include the effects and social/ecological contexts of stereotypes across various domains and the psychological effects of tokenism. Her numerous publications include a co-authored book, *Black Brown Relations and Stereotypes,* *and* notable chapters in *To Improve the Academy, The Handbook of Chicana/o Psychology and Mental health,* and *The Handbook of Racial and Ethnic Minority Psychology.* She has also published in numerous refereed journals, including *Journal of Applied Psychology, Journal of Applied Social Psychology, Sociological Perspectives, Personality and Social Psychology Bulletin, The Journal for the Theory of Social Behavior, Hispanic Journal of Behavioral Sciences,* and *Frontiers—A Journal of Women's Studies.* She was principal investigator of federal GEAR UP grants totaling twenty-six million dollars at Washington State University. These outreach grants prepare low socioeconomic students for success in higher education and currently serve more than ten thousand students in twenty-nine schools in Washington.

Carmen G. González is a professor of law at Seattle University School of Law. She holds a BA in political science from Yale University and a JD from Harvard Law School. Her scholarship focuses on the environmental justice implications of economic globalization. González's most recent articles have examined the impact of free trade agreements on global food security, the environment, and indigenous peoples; the developmental and environmental implications of China's growing economic influence in Latin America; and the ways that the legacy of colonialism in Latin America influences legal policy and practice. She has published articles in prominent human rights, international law, and environmental law journals (including Yale, Columbia, Georgetown, University of Pennsylvania, and Tulane) and policy papers on environmental justice. González is the co-editor of *Derecho, democracia y economía de mercado* with Colin Crawford and Daniel Bonilla Maldonado. She was a fellow at the US Supreme Court in 2004–5 and a visiting fellow at Cambridge University in the United Kingdom in the fall of 2006. She has served as chair of the Association of American Law Schools Section on Environmental Law, as member of the Research Committee of the International Union for the Conservation of Nature Academy of Environmental Law, and as member and vice-chair of the international subcommittee of the National Environmental Justice Advisory Council (an advisory body to the US Environmental Protection Agency on environmental justice issues). González practiced law for many years in the private sector and government before becoming a law professor.

Angela P. Harris received her JD from the University of Chicago and is a professor of law at the University of California, Davis School of Law. She has co-edited several casebooks for law students on race, gender, and class, including *Race and Races: Cases and Resources for a Diverse America* with Richard Delgado, Juan Perea, Stephanie Wildman, and Jean Stefancic; *Economic Justice: Race, Gender, Identity and Economics* with Emma Coleman Jordan; and *Gender and Law: Theory, Doctrine, Commentary* with Katherine Bartlett and Deborah Rhode. She has also written numerous articles on race, gender, and other forms of subordination based on social identity. Her work has been widely anthologized and is cited by scholars in feminist theory, ethnic and cultural studies, sociology, and history. Harris was one of the founding members of LatCrit, Inc., a coalition of progressive law faculty working within the intellectual framework of critical race theory. Her article, "Race and Essentialism in Feminist Legal Theory," published in 1989, identified her as one of the most influential legal scholars under the age of forty and has been translated into several languages.

Brenda J. Allen earned her PhD from Howard University, is an associate dean in the College of Liberal Arts and Sciences and a professor in the Department of Communication at the University of Colorado Denver (UCD). Her research and teaching areas are organizational communication, diversity, critical pedagogy, and computer-mediated communication. Among her numerous publications is *Difference Matters: Communicating*

Social Identity. She presents keynote speeches and conducts workshops on a range of topics, including diversity and higher education, teamwork, self-empowerment, and presentational speaking. Allen has received numerous awards and accolades, including the inaugural Award for Excellence in Faculty Mentoring from UCD in 2011 and Ohio University's 2011 Paul H. Boase Prize for Scholarship. She also was named a master teacher (2007–8) by the Western States Communication Association.

Bettina Aptheker is a distinguished professor of feminist studies at the University of California, Santa Cruz, where she has taught for more than thirty years. Her popular class, Introduction to Feminisms, is available on DVD. Her books include a memoir, *Intimate Politics: How I Grew Up Red, Fought for Free Speech, and Became a Feminist Rebel; The Morning Breaks: The Trial of Angela Davis; Tapestries of Life: Women's Work, Women's Consciousness, and the Meaning of Daily Experience;* and *Woman's Legacy: Essays on Race, Sex, and Class in American History.* She wrote the biography of Shirley Graham Du Bois for *Notable American Women* and the afterword for Jan Willis's memoir, *Dreaming Me: Black, Baptist, and Buddhist—One Woman's Spiritual Journey.* Aptheker gave the seventeenth annual W. E. B. Du Bois lecture at the University of Massachusetts and is currently working on a book, "Queering the History of the American Left." She co-led the Free Speech Movement at the University of California, Santa Cruz, 1964–65, and the National United Committee to Free Angela Davis (1970–72) and remains an activist committed to peace and social justice.

Nancy Cantor is chancellor and president of Syracuse University, where she is helping forge a new understanding of the role of universities in society as SU pursues its vision, Scholarship in Action. The breadth, depth, and success of these efforts earned SU the distinction of being among the first institutions to earn the Carnegie Foundation for the Advancement of Teaching's classification as a university committed to Community Engagement. They also earned Chancellor Cantor the 2008 Carnegie Corporation Academic Leadership Award. Chancellor Cantor lectures and writes extensively on the role of universities as anchor institutions in their communities, along with other crucial issues in higher education such as sustainability, liberal education and the creative campus, the status of women in the academy, and racial justice and diversity. Prior to her appointment at Syracuse, Chancellor Cantor served as chancellor of the University of Illinois at Urbana-Champaign; provost and executive vice president for academic affairs at the University of Michigan, prior to which she had been dean of its Horace H. Rackham School of Graduate Studies and vice provost for academic affairs. She was chair of the department of psychology at Princeton University. She also was professor of psychology and senior research scientist at the Institute for Social Research at Michigan. While at Michigan, she was closely involved in the university's defense of affirmative action in the *Grutter* and *Gratz* cases decided by the US Supreme Court in 2003.

An author of numerous books, chapters, and scientific journal articles, Chancellor Cantor holds an A.B. from Sarah Lawrence College and a Ph.D. in Psychology from Stanford University. She is a fellow of the American Academy of Arts and Sciences, a member of the Institute of Medicine of the National Academy of Sciences, and a member of the National Academies Roundtable on Science and Technology for Sustainability. She also has received the Distinguished Scientific Award for an Early Career Contribution to Psychology from the American Psychological Association, the Woman of Achievement Award from the Anti-Defamation League, the Making a Difference for Women Award from the National Council for Research on Women, and the Frank W. Hale Jr. Diversity Leadership Award from the National Association of Diversity Officers in Higher

Education. Chancellor Cantor is the past chair of the board of directors of the American Association for Higher Education and former chair of the board of the American Council on Education. She serves on the board of the American Institutes for Research and the advisory board of Future of Minority Studies, the Board of the Commission on Independent Colleges and Universities, the Board of Governors for the New York Academy of Sciences, the Paul Taylor Dance Foundation Board of Directors, and is an Honorary Trustee of the American Psychological Foundation. Chancellor Cantor is also national co-chair of Imagining America's Tenure Team Initiative.

John F. Dovidio, who is currently Professor of Psychology at Yale University, previously taught at Colgate University and at the University of Connecticut. At Colgate, he was the Charles A. Dana professor of psychology and served as provost and dean of the Faculty. His research interests are in stereotyping, prejudice, intergroup relations, and discrimination; social power and nonverbal communication; and altruism and helping. Dovidio has been president of the Society for Personality and Social Psychology, the Society for the Psychological Study of Social Issues, and of the Society of Experimental Social Psychology. He is currently Executive Officer of the Society for Personality and Social Psychology. Dovidio has been Editor of the *Journal of Personality and Social Psychology—Interpersonal Relations and Group Processes*, Editor of *Personality and Social Psychology Bulletin*, and Associate Editor of *Group Processes and Intergroup Relations*. He has published over 275 articles and chapters; is co-author of several books, including *Emergency Intervention; The Psychology of Helping and Altruism: Problems and Puzzles; The Social Psychology of Prosocial Behavior;* and *Reducing Intergroup Bias: The Common Ingroup Identity Model;* as well as co-editor of *Prejudice, Discrimination, and Racism; Power, Dominance, and Nonverbal Behavior; On the Nature of Prejudice: 50 Years After Allport;* and, *Intergroup Misunderstandings: Impact of Divergent Social Realities,* and the *Handbook of Prejudice, Stereotyping, and Discrimination.* Dovidio has been with co-recipient of the Kurt Lewin Award (with S.L. Gaertner), the Gordon Allport Prize, the APA Raymond A. Fowler Mentor Award, the APA Award for Distinguished Service to Psychological Science, and a Presidential Citation for his research on racism from the American Psychological Association.

Deena J. González is a professor of Chicano/a studies at Loyola Marymount University in Los Angeles, where she has spent the past decade chairing, mentoring, and participating in university governance. In 2010–11 she was selected as an American Council on Education (ACE) fellow and was hosted for the year at the University of California, Irvine, where she interned in academic personnel and planning, and budget and compliance. González is entering her twenty-ninth year in the professoriate. She was co-editor-in-chief of the award-winning encyclopedia, *The Oxford Encyclopedia of Latinos and Latinas in the United States,* and another forthcoming volume from Oxford, *Encyclopedia of Latino/as in Politics, Law, and Social Movements.* González is also the author of *Refusing the Favor: The Spanish-Mexican Women of Santa Fe, 1820–1880* and more than forty articles on Borderlands and Chicano/a history and women's studies.

Samuel H. Smith has enjoyed a distinguished career in higher education, first at the University of California, Berkeley, then at Pennsylvania State University. He subsequently served fifteen years as president of Washington State University. Strengthening undergraduate and graduate education, placing an international imprint on programs, and increasing opportunities for women and minorities were among his presidential priorities. Smith is well known in Washington for establishing Washington State University urban campuses in Spokane, the Tri-Cities, and Vancouver to serve place-bound and job-bound students. He also established learning centers and award-winning extended degree programs to expand access to higher education. He is a founding member of the Board of Trustees of the Western Governors University. Smith has chaired the Association of Public and Land-Grant Universities (APLU) Board of Directors, and chairs the Council of Presidents and its Commission on Information Technologies. He is currently serving his second term as a member of the Washington Higher Education Coordinating Board. In 1998 he was honored at the APLU annual meeting as the Justin Smith Morrill Memorial lecturer. He was the founding president of the Board of Directors of the Talaris Institute, which is devoted to the study of early learning. He is also a founding board member of the College Success Foundation, an organization that provides scholarships and mentoring to high-potential, low-income students. He has also served as chair of the Executive Committee of the National Collegiate Athletic Association.

Chapter Authors

Constance G. Anthony is an associate professor in the Department of Political Science at Seattle University. She received her PhD from the University of California, Berkeley and has also been a member of the faculty at Oberlin College and Boston College. She has published work on the politics of international aid and technology transfer in East Africa, US science policy in Africa, refugees, famine, theories of development, and the philosophical foundations of US intervention. Her current work focuses on challenging the objectification of the Third World in the study of north-south relationships and comparative development. Anthony served on Seattle University's rank-and-tenure committee for nine years and was president of the faculty senate in 2006–7. She has chaired her department twice, from 1994 to 1997 and from 2004 to 2008, directed women's studies for two years, and served as interim dean for the College of Arts and Sciences in 1998–99.

Margalynne Armstrong is an associate professor of law and the associate academic director of the Center for Social Justice and Public Service at Santa Clara University. She teaches courses on race and law, constitutional law, and property. Her scholarship in these areas has appeared in books, journals, and newspapers as well as online. Prior to teaching at Santa Clara, Armstrong practiced public employment law, was a staff attorney with the Legal Aid Society of Alameda County, and directed the Academic Support Program at the School of Law at the University of California, Berkeley.

Elvia R. Arriola is a professor of law at Northern Illinois University who identifies as a Latina, feminist, critical, legal theorist. She earned her Juris Doctor degree from the University of California, Berkeley and a postgraduate degree in American history from New York University. Arriola began her legal career as an ACLU attorney and her law teaching career at the University of Texas in 1991. She teaches courses on constitutional law, family law, gender and the law, and sexuality and the law, and a seminar titled Women, Law, and the Global Economy. Her scholarship focuses on gender, sexuality, and the law; Latina feminist theory; and the impact of global economics, free trade, and immigration policy on working women who live on the US/Mexico border. Arriola is executive director of Women on the Border, an educational nonprofit dedicated to advancing awareness of the impact of NAFTA and free trade on working women and children.

Diane A. Forbes Berthoud earned her PhD at Howard University and is an associate professor of organizational communication and the associate director for the practicum at the Sixth College of the University of California, San Diego. Most recently, she was an associate professor and the chair of the Department of Communication at Trinity

Washington University. Berthoud is also part-time faculty of leadership studies in the Elliott School of International Affairs at George Washington University. Her research focuses on gendered, raced, and sexualized processes of organizing. Her work also explores creative and concrete ways to expand pedagogy in leadership studies. Berthoud's scholarship has appeared in *Management Communication Quarterly*, *Communication Quarterly*, and *International and Intercultural Communication Annual*.

Deirdre M. Bowen, JD, PhD, is a professor at Seattle University School of Law. She writes on affirmative action and education, nontraditional families, and criminal plea bargaining. Bowen's work has been published in the *Indiana Law Journal*, *Denver University Law Review*, *University of Pittsburgh Law Review*, and *Justice Quarterly*. She is currently working on the third of a trilogy of articles that examine the benefits and challenges of the current diversity model of affirmative action for students of color. In addition, Bowen is writing an article examining whether the Defense of Marriage Act achieves the goals articulated by legislatures. She teaches courses on legal writing, family law, and criminal law. With her background in sociology and law, Bowen has also taught classes on law and society, statistics, research methods, and family and society in the Department of Sociology at Seattle University.

Beth A. Boyd is the director of the Psychology Service Center and a professor of psychology at the University of South Dakota (USD). She is an enrolled member of the Seneca Nation of Indians. Since completing her PhD in 1992, she has taught in the clinical psychology graduate program at USD. She is involved in a number of projects seeking to train culturally competent clinical psychologists and develop culturally responsive mental-health services for Native Americans in the USD Disaster Mental Health Institute and has responded to a number of disaster and crisis situations, particularly in Native communities. Boyd has served on a number of American Psychological Association (APA) governance groups and was the 1998 recipient of the APA Division 12 Early Career Award for outstanding contributions to professional clinical psychology, as well as the 1999 recipient of the APA Division 45 (Society for the Psychological Study of Ethnic Minority Issues) Distinguished Career Contributions to Service Award. She is the immediate past president of the Society for the Psychological Study of Ethnic Minority Issues.

Roe Bubar, JD, is an associate professor jointly appointed in the Department of Ethnic Studies and the School of Social Work, and is an affiliate faculty member in women's studies at Colorado State University. She teaches Indigenous studies and women's studies. Her current research examines sexual violence against women and children, health and justice disparities, Native youth and messaging on sexually transmitted disease and infection, and child maltreatment in tribal communities. She has taught courses in ethnicity, perspectives on conquest, federal Indian law and policy, Indigenous women and children, social-welfare policy, research methods, and human diversity practice.

Grace Chang is a writer and activist in struggles for immigrant, labor, and welfare rights of migrant women and women of color in the United States. Currently she is associate professor of feminist studies at the University of California, Santa Barbara. She teaches graduate and undergraduate courses on social science research methods and ethics; women resisting violence; women, globalization, and resistance; and grassroots, transnational, feminist movements for social justice. Her essays have appeared in *Radical America*, *Socialist Review*, the *Journal of Black Women*, *Gender & Families*, *Stanford Journal of Civil Rights & Civil Liberties*, and several anthologies. She co-edited *Mothering: Ideology*,

Experience and Agency with Evelyn Nakano Glenn and Linda Rennie Forcey and is the author of *Disposable Domestics: Immigrant Women Workers in the Global Economy*. She is also the founding director of WORD (Women of Color Revolutionary Dialogues), a spoken-word/political-theater group for women and queer people of color, who write, perform, and direct their work in a multimedia show each year. She is completing research for her book in progress, "Trafficking by Any Other Name: Transnational Feminist, Immigrant and Sex Worker Rights Responses."

Francisca de la Riva-Holly received her PhD from an Ivy League school and currently is a full professor at a liberal arts institution in the Midwest. She teaches in the Department of American Ethnic Studies. Her interests lie in situating Latin@ authors within the mainstream American literary canon. She is currently working on a book about Cuban American authors in the new millennium.

Delia D. Douglas is a black Canadian independent scholar who lives in Vancouver, British Columbia. She holds a PhD in sociology from the University of California, Santa Cruz. Her areas of interest include antiracism; equity and social justice in the academy; necropolitics: violence, everyday racism, and racial hostility; sociology of sport and culture; race and the law; and qualitative research. Douglas has taught classes on a range of topics in both Canada and the US; course titles include Women in Cross-Cultural Perspective: Speaking Truth to Power; Race, Gender, and Nation: Narratives from the Diaspora; Women: Sport and Culture; African/Black Women in the Americas; and Critical Race Theory in a Global Context. Douglas's work focuses on the continuing significance of the legacies of slavery, imperialism, and colonialism and the ways that they influence the social world.

Serena Easton is an assistant professor of sociology at a liberal arts college in New England. She holds a PhD in sociology and has been teaching courses on race, class, and gender inequality at several institutions across the country for the past fourteen years.

Kelly Ervin completed her Ph.D. in social psychology with a minor in industrial organization psychology from Michigan State University in 1993. She has taught a variety of psychology, ethnic studies, and cultural studies courses at Michigan State University, George Washington University, and Washington State University. These courses include social psychology, black social psychology, cross-cultural psychology, the social psychology of prejudice, and the psychology of diversity, and research methods for the social sciences, as well as African American studies, African American cinema, critical cultural studies, and a course on the intersection of race, class, and gender. Her academic research concentrates on diversity, social identity, the social psychology of minorities, racial self-esteem, racial attitudes, and intra/intergroup relations. Her publications have appeared in *Personality and Social Psychology Bulletin, Sex Roles, Journal of Applied Social Psychology, Journal of Social Psychology, Journal of Black Psychology, Journal of Research in Personality, Journal of Social Issues,* and the *Journal of Black Studies*. Ervin is currently employed with the US Army Research Institute as a senior research psychologist and is an adjunct professor with the University of Maryland University College.

May Fu, PhD, is an assistant professor jointly appointed in the Departments of Ethnic Studies and History at Colorado State University. Her current research examines the role of panethnic, interracial, and international affiliations in the development of Asian American political identities and activism during the late 1960s and early 1970s. She is a member of INCITE! Women of Color against Violence.

Cerise L. Glenn is an assistant professor in the Department of Communication Studies at the University of North Carolina at Greensboro. Her research interests center on social constructions of difference (diversity), particularly identity negotiation and representations of underrepresented groups in organizational, intercultural/international, and mass-mediated contexts. She completed a research postdoctoral position at Purdue University and earned her doctorate in intercultural communication and a graduate certificate in international affairs at Howard University. She also holds a master of science degree in organizational communication from North Carolina State University.

Ruth Gordon specializes in public international law. Her work has explored the role of the United Nation Security Council in ensuring international peace and security and humanitarian intervention, and climate change and its impact on low-income nations. Gordon has authored numerous articles on the Third World encounter with international law and has been influential in investigating the role of race in the international sphere. Her writing has appeared in the *National Black Law Journal, Inter Alia, American University Journal of International Law & Policy, Cornell International Law Journal, Michigan Journal of International Law, University of Pennsylvania Journal of Constitutional Law, Berkeley Journal of African-American Law & Policy, Wisconsin International Law Journal, Villanova Law Review*, and the *University of Colorado Law Review*. Gordon is a graduate of the London School of Economics and Political Science and the New York University School of Law. She has taught a variety of international law courses at Villanova University School of Law since 1990 and in 1994 was the first recipient of the Riesenfeld fellowship in public international law at the University of California, Berkeley. Before beginning her teaching career, Professor Gordon was a law clerk to US District Court Judge John L. Kane and an attorney at the renowned Lawyers' Committee for Civil Rights Under Law. She was also an assistant to former Ambassador Robert Van Lierop, where she assisted him in his role as the Ambassador for Vanuatu at the United Nations.

Heather E. Harris earned her PhD at Howard University and is an associate professor of business communication at Stevenson University. Her research focuses on representations of African women in media and women and interpersonal relationships. She is a co-editor of and contributor to *The Obama Effect: Multidisciplinary Renderings of the 2008 Campaign*. Her work has appeared in a number of edited volumes and in the *Journal of Black Studies* and *Business Communication Quarterly*.

Brenda G. Hart is a professor of engineering fundamentals and the director of student affairs at the J. B. Speed School of Engineering at the University of Louisville in Kentucky. Previously she served as the director of minority and women in engineering programs. She received her MEd in counseling and personnel services (college student personnel) from the College of Education and Human Development at the University of Louisville and her BA in French from Boston University. Her expertise includes special initiatives for historically underrepresented students in engineering, as well as orientation classes for first-year students. She has given professional presentations at regional and national conferences and has published articles in journals and conference proceedings. In addition, she has served on evaluation panels for the National Science Foundation's Graduate Research Fellowship Program (GRFP) and Scholarships in Science, Technology, Engineering, and Mathematics (S-STEM) program, as well as the Science, Mathematics, and Research for Transformation (SMART) scholarship program for the US Department of Defense.

Michelle A. Holling, PhD, is an associate professor in the Department of Communication at California State University, San Marcos. Previously she taught Chicano/a studies as a joint appointment in the Departments of Ethnic Studies and Communication at Colorado State University. Her scholarly interests include Chican@/Latin@ vernacular discourse, media representations of Chican@ identity, and Mexicana gendered violence. Her publications have appeared in various journals and edited book collections and examine border rhetoric, the state of Chican@/Latin@ communication, and representations of Chicano masculinity, among other topics. She recently published *Latina/o Discourse in Vernacular Spaces: Somos de una voz?*, co-edited by Bernadette M. Calafell. Over her career, she has taught courses on gender, rhetorical theory, and Chicano/a film, rhetoric, and argumentation, as well as graduate courses on feminist theory and rhetoric and race.

Michelle M. Jacob is a Yakama Indian and an associate professor of ethnic studies and affiliate faculty member in sociology at the University of San Diego, where she teaches courses in American Indian studies and ethnic identity. Her work has been published in several journals, including *Wicazo Sa Review, Social Justice, Societies Without Borders, International Feminist Journal of Politics*, and interdisciplinary anthologies. She engages in scholarly and activist work that seeks to understand and strive for a holistic sense of health and well-being within Indigenous communities. Her work has been funded by the Ford Foundation, American Sociological Association, National Institute of Mental Health, National Cancer Institute, National Institute on Aging, and University of San Diego faculty research grants. She is currently working on a book that analyzes models of grassroots activism on the Yakama Reservation to articulate a theory of Indigenous social change.

Angela Mae Kupenda is a professor at Mississippi College School of Law. She attended racially segregated schools in the Deep South and graduated as the first black valedictorian of her predominantly white high school. She received a bachelor's degree in finance from Jackson State University, summa cum laude, and an MBA from the Wharton School at the University of Pennsylvania as a Huebner fellow. After teaching in business schools at Jackson State University and the University of Mississippi, where she was the first African American faculty member, she graduated first in her class from the Mississippi College School of Law, clerked for two federal appellate judges, and practiced law in large firms in Washington, D.C., and Mississippi. Kupenda joined the faculty of Mississippi College School of Law in 1995. She worked on faculty diversity issues as the scholar in residence at Pine Manor College in Massachusetts and was the distinguished visiting professor of teaching excellence at the Franklin Pierce Law Center in New Hampshire. She also served as a visiting professor at Boston College and Notre Dame law schools.

Jessica Lavariega Monforti is an associate professor of political science and senior faculty research associate at the Center for Survey Research at the University of Texas–Pan American. She specializes in public-policy analysis, race, ethnicity, immigration and politics, and survey research. While much of her research focuses on the differential impact of public policy according to race, gender, and ethnicity, she is specifically interested in the political incorporation and representation of Latinos, immigrants, and women. Her latest research project surveys the political attitudes and behavior of Latinos and other minority groups. Recent publications include articles in *PS: Political Science & Politics, the Latino(a) Research Review, Social Science Quarterly*, and the *Journal of Women, Politics & Policy*. She also edited a book with William E. Nelson Jr. entitled *Black and Latino/a Politics: Issues in Political Development in the United States*.

Sylvia R. Lazos is the Justice Myron Leavitt professor of constitutional law at the William S. Boyd School of Law at the University of Nevada, Las Vegas (UNLV). Her academic expertise is as a critical race scholar, and her work focuses on the importance of diversity in the judiciary. She publishes in the areas of critical race theory, unconscious racial and gender bias, judicial diversity, and immigration. Her monograph, *Cambio de Colores (Change of Colors): Legal and Policy Challenges as Latinas/os Make Their Home in Missouri* covers issues ranging from education and health care to driver's licenses and racial profiling, and establishing a database for policy decision making in Missouri. Lazos is currently engaged in a research project on unconscious gender and racial bias in judicial performance evaluations. She is co-chair of the Research Center for Social Justice at UNLV, where faculty are working on immigrant civic incorporation research and educational achievement issues. In September 2009, Lazos gave a keynote address for Latino judges at the Hispanic National Bar Association convention. Also in 2009, she received the educator of the year award from the Las Vegas Latin Chamber of Commerce.

Kari Lerum holds a PhD in sociology and is an associate professor of interdisciplinary arts and sciences and cultural studies at the University of Washington Bothell and an adjunct professor in gender, women's, and sexuality studies at the University of Washington. Her scholarship centers on the critical study of social inequality, focusing on the intersections of race/class/gender/sexuality, institutions, and culture. Her articles have appeared in *Gender & Society, Sexuality & Culture,* and the *Journal of Sex Research,* and she is currently writing a book called "Sexuality: The Basics." Lerum teaches courses in inequality, sexuality education, sex work, sexual health, activism, culture and institutions, multimedia storytelling, and research methods. She serves on the board of directors for the Pat Graney prison transition program and is a blogger for *Ms.* magazine, *Sexuality & Society,* and *Rh Reality Check.*

Carmen R. Lugo-Lugo is an associate professor of comparative ethnic studies at Washington State University. She engages in research involving Latinos in the US, the War on Terror, and its links to popular culture. She has co-authored, with Mary K. Bloodsworth-Lugo, several articles on the rhetoric behind the War on Terror and its discourse on various marginalized groups. The two also have an edited volume, *A New Kind of Containment: "The War on Terror," Race, and Sexuality,* and a co-authored book, *Containing (Un)American Bodies: Race, Sexuality and Post 9/11 Constructions of Citizenship.* Lugo-Lugo has also published several articles on the representation of Latinos and other minority groups within United States popular culture. Along with C. Richard King and Mary K. Bloodsworth-Lugo, she coauthored *Animating Difference: Race, Gender, and Sexuality in Contemporary Films for Children.*

Kimberly R. Moffitt received her PhD from Howard University and is an assistant professor in the Department of American Studies at the University of Maryland, Baltimore County (UMBC). She conducts research on mediated representations of marginalized groups as well as sports icons. Her most recent work is a co-edited volume with Regina E. Spellers entitled *Blackberries and Redbones: Critical Articulations of Black Hair/Body Politics in Africana Communities.* Moffitt's latest project is a series of works analyzing the role of Princess Tiana in Disney's *The Princess and the Frog.* She often volunteers in Baltimore public schools facilitating critical race, media literacy programs for middle school children.

Sharon E. Moore is a professor of social work at the Raymond A. Kent School of Social Work at the University of Louisville in Kentucky. She received her PhD in social work from the University of Pittsburgh in 1992. Two of her most oft-cited works are "The ABCs of Tenure: What All African-American Faculty Should Know" with L. J. Cornelius and M. Gray in the *Western Journal of Black Studies* and "The Benefits, Challenges, and Strategies of African American Faculty Teaching at Predominantly White Institutions" with R. Alexander in the *Journal of African American Studies*. In addition, Moore co-edited *Dilemmas of Black Faculty at US Predominantly White Institutions: Issues in the Post-Multicultural Era* with R. Alexander and A. J. Lemelle Jr. and *Social Work Practice with Culturally Diverse People* with Surjit Singh Dhooper. Her clinical experience is in the fields of medical social work and substance abuse counseling. In 2006 Moore became only the second African American promoted to full professor at the Kent School since its founding in 1939.

Angela Onwuachi-Willig is Charles M. and Marion J. Kierscht professor of law at the University of Iowa. She joined the Iowa law faculty in 2006 after three years on the tenure track at the University of California, Davis School of Law. She graduated from Grinnell College, where she majored in American studies and was elected to Phi Beta Kappa. Onwuachi-Willig received her law degree from the University of Michigan Law School, where she was a Clarence Darrow scholar, a note editor on the Michigan Law Review, and an associate editor of the founding issue of the Michigan Journal of Race & Law. After law school, she clerked for the Honorable Solomon Oliver, US District Judge for the Northern District of Ohio, and the Honorable Karen Nelson Moore, US Circuit Judge for the Sixth Circuit Court of Appeals. Onwuachi-Willig researches and writes in employment discrimination, family law, and race and the law. Her recent articles have appeared in the *Michigan Law Review, California Law Review, Vanderbilt Law Review, Wisconsin Law Review, Minnesota Law Review*, and *Harvard Civil Rights-Civil Liberties Law Review*. In 2006 Onwuachi-Willig was honored by the Minority Groups Section of the Association of American Law Schools with the Derrick A. Bell Jr. Award. In 2010 she was elected to the American Law Institute and was invited to be a fellow of the American Bar Foundation in 2011.

Stephanie A. Shields is professor of psychology and women's studies at Pennsylvania State University–University Park (Penn State), where she coordinates the dual-title PhD in women's studies and psychology. She has served as director of women's studies at Penn State and the University of California, Davis. She was the founding director of the UC Davis Consortium for Women and Research. Shields works at the intersection of emotion, gender, and feminist psychology. She is also president-elect of the Society for the Psychology of Women. She is a two-time winner of the Association for Women in Psychology's Distinguished Publication Award, first for *Speaking from the Heart: Gender and the Social Meaning of Emotion* and then for a special issue of *Sex Roles* on the intersectionality of social identities. With NSF support, she developed an experiential learning demonstration on cumulative effects of subtle gender bias: http://wages.la.psu.edu/. Her editorial experience includes *Feminism & Psychology, Sex Roles,* and *Review of General Psychology, Psychology of Women Quarterly,* and *Teaching of Psychology*. She was the founding editor of the *Emotion Researcher* of the International Society for Research on Emotion. She is a fellow of the American Psychological Association, the American Psychological Society, and the Society of Experimental Social Psychology. Shields makes connections between her research work and people's practical concerns. Her research has been featured in newspapers and on the Web, including *Slate, Chicago Tribune,* the *Toronto Globe and Mail, USA Today,* the *Washington Post,* The *London Times,* and Chile's *La Tercera*.

Mary-Antoinette Smith, PhD, is an associate professor of eighteenth- and nineteenth-century British literature and director of women's studies at Seattle University. She also teaches African-American Literature and Society and Cultural Pluralism in Literature and Film, and her pedagogy infuses race, class, and gender theory as the primary lens to analyze literary and cultural works. Her recent publications include "Becoming Jane: Embedded Epistolarity in Jane Eyre's Writing Herself into Being," in a special issue of *Cycnos*; the edited *Thomas Clarkson and Ottobah Cugoano: Essays on the Slavery and Commerce of the Human Species*; and "The Battle of the Bell(e)s: The Sweet Labor of Working through It with bell hooks," the afterword in *Women and Work: The Labors of Self-Fashioning*. Smith also has a forthcoming chapter titled "'I am Heathcliff!' On Being a Paradoxically Enigmatic African-American Victorianist" in *Vexed by the Victorians: 21st-Century Reverberations of 19th-Century British Fiction*.

Dean Spade is an assistant professor at the Seattle University School of Law. In 2002 he founded the Sylvia Rivera Law Project, a nonprofit collective that provides free legal services to low-income trans and gender nonconforming people and people of color and works to build transresistance centered in racial and economic justice. He is the author of *Normal Life: Administrative Violence, Critical Trans Politics and the Limits of Law*.

Linda Trinh Võ is an associate professor and former chair of the Department of Asian American Studies at the University of California, Irvine (UCI). She received a PhD in sociology from the University of California, San Diego in 1995 and was a University of California, Berkeley chancellor's postdoctoral fellow (1994–96) and a UCI chancellor's fellow (2006–9). She is the author of *Mobilizing an Asian American Community*, and the co-editor of three books: *Contemporary Asian American Communities: Intersection and Divergences*; *Asian American Women: The Frontiers Reader*; and *Labor Versus Empire: Race, Gender, and Migration*. She also edited a special issue entitled "Vietnamese Americans: Diaspora & Dimensions" for *Amerasia Journal*; co-edited a special issue and co-wrote an article, "Mapping Comparative Studies of Racialization in the US," for *Ethnicities Journal*; and co-edited a special issue entitled "Asian American Women" for *Frontiers: A Journal of Women Studies*. She is a series editor for the Asian American Culture & History series published by Temple University Press.

Sherri L. Wallace is an associate professor in the Department of Political Science at the University of Louisville in Kentucky. She earned her PhD in government at Cornell University in 1995. She is the recipient of the competitive President's Council of Cornell Women's fellowship (1993), the William Wells Brown Award (2002) from the Afro-American Historical Association of the Niagara Frontier, and the Betty J. Cleckley Minority Issues Research Award finalist plaque of recognition from the Gerontological Health Section of the American Public Health Association (2002). Her research fields are African American politics, urban politics, public policy, community economic development, faith-based organizations, and college textbook diversity. She has published chapters in edited volumes, book reviews, and articles in a variety of scholarly journals, including *Economic Development Quarterly, Journal of Developmental Entrepreneurship, Community Development, Afro-Americans in New York Life and History, Review of Black Political Economy, Journal of African American Studies, National Political Science Review, PS: Political Science & Politics*, and the *Journal of Political Science Education*.

Stephanie M. Wildman received the 2007 Great Teacher Award from the Society of American Law Teachers. She was the founding director of the Center for Social Justice at the University of California, Berkeley School of Law (Boalt Hall). She taught for twenty-five years at the University of San Francisco School of Law. Wildman received her BA and her JD from Stanford University. She clerked for Judge Charles M. Merrill of the United States Court of Appeal for the Ninth Circuit and worked as a staff attorney for California Rural Legal Assistance. In 1983 she was elected to membership in the American Law Institute. She has been a visiting professor at U.C. Berkeley School of Law (Boalt Hall), U.C. Davis School of Law, Hastings College of the Law, Santa Clara University School of Law, and Stanford Law School. Wildman most recently published *Women and the Law Stories* with Elizabeth Schneider. Her book, *Privilege Revealed: How Invisible Preference Undermines America*, won the 1997 Outstanding Book Award from the Gustavus Meyers Center for the Study of Bigotry and Human Rights. Her books, *Race and Races: Cases and Resources for a Diverse America*, with Richard Delgado, Angela P. Harris, and Juan F. Perea, and *Social Justice: Professionals Communities and Law: Cases and Materials*, with Martha R. Mahoney and John O. Calmore, are popular textbooks. She is past co-president of the Society of American Law Teachers and served on the Association of American Law Schools' Executive Committee. Wildman teaches law and social justice, gender and law, and torts. Her scholarship emphasizes systems of privilege, gender, race, and classroom dynamics.

Linda L. Wilson is the associate director for administration and programming for the Asian studies program in the College of Arts and Sciences at the University of Louisville in Kentucky and an adjunct professor in the graduate School of Education at Indiana University Southeast. She received her PhD in counseling and personnel services (college student personnel) in the College of Education and Human Development at the University of Louisville in 2009. Her areas of expertise include diversity and multicultural education. Wilson has given professional presentations, written reports, and published research in these areas as well. She was the founding director of the Multicultural Center at the University of Louisville.

Sherrée Wilson is assistant dean of the faculties at Indiana University Purdue University Indianapolis (IUPUI), where she serves on the leadership team for academic affairs. She is also assistant clinical professor in Indiana University's Higher Education & Student Affairs program. She focuses on the recruitment and retention of less-represented faculty, collaborates with campus leadership to advance diversity, and provides career development consultation to graduate students. Wilson is co-director of Next Generation @ IUPUI, a leadership-development program for faculty from less-represented populations. She chairs the Steering and Advisory committees for the IUPUI-Crispus Attucks Medical Magnet High School early college program. Prior to her current appointment, Wilson served as Special Assistant to the Chancellor at IUPUI, where she worked along with senior campus leaders to develop plans and objectives for the campus. She also led a review of the campus' hiring practices for faculty and senior administrators. Her research focuses on the advancement of faculty of color in higher education. As director of IUPUI's Office for Multicultural Professional Development, Wilson led a team that developed IUPUI's first online *Multicultural Classroom Resource Guide*. She has a BS in speech pathology and audiology from Ball State University, an MS in college student personnel administration and counseling from Indiana University (IU), and a PhD in higher education administration from IU.

Adrien Katherine Wing is the Bessie Dutton Murray professor of law at the University of Iowa College of Law, where she has been teaching for twenty-five years. She is the former associate dean for faculty development. Her research areas include international human rights, law in the Muslim world, critical race theory, and US constitutional law. The author of more than one hundred publications, Wing is editor of *Global Critical Race Feminism* and *Critical Race Feminism*. She is the director of the London Law Consortium, a semester study abroad program, as well as the director of the summer abroad program in Arcachon, France. Wing has received numerous honors and held leadership positions in various organizations. She advised on constitutional options for South Africa, Palestine, and Rwanda. She is on the board of editors of the *American Journal of Comparative Law*. Her honors include the distinguished alumnus award from her high school, Newark Academy, and the Clyde Ferguson Award from the American Association of Law Schools. Wing is a life member of the New York–based Council on Foreign Relations and the American Law Institute and a member of the New York State Bar Association. She has been a visiting professor at the University of Michigan Law School. She holds a BA from Princeton, an MA in African studies from UCLA, and her JD from Stanford Law School.

INDEX